Leading Lives That Matter

Leading Lives That Matter

WHAT WE SHOULD DO

AND

WHO WE SHOULD BE

Edited by

Mark R. Schwehn & Dorothy C. Bass

William B. Eerdmans Publishing Company
Grand Rapids, Michigan

Wm. B. Eerdmans Publishing Co.
2140 Oak Industrial Drive NE, Grand Rapids, Michigan 49505
www.eerdmans.com

26 25 24 23 22 21 20 19   14 15 16 17 18 19

Library of Congress Cataloging-in-Publication Data

Leading lives that matter: what we should do and who we should be /
edited by Mark R. Schwehn & Dorothy C. Bass.
p.   cm.
ISBN 978-0-8028-2931-3 (pbk.: alk. paper)
ISBN 978-0-8028-3256-6 (cloth: alk. paper)
1. Vocation — Christianity.   2. Vocation.
3. Work — Religious aspects — Christianity.   4. Work — Religious life.
5. Meaning (Philosophy) — Religious aspects — Christianity.
6. Meaning (Philosophy) — Religious aspects.
I. Schwehn, Mark R., 1945-   II. Bass, Dorothy C.

BT738.5.L43 2006
248.4 — dc22

2006003736

For
John Steven Paul
and
Margaret Franson

Contents

Contents

Virtue

Vocation

PART II: QUESTIONS

1. Are Some Lives More Significant Than Others?   117

2. Must My Job Be the Primary Source of My Identity?

3. Is a Balanced Life Possible and Preferable to a Life Focused Primarily on Work?

Contents

6. Can I Control What I Shall Do and Become?

7. How Shall I Tell the Story of My Life?

Epilogue

Acknowledgments

Excerpts from *Nicomachean Ethics* by Aristotle. Translated by Terence Irwin, 2nd edition, Indianapolis: Hackett Publishing Company, 1999, pp. 7-29, 49-55, 147-148. Reprinted by permission of Hackett Publishing Company Inc. All rights reserved.

Excerpt from *The Way of Life: A Theology of Christian Vocation* by Gary D. Badcock. Copyright 1998. Reprinted by permission of Wm. B. Eerdmans Publishing Company.

"Sonny's Blues," copyright 1957 by James Baldwin. Originally published in the *Partisan Review*. Copyright renewed. Collected in *Going to Meet the Man*, published by Vintage Books. Reprinted by arrangement with the James Baldwin Estate.

"Composing a Life Story," from *Willing to Learn: Passages of Personal Discovery,* by Mary Catherine Bateson. Copyright 2004 by Mary Catherine Bateson. Used by permission of Mary Catherine Bateson.

Eulogy for Yitzhak Rabin from *In the Name of Sorrow* by Noa Ben Artzi-Pelossof, copyright 1996 by Editions Robert Laffont. Used by permission of Alfred A. Knopf, a division of Random House, Inc.

Excerpts from *Jayber Crow* by Wendell Berry. Copyright 2000 by Wendell Berry. Reprinted by permission of Counterpoint Press, a member of Perseus Books, L.L.C.

Excerpt by Dietrich Bonhoeffer reprinted with the permission of Scribner, an imprint of Simon & Schuster Adult Publishing Group, from ETHICS by Dietrich Bonhoeffer. Copyright 1955 by Macmillan Publishing Company.

Definition of "vocation" from *Wishful Thinking: A Theological ABC* by Frederick

Buechner. Copyright 1973 by Frederick Buechner. Reprinted by permission of HarperCollins Publishers.

"Vocation as Grace," by Will D. Campbell, in *Callings!* edited by James Y. Holloway and Will D. Campbell, 1974, Paulist Press (Deus Book). Reprinted by permission of Will D. Campbell.

"Iris Chang" 2004, *The Economist Newspaper,* Ltd. All rights reserved. Reprinted with permission.

Excerpt from *Good Will Hunting* by Matt Damon and Ben Affleck. Copyright 1997, Matt Damon and Ben Affleck. Reprinted by permission of Miramax Books. All rights reserved.

Excerpt from *Therese* by Dorothy Day, 1960, 1979 by Dorothy Day. Reprinted with the permission of Templegate Publishers (templegate.com).

"Living Like Weasels," from *Teaching a Stone to Talk: Expeditions and Encounters,* by Annie Dillard. Copyright 1982 by Annie Dillard. Reprinted by permission of HarperCollins Publishers and Macmillan, London, UK.

"The Last Hours," from *Different Hours* by Stephen Dunn. Copyright 2000 by Stephen Dunn. Used by permission of W. W. Norton & Company, Inc.

"Two Tramps in Mud Time," from *The Poetry of Robert Frost,* edited by Edward Connery Lathem. Copyright 1930, 1939, 1969 by Henry Holt and Company. Copyright 1958 by Robert Frost. Copyright 1967 by Lesley Frost Ballantine. Reprinted by permission of Henry Holt and Company, LLC.

"I Hear Them . . . Calling (And I Know What It Means)" by Vincent Harding, in *Callings!* edited by James Y. Holloway and Will D. Campbell, 1974, Paulist Press (Deus Book). Reprinted by permission of Vincent Harding.

"Making the Match: Career Choice," from *The Fabric of This World,* by Lee Hardy. Copyright 1990. Reprinted by permission of Wm. B. Eerdmans Publishing Company.

Excerpt from *The Sabbath: Its Meaning for Modern Man,* by Abraham Joshua Heschel. Copyright 1951 by Abraham Joshua Heschel. Copyright renewed 1979 by Sylvia Heschel. Reprinted by permission of Farrar, Straus and Giroux, LLC.

Excerpt from "There's No Place Like Work," by Arlie Russell Hochschild, in *The New York Times Magazine,* April 20, 1997. Reprinted with permission.

Excerpt from *The Iliad of Homer,* Book 9, lines 163-655, pp. 202-215, trans. Richard Lattimore. Used by permission of The University of Chicago Press.

Excerpt from *Foundations of the Metaphysics of Morals,* 3e (1993) by Immanuel Kant, translated by James Ellington, p. 31. Reprinted by permission of Hackett Publishing Company, Inc. All rights reserved.

"Robert McG. Thomas, 60, Chronicler of Unsung Lives," by Michael T. Kaufman. Copyright 2000 by The New York Times Co. Reprinted with permission.

Excerpt from *A Dresser of Sycamore Trees* by Garret Keizer. Reprinted by permission of David R. Godine, Publisher, Inc. Copyright 2001 by Garret Keizer.

LEARNING IN WAR-TIME by C. S. Lewis, copyright C. S. Lewis Pte. Ltd. Extract reprinted by permission.

Excerpt from *The Giver* by Lois Lowry. Copyright 1993 by Lois Lowry. Reprinted by permission of Houghton Mifflin Company. All rights reserved. Also reprinted by permission of HarperCollins Publishers Ltd.

"Passed On" by Thomas Lynch. Copyright 2004 *Christian Century*. Reprinted by permission from the July 13, 2004, issue of *Christian Century*.

Excerpt from *The Redemptive Self* by Dan P. McAdams. Copyright 2005 by Dan P. McAdams. Used by permission of Oxford University Press, Inc.

Excerpt from THE AUTOBIOGRAPHY OF MALCOLM X by Malcolm X and Alex Haley, copyright 1964 by Alex Haley and Malcolm X. Copyright 1965 by Alex Haley and Betty Shabazz. Used by permission of Random House, Inc., and The Random House Group Ltd.

"Friendship and Vocation" in *Friendship, A Study in Theological Ethics* by Gilbert C. Meilaender, Copyright 1981, University of Notre Dame Press. Used with permission.

"Generativity Crises of My Own," from *Also a Mother: Work and Family as Theological Dilemma* by Bonnie Miller-McLemore. Copyright 1994. Abingdon Press. Used by permission.

Interview of Martha Nussbaum from *Bill Moyers: A World of Ideas* by Bill Moyers, copyright 1989 by Public Affairs Television, Inc. Used by permission of Doubleday, a division of Random House, Inc.

Excerpt reprinted by permission of the publisher from *Just Work* by Russell Muirhead, pp. 26-29, Cambridge, Mass.: Harvard University Press, Copyright 2004 by the President and Fellows of Harvard College.

Excerpt from *The Martyrdom of Perpetua*, in *The Acts of the Christian Martyrs*, edited by Herbert Musurillo (translator), 1972. Oxford University Press. Reprinted with permission.

"Ray Kroc," by Jacques Pepin, in *Time 100: Builders and Titans*, ed. Kelly Knauer, New York: Time, Inc., 1999. Used by permission of Jacques Pepin.

"To be of use," by Marge Piercy. Copyright 1973, 1982 by Marge Piercy and Middlemarsh, Inc. From *Circles on the Water*, Alfred A. Knopf, 1982. Used by permission of Wallace Literary Agency, Inc. Also from *The Art of Blessing the Day* by Marge Piercy. Copyright 1999 by Middlemarsh, Inc. Used by permission of Alfred A. Knopf, a division of Random House, Inc.

"Why Work?" from *Creed or Chaos* by Dorothy L. Sayers, published in 1947 by Harcourt Brace. Used by permission of David Higham Associates Limited.

"I Resolve to Become a Jungle Doctor," from *Out of My Life and Thought* by Albert Schweitzer, English language translation copyright 1991 by Antje Bultmann Lemke. Reprinted by permission of Henry Holt and Company, LLC.

"Chapter 34," from *East of Eden* by John Steinbeck, copyright 1952 by John Steinbeck, renewed 1980 by Elaine Steinbeck, John Steinbeck IV, and Thom Steinbeck. Used by permission of Viking Penguin, a division of Penguin Group (USA) Inc., and Penguin Books Ltd.

"Two Kinds" from *The Joy Luck Club* by Amy Tan, copyright 1989 by Amy Tan. Used by permission of G. P. Putnam's Sons, a division of Penguin Group (USA) Inc. Reprinted with permission of the author and the Sandra Dijkstra Literary Agency.

"The Sources of Authenticity," reprinted by permission of the publisher from *The Ethics of Authenticity* by Charles Taylor, pp. 25-53, Cambridge, Mass.: Harvard University Press, copyright 1991 by Charles Taylor and the Canadian Broadcasting Company.

The Death of Ivan Ilych by Leo Tolstoy, trans. Aylmer Maude, reprinted by permission of Oxford University Press.

"The Undeclared Major," from *A Gravestone Made of Wheat*. Copyright 1989 by Will Weaver. Originally published by Simon & Schuster. Used by the permission of The Lazear Agency.

"The Changing Nature of Work in the United States," by Robert Wuthnow, originally appeared in *The Cresset*, a publication of Valparaiso University, 2003. Used by permission.

"The Choice," by William Butler Yeats. Reprinted by permission of A. P. Watts Ltd., on behalf of Michael B. Yeats, and with the permission of Scribner, an imprint of Simon & Schuster Adult Publishing Group, from THE COLLECTED WORKS OF W. B. YEATS, VOLUME I: THE POEMS, REVISED, edited by Richard J. Finneran. Copyright 1933 by The Macmillan Company; copyright renewed 1961 by Bertha Georgie Yeats.

"Weddings," by Yevgeny Yevtushenko in *Early Poems by Yevgeny Yevtushenko*, translated in 1955 by George Reavey. Reprinted in 1997 by Marion Boyars Publishers. Used by permission.

"Defining a Doctor," by Abigail Zuger. Copyright 2004 by The New York Times Co. Reprinted with permission.

Scripture quotations are from the *New Revised Standard Version* of the Bible, copyright 1989 by the National Council of the Churches of Christ in the USA. Used by permission. All rights reserved.

Preface

On October 19, 2005, we sent the manuscript of this anthology to the publisher. This date was also the twentieth birthday of our twin son and daughter. As second-year students in a liberal arts college, they were immersed that fall semester in a wide range of academic and non-academic pursuits. Yet they were also beginning to tire of the excess of options and to ponder more seriously than ever before the choices that will give shape and focus to what they do and become in the years after college. As of this writing, they do not yet know (or at least have not yet told us) what they hope to do to earn a living. At the same time, after a similar period of questioning, their older sister has discovered and embraced her calling as a writer and teacher of poetry. As we write, however, she is still searching for full-time employment.

The comparatively prolonged struggles of these and many other young adults to find their way in and through the process of figuring out what to do to earn a living are an important sign of our times, for the fluidity that characterizes their lives is also becoming increasingly common in the lives of older Americans. In this age of rapid economic, social, and cultural change, people of all ages and social classes can, and often do, experience unexpected unemployment, as well as other forms of personal or geographic displacement. Thus many people today are asking hard questions about how to make a living and what their work has to do with their identity.

We have composed this book not only for our children and their contemporaries but also for the many others who are asking these questions during this time of rapid social, cultural, and economic change. Although contemporary people bring special urgency to this set of questions, human beings have been asking them — and offering answers — for many centuries, and some have probed the heart of what gives a human life its shape, meaning, and significance. We have tried to capture in this book some of the wisdom that has found its way into words, by gathering texts from literature, philosophy, and everyday life that we believe may help readers to ponder these questions and to answer them well.

A few years ago the leaders of Lilly Endowment, a private family foundation in Indianapolis, noted this set of concerns and resolved to encourage students, faculty, and staff members in higher education to consider more deeply the insights inherent in the concept of *vocation*, a theological idea that also enjoys wide public use. The result was the Program for the Theological Exploration of Vocation (PTEV), which has given rise to exciting experiments at scores of colleges and universities in the United States and Canada. *Leading Lives That Matter* owes its origin to the new and vital interest in vocation sparked by PTEV but now evident far beyond its boundaries. In response to requests for material that could be used in campus settings as well as among parents and alums, Craig Dykstra and Chris Coble of the Lilly Endowment and Kim Maphis Early, coordinator of PTEV, invited the two of us and Professor William C. Placher of Wabash College to develop two complementary anthologies. *Callings: Twenty Centuries of Christian Wisdom about Vocation*, edited by Placher and published in the fall of 2005, includes theological texts that trace the development of the Christian idea of vocation over two millennia of history. *Living Lives That Matter*, the present volume, looks beyond the idea of vocation *per se*, includes texts from a wider range of fields, and takes its organization from contemporary concerns rather than historical sequence. Each of the two books can stand alone, but we hope many readers will choose to read them both. Study guides for these books, as well as many other resources designed to foster theological reflection on vocation, are available for free download at www.ptev.org.

While compiling this anthology we have been reminded again and again that the endeavor to understand "lives that matter," like the endeavor to live them, is a communal venture, requiring at every point many voices, hands, hearts, and minds. We are indebted to all those who have aided us in the preparation of *Leading Lives That Matter*. From the beginning, Kim Maphis Early, Chris Coble, and Craig Dykstra provided generous encouragement, support, and counsel. Special thanks to Bill Placher, who has been a wise counselor and a good friend throughout the process. Bill also administered the Lilly Endowment grant that supported this work.

During the spring of 2005 in Christ College, the honors college of

Valparaiso University, the students in Mark's seminar "What Makes a Life Significant?" helped to discover and shape some of the texts and questions that appear in this book. Special thanks therefore go to Sarah Benczik, Jeffrey Biebighauser, Julia Colbert, Katherine Hovsepian, Mark Koschmann, Nicole Kranich, Thomas Pichel, Jason Reinking, Amanda Schappler, Kendra Schmidt, Theodore Schultz, Jamie Stewart, and Joy Woellhart.

In August of 2005, the following students from Valparaiso University, St. Olaf College, Saint John's University, and the College of Saint Benedict reviewed a draft of part of the manuscript: Jeffrey Biebighauser, Hannah Bolt, Shaina Crotteau, Ben Durheim, Stephanie Mueller, Mike Reading, Martha Schwehn, Krista Senden, and Sarah Werner. Thanks to their criticisms, many of the introductions to sections and to specific texts were shortened and improved.

Many colleagues have suggested texts for inclusion and offered helpful comments on the shape of this anthology, including John Barbour, Kathleen Sprows Cummings, Sara Danger, John Feaster, Susan Felch, Darrell Jodock, Amy Kass, DeAne Lagerquist, and Dan McAdams. We benefited from challenging conversation about the issues explored here in sessions, at meals, and on the porches and trails of Holden Village. Our colleagues at the Collegeville Institute for Ecumenical and Cultural Studies and its director, Don Ottenhoff, asked hard questions and provided good company as we were finishing the work. The librarians at Valparaiso University, Saint John's University, and the College of Saint Benedict were patient and helpful. We are especially grateful for the diligence and perseverance of those who helped us with permissions and manuscript preparation: Doretta Kurzinski, Leslie Kurzinski, Sister Dolores Schuh, CHM, and Sarah Werner.

John Steven Paul, for many years chair of the Valparaiso University Theater Department and now the Program Director of the Lilly Fellows Program in Humanities and the Arts, and Margaret Franson, Associate Dean of Christ College, are remarkable educators who work daily to help others discern what they should do and who they should be. They are also godparents to one of our children, generous friends and guides to all three, and dear and faithful friends to the two of us. They lead lives that matter to us, to our children, to their colleagues and to hundreds of students and alumni of Valparaiso University. We dedicate this book to them with gratitude and affection.

MARK R. SCHWEHN
DOROTHY C. BASS

Introduction

In October of 1905, Albert Schweitzer wrote letters to several of his teachers, relatives, and friends informing them that he had decided to abandon his present employment in order to begin medical studies that would equip him to become a doctor in central Africa. Schweitzer was almost thirty years old and already the dean of a seminary and a successful scholar, organist, and organ builder. Even though he had a highly regarded job that suited his abilities well, he was restless. He longed to do work that would allow him to pursue his highest ideals.

Today many young people experience a similar yearning for work that is meaningful and significant. So do millions of somewhat older people who feel that their current employment is not satisfying in this regard. Moreover, many of these find, as Schweitzer did, that their search to discover the work that is right for them stretches over an extended period of struggle and uncertainty.

This anthology is designed for people such as these, people who want to lead lives that matter. The readings gathered here, which include Schweitzer's own story of his decision to become a "jungle doctor," have been selected because they can help us to think with greater clarity and depth about just what that might mean. Although most readers may not aspire to join Schweitzer as winners of the Nobel Peace Prize, in creating this book we have assumed that they do want to "make a difference" in the world, as our own students and friends put it. While creating this book, we have been guided by the belief that many people today desire, as we ourselves do, to lead lives that are meaningful but also significant, lives that manifest both personal integrity and social responsibility.

What We Do and Who We Are

In the United States, fundamental questions about ourselves and our purpose in life occur to many of us most forcefully when we are wondering what work we should do to earn a living. As many foreign observers have noticed, ours is a very practical and pragmatic culture. When we make new acquaintances, we ask them first about what they do, not about what they believe, or where they live, or what and whom they love. Those questions come later, if at all. Similarly, most of us are impatient to answer this same question for ourselves. Our eagerness to act can even prevent us from slowing down long enough to think carefully about what work would truly be best for ourselves and others.

Schweitzer's decision, which surprised and confounded many of his friends and family members, was by contrast the result of long and careful reflection. In his late teens he had decided that he would pursue the arts and scholarly subjects he loved until he was thirty and then he would devote the remainder of his life to humanitarian concerns. Few of us have laid down such elaborate life plans. And few of us make such radical alterations in our careers by choice rather than by necessity. Even so, we are like Schweitzer in this respect: we sense that what we do to earn a living somehow emerges from who we really are, and we also sense that what we do to earn a living will somehow shape who we will be. A person's thinking about what to do to earn a living, in other words, is entangled with her identity and how she understands it. A person's choice of livelihood is framed by a sense of who he is and what he hopes to become as a particular human being. (That is, when one *has* a choice in the matter, as many people do not; but more on this later.)

Leading Lives That Matter seeks to address a pragmatic society in a way that shows serious regard for ultimate concerns. Thus it invites readers into a set of questions and documents that attend both to immediate practical issues about what work we will do and to underlying religious and philosophical issues about identity and purpose. More important, the readings are arranged in a way that seeks to overcome the division between these two kinds of concerns. The essays, poems, stories, and biographies included here explore fundamental issues of human life and its meaning and purpose, to be sure. But they are clustered in chapters that respond directly to the practical questions that Americans who find themselves at important turning points in their lives most frequently ask.

In a sense, then, this book both yields to and resists Americans' obsession with work. Because jobs are such a focus of concern for people in our culture, the anthology considers the other vitally important parts of lives that matter — love and friendship, family and sexuality, leisure and play, study and worship — primarily in connection to paid employment. Yet many of the readings also challenge this way of thinking, leading us to wonder whether our jobs really are or should be such important indicators of meaning and significance. We will find ourselves asking again and again, "Do our jobs really define who we are? And if so, should they?"

Multiple Traditions

This book seeks to overcome another division as well. Popular media in the United States often feature events and stories that pit the religious against the secular, the pious and devout against the skeptical and irreverent. Much that happens in our common life warrants the prominence of these depictions of so-called culture wars. Nevertheless, over the course of Western history worldly and religious life, the secular and the sacred, have often informed, enriched, deepened, and constructively corrected one another. In this anthology, the readings are arranged in a way that will encourage that same dynamic of mutual correction and enrichment to happen here. Sources from both of these streams are intermingled, because wisdom and understanding from both are essential if we hope to explore together what it means to lead lives that matter.

All of the great religious traditions contain abundant wisdom about questions of who we are and what we should do. In this anthology, however, the religious authors and texts that are included come primarily, though not exclusively, from the Christian tradition. In part, the prominence of Christian texts reflects the editors' own home tradition, as well as the limited range of their knowledge. In addition, this imbalance reflects the fact that *Leading Lives That Matter* is a companion volume to another book focused entirely on the history of Christian thinking about vocation, William Placher's *Callings: Twenty Centuries of Christian Wisdom about Vocation*. The editors of both volumes hope that together these books will expand the treasury of wisdom on which contemporary readers can draw. We did not aim to exhaust this topic, and we hope that other authors will offer further resources from other traditions.

A similar restriction applies to the secular writings. Though secular culture, like Christianity, includes multiple and sometimes discordant modes of thought and reflection, most of the authors and texts in this volume belong loosely to what the philosopher Jeffrey Stout has recently identified as the "tradition of Democracy." Perhaps the dominant voice among the many secular voices that define our common life, the voice of Democracy emphasizes notions of equality, self-determination, and self-reliance. As we shall see, the Christian tradition and the democratic tradition sometimes clash. At other times, however, they have informed one another so closely that they are hard to distinguish from each other. In any event, we should take every opportunity in these frequently contentious times to engage people of religious conviction with those who do not share such conviction in the pursuit of common questions, ideas, and ideals like those that define what it means to lead a life that matters.

Indeed, in one particular case, many Christians share with many secular advocates of Democracy some deep suspicions about one of the basic inquiries that informs this anthology. The title question that governs Chapter 1 of Part II, "Are Some Lives More Significant Than Others?" makes people from both traditions profoundly uneasy, though for different reasons. Many Christians, along with those of other faiths, insist that all human beings are equally valued and valuable in the eyes of God. Protestant Christians have fervently maintained for centuries that, when we stand before God, we are not judged on the basis of our deeds but on the basis of our faith. So who are *we* ever to pass judgment upon the significance of the life of another? In the meanwhile, spokespersons for secular democratic traditions insist that since all are equal in nature and/or before the law, and since freely chosen paths in life are equally "valid" so long as they do not interfere with someone else's way of life, we had best refrain from judgment. Judgment, on this reckoning, is insidiously hierarchical, based on an implicit ranking of values from the higher to the lower. Judgment of relative significance suggests that some lives are "better" than others, and its practice is therefore undemocratic.

Whether or not we are comfortable admitting that we make judgments, however, it is clear that almost everyone does this every day; each of us finds some people more admirable, and their lives more choice-worthy, than others. We hope that *Leading Lives That Matter* will help all of us to become more articulate about the judgments we already make, while we also allow these judgments to be interrogated by a diverse group of readings and by those with whom we discuss them. Even so, part of the liveliness of this anthology may well mean that both of the major traditions that inform it, and other traditions as well, will sometimes question the book's own impulses and assumptions.

4

Fostering Conversations about Lives That Matter

The pragmatism and impatience that infuse American culture, insofar as these have shaped readers' expectations, have sustained for several decades a large market for self-help books. And so we must say: Readers beware! This is not a self-help book that provides ready answers or prefabricated exercises. Instead, the book is designed to lead readers to know their own minds better by encountering the minds of others who have gone before them. To read this book is to become another pilgrim along life's way, as we travel in the company of other pilgrims who have left behind them records of their own journeys or the journeys of others. Moreover, as those who have read Chaucer's *Canterbury Tales* know, pilgrims like to talk while they travel. Reading this book is therefore more like joining a conversation than it is like going to a paid consultant or therapist. We hope that the book will enable readers to join an ongoing conversation that reaches back to the Bible and ancient Greece. But beyond this, we also hope that it will engender actual conversations with others who share the concerns and questions each person brings to these readings. Such conversations with others different from ourselves not only help us to refine our opinions; they also help us to enlarge our moral imaginations. As we will learn especially in Chapter 7 of Part II, our ability to imagine more life-giving futures for ourselves and for the world can sometimes result from an honest resourcefulness in interpreting our own pasts.

Happily, there is reason to think that readers are ready and eager to enter the conversation. *Leading Lives That Matter* has arisen in a context within which multiple conversations and concerns are already alive. One group of conversations and concerns belongs to the young men and women in colleges or universities and graduate or professional schools who are struggling with questions of what they should do to earn a living and what that may mean for who they will become. Those who have been fortunate enough to attend institutions of higher education have long had the opportunity and burden of deciding what work to pursue — a privilege denied to most people in the past and one still denied to many in the U.S. and around the world. Our system of higher education, however, does not consistently encourage students to explore the kinds of basic questions this anthology raises. The vast majority of those who attend colleges and universities do so primarily in order to prepare themselves for jobs of one kind or another, not in order to gain greater clarity about who they are or simply to discover what is true about the worlds of nature and culture. To be sure, most post-secondary schools do require students to take "liberal education" courses, in which basic issues of meaning, significance, value, justice, identity, and purpose should be raised and explored, of course. However, these questions are often considered in isolation from the main concern that led most students to attend college in the first place: preparing for a job. Because of this division, which is structured by educators, many students come to believe that courses in literature or philosophy or history or religion are just academic requirements to be "gotten out of the way" until the "real" and more practical subjects can be studied. We hope that the readings gathered here will help students and recent graduates to retrieve the importance of questions about meaning and purpose and to include reflection on these questions in their thinking about what they hope to do and become.

Another group of conversations and concerns is taking place within and about higher education itself, as well as in the many fields of endeavor to which it is related. At colleges and universities, administrators and faculties are asking how "values," religious convictions, and ideals of service should influence education and scholarship. Meanwhile, at some hospitals, doctors and medical students are gathering to discuss literature and philosophy, in an effort to clarify and deepen their sense of the important human issues at stake in their profession. Those in other professions are engaging in similar explorations. In many cases, an effort to envision the work they do in relation to the kinds of philosophical and religious questions addressed by the readings gathered in this book is at the heart of their concern.

Beyond these arenas, a larger public comprised of serious-minded citizens is deeply interested in thinking together about how best to spend their lives in order to bring about a better world both for themselves and for others. The emergence of large numbers of reading groups that focus on challenging literature similar to the texts gathered in this anthology provides evidence of a widespread hunger for engagement with the issues surrounding what we should do and who we should be. Even popular culture has been exploring these issues in recent years. The enormous popularity of the three *Lord of the Rings* films may well arise from the films' capacity to visualize for a mass audience that is hungry for images of strenuous and significant lives a synthesis of both pagan and Christian stories about vocation, duty, devotion, and hope. The recent *Spiderman* movies address similar themes, as do popular television series like *Buffy the Vampire Slayer* and *Smallville*.

Though it is far too early to know whether these several developments amount to "straws in the wind" or a reconfiguration of public discourse, many of the social, material, economic, and even medical forces driving them will probably remain in place for the foreseeable future. The rising number of maladies that are at least to some degree culturally induced and that seem increasingly to afflict young people (depression, eating disorders, alcoholism) will continue to suggest that millions have come to feel a loss of significance and purpose. Global capitalism will continue to reshape the workforce, displace people, widen the gap between rich and poor, and saddle some with the burden of impossible choices. The stresses that two-career marriages and single-parent households place upon individuals, children, and institutions will doubtless remain. And finally, the still-popular equation between material prosperity and genuine fulfillment will continue to be challenged by the experience of millions, as will the worst forms of individualism.

How Can I Use This Book to Greatest Advantage?

This anthology seeks to make easily available to readers of all kinds some of the best thinking and writing that human beings have done over the centuries about the very questions that most trouble human beings when they wonder about how to lead lives of substance and significance. But not all readers are the same. For some, the most important question is, "What makes a life significant?" For others, the most urgent matter before them is, "Must my paid employment define who I am?" Still others are trying to sort out all of the conflicting advice they are receiving. For them, the question is, "To whom shall I listen?" For increasing numbers of middle-class people today, the most perplexing question is, "Is a balanced life possible and preferable to a life focused primarily upon work?"

Part II of this anthology is organized around exactly these questions and several more that are closely related to them. Those readers who come to the book with a particular, well-defined question are welcome to turn directly to the chapter in Part II that addresses just that question. Understanding and learning from the readings in any one chapter do not depend in any major way upon an understanding of the readings in another one. Often, however, the introductions to readings in one chapter will refer to readings in another chapter. We hope that this will lead readers to move in different directions away from their first question to consider other issues, which will in all likelihood set their initial question in a helpful, wider context.

Other readers will prefer to ponder the "big picture" before they attend to the more immediate and practical matters explored in Part II. These readers should turn to Part I, which addresses a broad and somewhat abstract question: "How Should I Think and Talk about My Life?" This section of the book addresses a concern that is actually quite urgent: many of us today have difficulty thinking about how to lead lives that matter because we are not able to express ourselves very clearly about what really matters to us. Part I endeavors to help readers make better judgments about their own lives and the lives of others by exploring three distinct "vocabularies" that people have used over the centuries to speak about lives that are choice-worthy and admirable. Most of us draw primarily upon one of these three vocabularies today, though many of us find creative ways to combine them. The key terms or ideas in each of the three vocabularies suggest what each of them will emphasize: authenticity and individualism; virtue and character; vocation and the divine.

Whether readers are initially drawn to Questions or to Vocabularies, however, we encourage all of them first to read the Prologue. This section begins, as does each chapter, with a brief essay by the editors that sets forth the key issues readers should consider. In the Prologue, this essay is followed by two wonderful readings that explore, in ways that we shall revisit throughout the book, the underlying question of what makes a life significant.

The Epilogue consists of only one reading, but it is arguably the most important one in the book: *The Death of Ivan Ilych,* by Leo Tolstoy. Because this short novel raises in a vivid and complete way all of the questions that the anthology addresses, it can serve readers in at least two ways. First, it can provide a rich opportunity to exercise some of the capacities for judgment that other readings in the anthology should strengthen and sharpen. And second, it can be itself a rich source of wisdom about what it means to lead a life that matters. Many readers will want to read this novel more than once, even perhaps at both the beginning and the conclusion of their engagement with the other treasures in this anthology. Engaging texts like *The Death of Ivan Ilych* in this way will be at one and the same time an exercise in liberal learning and an exercise in vocational preparation. Moreover, as we noted at the outset, the anthology as a whole is based upon the assumption that one cannot think very well or very long about practical matters without sustained attention to the fundamental questions that have preoccupied human beings from the time when they first began to think and talk together. We cannot ponder our livelihoods without at one and the same time thinking about the shape, the meaning, and the significance of our entire lives. We cannot decide what we should do without considering who we are and what we might become.

Prologue

During the spring semester of 2005, thirteen juniors and seniors in a college seminar pondered the following question: "What is the difference, if any, between a good life and a significant one?" Some students argued that a good life is a matter of character, having to do with the kind of person you are. A significant life, on the other hand, is simply a consequential life, they thought, a life that influences a great number of people. A person does not have to be morally good to be significant or influential.

Others strongly disagreed. A significant life, they insisted, must change the world for the better. Thus, Joseph Stalin, though he changed the lives of millions, did not lead a significant life, because the results of his often brutal and arbitrary actions were terrible, not beneficial, for humankind. Besides, Stalin was, so these students insisted, an ignoble human being, someone of bad character, perhaps mentally deranged, and therefore not worthy of admiration. A significant life must be a good life, *and* it must change the world for the better.

The students expressed other views, of course, but these were the two extremes. Students at one extreme thought significance is a purely quantitative measure: the more people influenced by someone, the more significant his or her life is. Students at the other extreme thought of significance as a mostly qualitative matter: people must lead good lives and change the world substantially for the better in order to lead significant lives. Students at both extremes agreed that significance had *something* to do with "making a difference," but

9

here again matters quickly grew complex. Who could tell how many lives a lo-cal high school teacher might touch? The instructor quoted Henry Adams: "A teacher touches eternity, for he never knows where his influence stops." Per-haps significance cannot be measured after all, unless we arbitrarily say that it pertains only to the number of people whose lives are changed for the better by a person during the course of his or her lifetime. Even so, measurements would be hard to make. How many lives did Dwight David Eisenhower change for the better during his lifetime, first as a general in the army during World War II, later as a two-term president of the United States?

Questions that forever elude precise answers are not for that reason trivial or "merely academic." On the contrary. Most of the students who were thinking and writing about the kind of life that is worth living were soon to graduate. They wanted to gain some clarity about what makes for a significant life, because most of them longed to make a difference in the world. Yet they hoped to do so in a way that would honor other aspirations as well. And they worried that endeavors to lead a good or virtuous life might sometimes conflict with efforts to lead a significant one.

Almost exactly a century ago, both William James and Albert Schweitzer, the authors of the two texts that follow, worried over the same questions about what they should do and who they should be that perplexed the stu-dents in the class. More important, both of them "lived" these questions. William James endured a long "vocational crisis," extending over a period of almost ten years and spanning the most terrible war in United States his-tory, the Civil War of the 1860s. Albert Schweitzer changed his vocation sev-eral times over the course of his life, often in the face of incomprehension and even opposition from family and friends. The writings that follow are in James's case the fruits of his questions and struggles; in Schweitzer's case, a record of them.

William James eventually became one of America's most distinguished psychologists as well as one of its most beloved philosophers. But his road to these achievements was not easy. He grew up in a large and accomplished family. His sister Alice was a troubled but very gifted writer. And his brother Henry became one of America's foremost novelists. His father and mother were by and large permissive and indulgent parents; they seldom interfered in their children's decisions about what they should do for a living. But Henry James, Sr., made an exception in William's case. For as long as Wil-liam could remember, he wanted to be an artist. His brother Henry remem-bered him "drawing, drawing, always drawing." But his father had other plans for William, insisting that he should become a scientist.

Though the reasons for William's father's efforts to manipulate his son's choice of career are far from clear, much of the evidence points to a motive that is not uncommon among parents. Henry James, Sr., had once hoped to be a scientist himself, but he gave up the effort. Instead, he tried to arrange matters so that his son William might realize Henry, Sr.'s, own ambitions. He therefore removed William, during the early 1860s, from the studio where he was learning to paint and transported him to Germany, where he exposed William to some of the most advanced scientific study in Europe at the time. Yielding to his father's wishes, William abandoned painting, a move he was to regret for at least ten years, and enrolled in the Lawrence Scientific School at Harvard in 1861.

The manifold conflicts between paternal expectations and William's own longings led to painful academic and psychological experiences. In today's parlance, we would say that William was a college student who was constantly changing his major. He enrolled in chemistry, soon changed to comparative anatomy and physiology, then resolved to study medicine, then decided that he preferred research to medicine, then took a trip to the Amazon on a specimen-collecting expedition to see whether he might pursue a career in natural history, then took another trip to Germany where his interests broadened to include literature and philosophy.

He had also gone to Germany to seek relief from a variety of physical and psychological symptoms — insomnia, digestive disorders, eye trouble, and acute back pains. But the various treatments he received had little positive effect. By the late 1860s, William James was deeply depressed, often unable to find the energy to work or to care about life. He grew to believe that his life was completely determined by physical and social forces beyond his control. On the verge of suicide, James happened to read works of poetry and philosophy that defended human freedom, and he came to believe that he was after all free to make his own choices. Or, as he put it, his first act of free will was to believe in free will, to believe "in my individual reality and creative power." James always believed that his "vocational crisis" was at one and the same time physical, psychological, philosophical, and spiritual. His essay below, originally delivered as a lecture to college students, shows many traces of his own struggles as a college student, given its emphases upon freedom, ideals, individual energy and initiative, and the belief that people can make a difference in the world.

Albert Schweitzer led a life that William James might have envied in certain respects. Like James, Schweitzer was a gifted artist, though his art was music, not painting. But unlike James, Schweitzer spent many years studying music, was recognized as one of the leading organists of his time, and later learned to build organs. Throughout a long and varied life, Schweitzer never lost his love for great music, and he continued to write about the compositions of J. S. Bach even while serving as a "jungle doctor." Again like James, Schweitzer studied philosophy, and he continued to write philosophical works throughout his life. Both Schweitzer and James loved both abstract speculation and practical affairs, though Schweitzer, unlike James, did finally decide to become a physician.

By comparison to James, Schweitzer was relatively free of mental illness. Indeed, he often gave thanks for his even temperament and his mental health, because these gifts enabled him to undertake the demanding work he loved. According to his own recollections, however, Schweitzer was not an especially strong student in his early years. And though he always applied himself diligently to his studies, he sometimes disappointed his examiners. In spite of minor setbacks, however, Schweitzer decided quite early upon a plan for his life that would include music, philosophy, theology, and humanitarianism. Remarkably, he stuck to that plan and carried it forward with great nobility and success.

The two men together represent, as well as any two people could, vital points of intersection between the two traditions that largely inform this anthology and that we discussed briefly in the general introduction — Democracy and Christianity. Although both James and Schweitzer remained deeply interested in and formed by religious concerns for their entire lives, they were suspicious of institutionalized religion, especially of most forms of institutionalized Christianity. Both of them, in different ways, were profoundly "spiritual" or "religious" without being conventionally Christian. James was never a regular churchgoer, but Schweitzer was. His father was a Protestant pastor in a Catholic region of Europe, and Schweitzer himself spent many years studying and preaching the Christian faith. From a very early age, James became deeply interested in religious experiences and affections, and he always believed that our own lives were suspended within a larger universe of religious meaning and purpose that was "congenial to powers that we possess." Schweitzer remained faithful to what he took to be the ethical core of Christianity, its emphasis upon self-giving love and care for those who are suffering. And though he remained very much a Christian, he developed a view of life that resulted in part from a synthesis of the great religions of the world, many of which he studied in depth.

Both James and Schweitzer belonged as much to traditions of Enlightenment and Democracy as they did to Christianity. Thought, reason, argument, criticism, and disciplined inquiry into the realms of nature and culture were just as important to both of them as reverence, devotion, and prayer. As such, they are very much the contemporaries of millions of Americans who are committed at one and the same time to democratic principles of equality and freedom, to Enlightenment ideals of rationality, and to spiritual ideals of humility and sacrificial love. Schweitzer put it this way in the book from which the excerpt below is taken:

> To become aware of its real self, Christianity needs thought. For centuries it treasured the great commandments of love and mercy as traditional truths without opposing slavery, witch burning, torture, and all the other ancient and medieval forms of inhumanity committed in its name. Only when it experienced Enlightenment was Christianity stirred up to enter the struggle for humanitarian principles. . . .
>
> Just as a stream is kept from gradually drying up because it flows along above underground water, so Christianity needs the underground water of elemental piety that issues from thinking. It can only attain real spiritual power when men no longer find the road from thought to religion barred.
>
> I know I myself owe it to thought that I was able to retain my faith in religion.

In an era of religious fanaticism and violence, many today are struggling to harmonize the same sometimes conflicting loyalties that shaped the lives of James and Schweitzer. Seeking to lead lives that matter, they want to think carefully about the world even as they retain their faith in ultimate and often mysterious powers to which they are obedient, which sometimes summon them to noble tasks, and which nurture within them aspirations that they do not fully understand. They want to remain faithful to their own religious traditions, even as they continue to honor and to learn from other religious traditions and from secular traditions like Democracy as well.

WILLIAM JAMES

"What Makes a Life Significant?"

William James (1842-1910) was a renowned psychologist, philosopher, and popular lecturer. He is probably remembered most for his 1905 Gifford Lectures, published as *The Varieties of Religious Experience*, and for his *Pragmatism*, one of the foundational works in a distinctively American school of philosophy that he helped to establish, along with his contemporary, Charles Saunders Peirce, and his heir, John Dewey. The following essay, "What Makes a Life Significant?" exhibits his characteristically exploratory and accessible style, having originally been delivered as a lecture to college students.

In the essay, James first suggests that a significant life must be one that overcomes great resistance in a struggle against malevolent forces, a life led by only a few heroes or heroines who attain immortal fame. Later, he revises that view to suggest that a significant life is possible for everyone, perhaps especially for those ordinary laborers who struggle daily to earn a living in ways that are often exemplary. Which of the two views seems more plausible to you? Later in the essay, James suggests that ideals are a large part, at least half, of what makes lives significant. Are some ideals more worthy of our life's devotion than others? Is there any way of distinguishing between admirable devotion to an ideal and dangerous fanaticism?

As an example of a struggle that incorporates ideals and that is large enough to engage human energies and efforts, James discusses the "labor question," the effort to provide fair wages and conditions for workers, which was very much alive during the period in which he wrote. Which issues, questions, or struggles are most worthy of human devotion and energy today?

From *The Writings of William James,* ed. John McDermott (Chicago: University of Chicago Press, 1977), pp. 645-660.

. . . A few summers ago I spent a happy week at the famous Assembly Grounds on the borders of Chautauqua Lake [a center for the arts and education in upstate New York]. The moment one treads that sacred enclosure, one feels one's self in an atmosphere of success. Sobriety and industry, intelligence and goodness, orderliness and ideality, prosperity and cheerfulness, pervade the air. It is a serious and studious picnic on a gigantic scale. Here you have a town of many thousands of inhabitants, beautifully laid out in the forest and drained, and equipped with means for satisfying all the necessary lower and most of the superfluous higher wants of man. You have a first-class college in full blast. You have magnificent music — a chorus of seven hundred voices, with possibly the most perfect open-air auditorium in the world. You have every sort of athletic exercise from sailing, rowing, swimming, bicycling, to the ball-field and the more artificial doings which the gymnasium affords. You have kindergartens and model secondary schools. You have general religious services and special club-houses for the several sects. You have perpetually running soda-water fountains, and daily popular lectures by distinguished men. You have the best of company, and yet no effort. You have no zymotic diseases, no poverty, no drunkenness, no crime, no police. You have culture, you have kindness, you have cheapness, you have equality, you have the best fruits of what mankind has fought and bled and striven for under the name of civilization for centuries. You have, in short, a foretaste of what human society might be, were it all in the light, with no suffering and no dark corners.

I went in curiosity for a day. I stayed for a week, held spell-bound by the charm and ease of everything, by the middle-class paradise, without a sin, without a victim, without a blot, without a tear. ·

And yet what was my own astonishment, on emerging into the dark and wicked world again, to catch myself quite unexpectedly and involuntarily saying: "Ouf! what a relief! Now for something primordial and savage, even though it were as bad as an Armenian massacre, to set the balance straight again. This order is too tame, this culture too second-rate, this goodness too uninspiring. This human drama without a villain or a pang; this community so refined that ice-cream soda-water is the utmost offering it can make to the brute animal in man; this city simmering in the tepid lakeside sun; this atrocious harmlessness of all things, — I cannot abide with them. Let me take my chances again in the big outside worldly wilderness with all its sins and sufferings. There are the heights and depths, the precipices and the steep ideals, the gleams of the awful and the infinite; and there is more hope and help a thousand times than in this dead level and quintessence of every mediocrity."

Such was the sudden right-about-face performed for me by my lawless fancy! There had been spread before me the realization — on a small, sample scale of course — of all the ideals for which our civilization has been striving: security, intelligence, humanity, and order; and here was the instinctive hostile reaction, not of the natural man, but of a so-called cultivated man upon such a Utopia. There seemed thus to be a self-contradiction and paradox somewhere, which I, as a professor drawing a full salary, was in duty bound to unravel and explain, if I could.

So I meditated. And, first of all, I asked myself what the thing was that was so lacking in this Sabbatical city, and the lack of which kept one forever falling short of the higher sort of contentment. And I soon recognized that it was the element that gives to the wicked outer world all its moral style, expressiveness and picturesqueness, — the element of precipitousness, so to call it, of strength and strenuousness, intensity and danger. What excites and interests the looker-on at life, what the romances and the statues celebrate and the grim civic monuments remind us of, is the everlasting battle of the powers of light with those of darkness; with heroism, reduced to its bare chance, yet ever and anon snatching victory from the jaws of death. But in this unspeakable Chautauqua there was no potentiality of death in sight anywhere, and no point of the compass visible from which danger might possibly appear. The ideal was so completely victorious already that no sign of any previous battle remained, the place just resting on its oars. But what our human emotions seem to require is the sight of the struggle going on. The moment the fruits are being merely eaten, things become ignoble. Sweat and effort, human nature strained to its uttermost and on the rack, yet getting through alive, and then turning its back on its success to pursue another more rare and arduous still — this is the sort of thing the presence of which inspires us, and the reality of which it seems to be the function of all the higher forms of literature and fine art to bring home to us and suggest. At Chautauqua there were no racks, even in the place's historical museum; and no sweat, except possibly the gentle moisture on the brow of some lecturer, or on the sides of some player in the ball-field.

Such absence of human nature *in extremis* anywhere seemed, then, a sufficient explanation for Chautauqua's flatness and lack of zest.

But was not this a paradox well calculated to fill one with dismay? It looks indeed, thought I, as if the romantic idealists with their pessimism about our civilization were, after all, quite right. An irremediable flatness is coming over the world. Bourgeoisie and mediocrity, church sociables and teachers' conventions, are taking the place of the old heights and depths and romantic chiaroscuro. And, to get human life in its wild intensity, we must

16

in future turn more and more away from the actual, and forget it, if we can, in the romancer's or the poet's pages. The whole world, delightful and sinful as it may still appear for a moment to one just escaped from the Chautauquan enclosure, is nevertheless obeying more and more just those ideals that are sure to make of it in the end a mere Chautauqua Assembly on an enormous scale. *Was in Gesang soll leben muss im Leben untergehn.* ["That which should live in song must perish in life."] Even now, in our own country, correctness, fairness, and compromise for every small advantage are crowding out all other qualities. The higher heroisms and the old rare flavors are passing out of life.

With these thoughts in my mind, I was speeding with the train toward Buffalo, when, near that city, the sight of a workman doing something on the dizzy edge of a sky-scaling iron construction brought me to my senses very suddenly. And now I perceived, by a flash of insight, that I had been steeping myself in pure ancestral blindness, and looking at life with the eyes of a remote spectator. Wishing for heroism and the spectacle of human nature on the rack, I had never noticed the great fields of heroism lying round about me, I had failed to see it present and alive. I could only think of it as dead and embalmed, labelled and costumed, as it is in the pages of romance. And yet there it was before me in the daily lives of the laboring classes. Not in clanging fights and desperate marches only is heroism to be looked for, but on every railway bridge and fire-proof building that is going up to-day. On freight-trains, on the decks of vessels, in cattle-yards and mines, on lumber-rafts, among the firemen and the policemen, the demand for courage is incessant; and the supply never fails. There, every day of the year somewhere, is human nature *in extremis* for you. And wherever a scythe, an axe, a pick, or a shovel is wielded, you have it sweating and aching and with its powers of patient endurance racked to the utmost under the length of hours of the strain.

As I awoke to all this unidealized heroic life around me, the scales seemed to fall from my eyes; and a wave of sympathy greater than anything I had ever before felt with the common life of common men began to fill my soul. It began to seem as if virtue with horny hands and dirty skin were the only virtue genuine and vital enough to take account of. Every other virtue poses; none is absolutely unconscious and simple, and unexpectant of decoration or recognition, like this. These are our soldiers, thought I, these our sustainers, these the very parents of our life. Many years ago, when in Vienna, I had had a similar feeling of awe and reverence in looking at the peasant-women, in from the country on their business at the market for the day. Old hags many of them were, dried and brown and wrinkled, kerchiefed and short-petticoated, with thick wool stockings on their bony shanks, stumping through the glittering thoroughfares, looking neither to the right nor the left, bent on duty, envying nothing, humble-hearted, remote; — and yet at bottom, when you came to think of it, bearing the whole fabric of the splendors and corruptions of that city on their laborious backs. For where would any of it have been without their unremitting, unrewarded labor in the fields? And so with us: not to our generals and poets, I thought, but to the Italian and Hungarian laborers in the Subway, rather, ought the monuments of gratitude and reverence of a city like Boston to be reared.

If any of you have been readers of Tolstoï [Leo Tolstoy, the Russian author], you will see that I passed into a vein of feeling similar to his, with its abhorrence of all that conventionally passes for distinguished, and its exclusive deification of the bravery, patience, kindliness, and dumbness of the unconscious natural man.

Where now is *our* Tolstoï, I said, to bring the truth of all this home to our American bosoms, fill us with a better insight, and wean us away from that spurious literary romanticism on which our wretched culture — as it calls itself — is fed? Divinity lies all about us, and culture is too hide-bound to even suspect the fact. Could a Howells or a Kipling [prominent authors of the time] be enlisted in this mission? or are they still too deep in the ancestral blindness, and not humane enough for the inner joy and meaning of the laborer's existence to be really revealed? Must we wait for some one born and bred and living as a laborer himself, but who, by grace of Heaven, shall also find a literary voice?

And there I rested on that day, with a sense of widening of vision, and with what it is surely fair to call an increase of religious insight into life. In God's eyes the differences of social position, of intellect, of culture, of cleanliness, of dress, which different men exhibit, and all the other rarities and exceptions on which they so fantastically pin their pride, must be so small as practically quite to vanish; and all that should remain is the common fact that here we are, a countless multitude of vessels of life, each of us pent in to peculiar difficulties, with which we must severally struggle by using whatever of fortitude and goodness we can summon up. The exercise of the courage, patience, and kindness, must be the significant portion of the whole business; and the distinctions of position can only be a manner of diversifying the phenomenal surface upon which these underground virtues may manifest their effects. At this rate, the deepest human life is everywhere, is eternal. And, if any human attributes exist only in particular individuals, they must belong to the mere trapping and decoration of the surface-show.

Thus are men's lives levelled up as well as levelled down, — levelled up in their common inner meaning, levelled down in their outer gloriousness and show. Yet always, we must confess, this levelling insight tends to be obscured again; and always the ancestral blindness returns and wraps us up, so that we end once more by thinking that creation can be for no other purpose than to develop remarkable situations and conventional distinctions and merits. And then always some new leveller in the shape of a religious prophet has to arise — the Buddha, the Christ, or some Saint Francis, some Rousseau or Tolstoï — to redispel our blindness. Yet, little by little, there comes one stable gain; for the world does get more humane, and the religion of democracy tends toward permanent increase.

This, as I said, became for a time my conviction, and gave me great content. I have put the matter into the form of a personal reminiscence, so that I might lead you into it more directly and completely, and so save time. But now I am going to discuss the rest of it with you in a more impersonal way.

Tolstoï's levelling philosophy began long before he had the crisis of melancholy commemorated in that wonderful document of his entitled 'My Confession,' which led the way to his more specifically religious works. In his masterpiece 'War and Peace,' — assuredly the greatest of human novels, — the rôle of the spiritual hero is given to a poor little soldier named Karataïeff, so helpful, so cheerful, and so devout that, in spite of his ignorance and filthiness, the sight of him opens the heavens, which have been closed, to the mind of the principal character of the book; and his example evidently is meant by Tolstoï to let God into the world again for the reader. Poor little Karataïeff is taken prisoner by the French; and, when too exhausted by hardship and fever to march, is shot as other prisoners were in the famous retreat from Moscow. The last view one gets of him is his little figure leaning against a white birch-tree, and uncomplainingly awaiting the end.

"The more," writes Tolstoï in the work 'My Confession,' "the more I examined the life of these laboring folks, the more persuaded I became that they veritably have faith, and get from it alone the sense and the possibility of life.... Contrariwise to those of our own class, who protest against destiny and grow indignant at its rigor, these people receive maladies and misfortunes without revolt, without opposition, and with a firm and tranquil confidence that all had to be like that, could not be otherwise, and that it is all right so.... The more we live by our intellect, the less we understand the meaning of life. We see only a cruel jest in suffering and death, whereas these people live, suffer, and draw near to death with tranquillity, and oftener than not with joy.... There are enormous multitudes of them happy

19

with the most perfect happiness, although deprived of what for us is the sole good of life. Those who understand life's meaning, and know how to live and die thus, are to be counted not by twos, threes, tens, but by hundreds, thousands, millions. They labor quietly, endure privations and pains, live and die, and throughout everything see the good without seeing the vanity. I had to love these people. The more I entered into their life, the more I loved them; and the more it became possible for me to live, too. It came about not only that the life of our society, of the learned and of the rich, disgusted me — more than that, it lost all semblance of meaning in my eyes. All our actions, our deliberations, our sciences, our arts, all appeared to me with a new significance. I understood that these things might be charming pastimes, but that one need seek in them no depth, whereas the life of the hard-working populace, of that multitude of human beings who really contribute to existence, appeared to me in its true light. I understood that there veritably is life, that the meaning which life there receives is the truth; and I accepted it."

In a similar way does [Robert Louis] Stevenson appeal to our piety toward the elemental virtue of mankind. "What a wonderful thing," he writes, "is this Man! How surprising are his attributes! Poor soul, here for so little, cast among so many hardships, savagely surrounded, savagely descended, irremediably condemned to prey upon his fellow-lives, — who should have blamed him, had be been of a piece with his destiny and a being merely barbarous? . . . [Yet] it matters not where we look, under what climate we observe him, in what stage of society, in what depth of ignorance, burdened with what erroneous morality; in ships at sea, a man inured to hardship and vile pleasures, his brightest hope a fiddle in a tavern, and a bedizened trull who sells herself to rob him, and he, for all that, simple, innocent, cheerful, kindly like a child, constant to toil, brave to drown, for others; . . . in the slums of cities, moving among indifferent millions to mechanical employments, without hope of change in the future, with scarce a pleasure in the present, and yet true to his virtues, honest up to his lights, kind to his neighbors, tempted perhaps in vain by the bright gin-palace, . . . often repaying the world's scorn with service, often standing firm upon a scruple; . . . everywhere some virtue cherished or affected, everywhere some decency of thought and courage, everywhere the ensign of man's ineffectual goodness, — ah! if I could show you this! If I could show you these men and women all the world over, in every stage of history, under every abuse of error, under every circumstance of failure, without hope, without help, without thanks, still obscurely fighting the lost fight of virtue, still clinging to some rag of honor, the poor jewel of their souls."

All this is as true as it is splendid, and terribly do we need our Tolstoïs and Stevensons to keep our sense for it alive. Yet you remember the Irishman who, when asked, "Is not one man as good as another?" replied, "Yes; and a great deal better, too!" Similarly (it seems to me) does Tolstoï overcorrect our social prejudices, when he makes his love of the peasant so exclusive, and hardens his heart toward the educated man as absolutely as he does. Grant that at Chautauqua there was little moral effort, little sweat or muscular strain in view. Still, deep down in the souls of the participants we may be sure that something of the sort was hid, some inner stress, some vital virtue not found wanting when required. And, after all, the question recurs, and forces itself upon us: Is it so certain that the surroundings and circumstances of the virtue do make so little difference in the importance of the result? Is the functional utility, the worth to the universe of a certain definite amount of courage, kindliness, and patience, no greater if the possessor of these virtues is in an educated situation, working out far-reaching tasks, than if he be an illiterate nobody, hewing wood and drawing water, just to keep himself alive? Tolstoï's philosophy, deeply enlightening though it certainly is, remains a false abstraction. It savors too much of that Oriental pessimism and nihilism of his, which declares the whole phenomenal world and its facts and their distinctions to be a cunning fraud.

A mere bare fraud is just what our Western common sense will never believe the phenomenal world to be. It admits fully that the inner joys and virtues are the *essential* part of life's business, but it is sure that *some* positive part is also played by the adjuncts of the show. If it is idiotic in romanticism to recognize the heroic only when it sees it labelled and dressed-up in books, it is really just as idiotic to see it only in the dirty boots and sweaty shirt of some one in the fields. It is with us really under every disguise: at Chautauqua; here in your college; in the stock-yards and on the freight-trains; and in the czar of Russia's court. But, instinctively, we make a combination of two things in judging the total significance of a human being. We feel it to be some sort of a product (if such a product only could be calculated) of his inner virtue *and* his outer place, — neither singly taken, but both conjoined. If the outer differences had no meaning for life, why indeed should all this immense variety of them exist? They *must* be significant elements of the world as well.

Just test Tolstoï's deification of the mere manual laborer by the facts. This is what Mr. Walter Wyckoff, after working as an unskilled laborer in the demolition of some buildings at West Point, writes of the spiritual condition of the class of men to which he temporarily chose to belong: —

"The salient features of our condition are plain enough. We are grown men, and are without a trade. In the labor-market we stand ready to sell to the highest bidder our mere muscular strength for so many hours each day. We are thus in the lowest grade of labor. And, selling our muscular strength in the open market for what it will bring, we sell it under peculiar conditions. It is all the capital that we have. We have no reserve means of subsistence, and cannot, therefore, stand off for a 'reserve price.' We sell under the necessity of satisfying imminent hunger. Broadly speaking, we must sell our labor or starve; and, as hunger is a matter of a few hours, and we have no other way of meeting this need, we must sell at once for what the market offers for our labor.

"Our employer is buying labor in a dear market, and he will certainly get from us as much work as he can at the price. The gang-boss is secured for this purpose, and thoroughly does he know his business. He has sole command of us. He never saw us before, and he will discharge us all when the debris is cleared away. In the mean time he must get from us, if he can, the utmost of physical labor which we, individually and collectively, are capable of. If he should drive some of us to exhaustion, and we should not be able to continue at work, he would not be the loser; for the market would soon supply him with others to take our places.

"We are ignorant men, but so much we clearly see, — that we have sold our labor where we could sell it dearest, and our employer has bought it where he could buy it cheapest. He has paid high, and he must get all the labor that he can; and, by a strong instinct which possesses us, we shall part with as little as we can. From work like ours there seems to us to have been eliminated every element which constitutes the nobility of labor. We feel no personal pride in its progress, and no community of interest with our employer. There is none of the joy of responsibility, none of the sense of achievement, only the dull monotony of grinding toil, with the longing for the signal to quit work, and for our wages at the end.

"And being what we are, the dregs of the labor-market, and having no certainty of permanent employment, and no organization among ourselves, we must expect to work under the watchful eye of a gang-boss, and be driven, like the wage-slaves that we are, through our tasks.

"All this is to tell us, in effect, that our lives are hard, barren, hopeless lives."

And such hard, barren, hopeless lives, surely, are not lives in which one ought to be willing permanently to remain. And why is this so? Is it because they are so dirty? Well, Nansen grew a great deal dirtier on his polar expedition; and we think none the worse of his life for that. Is it the insensibility? Our soldiers have to grow vastly more insensible, and we extol them to the skies. Is it the poverty? Poverty has been reckoned the crowning beauty of many a heroic career. Is it the slavery to a task, the loss of finer pleasures? Such slavery and loss are of the very essence of the higher fortitude, and are always counted to its credit, — read the records of missionary devotion all over the world. It is not anyone of these things, then, taken by itself, — no, nor all of them together, — that make such a life undesirable. A man might in truth live like an unskilled laborer, and do the work of one, and yet count as one of the noblest of God's creatures. Quite possibly there were some such persons in the gang that our author describes; but the current of their souls ran underground; and he was too steeped in the ancestral blindness to discern it.

If there *were* any such morally exceptional individuals, however, what made them different from the rest? It can only have been this, — that their souls worked and endured in obedience to some inner *ideal*, while their comrades were not actuated by anything worthy of that name. These ideals of other lives are among those secrets that we can almost never penetrate, although something about the man may often tell us when they are there. In Mr. Wyckoff's own case we know exactly what the self-imposed ideal was. Partly he had stumped himself, as the boys say, to carry through a strenuous achievement; but mainly he wished to enlarge his sympathetic insight into fellow-lives. For this his sweat and toil acquire a certain heroic significance, and make us accord to him exceptional esteem. But it is easy to imagine his fellows with various other ideals. To say nothing of wives and babies, one may have been a convert of the Salvation Army, and had a nightingale singing of expiation and forgiveness in his heart all the while he labored. Or there might have been an apostle like Tolstoï himself, or his compatriot Bondareff, in the gang, voluntarily embracing labor as their religious mission. Class-loyalty was undoubtedly an ideal with many. And who knows how much of that higher manliness of poverty, of which Phillips Brooks [a prominent Episcopal minister] has spoken so penetratingly, was or was not present in that gang?

"A rugged, barren land," says Phillips Brooks, "is poverty to live in, — a land where I am thankful very often if I can get a berry or a root to eat. But living in it really, letting it bear witness to me of itself, not dishonoring it all the time by judging it after the standard of the other lands, gradually there come out its qualities. Behold! no land like this barren and naked land of poverty could show the moral geology of the world. See how the hard ribs . . . stand out strong and solid. No life like poverty could so get one to the heart of things and make men know their meaning, could so let us feel life and the world with all the soft cushions stripped off and thrown away. . . .

Poverty makes men come very near each other, and recognize each other's human hearts; and poverty, highest and best of all, demands and cries out for faith in God. . . . I know how superficial and unfeeling, how like mere mockery, words in praise of poverty may seem. . . . But I am sure that the poor man's dignity and freedom, his self-respect and energy, depend upon his cordial knowledge that his poverty is a true region and kind of life, with its own chances of character, its own springs of happiness and revelations of God. Let him resist the characterlessness which often goes with being poor. Let him insist on respecting the condition where he lives. Let him learn to love it, so that by and by, [if] he grows rich, he shall go out of the low door of the old familiar poverty with a true pang of regret, and with a true honor for the narrow home in which he has lived so long."

The barrenness and ignobleness of the more usual laborer's life consist in the fact that it is moved by no such ideal inner springs. The backache, the long hours, the danger, are patiently endured — for what? To gain a quid of tobacco, a glass of beer, a cup of coffee, a meal, and a bed, and to begin again the next day and shirk as much as one can. This really is why we raise no monument to the laborers in the Subway, even though they be our conscripts, and even though after a fashion our city is indeed based upon their patient hearts and enduring backs and shoulders. And this is why we do raise monuments to our soldiers, whose outward conditions were even brutaller still. The soldiers are supposed to have followed an ideal, and the laborers are supposed to have followed none.

You see, my friends, how the plot now thickens; and how strangely the complexities of this wonderful human nature of ours begin to develop under our hands. We have seen the blindness and deadness to each other which are our natural inheritance; and, in spite of them, we have been led to acknowledge an inner meaning which passeth show, and which may be present in the lives of others where we least descry it. And now we are led to say that such inner meaning can be *complete* and *valid for us also*, only when the inner joy, courage, and endurance are joined with an ideal.

But what, exactly, do we mean by an ideal? Can we give no definite account of such a word? To a certain extent we can. An ideal, for instance, must be something intellectually conceived, something of which we are not unconscious, if we have it; and it must carry with it that sort of outlook, uplift, and brightness that go with all intellectual facts. Secondly, there must be *novelty* in an ideal, — novelty at least for him whom the ideal grasps. Sodden routine is incompatible with ideality, although what is sodden routine for one person may be ideal novelty for another. This shows that there is nothing absolutely ideal: ideals are relative to the lives that entertain them. To keep out of the gutter is for us here no part of consciousness at all, yet for many of our brethren it is the most legitimately engrossing of ideals.

Now, taken nakedly, abstractly, and immediately, you see that mere ideals are the cheapest things in life. Everybody has them in some shape or other, personal or general, sound or mistaken, low or high; and the most worthless sentimentalists and dreamers, drunkards, shirks and verse-makers, who never show a grain of effort, courage, or endurance, possibly have them on the most copious scale. Education, enlarging as it does our horizon and perspective, is a means of multiplying our ideals, of bringing new ones into view. And your college professor, with a starched shirt and spectacles, would, if a stock of ideals were all alone by itself enough to render a life significant, be the most absolutely and deeply significant of men. Tolstoï would be completely blind in despising him for a prig, a pedant and a parody; and all our new insight into the divinity of muscular labor would be altogether off the track of truth.

But such consequences as this, you instinctively feel, are erroneous. The more ideals a man has, the more contemptible, on the whole, do you continue to deem him, if the matter ends there for him, and if none of the laboring man's virtues are called into action on his part, no courage shown, no privations undergone, no dirt or scars contracted in the attempt to get them realized. It is quite obvious that something more than the mere possession of ideals is required to make a life significant in any sense that claims the spectator's admiration. Inner joy, to be sure, it may *have,* with its ideals; but that is its own private sentimental matter. To extort from us, outsiders as we are, with our own ideals to look after, the tribute of our grudging recognition, it must back its ideal visions with what the laborers have, the sterner stuff of manly virtue; it must multiply their sentimental surface by the dimension of the active will, if we are to have *depth,* if we are to have anything cubical and solid in the way of character.

The significance of a human life for communicable and publicly recognizable purposes is thus the offspring of a marriage of two different parents, either of whom alone is barren. The ideals taken by themselves give no reality, the virtues by themselves no novelty. And let the orientalists and pessimists say what they will, the thing of deepest — or, at any rate, of comparatively deepest — significance in life does seem to be its character of *progress,* or that strange union of reality with ideal novelty which it continues from one moment to another to present. To recognize ideal novelty is the task of what we call intelligence. Not every one's intelligence can tell which novelties are ideal. For many the ideal thing will always seem to cling still to the older more familiar good. In this case character, though not significant totally, may be still significant pathetically. So, if we are to choose which is the more essential factor of human character, the fighting virtue or the intellectual breadth, we must side with Tolstoï, and choose that simple faithfulness to his light or darkness which any common unintellectual man can show.

But, with all this beating and tacking on my part, I fear you take me to be reaching a confused result. I seem to be just taking things up and dropping them again. First I took up Chautauqua, and dropped that; then Tolstoï and the heroism of common toil, and dropped them; finally, I took up ideals, and seem now almost dropping those. But please observe in what sense it is that I drop them. It is when they pretend *singly* to redeem life from insignificance. Culture and refinement all alone are not enough to do so. Ideal aspirations are not enough, when uncombined with pluck and will. But neither are pluck and will, dogged endurance and insensibility to danger enough, when taken all alone. There must be some sort of fusion, some chemical combination among these principles, for a life objectively and thoroughly significant to result.

Of course, this is a somewhat vague conclusion. But in a question of significance, of worth, like this, conclusions can never be precise. The answer of appreciation, of sentiment, is always a more or a less, a balance struck by sympathy, insight, and good will. But it is an answer, all the same, a real conclusion. And, in the course of getting it, it seems to me that our eyes have been opened to many important things. Some of you are, perhaps, more livingly aware than you were an hour ago of the depths of worth that lie around you, hid in alien lives. And, when you ask how much sympathy you ought to bestow, although the amount is, truly enough, a matter of ideal on your own part, yet in this notion of the combination of ideals with active virtues you have a rough standard for shaping your decision. In any case, your imagination is extended. You divine in the world about you matter for a little more humility on your own part, and tolerance, reverence, and love for others; and you gain a certain inner joyfulness at the increased importance of our common life. Such joyfulness is a religious inspiration and an element of spiritual health, and worth more than large amounts of that sort of technical and accurate information which we professors are supposed to be able to impart.

To show the sort of thing I mean by these words, I will just make one brief practical illustration, and then close.

We are suffering to-day in America from what is called the labor-question; and, when you go out into the world, you will each and all of you be caught up in its perplexities. I use the brief term labor-question to cover all sorts of anarchistic discontents and socialistic projects, and the conservative resistances which they provoke. So far as this conflict is unhealthy and regrettable, — and I think it is so only to a limited extent, — the unhealthiness consists solely in the fact that one-half of our fellow-countrymen remain entirely blind to the internal significance of the lives of the other half. They miss the joys and sorrows, they fail to feel the moral virtue, and they do not guess the presence of the intellectual ideals. They are at cross-purposes all along the line, regarding each other as they might regard a set of dangerously gesticulating automata, or, if they seek to get at the inner motivation, making the most horrible mistakes. Often all that the poor man can think of in the rich man is a cowardly greediness for safety, luxury, and effeminacy, and a boundless affectation. What he is, is not a human being, but a pocket-book, a bank-account. And a similar greediness, turned by disappointment into envy, is all that many rich men can see in the state of mind of the dissatisfied poor. And, if the rich man begins to do the sentimental act over the poor man, what senseless blunders does he make, pitying him for just those very duties and those very immunities which, rightly taken, are the condition of his most abiding and characteristic joys! Each, in short, ignores the fact that happiness and unhappiness and significance are a vital mystery; each pins them absolutely on some ridiculous feature of the external situation; and everybody remains outside of everybody else's sight.

Society has, with all this, undoubtedly got to pass toward some newer and better equilibrium, and the distribution of wealth has doubtless slowly got to change: such changes have always happened, and will happen to the end of time. But if, after all that I have said, any of you expect that they will make any *genuine vital difference* on a large scale, to the lives of our descendants, you will have missed the significance of my entire lecture. The solid meaning of life is always the same eternal thing, — the marriage, namely, of some unhabitual ideal, however special, with some fidelity, courage, and endurance; with some man's or woman's pains. — And, whatever or wherever life may be, there will always be the chance for that marriage to take place. Fitz-James Stephen wrote many years ago words to this effect more eloquent than any I can speak: "The 'Great Eastern,' or some of her successors," he said, "will perhaps defy the roll of the Atlantic, and cross the seas without allowing their passengers to feel that they have left the firm land. The voyage from the cradle to the grave may come to be performed with similar facility. Progress and science may perhaps enable untold millions to live and die without a care, without a pang, without an anxiety. They will have a pleasant passage and plenty of brilliant conversation. They will wonder that men ever believed at all in clanging fights and blazing towns and sinking ships and praying hands; and, when they come to the end of their course, they will go their way, and the place thereof will know them no more. But it seems unlikely that they will have such a knowledge of the great ocean on which they sail, with its storms and wrecks, its currents and icebergs, its huge waves and mighty winds, as those who battled with it for years together in the little craft, which, if they had few other merits, brought those who navigated them full into the presence of time and eternity, their maker and themselves, and forced them to have some definite view of their relations to them and to each other."

In this solid and tridimensional sense, so to call it, those philosophers are right who contend that the world is a standing thing, with no progress, no real history. The changing conditions of history touch only the surface of the show. The altered equilibriums and redistributions only diversify our opportunities and open chances to us for new ideals. But, with each new ideal that comes into life, the chance for a life based on some old ideal will vanish; and he would needs be a presumptuous calculator who should with confidence say that the total sum of significances is positively and absolutely greater at any one epoch than at any other of the world.

I am speaking broadly, I know, and omitting to consider certain qualifications in which I myself believe. But one can only make one point in one lecture, and I shall be well content if I have brought my point home to you this evening in even a slight degree. *There are compensations:* and no outward changes of condition in life can keep the nightingale of its eternal meaning from singing in all sorts of different men's hearts. That is the main fact to remember. If we could not only admit it with our lips, but really and truly believe it, how our convulsive insistencies, how our antipathies and dreads of each other, would soften down! If the poor and the rich could look at each other in this way, *sub specie æternitatis,* how gentle would grow their disputes! what tolerance and good humor, what willingness to live and let live, would come into the world!

ALBERT SCHWEITZER

"I Resolve to Become a Jungle Doctor"

Albert Schweitzer (1875-1965) was an organist, organ-builder, philosopher, theologian, and, for many years, a doctor in equatorial Africa. An internationally famous lecturer and humanitarian, he wrote on subjects ranging from the music of J. S. Bach to the quest for the historical Jesus to world religions. Over time he developed a distinctive ethical and religious credo that he called simply "A Reverence for Life." In 1953, he was awarded the Nobel Peace Prize. His work below is chapter 9 from what he regarded as his most important work, the autobiographical *Out of My Life and Thought*, published in 1931. People of all ages and many nations still find this telling of his own story both instructive and inspiring.

Young people who say they hope to become doctors or missionaries in equatorial Africa or some other challenging and remote locale are often met with deep suspicion, today no less than in Schweitzer's time. Many people view such aspirations as stereotypically romantic or hopelessly idealistic or suspiciously paternalistic, even condescending. In this passage Schweitzer describes some of the arguments people made against his plans. Notice the reasons he gives for his decision, the steps he took in arriving at it, and the exchanges he had with those who criticized it. At what points do you agree or disagree with his critics? What do you make of the fact that Schweitzer almost always discouraged others from embarking on risky and exceptional ventures like the one he himself undertook?

On October 13, 1905, I dropped into a letter box on the avenue de la Grande Armée in Paris letters to my parents and to some of my closest friends tell-

---

From Albert Schweitzer, *Out of My Life and Thought* (Baltimore: The Johns Hopkins University Press, 1998), pp. 81-95; originally in English from (New York: Henry Holt and Company, 1933), pp. 102-118.

ing them that at the beginning of the winter term I would embark on the study of medicine with the idea of later going out to equatorial Africa as a doctor. In one letter I submitted my resignation from the post of principal of the Collegium Wilhelmitanum (the theological seminary of St. Thomas) because of the time my studies would require. The plan I hoped to realize had been in my mind for some time. Long ago in my student days I had thought about it. It struck me as inconceivable that I should be allowed to lead such a happy life while I saw so many people around me struggling with sorrow and suffering. Even at school I had felt stirred whenever I caught a glimpse of the miserable home surroundings of some of my classmates and compared them with the ideal conditions in which we children of the parsonage at Günsbach had lived. At the university, enjoying the good fortune of studying and even getting some results in scholarship and the arts, I could not help but think continually of others who were denied that good fortune by their material circumstances or their health.

One brilliant summer morning at Günsbach, during the Whitsuntide holidays — it was in 1896 — as I awoke, the thought came to me that I must not accept this good fortune as a matter of course, but must give something in return.

While outside the birds sang I reflected on this thought, and before I had gotten up I came to the conclusion that until I was thirty I could consider myself justified in devoting myself to scholarship and the arts, but after that I would devote myself directly to serving humanity. I had already tried many times to find the meaning that lay hidden in the saying of Jesus: "Whosoever would save his life shall lose it, and whosoever shall lose his life for My sake and the Gospel's shall save it." Now I had found the answer. I could now add outward to inward happiness.

What the character of my future activities would be was not yet clear to me. I left it to chance to guide me. Only one thing was certain, that it must be direct human service, however inconspicuous its sphere.

I naturally thought first of some activity in Europe. I formed a plan for taking charge of and educating abandoned or neglected children, then making them pledge to help children later on in a similar situation in the same way. When in 1903, as director of the theological seminary I moved into my roomy and sunny official quarters on the second floor of the College of St. Thomas, I was in a position to begin the experiment. I offered help now in one place, now in another, but always to no avail. The charters of the organizations that looked after destitute and abandoned children had made no provisions for accepting volunteers. For example, when the Strasbourg orphanage burned down, I offered to take in a few boys temporarily, but the superintendent did not even let me finish my sentence. I made similar attempts elsewhere also in vain.

For a time I thought I would someday devote myself to tramps and discharged convicts. To prepare myself for this I joined the Reverend Augustus Ernst at St. Thomas in an undertaking he had begun. Between one and two in the afternoon he remained at home ready to speak to anyone who came to him asking for help or a night's lodging. He did not, however, give the applicant money, nor did he make him wait until the information about his circumstances could be confirmed. Instead he would offer to look up the applicant in his home or shelter that very afternoon and verify the information he had been given about the situation. After this, he would give him all necessary assistance for as long as was needed. How many bicycle rides did we make into town or the suburbs, and quite often only to find that the applicant was unknown at the address he had given. In many cases, however, it provided an opportunity for giving appropriate help, with knowledge of the circumstances. I also had friends who kindly contributed money to this cause.

As a student, I had been active in social service as a member of the student association known as the Diaconate of St. Thomas, which held its meetings in the St. Thomas seminary. Each of us had a certain number of poor families assigned to him, which he was to visit every week, taking some aid and then reporting about their situation. The funds we thus distributed we collected from members of the old Strasbourg families who supported this undertaking, begun by earlier generations and now carried on by ourselves. Twice a year, if I remember correctly, each of us had to make a fixed number of financial appeals. For me, being shy and rather awkward in society, these visits were a torture. I believe that in this preparatory experience of soliciting funds, which I had to do much more of in later years, I sometimes showed myself extremely unskillful. However, I learned through them that soliciting with tact and restraint is better appreciated than any sort of aggressive approach, and also that correct soliciting methods include the friendly acceptance of refusal.

In our youthful inexperience we no doubt often failed, in spite of our best intentions, to use the money entrusted to us in the wisest way. The expectations of the givers were, however, fulfilled with respect to their purpose — that young men should devote themselves to serve the poor. For that reason I think with deep gratitude of those who met our efforts with so much understanding and generosity, and hope that many students may have the privilege of working as recruits in the struggle against poverty.

As I worried about the homeless and former convicts it became clear to me that they could only be effectively helped if many individuals devoted themselves to them. At the same time, however, I realized that in many cases individuals could only accomplish their tasks in collaboration with official organizations. But what I wanted was an absolutely personal and independent activity.

Although I was resolved to put my services at the disposal of some organization if it should become really necessary, I nonetheless never gave up the hope of finding an activity to which I could devote myself as an individual and as a wholly free agent. I have always considered it an ever renewed grace that I could fulfill this profound desire.

One morning in the autumn of 1904 I found on my writing table in the seminary one of the green-covered magazines in which the Paris Missionary Society (La Société Evangélique des Missions à Paris) reported on its activities every month. A Miss Scherdlin used to pass them on to me. She knew that in my youth I had been impressed by the letters from Mr. Casalis, one of the first missionaries of this society. My father had read them to us in his mission services.

Without paying much attention, I leafed through the magazine that had been put on my table the night before. As I was about to turn to my studies, I noticed an article with the headline "Les besoins de la Mission du Congo" ("The needs of the Congo Mission," in the *Journal des Missions Evangéliques*, June 1904). It was by Alfred Boegner, the president of the Paris Missionary Society, an Alsatian, who complained in it that the mission did not have enough people to carry on its work in the Gaboon, the northern province of the Congo colony. The writer expressed the hope that his appeal would bring some of those "on whom the Master's eyes already rested" to a decision to offer themselves for this urgent work. The article concluded: "Men and women who can reply simply to the Master's call, 'Lord, I am coming,' those are the people the Church needs." I finished my article and quietly began my work. My search was over.

I spent my thirtieth birthday a few months later like the man in the parable who, "desiring to build a tower, first calculates the cost of completion whether he has the means to complete it." The result was a resolve to realize my plan of direct human service in equatorial Africa.

Aside from one trustworthy friend, no one knew of my intention. When it became known through the letters I had sent from Paris, I had hard battles to fight with my relatives and friends. They reproached me more for not taking them into my confidence and discussing the decision with them than they did for the enterprise itself. With this secondary issue they tormented me beyond measure during those difficult weeks. That theological friends should outdo the others in their protests struck me as all the more absurd because they had no doubt all preached a fine sermon — perhaps a very fine one — that quoted Paul's declaration in his letter to the Galatians that he "did not confer with flesh or blood" before he knew what he would do for Jesus.

My relatives and friends reproached me for the folly of my enterprise. They said I was a man who was burying the talent entrusted to him and wanted to trade in false currency. I ought to leave work among Africans to those who would not thereby abandon gifts and achievements in scholarship and the arts. Widor, who loved me as a son, scolded me for acting like a general who, rifle in hand, insists on fighting in the firing line (there was no talk about trenches at that time). A lady who was filled with the modern spirit proved to me that I could do much more by lecturing on behalf of medical help for Africans than I could by the course of action I contemplated. The aphorism from Goethe's *Faust,* "In the beginning was the Deed," was now out of date, she said. "Today propaganda is the mother of events."

In the many adversarial debates I had to endure with people who passed for Christians, it amazed me to see them unable to perceive that the desire to serve the love preached by Jesus may sweep a man into a new course of life. They read in the New Testament that it can do so, and found it quite in order there.

I had assumed that familiarity with the sayings of Jesus would give a much better comprehension of what to popular logic is not rational. Several times, indeed, my appeal to the obedience that Jesus' command of love requires under certain circumstances earned me an accusation of conceit. How I suffered to see so many people assuming the right to tear open the doors and shutters of my inner self!

In general, neither allowing them to see that I was hurt nor letting them know the thought that had given birth to *my* resolution was of any use. They thought there must be something behind it all, and guessed at disappointment with the slow development of my career. For this there were no grounds at all, in that, even as a young man, I had received as much recognition as others usually get only after a whole life of toil and struggle. Unhappy love was another reason alleged for my decision.

The attitude of people who did not try to explore my feelings, but regarded me as a young man not quite right in the head and treated me with correspondingly affectionate ridicule, represented a real kindness.

I felt it to be quite natural in itself that family and friends should challenge the rationality of my plan. As one who demands that idealists should be sober in their views, I was aware that every venture down an untrodden path is a venture that looks sensible and likely to be successful only under unusual circumstances. In my own case I held the venture to be justified, because I had considered it for a long time and from every point of view, and I thought that I had good health, sound nerves, energy, practical common sense, toughness, prudence, very few wants, and everything else that might be necessary for the pursuit of my idea. I believed, further, that I had the inner fortitude to endure any eventual failure of my plan.

As a man of independent action, I have since that time been approached for my opinion and advice by many people who wanted to risk a similar venture. Only in comparatively few cases have I taken the responsibility of giving them encouragement. I often had to recognize that the need "to do something special" was born of a restless spirit. Such people wanted to dedicate themselves to larger tasks because those that lay nearest did not satisfy them. Often, too, it was evident that they were motivated by quite secondary considerations. Only a person who finds value in any kind of activity and who gives of himself with a full sense of service has the right to choose an exceptional task instead of following a common path. Only a person who feels his preference to be a matter of course, not something out of the ordinary, and who has no thought of heroism but only of a duty undertaken with sober enthusiasm, is capable of becoming the sort of spiritual pioneer the world needs. There are no heroes of action — only heroes of renunciation and suffering. Of these there are plenty. But few of them are known, and even they not to the crowd, but to the few. Carlyle's *On Heroes and Hero-Worship* is not a profound book.

The majority of those who feel the impulse and are actually capable of devoting their lives to independent action are compelled by circumstances to renounce that course. As a rule they have to provide for one or more dependents, or they have to stay with their profession in order to earn a living. Only a person who, thanks to his own efforts or the devotion of friends, is free from material needs can nowadays take the risk of undertaking such a personal task.

This was not so much the case in earlier times because anyone who gave up remunerative work could still hope to get through life somehow or other, but anyone thinking of doing such a thing in the difficult economic conditions of today runs the risk of coming to grief both materially and spiritually.

I know not only by what I have observed but also by experience that there are worthy and capable people who have had to renounce a course of independent action that would have been of great value to the world because of circumstances that made it impossible.

Those who are given the chance to embark on a life of independent action must accept their good fortune in a spirit of humility. They must often think of those who, though equally willing and capable, were not in a position to do the same. And as a rule, they must temper their own strong determination with humility. Almost always they must search and wait until they find a path that will permit the action they long to take. Fortunate are those who have received more years of creative work than years of searching and waiting. Fortunate those who succeed in giving themselves genuinely and completely.

These favored souls must also be humble so as not to get irritated by the resistance they encounter, but to accept it as inevitable. Anyone who proposes to do good must not expect people to roll any stones out of his way, and must calmly accept his lot even if they roll a few more into it. Only force that in the face of obstacles becomes stronger can win. Force that is used only to revolt wastes itself.

Of all the will toward the ideal in mankind only a small part can manifest itself in public action. All the rest of this force must be content with small and obscure deeds. The sum of these, however, is a thousand times stronger than the acts of those who receive wide public recognition. The latter, compared to the former, are like the foam on the waves of a deep ocean.

The hidden forces of goodness are alive in those who serve humanity as a secondary pursuit, those who cannot devote their full life to it. The lot of most people is to have a job, to earn their living, and to assume for themselves a place in society through some kind of nonfulfilling labor. They can give little or nothing of their human qualities. The problems arising from progressive specialization and mechanization of labor can only be partly resolved through the concessions society is willing to make in its economic planning. It is always essential that the individuals themselves not suffer their fate passively, but expend all their energies in affirming their own humanity through some spiritual engagement, even if the conditions are unfavorable.

One can save one's life as a human being, along with one's professional existence, if one seizes every opportunity, however unassuming, to act humanly toward those who need another human being. In this way we serve both the spiritual and the good. Nothing can keep us from this second job of direct human service. So many opportunities are missed because we let them pass by.

Everyone in his own environment must strive to practice true humanity toward others. The future of the world depends on it.

Great values are lost at every moment because we miss opportunities, but the values that are turned into will and action constitute a richness that must not be undervalued. Our humanity is by no means as materialistic as people claim so complacently.

Judging by what I have learned about men and women, I am convinced that far more idealistic aspiration exists than is ever evident. Just as the rivers we see are much less numerous than the underground streams, so the idealism that is visible is minor compared to what men and women carry in their hearts, unreleased or scarcely released. Mankind is waiting and longing for those who can accomplish the task of untying what is knotted and bringing the underground waters to the surface.

What to my friends seemed most irrational in my plan was that I wanted to go to Africa, not as a missionary, but as a doctor. Already thirty years of age, I would burden myself with long and laborious study. I never doubted for an instant that these studies would require an immense effort, and I anticipated the coming years with anxiety. But the reasons that made me determined to enter into the service I had chosen as a doctor weighed so heavily that other considerations were as dust in the balance and counted for nothing.

I wanted to be a doctor so that I might be able to work without having to talk. For years I had been giving of myself in words, and it was with joy that I had followed the calling of theological teacher and preacher. But this new form of activity would consist not in preaching the religion of love, but in practicing it. Medical knowledge would make it possible for me to carry out my intention in the best and most complete way, wherever the path of service might lead me.

Given my choice of equatorial Africa, acquiring this knowledge was especially appropriate because in the district to which I planned to go a doctor was, according to the missionaries' reports, the most urgent of all its needs. In their reports and magazines they always regretted that they could not provide help for the Africans who came in great physical pain. I was greatly motivated to study medicine and become, one day, the doctor whom these unhappy people needed. Whenever I was tempted to feel that the years I should have to sacrifice were too long, I reminded myself that Hamilcar and Hannibal had prepared for their march on Rome by their slow and tedious conquest of Spain.

There was still one more reason why it seemed to be my destiny to become a doctor. From what I knew of the Paris Missionary Society, I could not but feel very doubtful that they would accept me as a missionary. . . .

I

VOCABULARIES

"Be Like Mike!" A television commercial of recent popularity used this slogan to invite viewers to emulate Michael Jordan, perhaps the best basketball player who has ever played the game. Of course, the advertisement that featured the slogan suggested that one could be like Michael Jordan simply by purchasing the same brand of shoes he wore. This is rather like suggesting that one could be like Jesus of Nazareth simply by wearing sandals like his. Even so, on the basis of sales records, many people apparently did "buy" the idea that they would eventually be like Mike if only they wore his shoes.

We may nevertheless wonder whether the millions of people around the globe who actually do want to be like Mike wish merely to imitate his choice of footwear. Something more complicated seems to be going on here. A much deeper and more encouraging human aspiration explains both the appeal of Michael Jordan and the success of the slogan "Be Like Mike!" People wish that they were as gifted and as disciplined as Michael Jordan in *some* area of life. They want to excel at something, beyond consumerism. Human beings still have hopes and dreams that are fed and informed by real or imagined images of what they would like to become.

A second implication of the fact that so many millions of people apparently want to be like Mike is even more encouraging. In some fields of human endeavor people still believe that it is possible to recognize genuine excellence. They can say with great confidence, "Michael Jordan was a better basketball player than (to take a tough case) Magic Johnson." Basketball fans at least believe that they can be as certain about their judgments of better and worse basketball playing as chemists believe that they can be certain about judgments of whether a given compound is sugar or salt.

But are people as ready and able to judge the relative excellence of whole lives as they are to judge the exercise of particular skills? When it comes to assessing the relative worth or significance of lives, our culture seems both hesitant and confused. Hesitations arise primarily from the considerations we examined in the general introduction to this anthology: we are committed to various notions of human equality that seem to preclude our making judgments about relative worth or merit that imply that objective standards of worthiness or goodness exist. Meanwhile, confusions abound. How many of the people who admire Michael Jordan as a basketball player assume that excellence on the basketball court is the same thing as human excellence in general? Some believe that excelling in any skill leads directly to an excellent life overall. They want to "be like Mike" in every way simply because Mike plays basketball very well. Others act as though popularity and virtue were one and the same thing. They consult rock stars and movie actors for advice about politics and religion, apparently believing that mere fame evinces wisdom about everything that matters in human life. Many social observers think that the growth of such confusions in our culture has created a "cult of celebrity," the worshipful adulation of men and women whose only claim to honor and respect is popularity.

These confusions have created a somewhat desperate situation. We want to make good judgments about how we should live. We want to learn how to lead lives that really matter. But we don't know how to talk very well or think very well about these things. Strange as it may seem, we sometimes do not even know what we really think. We can't even give voice to our opinions, much less correct them if they prove to be mistaken. Our growing inability to articulate the point and importance of our own lives may go far to explain why many feel that their lives do not really have a point or that they do not finally matter at all.

Some of our best philosophers and social critics have thought that our troubles do indeed stem from our loss of any consistent and coherent way of talking about the things that matter most deeply to us. Instead, we have several "vocabularies" that have developed over the course of many years of thinking and speaking, and we cobble these words and ideas together to try to make sense of our lives, even though they sometimes conflict. So our confusions are built into this effort to think in several languages at the same time. It is like trying to speak French, Hindi, and English in the same sentence. No wonder we are confused!

Can we possibly become more clear about what we really think and about what really might be true in the midst of a given situation? More important, can we make genuine progress in helping one another determine whether some lives might really be more worth living than others? Yes, we can. First, we need to become aware of the various languages or "vocabularies" we are already using to make sense of these things. Second, we need to decide which of these languages or which combination of them will actually help us to make good judgments about how we might lead lives that matter.

The three following groups of readings in this part of the anthology represent and explore three different vocabularies — authenticity, virtue, and vocation — that people use today in their efforts to think and talk about the kind of life that they most admire and would therefore most like to lead.

Authenticity
Charles Taylor, *The Ethics of Authenticity*
Elizabeth Cady Stanton, *Solitude of Self*

Virtue
Aristotle, *Nicomachean Ethics*
Theodore Roosevelt, *An Autobiography*

Vocation
Matthew 20:20-28
Lee Hardy, *The Fabric of This World*
Gary Badcock, *A Way of Life*
Dietrich Bonhoeffer, *Ethics*
Frederick Buechner, *Wishful Thinking*
Will Campbell, "Vocation as Grace"

The philosopher Charles Taylor, perhaps more than anyone else among our contemporaries, has tried to help us understand how and why most people today speak the way they do about what they should do and how they should live. He describes this way of talking as "the ethics of authenticity," named after the central value that gives this manner of thinking its distinctively modern character. Authenticity simply means being true to ourselves. We must, according to this way of thinking, look within ourselves to find what authorizes our choices and thereby determine what we should do and what we should wish to become.

Does Taylor really capture the way most of us think? He claims that people in Western democracies like ours value free choice above almost anything else. So we are sometimes prone to talk as though a way of living is good or significant simply because we have freely chosen it. We worry over whether any choice that we have made is "really our choice" more than we worry over whether what we have chosen is really choice-worthy. So we try to help each other to "get in touch with ourselves." We want to be as sure as we can be that our life choices are not made for us by someone else — parents, friends, peers, or teachers. And we are very uneasy about the idea that someone who has really made a free choice might also have made a bad choice.

Is this the way you talk and think on your campuses or in your workplaces or around your dinner tables? Do you feel awkward about criticizing someone else's life choices? Do you doubt whether some free choices are better or worse than others? When you are asked to account for why your friend who is a very gifted science student has nonetheless decided to become a beach bum, do you defend him by saying that this is "just his thing"? Do you find yourself making choices by deciding against whatever others who are important to you recommend, just to show that your choices are really your own? If your answer to most of these questions is yes, you are probably manifesting what Taylor calls "soft relativism," a sloppy and ultimately trivial form of the ethics of authenticity.

Taylor wants not simply to show us how we think and talk about what matters in life these days. He also wants to help us see what assumptions are behind that particular way of talking. And he wants to show us how we came to talk the way we do. He wants us to reflect critically on the way we talk. Do we really believe that all ways of living are equally choice-worthy, equally significant? And when we look into ourselves, what do we find there? Do we find just one authentic voice, our own voice, or do we find many voices that together make up the selves that we are?

The ideal of authenticity has been very "liberating" for many and various oppressed groups over the course of American history. As Taylor has shown, the vocabulary of choice and the solitary self has been linked to ideas of individualism. Elizabeth Cady Stanton, speaking before a Congressional committee at the end of the nineteenth century, invoked ideals of the self, free choice, and individualism to defend and advance the cause of women's liberation in the United States. She argued then, following the logic that Taylor would describe a century later, that we are all sovereign, independent selves and that our relationships to others are secondary, often instrumental, to our personal choices and purposes. She also used another "vocabulary," however, when she began to sketch the kind of character that human beings need to have in order to live well and responsibly, suggesting that some "selves" might be more admirable than others and that some ways of living might be more choice-worthy than others.

When we begin to talk and think like people who believe that some choices really are better or worse than others and that some people's lives really are better or worse than those of other people, we are often using another vocabulary. That way of speaking does not include the idea of authenticity, but it does include words like "virtue," "excellence," and "choice-worthiness," and it goes back at least as far as 400 BCE. The ancient Greek philosopher Aristotle, for example, believed that there is only one way of living that is best for all human beings. He tried to provide a sketch of such a life and to show us why, if we are thinking honestly and carefully, we should all choose that way of life over others. He argued that such a life would have happiness as its end, but he meant something very different from what we mean by the word "happiness." For him, happiness was not a feeling; it was activity in accordance with virtue. Leading a life that mattered meant leading a life that exhibited a firm, admirable character. Like most of us, Aristotle admired people who live honestly, courageously, justly, wisely, moderately, and generously. He also admired people who enjoyed some very good and enduring friendships.

We are not, in other words, as far from Aristotle as we may think, even though we do sometimes use slogans that he would have disdained, like "do your own thing." As much as we may pretend that it is bad to "be judgmental," we are always making judgments about other people. Are they trustworthy? Should we befriend them? Can we rely upon them to help us in dangerous situations? Would we loan them money? Would we rather be like Jill or like Sarah? Our lives sometimes literally depend upon how well we make these judgments about others. These judgments always consist of two parts. First, what is this person really like? Second, is this person admirable? Is this a person of good character?

We might wonder why so many of us make judgments all of the time even as we insist that it is not good to be judgmental. Or why do so many of us say that one way of living is as good as any other even as we privately believe no such thing? It may be that we lack confidence in the judgments we make, so we refuse to make any. Or perhaps we don't want to offend people, and we think that most of our contemporaries would be offended by the idea that some people really do lead more admirable lives than others. Whatever the case, we cannot think very long or very well about how to lead lives that matter without *some* of Aristotle's vocabulary of virtue.

Nor can we think very well about the idea of *success* without some of Aristotle's vocabulary of virtue and character. Theodore Roosevelt, in his autobiography, wrote about two kinds of success, one that a few people achieve effortlessly through the exercise of extraordinary gifts, the other that all people can achieve through the diligent and arduous development of those gifts that they do possess. The former president counted himself as part of the latter group, and he, like Aristotle, spoke of the cultivation of aptitudes in terms of virtue and character. We should ask ourselves whether we think of success as something absolute and objective, involving the satisfaction of a common standard, or whether we think of it as something relative and partly subjective, involving a different level of achievement for each person, depending upon his or her natural talents and aptitudes.

Though many of us will agree with Aristotle when he argues that some lives are more virtuous or more excellent than others, and agree with Roosevelt when he argues that some lives are more successful than others, we may well doubt whether some genuinely virtuous or successful lives are more *significant* than others. Whom would we admire more: a generous person who gives ten percent of her $20,000 per year income anonymously to a campus beautification project or a person who gives ten percent of his

$500,000,000 fortune to fund on the same campus a concert hall that is named after him? When they recently discussed this question, almost all of the students in a college seminar admired the woman more than the man. First, they argued, she had less to give, so her ten percent was marginally more generous than the ten percent given by the multi-millionaire. Second, she was not at all moved by a desire for recognition or gratitude. The multi-millionaire *may* have been moved by such considerations, since the concert hall was named after him.

But were these students right? Aristotle would argue that the woman in this case is generous, whereas the man might well be both generous and magnificent. Should his gift, because of its magnitude and because it was given to what many would deem a worthier cause, be more admired than the woman's gift? If both the man and the woman were habitually and happily charitable, they would be equal in generosity. But only one of them could be, in addition, magnificent. Before we reject Aristotle's view, we should ask ourselves what we would do if we were choosing a basketball team. If we wanted to win games, would we choose people who tried hard but were relatively short, slow, and weak or people who tried hard and were relatively tall, fast, and strong? Which type of player would be more worthy of regard, more significant to the success of the team?

Now suppose that in thinking about whom to admire more, the generous man or the generous woman in the example above, our decision depended upon which one of them was more important to the functioning of a good college. Would that decision depend upon the *size* of the benefaction or upon its *objective* or upon its *motive* or upon some combination of these considerations? And when we are thinking about lives that matter, can we escape altogether the idea that one measure of a human life's significance is the number of people whose lives have been improved for the better by that life's actions and benefactions? Can we assess the relative significance of a life by inquiring into the relative importance of that life to a well-functioning society or political community?

Suppose now that our frame of reference for making such judgments expands from our society or state to a larger horizon of meaning and significance, to the "kingdom of heaven," for example. The reading that introduces the vocabulary of Christian vocation assumes exactly this frame of reference, and it stands in sharp contrast to Aristotle's notions of magnificence or greatness. Or does it? Does Jesus of Nazareth discuss greatness in the same way that Aristotle does in answer to the mother who is worried about her sons' relative standing in the kingdom of heaven?

For Christians, the vocabulary of vocation provides a way of thinking about how to live, both in terms of the different kinds of work they do and in terms of the overall character and point of their lives. Aristotle was not much interested in the various kinds of paid employment, since he believed that most forms of work were at best necessary and irksome, at worst slavish and degrading. Writing in the context of a slave society, Aristotle developed an ethics for a small percentage of the population, for free men. The arenas within which these men lived the life of virtue included the battlefield, the political assembly, and the bonds of friendship among citizens. Charles Taylor notes that with the Protestant Reformation and its reformulation of the idea of Christian vocation, the primary arenas for human achievement broadened to include two domains — the realm of production or paid employment and the realm of reproduction or the family. Thus, for Christians and non-Christians alike, the idea of vocation provides a vocabulary for thinking about the relationship between what human beings do to earn a living and what kind of life human beings should live. And the idea is far less exclusive than Aristotle's account, since ordinary women, tradesmen, and physical laborers, indeed all adult human beings, are included.

Christian writers have not been in agreement about the concept of vocation, however. Martin Luther, the first of the Reformers to formulate a radically new understanding of the Christian idea of vocation, argued that any kind of regular and legitimate work in the world — manual labor, parenting, and civic activity — could be a vocation or a calling so long as the Christian did that work out of love for God in service to humankind. Most Protestant Christian writers on the subject of vocation ever since have agreed with Luther on this point. Opinions soon diverge, however. Some writers, like the seventeenth-century Anglican divine, William Perkins, argued that all Christians have two callings, a general calling to the Christian life and a particular calling to some kind of productive work. Others have insisted that we have only one Christian calling, not two as Perkins believed. So, for example, the contemporary theologian Gary Badcock has argued that all Christians are called to share in Christ's mission of love and service to the world, but he does not believe that we should think of all particular jobs as callings. The contemporary philosopher Lee Hardy agrees with Luther in thinking that we have multiple callings as workers, children, neighbors, and citizens, but he also believes, like Perkins, that our primary, particular calling is our paid employment and that our problem is to discern and to help one another discern what kind of work we are really called by God to do.

Dietrich Bonhoeffer, a Christian theologian active in Germany before and during the Second World War, thought that the idea of vocation had been deeply misunderstood, especially by those among his fellow Lutherans who had used the concept as a way of vindicating the *status quo* and validating such institutions as marriage and wage labor as preferable to all other social or economic arrangements. Like Badcock, he stressed the "cost of discipleship" wherever we might find ourselves "stationed" in the world. Beyond this, Bonhoeffer also argued that God's call summons us into responsibility to and for our fellow human beings and for all of creation. Thus Christians are constantly summoned to break through the sometimes rigid circumscriptions of their roles as parents, citizens, or professionals. The responsibilities of a doctor, for example, might at some time include defending medical science itself, not simply caring for the patients immediately before her.

The contemporary theologian and novelist Frederick Buechner has tried to formulate the substance of vocation in a way that is exact yet flexible enough to take account of an almost infinite variety of gifts and circumstances. His short formulation of the nature of vocation is perhaps the most widely quoted one today. And the Christian novelist and preacher Will Campbell has reminded us that vocation is often as much a communal as it is an individual enterprise.

However much these writers disagree with one another, all of them can help us, Christian and non-Christian alike, to think carefully about the relationship between what we do to earn a living and the quality and significance of our lives overall.

Authenticity

CHARLES TAYLOR

The Ethics of Authenticity

Charles Taylor (1931-   ) is a Canadian philosopher who has written on a wide variety of subjects, especially on ethics and identity. His largest and most influential work, *Sources of the Self* (1989), examines the historical and philosophical backgrounds to the ways in which those of us living in modern, Western societies have come to think about who we are and how we should live. The reading below is from a shorter work, *The Ethics of Authenticity*, which critically examines the distinctively modern way in which a large number of people in the West, perhaps a majority of them, speak about and think about their own lives and the lives of others.

The selection begins in the third chapter, which is entitled "The Sources of Authenticity." How does Taylor's account help you to understand such frequently heard phrases as "do your own thing" and "deciding for myself"? It looks like American popular culture is constantly offering us images of people whom we should emulate, as in the case of Michael Jordan above. Yet, according to Taylor, moderns are reluctant even to "find models to live by outside of ourselves." Is Taylor right? Is there some way to explain this apparent contradiction?

In the middle part of the excerpt below, Taylor tries to do something very important for the purposes of this entire anthology. He shows us why and how we must talk and reason with each other about the many questions that perplex us about our lives. It is not enough just to express ourselves and move on, agreeing to "accept all points of view." How does Taylor describe or propose that we go about helping one another to reach deeper truth about who we really are and how we should live?

Taylor says that questions of identity provide the indispensable back-

---

From Charles Taylor, *The Ethics of Authenticity* (Cambridge: Harvard University Press, 1991), pp. 25-53.

ground for questions about our desires and aspirations. Indeed, he argues that our identities were first formed in dialogue with others and that our identities continue to be "dialogically" formed. When we listen to ourselves to try to discover what we should do and who we should be, we often find several voices speaking to us, not one. My self is not one voice struggling to be heard but a medley of voices that sometimes sing in unison, sometimes in discord. More important still, we continue to define and discover our identities in company with others. Identity formation is a collective project.

Taylor thinks that it is "crazy" to think that we can simply *decide* what is significant for us or for others. Yet many of us speak and think as though this were possible. Do you agree with Taylor that we are deeply mistaken if we believe that significance is simply a matter of personal choice? "I can define my own identity," he writes, "only against a background of things that matter." Matter to whom?

The ethic of authenticity is something relatively new and peculiar to modern culture. Born at the end of the eighteenth century, it builds on earlier forms of individualism, such as the individualism of disengaged rationality, pioneered by Descartes, where the demand is that each person think self-responsibly for him- or herself, or the political individualism of Locke, which sought to make the person and his or her will prior to social obligation. But authenticity also has been in some respects in conflict with these earlier forms. It is a child of the Romantic period, which was critical of disengaged rationality and of an atomism that didn't recognize the ties of community.

One way of describing its development is to see its starting point in the eighteenth-century notion that human beings are endowed with a moral sense, an intuitive feeling for what is right and wrong. The original point of this doctrine was to combat a rival view, that knowing right and wrong was a matter of calculating consequences, in particular those concerned with divine reward and punishment. The notion was that understanding right and wrong was not a matter of dry calculation, but was anchored in our feelings. Morality has, in a sense, a voice within.

The notion of authenticity develops out of a displacement of the moral accent in this idea. On the original view, the inner voice is important because it tells us what is the right thing to do. Being in touch with our moral feelings would matter here, as a means to the end of acting rightly. What I'm calling the displacement of the moral accent comes about when being in touch takes on independent and crucial moral significance. It comes to be something we have to attain to be true and full human beings.

To see what is new in this, we have to see the analogy to earlier moral views, where being in touch with some source — God, say, or the Idea of the Good — was considered essential to full being. Only now the source we have to connect with is deep in us. This is part of the massive subjective turn of modern culture, a new form of inwardness, in which we come to think of ourselves as beings with inner depths. At first, this idea that the source is within doesn't exclude our being related to God or the Ideas; it can be considered our proper way to them. In a sense, it can be seen just as a continuation and intensification of the development inaugurated by Saint Augustine, who saw the road to God as passing through our own reflexive awareness of ourselves.

The first variants of this new view were theistic, or at least pantheist. This is illustrated by the most important philosophical writer who helped to bring about this change, Jean-Jacques Rousseau. I think Rousseau is important not because he inaugurated the change; rather I would argue that his great popularity comes in part from his articulating something that was already happening in the culture. Rousseau frequently presents the issue of morality as that of our following a voice of nature within us. This voice is most often drowned out by the passions induced by our dependence on others, of which the key one is "amour propre" or pride. Our moral salvation comes from recovering authentic moral contact with ourselves. Rousseau even gives a name to the intimate contact with oneself, more fundamental than any moral view, that is a source of joy and contentment: "le sentiment de l'existence." Rousseau also articulated a closely related idea in a most influential way. This is the notion of what I want to call self-determining freedom. It is the idea that I am free when I decide for myself what concerns me, rather than being shaped by external influences. It is a standard of freedom that obviously goes beyond what has been called negative liberty, where I am free to do what I want without interference by others because that is compatible with my being shaped and influenced by society and its laws of conformity. Self-determining freedom demands that I break the hold of all such external impositions, and decide for myself alone. . . .

But to return to the ideal of authenticity: it becomes crucially important because of a development that occurs after Rousseau and that I associate with Herder — once again its major early articulator rather than its originator. Herder put forward the idea that each of us has an original way of being human. Each person has his or her own "measure" is his way of putting it. This idea has entered very deep into modern consciousness. It is also new.

51

Before the late eighteenth century no one thought that the differences between human beings had this kind of moral significance. There is a certain way of being human that is *my* way. I am called upon to live my life in this way, and not in imitation of anyone else's. But this gives a new importance to being true to myself. If I am not, I miss the point of my life, I miss what being human is for *me*.

This is the powerful moral ideal that has come down to us. It accords crucial moral importance to a kind of contact with myself, with my own inner nature, which it sees as in danger of being lost, partly through the pressures towards outward conformity, but also because in taking an instrumental stance to myself, I may have lost the capacity to listen to this inner voice. And then it greatly increases the importance of this self-contact by introducing the principle of originality: each of our voices has something of its own to say. Not only should I not fit my life to the demands of external conformity; I can't even find the model to live by outside myself. I can find it only within.

Being true to myself means being true to my own originality, and that is something only I can articulate and discover. In articulating it, I am also defining myself. I am realizing a potentiality that is properly my own. This is the background understanding to the modern ideal of authenticity, and to the goals of self-fulfillment or self-realization in which it is usually couched. This is the background that gives moral force to the culture of authenticity, including its most degraded, absurd, or trivialized forms. It is what gives sense to the idea of "doing your own thing" or "finding your own fulfillment."

IV
Inescapable Horizons

This is a very rapid sketch of the origins of authenticity. I shall have to fill in more detail later. But for the moment it is enough to see what is involved in reasoning here. And so I want to take up the second controversial claim that I made at the end of the last section. Can one say anything in reason to people who are immersed in the contemporary culture of authenticity? Can you talk in reason to people who are deeply into soft relativism, or who seem to accept no allegiance higher than their own development — say, those who seem ready to throw away love, children, democratic solidarity, for the sake of some career advancement?

Well, how do we reason? Reasoning in moral matters is always reasoning with somebody. You have an interlocutor, and you start from where that person is, or with the actual difference between you; you don't reason from the ground up, as though you were talking to someone who recognized no moral demands whatever. A person who accepted no moral demands would be as impossible to argue with about right and wrong as would a person who refused to accept the world of perception around us be impossible to argue with about empirical matters.

But we are imagining discussing with people who are in the contemporary culture of authenticity. And that means that they are trying to shape their lives in the light of this ideal. We are not left with just the bare facts of their preferences. But if we start from the ideal, then we can ask: What are the conditions in human life of realizing an ideal of this kind? And what does the ideal properly understood call for? The two orders of questions interweave, or perhaps shade into each other. In the second, we are trying to define better what the ideal consists in. With the first, we want to bring out certain general features of human life that condition the fulfillment of this or any other ideal.

In what follows, I want to work out two lines of argument that can illustrate what is involved in this kind of questioning. The argument will be very sketchy, more in the nature of a suggestion of what a convincing demonstration might look like. The aim will be to give some plausibility to my second claim, that you can argue in reason about these matters, and hence to show that there is indeed a practical point in trying to understand better what authenticity consists in.

The general feature of human life that I want to evoke is its fundamentally *dialogical* character. We become full human agents, capable of understanding ourselves, and hence of defining an identity, through our acquisition of rich human languages of expression. For purposes of this discussion, I want to take "language" in a broad sense, covering not only the words we speak but also other modes of expression whereby we define ourselves, including the "languages" of art, of gesture, of love, and the like. But we are inducted into these in exchange with others. No one acquires the languages needed for self-definition on their own. We are introduced to them through exchanges with others who matter to us — what George Herbert Mead called "significant others." The genesis of the human mind is in this sense not "monological," not something each accomplishes on his or her own, but dialogical.

Moreover, this is not just a fact about *genesis*, which can be ignored later on. It's not just that we learn the languages in dialogue and then can go on to use them for our own purposes on our own. This describes our situation to some extent in our culture. We are expected to develop our own opinions, outlook, stances to things, to a considerable degree through solitary reflection. But this is not how things work with important issues, such as the definition of our identity. We define this always in dialogue with, sometimes in struggle against, the identities our significant others want to recognize in us. And even when we outgrow some of the latter — our parents, for instance — and they disappear from our lives, the conversation with them continues within us as long as we live.

So the contribution of significant others, even when it occurs at the beginning of our lives, continues throughout. Some people might be following me up to here, but still want to hold on to some form of the monological ideal. True, we can never liberate ourselves completely from those whose love and care shaped us early in life, but we should strive to define ourselves on our own to the fullest degree possible, coming as best we can to understand and thus gain some control over the influence of our parents, and avoiding falling into any further such dependencies. We will need relationships to fulfill but not to define ourselves.

This is a common ideal, but I think it seriously underestimates the place of the dialogical in human life. It still wants to confine it as much as possible to the genesis. It forgets how our understanding of the good things in life can be transformed by our enjoying them in common with people we love, how some goods become accessible to us only through such common enjoyment. Because of this, it would take a great deal of effort, and probably many wrenching break-ups, to *prevent* our identity being formed by the people we love. Consider what we mean by "identity." It is "who" we are, "where we're coming from." As such it is the background against which our tastes and desires and opinions and aspirations make sense. If some of the things I value most are accessible to me only in relation to the person I love, then she becomes internal to my identity.

To some people this might seem a limitation, from which one might aspire to free oneself. This is one way of understanding the impulse behind the life of the hermit, or to take a case more familiar to our culture, the solitary artist. But from another perspective, we might see even this as aspiring to a certain kind of dialogicality. In the case of the hermit, the interlocutor is God. In the case of the solitary artist, the work itself is addressed to a future audience, perhaps still to be created by the work itself. The very form of a work of art shows its character as *addressed*. But however one feels about it, the making and sustaining of our identity, in the absence of a heroic effort to break out of ordinary existence, remains dialogical throughout our lives.

I want to indicate below that this central fact has been recognized in the growing culture of authenticity. But what I want to do now is take this dialogical feature of our condition, on one hand, and certain demands inherent in the ideal of authenticity on the other, and show that the more self-centered and "narcissistic" modes of contemporary culture are manifestly inadequate. More particularly, I want to show that modes that opt for self-fulfillment without regard (a) to the demands of our ties with others or (b) to demands of any kind emanating from something more or other than human desires or aspirations are self-defeating, that they destroy the conditions for realizing authenticity itself. I'll take these in reverse order, and start with (b), arguing from the demands of authenticity itself as an ideal.

(1) When we come to understand what it is to define ourselves, to determine in what our originality consists, we see that we have to take as background some sense of what is significant. Defining myself means finding what is significant in my difference from others. I may be the only person with exactly 3,732 hairs on my head, or be exactly the same height as some tree on the Siberian plain, but so what? If I begin to say that I define myself by my ability to articulate important truths, or play the Hammerklavier like no one else, or revive the tradition of my ancestors, then we are in the domain of recognizable self-definitions.

The difference is plain. We understand right away that the latter properties have human significance, or can easily be seen by people to have this, whereas the former do not — not, that is, without some special story. Perhaps the number 3,732 is a sacred one in some society; then having this number of hairs can be significant. But we get to this by linking it to the sacred.

We saw above in the second section how the contemporary culture of authenticity slides towards soft relativism. This gives further force to a general presumption of subjectivism about value: things have significance not of themselves but because people deem them to have it — as though people could determine what is significant, either by decision, or perhaps unwittingly and unwillingly by just feeling that way. This is crazy. I couldn't just *decide* that the most significant action is wiggling my toes in warm mud. Without a special explanation, this is not an intelligible claim (like the 3,732 hairs above). So I wouldn't know what sense to attribute to someone allegedly *feeling* that this was so. What could someone *mean* who said this?

But if it makes sense only with an explanation (perhaps mud is the element of the world spirit, which you contact with your toes), it is open to criticism. What if the explanation is wrong, doesn't pan out, or can be replaced with a better account? Your feeling a certain way can never be sufficient grounds for respecting your position, because your feeling can't *determine* what is significant. Soft relativism self-destructs.

Things take on importance against a background of intelligibility. Let us call this a horizon. It follows that one of the things we can't do, if we are to define ourselves significantly, is suppress or deny the horizons against which things take on significance for us. This is the kind of self-defeating move frequently being carried out in our subjectivist civilization. In stressing the legitimacy of choice between certain options, we very often find ourselves depriving the options of their significance. For instance, there is a certain discourse of justification of non-standard sexual orientations. People want to argue that heterosexual monogamy is not the only way to achieve sexual fulfillment, that those who are inclined to homosexual relations, for instance, shouldn't feel themselves embarked on a lesser, less worthy path. This fits well into the modern understanding of authenticity, with its notion of difference, originality, of the acceptance of diversity. I will try to say more about these connections below. But however we explain it, it is clear that a rhetoric of "difference," of "diversity" (even "multiculturalism"), is central to the contemporary culture of authenticity.

But in some forms this discourse slides towards an affirmation of choice itself. All options are equally worthy, because they are freely chosen, and it is choice that confers worth. The subjectivist principle underlying soft relativism is at work here. But this implicitly denies the existence of a pre-existing horizon of significance, whereby some things are worthwhile and others less so, and still others not at all, quite anterior to choice. But then the choice of sexual orientation loses any special significance. It is on a level with any other preferences, like that for taller or shorter sexual partners, or blonds or brunettes. No one would dream of making discriminating judgments about these preferences, but that's because they are all without importance. They really do just depend on how you feel. Once sexual orientation comes to be assimilated to these, which is what happens when one makes *choice* the crucial justifying reason, the original goal, which was to assert the *equal value* of this orientation, is subtly frustrated. Difference so asserted becomes *insignificant*.

Asserting the value of a homosexual orientation has to be done differently, more empirically, one might say, taking into account the actual nature of homo- and heterosexual experience and life. It can't just be assumed a priori, on the grounds that anything we choose is all right.

In this case, the assertion of value is contaminated by its connection with another leading idea, which I have mentioned above as closely interwoven with authenticity, that of self-determining freedom. This is partly responsible for the accent on choice as a crucial consideration, and also for the slide towards soft relativism. I will return to this below, in talking about how the goal of authenticity comes to deviate.

But for the moment, the general lesson is that authenticity can't be defended in ways that collapse horizons of significance. Even the sense that the significance of my life comes from its being chosen — the case where

56

authenticity is actually grounded on self-determining freedom — depends on the understanding that *independent of my will* there is something noble, courageous, and hence significant in giving shape to my own life. There is a picture here of what human beings are like, placed between this option for self-creation, and easier modes of copping out, going with the flow, conforming with the masses, and so on, which picture is seen as true, discovered, not decided. Horizons are given. . . .

So the ideal of self-choice supposes that there are *other* issues of significance beyond self-choice. The ideal couldn't stand alone, because it requires a horizon of issues of importance, which help define the *respects* in which self-making is significant. Following Nietzsche, I am indeed a truly great philosopher if I remake the table of values. But this means redefining values concerning important questions, not redesigning the menu at McDonald's, or next year's casual fashion.

The agent seeking significance in life, trying to define him- or herself meaningfully, has to exist in a horizon of important questions. That is what is self-defeating in modes of contemporary culture that concentrate on self-fulfillment *in opposition* to the demands of society, or nature, which *shut out* history and the bonds of solidarity. These self-centered "narcissistic" forms are indeed shallow and trivialized; they are "flattened and narrowed," as Bloom says. But this is not because they belong to the culture of authenticity. Rather it is because they fly in the face of its requirements. To shut out demands emanating beyond the self is precisely to suppress the conditions of significance, and hence to court trivialization. To the extent that people are seeking a moral ideal here, this self-immuring is self-stultifying; it destroys the condition in which the ideal can be realized.

Otherwise put, I can define my identity only against the background of things that matter. But to bracket out history, nature, society, the demands of solidarity, everything but what I find in myself, would be to eliminate all candidates for what matters. Only if I exist in a world in which history, or the demands of nature, or the needs of my fellow human beings, or the duties of citizenship, or the call of God, or something else of this order *matters* crucially, can I define an identity for myself that is not trivial. Authenticity is not the enemy of demands that emanate from beyond the self; it supposes such demands.

But if this is so, there is something you can say to those who are enmired in the more trivialized modes of the culture of authenticity. Reason is not powerless. Of course, we haven't got very far here; just to showing that *some* self-transcending issues are indispensable [issue (b) above]. We have not shown that any particular *one* has to be taken seriously. The argument so far is just a sketch, and I hope to take it (just a little) further in subsequent sections. But for the moment I want to turn to the other issue, (a), whether there is something self-defeating in a mode of fulfillment that denies our ties to others.

V
The Need for Recognition

(2) Another one of the common axes of criticism of the contemporary culture of authenticity is that it encourages a purely personal understanding of self-fulfillment, thus making the various associations and communities in which the person enters purely instrumental in their significance. At the broader social level, this is antithetical to any strong commitment to a community. In particular, it makes political citizenship, with its sense of duty and allegiance to political society, more and more marginal. On the more intimate level, it fosters a view of relationships in which these ought to subserve personal fulfillment. The relationship is secondary to the self-realization of the partners. On this view, unconditional ties, meant to last for life, make little sense. A relationship may last till death, if it goes on serving its purpose, but there is no point declaring a priori that it ought to.

This philosophy was articulated in a popular book of the mid-1970s: "You can't take everything with you when you leave on the midlife journey. You are moving away. Away from institutional claims and other people's agenda. Away from external valuations and accreditations. You are moving out of roles and into the self. If I could give everyone a gift for the send-off on this journey, it would be a tent. A tent for tentativeness. The gift of portable roots. . . . For each of us there is the opportunity to emerge reborn, *authentically* unique, with an enlarged capacity to love ourselves and embrace others. . . . The delights of self-discovery are always available. Though loved ones move in and out of our lives, the capacity to love remains." Authenticity seems once more to be defined here in a way that centers on the self, which distances us from our relations to others. And this has been seized on by the critics I quoted earlier. Can one say anything about this in reason?

Before sketching the direction of argument, it is important to see that the ideal of authenticity incorporates some notions of society, or at least of how people ought to live together. Authenticity is a facet of modern individualism, and it is a feature of all forms of individualism that they don't just emphasize the freedom of the individual but also propose models of society. We fail to see this when we confuse the two very different senses of individualism I distinguished earlier. The individualism of anomie and breakdown of course has no social ethic attached to it; but individualism as a moral principle or ideal must offer some view on how the individual should live with others.

So the great individualist philosophies also proposed models of society. Lockean individualism gave us the theory of society as contract. Later forms connected to notions of popular sovereignty. Two modes of social existence are quite evidently linked with the contemporary culture of self-fulfillment. The first is based on the notion of universal right: everyone should have the right and capacity to be themselves. This is what underlies soft relativism as a moral principle: no one has a right to criticize another's values. This inclines those imbued with this culture towards conceptions of procedural justice: the limit on anyone's self-fulfillment must be the safeguarding of an equal chance at this fulfillment for others.

Secondly, this culture puts a great emphasis on relationships in the intimate sphere, especially love relationships. These are seen to be the prime loci of self-exploration and self-discovery and among the most important forms of self-fulfillment. This view reflects the continuation in modern culture of a trend that is now centuries old and that places the centre of gravity of the good life not in some higher sphere but in what I want to call "ordinary life," that is, the life of production and the family, of work and love. Yet it also reflects something else that is important here: the acknowledgement that our identity requires recognition by others.

ELIZABETH CADY STANTON

"Solitude of Self"

The conviction that each individual possesses a unique self and deserves a degree of individual choice and autonomy is, as Taylor has shown, closely tied to the emergence of democratic philosophies and cultures

From Solitude of Self: An Address Delivered before the United States Congressional Committee on the Judiciary, Monday, January 18, 1892 [pamphlet, 1910]; also reprinted in *Elizabeth Cady Stanton and Susan B. Anthony: Correspondence, Writings, Speeches*, ed. Ellen Carol DuBois (New York: Schocken Books, 1981), pp. 247-250.

during the era of the French and American revolutions and the Romantic period that followed. Much of the history of the United States could be told as the history of struggles to widen the democratic principles evident in its founding, for example through the abolition of slavery, the expansion of suffrage to all male citizens, and the movement to attain women's rights. The following selection stands within this historic stream.

Elizabeth Cady Stanton (1815-1902), a founder and leader of the woman suffrage movement in the United States, delivered the following address before a Congressional committee in January 1892. Her long career in reform began in antislavery activity but focused on women's rights after the Seneca Falls Convention of 1848 issued its Declaration of the Rights of Woman, of which she was one of the authors. Gaining the right to vote was the most visible goal of the nineteenth-century women's movement, but this document suggests that far more was at stake, for Stanton, than political power. What elements of the ethics of authenticity do you see here? Do you think that the arguments Stanton makes on behalf of women's rights would apply as well to men, or to other social groups not defined by gender?

The point I wish plainly to bring before you on this occasion is the individuality of each human soul; our Protestant idea, the right of individual conscience and judgment — our republican idea, individual citizenship. In discussing the rights of woman, we are to consider, first, what belongs to her as an individual, in a world of her own, the arbiter of her own destiny, an imaginary Robinson Crusoe with her woman Friday on a solitary island. Her rights under such circumstances are to use all her faculties for her own safety and happiness.

Secondly, if we consider her as a citizen, as a member of a great nation, she must have the same rights as all other members, according to the fundamental principles of our Government.

Thirdly, viewed as a woman, an equal factor in civilization, her rights and duties are still the same — individual happiness and development.

Fourthly, it is only the incidental relations of life, such as mother, wife, sister, daughter, that may involve some special duties and training. . . .

The isolation of every human soul and the necessity of self-dependence must give each individual the right to choose his own surroundings. The strongest reason for giving woman all the opportunities for higher education, for the full development of her faculties, forces of mind and body; for giving her the most enlarged freedom of thought and action; a complete emancipation from all forms of bondage, of custom, dependence, superstition; from all the crippling influences of fear, is the solitude and personal responsibility of her own individual life. The strongest reason why we ask for woman a voice in the government under which she lives; in the religion she is asked to believe; equality in social life, where she is the chief factor; a place in the trades and professions, where she may earn her bread, is because of her birthright to self-sovereignty; because, as an individual, she must rely on herself. No matter how much women prefer to lean, to be protected and supported, nor how much men desire to have them do so, they must make the voyage of life alone, and for safety in an emergency they must know something of the laws of navigation. To guide our own craft, we must be captain, pilot, engineer; with chart and compass stand at the wheel; watch the wind and waves and know when to take in the sail, and read the signs in the firmament over all. It matters not whether the solitary voyager is man or woman. . . .

To appreciate the importance of fitting every human soul for independent action, think for a moment of the immeasurable solitude of self. We come into the world alone, unlike all who have gone before us, we leave it alone, under circumstances peculiar to ourselves. No mortal ever has been, no mortal ever will be like the soul just launched on the sea of life. There can never again be just such a combination of prenatal influences; never again just such environments as make up the infancy, youth and manhood of this one. Nature never repeats herself, and the possibilities of one human soul will never be found in another. No one has ever found two blades of ribbon grass alike, and no one will ever find two human beings alike. Seeing, then, what must be the infinite diversity in human character, we can in a measure appreciate the loss to a nation when any large class of the people is uneducated and unrepresented in the government.

We ask for the complete development of every individual, first, for his own benefit and happiness. In fitting out an army, we give each soldier his own knapsack, arms, powder, his blanket, cup, knife, fork and spoon. We provide alike for all their individual necessities; then each man bears his own burden.

Again, we ask complete individual development for the general good; for the consensus of the competent on the whole round of human interests, on all questions of national life; and here each man must bear his share of the general burden. It is sad to see how soon friendless children are left to bear their own burdens, before they can analyze their feelings; before they can even tell their joys and sorrows, they are thrown on their own resources.

The great lesson that nature seems to teach us at all ages is self-dependence, self-protection, self-support. . . .

The chief reason for opening to every soul the doors to the whole round of human duties and pleasures is the individual development thus attained, the resources thus provided under all circumstances to mitigate the solitude that at times must come to everyone. . . .

Inasmuch, then, as woman shares equally the joys and sorrows of time and eternity, is it not the height of presumption in man to propose to represent her at the ballot box and the throne of grace, to do her voting in the state, her praying in the church, and to assume the position of high priest at the family altar?

Nothing strengthens the judgment and quickens the conscience like individual responsibility. Nothing adds such dignity to character as the recognition of one's self-sovereignty; the right to an equal place, everywhere conceded — a place earned by personal merit, not an artificial attainment by inheritance, wealth, family and position. Seeing, then, that the responsibilities of life rest equally on man and woman, that their destiny is the same, they need the same preparation for time and eternity. The talk of sheltering woman from the fierce storms of life is the sheerest mockery, for they beat on her from every point of the compass, just as they do on man, and with more fatal results, for he has been trained to protect himself, to resist, and to conquer. Such are the facts in human experience, the responsibilities of individual sovereignty. Rich and poor, intelligent and ignorant, wise and foolish, virtuous and vicious, man and woman; it is ever the same, each soul must depend wholly on itself.

Whatever the theories may be of woman's dependence on man, in the supreme moments of her life, he cannot bear her burdens. Alone she goes to the gates of death to give life to every man that is born into the world. No one can share her fears, no one can mitigate her pangs; and if her sorrow is greater than she can bear, alone she passes beyond the gates into the vast unknown. From the mountain-tops of Judea long ago, a heavenly voice bade his disciples, "Bear ye one another's burdens"; but humanity has not yet risen to that point of self-sacrifice; and if ever so willing, how few the burdens are that one soul can bear for another! . . .

Virtue

Nicomachean Ethics

The many lectures that the ancient Greek philosopher Aristotle delivered on the nature of human excellence were gathered together by his students under the title *Nicomachean Ethics*. Nicomachus was the name of Aristotle's father and his son. Since Aristotle believed that the most important influence upon a person's character was good upbringing, the book was aptly named.

Aristotle sought to give an account of what the good life for humankind should look like. In order to do this, he consulted the opinions of "the many" and "the wise," believing that popular wisdom and expert advice would both have much to contribute to such an inquiry. Readers must therefore read actively if they are to understand the book rightly. In other words, we must consider Aristotle's own views in conversation with our own, testing whether we really think as he thinks we do or as he thinks we should. And if we differ with him, as we sometimes might, we must be able to show why our own views are superior to his.

As he sifted and critically examined many opinions, he developed a sketch of human excellence that has been remarkably durable throughout the many centuries since he taught. Why is a sketch by contrast to a highly detailed picture the best that should be expected of him when it comes to depiction of the good life for human beings, according to Aristotle? When he asks us readers to fill in the details, what kinds of details does he have in mind?

Human beings, Aristotle argued, aim at happiness or well-being above all other goods. Happiness was not, for Aristotle, a state of contentment or euphoria; it was rather an activity. Moreover, happiness was an

---

From Aristotle, *Nicomachean Ethics*, translated by Terence Irwin, 2nd edition (Indianapolis: Hackett Publishing Company, Inc., 1999), pp. 7-29, 49-55, 147-148.

activity in accordance with virtue, a life well performed, if you will. In the *Nicomachean Ethics* Aristotle offers an account of virtue, both what virtue is and how particular virtues develop in human beings. Virtues are states of character acquired through habituation, through acting repeatedly in the way that a virtuous person would act, until virtuous action becomes second nature.

Notice that though the repeated performance of virtuous actions might eventually make someone virtuous, the performance of these actions does not by itself mean that the person performing them *is* virtuous. The virtuous person must perform virtuous actions by choice and in the right way and in the proper spirit. A coward might perform a courageous action. Do you see why this is so? Aristotle also writes, "no one would call a person just, for instance, if he did not enjoy doing just actions, or generous if he did not enjoy generous actions, and similarly for the other virtues." Do you agree with this? Or do we think today that someone who performs a generous action, even though he would be more pleased to perform a selfish one, is more admirable for overcoming his base impulses than someone for whom acting generously is a pleasure? Aristotle himself suggests that acting virtuously or living well is "difficult." How can this be so, if living well is also pleasant? Do you think that the difficult can also be pleasant?

Book I
[Happiness — The Good for Man]

7
[An Account of the Human Good]

... §5 Now happiness, more than anything else, seems complete without qualification. For we always choose it because of itself, never because of something else. Honor, pleasure, understanding, and every virtue we certainly choose because of themselves, since we would choose each of them even if it had no further result; but we also choose them for the sake of happiness, supposing that through them we shall be happy. Happiness, by contrast, no one ever chooses for their sake, or for the sake of anything else at all. ...

§8 Moreover, we think happiness is most choiceworthy of all goods, [since] it is not counted as one good among many. [If it were] counted as one among many, then, clearly, we think it would be more choice-worthy if the smallest of goods were added; for the good that is added becomes an extra quantity of goods, and the larger of two goods is always more choice-worthy. Happiness, then, is apparently something complete and self-sufficient, since it is the end of the things achievable in action.

§9 But presumably the remark that the best good is happiness is apparently something [generally] agreed, and we still need a clearer statement of what the best good is. §10 Perhaps, then, we shall find this if we first grasp the function of a human being. For just as the good, i.e., [doing] well, for a flautist, a sculptor, and every craftsman, and, in general, for whatever has a function and [characteristic] action, seems to depend on its function, the same seems to be true for a human being, if a human being has some function.

§11 Then do the carpenter and the leather worker have their functions and actions, but has a human being no function? Is he by nature idle, without any function? Or, just as eye, hand, foot, and, in general, every [bodily] part apparently has its function, may we likewise ascribe to a human being some function apart from all of these?

§12 What, then, could this be? For living is apparently shared with plants, but what we are looking for is the special function of a human being; hence we should set aside the life of nutrition and growth. The life next in order is some sort of life of sense perception; but this too is apparently shared with horse, ox, and every animal.

§13 The remaining possibility, then, is some sort of life of action of the [part of the soul] that has reason. One [part] of it has reason as obeying reason; the other has it as itself having reason and thinking. Moreover, life is also spoken of in two ways [as capacity and as activity], and we must take [a human being's special function to be] life as activity, since this seems to be called life more fully. §14 We have found, then, that the human function is activity of the soul in accord with reason or requiring reason.

Now we say that the function of a [kind of thing] — of a harpist, for instance — is the same in kind as the function of an excellent individual of the kind — of an excellent harpist, for instance. And the same is true without qualification in every case, if we add to the function the superior achievement in accord with the virtue; for the function of a harpist is to play the harp, and the function of a good harpist is to play it well. Moreover, we take the human function to be a certain kind of life, and take this life to be activity and actions of the soul that involve reason; hence the function of the excellent man is to do this well and finely.

§15 Now each function is completed well by being completed in accord with the virtue proper [to that kind of thing]. And so the human good proves to be activity of the soul in accord with virtue, and indeed with the best and most complete virtue, if there are more virtues than one. §16 Moreover, it must be in a complete life. For one swallow does not make a spring, nor does one day; nor, similarly, does one day or a short time make us blessed and happy. . . .

13
[Introduction to the Virtues]

Since happiness is a certain sort of activity of the soul in accord with complete virtue, we must examine virtue; for that will perhaps also be a way to study happiness better. §2 Moreover, the true politician seems to have put more effort into virtue than into anything else, since he wants to make the citizens good and law-abiding. §3 We find an example of this in the Spartan and Cretan legislators and in any others who share their concerns. §4 Since, then, the examination of virtue is proper for political science, the inquiry clearly suits our decision at the beginning. . . .

Book II
[Virtue of Character]

1
[How a Virtue of Character Is Acquired]

Virtue, then, is of two sorts, virtue of thought and virtue of character. Virtue of thought arises and grows mostly from teaching; that is why it needs experience and time. Virtue of character [i.e., of *ethos*] results from habit [*ethos*]; hence its name "ethical," slightly varied from "ethos."

§2 Hence it is also clear that none of the virtues of character arises in us naturally. For if something is by nature in one condition, habituation cannot bring it into another condition. A stone, for instance, by nature moves downwards, and habituation could not make it move upwards, not even if you threw it up ten thousand times to habituate it; nor could habituation make fire move downwards, or bring anything that is by nature in one condition into another condition. §3 And so the virtues arise in us neither by nature nor against nature. Rather, we are by nature able to acquire them, and we are completed through habit.

§4 Further, if something arises in us by nature, we first have the capacity for it, and later perform the activity. This is clear in the case of the senses; for we did not acquire them by frequent seeing or hearing, but we already had them when we exercised them, and did not get them by exercising them. Virtues, by contrast, we acquire, just as we acquire crafts, by having first activated them. For we learn a craft by producing the same product that we must produce when we have learned it; we become builders, for instance, by building, and we become harpists by playing the harp. Similarly, then, we become just by doing just actions, temperate by doing temperate actions, brave by doing brave actions.

§5 What goes on in cities is also evidence for this. For the legislator makes the citizens good by habituating them, and this is the wish of every legislator; if he fails to do it well he misses his goal. Correct habituation distinguishes a good political system from a bad one.

§6 Further, the sources and means that develop each virtue also ruin it, just as they do in a craft. For playing the harp makes both good and bad harpists, and it is analogous in the case of builders and all the rest; for building well makes good builders, and building badly makes bad ones. §7 Otherwise no teacher would be needed, but everyone would be born a good or a bad craftsman.

It is the same, then, with the virtues. For what we do in our dealings with other people makes some of us just, some unjust; what we do in terrifying situations, and the habits of fear or confidence that we acquire, make some of us brave and others cowardly. The same is true of situations involving appetites and anger; for one or another sort of conduct in these situations makes some temperate and mild, others intemperate and irascible. To sum it up in a single account: a state [of character] results from [the repetition of] similar activities.

§8 That is why we must perform the right activities, since differences in these imply corresponding differences in the states. It is not unimportant, then, to acquire one sort of habit or another, right from our youth. On the contrary, it is very important, indeed all-important.

2

[Habituation]

Our present discussion does not aim, as our others do, at study; for the purpose of our examination is not to know what virtue is, but to become good, since otherwise the inquiry would be of no benefit to us. And so we must examine the right ways of acting; for, as we have said, the actions also control the sorts of states we acquire.

§2 First, then, actions should accord with the correct reason. That is a common [belief], and let us assume it. We shall discuss it later, and say what the correct reason is and how it is related to the other virtues.

§3 But let us take it as agreed in advance that every account of the actions we must do has to be stated in outline, not exactly. As we also said at the beginning, the type of accounts we demand should accord with the subject matter; and questions about actions and expediency, like questions about health, have no fixed answers.

§4 While this is the character of our general account, the account of particular cases is still more inexact. For these fall under no craft or profession; the agents themselves must consider in each case what the opportune action is, as doctors and navigators do. §5 The account we offer, then, in our present inquiry is of this inexact sort; still, we must try to offer help.

§6 First, then, we should observe that these sorts of states naturally tend to be ruined by excess and deficiency. We see this happen with strength and health — for we must use evident cases [such as these] as witnesses to things that are not evident. For both excessive and deficient exercise ruin bodily strength, and, similarly, too much or too little eating or drinking ruins health, whereas the proportionate amount produces, increases, and preserves it.

§7 The same is true, then, of temperance, bravery, and the other virtues. For if, for instance, someone avoids and is afraid of everything, standing firm against nothing, he becomes cowardly; if he is afraid of nothing at all and goes to face everything, he becomes rash. Similarly, if he gratifies himself with every pleasure and abstains from none, he becomes intemperate; if he avoids them all, as boors do, he becomes some sort of insensible person. Temperance and bravery, then, are ruined by excess and deficiency, but preserved by the mean.

§8 But these actions are not only the sources and causes both of the emergence and growth of virtues and of their ruin; the activities of the virtues [once we have acquired them] also consist in these same actions. For this is also true of more evident cases; strength, for instance, arises from eating a lot and from withstanding much hard labor, and it is the strong person who is most capable of these very actions. §9 It is the same with the virtues. For abstaining from pleasures makes us become temperate, and once we have become temperate we are most capable of abstaining from pleasures. It is similar with bravery; habituation in disdain for frightening situations and in standing firm against them makes us become brave, and once we have become brave we shall be most capable of standing firm. . . .

4
[Virtuous Actions versus Virtuous Character]

Someone might be puzzled, however, about what we mean by saying that we become just by doing just actions and become temperate by doing temperate actions. For [one might suppose that] if we do grammatical or musical actions, we are grammarians or musicians, and, similarly, if we do just or temperate actions, we are thereby just or temperate.

§2 But surely actions are not enough, even in the case of crafts; for it is possible to produce a grammatical result by chance, or by following someone else's instructions. To be grammarians, then, we must both produce a grammatical result and produce it grammatically — that is to say, produce it in accord with the grammatical knowledge in us.

§3 Moreover, in any case, what is true of crafts is not true of virtues. For the products of a craft determine by their own qualities whether they have been produced well; and so it suffices that they have the right qualities when they have been produced. But for actions in accord with the virtues to be done temperately or justly it does not suffice that they themselves have the right qualities. Rather, the agent must also be in the right state when he does them. First, he must know [that he is doing virtuous actions]; second, he must decide on them, and decide on them for themselves; and, third, he must also do them from a firm and unchanging state.

As conditions for having a craft, these three do not count, except for the bare knowing. As a condition for having a virtue, however, the knowing counts for nothing, or [rather] for only a little, whereas the other two conditions are very important, indeed all-important. And we achieve these other two conditions by the frequent doing of just and temperate actions.

§4 Hence actions are called just or temperate when they are the sort that a just or temperate person would do. But the just and temperate person is not the one who [merely] does these actions, but the one who also does them in the way in which just or temperate people do them.

§5 It is right, then, to say that a person comes to be just from doing just actions and temperate from doing temperate actions; for no one has the least prospect of becoming good from failing to do them.

§6 The many, however, do not do these actions. They take refuge in arguments, thinking that they are doing philosophy, and that this is the way to become excellent people. They are like a sick person who listens attentively to the doctor, but acts on none of his instructions. Such a course of treatment will not improve the state of the sick person's body; nor will the many improve the state of their souls by this attitude to philosophy. . . .

6
[Virtue of Character: Its Differentia]

§2 It should be said, then, that every virtue causes its possessors to be in a good state and to perform their functions well. The virtue of eyes, for instance, makes the eyes and their functioning excellent, because it makes us see well; and similarly, the virtue of a horse makes the horse excellent, and thereby good at galloping, at carrying its rider, and at standing steady in the face of the enemy. §3 If this is true in every case, the virtue of a human being will likewise be the state that makes a human being good and makes him perform his function well.

§4 We have already said how this will be true, and it will also be evident from our next remarks, if we consider the sort of nature that virtue has.

In everything continuous and divisible we can take more, less, and equal, and each of them either in the object itself or relative to us; and the equal is some intermediate between excess and deficiency. §5 By the intermediate in the object I mean what is equidistant from each extremity; this is one and the same for all. But relative to us the intermediate is what is neither superfluous nor deficient; this is not one, and is not the same for all.

§6 If, for instance, ten are many and two are few, we take six as intermediate in the object, since it exceeds [two] and is exceeded [by ten] by an equal amount, [four]. §7 This is what is intermediate by numerical proportion. But that is not how we must take the intermediate that is relative to us. For if ten pounds [of food], for instance, are a lot for someone to eat, and two pounds a little, it does not follow that the trainer will prescribe six, since this might also be either a little or a lot for the person who is to take it — for Milo [the athlete] a little, but for the beginner in gymnastics a lot; and the same is true for running and wrestling. §8 In this way every scientific expert avoids excess and deficiency and seeks and chooses what is intermediate — but intermediate relative to us, not in the object.

§9 This, then, is how each science produces its product well, by focusing on what is intermediate and making the product conform to that. This, indeed, is why people regularly comment on well-made products that nothing could be added or subtracted; they assume that excess or deficiency ruins a good [result], whereas the mean preserves it. Good craftsmen also, we say, focus on what is intermediate when they produce their product. And since virtue, like nature, is better and more exact than any craft, it will also aim at what is intermediate.

§10 By virtue I mean virtue of character; for this is about feelings and actions, and these admit of excess, deficiency, and an intermediate condition.

We can be afraid, for instance, or be confident, or have appetites, or get angry, or feel pity, and in general have pleasure or pain, both too much and too little, and in both ways not well. §11 But having these feelings at the right times, about the right things, toward the right people, for the right end, and in the right way, is the intermediate and best condition, and this is proper to virtue. §12 Similarly, actions also admit of excess, deficiency, and an intermediate condition.

Now virtue is about feelings and actions, in which excess and deficiency are in error and incur blame, whereas the intermediate condition is correct and wins praise, which are both proper to virtue. §13 Virtue, then, is a mean, insofar as it aims at what is intermediate.

§14 Moreover, there are many ways to be in error — for badness is proper to the indeterminate, as the Pythagoreans pictured it, and good to the determinate. But there is only one way to be correct. That is why error is easy and correctness is difficult, since it is easy to miss the target and difficult to hit it. And so for this reason also excess and deficiency are proper to vice, the mean to virtue; "for we are noble in only one way, but bad in all sorts of ways."

§15 Virtue, then, is a state that decides, consisting in a mean, the mean relative to us, which is defined by reference to reason, that is to say, to the reason by reference to which the prudent person would define it. It is a mean between two vices, one of excess and one of deficiency.

§16 It is a mean for this reason also: Some vices miss what is right because they are deficient, others because they are excessive, in feelings or in actions, whereas virtue finds and chooses what is intermediate.

§17 That is why virtue, as far as its essence and the account stating what it is are concerned, is a mean, but, as far as the best [condition] and the good [result] are concerned, it is an extremity. . . .

7
[The Particular Virtues of Character]

However, we must not only state this general account but also apply it to the particular cases. For among accounts concerning actions, though the general ones are common to more cases, the specific ones are truer, since actions are about particular cases, and our account must accord with these. Let us, then, find these from the chart.

§2 First, then, in feelings of fear and confidence the mean is bravery. The excessively fearless person is nameless (indeed many cases are nameless), and the one who is excessively confident is rash. The one who is excessive in fear and deficient in confidence is cowardly.

§3 In pleasures and pains — though not in all types, and in pains less than in pleasures — the mean is temperance and the excess intemperance. People deficient in pleasure are not often found, which is why they also lack even a name; let us call them insensible.

§4 In giving and taking money the mean is generosity, the excess wastefulness and the deficiency ungenerosity. Here the vicious people have contrary excesses and defects; for the wasteful person is excessive in spending and deficient in taking, whereas the ungenerous person is excessive in taking and deficient in spending. §5 At the moment we are speaking in outline and summary, and that is enough; later we shall define these things more exactly.

§6 In questions of money there are also other conditions. Another mean is magnificence; for the magnificent person differs from the generous by being concerned with large matters, while the generous person is concerned with small. The excess is ostentation and vulgarity, and the deficiency is stinginess. These differ from the vices related to generosity in ways we shall describe later.

§7 In honor and dishonor the mean is magnanimity, the excess something called a sort of vanity, and the deficiency pusillanimity. §8 And just as we said that generosity differs from magnificence in its concern with small matters, similarly there is a virtue concerned with small honors, differing in the same way from magnanimity, which is concerned with great honors. For honor can be desired either in the right way or more or less than is right. If someone desires it to excess, he is called an honor-lover, and if his desire is deficient he is called indifferent to honor, but if he is intermediate he has no name. The corresponding conditions have no name either, except the condition of the honor-lover, which is called honor-loving. . . .

9
[How Can We Reach the Mean?]

We have said enough, then, to show that virtue of character is a mean and what sort of mean it is; that it is a mean between two vices, one of excess and one of deficiency; and that it is a mean because it aims at the intermediate condition in feelings and actions.

§2 That is why it is also hard work to be excellent. For in each case it is hard work to find the intermediate; for instance, not everyone, but only one who knows, finds the midpoint in a circle. So also getting angry, or giving and spending money, is easy and everyone can do it; but doing it to the right person, in the right amount, at the right time, for the right end, and in the right way is no longer easy, nor can everyone do it. Hence doing these things well is rare, praiseworthy, and fine.

§3 That is why anyone who aims at the intermediate condition must first of all steer clear of the more contrary extreme, following the advice that Calypso also gives: "Hold the ship outside the spray and surge." For one extreme is more in error, the other less. §4 Since, therefore, it is hard to hit the intermediate extremely accurately, the second-best tack, as they say, is to take the lesser of the evils. We shall succeed best in this by the method we describe.

We must also examine what we ourselves drift into easily. For different people have different natural tendencies toward different goals, and we shall come to know our own tendencies from the pleasure or pain that arises in us. §5 We must drag ourselves off in the contrary direction; for if we pull far away from error, as they do in straightening bent wood, we shall reach the intermediate condition.

§6 And in everything we must beware above all of pleasure and its sources; for we are already biased in its favor when we come to judge it. Hence we must react to it as the elders reacted to Helen, and on each occasion repeat what they said; for if we do this, and send it off, we shall be less in error.

§7 In summary, then, if we do these things we shall best be able to reach the intermediate condition. But presumably this is difficult, especially in particular cases, since it is not easy to define the way we should be and with whom, about what, for how long. For sometimes, indeed, we ourselves praise deficient people and call them mild, and sometimes praise quarrelsome people and call them manly.

§8 Still, we are not blamed if we deviate a little in excess or deficiency from doing well, but only if we deviate a long way, since then we are easily noticed. But how great and how serious a deviation receives blame is not easy to define in an account; for nothing else perceptible is easily defined either. Such things are among particulars, and the judgment depends on perception.

§9 This is enough, then, to make it clear that in every case the intermediate state is praised, but we must sometimes incline toward the excess, sometimes toward the deficiency; for that is the easiest way to hit the intermediate and good condition. . . .

Book IV

Aristotle discusses several of the virtues at length, for example courage, temperance, justice, and practical wisdom. The passages below discuss two other virtues — generosity and magnificence. Studying these passages should sharpen our own ability to speak and think together about what kinds of people and what kinds of lives we admire. And once we decide that issue, we should be well on the way to deciding how we should try to live. We have selected the virtues of generosity and magnificence for presentation here because many people believe that leading a life that matters involves both what we do to earn a living and what we do with the earnings we receive.

Aristotle suggests that the generous person will give "to the right people." Who are these people? Aristotle does not tell us. Do you think that a person is ungenerous if he or she gives money regularly to panhandlers on the street, knowing that some of them will use the money to buy alcohol? Should we, in other words, give only to those who will use our money well?

Anyone can be generous, but can anyone be magnificent? The virtue of magnificence would seem to depend both upon having a particular character (a generous one) and upon possessing certain material goods (many of them). Does it seem plausible to you that some virtues are possible for only a few?

Do you think that someone could lead a life that matters without being generous?

―――――――――――

1

[Generosity]

Next let us discuss generosity. It seems, then, to be the mean about wealth; for the generous person is praised not in conditions of war, nor in those in which the temperate person is praised, nor in judicial verdicts, but in the giving and taking of wealth, and more especially in the giving. §2 By wealth we mean anything whose worth is measured by money.

§3 Both wastefulness and ungenerosity are excesses and deficiencies about wealth. Ungenerosity is always ascribed to those who take wealth more seriously than is right. But when wastefulness is attributed to someone, several vices are sometimes combined. For incontinent people and those who spend money on intemperance are called wasteful. §4 Since these have many vices at the same time, they make wasteful people seem the basest.

These people, however, are not properly called wasteful. §5 For the wasteful person is meant to have the single vicious feature of ruining his property; for someone who causes his own destruction ["lays waste" to himself, and so] is wasteful, and ruining one's own property seems to be a sort of self-destruction, on the assumption that our living depends on our property. This, then, is how we understand wastefulness.

§6 Whatever has a use can be used either well or badly; riches are something useful; and the best user of something is the person who has the virtue concerned with it. Hence the best user of riches will be the person who has the virtue concerned with wealth; and this is the generous person.

§7 Using wealth seems to consist in spending and giving, whereas taking and keeping seem to be possessing rather than using. That is why it is more proper to the generous person to give to the right people than to take from the right sources and not from the wrong sources.

For it is more proper to virtue to do good than to receive good, and more proper to do fine actions than not to do shameful ones; §8 and clearly [the right sort of] giving implies doing good and doing fine actions, while [the right sort of] taking implies receiving well or not doing something shameful. Moreover, thanks go to the one who gives, not to the one who fails to take, and praise goes more [to the giver]. §9 Besides, not taking is easier than giving, since people part with what is their own less readily than they avoid taking what is another's. §10 Further, those who are called generous are those who give [rightly]. Those who avoid taking [wrongly] are not praised for generosity, though they are praised nonetheless for justice, while those who take [rightly] are not much praised at all. §11 Besides, generous people are loved more than practically any others who are loved because of their virtue; that is because they are beneficial; and they are beneficial in their giving.

§12 Actions in accord with virtue are fine, and aim at the fine. Hence the generous person will also aim at the fine in his giving, and will give correctly; for he will give to the right people, the right amounts, at the right time, and all the other things that are implied by correct giving. §13 Moreover, he will do this with pleasure, or at any rate without pain; for action in accord with virtue is pleasant or at any rate painless, and least of all is it painful.

§14 If someone gives to the wrong people, or does not aim at the fine, but gives for some other reason, he will not be called generous, but some other sort of person. Nor will he be called generous if he finds it painful to give; for such a person would choose wealth over fine action, and that is not how the generous person chooses.

§15 Nor will the virtuous person take wealth from the wrong sources; since he does not honor wealth, this way of taking it is not for him. §16 Nor will he be ready to ask for favors; since he is the one who benefits others, receiving benefits readily is not for him.

§17 He will, however, acquire wealth from the right sources — from his own possessions, for instance — regarding taking not as fine, but as necessary to provide something to give. Nor will he neglect his own possessions, since he wants to use them to assist people. And he will avoid giving to just anyone, so that he will have something to give to the right people, at the right time, and where it is fine.

§18 It is also very definitely proper to the generous person to exceed so much in giving that he leaves less for himself, since it is proper to a generous person not to look out for himself. §19 However, ["exceed" must be explained;] in speaking of generosity we refer to what accords with one's means. For what is generous does not depend on the quantity of what is given, but on the state [of character] of the giver, and the generous state gives in accord with one's means. Hence one who gives less than another may still be more generous, if he has less to give.

§20 Those who have not acquired their means by their own efforts, but have inherited it, seem to be more generous; for they have had no experience of shortage, and, besides, everyone likes his own work more than [other people's], as parents and poets do.

It is not easy for a generous person to grow rich, since he is ready to spend, not to take or keep, and honors wealth for the sake of giving, not for itself. §21 Indeed, that is why fortune is denounced, because those who most deserve to grow rich actually do so least. This is only to be expected, however, since someone cannot possess wealth, any more than other things, if he pays no attention to possessing it.

§22 Still, he does not give to the wrong people, at the wrong time, and so on. For if he did, he would no longer be acting in accord with generosity, and if he spent his resources on the wrong sort of giving, he would have nothing left to spend for the right purposes. §23 For, as we have said, the generous person is the one who spends in accord with his means, and for the right purposes, whereas the one who exceeds his means is wasteful. That is why tyrants are not called wasteful, since it seems they will have difficulty exceeding their possessions in giving and spending.

§24 Since generosity, then, is a mean concerned with the giving and the taking of wealth, the generous person will both give and spend the right amounts for the right purposes, in small and large matters alike, and do this with pleasure. He will also take the right amounts from the right sources.

For since the virtue is a mean about both giving and taking, he will do both in the right way; for decent giving implies decent taking, and the other sort of taking is contrary to the decent sort. Hence the states that imply each other are present at the same time in the same subject, whereas the contrary states clearly are not.

§25 If the generous person finds that his spending deviates from what is fine and right, he will feel pain, but moderately and in the right way; for it is proper to virtue to feel both pleasure and pain in the right things and in the right way.

§26 The generous person is also an easy partner to have common dealings with matters of money; §27 for he can easily be treated unjustly, since he does not honor money, and is more grieved if he has failed to spend what it was right to spend than if he has spent what it was wrong to spend — here he does not please Simonides.

§28 The wasteful person is in error here too, since he feels neither pleasure nor pain at the right things or in the right way; this will be more evident as we go on.

§29 We have said, then, that wastefulness and ungenerosity are excesses and deficiencies in two things, in giving and taking — for we also count spending as giving. Now wastefulness is excessive in giving and not taking, but deficient in taking. Ungenerosity is deficient in giving and excessive in taking, but in small matters.

§30 Now the different aspects of wastefulness are not very often combined; for it is not easy to take from nowhere and give to everyone, since private citizens soon outrun their resources in giving, and private citizens are the ones who seem to be wasteful. §31 However, such a person seems to be quite a lot better than the ungenerous person, since he is easily cured, both by growing older and by poverty, and is capable of reaching the intermediate condition. For he has the features proper to the generous person, since he gives and does not take, though he does neither rightly or well. If, then, he is changed, by habituation or some other means, so that he does them rightly and well, he will be generous; for then he will give to the right people and will not take from the wrong sources. This is why the wasteful person seems not to be base in his character; for excess in giving without taking is proper to a foolish person, not to a vicious or ignoble one. §32 Someone who is wasteful in this way seems to be much better than the ungenerous person, both for the reasons just given and because he benefits many, whereas the ungenerous person benefits no one, not even himself.

§33 Most wasteful people, however, as we have said, [not only give wrongly, but] also take from the wrong sources, and to this extent are ungenerous. §34 They become acquisitive because they wish to spend, but cannot do this readily, since they soon exhaust all they have; hence they are compelled to provide from elsewhere. At the same time they care nothing for the fine, and so take from any source without scruple; for they have an urge to give, and the way or source does not matter to them.

§35 This is why their ways of giving are not generous either, since they are not fine, do not aim at the fine, and are not done in the right way. Rather, these people sometimes enrich people who ought to be poor, and would give nothing to people with sound characters, but would give much to flatterers or to those providing some other pleasure. That is why most of these people are also intemperate. For since they part with money readily, they also spend it lavishly on intemperance; and because their lives do not aim at the fine, they decline toward pleasures.

§36 If, then, the wasteful person has been left without a guide, he changes into this; but if he receives attention, he might reach the intermediate and the right state.

§37 Ungenerosity, however, is incurable, since old age and every incapacity seem to make people ungenerous. And it comes more naturally to human beings than wastefulness; for the many are money-lovers rather than givers. §38 Moreover, it extends widely and has many species, since there seem to be many ways of being ungenerous. For it consists in two conditions, deficiency in giving and excess in taking; but it is not found as a whole in all cases. Sometimes the two conditions are separated, and some people go to excess in taking, whereas others are deficient in giving.

§39 For the people called misers, tightfisted, skinflints and so on, are all deficient in giving, but they do not go after other people's goods and do not wish to take them. With some people the reason for this is some sort of decency in them, and a concern to avoid what is shameful. For some people seem — at least, this is what they say — to hold on to their money so that they will never be compelled to do anything shameful. These include the cheeseparer, and everyone like that; he is so called from his excessive refusal to give anything. Others keep their hands off other people's property because they are afraid, supposing that it is not easy for them to take other people's property without other people taking theirs too; hence, they say, they are content if they neither take from others nor give to them.

§40 Other people, by contrast, go to excess in taking, by taking anything from any source — those, for instance, who work at degrading occupations, pimps and all such people, and usurers who lend small amounts at high interest; for all of these take the wrong amounts from the wrong sources.

§41 Shameful love of gain is apparently their common feature, since they all put up with reproaches for some gain — more precisely, for a small gain. §42 For those who take the wrong things from the wrong sources on a large scale — such as tyrants who sack cities and plunder temples — are called wicked, impious, and unjust, but not ungenerous. §43 The ungenerous, however, include the gambler and the robber, since these are shameful lovers of gain. For in pursuit of gain both go to great efforts and put up with reproaches; the robber faces the greatest dangers to get his haul, while the gambler takes his gains from his friends, the very people he ought to be giving to. Both of them, then, are shameful lovers of gain, because they wish to acquire gains from the wrong sources; and all these methods of acquisition are ungenerous.

§44 It is plausibly said that ungenerosity is contrary to generosity. For it is a greater evil than wastefulness; and error in this direction is more common than the error of wastefulness, as we have described it. §45 So much, then, for generosity and the vices opposed to it.

2

[Magnificence]

Next, it seems appropriate to discuss magnificence also. For it seems to be, like generosity, a virtue concerned with wealth, but it does not extend, as generosity does, to all the actions involving wealth, but only to those involving heavy expenses, and in them it exceeds generosity in its large scale. For, just as the name [*megaloprepeia*] itself suggests, magnificence is expenditure that is fitting [*prepousa*] in its large scale [*megethos*]. §2 But large scale is large relative to something; for the expenses of the captain of a warship and of the leader of a delegation are not the same. Hence what is fitting is also relative to oneself, the circumstances, and the purpose.

§3 Someone is called magnificent only if he spends the worthy amount on a large purpose, not on a trivial or an ordinary purpose like the one who "gave to many a wanderer"; for the magnificent person is generous, but generosity does not imply magnificence.

§4 The deficiency falling short of this state is called stinginess. The excess is called vulgarity, poor taste, and such things. These are excesses not because they spend an excessively great amount on the right things, but because they show off in the wrong circumstances and in the wrong way. We shall discuss these vices later.

§5 The magnificent person, in contrast to these, is like a scientific expert, since he is able to observe what will be the fitting amount, and to spend large amounts in an appropriate way. §6 For, as we said at the start, a state is defined by its activities and its objects; now the magnificent person's expenditures are large and fitting; so also, then, must the results be, since that is what makes the expense large and fitting to the result. Hence the result must be worthy of the expense, and the expense worthy of, or even in excess of, the result.

§7 In this sort of spending the magnificent person will aim at the fine; for that is a common feature of the virtues. §8 Moreover, he will spend gladly and readily, since it is stingy to count every penny. §9 He will think more about the finest and most fitting way to spend than about the cost or about the cheapest way to do it.

§10 Hence the magnificent person must also be generous; for the generous person will also spend what is right in the right way. But it is in this spending that the large scale of the magnificent person, his greatness, is found, since his magnificence is a sort of large scale of generosity in these things; and from an expense that is equal [to a nonmagnificent person's] he will make the result more magnificent. For a possession and a result have different sorts of excellence; the most honored [and hence most excellent] possession is the one worth most — for example, gold — but the most honored result is the one that is great and fine, since that is what is admirable to behold. Now what is magnificent is admirable, and the excellence of the result consists in its large scale.

§11 This sort of excellence is found in the sorts of expenses called honorable, such as expenses for the gods — dedications, temples, sacrifices, and so on, for everything divine — and in expenses that provoke a good competition for honor, for the common good, if, for instance, some city thinks a splendid chorus or warship or a feast for the city must be provided.

§12 But in all cases, as we have said, we fix the right amount by reference to the agent [as well as the task] — by who he is and what resources he has; for the amounts must be worthy of these, fitting the producer as well as the result.

§13 That is why a poor person could not be magnificent; he lacks the means for large and fitting expenditures. If he tries to be magnificent, he is foolish; for he spends more than what is worthy and right for him, whereas correct spending accords with virtue. §14 Large spending befits those who have the means, acquired through their own efforts or their ancestors or connections, or are well born or reputable, and so on; for each of these conditions includes greatness and reputation for worth.

§15 This, then, above all is the character of the magnificent person, and magnificence is found in these sorts of expenses, as we have said, since these are the largest and most honored.

It is found also in those private expenses that arise only once, such as a wedding and the like, and in those that concern the whole city, or the people in it with a reputation for worth — the receiving of foreign guests and sending them off, gifts and exchanges of gifts. For the magnificent person spends money on the common good, not on himself, and the gifts have some similarity to dedications.

§16 It is also proper to the magnificent person to build a house befitting his riches, since this is also a suitable adornment. He spends more readily on long-lasting results, since these are the finest. In each case he spends on what is fitting. §17 For what suits gods does not suit human beings, and what suits a temple does not suit a tomb.

And since each great expense is great in relation to a particular kind of object, the most magnificent will be a great expense on a great object, and the [magnificent] in a particular area will be what is great in relation to the particular kind of object. §18 Moreover, greatness in the results is not the same as greatness in an expense, since the finest ball or oil bottle has the magnificence proper to a gift for a child, but its value is small and paltry. §19 That is why it is proper to the magnificent person, whatever kind of thing he produces, to produce it magnificently, since this is not easily exceeded, and to produce something worthy of the expense.

§20 This, then, is the character of the magnificent person. . . .

THEODORE ROOSEVELT

"The Vigor of Life"

Theodore Roosevelt attained national prominence as the leader of the Rough Riders during the Spanish-American War. Elected to the vice presidency in 1900, he went on to become president of the United States after the assassination of William McKinley, and he was then elected president

From Theodore Roosevelt, *An Autobiography* (1913; Library of America edition, 2004), pp. 305-307.

in his own right, serving for most of the first decade of the twentieth century. He entitled the chapter of his autobiography from which the following selection is taken "The Vigor of Life," and in it he speaks of two kinds of success. Do you think that success should be measured according to a common standard, or do you think that success is relative to the gifts and aptitudes each person has? In other words, is a person's success something we can determine simply on the basis of his or her achievements, or must we determine it on the basis of the relationship between those achievements and the person's capacities for realizing them?

Both Aristotle and Roosevelt admired military men, and they stressed courage as a virtue. Does their ethical writing exclude women? Many women ethicists believe that even though Aristotle's biological views of the inferiority of women were unfounded, and even though he appealed only to men in his writing, as Roosevelt would also do, his account of virtue and human excellence can and should apply equally well to both genders. Do you agree? Or do you think that there should be separate and distinct accounts of a life in accordance with virtue for men and for women?

───────────────

There are two kinds of success, or rather two kinds of ability displayed in the achievement of success. There is, first, the success either in big things or small things which comes to the man who has in him the natural power to do what no one else can do, and what no amount of training, no perseverance or will power, will enable any ordinary man to do. This success, of course, like every other kind of success, may be on a very big scale or on a small scale. The quality which the man possesses may be that which enables him to run a hundred yards in nine and three-fifths seconds, or to play ten separate games of chess at the same time blindfolded, or to add five columns of figures at once without effort, or to write the "Ode to a Grecian Urn," or to deliver the Gettysburg speech, or to show the ability of Frederick at Leuthen or Nelson at Trafalgar. No amount of training of body or mind would enable any good ordinary man to perform anyone of these feats. Of course the proper performance of each implies much previous study or training, but in no one of them is success to be attained save by the altogether exceptional man who has in him the something additional which the ordinary man does not have.

This is the most striking kind of success, and it can be attained only by the man who has in him the quality which separates him in kind no less than in degree from his fellows. But much the commoner type of success in every walk of life and in every species of effort is that which comes to the man who differs from his fellows not by the kind of quality which he possesses but by the degree of development which he has given that quality. This kind of success is open to a large number of persons, if only they seriously determine to achieve it. It is the kind of success which is open to the average man of sound body and fair mind, who has no remarkable mental or physical attributes, but who gets just as much as possible in the way of work out of the aptitudes that he does possess. It is the only kind of success that is open to most of us. Yet some of the greatest successes in history have been those of this second class — when I call it second class I am not running it down in the least, I am merely pointing out that it differs in kind from the first class. To the average man it is probably more useful to study this second type of success than to study the first. From the study of the first he can learn inspiration, he can get uplift and lofty enthusiasm. From the study of the second he can, if he chooses, find out how to win a similar success himself.

I need hardly say that all the successes I have ever won have been of the second type. I never won anything without hard labor and the exercise of my best judgment and careful planning and working long in advance. Having been a rather sickly and awkward boy, I was as a young man at first both nervous and distrustful of my own prowess. I had to train myself painfully and laboriously not merely as regards my body but as regards my soul and spirit.

When a boy I read a passage in one of Marryat's books which always impressed me. In this passage the captain of some small British man-of-war is explaining to the hero how to acquire the quality of fearlessness. He says that at the outset almost every man is frightened when he goes into action, but that the course to follow is for the man to keep such a grip on himself that he can act just as if he was not frightened. After this is kept up long enough it changes from pretense to reality, and the man does in very fact become fearless by sheer dint of practicing fearlessness when he does not feel it. (I am using my own language, not Marryat's.) This was the theory upon which I went. There were all kinds of things of which I was afraid at first, ranging from grizzly bears to "mean" horses and gun-fighters; but by acting as if I was not afraid I gradually ceased to be afraid. Most men can have the same experience if they choose. They will first learn to bear themselves well in trials which they anticipate and which they school themselves in advance to meet. After a while the habit will grow on them, and they will behave well in sudden and unexpected emergencies which come upon them unawares.

It is of course much pleasanter if one is naturally fearless, and I envy and respect the men who are naturally fearless. But it is a good thing to remember that the man who does not enjoy this advantage can nevertheless stand beside the man who does, and can do his duty with the like efficiency, *if he chooses to.* Of course he must not let his desire take the form merely of a daydream. Let him dream about being a fearless man, and the more he dreams the better he will be, always provided he does his best to realize the dream in practice. He can do his part honorably and well provided only he sets fearlessness before himself as an ideal, schools himself to think of danger merely as something to be faced and overcome, and regards life itself as he should regard it, not as something to be thrown away, but as a pawn to be promptly hazarded whenever the hazard is warranted by the larger interests of the great game in which we are all engaged.

Vocation

Matthew 20:20-28

A biblical text that addresses the issues of honor and greatness from the vantage point of the kingdom of heaven introduces our readings on the vocabulary of vocation. At first glance, the passage seems to turn Aristotle's vocabulary of virtue upside down. For Aristotle, slaves could not become virtuous, because their souls were slaves to their appetites and because they lacked the freedom of choice essential to the cultivation and practice of virtue. By contrast, Jesus tells the disciples that those who would win the first place of honor must imitate him in becoming slaves to others. In a passage from the *Nicomachean Ethics* that appears later in this anthology, however, Aristotle praises those who sacrifice themselves for their friends or their country (see Part II, Chapter 1). Perhaps the contrast between Aristotle and Jesus is not as great as it might seem at first. Is there a difference between serving someone and being slavishly responsive to their every desire? If so, might this also soften the apparent contrast between Aristotle and Jesus?

Then the mother of the sons of Zebedee came to [Jesus] with her sons, and kneeling before him, she asked a favor of him. And he said to her, "What do you want?" She said to him, "Declare that these two sons of mine will sit, one at your right hand and one at your left, in your kingdom." But Jesus answered, "You do not know what you are asking. Are you able to drink the cup that I am about to drink?" They said to him, "We are able." He said to them, "You will indeed drink my cup, but to sit at my right hand and at my left, this is not mine to grant, but it is for those for whom it has been prepared by my Father."

From the New Revised Standard Version of the Bible.

When the ten heard it, they were angry with the two brothers. But Jesus called them to him and said, "You know that the rulers of the Gentiles lord it over them, and their great ones are tyrants over them. It will not be so among you; but whoever wishes to be great among you must be your servant, and whoever wishes to be first among you must be your slave; just as the Son of Man came not to be served but to serve, and to give his life a ransom for many."

LEE HARDY

"Making the Match: Career Choice"

In this selection, Lee Hardy, who has taught philosophy at Calvin College for more than twenty years, recounts his own somewhat prolonged struggle to find his vocation — not only, as he explains at the outset, the "general" calling to discipleship, but also the "particular" calling "to do certain kinds of things." Hardy changed occupations several times before he discovered his calling as a philosopher. A life that included several changes of occupation would have been extremely rare during the period in which the Protestant idea of vocation was first developed in the sixteenth century, but in our own time, among relatively affluent people in Western, post-industrial societies, the prospect of "changing jobs three or four times" has become increasingly expected. What counsel does Hardy provide to enable us to live through these times of uncertainty and change with integrity and a sense of overall purpose?

Hardy suggests that without an understanding of and belief in God's providential care for the world, we are apt to think that our occupational roles are mere accidents and that our task is therefore to *create* a significant life from circumstances that are arbitrary and without intrinsic meaning. If, on the other hand, we believe that our own lives are part of a divine

---

From Lee Hardy, *The Fabric of This World* (Grand Rapids: William B. Eerdmans Publishing Company, 1990), pp. 80-93.

plan for the redemption and transformation of the world, our task is to *discover* what exactly our role is in that plan. Hardy elsewhere states that there may not be only one thing we are called to do. Is our challenge then to discern what our occupational calling really is, or is it to accept and interpret whatever we find ourselves doing to earn a living as part of a larger, perhaps a divinely ordained, plan?

How exactly does the Christian concept of work as a divine calling bear upon the problem of choosing a vocation? Before we answer this question, we would do well to make two preliminary observations. First, to those of us who are familiar with the language of the Bible, there is something odd about the phrase "choosing a vocation." For in the New Testament the primary, if not exclusive, meaning of the term "vocation" — or calling *(klēsis)* — pertains to the call of the gospel, pure and simple. We are called to repentance and to faith (Acts 2:38); we are called into fellowship with Jesus Christ (1 Cor. 1:9); we are called out of the darkness and into the light (1 Pet. 2:9); we are called to be holy (1 Pet. 1:15, 1 Cor. 1:2); indeed, we are called to be saints (Rom. 1:7). Here we are not being asked to choose from a variety of callings, to decide which one is "right" for us. Rather, one call goes out to all — the call of discipleship. For it is incumbent upon all Christians to follow Christ, and, in so doing, to become the kind of people God wants us to be. The call of the gospel is not to a particular occupation, but to sainthood.

Yet we are also as Christians commanded, and therefore called, to love and serve our neighbors with the gifts that God has given to us. Each one of us, writes St. Peter, "should use whatever gift he has received to serve others, faithfully administering God's grace in its various forms" (1 Pet. 4:10). For each of us has certain gifts, certain talents and abilities. Those gifts were not given that we might heap up fame and fortune for ourselves. Rather, the possession of those gifts places an obligation upon us to use them for the building up of the community of faith and the human community at large (Rom. 12:4-21). We are called, then, not only to be certain kinds of persons, but also to do certain kinds of things.

Because of this twofold character of God's call, the Puritans used to distinguish between the "general" and the "particular" calling. The general calling is the call to be a Christian, that is, to take on the virtues appropriate to followers of Christ, whatever one's station in life. St. Paul refers to these virtues as the "fruit" of the Spirit: love, joy, peace, patience, kindness, goodness, faithfulness, gentleness, and self-control (Gal. 5:22-23). It is not for us to pick and choose among these virtues. When it comes to being a Christian, the virtues come in one package. They are the fruition of the work of the Spirit in our lives.

The particular calling, on the other hand, is the call to a specific occupation — an occupation to which not all Christians are called. With respect to occupations within the church, St. Paul refers to such particular callings as the "gifts" of the Spirit: to be an apostle, a prophet, a teacher, a worker of miracles, an administrator, and the like (1 Cor. 12:28-31). Not all are called to be apostles, prophets, or teachers. For here the Spirit fits each member of the body of Christ differently for a specific work: we are not expected or able to do all things, but only the things which God has enabled and called us to do. In the discharge of our various particular callings we together build up the interdependent society of the saints, which finds its unity in Christ, the head of the church.

With the distinction between the general and the particular calling in mind, talk about "vocational choice" — in the sense of choosing a particular occupation in which we will exercise our gifts — is both biblically appropriate and religiously important. At certain junctures in our lives we are confronted with the need to identify our gifts and choose an occupation; and an occupation can provide us with the concrete opportunity to employ our gifts in the service of our neighbor, as God commanded us to do. This holds not only for the occupations within the church, but in society as well. For although the Bible concentrates on the spiritual gifts and their employment in the community of faith, the Christian tradition has generally extended the Biblical principle, confessing that our "natural" gifts also come from God and are to be employed for the benefit of the wider human community.

As a second preliminary observation, lest we move too quickly from the question of vocation to that of paid occupation, we ought to remind ourselves that vocation is the wider concept. One need not have a paid occupation in order to have a vocation. Indeed all of us have, at any one time, a number of vocations — and only one of them might be pursued as a paid occupation. To put it in Luther's language, at any given time we occupy a number of stations: parent, child, citizen, parishioner, and so on. Each one of these stations entails a specific vocation. As a parent it is my vocation to love, discipline, and care for my children; as a child it is my vocation to honor and obey my parents; as a citizen it is my vocation to participate in the political process and abide by the decisions and rulings of the government; as a parishioner it is my vocation to exercise my spiritual gifts for the edification of the body of Christ. I may not have a paid occupation. But that doesn't mean I have no calling in life.

Furthermore, it follows from the broad concept of vocation that we will always have a number of vocations as a result of certain social relations and historical circumstances which we ourselves have not chosen. I, for instance, was born in a modern nation state known as the United States of America in the mid-twentieth century of white Anglo-Saxon Protestant parentage. I did not ask or choose to be so born. I just was. From the purely human perspective it seems almost accidental that I should be who I am. Could I not just as well have been a Chinese woman born during the Ming dynasty, or a Nicaraguan *campesino* born during the glory days of William Walker? Why was I born of this particular race and nationality, with this particular body and temperament? It's hard to say.

Existential philosophers of atheist persuasion have dwelt upon the apparently accidental nature of our identities, and refer to such as the brute "facticity" or "thrownness" of human existence. We find ourselves thrown into a particular situation with no apparent rhyme or reason, and our task as human beings is to appropriate our absurd circumstances into a meaningful life project which we ourselves freely choose.

But from a theistic point of view things look quite different. That I am who I am is not a result of chance, a mere cosmic accident. Rather it is the result of God's intention. There is a reason why I am who I am, although that reason may not be immediately apparent to me. I was placed here for a purpose, and that purpose is one which I am, in part, to discover, not invent. The facts about me are indicators of the divine intent for my life, indicators which are to be interpreted in the light of God's revealed Word. Perhaps, through no choice of my own, I inherit a vast family fortune and suddenly find myself wealthy to the point of embarrassment. An absurd event? No. A providential one in which I am to discern God's will for the shape and direction of my life. For the rich have at least one divine vocation just by virtue of being rich, namely to use their money to benefit others. Many things about me I did not choose. But that does not mean that they are not meaningful, or that they have to be made meaningful through other choices that I make.

Even a vocation as a paid occupation may not be a matter of choice. In fact, for most people it never has been. Down through the ages and in many parts of the world today people did and do not have much choice in the kind of work they do. Their work was and is simply imposed upon them by circumstances beyond their control: the economic niche of the family into which they were born, or a combination of financial necessity and the existing job market. One is born a rice farmer or becomes a factory worker because that is the only line of work open at the time. "Today we consider it an imperfection of society for people to be fixed in their opportunities and jobs by class and birth," management theorist Peter Drucker observes, "where only yesterday this was the natural and apparently inescapable condition of mankind." Freedom of choice regarding occupation is a relatively novel social phenomenon. Those of us who are faced with such a choice are, historically speaking, a very small minority indeed.

It shouldn't come as a surprise, then, that guidelines for the responsible choice of an occupation have not been thoroughly worked out by the Christian community at large. The fact that in many parts of Christendom today work is still considered a secular matter, with little or no connection to religion, has not helped either.

But an initial attempt to formulate the principles of vocational choice was made by the Protestant reformers of the sixteenth and seventeenth centuries. They were, on the one hand, firmly convinced that all of life, even the life of everyday work, ought to be lived to the glory of God. On the other hand, they were aware that in their time people were being granted a greater measure of freedom in the choice of occupations. The rigid structures of medieval society were crumbling around them and social life was opening up, differentiating, and becoming more flexible. Higher education was no longer the prerogative of the aristocracy alone. As a direct result, an increasing number of people had access to an increasingly wider range of occupational options. Thus it was given to them to work out the principles of vocational choice in the light of the Word of God.

How did they go about this? Taking their initial bearings from the biblical witness together with a reflection upon the human condition, they began with a definition of work that went something like this: work is the social place where people can exercise the gifts that God has given them in the service of others. For God did not create us as self-sufficient individuals. We all have needs which we alone cannot meet. By necessity we live in communities of interdependent individuals. And we are to make use of what talents we do have to serve others as they, in turn, serve us. Together we build up society as a mutual support system.

With this concept of work, two practical items immediately arise: the gifts God has given me, and the exercise of those gifts for the sake of others. The first step then, in making a responsible choice of vocation, is ascertaining precisely which gifts God has bestowed upon me.

This in itself can be a difficult, painful, and protracted process. We were not born with job descriptions taped to our backs. Our vocational aptitudes have to be discovered in that process by which we come to know ourselves. But the road to self-knowledge can be a long one, and often we don't possess a clear idea of exactly what our talents are at the time we must make vocational decisions. If we are not sure what we are good at, it often pays to reflect upon our past experience with precisely that question in mind. What have I done, and done well? What kind of skills did I make use of? Planning, investigating, implementing, building, repairing, creating, writing, teaching, supervising? What kind of knowledge did I acquire? Knowledge about cars, computers, finance, administration, food, flowers, music, mathematics? What kind of objects did I work with? Numbers, words, people, mechanical things, living things, programs, institutions? In what capacity was I relating to others? As a team member, team leader, lone ranger, coach, manager, expert? Was I in a position with a lot of freedom and responsibility, or was I working in a highly structured situation, where my activity was thoroughly specified? With an autobiographical grasp of my talents I can begin, perhaps with some additional guidance, to see what kind of work I could do well.

Beside reflecting on past experience, remaining open to future experience is equally important. For self-knowledge is an open-ended process, a fact twentieth-century theologian Karl Barth underscored in his *Church Dogmatics*:

> In relation to the personal presuppositions which he himself brings, the action of man must be one which always and in all directions is open, eager to learn, capable of modification, perpetually ready, in obedience to the exclusively sovereign command of God, to allow itself to be orientated afresh and in very different ways from those which might have seemed possible and necessary on the basis of man's own ideas of his ability and capacity. In the last analysis man has no more knowledge of himself than mastery over himself. Again and again he must let himself be shown who he is. His faithfulness to himself, then, [consists] only in constant attention and openness to that which, as God claims him, will be continually disclosed to him as his true self, as the real aptitude which he has been given together with its limits, and then in the corresponding decision for perhaps a much more daring or possibly a much more humble action than that to which he has hitherto considered himself called.

Some experimentation, then, may be required in the process of career choice. If several occupational options lie before me, and they all look equally valid and interesting, rather than allowing myself to be paralyzed by the lack of a deciding factor, it would be better simply to choose one and pursue it. In the course of pursuing that occupation I will inevitably learn something I couldn't have known prior to its pursuit. I may become convinced that I had in fact made the right choice. On the other hand, I might find out in no uncertain terms that I made the "wrong" choice. Not to worry. I can still benefit from that. I have learned something about myself. And I can cross one occupational option off my list.

Besides, career decisions are rarely irrevocable. Most people nowadays go through four or five career changes in the course of a lifetime. When I was in high school I wanted to go into cinematography. I loved movies, and I wanted to make some. Instead I became an advertising artist. But later, while working in an art studio in the San Francisco Bay area, I found myself drawn into the discipline of philosophy. I needed to clarify certain issues in life. Today I am a professor of philosophy at a liberal arts college. And I suspect most people past their twenties have similarly crooked accounts of how they came to their present occupations. Career paths are rarely straight. Typically they are afflicted by detours, unmarked intersections, forced exits, blind alleys, and cul-de-sacs. When the philosophy majors I advise at Calvin College hesitate to go to graduate school because they are not sure if philosophy is their calling, I usually tell them that going to graduate school is the best way to find out if philosophy is their calling. We can't know everything before we act. An element of trial and error is unavoidable in the carving out of a niche for oneself in the world of work. Barth was entirely correct when he said that "a man can really learn to know his sphere of operation only as he sets to work in it."

Vocational counseling and testing can also help here. Not that the results of a vocational test are to count as the last word. The validity of the results depends upon how well the test was designed, how accurately and honestly you were able to answer the questions, and how carefully the results are interpreted. But a vocational test can at least do this: it can comfort you by confirming what you already thought you knew about yourself, but weren't sure; or it can challenge you by suggesting occupational possibilities you had never considered before.

An honest lack of self-knowledge is not the only problem in making a career choice. The sins of greed, pride, envy, and fear can enter into the picture too, clouding our vision of who we are and what we were cut out to do. We might have our eye on a certain career because of the salary. We approach our career as a means to untold riches and material delights. Or perhaps we find ourselves attracted to a certain career because of its social prestige. We want to prove to others — and perhaps to ourselves — that we are much more talented and capable than either thought. We treat our prospective career as a wand to wave before the crowds to command their respect, awe, and admiration. Or perhaps we are unhappy with the way God has made us, and we are envious of another person's gifts and accomplishments. In the course of our prospective career, we resolve to become just like her and excel where she has excelled. Our career becomes the tool of our covetousness. Or we begin by being aimed at certain careers due to family expectations about what we are going to do with our lives, and we are afraid to disappoint our parents. We live in fear of what others would think of us were we to strike out on our own. Our career becomes a place where we hide from others, and especially ourselves. On the basis of these and similarly errant motives, we can convince ourselves that we are qualified for certain careers, while what led us to choose those careers had very little to do with our particular gifts or the human needs around us.

Perhaps I have been raised in a community where intellectual prowess is held in high esteem. Perhaps other features of my upbringing led to an overwhelming psychological need to be highly esteemed by others. Or, I may have been raised in a community with a substantial anti-intellectual bias and, due to other features of my upbringing, I have an overwhelming psychological need to distinguish myself over against that community, thereby establishing my social independence. At any rate, on the basis of some subterranean motive of which I am not fully aware, I find myself quite naturally drawn in the direction of intellectual pursuits. When I get to college I might even boldly stage a direct assault on the very pinnacle of mental achievement, surrounded by the chill, thin air of theoretical abstraction — I declare a philosophy major.

Thus I become convinced that in philosophy I have found my true calling. But have I? Has God really given me the appropriate intellectual gifts and a genuine zeal for the truth? Or am I just fooling myself? These are difficult questions to answer on the basis of private self-examination. The opportunities for self-deception along these lines are almost limitless. Even if I received lousy grades in all my philosophy courses — enough to thoroughly discourage the average mortal — I could still convince myself that this failure was wholly due to the clumsy pedagogy of my professors, or their inability to detect the secret genius of my work. Resolute in purpose, I go on to graduate school against the advice of my mentors. No one will deny me the glory associated with my chosen field — and I proceed to make a total fool of myself trying to prove to everyone else that I am not a complete idiot.

Because of the innate human talent for self-deception, it is a good idea to seek the advice of others known for mature and balanced judgment. I may be convinced that God has especially called me to a particular occupation. But do others recognize in me the gifts I think I possess? Can my friends detect in the pattern of my life the passions, the interests, and the concerns I claim to have? Do my teachers take me to be mentally competent and personally well-suited for the career of my own choosing? Their counsel may be encouraging. Or devastating. But it must be sought. Often I must seek the help of others if I am to be honest with myself before God.

It seems, then, that perceived social status combined with certain psychological needs can push people into occupations for which they are not at all qualified. But it can work the other way too. Low social status plus similar psychological needs can drive people away from an occupation for which they are eminently qualified. I may have formidable mechanical abilities and a genuine love for the automobile as an engineered system of intake and exhaust manifolds, regulators and alternators, camshafts and crankshafts. In the world of car repair, infested as it is by rip-off artists, I may be able to perform a genuine service to the community as a mechanic. But I chafe at the suggestion. After all, who wants to be a "grease monkey"? What would my parents think? My friends?

Finding our niche in life may not only require that we be honest with ourselves. It may also require a stiff dose of humility. Yet, as John Calvin said, "No task will be so sordid and base . . . that it will not shine and be reckoned very precious in God's sight." An occupation held to be of no account in the eyes of the world can nonetheless be important to God. The ranking of occupations in our society and in the kingdom of God are often two very different things. And it's important to keep the difference in mind. The garbage collector performs an infinitely more valuable social service than the advertising executive about to launch a campaign to convince the American homemaker that Pink Froth dish detergent is indispensable to gracious living. But the latter, for reasons difficult to fathom, enjoys more social status.

The first step, then, in responsible vocational choice is to identify the abilities and talents God has given us. Those talents and abilities, however, will probably not be unique. For that reason they will not, by themselves, lead a person to a unique job. That is especially true if we consider such things as the ability to grasp objects between the thumb and fingers. That ability is regularly exercised by the dentist, the electrician, and the surgeon — as well as the paperboy. Even rarer gifts, like a lightning-quick analytical mind, do not suggest only one profession. One could use such a mind in law, philosophy, or the CIA.

Although the absence of a unique gift may leave us in the lurch when it comes to choosing a specific career, we can take positive comfort in the fact that as generic human beings we already possess a wide range of abilities. And we can meaningfully put these ordinary abilities to use in a number of perfectly acceptable occupations. What is lost by way of unambiguous guidance is made up by flexibility. And we are thereby relieved of the frustrating and ultimately self-defeating quest for "the right job," as if there were only one per person. As a simple matter of fact, we are qualified to do a number of things. And a number of the things we are qualified to do would be good things to do.

Nonetheless, God can give us two other things that will narrow down the field considerably. First, he can give us a concern. Of course, we are all concerned about ourselves and how we will fare in this life. No special work of God is required for that. But if we can detect within a growing concern for others, then we can be sure God is at work within us. But not all of us will be concerned for others in the same way. Some may be concerned for their health. Others may be concerned for their emotional well-being, their spiritual condition, or the integrity of their natural or cultural environment. Once we become aware of the specific concern God has given us, we can go about cultivating the skills required to follow through on that concern effectively.

Furthermore, God may have endowed us with certain lively interests apart from any other-directed concerns — interests in mathematics, music, or microbiology. Those interests lead us to cultivate skills which we can in turn use in the service of others. For example, based on an innate love of literature I might acquire the skills of appreciation and criticism that would later qualify me, as an English teacher, to introduce others to the wonders of the written word. Or I might become a writer myself, and proceed to open up God's world to others through the medium of language.

The assumption behind these recommendations is that discovering God's will for one's life is not so much a matter of seeking out miraculous signs and wonders as it is being attentive to who and where we are. It is not as if our abilities, concerns, and interests are just there, as an accident of nature, and then God has to intervene in some special way in order to make his will known to us in a completely unrelated manner. Rather, in making a career choice, we ought to take seriously the doctrine of divine providence: God himself gives us whatever legitimate abilities, concerns, and interests we in fact possess. These are his gifts, and for that very reason they can serve as indicators of his will for our lives. In coming to know ourselves and our situation, we come to know God's will. The Protestant theologian Emil Brunner claims, in fact, that "the idea of the Calling and of the Call is unintelligible apart from that of Divine Providence. The God who says to me here and now: 'Act where you are, as you are,' is not One who comes on the scene after all that has been done previously has been done without His knowledge. Nothing can happen apart from Him. . . . To Him it is no accident that you are what you are here and now, an accident with which He must come to terms. He Himself places you where you are." Too often our search for God's will in our lives has been skewed by a highly secularized view of the world. We don't really believe that God is present and at work in the concrete events and circumstances of this world. Rather we think of Him as distant, removed, putting in only occasional appearances here on earth. If God speaks to us at all, he must speak to us in the freakish and miraculous, but not in the normal, everyday course of affairs.

At this point, however, we might step back and wonder if doing what God is calling us to do is always a matter of doing that for which we are best qualified. Certainly the Bible records numerous instances in which this was emphatically not the case. Are we developing a truly biblical approach to career choice? After all, a stuttering Moses was called by God to speak before Pharaoh; Jonah was instructed to call the city of Nineveh to repentance, a city he himself would have liked to see burn under God's judgment; and the personally unimpressive Paul was prevailed upon to present the gospel to the entire Gentile world. It seems unlikely that a modern vocational counseling agency would have directed these biblical characters to their respective tasks on the basis of their native interests and talents.

True. And the point is well taken. God does sometimes call people to do that for which they are outstandingly unqualified; and sometimes he calls people to do what they are entirely disinclined to do. But when he does that, it is because he is about to give a special demonstration of his power. That is, he is about to perform a miracle — which is, by definition, a departure from the normal course of affairs. As a rule people are to do that for which they are qualified. Of course, there are exceptions to the rule. And we must remain open to the possibility of an exception in our own case through prayer and awareness of God's leading hand.

GARY D. BADCOCK

"Choosing"

Gary Badcock is a Christian ethicist who wrote the book from which the excerpt below has been taken in order to correct what he took to be some unwarranted claims in writers like Lee Hardy. Like Hardy, Badcock addresses the whole matter of career choice from a theological point of view. Like Hardy, Badcock believes that issues of personal identity (who am I, and what sort of person should I become?) are closely related to decisions about what we should do to earn a living. Yet their conclusions are different. "The will of God," says Badcock, "does not extend down to the details of career choice." He claims that this view is more "liberating" than a view like Hardy's, which does insist that God's will includes the details of our choices of careers. Do you think Badcock is right?

Both Hardy and Badcock include autobiographical material in their accounts of Christian vocation. Hardy tells us about the many occupations he actually held, whereas Badcock compares what he finally wound up doing with two other occupations he *might* have chosen. How are these two very different strategies of self-disclosure linked to the different accounts of vocation that the two men develop?

Badcock directly compares and contrasts his own account of the meaningful and significant life to Aristotle's. What kinds of ideal characters emerge from the two accounts?

Individual people usually struggle with the question of career choice. The adolescent, encouraged, perhaps, by a fond parent, may well have a set view of what the future holds, but the transition to adulthood often brings into play serious doubts about formerly cherished ambitions. The young man

From Gary D. Badcock, *The Way of Life: A Theology of Christian Vocation* (Grand Rapids: William B. Eerdmans Publishing Company, 1998), pp. 134-142.

who decides to marry, similarly, will inevitably reflect carefully on his choice of partner, but he will most likely be able to carry through with his commitment only in fear and trembling — sometimes quite literally at the altar on the "day of reckoning." Doubt is oftentimes a necessary ingredient in the quest for certainty, doubt that arises "out of the depths," *de profundis.*

Such considerations are prominent in a recent study by the Canadian philosopher James Horne, in which the relevance of mysticism to the question of career choice is highlighted. Horne notes that the typical experience of the mystic in the Christian tradition (among others) involves a path through darkness into light. The darkness is a necessary stage within the whole journey of spiritual development. Horne attempts to draw a parallel between such mystical experience and the psychological processes by which individuals make decisions concerning their future. There is, he suggests, much to be gained from such an analysis. The feeling of being "at sea," and even of lacking an integrated self-image and of wishing to have one, is common currency in many young people's experience. We cannot choose for the future without a sense of identity in the present and without a realistic sense of what we may become. Horne's treatment of mysticism and vocation allows us to understand this as a necessary part of the process by which such a decision is made — to give it a name, to "baptize" the apparent meaninglessness as something religiously and psychologically necessary. Yet the essential thing for those who wrestle with career choice in such an existential way is finally to transcend the darkness in such a way as to lay plans for the future, to have a project in life.

One must, of course, distinguish between what is theoretically possible and what is pragmatically possible, between the tentative decisions made at some earlier stage in life and what actually becomes possible on the basis of decisions already made. I may wish to work at such and such an occupation in some geographical area; in the event, I may be able to realize the first ambition, but not the second. I may even discover as life goes on that the second rather than the first ambition was closer to my heart. It may be that living "in exile" will be what pains me most about my circumstances as I mature; my children, for example, may thus grow up without knowing their grandparents. A sense of place, of location in the world, can be extremely important, whereas the working role assumed is less important. The potential variety of factors to consider is enormous, so much so that, in the final analysis, there is no escaping the conclusion that any career choice will inevitably be a risky venture, undertaken "in faith," or in a kind of faith, in relation to what is as yet unseen and unknown.

Vocation and Mission

For the Christian, however, the decisive consideration is that a life project must be capable of being integrated into the overall mission of Christ. Christ's mission is a mission of love, of self-giving service, and of obedience to God. My argument has been that the question "What ought I to do?" really leads to another: "What kind of person ought I to be?" There is no clear answer to the first — insofar, at least, as it is a question concerned solely with career choice. However, much clearer answers can be given to the second question. I ought to be a person for whom love, service, and obedience to God are the major priorities. The Christian ethic is flexible insofar as it allows a multitude of possibilities by which one can fulfill such goals, but there is nevertheless an irreducible core concern within it, which can never be relinquished.

Let me illustrate this by outlining three possible paths that I might have taken in life. The first option requires some reference to my own family background. For centuries my ancestors have made a living from the sea. I also might have done so. I come from a region in which the fishing industry is a major source of wealth, and in which there were opportunities for a young man such as I was when I left school. Had I become a fisherman, my life would certainly have been very different from what it is today: I would, for example, most probably have remained a member of the local community within which I was born and grew up and thus maintained the link between my family and that place, a link that has lasted (until now) for some three centuries. The friends of youth would have remained the friends of adult life, and I would have been at hand for my aging parents. The commandment to honor one's father and mother would have been fulfilled in this way. I would also have been able to maintain contact with people and with a place that I love. No doubt there would have been opportunities to become involved locally in community and church work. I would have taken up a useful role in relation to the rest of society providing food for others. Had I married and raised a family, I could have shown love in that context; the monotony of early mornings and days at sea would have been offset by the knowledge that a family was cared for. My Christian faith would no doubt have remained simpler than it is now, for I would probably have read little theology, but this would not have been a great burden or hindrance to my fulfillment, which would have come in other ways. I am, in fact, attracted to such a life still, punctuated as it is by the rhythm of the seasons and based as it is on strong ties with the sea and the land.

Would any of this been incompatible with sharing in the mission of

Christ? I do not think so. Some of it would have been much more compatible with it than the path I finally took in life. For one surely owes a debt to one's own society and people, to those, for example, who provided an education, and to the Christian community that nurtured one's faith. The people whose lives might have been affected by my own were very much as real in that world as they are in my situation today. And for me, an especially important consideration is that my own father would not have died while I worked far away.

Another alternative was available. I might well have gone into business. Suppose, for the sake of argument, that the business had been successful and that I had gone on to build up a modest company which, after twenty years, employed twenty people and looked set to make me modestly wealthy. Would this have been compatible with the mission of Christ? The answer, I believe, is yes — especially in my home context. In resource-based economies, there is often insufficient secondary industry. The result is that there is much unemployment and sometimes surprising poverty. In such a context, the creation of wealth in business would have been more than self-service or worship at the altar of greed, even were such sins a factor in the whole story. For the creation of wealth can be the creation of new possibilities for an entire community, with prospects of work for young people and a prosperity that enables social as well as economic well-being. For a few people, at least, the cycle of welfare dependency might have been broken. Economic prospects can generate hope as well as wealth, sustaining communities and helping people to live a full life. And along the way, opportunities for service, for living in love within a family, or for participating constructively in the life of a Christian congregation would also have been present.

In the event, of course, I became a scholar. Contrary to my own expectation, which was that I would enter the Christian ministry and work with my own people in a pastoral way, I was drawn more and more deeply into academic issues and into an academic culture far from my original goals. It has been a surprising journey for me, going against my own plans at a number of crucial junctures. However, I find that the needs of my neighbor are much the same here as elsewhere, and that the so-called "ivory tower" of higher education has as much genuine reality in it as does any other sphere of life. As well as the usual grind that is the warp and woof of most occupations, ample opportunities for serving others and even for preaching and pastoral care arise. In the meantime, I have a wife and family, and within the home I am sustained and I help to sustain other human lives in dignity and in love.

Which of the three paths "ought" I to have taken? There is no clear answer to such a question, for there is no clear moral imperative governing the situation. In each case, the opportunity to participate in one way or another in the mission of Christ was open to me. I would go further, in fact, and say that it was *equally* open to me under any of the scenarios presented, for there is nothing especially saintly about my present work as a theologian, nothing intrinsic to it to lift it beyond the possibility of self-centeredness or faithlessness. The calling to be faithful and loving is one that extends to any and all walks of life and that cannot be identified with any one of them. And it is this calling to faithfulness and love with which Christian vocation is really concerned, the calling to follow the one who obeyed the Father to the end, who laid down his life for his friends — the one who, as such, was raised from the dead and exalted to the right hand of the Father.

The Way of Life

Psychological studies have demonstrated that people with a clear sense of direction are often also more integrated as persons. It is only what might be expected, though one has to add to this the qualification that some who *appear* to be most certain are also sometimes the most vulnerable should doubts about their chosen path ever arise. Nevertheless, there is a sense in which one constantly lives, and can only live, with a view to the future, to what one may become. Only thus can one be a full human being. The acorn becomes an oak, and in the same way the youth becomes an adult, while adulthood brings with it special opportunities and responsibilities; the adult, finally, grows old, enters into a period of retirement, and at last dies. Life itself is organic, being fundamentally characterized by growth and movement. Religious life is similar: one of the pervasive metaphors found within it is the "journey," the "pilgrimage," by which one travels along life's way into the light and love of God. Here as elsewhere, without such orientation to the future life itself would be inconceivable.

The philosopher Aristotle, who saw the entire universe in such developmental terms, once observed that we are likely to develop to our full potential only if we have sight of our goal. Like archers who have a mark to aim at, it is obviously more likely that we will hit the target if we can actually see it than if we do not. Aristotle himself construed the goal of human life as happiness, by which he meant a general state of well-being corresponding to the fulfillment of various aspects of "natural" human potentiality, rather than a purely emotional state. He then went on to develop a moral philosophy of the virtues — that is, those qualities "by virtue of which" a person can attain to the human goal. Thus the human acorn becomes the adult oak.

There is, I believe, a great deal of truth in this. A life is "full" to the extent that a person has reached a goal that is appropriate to a human being, and to this extent such a person will achieve "happiness" in the sense of well-being. What is entirely missing from Aristotle's account of the moral life, however, is any reference to the human relation to God as the context of such development. And at this point, I want to say, his position is badly flawed.

Jesus speaks of the human goal in two ways. The first is in terms of the great commandments. The human goal and the divine imperative here coalesce: "you shall love the Lord your God with all your heart . . . ; you shall love your neighbor as yourself" (Mark 12:30-31 par.). From the standpoint of the spiritual life, the human goal is succinctly summed up in these key statements. The second, and literally crucial way in which Jesus speaks of the goal of life is in terms of discipleship: "If any want to become my followers, let them deny themselves and take up their cross and follow me" (Mark 8:34 par.). According to this teaching, we find life by relinquishing it, by sacrificing our small goods to the overriding good of the gospel of the kingdom and for the sake of the name of Christ. I have chosen the title *The Way of Life* for this book with this in view: the "way of life," according to the Christian gospel, is a paradoxical "way" that involves self-denial and often leads through suffering. There is no other "way," in this sense, to our goal. Nevertheless, within this one "way" are a multiplicity of individual paths that we tread. But we navigate by means of the same signs, following the same rules, living one life of love and discipleship.

At the beginning of this book, I wrote of my own childish belief that God had a plan for each life, a plan that a given individual might miss if he or she was not attentive to God's call and obedient to his voice. As a youth, I took such a view. It was as if I were waiting for a bus, or a "streetcar named vocation"; if I became bored and decided to wander away from the street, it would pass me by. But is it really possible to miss the will of God in this way? I have found such a vision of the Christian vocation to be extremely unhelpful, and because I am convinced that there are many people (especially young people) who are similarly mistaken, I have sought to develop a different understanding of the Christian vocation. Christian vocation is not reducible to the acquisition of a career goal or to its realization in time. It is, rather, something relating to the great issues of the spiritual life. It has to do with what one lives "for" rather than with what one does.

Such an understanding, once developed, can liberate us from the tyranny of such notions as the one that some have vocations whereas others do not, from the idea that having a vocation is incompatible with being unemployed or retired, from despair over not being able to "hear" God's voice when looking into the future at turning points in life. The human vocation is to do the will of God and so to live life "abundantly" (John 10:10), but the will of God does not extend down to the details of career choice. And once this is realized, I believe, then it becomes possible for us to live more adventurously, more freely, breathing in an atmosphere of love rather than law, looking for *our own* way to share the good news of the gospel in daily life, whether in career choices or in business or in the ordinary transactions of the daily round. Here, new possibilities open for the creating of Christian lifestyle and modes of spirituality that reflect the generosity of God in Christ. For this, at heart, is the Christian's vocation.

DIETRICH BONHOEFFER

"The Place of Responsibility"

Dietrich Bonhoeffer (1906-1945) was a German Lutheran pastor and theologian who was executed by the Nazis in the last days of World War II in Europe. He grew up in a very accomplished extended family, and he inherited from his parents a deep sense of social responsibility. During the course of his ministry in the 1930s, the Nazis relentlessly persecuted those churches and seminaries that were critical of their regime, including the Confessing Church seminary that Bonhoeffer headed in Finkenwalde. Because of his own public statements and affiliations, the Nazis withdrew his authorization for academic teaching in 1936, prohibited him from speaking publicly anywhere in the German Reich in 1940, and forbade him to write for publication in 1941.

The Nazis' suspicions of Bonhoeffer were not without foundation. As all avenues of more conventional protest and opposition were closed off, he became involved in a conspiracy to kill Hitler. He did so in full recognition that such an action was a lesser evil, but an evil nonetheless. He

From *Ethics*, in Dietrich Bonhoeffer Works, volume 6 (Minneapolis: Fortress Press, 2005), pp. 289-297.

wrote the many papers later assembled as his *Ethics* during the period of the most intense military engagements of World War II, from 1941 through 1944, when he was himself most active in the conspiracy. For him, questions of vocation and responsibility were urgent matters of life and death. Did his calling as a pastor and theologian require him to attend first and last to his immediate, circumscribed duties to his parishioners and students, he wondered, or did it require something more of him?

Because Bonhoeffer's understanding of vocation was forged in the midst of a hideous regime that had incorporated almost all of those "places" or "orders" in which human beings find themselves stationed — family, church, state, work — into an evil, totalitarian system, Bonhoeffer's account of vocation has a decidedly critical and countercultural edge to it. Like Lee Hardy, Bonhoeffer argues that we all are stationed in many places concurrently, but he is much more alert than Hardy to how these places or orders can themselves be corrupted and how their various duties can and often do conflict with one another. And like Gary Badcock, Bonhoeffer insists that Christians are called above all things to a life of radical discipleship, but he is much more concerned than Badcock to specify what such discipleship actually means within our workplaces, families, churches, and polities.

For Bonhoeffer, radical obedience to Christ's call meant radical freedom to be fully responsible to and for others. Both because of his courage and because of the character of his witness, Bonhoeffer's account of Christian vocation has found wide admiration from both Christians and non-Christians. How might your own work and the character of your own relationships to others change if you were to adopt Bonhoeffer's view of vocation and responsibility?

———

In encounter with Jesus Christ, a person experiences God's call [*Ruf*], and in it the calling [*Berufung*] to a life in community with Jesus Christ. Human beings experience the divine grace that claims them. It is not human beings who seek out grace in its place, for God lives in unapproachable light (1 Tim. 6:16). Instead, grace seeks out and finds human beings in their place — the Word became flesh (John 1:14) — and claims them precisely there. It is a place that in every case and in every respect is burdened with sin and guilt, be it a royal throne, the home of a respected citizen, or a shanty of misery. It is a place of this world. This visitation by grace took place in Jesus Christ becoming human, and still occurs in the word about Jesus Christ that the Holy

Spirit brings. The call reaches us as Gentile or Jew, slave or free, man or woman, married or unmarried. Right where they happen to be, human beings ought to hear the call and allow themselves to be claimed by it. It is not as if this would imply a justification of slavery, marriage, or singleness as such. Instead, those who are called may belong to God in one state or the other. Only by the call of grace heard in Jesus Christ, by which I am claimed, may I live justified before God as slave or free, married or single. From Christ's perspective this life is now my vocation; from my own perspective it is my responsibility.

. . . People do not fulfill the responsibility laid on them by faithfully performing their earthly vocational obligations as citizens, workers, and parents, but by hearing the call of Jesus Christ that, although it leads them also into earthly obligations, is never synonymous with these, but instead always transcends them as a reality standing before and behind them. Vocation in the New Testament sense is never a sanctioning of the worldly orders as such. Its Yes always includes at the same time the sharpest No, the sharpest protest against the world. Luther's return from the monastery into the world, into a "vocation," is, in the genuine spirit of the New Testament, the fiercest attack that has been launched and the hardest blow that has been struck against the world since the time of early Christianity. Now a stand against the world is taken *within* the world. Vocation is the place at which one responds to the call of Christ and thus lives responsibly. The task given to me by my vocation is thus limited; but my responsibility to the call of Jesus Christ knows no bounds. . . .

The question of the place and the limit of responsibility has led us to the concept of vocation. However, this answer is valid only where vocation is understood simultaneously in all its dimensions. The call of Jesus Christ is the call to belong to Christ completely; it is Christ's address and claim at the place at which this call encounters me; vocation comprises work with things and issues [*sachliche Arbeit*] as well as personal relations; it requires a definite "field of activity," though never as a value in itself but only in responsibility to Jesus Christ. By being related to Jesus Christ, the "definite field of activity" is set free from any isolation. The boundary of vocation has been broken open not only vertically, through Christ, but horizontally, with regard to the extent of responsibility. Let us say I am a medical doctor, for example. In dealing with a concrete case I serve not only my patient, but also the body of scientific knowledge, and thus science and knowledge of truth in general. Although in practice I render this service in my concrete situation — for example, at a patient's bedside — I nevertheless remain aware of my responsibility toward the whole, and only thus fulfill my vocation. In so doing, it may come to the point that in a particular case I must recognize and fulfill my concrete responsibility as a physician no longer only at a patient's bedside, but, for example, in taking a public stance against a measure that poses a threat to medical science, or human life, or science in general. Vocation is responsibility, and responsibility is the whole response of the whole person to reality as a whole. This is precisely why a myopic self-limitation to one's vocational obligation in the narrowest sense is out of the question; such a limitation would be irresponsibility. The nature of free responsibility rules out any legal regulation of when and to what extent human vocation and responsibility entail breaking out [*Durchbrechen*] of the "definite field of activity." This can happen only after seriously considering one's immediate vocational obligations, the dangers of encroaching on the responsibilities of others, and finally the total picture of the issue at hand. It will then be my free responsibility in response to the call of Jesus Christ that leads me in one direction or the other. Responsibility in a vocation follows the call of Christ alone. . . .

But now is it not the case that the law of God as revealed in the Decalogue, and the divine mandates of marriage, work, and government, establish an inviolable boundary for any responsible action in one's vocation? Would any transgressing [*Durchbrechung*] of this boundary not amount to insubordination against the revealed will of God? Here the recurring problem of law and freedom presents itself with ultimate urgency. It now threatens to introduce a contradiction into the will of God itself. Certainly no responsible activity is possible that does not consider with ultimate seriousness the boundary that God established in the law. Nevertheless, precisely as responsible action it will not separate this law from its giver. Only as the Redeemer in Jesus Christ will it be able to recognize the God by whose law the world is held in order; it will recognize Jesus Christ as the ultimate reality to whom it is responsible, and precisely through Christ it will be freed from the law for the responsible deed. For the sake of God and the neighbor, which means for Christ's sake, one may be freed from keeping the Sabbath holy, honoring one's parents, indeed from the entire divine law. It is a freedom that transgresses this law, but only in order to affirm it anew. The suspension of the law must only serve its true fulfillment. In war, for example, there is killing, lying, and seizing of property solely in order to reinstate the validity of life, truth, and property. Breaking the law must be *recognized* in all its gravity — "blessed are you if you know what you are doing; however, if you do not know what you are doing you are cursed and a transgressor of the law." Whether an action springs from responsibility or cynicism can become evident only in whether the objective guilt one incurs by breaking the law is recognized and borne, and whether by the very act of breaking it the law is truly sanctified. The will of God is thus sanctified in the deed that arises out of freedom. Precisely because we are dealing with a deed that arises from freedom, the one who acts is not torn apart by destructive conflict, but instead can with confidence and inner integrity do the unspeakable, namely, in the very act of breaking the law to sanctify it.

FREDERICK BUECHNER

"Vocation"

Frederick Buechner is a contemporary novelist and theologian whose facility with the English language and whose ability to condense complex issues into memorable aphorisms have made many of his theological formulations especially quotable. Indeed, his special gift for verbal economy may have encouraged him to produce a kind of dictionary of Christian theological terms in the book from which the selection below has been taken, *Wishful Thinking: A Theological ABC*. The term that appeared under the letter V in that volume was, of course, "vocation."

The conclusion of Buechner's short discussion of vocation is perhaps the most widely quoted formulation of vocation among contemporary American Christians. "The place God calls you to is the place where your deep gladness and the world's deep hunger meet." By "deep gladness," do you suppose that Buechner means "contentment," or does he mean the kind of joy that can be present even in the midst of suffering? Which of those two understandings would be more consonant with the ideas of vocation set forth by the other writers in this anthology?

From Frederick Buechner, *Wishful Thinking: A Theological ABC* (New York: Harper and Row, 1973), p. 95.

[Vocation] comes from the Latin *vocare*, to call, and means the work a person is called to by God.

There are all different kinds of voices calling you to all different kinds of work, and the problem is to find out which is the voice of God rather than of Society, say, or the Superego, or Self-Interest.

By and large a good rule for finding out is this: The kind of work God usually calls you to is the kind of work (a) that you need most to do and (b) that the world most needs to have done. If you really get a kick out of your work, you've presumably met requirement (a), but if your work is writing cigarette ads, the chances are you've missed requirement (b). On the other hand, if your work is being a doctor in a leper colony, you have probably met requirement (b), but if most of the time you're bored and depressed by it, the chances are you have not only bypassed (a), but probably aren't helping your patients much either.

Neither the hair shirt nor the soft berth will do. The place God calls you to is the place where your deep gladness and the world's deep hunger meet.

WILL CAMPBELL

"Vocation as Grace"

Will Campbell, who lives on a farm in Tennessee, has been upsetting Christian complacencies for many years as a preacher, activist, essayist, and novelist. Like Bonhoeffer, Campbell believes that "when Christ calls a man, he bids him come and die." Campbell therefore has no patience for the idea of vocation as something that simply gives a spiritual gloss to what we have chosen to do for ourselves by ourselves in any case.

In the story that he recounts below, Campbell challenges the conventional Christian notion that vocation is a purely individual matter. He suggests that our callings are best negotiated in community with others,

From William D. Campbell, "Vocation as Grace," in *Callings!* ed. James Y. Holloway and Will D. Campbell (New York: Paulist Press, 1974), pp. 279-280.

through a process that leads us to discern not only our own gifts but also our own needs and weaknesses, not only the rich potentials of the world but also its poverty. Do you agree with Campbell in thinking that we cannot rightly hear our own call unless and until we recognize both others' dependence on us and our dependence on them?

———————————————

Long before the process of my vocational self-examination (justification) began I once cornered and talked to a high wire artist in a small traveling circus. I asked him why he chose that particular way of making a living. The first few minutes were filled with circus romance — the thrill of hurling through space, feeling at the last instant that pasty flesh of two always welcomed hands pressing around the wrists, swinging you forward to the next set of pasty hands which in turn deliver you safely back to the starting platform; the joy of laughter and approval and applause in the eyes of "children of all ages," the clanking of train wheels moving you on to the next city; even the part about it being a comfortable life with good pay. But finally he said what I had not expected him to say. "Now you really want to know why I go up there on that damned thing night after night after night?" I said I did. "Man, I would have quit it a long time ago. But my sister is up there. And my wife and my father are up there. My sister has more troubles than Job. My wife is a devil-may-care nut and my old man is getting older. If I wasn't up there, some bad night, man . . . smash!" His foot stomped the floor with a bone cracking thud.

"H'mmm."

He started to walk away but I had one more question to ask and ran after him. "But why do *they* stay up there?" He looked like he didn't want to answer, wasn't going to answer. But then he did. Turning from the door of the boy's locker room in the county seat high school, with a brown craft cardboard box and heavy crayola sign: MEN'S COSTUMES above it for the evening's performance, he looked me up and down and then, as he disappeared, blurted it out: "Because I drink too much!"

II

QUESTIONS

1

Are Some Lives
More Significant Than Others?

Of all the old Hollywood films regularly rerun on television, the one that investigates the question at the heart of this chapter is in a class by itself. Frank Capra's *It's a Wonderful Life* (1946) may have been seen by more Americans than any other film — or at least by more than any made before the age of the blockbusters. Because it usually appears several times during the Christmas season, millions of families have incorporated it into their holiday rituals, and even those who have never seen it are unwittingly familiar with it, since its plot has been imitated, adapted, and satirized in countless television shows and series. It is hard to think of another piece of popular culture that so clearly joins the two traditions that inform this anthology: Democracy and Christianity. Moreover, as its title suggests, the film explores the very question implied by this anthology's title: What would a "life that matters" look like?

It's a Wonderful Life also demonstrates what makes this chapter's question — "Are some lives more significant than others?" — at one and the same time so important and so impossible to answer conclusively. The film's central character, George Bailey, was born and raised in Bedford Falls, which could be almost any small town in America. As he grew up, he planned to leave Bedford Falls, go to college, see the world, and achieve great things, things on a par with the feats of valor his older brother performed during World War II. At every turn, however, something happens to frustrate George's ambitions. Just as he is about to leave for college, for example, his father suddenly dies, and George feels obliged to postpone his college admission in order to take over the family building and loan business. Time and again, George yields to a sense of civic duty or to claims made by loved ones upon his time and energies, deferring the fulfillment of his own dreams.

The action of the movie turns on a mistake made by a beloved associate of George — a mistake that threatens to ruin his business and to place the entire town's future in the hands of the miserly villain, Mr. Potter, who has been for years plotting to undo George's good deeds. This impending chain of events, which George feels powerless to stop, drives George to the verge of suicide. He concludes that his life has been a failure, and he bitterly regrets having sacrificed his own aspirations to satisfy the needs of others. All of his efforts have come to nothing, he concludes; he seems to have led a life that did not really matter to anyone, least of all to himself. At this point, a fledgling angel who has not yet "earned his wings" appears to George. He invites George to reexamine his belief that his life was of relatively little or no significance by showing him what the town of Bedford Falls would have been like if George had not been an integral part of its common life. As the hypothetical flashback unfolds without George in it, we see along with him that Bedford Falls would have become the American nightmare, a company town controlled by the malevolent Mr. Potter, a town without pity, without spirit, without hope, without faith, and without love. It would not even have been Bedford Falls; it would have been "Pottersville." The portrayal of Pottersville may be melodrama, but it is melodrama that makes a crucially important point: George's life did matter.

Whatever one might think about the aesthetic merits of the film, a story such as this does complicate the question of whether some lives are more significant than others. In order to determine the relative significance of George's life, the film suggests, one would have to know not just what George actually *did* accomplish; one would have to know as well everything that *would* have happened if George had not been a presence within his community. Without an "angelic" perspective or a "God's eye point of view," it would seem impossible to know whether and to what extent George's life was a life that mattered. And indeed, some Christians have thought that this film vindicates their view that the significance of our lives lies not in our own hands but in God's, both because we cannot by ourselves control the consequences of our actions and because only God can know the real differences each of us has made in the world. Better therefore to carry out virtuously the tasks that have been given to us, no matter how humble they may seem, than to seek glorious achievements elsewhere. Better faithfully to fulfill your duties as manager of the Bailey Building and Loan than to long for your brother's heroic life as a fighter pilot in World War II.

The sermon that introduces this chapter's readings includes a similar argument made by C. S. Lewis, perhaps the best-known Christian writer of the twentieth century, to a group of young men who were students at Oxford University in the autumn of 1939. With their country at war with Germany and their brothers heading off to battle, these young men were facing, in real life, exactly the same dilemma that the fictional George Bailey would face in the film made shortly after that same war ended. Longing to take part in what seemed to be more important action by fighting for their country, they were tempted to despise their quiet and ordinary lives at the university. Lewis's sermon, "Learning in War-Time," addressed this temptation in part by arguing that study is itself a kind of work with its own dignity and purposes, a pursuit that needs to be honored no more and no less than piloting an airplane or wiring a house. (Or, to put this in Lewis's own Christian vocabulary, study at a university or college *is* a vocation, not merely a preparation for one.) Lewis also pointed out that, although war makes death more visible, real matters of life and death are always close at hand, even for students.

Lewis's sermon reminds us that, though questions about the relative significance of different paths of life may be impossible to answer definitively, we nevertheless cannot escape them. Such questions will sooner or later "find" us, whether in the large, sudden, and dramatic way they found the young men at Oxford in 1939 or in the small, persistent, but unobtrusive way they found George Bailey as he was growing up in Bedford Falls. We've already explored (in the general introduction to this anthology) some of the reasons why contemporary Americans are suspicious of making relative judgments about the worth or merit or significance of the lives of their fellow citizens. And indeed, some critics have explained the appeal of *It's a Wonderful Life* by suggesting that it reinforces the democratic conviction that millions of ordinary men like George Bailey are every bit as noble and worthy of praise as their alleged "betters," who have apparently achieved much more in life than George Bailey did. On the other hand, the enduring appeal of the film also suggests that questions of relative significance continue to haunt us.

When life's choices and questions suddenly come upon us with irresistible force, having thought through such questions may prove to be important preparation. The readings that follow can help us to do such thinking. As the fantastic plot of *It's a Wonderful Life* demonstrates, one helpful way to explore questions of significance is to reflect on the life of someone caught in extreme circumstances that dramatize alternatives with unusual clarity. At the same time, the film's detailed examination of the ordinary life of one man demonstrates the value of looking in some detail at the complete lives of human beings who don't stand out as heroic. Considering a variety of lives, moreover, will enable us to compare their relative significance or choice-worthiness. And so the texts gathered in this chapter portray both extraordinary lives and lives that are apparently less outstanding, including the following:

- Aristotle's argued preference for the short but splendid life
- A scene from Homer's *Iliad*
- *The Martyrdom of Perpetua*
- Dorothy Day's tribute to St. Therese of Lisieux
- Three biographical sketches
- Thomas Gray's "Elegy Written in a Country Churchyard"

We have encountered the writings of Aristotle before, in Part I, where his *Nicomachean Ethics* served as the premier instance of the vocabulary of virtue. Here, in a short passage from that same work, Aristotle wonders about a hypothetical situation. Suppose you were given the following choice: either you could live a short life of heroic splendor, sacrificing yourself for the sake of a noble cause, or you could live a long life of steady but unremarkable accomplishment in any honorable occupation, serving concurrently as a good parent and a reliable friend and neighbor to others. Which would be more choice-worthy? Which life would be the more significant one?

Aristotle thought that the more choice-worthy life would be the extraordinary life of noble sacrifice. It is clear, however, that not everyone would agree. For example, in J. D. Salinger's *A Catcher in the Rye*, an American novel that has been a persistent favorite of high school and college students for the last half-century, a teacher offers the principal character the following counsel: "It is the mark of the immature man to want to die nobly for a cause; it is the mark of the mature man to want to live humbly for one." The teacher meant to be speaking in favor of the longer, more modest life, in opposition to the short, splendid one commended by Aristotle. But in fact is it always so evident which path is which? At first it might seem that George Bailey chose to follow the advice of the teacher, whereas his brother chose to heed Aristotle's counsel. But on second thought, perhaps George (nobly) sacrificed the life he hoped to live for the sake of others, while his brother (humbly) chose to place his own life in jeopardy for the same reasons.

Few of us will be presented with a clear moment of choice between Aristotle's sharply defined alternatives. We can nevertheless learn a great deal from pondering our own reactions to characters who were. One such character was the Greek warrior Achilles in Homer's epic poem the *Iliad*. Another was the young woman Vibia Perpetua, a North African Christian who in the year 203 CE chose to face martyrdom at the hands of the Romans rather than return to the safety of her father's house. In the course of discovering to what extent and why we admire such characters, we may also gain insight into what matters most deeply to us about our own present lives and the lives we might choose to live.

Achilles, a human warrior whose mother is the goddess Thetis, tells his friends in Book IX of the *Iliad* what his mother had told him: not one but two fates governed his destiny. He could choose a long life of mild satisfaction in his homeland, the ancient Greek equivalent of the one that George Bailey led in the town of Bedford Falls; *or* he could choose a short but heroic life that would bring him lasting fame, a life not unlike that of George's brother. For our purposes here, the most pertinent portions of the selection from the *Iliad* are the arguments Achilles' friends advance to persuade him to choose to fight for his country rather than to retreat to the comparatively secure life he might enjoy at home. Do you agree with these arguments? Why or why not? In the world of ancient Greece, of course, a choice like this was available only to men, and the only setting for heroism was war. In our present situation, however, both men and women may have to decide whether to embrace activities that put one's life in peril or that shorten it in the course of achieving worthy goals for the sake of others — activities of which war is simply the most vivid example.

The example of Vibia Perpetua, a real-life character who faced a choice between "dying nobly for a cause and living humbly for one," raises another set of questions. To what extent are we justified in making others suffer for the sake of our own favored causes and convictions? We know from the text that Perpetua's father was devastated by her choice, and we can only imagine what her young child experienced while growing up without his mother. Choosing the short and splendid life over the long and undistinguished one may bring lasting fame and other goods, but it may at the same time impose lasting sorrow on others. What are we to make of this latter possibility?

Before we jump to the conclusion that this question about the relative merits of a short, heroic life and a long, ordinary one is merely "academic," we should notice that it is akin to a somewhat less momentous question that many people today must sooner or later face. We will encounter this question in a later chapter, when we consider whether an unbalanced life, marked by extraordinary achievement in one field of human endeavor, is preferable to a balanced life that is marked by solid but relatively ordinary achievements in many. Do I devote myself entirely to finding the cure for cancer, ignoring my family and immediate community, or do I settle for work as a medical technician in part because I want to have plenty of time to raise my children, care for my aging parents, and be a good neighbor and citizen?

Such stark alternatives rarely present themselves in pure form, to be sure. Indeed, elements of the ordinary and the extraordinary, the balanced and the unbalanced, are no doubt commingled in the lives of many, where they may be woven together in all kinds of ways. One remarkable example appears in the life of one of the most widely known saints of the modern period, a saint familiar and beloved to millions of Roman Catholics around the world as "The Little Flower," Therese of Lisieux. We will meet Saint Therese through the words of Dorothy Day, an American Catholic who founded the Catholic Worker Movement in 1933 and later wrote a book in tribute to Therese's role in Day's own spiritual and moral formation. In Day's account, Therese is at once a spiritual heroine and a model of humility; a person who both sacrificed everything and attained everything worth having; a saint who entered the extraordinary realm of God through the ordinary doorways of housework, illness, and prayer.

After encountering Day's sketch of Saint Therese on the heels of the ancient stories of Achilles and Perpetua, some readers may be relieved to turn to sources that depict lives in times and places more like our own. An entrepreneur who developed a single fast food restaurant into a global business; a mail handler and bus attendant who sustained his wife in her political activity; a writer who became obsessed with discovering and publishing the truth about a terrible injustice in recent history: these three very different lives, described in the readings below, invite us both to marvel at human diversity and to wonder about which of the three was most choice-worthy.

Though different one from another, all three of these lives were at least considered worthy of notice upon their death; all were honored at the end in that they were remembered, even celebrated, by eulogists or obituary writers. By contrast, what should we think and say about the "short and simple annals of the poor," about the obituaries that weren't, about the significance of those whose "lot forbade" them to distinguish themselves in public memory and who therefore led lives of almost complete anonymity? Were these lives that mattered? Did they matter by comparison to those, like Achilles, who earned honor, glory, and everlasting fame? How significant do these anonymous lives seem in comparison to the three actual lives that were remembered and memorialized in the readings?

One of the great poems of the English language, Thomas Gray's "Elegy Written in a Country Churchyard," raises these latter questions in a powerful and poignant way, concluding with the poet's own epitaph. The literary forms that celebrate or summarize a full life — the obituary, the eulogy, the elegy, and the epitaph — are perhaps most ideally suited to raise questions about the substance and the relative significance of human lives. In addition to reading and discussing the ones that follow, it might be a good spiritual and intellectual exercise to try to write your own obituary or epitaph. What kind of life do you hope you will have lived when you come to die? How would you like to be remembered? What difference do you hope your life might make in the world?

C. S. LEWIS

"Learning in War-Time"

Clive Staples Lewis (1898-1963) taught literature for many years at Oxford University in England. This selection is a sermon he delivered to students in a chapel service there on October 22, 1939. The Second World War had begun less than two months earlier. These students surely knew many classmates and relatives who had enlisted in the armed forces, and they must have felt that they should do so, too. At the beginning of the sermon, in fact, Lewis articulates the question on their minds: "Why should we — indeed how can we — continue to take an interest in these placid occupations when the lives of our friends and the liberties of Europe are in the balance?" They were questioning whether their daily lives as students had any significance during a time of historic struggle.

At this intense moment of national emergency and individual confusion, Lewis urged these students to "see the present calamity in a true perspective." Human beings always live on the precipice of calamity, he noted; and though war makes this reality more visible, the question of whether being a student can be justified is applicable even in peacetime, when students might also be asked why they "spend any fraction of the little time allowed them in this world on such comparative trivialities as literature or art, mathematics or biology." In the selection that follows, Lewis provides a justification for study, both in war and in peace, and encourages the students in front of him to embrace this as their calling at the present time.

Lewis himself had been a student at Oxford during the First World War. He left his studies, was commissioned as an officer at the age of nineteen, and was wounded in battle. He became a Christian several years later. Lewis is probably best known as the author of the Chronicles of

From C. S. Lewis, *The Weight of Glory* (1949; New York: HarperCollins, 2001), pp. 55-63.

Narnia, a seven-volume work of fiction for young people that features a number of stirring battles while also imparting a Christian vision of the world. Many of his more explicitly theological books, which are notable for making accessible a challenging ecumenical version of Christian faith, continue to be widely read as well.

What was it about Lewis's Christian view of life that led him to urge the students in his congregation to follow a course of action different from the one that he himself followed in an earlier war, before he became a Christian? If his arguments are sound here, could we ever justify abandoning our present pursuits for the sake of what we regard as "higher purposes"?

We are now in a position to answer the view that human culture is an inexcusable frivolity on the part of creatures loaded with such awful responsibilities as we. I reject at once an idea which lingers in the mind of some modern people that cultural activities are in their own right spiritual and meritorious — as though scholars and poets were intrinsically more pleasing to God than scavengers and bootblacks. I think it was Matthew Arnold who first used the English word *spiritual* in the sense of the German *geistlich,* and so inaugurated this most dangerous and most anti-Christian error. Let us clear it forever from our minds. The work of a Beethoven and the work of a charwoman become spiritual on precisely the same condition, that of being offered to God, of being done humbly "as to the Lord." This does not, of course, mean that it is for anyone a mere toss-up whether he should sweep rooms or compose symphonies. A mole must dig to the glory of God and a cock must crow. We are members of one body, but differentiated members, each with his own vocation. A man's upbringing, his talents, his circumstances, are usually a tolerable index of his vocation. If our parents have sent us to Oxford, if our country allows us to remain there, this is *prima facie* evidence that the life which we, at any rate, can best lead to the glory of God at present is the learned life. By leading that life to the glory of God I do not, of course, mean any attempt to make our intellectual inquiries work out to edifying conclusions. That would be, as Bacon says, to offer to the author of truth the unclean sacrifice of a lie. I mean the pursuit of knowledge and beauty, in a sense, for their own sake, but in a sense which does not exclude their being for God's sake. An appetite for these things exists in the human mind, and God makes no appetite in vain. We can therefore pursue knowledge as such, and beauty as such, in the sure confidence that by so doing we are either advancing to the vision of God ourselves or indirectly helping others to do so. Humility, no less than the appetite, encourages us to concentrate simply on the knowledge or the beauty, not too much concerning ourselves with their ultimate relevance to the vision of God. That relevance may not be intended for us but for our betters — for men who come after and find the spiritual significance of what we dug out in blind and humble obedience to our vocation. This is the teleological argument that the existence of the impulse and the faculty prove that they must have a proper function in God's scheme — the argument by which Thomas Aquinas proves that sexuality would have existed even without the Fall. The soundness of the argument, as regards culture, is proved by experience. The intellectual life is not the only road to God, nor the safest, but we find it to be a road, and it may be the appointed road for us. Of course, it will be so only so long as we keep the impulse pure and disinterested. That is the great difficulty. As the author of the *Theologia Germanica* says, we may come to love knowledge — our knowing — more than the thing known: to delight not in the exercise of our talents but in the fact that they are ours, or even in the reputation they bring us. Every success in the scholar's life increases this danger. If it becomes irresistible, he must give up his scholarly work. The time for plucking out the right eye has arrived.

That is the essential nature of the learned life as I see it. But it has indirect values which are especially important today. If all the world were Christian, it might not matter if all the world were uneducated. But, as it is, a cultural life will exist outside the Church whether it exists inside or not. To be ignorant and simple now — not to be able to meet the enemies on their own ground — would be to throw down our weapons, and to betray our uneducated brethren who have, under God, no defence but us against the intellectual attacks of the heathen. Good philosophy must exist, if for no other reason, because bad philosophy needs to be answered. The cool intellect must work not only against cool intellect on the other side, but against the muddy heathen mysticisms which deny intellect altogether. Most of all, perhaps, we need intimate knowledge of the past. Not that the past has any magic about it, but because we cannot study the future, and yet need something to set against the present, to remind us that the basic assumptions have been quite different in different periods and that much which seems certain to the uneducated is merely temporary fashion. A man who has lived in many places is not likely to be deceived by the local errors of his native village; the scholar has lived in many times and is therefore in some degree immune from the great cataract of nonsense that pours from the press and the microphone of his own age.

The learned life then is, for some, a duty. At the moment it looks as if it were your duty. I am well aware that there may seem to be an almost comic discrepancy between the high issues we have been considering and the immediate task you may be set down to, such as Anglo-Saxon sound laws or chemical formulae. But there is a similar shock awaiting us in every vocation — a young priest finds himself involved in choir treats and a young subaltern in accounting for pots of jam. It is well that it should be so. It weeds out the vain, windy people and keeps in those who are both humble and tough. On that kind of difficulty we need waste no sympathy. But the peculiar difficulty imposed on you by the war is another matter, and of it I would again repeat what I have been saying in one form or another ever since I started — do not let your nerves and emotions lead you into thinking your predicament more abnormal than it really is. Perhaps it may be useful to mention the three mental exercises which may serve as defences against the three enemies which war raises up against the scholar.

The first enemy is excitement — the tendency to think and feel about the war when we had intended to think about our work. The best defence is a recognition that in this, as in everything else, the war has not really raised up a new enemy but only aggravated an old one. There are always plenty of rivals to our work. We are always falling in love or quarrelling, looking for jobs or fearing to lose them, getting ill and recovering, following public affairs. If we let ourselves, we shall always be waiting for some distraction or other to end before we can really get down to our work. The only people who achieve much are those who want knowledge so badly that they seek it while the conditions are still unfavourable. Favourable conditions never come. There are, of course, moments when the pressure of the excitement is so great that only superhuman self-control could resist it. They come both in war and peace. We must do the best we can.

The second enemy is frustration — the feeling that we shall not have time to finish. If I say to you that no one has time to finish, that the longest human life leaves a man, in any branch of learning, a beginner, I shall seem to you to be saying something quite academic and theoretical. You would be surprised if you knew how soon one begins to feel the shortness of the tether, of how many things, even in middle life, we have to say "No time for that," "Too late now," and "Not for me." But Nature herself forbids you to share that experience. A more Christian attitude, which can be attained at any age, is that of leaving futurity in God's hands. We may as well, for God will certainly retain it whether we leave it to Him or not. Never, in peace or war, commit your virtue or your happiness to the future. Happy work is best done by the man who takes his long-term plans somewhat lightly and works from moment to moment "as to the Lord." It is only our *daily* bread that we are encouraged to ask for. The present is the only time in which any duty can be done or any grace received.

The third enemy is fear. War threatens us with death and pain. No man — and specially no Christian who remembers Gethsemane — need try to attain a stoic indifference about these things, but we can guard against the illusions of the imagination. We think of the streets of Warsaw and contrast the deaths there suffered with an abstraction called Life. But there is no question of death or life for any of us, only a question of this death or of that — of a machine gun bullet now or a cancer forty years later. What does war do to death? It certainly does not make it more frequent; 100 percent of us die, and the percentage cannot be increased. It puts several deaths earlier, but I hardly suppose that that is what we fear. Certainly when the moment comes, it will make little difference how many years we have behind us. Does it increase our chances of a painful death? I doubt it. As far as I can find out, what we call natural death is usually preceded by suffering, and a battlefield is one of the very few places where one has a reasonable prospect of dying with no pain at all. Does it decrease our chances of dying at peace with God? I cannot believe it. If active service does not persuade a man to prepare for death, what conceivable concatenation of circumstances would? Yet war does do something to death. It forces us to remember it. The only reason why the cancer at sixty or the paralysis at seventy-five do not bother us is that we forget them. War makes death real to us, and that would have been regarded as one of its blessings by most of the great Christians of the past. They thought it good for us to be always aware of our mortality. I am inclined to think they were right. All the animal life in us, all schemes of happiness that centred in this world, were always doomed to a final frustration. In ordinary times only a wise man can realise it. Now the stupidest of us knows. We see unmistakably the sort of universe in which we have all along been living, and must come to terms with it. If we had foolish unChristian hopes about human culture, they are now shattered. If we thought we were building up a heaven on earth, if we looked for something that would turn the present world from a place of pilgrimage into a permanent city satisfying the soul of man, we are disillusioned, and not a moment too soon. But if we thought that for some souls, and at some times, the life of learning, humbly offered to God, was, in its own small way, one of the appointed approaches to the Divine reality and the Divine beauty which we hope to enjoy hereafter, we can think so still.

EXTRAORDINARY LIVES

ARISTOTLE

Nicomachean Ethics

In this brief but famous passage, Aristotle argues that a person of noble character will and should prefer a short but splendid life to a long life of steady accomplishment and satisfaction. Aristotle might well have had Achilles, the principal character in the subsequent reading from the *Iliad*, in mind when he made this argument. Do you agree with Aristotle? Would you make a similar choice if given the opportunity?

At other points in this anthology, we have been tempted to draw sharp contrasts between the vocabularies of virtue and Christian vocation, between the pagan ethos of the ancient Greeks and the Christian way of life. The passage below should give us pause. How different is the pagan life of heroic sacrifice sketched below from the life of self-giving love led by Jesus of Nazareth? Compare Gary Badcock's account of the Christian life in Part I to Aristotle's account of the splendid life below. Does Badcock argue that in dying for others, Christians are "choosing something great and fine" for themselves? These inquiries should be pursued in greater depth and detail by comparing, in the two readings following the one below, the reasons that Achilles' comrades put forward to persuade him to risk his life for the Greeks to the reasons that Perpetua puts forward to explain her decision to die for her faith.

From Aristotle, *Nicomachean Ethics*, trans. Terence Irwin, 2nd edition (Indianapolis: Hackett Publishing Company, Inc., 1999), pp. 147-148.

Book IX.8

§9 It is quite true that, as they say, the excellent person labors for his friends and for his native country, and will die for them if he must; he will sacrifice money, honors, and contested goods in general, in achieving the fine for himself. For he will choose intense pleasure for a short time over slight pleasure for a long time; a year of living finely over many years of undistinguished life; and a single fine and great action over many small actions. This is presumably true of one who dies for others; he does indeed choose something great and fine for himself. He is also ready to sacrifice money as long as his friends profit; for the friends gain money, while he gains the fine, and so he awards himself the greater good.

§10 He treats honors and offices in the same way; for he will sacrifice them all for his friends, since this is fine and praiseworthy for himself. It is not surprising, then, that he seems to be excellent, since he chooses the fine at the cost of everything. It is also possible, however, to sacrifice actions to his friend, since it may be finer to be responsible for his friend's doing the action than to do it himself.

§11 In everything praiseworthy, then, the excellent person awards himself the fine. In this way, then, we must be self-lovers, as we have said. But in the way the many are, we ought not to be.

HOMER

The Iliad

The *Iliad* is a poem about the anger of Achilles. In the scene below, three of his closest friends, Ajax and Odysseus — comrades in arms — and Phoenix, the teacher who trained him in the arts of war and speech, attempt to persuade Achilles to set aside his anger and join them in the bat-

From Homer, *The Iliad*, trans. Richmond Lattimore (Chicago: The University of Chicago Press, 1974), pp. 202-215.

tle against the Trojans, who threaten to overwhelm them without him. When we consider in Chapter 5 the question of whom we should heed when we are trying to decide what we should do with our lives, we will want to revisit this scene, since from one point of view these friends and mentors are advising Achilles about what his job and, beyond that, his destiny really are. For now, we should notice that Achilles was told by his mother, the goddess Thetis, that *two* fates would await him until the day of his death. "If I hold out here and I lay siege to Troy, my journey home is gone, but my glory never dies. If I voyage back to the fatherland I love, my pride, my glory dies . . . true, but the life that's left me will be long, the stroke of death will not come on me quickly."

What arguments do the three ambassadors advance to persuade Achilles that he should not choose to abandon them and seek a long and unsung life back in Argos? Which of these arguments, if any, do you find persuasive? Eventually, Achilles does fight, and he is killed. But he is moved to battle not because he has been persuaded by any of the arguments advanced in the scene below. He fights instead to avenge the death of his beloved Patroclus, who has been killed by Hector, the great Trojan hero. Is this thirst for vengeance a more admirable motive than those that his friends attempt to arouse within him — patriotism, fame, honor, wealth, and loyalty to friends? Is self-sacrifice ever "sensible"? If it is sensible, if the noble human being, in sacrificing for others, really is "choosing the best part for himself," as Aristotle thought, is he really sacrificing?

Book IX, "The Embassy to Achilles"

Thereupon the Gerenian horseman Nestor answered him:
'Son of Atreus, most lordly and king of men, Agamemnon,
none could scorn any longer these gifts you offer to Achilleus
the king. Come, let us choose and send some men, who in all speed   165
will go to the shelter of Achilleus, the son of Peleus;
or come, the men on whom my eye falls, let these take the duty.
First of all let Phoinix, beloved of Zeus, be their leader,
and after him take Aias the great, and brilliant Odysseus,
and of the heralds let Odios and Eurybates go with them.   170
Bring also water for their hands, and bid them keep words of good omen,
so we may pray to Zeus, son of Kronos, if he will have pity.'
    So he spoke, and the word he spoke was pleasing to all of them.

And the heralds brought water at once, and poured it over
their hands, and the young men filled the mixing-bowl with pure wine   175
and passed it to all, pouring first a libation in goblets.
Then when they had poured out wine, and drunk as much as their
          hearts wished,
they set out from the shelter of Atreus' son, Agamemnon.
And the Gerenian horseman Nestor gave them much instruction,
looking eagerly at each, and most of all at Odysseus,   180
to try hard, so that they might win over the blameless Peleion.
     So these two walked along the strand of the sea deep-thundering
with many prayers to the holder and shaker of the earth, that they
might readily persuade the great heart of Aiakides.
Now they came beside the shelters and ships of the Myrmidons   185
and they found Achilleus delighting his heart in a lyre, clear-sounding,
splendid and carefully wrought, with a bridge of silver upon it,
which he won out of the spoils when he ruined Eëtion's city.
With this he was pleasuring his heart, and singing of men's fame,
as Patroklos was sitting over against him, alone, in silence,   190
watching Aiakides and the time he would leave off singing.
Now these two came forward, as brilliant Odysseus led them,
and stood in his presence. Achilleus rose to his feet in amazement
holding the lyre as it was, leaving the place where he was sitting.
In the same way Patroklos, when he saw the men come, stood up.   195
And in greeting Achilleus the swift of foot spoke to them:
'Welcome. You are my friends who have come, and greatly I need you,
who even to this my anger are dearest of all the Achaians.'
     So brilliant Achilleus spoke, and guided them forward,
and caused them to sit down on couches with purple coverlets   200
and at once called over to Patroklos who was not far from him:
'Son of Menoitios, set up a mixing-bowl that is bigger,
and mix us stronger drink, and make ready a cup for each man,
since these who have come beneath my roof are the men that I love best.'
     So he spoke, and Patroklos obeyed his beloved companion,   205
and tossed down a great chopping-block into the firelight,
and laid upon it the back of a sheep, and one of a fat goat,
with the chine of a fatted pig edged thick with lard, and for him
Automedon held the meats, and brilliant Achilleus carved them,
and cut it well into pieces and spitted them, as meanwhile   210
Menoitios' son, a man like a god, made the fire blaze greatly.
But when the fire had burned itself out, and the flames had died down,

he scattered the embers apart, and extended the spits across them
lifting them to the andirons, and sprinkled the meats with divine salt.
Then when he had roasted all, and spread the food on the platters,   215
Patroklos took the bread and set it out on a table
in fair baskets, while Achilleus served the meats. Thereafter
he himself sat over against the godlike Odysseus
against the further wall, and told his companion, Patroklos,
to sacrifice to the gods; and he threw the firstlings in the fire.   220
They put their hands to the good things that lay ready before them.
But when they had put aside their desire for eating and drinking,
Aias nodded to Phoinix, and brilliant Odysseus saw it,
and filled a cup with wine, and lifted it to Achilleus:
'Your health, Achilleus. You have no lack of your equal portion   225
either within the shelter of Atreus' son, Agamemnon,
nor here now in your own. We have good things in abundance
to feast on; here it is not the desirable feast we think of,
but a trouble all too great, beloved of Zeus, that we look on
and are afraid. There is doubt if we save our strong-benched vessels   230
or if they will be destroyed, unless you put on your war strength.
The Trojans in their pride, with their far-renowned companions,
have set up an encampment close by the ships and the rampart,
and lit many fires along their army, and think no longer
of being held, but rather to drive in upon the black ships.   235
And Zeus, son of Kronos, lightens upon their right hand, showing them
portents of good, while Hektor in the huge pride of his strength rages
irresistibly, reliant on Zeus, and gives way to no one
neither god nor man, but the strong fury has descended upon him.
He prays now that the divine Dawn will show most quickly,   240
since he threatens to shear the uttermost horns from the ship-sterns,
to light the ships themselves with ravening fire, and to cut down
the Achaians themselves as they stir from the smoke beside them.
All this I fear terribly in my heart, lest immortals
accomplish all these threats, and lest for us it be destiny   245
to die here in Troy, far away from horse-pasturing Argos.
Up, then! if you are minded, late though it be, to rescue
the afflicted sons of the Achaians from the Trojan onslaught.
It will be an affliction to you hereafter, there will be no remedy
found to heal the evil thing when it has been done. No, beforehand   250
take thought to beat the evil day aside from the Danaans.
Dear friend, surely thus your father Peleus advised you

that day when he sent you away to Agamemnon from Phthia:
"My child, for the matter of strength, Athene and Hera will give it
if it be their will, but be it yours to hold fast in your bosom   255
the anger of the proud heart, for consideration is better.
Keep from the bad complication of quarrel, and all the more for this
the Argives will honour you, both their younger men and their elders."
So the old man advised, but you have forgotten. Yet even now
stop, and give way from the anger that hurts the heart. Agamemnon   260
offers you worthy recompense if you change from your anger.
Come then, if you will, listen to me, while I count off for you
all the gifts in his shelter that Agamemnon has promised:
Seven unfired tripods; ten talents' weight of gold; twenty
shining cauldrons; and twelve horses, strong, race-competitors   265
who have won prizes in the speed of their feet. That man would not be
poor in possessions, to whom were given all these have won him,
nor be unpossessed of dearly honoured gold, were he given
all the prizes Agamemnon's horses won in their speed for him.
He will give you seven women of Lesbos, the work of whose hands   270
is blameless, whom when you yourself captured strong-founded Lesbos
he chose, and who in their beauty surpassed the races of women.
He will give you these, and with them shall go the one he took from you,
the daughter of Briseus. And to all this he will swear a great oath
that he never entered into her bed and never lay with her   275
as is natural for human people, between men and women.
All these gifts shall be yours at once; but again, if hereafter
the gods grant that we storm and sack the great city of Priam,
you may go to your ship and load it deep as you please with
gold and bronze, when we Achaians divide the war spoils,   280
and you may choose for yourself twenty of the Trojan women,
who are the loveliest of all after Helen of Argos.
And if we come back to Achaian Argos, pride of the tilled land,
you could be his son-in-law; he would honour you with Orestes,
his growing son, who is brought up there in abundant luxury.   285
Since, as he has three daughters there in his strong-built castle,
Chrysothemis and Laodike and Iphianassa,
you may lead away the one of these that you like, with no bride-price,
to the house of Peleus; and with the girl he will grant you as dowry
many gifts, such as no man ever gave with his daughter.   290
He will grant you seven citadels, strongly settled:
Kardamyle and Enope and Hire of the grasses,

Pherai the sacrosanct, and Antheia deep in the meadows,
with Aipeia the lovely, and Pedasos of the vineyards.
All these lie near the sea, at the bottom of sandy Pylos, 295
and men live among them rich in cattle and rich in sheepflocks,
who will honour you as if you were a god with gifts given
and fulfil your prospering decrees underneath your sceptre.
All this he will bring to pass for you, if you change from your anger.
But if the son of Atreus is too much hated in your heart, 300
himself and his gifts, at least take pity on all the other
Achaians, who are afflicted along the host, and will honour you
as a god. You may win very great glory among them.
For now you might kill Hektor, since he would come very close to you
with the wicked fury upon him, since he thinks there is not his equal 305
among the rest of the Danaans the ships carried hither.'
    Then in answer to him spoke Achilleus of the swift feet:
'Son of Laertes and seed of Zeus, resourceful Odysseus:
without consideration for you I must make my answer,
the way I think, and the way it will be accomplished, that you may not 310
come one after another, and sit by me, and speak softly.
For as I detest the doorways of Death, I detest that man, who
hides one thing in the depths of his heart, and speaks forth another.
But I will speak to you the way it seems best to me: neither
do I think the son of Atreus, Agamemnon, will persuade me, 315
nor the rest of the Danaans, since there was no gratitude given
for fighting incessantly forever against your enemies.
Fate is the same for the man who holds back, the same if he fights hard.
We are all held in a single honour, the brave with the weaklings.
A man dies still if he has done nothing, as one who has done much. 320
Nothing is won for me, now that my heart has gone through its afflictions
in forever setting my life on the hazard of battle.
For as to her unwinged young ones the mother bird brings back
morsels, wherever she can find them, but as for herself it is suffering,
such was I, as I lay through all the many nights unsleeping, 325
such as I wore through the bloody days of the fighting,
striving with warriors for the sake of these men's women.
But I say that I have stormed from my ships twelve cities
of men, and by land eleven more through the generous Troad.
From all these we took forth treasures, goodly and numerous, 330
and we would bring them back, and give them to Agamemnon,
Atreus' son; while he, waiting back beside the swift ships,

would take them, and distribute them little by little, and keep many.
All the other prizes of honour he gave the great men and the princes
are held fast by them, but from me alone of all the Achaians   335
he has taken and keeps the bride of my heart. Let him lie beside her
and be happy. Yet why must the Argives fight with the Trojans?
And why was it the son of Atreus assembled and led here
these people? Was it not for the sake of lovely-haired Helen?
Are the sons of Atreus alone among mortal men the ones   340
who love their wives? Since any who is a good man, and careful,
loves her who is his own and cares for her, even as I now
loved this one from my heart, though it was my spear that won her.
Now that he has deceived me and taken from my hands my prize of honour,
let him try me no more. I know him well. He will not persuade me.   345
Let him take counsel with you, Odysseus, and the rest of the princes
how to fight the ravening fire away from his vessels.
Indeed, there has been much hard work done even without me;
he has built himself a wall and driven a ditch about it,
making it great and wide, and fixed the sharp stakes inside it.   350
Yet even so he cannot hold the strength of manslaughtering
Hektor; and yet when I was fighting among the Achaians
Hektor would not drive his attack beyond the wall's shelter
but would come forth only so far as the Skaian gates and the oak tree.
There once he endured me alone, and barely escaped my onslaught.   355
But, now I am unwilling to fight against brilliant Hektor,
tomorrow, when I have sacrificed to Zeus and to all gods,
and loaded well my ships, and rowed out on to the salt water,
you will see, if you have a mind to it and if it concerns you,
my ships in the dawn at sea on the Hellespont where the fish swarm   360
and my men manning them with good will to row. If the glorious
shaker of the earth should grant us a favouring passage
on the third day thereafter we might raise generous Phthia.
I have many possessions there that I left behind when I came here
on this desperate venture, and from here there is more gold,
      and red bronze,   365
and fair-girdled women, and grey iron I will take back;
all that was allotted to me. But my prize: he who gave it,
powerful Agamemnon, son of Atreus, has taken it back again
outrageously. Go back and proclaim to him all that I tell you,
openly, so other Achaians may turn against him in anger   370
if he hopes yet one more time to swindle some other Danaan,

wrapped as he is forever in shamelessness; yet he would not,
bold as a dog though he be, dare look in my face any longer.
I will join with him in no counsel, and in no action.
He cheated me and he did me hurt. Let him not beguile me   375
with words again. This is enough for him. Let him of his own will
be damned, since Zeus of the counsels has taken his wits away from him.
I hate his gifts. I hold him light as the strip of a splinter.
Not if he gave me ten times as much, and twenty times over
as he possesses now, not if more should come to him from elsewhere,   380
or gave all that is brought in to Orchomenos, all that is brought in
to Thebes of Egypt, where the greatest possessions lie up in the houses,
Thebes of the hundred gates, where through each of the gates two hundred
fighting men come forth to war with horses and chariots;
not if he gave me gifts as many as the sand or the dust is,   385
not even so would Agamemnon have his way with my spirit
until he had made good to me all this heartrending insolence.
Nor will I marry a daughter of Atreus' son, Agamemnon,
not if she challenged Aphrodite the golden for loveliness,
not if she matched the work of her hands with grey-eyed Athene;   390
not even so will I marry her; let him pick some other Achaian,
one who is to his liking and is kinglier than I am.
For if the gods will keep me alive, and I win homeward,
Peleus himself will presently arrange a wife for me.
There are many Achaian girls in the land of Hellas and Phthia,   395
daughters of great men who hold strong places in guard. And of these
any one that I please I might make my beloved lady.
And the great desire in my heart drives me rather in that place
to take a wedded wife in marriage, the bride of my fancy,
to enjoy with her the possessions won by aged Peleus. For not   400
worth the value of my life are all the possessions they fable
were won for Ilion, that strong-founded citadel, in the old days
when there was peace, before the coming of the sons of the Achaians;
not all that the stone doorsill of the Archer holds fast within it,
of Phoibos Apollo in Pytho of the rocks. Of possessions   405
cattle and fat sheep are things to be had for the lifting,
and tripods can be won, and the tawny high heads of horses,
but a man's life cannot come back again, it cannot be lifted
nor captured again by force, once it has crossed the teeth's barrier.
For my mother Thetis the goddess of the silver feet tells me   410
I carry two sorts of destiny toward the day of my death. Either,

if I stay here and fight beside the city of the Trojans,
my return home is gone, but my glory shall be everlasting;
but if I return home to the beloved land of my fathers,
the excellence of my glory is gone, but there will be a long life   415
left for me, and my end in death will not come to me quickly.
And this would be my counsel to others also, to sail back
home again, since no longer shall you find any term set
on the sheer city of Ilion, since Zeus of the wide brows has strongly
held his own hand over it, and its people are made bold.   420
    Do you go back therefore to the great men of the Achaians,
and take them this message, since such is the privilege of the princes:
that they think out in their minds some other scheme that is better,
which might rescue their ships, and the people of the Achaians
who man the hollow ships, since this plan will not work for them   425
which they thought of by reason of my anger. Let Phoinix
remain here with us and sleep here, so that tomorrow
he may come with us in our ships to the beloved land of our fathers,
if he will; but I will never use force to hold him.'
    So he spoke, and all of them stayed stricken to silence   430
in amazement at his words. He had spoken to them very strongly.
But at long last Phoinix the aged horseman spoke out
in a stormburst of tears, and fearing for the ships of the Achaians:
'If it is going home, glorious Achilleus, you ponder
in your heart, and are utterly unwilling to drive the obliterating   435
fire from the fast ships, since anger has descended on your spirit,
how then shall I, dear child, be left in this place behind you
all alone? Peleus the aged horseman sent me forth with you
on that day when he sent you from Phthia to Agamemnon
a mere child, who knew nothing yet of the joining of battle   440
nor of debate where men are made pre-eminent. Therefore
he sent me along with you to teach you of all these matters,
to make you a speaker of words and one who accomplished in action.
Therefore apart from you, dear child, I would not be willing
to be left behind, not were the god in person to promise   445
he would scale away my old age and make me a young man blossoming
as I was that time when I first left Hellas, the land of fair women,
running from the hatred of Ormenos' son Amyntor,
my father; who hated me for the sake of a fair-haired mistress.
For he made love to her himself, and dishonoured his own wife,   450
my mother; who was forever taking my knees and entreating me

to lie with this mistress instead so that she would hate the old man.
I was persuaded and did it; and my father when he heard of it straightway
called down his curses, and invoked against me the dreaded furies
that I might never have any son born of my seed to dandle   455
on my knees; and the divinities, Zeus of the underworld
and Persephone the honoured goddess, accomplished his curses.
Then I took it into my mind to cut him down with the sharp bronze,
but some one of the immortals checked my anger, reminding me
of rumour among the people and men's maledictions repeated,   460
that I might not be called a parricide among the Achaians.
But now no more could the heart in my breast be ruled entirely
to range still among these halls when my father was angered.
Rather it was the many kinsmen and cousins about me
who held me closed in the house, with supplications repeated,   465
and slaughtered fat sheep in their numbers, and shambling horn-curved
cattle, and numerous swine with the fat abundant upon them
were singed and stretched out across the flame of Hephaistos,
and much wine was drunk that was stored in the jars of the old man.
Nine nights they slept nightlong in their places beside me,   470
and they kept up an interchange of watches, and the fire was never
put out; one below the gate of the strong-closed courtyard,
and one in the ante-chamber before the doors of the bedroom.
But when the tenth night had come to me in its darkness,
then I broke the close-compacted doors of the chamber   475
and got away, and overleapt the fence of the courtyard
lightly, unnoticed by the guarding men and the women servants.
Then I fled far away through the wide spaces of Hellas
and came as far as generous Phthia, mother of sheepflocks,
and to lord Peleus, who accepted me with a good will   480
and gave me his love, even as a father loves his own son
who is a single child brought up among many possessions.
He made me a rich man, and granted me many people,
and I lived, lord over the Dolopes, in remotest Phthia,
and, godlike Achilleus, I made you all that you are now,   485
and loved you out of my heart, for you would not go with another
out to any feast, nor taste any food in your own halls
until I had set you on my knees, and cut little pieces
from the meat, and given you all you wished, and held the wine for you.
And many times you soaked the shirt that was on my body   490
with wine you would spit up in the troublesomeness of your childhood.

So I have suffered much through you, and have had much trouble,
thinking always how the gods would not bring to birth any children
of my own; so that it was you, godlike Achilleus, I made
my own child, so that some day you might keep hard affliction from me. 495
Then, Achilleus, beat down your great anger. It is not
yours to have a pitiless heart. The very immortals
can be moved; their virtue and honour and strength are greater
       than ours are,
and yet with sacrifices and offerings for endearment,
with libations and with savour men turn back even the immortals 500
in supplication, when any man does wrong and transgresses.
For there are also the spirits of Prayer, the daughters of great Zeus,
and they are lame of their feet, and wrinkled, and cast their eyes sidelong,
who toil on their way left far behind by the spirit of Ruin:
but she, Ruin, is strong and sound on her feet, and therefore 505
far outruns all Prayers, and wins into every country
to force men astray; and the Prayers follow as healers after her.
If a man venerates these daughters of Zeus as they draw near,
such a man they bring great advantage, and hear his entreaty;
but if a man shall deny them, and stubbornly with a harsh word 510
refuse, they go to Zeus, son of Kronos, in supplication
that Ruin may overtake this man, that he be hurt, and punished.
So, Achilleus: grant, you also, that Zeus' daughters be given
their honour, which, lordly though they be, curbs the will of others.
Since, were he not bringing gifts and naming still more hereafter, 515
Atreus' son; were he to remain still swollen with rancour,
even I would not bid you throw your anger aside, nor
defend the Argives, though they needed you sorely. But see now,
he offers you much straightway, and has promised you more hereafter;
he has sent the best men to you to supplicate you, choosing them 520
out of the Achaian host, those who to yourself are the dearest
of all the Argives. Do not you make vain their argument
nor their footsteps, though before this one could not blame your anger.
Thus it was in the old days also, the deeds that we hear of
from the great men, when the swelling anger descended upon them. 525
The heroes would take gifts; they would listen, and be persuaded.
For I remember this action of old, it is not a new thing,
and how it went; you are all my friends, I will tell it among you.
    The Kouretes and the steadfast Aitolians were fighting
and slaughtering one another about the city of Kalydon, 530

the Aitolians in lovely Kalydon's defence, the Kouretes
furious to storm and sack it in war. For Artemis,
she of the golden chair, had driven this evil upon them,
angered that Oineus had not given the pride of the orchards
to her, first fruits; the rest of the gods were given due sacrifice,   535
but alone to this daughter of great Zeus he had given nothing.
He had forgotten, or had not thought, in his hard delusion,
and in wrath at his whole mighty line the Lady of Arrows
sent upon them the fierce wild boar with the shining teeth, who
after the way of his kind did much evil to the orchards of Oineus.   540
For he ripped up whole tall trees from the ground and scattered them
        headlong
roots and all, even to the very flowers of the orchard.
The son of Oineus killed this boar, Meleagros, assembling
together many hunting men out of numerous cities
with their hounds; since the boar might not have been killed by a
        few men,   545
so huge was he, and had put many men on the sad fire for burning.
But the goddess again made a great stir of anger and crying
battle, over the head of the boar and the bristling boar's hide,
between Kouretes and the high-hearted Aitolians. So long
as Meleagros lover of battle stayed in the fighting   550
it went the worse for the Kouretes, and they could not even
hold their ground outside the wall, though they were so many.
But when the anger came upon Meleagros, such anger
as wells in the hearts of others also, though their minds are careful,
he, in the wrath of his heart against his own mother, Althaia,   555
lay apart with his wedded bride, Kleopatra the lovely,
daughter of sweet-stepping Marpessa, child of Euenos,
and Idas, who was the strongest of all men upon earth
in his time; for he even took up the bow to face the King's onset,
Phoibos Apollo, for the sake of the sweet-stepping maiden;   560
a girl her father and honoured mother had named in their palace
Alkyone, sea-bird, as a by-name, since for her sake
her mother with the sorrow-laden cry of a sea-bird
wept because far-reaching Phoibos Apollo had taken her;
with this Kleopatra he lay mulling his heart-sore anger,   565
raging by reason of his mother's curses, which she called down
from the gods upon him, in deep grief for the death of her brother,
and many times beating with her hands on the earth abundant

she called on Hades and on honoured Persephone, lying
at length along the ground, and the tears were wet on her bosom,   570
to give death to her son; and Erinys, the mist-walking,
she of the heart without pity, heard her out of the dark places.
Presently there was thunder about the gates, and the sound rose
of towers under assault, and the Aitolian elders
supplicated him, sending their noblest priests of the immortals,   575
to come forth and defend them; they offered him a great gift:
wherever might lie the richest ground in lovely Kalydon,
there they told him to choose out a piece of land, an entirely
good one, of fifty acres, the half of it to be vineyard
and the half of it unworked ploughland of the plain to be furrowed.   580
And the aged horseman Oineus again and again entreated him,
and took his place at the threshold of the high-vaulted chamber
and shook against the bolted doors, pleading with his own son.
And again and again his honoured mother and his sisters
entreated him, but he only refused the more; then his own friends   585
who were the most honoured and dearest of all entreated him;
but even so they could not persuade the heart within him
until, as the chamber was under close assault, the Kouretes
were mounting along the towers and set fire to the great city.
And then at last his wife, the fair-girdled bride, supplicated   590
Meleagros, in tears, and rehearsed in their numbers before him
all the sorrows that come to men when their city is taken:
they kill the men, and the fire leaves the city in ashes,
and strangers lead the children away and the deep-girdled women.
And the heart, as he listened to all this evil, was stirred within him,   595
and he rose, and went, and closed his body in shining armour.
So he gave way in his own heart, and drove back the day of evil
from the Aitolians; yet these no longer would make good
their many and gracious gifts; yet he drove back the evil from them.
     Listen, then; do not have such a thought in your mind; let not   600
the spirit within you turn you that way, dear friend. It would be worse
to defend the ships after they are burning. No, with gifts promised
go forth. The Achaians will honour you as they would an immortal.
But if without gifts you go into the fighting where men perish,
your honour will no longer be as great, though you drive back
          the battle.'   605
     Then in answer to him spoke Achilleus of the swift feet:
'Phoinix my father, aged, illustrious, such honour is a thing

142

I need not. I think I am honoured already in Zeus' ordinance
which will hold me here beside my curved ships as long as life's wind
stays in my breast, as long as my knees have their spring beneath me.   610
And put away in your thoughts this other thing I tell you.
Stop confusing my heart with lamentation and sorrow
for the favour of great Atreides. It does not become you
to love this man, for fear you turn hateful to me, who love you.
It should be your pride with me to hurt whoever shall hurt me.   615
Be king equally with me; take half of my honour.
These men will carry back the message; you stay here and sleep here
in a soft bed, and we shall decide tomorrow, as dawn shows,
whether to go back home again or else to remain here.'

He spoke, and, saying nothing, nodded with his brows to Patroklos   620
to make up a neat bed for Phoinix, so the others might presently
think of going home from his shelter. The son of Telamon,
Aias the godlike, saw it, and now spoke his word among them:
'Son of Laertes and seed of Zeus, resourceful Odysseus:
let us go. I think that nothing will be accomplished   625
by argument on this errand; it is best to go back quickly
and tell this story, though it is not good, to the Danaans
who sit there waiting for us to come back, seeing that Achilleus
has made savage the proud-hearted spirit within his body.
He is hard, and does not remember that friends' affection   630
wherein we honoured him by the ships, far beyond all others.
Pitiless. And yet a man takes from his brother's slayer
the blood price, or the price for a child who was killed, and the guilty
one, when he has largely repaid, stays still in the country,
and the injured man's heart is curbed, and his pride, and his anger   635
when he has taken the price; but the gods put in your breast a spirit
not to be placated, bad, for the sake of one single
girl. Yet now we offer you seven, surpassingly lovely,
and much beside these. Now make gracious the spirit within you.
Respect your own house; see, we are under the same roof with you,   640
from the multitude of the Danaans, we who desire beyond all
others to have your honour and love, out of all the Achaians.'

Then in answer to him spoke Achilleus of the swift feet:
'Son of Telamon, seed of Zeus, Aias, lord of the people:
all that you have said seems spoken after my own mind.   645
Yet still the heart in me swells up in anger, when I remember
the disgrace that he wrought upon me before the Argives,

the son of Atreus, as if I were some dishonoured vagabond.
Do you then go back to him, and take him this message:
that I shall not think again of the bloody fighting   650
until such time as the son of wise Priam, Hektor the brilliant,
comes all the way to the ships of the Myrmidons, and their shelters,
slaughtering the Argives, and shall darken with fire our vessels.
But around my own shelter, I think, and beside my black ship
Hektor will be held, though he be very hungry for battle.'   655

<hr />

The Martyrdom of Perpetua

Vibia Perpetua was a North African Christian who was martyred in 203 CE along with several catechumens (new converts still studying to become Christians). The story of her imprisonment, torture, and death was written shortly after the event (possibly by Tertullian) and includes an account of the imprisonment apparently written by Perpetua herself.

From one vantage point, Perpetua's situation seems totally opposite to the one faced by Achilles in the scene above. She is willing, perhaps even eager, to sacrifice her life for the sake of her faith, even rejoicing in her suffering. Moreover, the main conflict in the scene below is between Perpetua and her father, who repeatedly tries to persuade her to choose the long and ordinary life over the short but glorious one that she contemplates. Perpetua is simply refusing to make sacrifices to the emperor under pain of death; thus, she is faced with the question of whether she will endure suffering, not with the question of whether she will inflict suffering upon others. The glory that Achilles contemplates is very much of this world; the glory that Perpetua seeks is of a different kind altogether.

But are Achilles and Perpetua really so different? Perpetua's struggle may be spiritual, but it is a life-and-death battle nonetheless. And she, like Achilles, is regarded by many as being proud and stubborn, impervious to

<hr />

From *The Martyrdom of Perpetua*, in *The Acts of the Christian Martyrs*, ed. and trans. Herbert Musurillo (Oxford: Oxford University Press, 1972), pp. 109-115, 117-119, 123-131.

the pleas of those closest to her. And also like Achilles, Perpetua shows no fear of death. Is this fearlessness a kind of courage or a kind of fanaticism?

This last question raises in turn a whole host of issues that need to be addressed if we are to choose well how to live. If we choose a life of sacrifice, to what extent does the worthiness of that life depend upon the worthiness of the cause or the people for whom we are giving up our own lives? To what extent should we consider the grief and suffering that others might have to bear if we sacrifice our own lives for a cause or a conviction that they do not share?

A number of young catechumens were arrested, Revocatus and his fellow slave Felicitas, Saturninus and Secundulus, and with them Vibia Perpetua, a newly married woman of good family and upbringing. Her mother and father were still alive and one of her two brothers was a catechumen like herself. She was about twenty-two years old and had an infant son at the breast. (Now from this point on the entire account of her ordeal is her own, according to her own ideas and in the way that she herself wrote it down.)

While we were still under arrest (she said), my father out of love for me was trying to persuade me and shake my resolution. "Father," said I, "do you see this vase here, for example, or waterpot or whatever?" "Yes, I do," said he. And I told him, "Could it be called by any other name than what it is?" And he said, "No." "Well, so too I cannot be called anything other than what I am, a Christian."

At this my father was so angered by the word "Christian" that he moved towards me as though he would pluck my eyes out. But he left it at that and departed, vanquished along with his diabolical arguments. For a few days afterwards I gave thanks to the Lord that I was separated from my father, and I was comforted by his absence. During these few days I was baptized, and I was inspired by the Spirit not to ask for any other favor after the water but simply the perseverance of the flesh. A few days later we were lodged in the prison; and I was terrified, as I had never before been in such a dark hole. What a difficult time it was! With the crowd the heat was stifling; then there was the extortion of the soldiers; and to crown all, I was tortured with worry for my baby there. Then Tertius and Pomponius, those blessed deacons who tried to take care of us, bribed the soldiers to allow us to go to a better part of the prison to refresh ourselves for a few hours.

Everyone then left that dungeon and shifted for himself. I nursed my baby, who was faint from hunger. In my anxiety I spoke to my mother about the child, I tried to comfort my brother, and I gave the child in their charge. I was in pain because I saw them suffering out of pity for me. These were the trials I had to endure for many days. Then I got permission for my baby to stay with me in prison. At once I recovered my health, relieved as I was of my worry and anxiety over the child. My prison had suddenly become a palace, so that I wanted to be there rather than anywhere else. Then my brother said to me: "Dear sister, you are greatly privileged; surely you might ask for a vision to discover whether you are to be condemned or freed." Faithfully I promised that I would, for I knew that I could speak with the Lord, whose great blessings I had come to experience. And so I said: "I shall tell you tomorrow." Then I made my request and this was the vision I had:

> I saw a ladder of tremendous height made of bronze, reaching all the way to the heavens, but it was so narrow that only one person could climb up at a time. To the sides of the ladder were attached all sorts of metal weapons: there were swords, spears, hooks, daggers, and spikes; so that if anyone tried to climb up carelessly or without paying attention, he would be mangled and his flesh would adhere to the weapons.
>
> At the foot of the ladder lay a dragon of enormous size, and it would attack those who tried to climb up and try to terrify them from doing so. And Saturus was the first to go up, he who was later to give himself up of his own accord. He had been the builder of our strength, although he was not present when we were arrested. And he arrived at the top of the staircase and he looked back and said to me: "Perpetua, I am waiting for you. But take care; do not let the dragon bite you."
>
> "He will not harm me," I said, "in the name of Christ Jesus."
>
> Slowly, as though he were afraid of me, the dragon stuck his head out from underneath the ladder.
>
> Then, using it as my first step, I trod on his head and went up. Then I saw an immense garden, and in it a gray-haired man sat in shepherd's garb; tall he was, and milking sheep. And standing around him were many thousands of people clad in white garments. He raised his head, looked at me, and said: "I am glad you have come, my child."
>
> He called me over to him and gave me, as it were, a mouthful of the milk he was drawing; and I took it into my cupped hands and consumed it. And all those who stood around said: "Amen!"

At the sound of this word I came to, with the taste of something sweet still in my mouth. I at once told this to my brother, and we realized that we would have to suffer, and that from now on we would no longer have any hope in this life.

A few days later there was a rumor that we were going to be given a hearing. My father also arrived from the city, worn with worry, and he came to see me with the idea of persuading me.

"Daughter," he said, "have pity on my gray head — have pity on me your father, if I deserve to be called your father, if I have favored you above all your brothers, if I have raised you to reach this prime of your life. Do not abandon me to be the reproach of men. Think of your brothers, think of your mother and your aunt, think of your child, who will not be able to live once you are gone. Give up your pride! You will destroy all of us! None of us will ever be able to speak freely again if anything happens to you."

This was the way my father spoke out of love for me, kissing my hands and throwing himself down before me. With tears in his eyes he no longer addressed me as his daughter but as a woman. I was sorry for my father's sake, because he alone of all my kin would be unhappy to see me suffer.

I tried to comfort him saying: "It will all happen in the prisoner's dock as God wills; for you may be sure that we are not left to ourselves but are all in his power."

And he left me in great sorrow.

One day while we were eating breakfast we were suddenly hurried off for a hearing. We arrived at the forum, and straight away the story went about the neighborhood near the forum and a huge crowd gathered. We walked up to the prisoner's dock. All the others when questioned admitted their guilt. Then, when it came my turn, my father appeared with my son, dragged me from the step, and said: "Perform the sacrifice — have pity on your baby!"

Hilarianus the governor, who had received his judicial powers as the successor of the late proconsul Minucius Timinianus, said to me: "Have pity on your father's gray head; have pity on your infant son. Offer the sacrifice for the welfare of the emperors."

"I will not," I retorted.

"Are you a Christian?" said Hilarianus.

And I said: "Yes, I am."

When my father persisted in trying to dissuade me, Hilarianus ordered him to be thrown to the ground and beaten with a rod. I felt sorry for father, just as if I myself had been beaten. I felt sorry for his pathetic old age.

Then Hilarianus passed sentence on all of us: we were condemned to the beasts, and we returned to prison in high spirits. But my baby had got used to being nursed at the breast and to staying with me in prison. So I sent the deacon Pomponius straight away to my father to ask for the baby. But father refused to give him over. But as God willed, the baby had no further desire for the breast, nor did I suffer any inflammation; and so I was relieved of any anxiety for my child and of any discomfort in my breasts. . . .

Some days later, an adjutant named Pudens, who was in charge of the prison, began to show us great honor, realizing that we possessed some great power within us. And he began to allow many visitors to see us for our mutual comfort.

Now the day of the contest was approaching, and my father came to see me overwhelmed with sorrow. He started tearing the hairs from his beard and threw them on the ground; he then threw himself on the ground and began to curse his old age and to say such words as would move all creation. I felt sorry for his unhappy old age.

The day before we were to fight with the beasts I saw the following vision:

Pomponius the deacon came to the prison gates and began to knock violently. I went out and opened the gate for him. He was dressed in an unbelted white tunic, wearing elaborate sandals. And he said to me: "Perpetua, come; we are waiting for you."

Then he took my hand and we began to walk through rough and broken country. At last we came to the amphitheatre out of breath, and he led me into the centre of the arena.

Then he told me: "Do not be afraid. I am here, struggling with you." Then he left.

I looked at the enormous crowd who watched in astonishment. I was surprised that no beasts were let loose on me; for I knew that I was condemned to die by the beasts. Then out came an Egyptian against me, of vicious appearance, together with his seconds, to fight with me. There also came up to me some handsome young men to be my seconds and assistants.

My clothes were stripped off, and suddenly I was a man. My seconds began to rub me down with oil (as they are accustomed to do before a contest). Then I saw the Egyptian on the other side rolling in the dust. Next there came forth a man of marvelous stature, such that he rose above the top of the amphitheatre. He was clad in a beltless purple tunic with two stripes (one on either side) running down the middle of his chest. He wore sandals that were wondrously made of gold and silver, and he carried a wand like an athletic trainer and a green branch on which there were golden apples.

148

And he asked for silence and said: "If this Egyptian defeats her he will slay her with the sword. But if she defeats him, she will receive this branch." Then he withdrew.

We drew close to one another and began to let our fists fly. My opponent tried to get hold of my feet, but I kept striking him in the face with the heels of my feet. Then I was raised up into the air, and I began to pummel him without as it were touching the ground. Then when I noticed there was a lull, I put my two hands together, linking the fingers of one hand with those of the other, and thus I got hold of his head. He fell flat on his face and I stepped on his head.

The crowd began to shout and my assistants started to sing psalms. Then I walked up to the trainer and took the branch. He kissed me and said to me: "Peace be with you, my daughter!" I began to walk in triumph towards the Gate of Life.

Then I awoke. I realized that it was not with wild animals that I would fight but with the Devil, but I knew that I would win the victory. So much for what I did up until the eve of the contest. About what happened at the contest itself, let him write of it who will. . . .

Such were the remarkable visions of these martyrs, Saturus and Perpetua, written by themselves. As for Secundulus, God called him from this world earlier than the others while he was still in prison, by a special grace that he might not have to face the animals. Yet his flesh, if not his spirit, knew the sword.

As for Felicitas, she too enjoyed the Lord's favor in this respect. She had been pregnant when she was arrested, and was now in her eighth month. As the day of the spectacle drew near she was very distressed that her martyrdom would be postponed because of her pregnancy; for it is against the law for women with child to be executed. Thus she might have to shed her holy, innocent blood afterwards along with others who were common criminals. Her comrades in martyrdom were also saddened; for they were afraid that they would have to leave behind so fine a companion to travel alone on the same road to hope. And so, two days before the contest, they poured forth a prayer to the Lord in one torrent of common grief. And immediately after their prayer the birth pains came upon her. She suffered a good deal in her labor because of the natural difficulty of an eight months' delivery.

Hence one of the assistants of the prison guards said to her: "You suffer so much now — what will you do when you are tossed to the beasts? Little did you think of them when you refused to sacrifice."

"What I am suffering now," she replied, "I suffer by myself. But then another will be inside me who will suffer for me, just as I shall be suffering for him." And she gave birth to a girl; and one of her sisters brought her up as her own daughter.

Therefore, since the Holy Spirit has permitted the story of this contest to be written down and by so permitting has willed it, we shall carry out the command or, indeed, the commission of the most saintly Perpetua, however unworthy I might be to add anything to this glorious story. At the same time I shall add one example of her perseverance and nobility of soul.

The military tribune had treated them with extraordinary severity because on the information of certain very foolish people he became afraid that they would be spirited out of the prison by magical spells.

Perpetua spoke to him directly. "Why can you not even allow us to refresh ourselves properly? For we are the most distinguished of the condemned prisoners, seeing that we belong to the emperor; we are to fight on his very birthday. Would it not be to your credit if we were brought forth on the day in a healthier condition?"

The officer became disturbed and grew red. So it was that he gave the order that they were to be more humanely treated; and he allowed her brothers and other persons to visit, so that the prisoners could dine in their company. By this time the adjutant who was head of the jail was himself a Christian.

On the day before, when they had their last meal, which is called the free banquet, they celebrated not a banquet but rather a love feast. They spoke to the mob with the same steadfastness, warned them of God's judgment, stressing the joy they would have in their suffering, and ridiculing the curiosity of those that came to see them. Saturus said: "Will not tomorrow be enough for you? Why are you so eager to see something that you dislike? Our friends today will be our enemies on the morrow. But take careful note of what we look like so that you will recognize us on the day." Thus everyone would depart from the prison in amazement, and many of them began to believe.

The day of their victory dawned, and they marched from the prison to the amphitheater joyfully as though they were going to heaven, with calm faces, trembling, if at all, with joy rather than fear. Perpetua went along with shining countenance and calm step, as the beloved of God, as a wife of Christ, putting down everyone's stare by her own intense gaze. With them also was Felicitas, glad that she had safely given birth so that now she could fight the beasts, going from one blood bath to another, from the midwife to the gladiator, ready to wash after childbirth in a second baptism.

They were then led up to the gates and the men were forced to put on the robes of priests of Saturn, the women the dress of the priestesses of Ceres. But the noble Perpetua strenuously resisted this to the end.

"We came to this of our own free will, that our freedom should not be violated. We agreed to pledge our lives provided that we would do no such thing. You agreed with us to do this."

Even injustice recognized justice. The military tribune agreed. They were to be brought into the arena just as they were. Perpetua then began to sing a psalm: she was already treading on the head of the Egyptian. Revocatus, Saturninus, and Saturus began to warn the onlooking mob. Then when they came within sight of Hilarianus, they suggested by their motions and gestures, "You have condemned us, but God will condemn you."

At this the crowds became enraged and demanded that they be scourged before a line of gladiators. And they rejoiced at this that they had obtained a share in the Lord's sufferings.

But he who said, "Ask and you shall receive," [Matt. 7:7] answered their prayer by giving each one the death he had asked for. For whenever they would discuss among themselves their desire for martyrdom, Saturninus indeed insisted that he wanted to be exposed to all the different beasts, that his crown might be all the more glorious. And so at the outset of the contest he and Revocatus were matched with a leopard, and then while in the stocks they were attacked by a bear. As for Saturus, he dreaded nothing more than a bear, and he counted on being killed by one bite of a leopard. Then he was matched with a wild boar; but the gladiator who had tied him to the animal was gored by the boar and died a few days after the contest, whereas Saturus was only dragged along. Then when he was bound in the stocks awaiting the bear, the animal refused to come out of the cages, so that Saturus was called back once more unhurt.

For the young women, however, the Devil had prepared a mad heifer. This was an unusual animal, but it was chosen that their sex might be matched with that of the beast. So they were stripped naked, placed in nets and thus brought out into the arena. Even the crowd was horrified when they saw that one was a delicate young girl and the other was a woman fresh from childbirth with the milk still dripping from her breasts. And so they were brought back again and dressed in unbelted tunics.

First the heifer tossed Perpetua and she fell on her back. Then sitting up she pulled down the tunic that was ripped along the side so that it covered her thighs, thinking more of her modesty than of her pain. Next she asked for a pin to fasten her untidy hair: for it was not right that a martyr should die with her hair in disorder, lest she might seem to be mourning in her hour of triumph.

Then she got up. And seeing that Felicitas had been crushed to the ground, she went over to her, gave her hand, and lifted her up. Then the two stood side by side. But the cruelty of the mob was by now appeased, and so they were called back through the Gate of Life.

There Perpetua was held up by a man named Rusticus who was at the time a catechumen and kept close to her. She awoke from a kind of sleep (so absorbed had she been in ecstasy in the Spirit) and she began to look about her. Then to the amazement of all she said: "When are we going to be thrown to that heifer or whatever it is?"

When told that this had already happened, she refused to believe it until she noticed the marks of her rough experience on her person and her dress. Then she called for her brother and spoke to him together with the catechumens and said: "You must all stand fast in the faith and love one another, and do not be weakened by what we have gone through."

At another gate Saturus was earnestly addressing the soldier Pudens. "It is exactly," he said, "as I foretold and predicted. So far not one animal has touched me. So now you may believe me with all your heart: I am going in there and I shall be finished off with one bite of the leopard." And immediately as the contest was coming to a close a leopard was let loose, and after one bite Saturus was so drenched with blood that as he came away the mob roared in witness to his second baptism: "Well washed! Well washed!" For well washed indeed was one who had been bathed in this manner.

Then he said to the soldier Pudens: "Good-bye. Remember me, and remember the faith. These things should not disturb you but rather strengthen you."

And with this he asked Pudens for a ring from his finger, and dipping it into his wound he gave it back to him again as a pledge and as a record of his bloodshed.

Shortly after he was thrown unconscious with the rest in the usual spot to have his throat cut. But the mob asked that their bodies be brought out into the open that their eyes might be the guilty witnesses of the sword that pierced their flesh. And so the martyrs got up and went to the spot of their own accord as the people wanted them to, and kissing one another they sealed their martyrdom with the ritual kiss of peace. The others took the sword in silence and without moving, especially Saturus, who being the first to climb the stairway was the first to die. For once again he was waiting for Perpetua. Perpetua, however, had yet to taste more pain. She screamed as she was struck on the bone; then she took the trembling hand of the young gladiator and guided it to her throat. It was as though so great a woman, feared as she was by the unclean spirit, could not be dispatched unless she herself were willing.

Ah, most valiant and blessed martyrs! Truly are you called and chosen for the glory of Christ Jesus our Lord! And any man who exalts, honors, and worships his glory should read for the consolation of the Church these new deeds of heroism which are no less significant than the tales of old. For these new manifestations of virtue will bear witness to one and the same Spirit who still operates, and to God the Father almighty, to his Son Jesus Christ our Lord, to whom is splendor and immeasurable power for all the ages. Amen.

———

DOROTHY DAY

Therese

Both the author and the subject of the biography from which this selection is taken are widely admired, even venerated, as having lived lives of exceptional holiness. Dorothy Day (1897-1980) was a lifelong activist on behalf of peace and economic justice who converted to Catholicism shortly after the birth of her daughter. She would later found the Catholic Worker Movement and become an inspiring and influential advocate for social justice and compassion grounded in Catholic social thought and sustained by Catholic sacraments and prayer. Therese of Lisieux, a French nun who died in 1897 at the age of twenty-four, led a far more secluded and outwardly uneventful life. Yet the "little way" of love and attentiveness she explored in her living and expressed in her writing became a strong influence on the spirituality of Day and millions of other believers.

As you consider the significance of Therese's life, consider Matthew 20:20-28, which is included among the "vocation" readings in Part I. Although the following passage does not refer explicitly to this biblical text,

---

From Dorothy Day, *Therese* (Springfield, IL: Templegate Publishers, 1960), pp. v-x, 69-72, 81-83, 106-107, 126-127, 162-166, and 173-176.

both it and Day's account of Therese's life seem to turn notions of "signif-icance" upside down. Why do you think Day so admired "The Little Flower"? Do you consider Therese's life "extraordinary" or "ordinary"?

———————————————

The first time I heard the name of St. Therese of the Child Jesus and of the Holy Face (to give her her whole title), also known as Therese of Lisieux, the Little Flower, was when I lay in the maternity ward of Bellevue Hospital in New York. Bellevue is the largest hospital in the world, and doctors from all over the world come there. If you are poor you can have free hospital care. At that time, if you could pay anything there was a flat rate for having a baby — thirty dollars for a ten days' stay, in a long ward with about sixty beds. I was so fortunate as to have a bed next to the window looking out over the East River, so that I could see the sun rise in the morning and light up the turgid water and make gay the little tugs and the long tankers that went by the window. When there was fog it seemed as though the world ended outside my window, and the sound of fog horns haunted the day and the night.

As a matter of fact, my world did end at the window those ten days that I was in the hospital, because I was supremely happy. If I had written the greatest book, composed the greatest symphony, painted the most beautiful painting, or carved the most exquisite figure, I could not have felt more the exalted creator than I did when they placed my child in my arms. To think that this thing of beauty, sighing gently in my arms, reaching her little mouth for my breast, clutching at me with her tiny beautiful hands, had come from my flesh, was my own child! Such a great feeling of happiness and joy filled me that I was hungry for Someone to thank, to love, even to worship, for so great a good that had been bestowed upon me. That tiny child was not enough to contain my love, nor could the father, though my heart was warm with love for both.

We were radicals and had no particular religious affiliations. If I was drawn to any "organized church," it was to the Catholic. I knew of such saints as St. Francis of Assisi and St. Augustine, and William James, in his *Varieties of Religious Experience*, had introduced me to St. Teresa of Avila, that well-traveled yet cloistered contemplative, with her vigorous writing and her sense of humor.

"What are you going to name your baby?" the girl in the next bed to mine asked me.

"Teresa," I told her. "Tamar Teresa. I have a dear friend whose husband is a Zionist, and she has a little girl named Tamar. It means little palm tree, in Hebrew."

"And Teresa is after the Little Flower?"

I had never heard of the Little Flower and she had never heard of Teresa of Avila. She was a Catholic, and although she didn't read much, she knew the outlines of the life of St. Therese of Lisieux. In her pocketbook, where she kept her powder and lipstick, tissues and rosary beads, money to buy candy and the *Daily News* when the boy made his rounds, she also had a medal of the Little Flower. "Here, I will give it to you for your baby," she said. "Pin it on her."

I was some years from being a Catholic and I shied away from this man-ifestation of superstition and charm-wearing. I wanted no such talisman. Besides, the baby might swallow it. The pin might come unloosed and pierce that tender flesh.

"But if you love someone, you want something around you to remind you of them," the girl protested. So I took the medal, and after hearing of St. Therese as the young novice mistress of a far-off convent of Lisieux in Nor-mandy, who had died the year I was born, and whose sisters were still alive, I decided that although I would name my child after the older saint, the new one would be my own Teresa's novice mistress, to train her in the spiritual life. I knew that I wanted to have the child baptized a Catholic and I wanted both saints to be taking care of her. One was not enough.

The next time I heard of St. Therese of Lisieux was in 1928, a year after I had been baptized a Catholic. I was thirty years old. I had read the New Testa-ment, the *Imitation of Christ,* St. Augustine, and had dipped into the writings of some of the saints William James had introduced me to. I had a daily mis-sal, too, which presented a little biography of the saint of the day, commem-orated in the Mass. I still knew nothing of modern saints. Perhaps, I thought, the days of saints had passed.

At that time I did not understand that we are all "called to be saints," as St. Paul puts it. Most people nowadays, if they were asked, would say diffi-dently that they do not profess to be saints, indeed they do not want to be saints. And yet the saint is the holy man, the "whole man," the integrated man. We all wish to be that, but in these days of stress and strain we are not developing our spiritual capacities as we should and most of us will admit that. We want to grow in love but we do not know how. Love is a science, a knowledge, and we lack it.

My confessor at the time was Father Zachary, an Augustinian Father of the Assumption, stationed at the Church of Our Lady of Guadalupe on West

Fourteenth Street. He was preparing me for Confirmation, giving me a weekly evening of instruction.

One day Father Zachary said to me, "Here is a book that will do you good." He had already given me Challoner's *Meditations* and the St. Andrew Missal. The book he now handed me was *The Little White Flower: The Story of a Soul,* an unbound book which had a tan cover with a not too attractive picture of a young nun with a sweet insipid face, holding a crucifix and a huge bouquet of roses. I was by now familiar with the statues of this little Sister which were to be seen in every church. They always called her little, although it is said she was very tall, and completely emaciated when the last photographs of her were taken. She had a proud face, however, and her habit and cloak concealed how thin she was. She was very young and her writing seemed to me like that of a schoolgirl. I wasn't looking for anything so simple and felt slightly aggrieved at Father Zachary. Men, even priests, were very insulting to women, I thought, handing out what they felt suited their intelligence — in other words, pious pap.

I dutifully read *The Story of a Soul* and am ashamed to confess that I found it colorless, monotonous, too small in fact for my notice. What kind of a saint was this who felt that she had to practice heroic charity in eating what was put in front of her, in taking medicine, enduring cold and heat, restraint, enduring the society of mediocre souls, in following the strict regime of the convent of Carmelite nuns which she had joined at the age of fifteen? A splash of dirty water from the careless washing of a nun next to her in the laundry was mentioned as a "mortification," when the very root of the word meant death. And I was reading in my Daily Missal of saints stretched on the rack, burnt by flames, starving themselves in the desert, and so on.

Joan of Arc leading an army fitted more into my concept of a saint, familiar as I was with the history of labor with its martyrs in the service of their brothers. "Love of brothers is to lay down one's life on the barricades, in revolt against the hunger and injustice in the world," I told Father Zachary, trying to convert him to my point of view. Living as we were in a time of world revolution, when, as I felt, the people of the world were rising to make a better world for themselves, I wondered what this new saint had to offer.

As a matter of fact, I was working at the time for the Anti-Imperialist League, a Communist Party affiliate with offices on Union Square. I had been given the job by a young Jewish intellectual whom I had known when he went to Columbia University and took part in the anti-conscription campaign of the First World War, who went to Russia to attend the Third International, was active in the Party for some years, and was dismissed in one of the frequent Party purges some years later. My companions were two women, both of them former Catholics, who looked on me indulgently and felt that my "faith" was a neurotic aspect of my character and something quite divorced from my daily life.

The work that we were engaged in was to publicize and raise funds for General Sandino, who was resisting American aggression in Nicaragua. Our marines were hunting him in the mountains, and the work of our committee was to raise funds and medical supplies. I did the publicity.

I was so new a Catholic that I was still working for this committee for some months after my Baptism, and I talked to Father Zachary about the work. "I am in agreement with it," I told him. "We should not be sending our marines to Nicaragua. I am in agreement with many of the social aims of Communism. 'From each according to his ability and to each according to his need.'"

Father Zachary could only quote Lenin to me, saying, "Atheism is basic to Marxism." He was the gentlest of confessors with me, who, at that time, was a female counterpart of Graham Greene's Quiet American, wanting to do good by violence.

But I did not feel he understood me when he gave me the life of St. Therese to read. What did she have to do with this world conflict, in which I in my way was involved?

I obtained other work which took me out of the Party work. I was engrossed with my child, and with earning a living. I saw more and more the basic oppositions between Catholicism and Marxism. But it took me a longer time to realize the unique position of Therese of Lisieux in the Church today.

*   *   *

Therese remembers a dream she had at the age of three which, she said, left a very deep impression. She was walking alone in the garden and suddenly she saw "two horrible little devils near the arbor, dancing on a barrel of lime with amazing agility in spite of having heavy irons on their feet." They looked at her with flaming eyes and then, as if overcome by fear, threw themselves in the twinkling of an eye to the bottom of the barrel. They escaped in some mysterious way, and ran off to hide in the linen room, which opened onto the garden. "When I saw how cowardly they were I put my fears aside and went over to the window to see what they were up to. There the little wretches were, running around and around the table, and not knowing how to escape my gaze. From time to time they came nearer, still very agitated, to peep through the window; then when they saw that I was still there, they began racing about again in abject misery."

She does not give much importance to this dream but she says she felt that God made use of it to show her that anyone in a state of grace had no need to fear.

She was beginning, even at that very early age, to see what the spiritual life meant, the series and successions of definite choices, the preference which means the life of love, the ordering of every little thing in life as though we were "practicing the presence of God." "What would He have me to do?" "Speak Lord, for Thy servant heareth." Samuel, St. Paul, all the saints had that attitude, that attraction to the good, that sense of the importance of the present moment.

Those were sunny years of childhood with delightful memories. Her father used to take the children to the pavilion where he kept his fishing tackle and books; he took them for walks on Sunday and then her mother was with them. She remembers the wheat fields studded with poppies and cornflowers and daisies. She loved, she said — she who was to wall herself in at the age of fifteen in a severely cloistered order — she loved "far distances, wide spaces and trees." Her whole soul was steeped in beauty and love, and her own happy nature made life all the more delightful. For four and a half years, the whole world was sunny for her.

And then came her mother's illness and death.

Now Therese's natural gaiety left her, and the second part of her life — the saddest she calls it — was to begin. This lasted from the time she was four and a half until she was fourteen. She was no longer lively and open, but diffident and oversensitive, crying if anyone looked at her. She could not bear to be anywhere but in the intimacy of her own family, where she could be herself. Her father and her two oldest sisters overwhelmed her with loving-kindness.

The very fact that children come face to face with death and suffering early, makes for that paradox, "rejoicing in tribulation," that the New Testament speaks of. Therese suffered, hovered on the verge of tears, could not bear to go abroad, was hypersensitive. The light of life seemed to have gone out with her mother, and yet she spoke of delightful times in their new home, of visiting their cousins and going on holidays.

"I die, yet behold I live," St. Paul says. One has to experience this to write about it. In cold words, it is hard to convey this sense of tears and joy, soft rain and sunshine.

Every afternoon Mr. Martin took his youngest daughter for a walk, to pay a visit to the Blessed Sacrament in each of the churches in the town. When she was five she visited Carmel for the first time and heard her father tell how the holy nuns spent their time in prayer behind the grille, and never went out for walks, never set foot outside their walls.

Therese learned much at an early age and this child knew what evil was. She herself spoke of the goodness of the Father who had removed all obstacles from the path of His child, knowing her capacity for sin, her danger of falling. She well knew her weakness, she well knew the world. She recognized and said over and over again that it was because of her parents, her sisters, her home life, the training she had received, and finally her life in the convent that she had been saved from falling into the most appalling depths of sin.

But she also suffered intensely from scruples and for so long that it was a neurosis, like the need to be forever washing one's hands. She was tempted to vanity and wept, and then wept because she had wept. Vanity may seem to be only a slight sin, but to what depths vanity has led many a woman, perhaps only a woman can know. The vanity of Eve, that desire to exercise power, to seduce, to drag down!

Just as this child longed for the martyrdom of a Joan of Arc, an Ignatius of Antioch, as an atonement, as a way of showing her love, so also she recognized the capacity to sin which she possessed. Her love, she felt, should be greater than that of a Magdalene, because she had been prevented from sin by a loving Father who knew her weakness, knew to what depths she could have fallen. She gave up, too, her desire for great and noble deeds.

In other words, she expected nothing of herself, she was "the little grain of sand," trampled underfoot, forgotten, and God would do it all in making her a saint, because He wanted it. He wanted just such a saint as she was to become, because she was ordinary, just like many another girl, a child of comfortably situated, hard-working parents. She was one of "the people." When she spoke of herself as a "little flower," a comparison her father had made, it was of a common, ordinary, and fragile little flower of the spring, common as grass, that she was thinking.

In Therese's world, she was faced with only three choices. She could look forward to marriage, or to living at home as a single woman and caring for her father, or to entering the convent. The atmosphere of this home was one of such liberty that the girls were always free to decide what they wanted, what they themselves thought was God's will for them.

On the feast of Pentecost, Therese told her father of her desires. She did it in fear and trembling, at the close of the day, after they had come home from Vespers. Her father was sitting in the garden; it was sunset at the end of a most beautiful day. She had prayed to the Holy Spirit and to the Apostles to help her to speak, to ask her father's permission. After all, she was only fourteen.

The very words she uses in her autobiography show how important she considered her vocation, how out of the ordinary, not in the least like that of others. She felt herself to be, she wrote, "a child destined by God to be, by means of prayer and sacrifice, an apostle of apostles." Already once before, when out walking with her father, she had pointed to the large T made by the configuration of the stars and said childishly, "Look, my name is written in heaven." She felt her vocation to be a saint — and a special kind of saint for our times.

When she told her father, he wept at first. He tried to tell her she was too young to leave him, to take such a step into a harsh and rigorous life. But they continued to talk as they walked up and down the garden path, and her heart grew light with joy when she realized that he had consented. After they had walked for some time together, he stooped down to a little rock garden and picked a small white flower, which came out by the roots. Then he spoke to her of her sheltered life, and how God had chosen her, a little flower, preserving her in her fragility and obscurity. From then on she thought of herself as "a little white flower" — the name she first gave to her book. She took the flower and pressed it in her prayer book and since the roots had come up with the stem, she thought of herself as being transplanted to Carmel. Later, when the stem broke, she took it as a sign that she was going to die young, as she did.

There is no question but that the Carmelite cloister was a fervent one. The life was hard. Therese said that when her dream of gaining admittance was at last realized, "peace flooded my soul, a deep, sweet, inexpressible peace; an inward peace which has been my lot these eight and a half years. It has never left me, not even when trials were at their height. Everything here delighted me, our little cell most of all; it was as though I had been transported to my faraway desert."

She kept saying to herself that at last she was where she wanted to be. "I am here forever now." It had been so hard those last months; there had been the long period of waiting and then the last days of farewell to the family, the last Holy Communion together, the last breakfast in that much-loved dining room, the parting with father and uncle and aunt, cousins and sisters. They went with her to Carmel and after Mass said goodbye to her at the door. She felt at that moment as though her heart would burst and that she would die. It was a truly terrible moment, a fearful moment, but she was always sure of just what she wanted. Her will was set on God. God alone!

"Illusions!" she was to write later. "Thanks to God's mercy I had none at all; the religious life was just what I had expected."

Always she was praying that she would see things as they were, that she would live in reality, not in dreams.

Certainly she had little time to dream. According to the Benedictine Rule, the *Opus Dei* — the work of God which must come before all other work — is that of offering up the Holy Sacrifice of the Mass and reciting the Divine Office. So the prime work of the Carmelite is to acquire a love for and a knowledge of God as well as to praise Him. This Rule obliges her to recite the Breviary. The Carmelite also fits reading and meditation into her schedule.

Six or seven hours of prayer, a life of hard work in silence the rest of the time, two brief periods of recreation when there was permission to talk, sew, paint, or take up the "busy work" all women delight in. In addition to the works of the community, whether it was laundry, kitchen, dining room, sacristy, much of the work was done alone. When it came to the sewing, the fine embroidery done by the community, the tradition was to work in one's cell.

Therese's habit was of coarse serge, her stockings of rough muslin, and on her feet she wore rope sandals. Her bed was made of three planks, covered by a thin pad and one woolen blanket. There was scarcity of food, inadequate bedding, no heat in the convent except for one small stove in one room. Prayer and penance! These are indeed spiritual works, spiritual weapons to save souls, penance for luxury when the destitute suffer, a work to increase the sum total of love and peace in the world.

By the time she was twenty, Therese had gone through many intense experiences, losing father and mother, feeling an orphan, but emphasizing for that reason her dependence on God as a Father. Over and over again through her writings "God appears to her understanding," writes Father Liagre, "and above all to her heart (for she lived much more by her heart than her understanding) as a Father, as her Father, as the most affectionate and tender of fathers; in a word, as fatherly love, and that at its very highest perfection."

Her familiarity with God the Father, God the Son, and God the Holy Spirit might be called her recognition of the immanence of God, and this very familiarity which leads her to liken herself to a little plaything, a ball, a little grain of dust to be trampled underfoot, points to God's transcendence, to the infinite distance between God and creatures. On the one hand He is closer than the air we breathe, and on the other hand we are the grain of sand on the seashore, lost in the nothingness before the All-Powerful.

It was in the spring of 1896, in April, that she received the first warning of the sickness that caused her death. Therese tells the story of the beginning of her illness, how on going to her cell one night in the bitter cold, and undressing in the dark, she suffered a hemorrhage from the lungs which soaked her handkerchief with blood. She did not even light her lamp, but lay down on her hard pallet to take the few hours of sleep allowed Good Friday night. She says she was overwhelmed with joy at the thought that she was going to go soon to God. She did not lie awake, since it was already midnight, but she woke with a sense of expectation, as though she had something good and exciting to look forward to, and going to the window, saw that her handkerchief was all stained with blood.

She knew with a certainty beyond doubt that she was teaching the way of the early Christians, the way Jesus Himself spoke of when He said, "I am the Way, the Truth and the Life."

She knew with a certainty that is heaven itself, or a foretaste of heaven, that she had been taught the secret, the "science of love." She died saying, "Love alone matters." She died saying that she did not regret having given herself up to love.

Her secret is generally called the Little Way, and is so known by the Catholic world. She called it little because it partakes of the simplicity of a child, a very little child, in its attitude of abandonment, of acceptance.

We know of course that not all children, not even infants, are so gifted. But generally speaking, the little child is dependent and trustful, ready to accept everything from the hand of its parent, with no knowledge of prideful independence. Therese is content to be considered always the little child, the little grain of sand, the creature who can give nothing to its Creator but the willing acceptance of this status, taking from the hand of its Creator all that comes in daily life.

To the community she gave every appearance of serenity and peace, and yet "in peace is my bitterness most bitter," she quotes. On another occasion she says, "Let us suffer, if need be, with bitterness." She, the realist, well knew that suffering of body and soul is not lofty and exalted, but mean and cruel, a reflection of the blackness of hell. It was not suffering for itself that she embraced. It was a means to an end; the very means used by Jesus Himself.

In order to hide this suffering from others, she wrote poems about the joys of faith, hope, and charity, and yet in the night of sense and soul that she was passing through, she felt none of these joys. She wanted her suffering to be hidden even from God, if that were possible, in order to atone for lack of faith in the world. She asked consolation from no one, not even from God. She had wanted martyrdom, and this heavy weight of despair is martyrdom.

She says that she wants to offer this blackness for all those in the world today who do not believe, who "have lost the precious treasures of faith and hope and with them all joy that is pure and true." She says she has no sense of joy whatever, and yet she can still say, "Thou hast given me, O Lord, a delight in Thy doings." Since it is suffering of a most cruel kind that she is laboring under, a blackness of the mind and soul, she "wills" a delight in this suffering. If suffering is a part of love, suffering then will become her delight.

Before the end, she became skin and bones. Father Petitot said that she became so thin that her bones protruded through her skin. Tuberculosis of the intestines set in and gangrene, and when she was raised up in bed to get her breath, she gasped that it was as though she were sitting on spikes.

The flies tormented her very much during the last hot summer. It must have been no little part of the suffering of Christ on the Cross, nailed and enduring the crawling of flies on His eyes, His wounds, His flesh. "They are my only enemies," Therese said when she was tormented by them. "God commanded us to forgive our enemies, and I am glad I have some occasion to do so. That is why I spare them."

When her sister Celine sat reading her a conference on eternal beatitude, suddenly Therese interrupted her — "It is not that which attracts me. It is love! To love and be loved!, and to return to earth to make Love to be loved!"

It was on July 17 that she said, "I feel that my mission is about to begin; my mission of making souls love the good God as I love Him, to teach my little way to souls. If my desires receive fulfillment, I shall spend my heaven on earth even until the end of time. Yes, I will spend my heaven doing good upon earth."

"It is the way of spiritual childhood," she said in response to a question about her "little way." "It is the path of total abandonment and confidence. I would show them the little method I have found so perfectly successful and tell them there is but one thing to do on earth; to cast before Jesus the flowers of little sacrifices. That is what I have done and that is why I shall be so well received."

There has been so much discussion of the diminutive "little" which Therese used constantly that it is good to remember her words of explanation of August 6. "To be little . . . is . . . not to attribute to ourselves the virtues we practice, nor to believe ourselves capable of practicing virtue at all. It is rather to recognize the fact that God puts treasures of virtue into the hands of his little children to make use of them in time of need, but they remain always treasures of the good God. Finally, to be little means that we must never be discouraged over our faults, for children often fall but they are too small to harm themselves very much."

*   *   *

Therese Martin died on September 30, 1897. Only seventeen years later, when those who had been born in the same year with her were just forty-one years of age, the fame of her sanctity had so spread among the people that her cause was introduced at Rome. She was beatified on April 29, 1923, and canonized on May 17, 1925, an unusually rapid process for the Church in modern times.

So many books have been written about St. Therese, books of all kinds, too, so why, I ask myself again, have I written one more? There are popular lives, lives written for children, travelogue lives following her footsteps, lives for the extrovert, the introvert, the contemplative, the activist, the scholar, and the theologian.

Yet it was the "worker," the common man, who first spread her fame by word of mouth. It was the masses who first proclaimed her a saint. It was the "people."

What was there about her to make such an appeal? Perhaps because she was so much like the rest of us in her ordinariness. In her lifetime there are no miracles recounted; she was just good, good as the bread which the Normans bake in huge loaves. Good as the pale cider which takes the place of the wine of the rest of France, since Normandy is an apple country. "Small beer," one might say. She compares to the great saints as cider compares with wine, others might complain. But it is the world itself which has canonized her, it is the common people who have taken her to their hearts. And now the theologians are writing endlessly to explain how big she was, and not little, how mature and strong she was, not childlike and dependent. They are tired of hearing people couple her name with that of Teresa of Avila, whom they call the "Great Teresa" as distinguished from the "Little Therese."

What did she do? She practiced the presence of God and she did all things — all the little things that make up our daily life and contact with others — for His honor and glory. She did not need much time to expound what she herself called her "little way." She wrote her story, and God did the rest. God and the people. God chose for the people to clamor for her canonization.

What stands out in her life? Her holiness, of course, and the holiness of her entire family. That is not an ordinary thing in this day of post-war materialism, delinquency, and all those other words which indicate how dissatisfied the West is with its economy of abundance while the East sits like Lazarus at the gate of Dives.

With governments becoming stronger and more centralized, the common man feels his ineffectiveness. When the whole world seems given over to preparedness for war and the show of force, the message of Therese is quite a different one.

She speaks to our condition. Is the atom a little thing? And yet what havoc it has wrought. Is her little way a small contribution to the life of the spirit? It has all the power of the spirit of Christianity behind it. It is an explosive force that can transform our lives and the life of the world, once put into effect. In the homily he gave after the Gospel at the Mass of her canonization, Pope Pius XI said: "If the way of spiritual childhood became general, who does not see how easily would be realized the reformation of human society. . . ."

The seeds of this teaching are being spread, being broadcast, to be watered by our blood perhaps, but with a promise of a harvest. God will give the increase. At a time when there are such grave fears because of the radioactive particles that are sprinkled over the world by the hydrogen bomb tests, and the question is asked, what effect they are going to have on the physical life of the universe, one can state that this saint, of this day, is releasing a force, a spiritual force upon the world, to counteract that fear and that disaster. We know that one impulse of grace is of infinitely more power than a cobalt bomb. Therese has said, "All is grace."

She declared, "I will spend my heaven doing good upon earth." "I will raise up a mighty host of little saints." "My mission is to make God loved, to make Love loved."

And one can only remember the story of Abraham and how he asked, "Wilt Thou destroy the just with the wicked? If there be fifty just men in the city, shall they perish withal? And wilt Thou not spare that place for the sake of the fifty just, if they be therein? Far be it from Thee to do this thing, and to slay the just with the wicked, and for the just to be in like case as the wicked. This is not beseeming Thee: Thou, who judgest all the earth, wilt not make this judgment."

The mystery of suffering has a different aspect under the New Covenant, since Christ died on the Cross and took on Himself men's sins. Now St. Paul teaches that we can fill up the sufferings of Christ, that we must share in the sufferings of the world to lessen them, to show our love for our brothers. But God does not change, so we can trust with Abraham that for even ten just men, He will not destroy the city. We can look with faith and hope to that *mighty army of little ones* that St. Therese has promised us and which is present now among us.

THREE BIOGRAPHICAL SKETCHES

The three readings that follow represent the most common short, literary forms in which whole lives are briefly composed for the general public. These forms call forth different kinds of rhetoric suitable for different occasions and audiences. The first one is a biographical sketch of Ray Kroc, the past chairman of McDonald's Corporation, written by Jacques Pepin, a chef, author, and host of a popular PBS television series on cooking. The second reading is an obituary that appeared in the *Economist* magazine. The third is a funeral eulogy delivered by Amiri Baraka, the poet and activist formerly known as Leroi Jones.

Consider the three lives together. Which of them do you admire the most and the least? All life stories, even much longer ones, are highly selective in what they present. Figuring out what you need to know about someone before you can make judgments about them is a good way of figuring out what makes for lives that matter. It is therefore worth considering what additional facts about any one of these people would be most likely to alter your initial judgments about them. Information about their motives, their upbringing, the obstacles they had to overcome, and their overall views of life might all be important.

Consider Ray Kroc. According to Pepin, Kroc provided places for "eating" rather than "dining." Does such provision enhance human flourishing or diminish it? Ray Kroc's widow has given an enormous amount of the money he made to various charities and projects for the promotion of international peace. Assuming that she has acted according to Ray's own wishes, does this fact alter your assessment of the worthiness and significance of Kroc's life? As Pepin tells the story, Kroc's life becomes the archetypically American "rags to riches" tale, full of success due to "pluck and luck." Do you admire Kroc's life more because of the serious physical obstacles he had to overcome than you would if he had been perfectly healthy during his entire life?

Ray Kroc lived a long life, Iris Chang a very short one. Indeed, her death at her own hand at an early age seems to have come about as the direct result of her work. Do you think that Aristotle would have thought of her as someone who had chosen well a short but splendid and self-sacrificial life over a long and comparatively undistinguished one? If so, would you share that judgment? How important are the quality and benefits of the products of a life (fast food restaurants for Kroc; history books for Chang) in assessing the overall significance of a life?

Aristotle concluded the passage at the beginning of this chapter as follows: "It is also possible, however, to sacrifice actions to [the excellent human being's] friend, since it may be finer to be responsible for his friend's doing the action than to do it himself." This would appear to be one of the primary themes in the life of Joe Landrum, because Landrum, according to this eulogy delivered at his funeral, worked at two jobs in part to support his wife's commendable political activities. Indeed, Landrum's life, as it is presented here, seems more multidimensional than either Kroc's or Chang's. We see him as postal worker, bus attendant, union organizer, husband, lover, neighbor, father, and grandfather. He worked so that others might live well; Kroc and Chang seem to have lived in order to work. Moreover, Landrum seems to have been a working man like those who commanded so much respect from William James in his essay on what makes a life significant from the Prologue to this anthology. We do not know, of course, what Kroc and Chang did outside of their work. Assuming, however, that they really did sacrifice all other goods and human relationships for the sake of the products they produced, how would you compare the worthiness and significance of their lives to Landrum's?

Ray Kroc

Among the army of burger flippers at work across America in the 1960s was a French chef putting his training to use at Howard Johnson's on Queens Boulevard in New York City. I worked for HoJo's from the summer of 1960 to the spring of 1970, doing my American apprenticeship, learning about mass production and marketing. The company had been started in 1925 in Massachusetts by Howard Deering Johnson, and by the mid-1960s its sales exceeded that of Burger King, Kentucky Fried Chicken and McDonald's combined. There would be more than 1,000 Howard Johnson restaurants and 500 motor lodges. Yet after Johnson's death in 1972, the company lost its raison d'etre. The restaurants became obsolete; the food quality deteriorated. You underestimate the clientele at your peril. The late restaurateur Joe Baum used to say, "There is no victory over a customer."

As the Howard Johnson Co. went to pieces, Ray Kroc's obsession with Quality, Service, Cleanliness and Value — the unwavering mission of McDonald's — was gathering momentum. Kroc was adroit and perceptive in identifying popular trends. He sensed that America was a nation of people who ate out, as opposed to the Old World tradition of eating at home. Yet he also knew that people here wanted something different. Instead of a structured, ritualistic restaurant with codes and routine, he gave them a simple, casual and identifiable restaurant with friendly service, low prices, no waiting and no reservations. The system eulogized the sandwich — no tableware to wash. One goes to McDonald's to eat, not to dine.

Kroc gave people what they wanted or, maybe, what he wanted. As he said, "The definition of salesmanship is the gentle art of letting the customer have it your way." He would remain the ultimate salesman, serving as a chairman of McDonald's Corp., the largest restaurant company in the world, from 1968 until his death in 1984.

In 1917, Ray Kroc was a brash 15-year-old who lied about his age to join the Red Cross as an ambulance driver. Sent to Connecticut for training, he never left for Europe because the war ended. So the teen had to find work, which he did, first as a piano player and then, in 1922, as a salesman for the Lily Tulip Cup Co.

Although he sold paper cups by day and played the piano for a radio sta-

From Jacques Pepin, "Ray Kroc," in *Time 100: Builders and Titans*, ed. Kelly Knauer (New York: Time, Inc., 1999), pp. 62-64.

tion at night, Kroc had an ear better tuned to the rhythms of commerce. In the course of selling paper cups he encountered Earl Prince, who had invented a five-spindle multimixer and was buying Lily cups by the truckload. Fascinated by the speed and efficiency of the machine, Kroc obtained exclusive marketing rights from Prince. Indefatigable, for the next 17 years he crisscrossed the country peddling the mixer.

On his travels he picked up the beat of a remarkable restaurant in San Bernardino, Calif., owned by two brothers, Dick and Mac McDonald, who had ordered eight mixers and had them churning away all day. Kroc saw the restaurant in 1954 and was entranced by the effectiveness of the operation. It was a hamburger restaurant, though not of the drive-in variety popular at the time. People had to get out of their cars to be served. The brothers had produced a very limited menu, concentrating on just a few items: hamburgers, cheeseburgers, french fries, soft drinks and milk shakes, all at the lowest possible prices.

Kroc, ever the instigator, started thinking about building McDonald's stores all over the U.S. — each of them equipped with eight multimixers whirring away, spinning off a steady stream of cash. The following day he pitched the idea of opening several restaurants to the brothers. They asked, "Who could we get to open them for us?" Kroc was ready: "Well, what about me?"

The would-be Great War veteran would grow rich serving the children of World War II vets. His confidence in what he had seen was unshakable. As he noted later, "I was 52 years old. I had diabetes and incipient arthritis. I had lost my gall bladder and most of my thyroid gland in earlier campaigns, but I was convinced that the best was ahead of me." He was even more convinced than the McDonalds and eventually cajoled them into selling out to him in 1961 for a paltry $2.7 million.

He was now free to run the business his own way, but he never changed the fundamental format that had been devised by the brothers. Kroc added his own wrinkles, certainly. He was a demon for cleanliness. From the overall appearance, to the parking lot, to the kitchen floor, to the uniforms, cleanliness was foremost and essential. "If you have time to lean, you have time to clean," was one of his favorite axioms. He was dead on, of course. The first impression you get from a restaurant through the eyes and nose is often what determines whether you'll go back.

By 1963 more than 1 billion hamburgers had been sold, a statistic that was displayed on a neon sign in front of each restaurant. That same year, the 500th McDonald's restaurant opened and the famous clown, Ronald McDonald, made his debut. He soon became known to children throughout the country, and kids were critical in determining where the family ate. According to John Mariani in his remarkable book *America Eats Out*, "Within six years of airing his first national TV ad in 1965, the Ronald McDonald clown character was familiar to 96% of American children, far more than knew the name of the President of the United States." Being a baby-boom company, McDonald's has found maturity a bit difficult. Its food today is as consistent as ever. But Americans are different, much surer of their tastes today. They no longer need the security McDonald's provides. So the same assets that had made the restaurants so great started to turn against the company, especially after Kroc died in 1984. People looked at uniformity as boring, insipid and controlling, the Golden Arches as a symbol of junk-food pollution. Franchisees began to feel increasingly alienated from top management, especially in its aggressive expansion policies.

Ironically, no adjustments are needed outside the U.S. With restaurants in more than 114 countries, McDonald's still represents Americana. When I return to France, my niece's children, who are wild about what they call "Macdo," clamor to go there. It has a somewhat snobbish appeal for the young, who are enamored of the American life-style.

Still, it's likely Ray Kroc would have moved on to something else if he had found a better idea. Even after McDonald's was well established, Kroc still tried, often with dismal results, to move forward with upscale hamburger restaurants, German-tavern restaurants, pie shops and even theme parks, like Disneyland. He always had a keen sense of the power of novelty and a strong belief in himself and his vision.

Like many of America's great entrepreneurs, Kroc was not a creator — convenience food already existed in many forms, from Howard Johnson's to White Castle — but he had the cunning ability to grasp a concept with all its complexities and implement it in the best possible way. And that's as American as a cheeseburger.

Iris Chang

Among the many issues that bedevil relations between China and Japan, the most intractable occurred almost 70 years ago. In 1937 around 50,000 Japanese troops descended on Nanking, China's former capital, and took charge there. What happened next is a matter of lasting controversy. The Chinese say that more than 300,000 civilians were killed, and 80,000 girls and women raped. The Japanese divide into different schools of thought. At one extreme, the "Great Illusion" school argues that almost no civilians were killed, and that most of the deaths were legal killings of soldiers in plain clothes. At the other, the "Great Massacre" school thinks as many as 200,000 Chinese may have died. Scholars on both sides continue to revile each other either as Japan-bashers, or as apologists for imperialism.

In Japan, the Nanking "Incident" — still too controversial even to have a settled name — is central to a wider debate about history teaching in Japanese schools. In China, it is crucial to the nation's modern identity. After the war, the atrocity was played down: Japan, seared by Hiroshima and Nagasaki, was seen as a victim nation, not as an aggressor, and the Americans were keen to cultivate it as a counterweight to dangerous Red China. To deny the Chinese version of Nanking, therefore, is to continue to gang up on China and to stifle its account of history.

Into this maelstrom of nationalist pride and pain stepped, in the 1990s, a 29-year-old Chinese-American. Iris Chang was not an historian by training. She had studied journalism at the University of Illinois, then taken a master's in science writing, and had worked for a while on the *Chicago Tribune*. Her interest in Nanking was aroused incidentally, by hearing her grandparents talk about it. Like many others, they had fled the city before the Japanese arrived; what they knew was hearsay. But it was sufficiently terrible for Miss Chang to spend a day "walking around in a state of shock," before deciding to devote herself to making the massacre known.

For two years she did research in China, rifling the archives and talking to survivors. She pinned a map of Nanking on her study wall, covering it

---

Obituary from *The Economist* Magazine, November 27, 2004.

with pictures of tortures and killing in the places where they had happened. Some civilians had been mutilated with broken beer bottles, some impaled on bamboo. Women's breasts had been cut off and nailed to walls. The Japanese killed so many men that they found it quicker to bayonet them as they stood in a line, rather than behead them.

As the grim stories accumulated, Miss Chang lost weight and broke down. She went on, defying exhaustion. When her book on Nanking came out, in 1997, she spent a year on the road talking about it. More than half a million copies were sold in America alone; she became a celebrity, leaving audiences astonished that this pretty, smiling girl could tell such tales of horror. But she did not care, she said, whether she made a cent from it. All she wanted to do was get the story out.

Facing the Ambassador

"Proper" historians cavilled, and with some reason. Her book, several said, was too polemical, and was riddled with mistakes which she refused to correct. Her reliance on oral history, especially the fading memories of Chinese witnesses, was unwise. Even her use of the invaluable diaries of foreign "bystanders" in Nanking was suspect, for these people — who had organised a "safety zone" both for foreigners and Chinese — had no idea of the actual numbers killed. When her book was translated into Japanese, supporters of the Great Massacre school found they could not defend her figures, which were higher even than those claimed in China.

Miss Chang could not bear this nit-picking. A great injustice had occurred, and had been all but covered up. There was no doubt at all that it had happened, with immense human suffering. She had no time for semantics: whether to include deaths outside the city walls, whether the plainclothes soldiers had been billetted with civilians, and so on. What she wanted, at the very least, was an official Japanese apology. Face to face on television with the Japanese ambassador to America, she demanded one. When he muttered that there had been "perhaps some unfortunate incidents," she was outraged.

When she died — apparently by shooting herself in the head, on a rural road in California — she had started work on a book on the Bataan Death March and the abuse of American prisoners-of-war by the Japanese. Again, the stories were affecting her: she had been taken to hospital, suffering from depression.

She had been planning, too, to publish the diaries of Minnie Vautrin, an

American missionary in Nanking during the massacre. Vautrin, like her, came from Illinois. She had saved thousands of Chinese civilians from the Japanese, sometimes giving them her own last ration of rice. In 1941, however, a year to the day after leaving Nanking, she had committed suicide, convinced that she had done too little.

Friends wondered whether Miss Chang had felt the same. This was certainly likely. But she was also aware that her writings had played into the hands of the massacre's deniers: that she had perhaps not only done too little, but protested too much.

Joseph S. ("Smiley") Landrum

Joseph "Smiley" Landrum was one of those solid rock working people of which our Newark community and indeed the American and African American nation are fundamentally composed. They are the basic creators, the production movers and shakers upon which all nations depend for their sustenance and development.

In the U.S., a great deal is made of the "rich & famous." There are tv shows, countless films, unending magazine and newspaper accounts of the folks with the big bux or high finance lifestyles or media-created superstars. We are trained publicly to worship, to envy, to be controlled by, the wealthy. To aspire to their lives, and take on, to the extent this is possible, their world view. . . .

But the basic, the most common fabric of our society are the working people, and they are still largely anonymous and unsung. Joe Landrum was such a man and while this brief moment is also something of a song for him, so that even in this form he will no longer be totally unsung, still there is something deeper you should know. About Joe, why finally he was important, not just to our long time sister-in-arms, Tina Johnson, Takalifu, but to us all.

From "Joseph S. ('Smiley') Landrum: 'My Joe' Funeral Oration," in *Eulogies*, ed. Imamu Amiri Baraka (New York: Marsilio Publishers, 1996), pp. 118-121.

You see part of Joe's song was Takalifu, that's Sister Tina Johnson's swahili name[,] for any Johnny-come-latelies in the house. Takalifu, and the entire family is also part of Joe's song. You see, for working people, the real creators of society, of both people and objects and relationships, they are sung, realized, by those creations. . . .

Takalifu was the swingingest part of Joe's song. And even though some of us did not know Joe well, the laughing jovial brother, always spreading that little light of his around so all of us could get a little, chances are if we were educated to the politics of Newark education, we knew or know of Tina/Takalifu, that little laughing ball of dynamism and community activism.

Tina has headed up the *Peoples' Democratic Council Committee to Save The Children* for several years, and even ran for the Newark Board of Education. She is always in the thick of the good fight, both seen and heard. What is so important for us to understand is that her husband and lover for 26 years, Joseph Landrum, backed all of her activities to the max.

Joe Landrum, like many working people, had two jobs. Maybe that's what helped kill him so young, at 53. A life of hard work and maximum stress. He worked for the post office as a mail handler, he also worked for the Newark Board of Education as a bus attendant for handicapped children. And Joe was a father, a grandfather, and recently even a great grandfather.

Born in that part of the city we used to call "Down Neck," on Bruen St., Joe Landrum made many many friends in the post office and board of education over the years and throughout the city. He was a good union man as well, and served as a group leader and spent many hours on the phone and in meetings counciliating [sic] workers' disputes. In other words, Joe was a class-conscious worker, one of the advanced, whose efforts make the whole movement go forward.

Joe and Tina's is a real love story. And even though he could not be present at the interminable round of meetings and rallies and marches that Tina/Takalifu was always at the head of, he was the bedrock, the solid foundation upon which any lasting structure must be built.

Tina could be at all these manifestations of progressive African American political motion because Joe provided the means, the backup, not just economic, but the spritiual [sic] support, the human encouragement, that bonding of will to will that makes a larger more forceful will. What keeps so many of us who are out front going. Without that solid backup, that spiritual nourishing back home, we could do nothing but stutter and stumble, and instead of being heroes, we would be very very humble.

One thing the detractors of working people and detractors of African American people, specifically those who are always putting down black and latino men for not being present at different political struggles, while the women are. There is some truth to this accusation, but we should also keep in mind Joe Landrum, bcause [sic] there are a bunch of Joe Landrums or José Landrums, who are the homefront, solid as a rock, backups. Whose wives or female companions might be out front battling but who support their wives' work, who support our community's development. The Joes who make the Tinas possible. It used to be we would say behind every great man there is a woman; now we can say, as well, behind every great woman there is a great man.

Joe even enabled Tina to go back to school at the middle age of her life, and get her degree. Joseph Landrum was no male chauvinist; he had got beyond Macho Man to Revolutionary Man.

So we must now sing Joseph Landrum. He cannot be unsung any longer. When we see Tina or any of the children — moving through or doing progressive work in the community, remember it is part of Joe's song. Now all of us need to help sing that song, ever louder and ever stronger. Along with Tina/Takalifu. . . .

〜〜〜

THOMAS GRAY

"Elegy Written in a Country Churchyard"

Thomas Gray (1716-1771) lived most of his life at Cambridge University, where he became one of the most learned men of his generation. Solitary and somewhat reclusive, he worked steadily but very deliberately at both his poetry and his scholarship. He labored over the *Elegy* for more than five years. Ironically, given the subject of the poem, its publication brought him immediate and overwhelming fame. And it remains even today one of the most widely known and dearly beloved poems of the English language.

From *Immortal Poems of the English Language,* ed. Oscar Williams (New York: Pocket, 1983), pp. 187-190.

The speaker of this poem has been thinking about many of the same questions that we have been wondering about throughout this anthology — for example, Are some lives more significant than others? Are the most choice-worthy and significant lives attended by fame and glory? Isn't there something wrong, or at least unsettling, about suggesting that one life is better or more significant than another one? Are we not all equal before God?

The speaker addresses these large questions in a very concrete situation. He is in a country churchyard wondering about the local people who are buried there. He wonders whether they are any more or less worthy of being remembered than the famous men of England like John Milton or Oliver Cromwell. We might wonder whether Gray's own effort to commemorate the rural poor in words is also a defense of their lives relative to the lives of the great and the famous. If so, how does he go about framing such a defense?

Like us, the speaker of this poem concerns himself with the relative significance of other lives in part because he is concerned about the meaning and the significance of his own. During the last stanzas of the poem, the situation of the first several stanzas is reversed. Instead of the speaker defending those buried in the country churchyard, he imagines some "hoary headed swain" defending him one day by telling the story of his life to a curious wanderer. On the basis of his epitaph and the poem as a whole, does our speaker finally belong to the tradition of Democracy, highly suspicious of any qualitative distinctions drawn between people and deeply committed to equality in every sense of the word, or does he finally belong to the Christian tradition, devoted to humility and charity as supreme virtues?

The curfew tolls the knell of parting day,
  The lowing herd wind slowly o'er the lea,
The plowman homeward plods his weary way,
  And leaves the world to darkness and to me.

Now fades the glimmering landscape on the sight,
  And all the air a solemn stillness holds,
Save where the beetle wheels his droning flight,
  And drowsy tinklings lull the distant folds;

Save that from yonder ivy-mantled tow'r
    The moping owl does to the moon complain
Of such as, wand'ring near her secret bow'r,
    Molest her ancient solitary reign.

Beneath those rugged elms, that yew-tree's shade,
    Where heaves the turf in many a mould'ring heap,
Each in his narrow cell for ever laid,
    The rude Forefathers of the hamlet sleep.

The breezy call of incense-breathing morn,
    The swallow twitt'ring from the straw-built shed,
The cock's shrill clarion, or the echoing horn,
    No more shall rouse them from their lowly bed.

For them no more the blazing hearth shall burn,
    Or busy housewife ply her evening care:
No children run to lisp their sire's return,
    Or climb his knees the envied kiss to share.

Oft did the harvest to their sickle yield,
    Their furrow oft the stubborn glebe has broke:
How jocund did they drive their team afield!
    How bow'd the woods beneath their sturdy stroke!

Let not Ambition mock their useful toil,
    Their homely joys, and destiny obscure;
Nor Grandeur hear with a disdainful smile
    The short and simple annals of the poor.

The boast of heraldry, the pomp of pow'r,
    And all that beauty, all that wealth e'er gave,
Awaits alike th' inevitable hour:
    The paths of glory lead but to the grave.

Nor you, ye Proud, impute to these the fault,
    If Memory o'er their tomb no trophies raise,
Where through the long-drawn aisle and fretted vault
    The pealing anthem swells the note of praise.

Can storied urn or animated bust
      Back to its mansion call the fleeting breath?
Can Honour's voice provoke the silent dust,
      Or Flatt'ry soothe the dull cold ear of death?

Perhaps in this neglected spot is laid
      Some heart once pregnant with celestial fire;
Hands, that the rod of empire might have sway'd,
      Or waked to ecstasy the living lyre.

But Knowledge to their eyes her ample page
      Rich with the spoils of time did ne'er unroll;
Chill Penury repress'd their noble rage,
      And froze the genial current of the soul.

Full many a gem of purest ray serene
      The dark unfathom'd caves of ocean bear:
Full many a flower is born to blush unseen,
      And waste its sweetness on the desert air.

Some village Hampden that with dauntless breast
      The little tyrant of his fields withstood,
Some mute inglorious Milton, here may rest,
      Some Cromwell guiltless of his country's blood.

Th' applause of list'ning senates to command,
      The threats of pain and ruin to despise,
To scatter plenty o'er a smiling land,
      And read their history in a nation's eyes,

Their lot forbade: nor circumscribed alone
      Their growing virtues, but their crimes confined;
Forbade to wade through slaughter to a throne,
      And shut the gates of mercy on mankind,

The struggling pangs of conscious truth to hide,
      To quench the blushes of ingenuous shame,
Or heap the shrine of Luxury and Pride
      With incense kindled at the Muse's flame.

Far from the madding crowd's ignoble strife
    Their sober wishes never learn'd to stray;
Along the cool sequester'd vale of life
    They kept the noiseless tenor of their way.

Yet ev'n these bones from insult to protect
    Some frail memorial still erected nigh,
With uncouth rhymes and shapeless sculpture deck'd,
    Implores the passing tribute of a sigh.

Their name, their years, spelt by th' unletter'd muse,
    The place of fame and elegy supply:
And many a holy text around she strews,
    That teach the rustic moralist to die.

For who, to dumb Forgetfulness a prey,
    This pleasing anxious being e'er resign'd,
Left the warm precincts of the cheerful day,
    Nor cast one longing ling'ring look behind?

On some fond breast the parting soul relies,
    Some pious drops the closing eye requires;
E'en from the tomb the voice of Nature cries,
    E'en in our ashes live their wonted fires.

For thee, who, mindful of th' unhonour'd dead,
    Dost in these lines their artless tale relate;
If chance, by lonely contemplation led,
    Some kindred spirit shall inquire thy fate,

Haply some hoary-headed Swain may say,
    "Oft have we seen him at the peep of dawn
Brushing with hasty steps the dews away
    To meet the sun upon the upland lawn.

"There at the foot of yonder nodding beech
    That wreathes its old fantastic roots so high,
His listless length at noontide would he stretch,
    And pore upon the brook that babbles by.

"Hard by yon wood, now smiling as in scorn,
　　Mutt'ring his wayward fancies he would rove,
Now drooping, woeful wan, like one forlorn,
　　Or crazed with care, or cross'd in hopeless love.

"One morn I miss'd him on the custom'd hill,
　　Along the heath and near his fav'rite tree;
Another came, nor yet beside the rill,
　　Nor up the lawn, nor at the wood was he;

"The next with dirges due in sad array
　　Slow through the church-way path we saw him borne.
Approach and read (for thou canst read) the lay
　　Graved on the stone beneath yon aged thorn."

The Epitaph

Here rests his head upon the lap of Earth
　　A Youth to Fortune and to Fame unknown.
Fair Science frown'd not on his humble birth,
　　And Melancholy mark'd him for her own.

Large was his bounty, and his soul sincere,
　　Heav'n did a recompense as largely send:
He gave to Mis'ry all he had, a tear,
　　He gain'd from Heav'n ('twas all he wish'd) a friend.

No farther seek his merits to disclose,
　　Or draw his frailties from their dread abode,
(There they alike in trembling hope repose,)
　　The bosom of his Father and his God.

2

Must My Job Be
the Primary Source of My Identity?

What question do college students most dread? Perhaps the one they get most often: "So, what are you going to *do* after you graduate?" Relatives have an irksome way of raising this question repeatedly. Adults of all ages are frequently subject to similar, abrupt interrogations about what they do to earn a living. Indeed, social observers have long noticed that in the United States people typically open a conversation with strangers by asking them what they *do*, a question that seems especially discomfiting to those who are unemployed or working at a job that they do not especially enjoy or respect.

These everyday queries are worth pondering, since they are not common everywhere. People in other countries find it offensive to be asked straight away what they do to earn a living, rather like the way we might feel if people began a conversation with us by asking how much money we make. And even in this country, some people invite others to identify themselves by asking different questions. What tribe are you from? Tell me about your family, about your place of birth, or about how you came to be where you are now. In other words, there are many other ways in which people here and elsewhere can and do begin to become acquainted with one another.

Why do questions about our actual or prospective jobs sometimes agitate us? If we are made uncomfortable by them, is this only because we are unsure about the answer or unhappy with the one we must give? We would probably not be embarrassed or irked by questions about where we plan to settle down eventually or about what kind of car we plan to buy, even if we were not clear about the answers. Many of us are, however, rankled by questions about our occupations because we really do believe that the answers to them reveal something vitally important about who we are. Some of us are uncomfortable about being so quickly self-revealing, whereas others of us are quite eager to respond because we are proud of what we do and proud as well of what we believe this indicates about our overall character and standing in the world. In this country, for better or for worse, our sense of who we are and our sense of what we do for a living or plan to do for a living are deeply bound up with one another.

If we think that human beings have always thought of their work as the most important thing about them, we would be mistaken, however. Such an exalted view of work is itself the result of complex social and economic processes that have been most pronounced in Western, capitalist countries over the last three or four hundred years. Professor Gilbert Meilaender, in an anthology that he edited on the subject of work, showed that many people throughout history have regarded paid employment as merely "necessary for leisure," not as a primary source of fulfillment and identity. Many others have regarded their work as, at best, "dignified but irksome." And for the majority of people around the globe, making a living has involved and still does involve work that is "ugly, crippling, and dangerous." These historical and social realities have often escaped Americans who have tended to elevate paid employment to a position of premier importance both for individuals and for the society as a whole.

The following readings should help us think about why paid employment has become, for millions of U.S. citizens, so vitally, even centrally, important to their sense of who they are:

- a selection from a book on work and liberal democracy (Muirhead)
- an essay arguing that we live in order to work (Sayers)
- two poems that celebrate the importance of work (Frost and Piercy).

Readings that follow immediately after these will address the question, "What are some other sources of identity?" They invite us to wonder whether our jobs really *should* be so central to our identities by proposing important alternative sources of human meaning and significance:

- a short story by H. G. Wells
- a discussion of Sabbath by Abraham Heschel
- two poems by William Wordsworth on nature
- an essay by Gilbert Meilaender on tensions between vocation and friendship.

The first two readings help us to see that having the right kind of job has been of great concern both to those who care about what makes for a healthy democracy and to those who care about what makes for faithful Christian living. From the earliest years of American history, political life was closely tied to economic life. The right to vote, for example, was for a long time restricted to adult, male property owners. This limitation of the franchise was based upon the seemingly unshakeable conviction that, in order to make wise political decisions, one had to be economically independent, not overly beholden to others for economic security. Holding property not only gave a man a stake in society; it also gave him a measure of freedom from the demands of others who might use their economic power over him to dictate his political preferences. Economic, social, and political identities were closely linked together in many ways, leading some historians to maintain that economic equality is a precondition for political equality.

The central importance of work in human life is as deeply embedded within Christian and Jewish stories of the beginnings of humankind as it is within secular accounts of the origins and social conditions of democracy. Dorothy Sayers argues that in and through our work we should be expressing our nature as beings who were created in the image of God. And Sayers is by no means the only religious thinker who suggests that "in the beginning" human beings were made to labor and that their labor gave dignity, meaning, and purpose to their lives. Sayers goes farther than most religious thinkers, however, when she insists that we live in order to work. For example, Abraham Heschel, the great Jewish writer whose work is also excerpted in this chapter, agrees that God intended that we should labor, but he insists that we were finally made for rest, not for work.

The poet Robert Frost agrees with Sayers in worrying over whether working primarily for pay does not demean the intrinsic meaning and pleasure that labor might give to a human life. For the speaker in Frost's poem, working in order to live and living in order to work are in tension with one another. The relationship between jobs within a capitalist economy with its "cash nexus" and the place of work within the order that God intended for humankind would seem to be in tension, not in harmony. By contrast, the other poet in the first group of readings, Marge Piercy, stresses the "usefulness" of work, a theme that was dear to the heart of such pillars of American democracy as Benjamin Franklin, whose very definition of a life that mattered was a life of labor that was useful to his fellow citizens and to his country.

The great difficulty with all of the views that celebrate work and working men and women, regardless of how different these views may be from one another, was perhaps best summed up in the opening sentence of a chapter from James Galvin's novel *The Meadow*. "In the Depression a lot of people lost their lives," Galvin wrote, "if your life is what you do." Galvin was right. Unemployment during the Depression brought not only poverty; it also brought despair and suicide. If we live in order to work, we may die if we have no work. If work is all that matters in life, then a life without work might not matter at all.

The second group of readings in this chapter not only suggest that there is more besides work that matters in life; they suggest as well that what should matter most in human life is not work but something else. To lead a life that matters is to attend to these other things — to rest, to the divine, to nature, and to the love of others. The most alluring yet perplexing reading in this group, the short story by H. G. Wells, dramatizes very forcefully a complicated sentiment that has been expressed countless times in fiction and film, the sense that what really matters in life lies somewhere other than those working places and pursuits that claim most of our energies. But is this dreamy, recurrent intuition that an elusive "something" actually matters a great deal to us, so much so that our work and our ordinary life should be understood as unfortunate distractions, a life-giving insight or a dangerous illusion? That really is the question behind "The Door in the Wall."

Abraham Heschel's work on Sabbath does double duty for our purposes. Of all the alternative candidates to work that have served as the primary source of meaning and identity in people's lives, religion is surely foremost. Since even a small sampling of the immense variety of religious experience and conviction would be impossible to offer here, one religious meditation on the subject of work itself and its proper place in our lives will have to suffice. Any serious religious thinker would seek to place our jobs within a larger, often transcendent, framework of meaning and significance. Heschel does this with great eloquence. He also locates work within a set of very specific Jewish rituals and practices that are designed to honor, to display, and to re-create basic spiritual truths about, for example, the relationship between labor and rest, between "our own work" and the work that God has done for us. Readers do not have to share Heschel's religious tradition in order to ponder with him the differences between labor and toil and the question of whether our leisure should be seen as a way of strengthening us for more work or our work should be seen, in a life that matters, as a way of sustaining us for and pointing us toward larger purposes.

Perhaps the greatest secular counterpart to religious truth as a primary source of meaning and significance in a human life is natural beauty. Many would say that poets like Wordsworth are high priests of the "religion of nature." In our contemporary world, this powerful alternative to work as the source of our identity has assumed many forms, ranging from some parts of the environmental movement to a resurgent interest in "nature films" to the burgeoning outdoor recreational industry. Though some of these activities are highly commercialized, most of them appeal to our sense that nature, properly understood and recalled, connects us to something deep and basic about who we are. In other words, like contemplation of the divine, contemplation of the natural world might be a surer path to the discovery and even to the constitution of our identities than our daily labors. "Getting and spending," as Wordsworth writes, "we lay waste our powers" of feeling and insight that would lead us to a recovery of who we truly are as human beings. Those powers are best restored to us, according to some of our wisest and most eloquent writers, in the recollection of natural beauty.

Gilbert Meilaender discusses another love, friendship, which, in addition to the love of God or the love of natural beauty, might serve as a powerful alternative to our jobs as the primary source of our identities. For Meilaender, as for many of those who have written on the subject before him, friendship includes not only our close acquaintances but also our lifelong partners, in short, all of those people whom we have chosen to love in a reciprocal way. And he sets up his discussion of friendship, its demands, its pleasures, and its rewards, as often being in some tension with the demands, pleasures, and rewards of our jobs or vocations. Thus, he suggests, we cannot really come fully to terms with the proper place of friendship in a life that matters without at the same time coming to terms with the proper place of our jobs, especially if we think of those jobs as vocations.

Paid employment, religious practice, love of the natural world, and friendship, all of them to some extent the sources of our identities, are not in life so neatly compartmentalized as they may seem at first in these readings. As we saw in Part I, we may think of our jobs religiously, as vocations. Or, we may choose to work as a forest ranger because of our love of the natural world. And we may find our jobs, the natural world, or our religious communities all the more formative and life-giving for us because we enjoy them in the company of friends. None of the writers in this section would deny the importance of all of these things in a life that matters; indeed, most of their writings cut across several of these different sources of meaning and identity.

This fluid character of our lives should discourage us from the kind of thinking and speaking that almost always follows closely upon the discovery that there are sometimes several worthy but competing, even conflicting, goods set before us. When faced with a range of goods that seem important to a life that matters, most people insist that we must rank them somehow. Thus, one says, "my family comes first; my job second." And another says, "You must establish priorities! Then you will be fine." Some religious counsel seems to follow a similar pattern. St. Augustine thought, for example, that leading a choice-worthy life depended upon the right ordering of our loves. Size up, prioritize, and solve. This would seem to be the American way of deciding how to lead a life that matters.

When Augustine advocated the right ordering of our loves, however, he did not mean that we should love God first, friends second, and jobs third. He meant instead that, in loving God first, we should come to love everything else "in God" who is the source and end of all the other goods in life. Some secular views of the all-encompassing importance of jobs have the same form. According to these accounts, our jobs not only define us more than anything else; they make everything else subservient to them. Families support us, friends are useful to us, and leisure time refreshes us so that we can do our jobs well. Whatever we may come to think about what matters most in a significant life, we should probably resist the temptation to think about it simply as something that we place at the top of a list of unrelated goods, ranked in order of importance. We should instead begin to study the complex connections among the various goods in our lives, including our jobs. The readings below, contrary to any initial impressions that they segregate jobs, religion, natural beauty, and friendship, invite us to consider the several relationships among them.

The blurring of the boundaries between the different goods in our lives and the discovery that it might not be possible simply to "prioritize" them may seem at first to spare us the need for difficult thinking and difficult choices. But on second thought, our dilemmas might only become more acute if we come to think that all of these goods are of a piece or are somehow equally important in a life that matters. For one thing, most of us have limited choices about how much of our time and energy we will devote to our jobs. And, as we have seen, we live in a culture that gives primary importance to our jobs as the sources of our identity. If we deny this cultural claim upon us and seek to live some other way, we will be doing so "against the grain." And this may prove difficult both practically and psychologically, robbing some of the goods that we seek of their potential to nourish us. For another thing, even if we were to sort out for ourselves the relative importance of our job, our religious practice, our recreation, and our friendships, and then be able to live in accordance with our preferences, we might still wonder whether our life really "matters" to anyone but ourselves. The nagging question of the relationship between meaning and significance may grow even more perplexing: *To whom* should a life that matters really matter?

The discovery that what we do for a living need not completely determine who we are does not take place in an economic and cultural vacuum. We simply cannot evade for very long the widespread sense that the question of what it means to lead a life that matters should at least *begin* with the question of our livelihoods. Coming to understand *why* this is so is not the same thing, however, as coming to a conviction that it should be. Increasing attentiveness to other sources of identity has led, especially among young adults, to two different projects. One project is the one undertaken in this present chapter, namely an effort to challenge the prevailing ideology of work even as we acknowledge its power and even to some extent its cogency. The other project, explored in the next chapter, is the quest for a "balanced life," for one that can in some sense make room for the sources of meaning and identity examined below and for some others as well.

RUSSELL MUIRHEAD

Just Work

In this early selection from his 2004 book, *Just Work*, entitled "Democracy and the Value of Work," the Harvard political theorist Russell Muirhead explores the question of why our work is so closely bound up with our identities in democratic societies. Muirhead is writing from within what we have described as the tradition of Democracy, and he is at the same time seeking to advance that tradition. He offers us here intimations of what makes for "just work" in a democracy in the form of several points that he later elaborates through careful argument during the course of his book.

Muirhead begins his discussion by reminding us of a theme that will run through many of the readings in this anthology: our freedom to forge an identity is constrained. Thus, though we can, within limits that differ from person to person, choose from a variety of roles the ones we wish to play in life, we ourselves did not create or select the roles themselves. Rather, the repertoire of roles set before us was created through long, historical processes that we simply inherited. We must remember this when we consider the proper place of work in our lives.

Muirhead also challenges us to recognize that the relationship between who we are and what we do to earn a living is more complicated than it may at first seem. On the one hand, our character determines to a great degree our choice of occupation. But on the other hand, what we do to earn a living will determine to a great extent our character. Can you think of concrete ways in which, say, practicing law makes a lawyer into a certain kind of human being? Can you think of ways in which some of the jobs you have done have begun to shape you into a certain kind of human being?

From Russell Muirhead, *Just Work* (Cambridge: Harvard University Press, 2004), pp. 26-29.

Politics in the largest sense is about the lives individuals can choose under particular conditions, and the lives they are impelled to live or even choose in a particular society and regime. These lives are composed of roles: parent, spouse, worker, to name a few. It matters that we choose these roles for ourselves. But the choices we make run only so deep, for the roles themselves exist independent of our choice. They come to us on a limited menu, one that is carried by social conventions and beliefs that in turn are sustained and buttressed by families, voluntary associations, traditions, and laws. From the perspective of consent, what matters most is that these roles are open to all, that no one is either forced into them or excluded from them. Thus we need to ensure that people have the freedom to choose among roles and to exit, when they wish, those they have assumed. But this does not exhaust the questions we ought to ask about such roles, even from a concern with justice. We ought to inquire, too, about the conditions of choice, the sorts of choices individuals are impelled to make under constraints, as well as the quality and variety of the options available for people to choose from.

This is especially so when it comes to work. As a descriptive matter and (if we reject a guaranteed minimum income as parasitic) as a normative matter, the working life is something that citizens necessarily share. The working life is *our* life. As we have seen, the necessity or obligatory character of work is in tension with the liberal ideal that citizens should be free (not only formally but effectively) to form and act from their own conception of the good. Yet work is one of the most common and inescapable constraints on our freedom. This raises a crucial question: can the regulative ideals that concern work be modeled entirely on the liberal values of freedom and equality? Or will they at times follow a different cue, one that more fully recognizes the reality that work itself is a kind of restraint, a sort of discipline?

Any full account of the justice of work would certainly need somehow to reconcile the work people do (and at some level *have* to do) with their freedom. It would take stock of how work might look if its form resulted solely from our choices. Yet since work as it appears in the world will reflect not only our freedom but also our need, since it does not and probably cannot reflect our choices precisely, it remains something to which we often need to attune or accommodate or even reconcile ourselves. The ideal of fitting work recognizes the constrained character of freedom. It acknowledges our freedom, since fitting work is work we might more likely endorse. At the same time, the concept of fit acknowledges that freedom in the world of work is always circumscribed. The category of fit thus allows for the possibility that even when work is good, it is something we have to make our peace with.

The ideal of fitting work also acknowledges the special kind of relationship that work involves. Along with family and religion, work remains one of the central activities constituting everyday life. Work is instrumental (we work to earn and spend), but is rarely only that: it is also formative. Devoting the bulk of our waking hours to a particular activity over many years has an effect on who we are, whether we like it or not. In a limited but crucial way, we are what we do ("What do you do?" is a kind of shorthand for "Who are you?"). In one sense, this reflects the way work positions us in a kind of hierarchy — both in the hierarchy of authority within organizations and in the larger social hierarchy represented by differences in income and wealth. If it is often inexplicit, it is no secret that some jobs are admired for their authority, command, glamour, compensation — in short, their prestige. And others are scorned. Our work makes manifest where we fall — or where we have climbed — in the social hierarchy. Yet we are also what we do in a more constitutive sense. What we do all day habituates and orients us in profound ways that over time impress a pattern on our emotional and intellectual life. Work might make us more compassionate or more stern, more decisive or more resentful, more deft or more argumentative. The way we spend the bulk of our waking energy can even come to inform our larger posture toward the world, depending on whether work prods us to experience the world as hostile or alien, compliant or beneficent. This is why for many work cannot be merely another of life's routines but is rather a key source of their identity.

The aspiration to work that fits us, as both individuals and as human beings, is one I locate in the public culture of American life, in the way many evaluate work. This aspiration, widely if not universally shared, in turn points to an ancient understanding of justice, where justice addresses what we as individuals morally deserve, and what we deserve depends on what fits us. Because it focuses on what we deserve, the justice of fit is distinct from Rawls's justice as fairness, which concerns what we would accept under impartial conditions. Yet if they are in tension with each other, they are not quite face-to-face rivals because they apply at different levels. Justice as fairness most directly addresses constitutional essentials, while the justice of fit concerns "middle level" regulative ideals that operate in civil society. Each might influence legislation, though in different ways. Justice as fairness, in its way, addresses legislation from above by offering a model of impartiality that legislators can follow when basic principles of justice are at stake. It is most relevant when legislation is directly and obviously coercive. Regulative ideals like justice as fit influence legislation from below, when legislators represent and advance the sort of ethical notions that their constituents endorse. It is most relevant when legislation addresses not constitutional essentials but the circumstances of everyday life.

The regulative ideal of fit reflects the aspirations people bring to the world of work, as it also elucidates the common opinion that work somehow supports human dignity. What would be required of us to fit our work? What would be required of work? What is the difference between a good fit and a bad one? Are there some useful jobs that cannot be said to fit anyone very well? And if so, how should these be allocated? This book will engage these questions and others in a way that will be at times uncomfortable, for I do not presuppose that the familiar terms of equal opportunity and free choice exhaust the categories with which we might evaluate the world of work. Yet uncomfortable categories are necessary if we are to understand the sources of pride and disappointment (and the sense of dignity and justice) that our way of life contains.

DOROTHY L. SAYERS

"Why Work?"

Dorothy L. Sayers (1893-1957) was a British author and churchwoman who published plays, translations of medieval literature, a delightful series of detective novels, and theological essays like the one included here. It is said that she loved her work so much that writing filled almost all her waking hours. It is possible that the creative character of her own work had a strong influence on her thinking about work in general.

More than most other essays in this anthology, this one makes a powerful case for our identities being wholly determined by our occupations. Sayers argues that we live in order to work, suggesting that those who work merely in order to live have, by choice or necessity, distorted the meaning and significance of work in their lives. On what basis does she make such an argument? Is she writing in the language of authenticity, suggesting that our work must be an authentic expression of our true

---

From Dorothy L. Sayers, "Why Work?" in *Creed or Chaos?* (London: Methuen & Co., 1947), pp. 47-64.

selves? Is she making the same kind of argument as Muirhead, suggesting that our work should fit our own personal preferences and skills and fit the needs of society as well? How does her argument, which she locates within the tradition of Christianity, compare to the other Christian readings in this book, such as those in the "vocation" section of Part I?

One of Sayers's other points also stands out as unusual: her argument that the first and perhaps the only obligation of Christians in their work is to "serve the work." She is probably right in thinking that Christian talk about work has overemphasized, often mindlessly, the idea of "service." So we should pay special attention to any effort to challenge conventional wisdom on this matter, while also wondering what form that service might take in the work we do as students or in the kinds of work that are emerging in the twenty-first-century economy.

I have already, on a previous occasion, spoken at some length on the subject of work and vocation. What I urged then was a thorough-going revolution in our whole attitude to work. I asked that it should be looked upon — not as a necessary drudgery to be undergone for the purpose of making money, but as a way of life in which the nature of man should find its proper exercise and delight and so fulfil itself to the glory of God. That it should, in fact, be thought of as a creative activity undertaken for the love of the work itself; and that man, made in God's image, should make things, as God makes them, for the sake of doing well a thing that is well worth doing. . . .

What is the Christian understanding of work? . . . I should like to put before you two or three propositions arising out of the doctrinal position which I stated at the beginning: namely, that work is the natural exercise and function of man — the creature who is made in the image of his Creator. You will find that any one of them, if given in effect everyday practice, is so revolutionary (as compared with the habits of thinking into which we have fallen), as to make all political revolutions look like conformity.

The first, stated quite briefly, is that work is not, primarily, a thing one does to live, but the thing one lives to do. It is, or it should be, the full expression of the worker's faculties, the thing in which he finds spiritual, mental, and bodily satisfaction, and the medium in which he offers himself to God.

Now the consequences of this are not merely that the work should be performed under decent living and working conditions. That is a point we have begun to grasp, and it is a perfectly sound point. But we have tended to concentrate on it to the exclusion of other considerations far more revolutionary.

(a) There is, for instance, the question of profits and remuneration. We have all got it fixed in our heads that the proper end of work is to be paid for — to produce a return in profits or payment to the worker which fully or more than compensates the effort he puts into it. But if our proposition is true, this does not follow at all. So long as society provides the worker with a sufficient return in real wealth to enable him to carry on the work properly, then he has his reward. For his work is the measure of his life, and his satisfaction is found in the fulfilment of his own nature, and in contemplation of the perfection of his work. That, in practice, there is this satisfaction, is shown by the mere fact that a man will put loving labour into some hobby which can never bring him in any economically adequate return. His satisfaction comes, in the god-like manner, from looking upon what he has made and finding it very good. He is no longer bargaining with his work, but serving it. It is only when work has to be looked on as a means to gain that it becomes hateful; for then, instead of a friend, it becomes an enemy from whom tolls and contributions have to be extracted. What most of us demand from society is that we should always get out of it a little more than the value of the labour we give to it. By this process, we persuade ourselves that society is always in our debt — a conviction that not only piles up actual financial burdens, but leaves us with a grudge against society.

(b) Here is the second consequence. At present we have no clear grasp of the principle that every man should do the work for which he is fitted by nature! The employer is obsessed by the notion that he must find cheap labour, and the worker by the notion that the best-paid job is the job for him. Only feebly, inadequately, and spasmodically do we ever attempt to tackle the problem from the other end, and inquire: What type of worker is suited to this type of work? People engaged in education see clearly that this is the right end to start from; but they are frustrated by economic pressure, and by the failure of parents on the one hand and employers on the other to grasp the fundamental importance of this approach. And that the trouble results far more from a failure of intelligence than from economic necessity is seen clearly under war conditions, when, though competitive economics are no longer a governing factor, the right men and women are still persistently thrust into the wrong jobs, through sheer inability on everybody's part to imagine a purely vocational approach to the business of fitting together the worker and his work.

(c) A third consequence is that, if we really believed this proposition and arranged our work and our standard of values accordingly, we should no longer think of work as something that we hastened to get through in order to enjoy our leisure; we should look on our leisure as the period of changed rhythm that refreshed us for the delightful purpose of getting on with our work. And, this being so, we should tolerate no regulations of any sort that prevented us from working as long and as well as our enjoyment of work demanded. We should resent any such restrictions as a monstrous interference with the liberty of the subject. How great an upheaval of our ideas that would mean I leave you to imagine. It would turn topsy-turvy all our notions about hours of work, rates of work, unfair competition, and all the rest of it. We should all find ourselves fighting, as now only artists and the members of certain professions fight, for precious time in which to get on with the job — instead of fighting for precious hours saved from the job.

(d) A fourth consequence is that we should fight tooth and nail, not for mere employment, but for the quality of the work that we had to do. We should clamour to be engaged on work that was worth doing, and in which we could take a pride. The worker would demand that the stuff he helped to turn out should be good stuff — he would no longer be content to take the cash and let the credit go. Like the shareholders in the brewery, he would feel a sense of personal responsibility, and clamour to know, and to control, what went into the beer he brewed. There would be protests and strikes — not only about pay and conditions, but about the quality of the work demanded and the honesty, beauty, and usefulness of the goods produced. The greatest insult which a commercial age has offered to the worker has been to rob him of all interest in the end-product of the work and to force him to dedicate his life to making badly things which were not worth making.

This first proposition chiefly concerns the worker as such. My second proposition directly concerns Christians as such, and it is this: It is the business of the Church to recognize that the secular vocation, as such, is sacred. Christian people, and particularly perhaps the Christian clergy, must get it firmly into their heads that when a man or woman is called to a particular job of secular work, that is as true a vocation as though he or she were called to specifically religious work. The Church must concern herself not only with such questions as the just price and proper working conditions: she must concern herself with seeing that the work itself is such as a human being can perform without degradation — that no one is required by economic or any other considerations to devote himself to work that is contemptible, soul-destroying, or harmful. It is not right for her to acquiesce in the notion that a man's life is divided into the time he spends on his work and the time he spends in serving God. He must be able to serve God in his work, and the work itself must be accepted and respected as the medium of divine creation. . . .

The Church's approach to an intelligent carpenter is usually confined to exhorting him not to be drunk and disorderly in his leisure hours, and to come to church on Sundays. What the Church should be telling him is this: that the very first demand that his religion makes upon him is that he should make good tables. . . .

Let the Church remember this: that every maker and worker is called to serve God in his profession or trade — not outside it. The Apostles complained rightly when they said it was not meet [meant] they should leave the word of God and serve tables; their vocation was to preach the word. But the person whose vocation it is to prepare the meals beautifully might with equal justice protest: It is not meet for us to leave the service of our tables to preach the word. The official Church wastes time and energy, and, moreover, commits sacrilege, in demanding that secular workers should neglect their proper vocation in order to do Christian work — by which she means ecclesiastical work. The only Christian work is good work well done. Let the Church see to it that the workers are Christian people and do their work well, as to God: then all the work will be Christian work, whether it is Church embroidery, or sewage-farming. . . .

This brings me to my third proposition; and this may sound to you the most revolutionary of all. It is this: the worker's first duty is to *serve the work*. The popular 'catch' phrase of to-day is that it is everybody's duty to serve the community. It is a well-sounding phrase, but there is a catch in it: It is the old catch about the two great commandments. 'Love God — and your neighbour; on those two commandments hang all the Law and the Prophets.' The catch in it, which nowadays the world has largely forgotten, is that the second commandment depends upon the first, and that without the first, it is a delusion and a snare. Much of our present trouble and disillusionment have come from putting the second commandment before the first. If we put our neighbour first, we are putting man above God, and that is what we have been doing ever since we began to worship humanity and make man the measure of all things. Whenever man is made the centre of things, he becomes the storm-centre of trouble — and that is precisely the catch about serving the community. It ought perhaps to make us suspicious of that phrase when we consider that it is the slogan of every commercial scoundrel and swindler who wants to make sharp business practice pass muster as social improvement. 'Service' is the motto of the advertiser, of big business, and of fraudulent finance. . . .

There is, in fact, a paradox about working to serve the community, and it is this: that to aim directly at serving the community is to falsify the work; the only way to serve the community is to forget the community and serve the work.

ROBERT FROST

"Two Tramps in Mud Time"

Robert Frost may be the most famous and beloved American poet of the twentieth century. He used simple and easily accessible diction, combined with beguiling rhythms and rhyme schemes, to achieve remarkably complex effects and affects. The poem below may be the most searching twentieth-century poem about work, vocation, and avocation. It contains many contrasts, some of them in tension with one another, others complementing one another. Work and play, physical effort for enjoyment and physical effort for pay, avocation and vocation — these are just some of the contrasting pairs that need to be understood in order to appreciate the poem.

Sometimes the treatment of the main subject of the poem can best be understood obliquely, by thinking about something that does not at first appear central to it. Notice that the title includes a temporal reference, "mud time." Notice as well that the central part of the poem is taken up with characterizing the time of the day and the time of the year in great and telling detail. These temporal descriptions, showing how a day in April can feel, from one minute to the next, like winter or like spring, prepare us for understanding how the "same" physical activity, chopping wood, can be two very different things, perhaps both of them alternately, even both of them at one and the same time.

The interactions that take place between the tramps and the speaker should show us and enable us to talk about two very different views of work and its proper place in a human life. The tramps are the title characters, and they work "for need," to earn a living. The speaker of the poem works "for love," for the sheer pleasure of physical exertion. The poem itself invites us to wonder which of the two views of work is the better one and whether they can ever be brought together and if so how. This very

From Robert Frost, "Two Tramps in Mud Time," in *A Further Range* (New York: Henry Holt, 1936), pp. 16-18.

complex drama between two views of work takes place within a cosmic framework. The poem begins with human origins expressed in a way that has a biblical resonance ("Out of the mud two strangers came") and concludes with references to heaven and the future. How important is this "frame" for understanding the way the whole poem works in its effort to educate our own imaginations about the proper place of work in our lives?

Out of the mud two strangers came
And caught me splitting wood in the yard.
And one of them put me off my aim
By hailing cheerily "Hit them hard!"
I knew pretty well why he dropped behind   5
And let the other go on a way.
I knew pretty well what he had in mind:
He wanted to take my job for pay.

Good blocks of oak it was I split,
As large around as the chopping block;   10
And every piece I squarely hit
Fell splinterless as a cloven rock.
The blows that a life of self-control
Spares to strike for the common good,
That day, giving a loose to my soul,   15
I spent on the unimportant wood.

The sun was warm but the wind was chill.
You know how it is with an April day
When the sun is out and the wind is still,
You're one month on in the middle of May.   20
But if you so much as dare to speak,
A cloud comes over the sunlit arch,
A wind comes off a frozen peak,
And you're two months back in the middle of March.

A bluebird comes tenderly up to alight   25
And fronts the wind to unruffle a plume,
His song so pitched as not to excite
A single flower as yet to bloom.

It is snowing a flake: and he half knew
Winter was only playing possum.   30
Except in color he isn't blue,
But he wouldn't advise a thing to blossom.

The water for which we may have to look
In summertime with a witching wand,
In every wheelrut's now a brook,   35
In every print of a hoof a pond.
Be glad of water, but don't forget
The lurking frost in the earth beneath
That will steal forth after the sun is set
And show on the water its crystal teeth.   40

The time when most I loved my task
These two must make me love it more
By coming with what they came to ask.
You'd think I never had felt before
The weight of an ax-head poised aloft,   45
The grip on earth of outspread feet,
The life of muscles rocking soft
And smooth and moist in vernal heat.

Out of the woods two hulking tramps
(From sleeping God knows where last night,   50
But not long since in the lumber camps).
They thought all chopping was theirs of right.
Men of the woods and lumberjacks,
They judged me by their appropriate tool.
Except as a fellow handled an ax   55
They had no way of knowing a fool.

Nothing on either side was said.
They knew they had but to stay their stay
And all their logic would fill my head:
As that I had no right to play   60
With what was another man's work for gain.
My right might be love but theirs was need.
And where the two exist in twain
Theirs was the better right — agreed.

But yield who will to their separation,   65
My object in living is to unite
My avocation and my vocation
As my two eyes make one in sight.
Only where love and need are one,
And the work is play for mortal stakes,   70
Is the deed ever really done
For Heaven and the future's sakes.

MARGARET PIERCY

"To be of use"

This poem by Marge Piercy, first published in 1973, is widely read and frequently anthologized. Perhaps it resonates because so many people feel that their work is not "of use," or because so many long for work that is "real," as the poem concludes. The title of this poem suggests that the meaning and significance of our work might best be understood in terms of its usefulness. However, the idea of usefulness begs a series of questions. Useful to whom? Useful for what? Consider how the poem answers these questions, how Piercy understands usefulness and why she commends it to us.

The poem begins by portraying "the people I love" and their way of approaching work, and the poem's images seem at some points to suggest that how people work is as important as what they do. Do the images invite us to think of the people whom the speaker "loves best" as those whose work and identity merge or as those whose work and identity remain distinct?

Would it be fair to say that the workers Piercy admires are, as Sayers might say, "serving the work"? Do they "live to work"?

From Margaret Piercy, *The Art of Blessing the Day: Poems with a Jewish Theme* (New York: Alfred A. Knopf, 1999), pp. 73-74.

In addition to writing poetry, Piercy, who was born in 1936, has written several novels and books of essays.

The people I love the best
jump into work head first
without dallying in the shallows
and swim off with sure strokes almost out of sight.
They seem to become natives of that element,
the black sleek heads of seals
bouncing like half-submerged balls.

I love people who harness themselves, an ox to a heavy cart,
who pull like water buffalo, with massive patience,
who strain in the mud and the muck to move things forward,
who do what has to be done, again and again.

I want to be with people who submerge
in the task, who go into the fields to harvest
and work in a row and pass the bags along,
who are not parlor generals and field deserters
but move in a common rhythm
when the food must come in or the fire be put out.

The work of the world is common as mud.
Botched, it smears the hands, crumbles to dust.
But the thing worth doing well done
has a shape that satisfies, clean and evident.
Greek amphoras for wine or oil,
Hopi vases that held corn, are put in museums
but you know they were made to be used.
The pitcher cries for water to carry
and a person for work that is real.

———

H. G. WELLS

"The Door in the Wall"

Human beings have discovered the sources of their common humanity and their particular identities in many places other than their work. Part of leading a life that matters involves attaining clarity about what finally matters to us, not simply about what we value and cherish but also about what we regard as the sources of ourselves. In the three readings that follow Wells's story, we offer a small sampling of three of the main places human beings have looked over time to find themselves: religion, nature, and love of others.

Before turning to these particular "sources of the self," we should remark upon a powerful feeling or conviction that is common to many human beings at some times and to some human beings all of the time. In its negative form, this is called world weariness or *Weltschmertz*; in its positive form, it consists of the overwhelming sentiment that one's deepest self, the source of everything that is most beautiful, most true, most genuine, and most joyful, is to be found in a "world elsewhere," in some place or time far distant from the demands of work and the routines of daily life. Whether such sentiments provide momentary glimpses into an ideal world that really does enfold our quotidian lives or whether they provide comforting illusions at best and crippling escapes from responsibility at worst has been a persistent matter of debate in a good deal of world literature. "The Door in the Wall" powerfully dramatizes this sentiment in the life of one man. Whether what lies behind the door is life-giving or death-dealing in the judgment of the narrator and the principal character must be left to the reader to decide.

Consider these four people: the author, H. G. Wells; the narrator of the story who claims to be recounting what someone else told him; Lionel Wallace, the subject of the story as he told it to the narrator; and you, the

---

From *The Complete Short Stories of H. G. Wells* (New York: St Martin's Press, 1971), pp. 144-161.

reader. What do each of these four people make of the meaning and significance of the green door? How do their opinions differ and why?

<hr>

1

One confidential evening, not three months ago, Lionel Wallace told me this story of the Door in the Wall. And at the time I thought that so far as he was concerned it was a true story.

He told it to me with such a direct simplicity of conviction that I could not do otherwise than believe in him. But in the morning, in my own flat, I woke to a different atmosphere, and as I lay in bed and recalled the things he had told me, stripped of the glamour of his earnest slow voice, denuded of the focused shaded table light, the shadowy atmosphere that wrapped about him and the pleasant bright things, the dessert and glasses and napery of the dinner we had shared, making them for the time a bright little world quite cut off from every-day realities, I saw it all as frankly incredible. "He was mystifying!" I said, and then: "How well he did it! . . . It isn't quite the thing I should have expected him, of all people, to do well."

Afterwards, as I sat up in bed and sipped my morning tea, I found myself trying to account for the flavour of reality that perplexed me in his impossible reminiscences, by supposing they did in some way suggest, present, convey — I hardly know which word to use — experiences it was otherwise impossible to tell.

Well, I don't resort to that explanation now. I have got over my intervening doubts. I believe now, as I believed at the moment of telling, that Wallace did to the very best of his ability strip the truth of his secret for me. But whether he himself saw, or only thought he saw, whether he himself was the possessor of an inestimable privilege, or the victim of a fantastic dream, I cannot pretend to guess. Even the facts of his death, which ended my doubts forever, throw no light on that.

That much the reader must judge for himself.

I forget now what chance comment or criticism of mine moved so reticent a man to confide in me. He was, I think, defending himself against an imputation of slackness and unreliability I had made in relation to a great public movement in which he had disappointed me. But he plunged suddenly. "I have," he said, "a preoccupation —"

"I know," he went on, after a pause that he devoted to the study of his cigar ash, "I have been negligent. The fact is — it isn't a case of ghosts or apparitions — but — it's an odd thing to tell of, Redmond — I am haunted. I am haunted by something — that rather takes the light out of things, that fills me with longings. . . ."

He paused, checked by that English shyness that so often overcomes us when we would speak of moving or grave or beautiful things. "You were at Saint Athelstan's all through," he said, and for a moment that seemed to me quite irrelevant. "Well" — and he paused. Then very haltingly at first, but afterwards more easily, he began to tell of the thing that was hidden in his life, the haunting memory of a beauty and a happiness that filled his heart with insatiable longings that made all the interests and spectacle of worldly life seem dull and tedious and vain to him.

Now that I have the clue to it, the thing seems written visibly in his face. I have a photograph in which that look of detachment has been caught and intensified. It reminds me of what a woman once said of him — a woman who had loved him greatly. "Suddenly," she said, "the interest goes out of him. He forgets you. He doesn't care a rap for you — under his very nose. . . ."

Yet the interest was not always out of him, and when he was holding his attention to a thing Wallace could contrive to be an extremely successful man. His career, indeed, is set with successes. He left me behind him long ago; he soared up over my head, and cut a figure in the world that I couldn't cut — anyhow. He was still a year short of forty, and they say now that he would have been in office and very probably in the new Cabinet if he had lived. At school he always beat me without effort — as it were by nature. We were at school together at Saint Athelstan's College in West Kensington for almost all our school time. He came into the school as my co-equal, but he left far above me, in a blaze of scholarships and brilliant performance. Yet I think I made a fair average running. And it was at school I heard first of the Door in the Wall — that I was to hear of a second time only a month before his death.

To him at least the Door in the Wall was a real door leading through a real wall to immortal realities. Of that I am now quite assured.

And it came into his life early, when he was a little fellow between five and six. I remember how, as he sat making his confession to me with a slow gravity, he reasoned and reckoned the date of it. "There was," he said, "a crimson Virginia creeper in it — all one bright uniform crimson in a clear amber sunshine against a white wall. That came into the impression somehow, though I don't clearly remember how, and there were horse-chestnut leaves upon the clean pavement outside the green door. They were blotched yellow and green, you know, not brown nor dirty, so that they must have been new fallen. I take it that means October. I look out for horse-chestnut leaves every year, and I ought to know.

"If I'm right in that, I was about five years and four months old."

He was, he said, rather a precocious little boy — he learned to talk at an abnormally early age, and he was so sane and "old-fashioned," as people say, that he was permitted an amount of initiative that most children scarcely attain by seven or eight. His mother died when he was born, and he was under the less vigilant and authoritative care of a nursery governess. His father was a stern, preoccupied lawyer, who gave him little attention, and expected great things of him. For all his brightness he found life a little grey and dull, I think. And one day he wandered.

He could not recall the particular neglect that enabled him to get away, nor the course he took among the West Kensington roads. All that had faded among the incurable blurs of memory. But the white wall and the green door stood out quite distinctly.

As his memory of that remote childish experience ran, he did at the very first sight of that door experience a peculiar emotion, an attraction, a desire to get to the door and open it and walk in. And at the same time he had the clearest conviction that either it was unwise or it was wrong of him — he could not tell which — to yield to this attraction. He insisted upon it as a curious thing that he knew from the very beginning — unless memory has played him the queerest trick — that the door was unfastened, and that he could go in as he chose.

I seem to see the figure of that little boy, drawn and repelled. And it was very clear in his mind, too, though why it should be so was never explained, that his father would be very angry if he went through that door.

Wallace described all these moments of hesitation to me with the utmost particularity. He went right past the door, and then, with his hands in his pockets, and making an infantile attempt to whistle, strolled right along beyond the end of the wall. There he recalls a number of mean, dirty shops, and particularly that of a plumber and decorator, with a dusty disorder of earthenware pipes, sheet lead ball taps, pattern books of wall paper, and tins of enamel. He stood pretending to examine these things, and coveting, passionately desiring the green door.

Then, he said, he had a gust of emotion. He made a run for it, lest hesitation should grip him again; he went plump with outstretched hand through the green door and let it slam behind him. And so, in a trice, he came into the garden that has haunted all his life.

It was very difficult for Wallace to give me his full sense of that garden into which he came.

There was something in the very air of it that exhilarated, that gave one a sense of lightness and good happening and well being; there was something in the sight of it that made all its colour clean and perfect and subtly luminous. In the instant of coming into it one was exquisitely glad — as only in rare moments and when one is young and joyful one can be glad in this world. And everything was beautiful there. . . .

Wallace mused before he went on telling me. "You see," he said, with the doubtful inflection of a man who pauses at incredible things, "there were two great panthers there. . . . Yes, spotted panthers. And I was not afraid. There was a long wide path with marble-edged flower borders on either side, and these two huge velvety beasts were playing there with a ball. One looked up and came towards me, a little curious as it seemed. It came right up to me, rubbed its soft round ear very gently against the small hand I held out and purred. It was, I tell you, an enchanted garden. I know. And the size? Oh! it stretched far and wide, this way and that. I believe there were hills far away. Heaven knows where West Kensington had suddenly got to. And somehow it was just like coming home.

"You know, in the very moment the door swung to behind me, I forgot the road with its fallen chestnut leaves, its cabs and tradesmen's carts, I forgot the sort of gravitational pull back to the discipline and obedience of home, I forgot all hesitations and fear, forgot discretion, forgot all the intimate realities of this life. I became in a moment a very glad and wonder-happy little boy — in another world. It was a world with a different quality, a warmer, more penetrating and mellower light, with a faint clear gladness in its air, and wisps of sun-touched cloud in the blueness of its sky. And before me ran this long wide path, invitingly, with weedless beds on either side, rich with untended flowers, and these two great panthers. I put my little hands fearlessly on their soft fur, and caressed their round ears and the sensitive corners under their ears, and played with them, and it was as though they welcomed me home. There was a keen sense of home-coming in my mind, and when presently a tall, fair girl appeared in the pathway and came to meet me, smiling, and said 'Well?' to me, and lifted me, and kissed me, and put me down, and led me by the hand, there was no amazement, but only an impression of delightful rightness, of being reminded of happy things that had in some strange way been overlooked. There were broad steps, I remember, that came into view between spikes of delphinium, and up these we went to a great avenue between very old and shady dark trees. All down this avenue, you know, between the red chapped stems, were marble seats of honour and statuary, and very tame and friendly white doves. . . .

"And along this avenue my girl-friend led me, looking down — I recall the pleasant lines, the finely-modelled chin of her sweet kind face — asking me questions in a soft, agreeable voice, and telling me things, pleasant things I know, though what they were I was never able to recall. . . . And presently a little Capuchin monkey, very clean, with a fur of ruddy brown and kindly hazel eyes, came down a tree to us and ran beside me, looking up at me and grinning, and presently leapt to my shoulder. So we went on our way in great happiness. . . ."

He paused.

"Go on," I said.

"I remember little things. We passed an old man musing among laurels, I remember, and a place gay with parakeets, and came through a broad shaded colonnade to a spacious cool palace, full of pleasant fountains, full of beautiful things, full of the quality and promise of heart's desire. And there were many things and many people, some that still seem to stand out clearly and some that are a little vague, but all these people were beautiful and kind. In some way — I don't know how — it was conveyed to me that they all were kind to me, glad to have me there, and filling me with gladness by their gestures, by the touch of their hands, by the welcome and love in their eyes. Yes — "

He mused for awhile. "Playmates I found there. That was very much to me, because I was a lonely little boy. They played delightful games in a grass-covered court where there was a sun-dial set about with flowers. And as one played one loved. . . .

"But — it's odd — there's a gap in my memory. I don't remember the games we played. I never remembered. Afterwards, as a child, I spent long hours trying, even with tears, to recall the form of that happiness. I wanted to play it all over again — in my nursery — by myself. No! All I remember is the happiness and two dear playfellows who were most with me. . . . Then presently came a sombre dark woman, with a grave, pale face and dreamy eyes, a sombre woman wearing a soft long robe of pale purple, who carried a book and beckoned and took me aside with her into a gallery above a hall — though my playmates were loth to have me go, and ceased their game and stood watching as I was carried away. 'Come back to us!' they cried. 'Come back to us soon!' I looked up at her face, but she heeded them not at all. Her face was very gentle and grave. She took me to a seat in the gallery, and I stood beside her, ready to look at her book as she opened it upon her knee. The pages fell open. She pointed, and I looked, marvelling, for in the living pages of that book I saw myself; it was a story about myself, and in it were all the things that had happened to me since ever I was born. . . .

"It was wonderful to me, because the pages of that book were not pictures, you understand, but realities."

Wallace paused gravely — looked at me doubtfully.

"Go on," I said. "I understand."

"They were realities — yes, they must have been; people moved and things came and went in them; my dear mother, whom I had near forgotten; then my father, stern and upright, the servants, the nursery, all the familiar things of home. Then the front door and the busy streets, with traffic to and fro: I looked and marvelled, and looked half doubtfully again into the woman's face and turned the pages over, skipping this and that, to see more of this book, and more, and so at last I came to myself hovering and hesitating outside the green door in the long white wall, and felt again the conflict and the fear.

"'And next?' I cried, and would have turned on, but the cool hand of the grave woman delayed me.

"'Next?' I insisted, and struggled gently with her hand, pulling up her fingers with all my childish strength, and as she yielded and the page came over she bent down upon me like a shadow and kissed my brow.

"But the page did not show the enchanted garden, nor the panthers, nor the girl who had led me by the hand, nor the playfellows who had been so loth to let me go. It showed a long grey street in West Kensington, on that chill hour of afternoon before the lamps are lit, and I was there, a wretched little figure, weeping aloud, for all that I could do to restrain myself, and I was weeping because I could not return to my dear playfellows who had called after me, 'Come back to us! Come back to us soon!' I was there. This was no page in a book, but harsh reality; that enchanted place and the restraining hand of the grave mother at whose knee I stood had gone — whither have they gone?"

He halted again, and remained for a time, staring into the fire.

"Oh! the wretchedness of that return!" he murmured.

"Well?" I said after a minute or so.

"Poor little wretch I was — brought back to this grey world again! As I realised the fullness of what had happened to me, I gave way to quite ungovernable grief. And the shame and humiliation of that public weeping and my disgraceful homecoming remain with me still. I see again the benevolent-looking old gentleman in gold spectacles who stopped and spoke to me — prodding me first with his umbrella. 'Poor little chap,' said he; 'and are you lost then?' — and me a London boy of five and more! And he must needs bring in a kindly young policeman and make a crowd of me, and so march me home. Sobbing, conspicuous and frightened, I came from the enchanted garden to the steps of my father's house.

"That is as well as I can remember my vision of that garden — the garden that haunts me still. Of course, I can convey nothing of that indescribable quality of translucent unreality, that difference from the common things of experience that hung about it all; but that — that is what happened. If it was a dream, I am sure it was a day-time and altogether extraordinary dream. . . . H'm! — naturally there followed a terrible questioning, by my aunt, my father, the nurse, the governess — everyone. . . .

"I tried to tell them, and my father gave me my first thrashing for telling lies. When afterwards I tried to tell my aunt, she punished me again for my wicked persistence. Then, as I said, everyone was forbidden to listen to me, to hear a word about it. Even my fairy tale books were taken away from me for a time — because I was 'too imaginative.' Eh? Yes, they did that! My father belonged to the old school. . . . And my story was driven back upon myself. I whispered it to my pillow — my pillow that was often damp and salt to my whispering lips with childish tears. And I added always to my official and less fervent prayers this one heartfelt request: 'Please God I may dream of the garden. Oh! take me back to my garden! Take me back to my garden!'

"I dreamt often of the garden. I may have added to it, I may have changed it; I do not know. . . . All this you understand is an attempt to reconstruct from fragmentary memories a very early experience. Between that and the other consecutive memories of my boyhood there is a gulf. A time came when it seemed impossible I should ever speak of that wonder glimpse again."

I asked an obvious question.

"No," he said. "I don't remember that I ever attempted to find my way back to the garden in those early years. This seems odd to me now, but I think that very probably a closer watch was kept on my movements after this misadventure to prevent my going astray. No, it wasn't until you knew me that I tried for the garden again. And I believe there was a period — incredible as it seems now — when I forgot the garden altogether — when I was about eight or nine it may have been. Do you remember me as a kid at Saint Athelstan's?"

"Rather!"

"I didn't show any signs, did I, in those days of having a secret dream?"

2

He looked up with a sudden smile.

"Did you ever play North-West Passage with me? . . . No, of course you didn't come my way!"

"It was the sort of game," he went on, "that every imaginative child plays all day. The idea was the discovery of a North-West Passage to school. The way to school was plain enough; the game consisted in finding some way that wasn't plain, starting off ten minutes early in some almost hopeless direction, and working one's way round through unaccustomed streets to my goal. And one day I got entangled among some rather low-class streets on the other side of Campden Hill, and I began to think that for once the game would be against me and that I should get to school late. I tried rather desperately a street that seemed a cul-de-sac, and found a passage at the end. I hurried through that with renewed hope. 'I shall do it yet,' I said, and passed a row of frowsy little shops that were inexplicably familiar to me, and behold! there was my long white wall and the green door that led to the enchanted garden!

"The thing whacked upon me suddenly. Then, after all, that garden, that wonderful garden, wasn't a dream!"

He paused.

"I suppose my second experience with the green door marks the world of difference there is between the busy life of a schoolboy and the infinite leisure of a child. Anyhow, this second time I didn't for a moment think of going in straight away. You see.... For one thing my mind was full of the idea of getting to school in time — set on not breaking my record for punctuality. I must surely have felt *some* little desire at least to try the door — yes, I must have felt that.... But I seem to remember the attraction of the door mainly as another obstacle to my overmastering determination to get to school. I was immediately interested by this discovery I had made, of course — I went on with my mind full of it — but I went on. It didn't check me. I ran past tugging out my watch, found I had ten minutes still to spare, and then I was going downhill into familiar surroundings. I got to school, breathless, it is true, and wet with perspiration, but in time. I can remember hanging up my coat and hat.... Went right by it and left it behind me. Odd, eh?"

He looked at me thoughtfully. "Of course, I didn't know then that it wouldn't always be there. Schoolboys have limited imaginations. I suppose I thought it was an awfully jolly thing to have it there, to know my way back to it, but there was the school tugging at me. I expect I was a good deal distraught and inattentive that morning, recalling what I could of the beautiful strange people I should presently see again. Oddly enough I had no doubt in my mind that they would be glad to see me.... Yes, I must have thought of the garden that morning just as a jolly sort of place to which one might resort in the interludes of a strenuous scholastic career.

"I didn't go that day at all. The next day was a half-holiday, and that may have weighed with me. Perhaps, too, my state of inattention brought down impositions upon me and docked the margin of time necessary for the detour. I don't know. What I do know is that in the meantime the enchanted garden was so much upon my mind that I could not keep it to myself.

"I told — What was his name? — a ferrety-looking youngster we used to call Squiff."

"Young Hopkins," said I.

"Hopkins it was. I did not like telling him. I had a feeling that in some way it was against the rules to tell him, but I did. He was walking part of the way home with me; he was talkative, and if we had not talked about the enchanted garden we should have talked of something else, and it was intolerable to me to think about any other subject. So I blabbed.

"Well, he told my secret. The next day in the play interval I found myself surrounded by half a dozen bigger boys, half teasing and wholly curious to hear more of the enchanted garden. There was that big Fawcett — you remember him? — and Carnaby and Morley Reynolds. You weren't there by any chance? No, I think I should have remembered if you were. . . .

"A boy is a creature of odd feelings. I was, I really believe, in spite of my secret self-disgust, a little flattered to have the attention of these big fellows. I remember particularly a moment of pleasure caused by the praise of Crawshaw — you remember Crawshaw major, the son of Crawshaw the composer? — who said it was the best lie he had ever heard. But at the same time there was a really painful undertow of shame at telling what I felt was indeed a sacred secret. That beast Fawcett made a joke about the girl in green —"

Wallace's voice sank with the keen memory of that shame. "I pretended not to hear," he said. "Well, then Carnaby suddenly called me a young liar and disputed with me when I said the thing was true. I said I knew where to find the green door, could lead them all there in ten minutes. Carnaby became outrageously virtuous, and said I'd have to — and bear out my words or suffer. Did you ever have Carnaby twist your arm? Then perhaps you'll understand how it went with me. I swore my story was true. There was nobody in the school then to save a chap from Carnaby, though Crawshaw put in a word or so. Carnaby had got his game. I grew excited and red-eared, and a little frightened, I behaved altogether like a silly little chap, and the outcome of it all was that instead of starting alone for my enchanted garden, I led the way presently — cheeks flushed, ears hot, eyes smarting, and my soul one burning misery and shame — for a party of six mocking, curious and threatening school-fellows.

"We never found the white wall and the green door. . . ."

"You mean? —"

"I mean I couldn't find it. I would have found it if I could.

"And afterwards when I could go alone I couldn't find it. I never found it. I seem now to have been always looking for it through my school-boy days, but I've never come upon it again."

"Did the fellows — make it disagreeable?"

"Beastly. . . . Carnaby held a council over me for wanton lying. I remember how I sneaked home and upstairs to hide the marks of my blubbering. But when I cried myself to sleep at last it wasn't for Carnaby, but for the garden, for the beautiful afternoon I had hoped for, for the sweet friendly women and the waiting playfellows and the game I had hoped to learn again, that beautiful forgotten game. . . .

"I believed firmly that if I had not told — . . . I had bad times after that — crying at night and wool-gathering by day. For two terms I slackened and had bad reports. Do you remember? Of course you would! It was *you* — your beating me in mathematics that brought me back to the grind again."

3

For a time my friend stared silently into the red heart of the fire. Then he said: "I never saw it again until I was seventeen.

"It leapt upon me for the third time — as I was driving to Paddington on my way to Oxford and a scholarship. I had just one momentary glimpse. I was leaning over the apron of my hansom smoking a cigarette, and no doubt thinking myself no end of a man of the world, and suddenly there was the door, the wall, the dear sense of unforgettable and still attainable things.

"We clattered by — I too taken by surprise to stop my cab until we were well past and round a corner. Then I had a queer moment, a double and divergent movement of my will: I tapped the little door in the roof of the cab, and brought my arm down to pull out my watch. 'Yes, sir!' said the cabman, smartly. 'Er — well — it's nothing,' I cried. 'My mistake! We haven't much time! Go on!' and he went on. . . .

"I got my scholarship. And the night after I was told of that I sat over my fire in my little upper room, my study, in my father's house, with his praise — his rare praise — and his sound counsels ringing in my ears, and I smoked my favourite pipe — the formidable bulldog of adolescence — and thought of that door in the long white wall. 'If I had stopped,' I thought, 'I should have missed my scholarship, I should have missed Oxford — muddled all the fine career before me! I begin to see things better!' I fell musing deeply, but I did not doubt then this career of mine was a thing that merited sacrifice.

"Those dear friends and that clear atmosphere seemed very sweet to me, very fine, but remote. My grip was fixing now upon the world. I saw another door opening — the door of my career."

He stared again into the fire. Its red lights picked out a stubborn strength in his face for just one flickering moment, and then it vanished again.

"Well," he said and sighed, "I have served that career. I have done — much work, much hard work. But I have dreamt of the enchanted garden a thousand dreams, and seen its door, or at least glimpsed its door, four times since then. Yes — four times. For a while this world was so bright and interesting, seemed so full of meaning and opportunity that the half-effaced charm of the garden was by comparison gentle and remote. Who wants to pat panthers on the way to dinner with pretty women and distinguished men? I came down to London from Oxford, a man of bold promise that I have done something to redeem. Something — and yet there have been disappointments. . . .

"Twice I have been in love — I will not dwell on that — but once, as I went to someone who, I know, doubted whether I dared to come, I took a short cut at a venture through an unfrequented road near Earl's Court, and so happened on a white wall and a familiar green door. 'Odd!' said I to myself, 'but I thought this place was on Campden Hill. It's the place I never could find somehow — like counting Stonehenge — the place of that queer day dream of mine.' And I went by it intent upon my purpose. It had no appeal to me that afternoon.

"I had just a moment's impulse to try the door, three steps aside were needed at the most — though I was sure enough in my heart that it would open to me — and then I thought that doing so might delay me on the way to that appointment in which I thought my honour was involved. Afterwards I was sorry for my punctuality — I might at least have peeped in I thought, and waved a hand to those panthers, but I knew enough by this time not to seek again belatedly that which is not found by seeking. Yes, that time made me very sorry. . . .

"Years of hard work after that and never a sight of the door. It's only recently it has come back to me. With it there has come a sense as though some thin tarnish had spread itself over my world. I began to think of it as a sorrowful and bitter thing that I should never see that door again. Perhaps I was suffering a little from overwork — perhaps it was what I've heard spoken of as the feeling of forty. I don't know. But certainly the keen brightness that makes effort easy has gone out of things recently, and that just at a time with all these new political developments — when I ought to be working. Odd, isn't it? But I do begin to find life toilsome, its rewards, as I come near

them, cheap. I began a little while ago to want the garden quite badly. Yes —
and I've seen it three times."

"The garden?"

"No — the door! And I haven't gone in!"

He leaned over the table to me, with an enormous sorrow in his voice as
he spoke. "Thrice I have had my chance — *thrice!* If ever that door offers itself
to me again, I swore, I will go in out of this dust and heat, out of this dry glit-
ter of vanity, out of these toilsome futilities. I will go and never return. This
time I will stay. . . . I swore it and when the time came — *I didn't go.*

"Three times in one year have I passed that door and failed to enter.
Three times in the last year.

"The first time was on the night of the snatch division on the Tenants'
Redemption Bill, on which the Government was saved by a majority of
three. You remember? No one on our side — perhaps very few on the opposite side — expected the end that night. Then the debate collapsed like egg-
shells. I and Hotchkiss were dining with his cousin at Brentford, we were
both unpaired, and we were called up by telephone, and set off at once in his
cousin's motor. We got in barely in time, and on the way we passed my wall
and door — livid in the moonlight, blotched with hot yellow as the glare of
our lamps lit it, but unmistakable. 'My God!' cried I. 'What?' said Hotchkiss.
'Nothing!' I answered, and the moment passed.

"'I've made a great sacrifice,' I told the whip as I got in. 'They all have,' he
said, and hurried by.

"I do not see how I could have done otherwise then. And the next occasion was as I rushed to my father's bedside to bid that stern old man farewell. Then, too, the claims of life were imperative. But the third time was different; it happened a week ago. It fills me with hot remorse to recall it. I was
with Gurker and Ralphs — it's no secret now you know that I've had my talk
with Gurker. We had been dining at Frobisher's, and the talk had become intimate between us. The question of my place in the reconstructed ministry
lay always just over the boundary of the discussion. Yes — yes. That's all settled. It needn't be talked about yet, but there's no reason to keep a secret
from you. . . . Yes — thanks! thanks! But let me tell you my story.

"Then, on that night things were very much in the air. My position was a
very delicate one. I was keenly anxious to get some definite word from
Gurker, but was hampered by Ralphs' presence. I was using the best power
of my brain to keep that light and careless talk not too obviously directed to
the point that concerns me. I had to. Ralphs' behaviour since has more than
justified my caution. . . . Ralphs, I knew, would leave us beyond the
Kensington High Street, and then I could surprise Gurker by a sudden frank-

ness. One has sometimes to resort to these little devices. . . . And then it was that in the margin of my field of vision I became aware once more of the white wall, the green door before us down the road.

"We passed it talking. I passed it. I can still see the shadow of Gurker's marked profile, his opera hat tilted forward over his prominent nose, the many folds of his neck wrap going before my shadow and Ralphs' as we sauntered past.

"I passed within twenty inches of the door. 'If I say good-night to them, and go in,' I asked myself, 'what will happen?' And I was all a-tingle for that word with Gurker.

"I could not answer that question in the tangle of my other problems. 'They will think me mad,' I thought. 'And suppose I vanish now! — Amazing disappearance of a prominent politician!' That weighed with me. A thousand inconceivably petty worldlinesses weighed with me in that crisis."

Then he turned on me with a sorrowful smile, and, speaking slowly; "Here I am!" he said.

"Here I am!" he repeated, "and my chance has gone from me. Three times in one year the door has been offered me — the door that goes into peace, into delight, into a beauty beyond dreaming, a kindness no man on earth can know. And I have rejected it, Redmond, and it has gone — "

"How do you know?"

"I know. I know. I am left now to work it out, to stick to the tasks that held me so strongly when my moments came. You say, I have success — this vulgar, tawdry, irksome, envied thing. I have it." He had a walnut in his big hand. "If that was my success," he said, and crushed it, and held it out for me to see.

"Let me tell you something, Redmond. This loss is destroying me. For two months, for ten weeks nearly now, I have done no work at all, except the most necessary and urgent duties. My soul is full of inappeasable regrets. At nights — when it is less likely I shall be recognised — I go out. I wander. Yes. I wonder what people would think of that if they knew. A Cabinet Minister, the responsible head of that most vital of all departments, wandering alone — grieving — sometimes near audibly lamenting — for a door, for a garden!"

4

I can see now his rather pallid face, and the unfamiliar sombre fire that had come into his eyes. I see him very vividly to-night. I sit recalling his words, his tones, and last evening's Westminster Gazette still lies on my sofa, containing the notice of his death. At lunch to-day the club was busy with him and the strange riddle of his fate.

They found his body very early yesterday morning in a deep excavation near East Kensington Station. It is one of two shafts that have been made in connection with an extension of the railway southward. It is protected from the intrusion of the public by a hoarding upon the high road, in which a small doorway has been cut for the convenience of some of the workmen who live in that direction. The doorway was left unfastened through a misunderstanding between two gangers, and through it he made his way. . . .

My mind is darkened with questions and riddles.

It would seem he walked all the way from the House that night — he has frequently walked home during the past Session — and so it is I figure his dark form coming along the late and empty streets, wrapped up, intent. And then did the pale electric lights near the station cheat the rough planking into a semblance of white? Did that fatal unfastened door awaken some memory?

Was there, after all, ever any green door in the wall at all?

I do not know. I have told his story as he told it to me. There are times when I believe that Wallace was no more than the victim of the coincidence between a rare but not unprecedented type of hallucination and a careless trap, but that indeed is not my profoundest belief. You may think me superstitious if you will, and foolish; but, indeed, I am more than half convinced that he had in truth, an abnormal gift, and a sense, something — I know not what — that in the guise of wall and door offered him an outlet, a secret and peculiar passage of escape into another and altogether more beautiful world. At any rate, you will say, it betrayed him in the end. But did it betray him? There you touch the inmost mystery of these dreamers, these men of vision and the imagination.

We see our world fair and common, the hoarding and the pit. By our daylight standard he walked out of security into darkness, danger and death.

But did he see like that?

SABBATH

ABRAHAM JOSHUA HESCHEL

The Sabbath

Abraham Joshua Heschel (1907-1972) was born in Warsaw, Poland, and studied and taught in Germany and England before immigrating to the United States in 1940. As Professor of Jewish Ethics and Mysticism at the Jewish Theological Seminary of America from 1945 to 1972, he was an influential and beloved teacher within the Jewish community. His books were and continue to be read and admired by many Christians and secular intellectuals. In this passage, he considers the meaning of the Sabbath, the weekly day of rest that has been a central aspect of Jewish life for many centuries. Drawing on the history of his tradition and his belief that "the likeness of God can be found in time," he vividly portrays the holiness of this day and the urgently needed shift in perception it offers to contemporary people.

In Heschel's view, how does the Sabbath answer the question that frames this chapter of *Leading Lives That Matter:* "Must work be the primary source of my identity?" What criticisms of the place of work in contemporary life are built into this account of Sabbath?

He who wants to enter the holiness of the day must first lay down the profanity of clattering commerce, of being yoked to toil. He must go away from the screech of dissonant days, from the nervousness and fury of acquisitive-

---

From Abraham Joshua Heschel, *The Sabbath: Its Meaning for Modern Man* (New York: Farrar, Straus and Company, 1951, 1952), pp. 13-21.

ness and the betrayal in embezzling his own life. He must say farewell to manual work and learn to understand that the world has already been created and will survive without the help of man. Six days a week we wrestle with the world, wringing profit from the earth; on the Sabbath we especially care for the seed of eternity planted in the soul. The world has our hands, but our soul belongs to Someone Else. Six days a week we seek to dominate the world, on the seventh day we try to dominate the self.

When the Romans met the Jews and noticed their strict adherence to the law of abstaining from labor on the Sabbath, their only reaction was contempt. The Sabbath is a sign of Jewish indolence, was the opinion held by Juvenal, Seneca and others.

In defense of the Sabbath, Philo, the spokesman of the Greek-speaking Jews of Alexandria, says: "On this day we are commanded to abstain from all work, not because the law inculcates slackness. . . . Its object is rather to give man relaxation from continuous and unending toil and by refreshing their bodies with a regularly calculated system of remissions to send them out renewed to their old activities. For a breathing spell enables not merely ordinary people but athletes also to collect their strength with a stronger force behind them to undertake promptly and patiently each of the tasks set before them."

Here the Sabbath is represented not in the spirit of the Bible but in the spirit of Aristotle. According to the Stagirite, "we need relaxation, because we cannot work continuously. Relaxation, then, is not an end"; it is "for the sake of activity," for the sake of gaining strength for new efforts. To the biblical mind, however, labor is the means toward an end, and the Sabbath as a day of rest, as a day of abstaining from toil, is not for the purpose of recovering one's lost strength and becoming fit for the forthcoming labor. The Sabbath is a day for the sake of life. Man is not a beast of burden, and the Sabbath is not for the purpose of enhancing the efficiency of his work. "Last in creation, first in intention," the Sabbath is "the end of the creation of heaven and earth."

The Sabbath is not for the sake of the weekdays; the weekdays are for the sake of Sabbath. It is not an interlude but the climax of living.

Three acts of God denoted the seventh day: He rested, He blessed and He hallowed the seventh day (Genesis 2:2-3). To the prohibition of labor is, therefore, added the blessing of delight and the accent of sanctity. Not only the hands of man celebrate the day, the tongue and the soul keep the Sabbath. One does not talk on it in the same manner in which one talks on weekdays. Even thinking of business or labor should be avoided.

Labor is a craft, but perfect rest is an art. It is the result of an accord of body, mind and imagination. To attain a degree of excellence in art, one must accept its discipline, one must adjure slothfulness. The seventh day is a *palace in time* which we build. It is made of soul, of joy and reticence. In its atmosphere, a discipline is a reminder of adjacency to eternity. Indeed, the splendor of the day is expressed in terms of *abstentions*, just as the mystery of God is more adequately conveyed *via negationis*, in the categories of *negative theology* which claims that we can never say what He is, we can only say what He is not. We often feel how poor the edifice would be were it built exclusively of our rituals and deeds which are so awkward and often so obtrusive. How else express glory in the presence of eternity, if not by the silence of abstaining from noisy acts? . . .

What is so luminous about a day? What is so precious to captivate the hearts? It is because the seventh day is a mine where spirit's precious metal can be found with which to construct the palace in time, a dimension in which the human is at home with the divine; a dimension in which man aspires to approach the likeness of the divine.

For where shall the likeness of God be found? There is no quality that space has in common with the essence of God. There is not enough freedom on the top of the mountain; there is not enough glory in the silence of the sea. Yet the likeness of God can be found in time, which is eternity in disguise.

The art of keeping the seventh day is the art of painting on the canvas of time the mysterious grandeur of the climax of creation: as He sanctified the seventh day, so shall we. The love of the Sabbath is the love of man for what he and God have in common. Our keeping the Sabbath day is a paraphrase of His sanctification of the seventh day.

What would be a world without Sabbath? It would be a world that knew only itself or God distorted as a thing or the abyss separating Him from the world; a world without the vision of a window in eternity that opens into time.

For all the idealization, there is no danger of the idea of the Sabbath becoming a fairy-tale. With all the romantic idealization, the Sabbath remains a concrete fact, a legal institution and a social order. There is no danger of its becoming a disembodied spirit, for the spirit of the Sabbath must always be in accord with actual deeds, with definite actions and abstentions. The real and the spiritual are one, like body and soul in a living man. It is for the law to clear the path; it is for the soul to sense the spirit.

This is what the ancient rabbis felt: the Sabbath demands all of man's attention, the service and single-minded devotion of total love. The logic of such a conception compelled them to enlarge constantly the system of laws and rules of observance. They sought to ennoble human nature and make it worthy of being in the presence of the royal day.

Yet law and love, discipline and delight, were not always fused. In their illustrious fear of desecrating the spirit of the day, the ancient rabbis established a level of observance which is within the reach of exalted souls but not infrequently beyond the grasp of ordinary men.

The glorification of the day, the insistence upon strict observance, did not, however, lead the rabbis to a deification of the law. "The Sabbath is given unto you, not you unto the Sabbath." The ancient rabbis knew that excessive piety may endanger the fulfillment of the essence of the law. "There is nothing more important, according to the Torah, than to preserve human life. . . . Even when there is the slightest possibility that a life may be at stake one may disregard every prohibition of the law." One must sacrifice mitzvot *for the sake of man* rather than sacrifice man *"for the sake of mitzvot."* The purpose of the Torah is "to bring life to Israel, in this world and in the world to come."

Continuous austerity may severely dampen, yet levity would certainly obliterate the spirit of the day. One cannot modify a precious filigree with a spear or operate on a brain with a plowshare. It must always be remembered that the Sabbath is not an occasion for diversion or frivolity; not a day to shoot fireworks or to turn somersaults, but an opportunity to mend our tattered lives; to collect rather than to dissipate time. Labor without dignity is the cause of misery; rest without spirit the source of depravity. Indeed, the prohibitions have succeeded in preventing the vulgarization of the grandeur of the day. . . .

The seventh day is like a palace in time with a kingdom for all. It is not a date but an atmosphere.

It is not a different state of consciousness but a different climate; it is as if the appearance of all things somehow changed. The primary awareness is one of our being *within* the Sabbath rather than of the Sabbath being within us. We may not know whether our understanding is correct, or whether our sentiments are noble, but the air of the day surrounds us like spring which spreads over the land without our aid or notice.

"How precious is the Feast of Booths! Dwelling in the Booth, even our body is surrounded by the sanctity of the Mitzvah," said once a rabbi to his friend. Whereupon the latter remarked: "The Sabbath Day is even more than that. On the Feast you may leave the Booth for a while, whereas the Sabbath surrounds you wherever you go."

The difference between the Sabbath and all other days is not to be noticed in the physical structure of things, in their spatial dimension. Things do not change on that day. There is only a difference in the dimension of time, in the relation of the universe to God. The Sabbath preceded creation and the Sabbath completed creation; it is all of the spirit that the world can bear. . . .

Technical civilization is the product of labor, of man's exertion of power for the sake of gain, for the sake of producing goods. It begins when man, dissatisfied with what is available in nature, becomes engaged in a struggle with the forces of nature in order to enhance his safety and to increase his comfort. To use the language of the Bible, the task of civilization is to subdue the earth, to have dominion over the beast.

How proud we often are of our victories in the war with nature, proud of the multitude of instruments we have succeeded in inventing, of the abundance of commodities we have been able to produce. Yet our victories have come to resemble defeats. In spite of our triumphs, we have fallen victims to the work of our hands; it is as if the forces we had conquered have conquered us.

Is our civilization a way to disaster, as many of us are prone to believe? Is civilization essentially evil, to be rejected and condemned? The faith of the Jew is not a way out of this world, but a way of being within and above this world; not to reject but to surpass civilization. The Sabbath is the day on which we learn the art of *surpassing* Civilization.

Adam was placed in the Garden of Eden "to dress it and to keep it" (Genesis 2:15). Labor is not only the destiny of man; it is endowed with divine dignity. However, after he ate of the tree of knowledge he was condemned to toil, not only to labor. "In toil shalt thou eat . . . all the days of thy life" (Genesis 3:17). Labor is a blessing, toil is the misery of man.

The Sabbath as a day of abstaining from work is not a depreciation but an affirmation of labor, a divine exaltation of its dignity. Thou shalt abstain from labor on the seventh day is a sequel to the command: *Six days shalt thou labor, and do all thy work.*

"Six days shalt thou labor and do all thy work; but the seventh day is Sabbath unto the Lord thy God." Just as we are commanded to keep the Sabbath, we are commanded to labor. "Love work. . . ." The duty to work for six days is just as much a part of God's covenant with man as the duty to abstain from work on the seventh day.

To set apart one day a week for freedom, a day on which we would not use the instruments which have been so easily turned into weapons of destruction, a day for being with ourselves, a day of detachment from the vulgar, of independence of external obligations, a day on which we stop worshipping the idols of technical civilization, a day on which we use no money, a day of armistice in the economic struggle with our fellow men and the forces of nature — is there any institution that holds out a greater hope for man's progress than the Sabbath?

The solution of mankind's most vexing problem will not be found in renouncing technical civilization, but in attaining some degree of independence of it.

In regard to external gifts, to outward possessions, there is only one proper attitude — to have them and to be able to do without them. On the Sabbath we live, as it were, *independent of technical civilization:* we abstain primarily from any activity that aims at remaking or reshaping the things of space. Man's royal privilege to conquer nature is suspended on the seventh day.

What are the kinds of labor not to be done on the Sabbath? They are, according to the ancient rabbis, all those acts which were necessary for the construction and furnishing of the Sanctuary in the desert. The Sabbath itself is a sanctuary which we build, *a sanctuary in time.*

It is one thing to race or be driven by the vicissitudes that menace life, and another thing to stand still and to embrace the presence of an eternal moment.

The seventh day is the armistice in man's cruel struggle for existence, a truce in all conflicts, personal and social, peace between man and man, man and nature, peace within man; a day on which handling money is considered a desecration, on which man avows his independence of that which is the world's chief idol. The seventh day is the exodus from tension, the liberation of man from his own muddiness, the installation of man as a sovereign in the world of time.

NATURE

WILLIAM WORDSWORTH

"The World Is Too Much with Us"

In the English-speaking world, William Wordsworth (1770-1850) may be *the* poet of nature. One of his great subjects was the relationship between humanity and the natural world, especially with respect to the interplay of memory, imagination, and the experience of nature in forming human sentiments, character, and identity. Both of the poems below suggest that human beings find themselves most authentically when they are away from the workaday world and its cares and routines, especially its sometimes brutal tendency to alienate us from the true source of ourselves, the world of nature.

What is "the world" in the poem below, and what does it mean to say that "the world is too much *with* us"? In Part I, we learned from Aristotle that generosity is the virtue that governs "getting and spending" and that "wastefulness" is a vice. Does the speaker below mean to suggest that our wastefulness has led to a loss of a capacity to see certain things, or does he suggest that getting and spending themselves lead us to waste our powers and to "give" the wrong things away? When the poet says, "Little we see in nature that is ours," does he mean (a) that we see little in nature though it belongs to us; (b) that we see little in nature that we ourselves own or possess; or (c) that we see little of ourselves in nature any longer? Which of the three readings is most consistent with the rest of the poem? Or does the most compelling interpretation of the poem depend upon two or more meanings of the statement?

From *The Complete Poetical Works of William Wordsworth* (New York: Thomas Y. Crowell & Co., 1888), p. 398.

The world is too much with us; late and soon,
Getting and spending, we lay waste our powers:
Little we see in Nature that is ours;
We have given our hearts away, a sordid boon!
The Sea that bares her bosom to the moon;
The Winds that will be howling at all hours,
And are up-gathered now like sleeping flowers;
For this, for everything, we are out of tune;
It moves us not. — Great God! I'd rather be
A Pagan suckled in a creed outworn;
So might I, standing on this pleasant lea,
Have glimpses that would make me less forlorn;
Have sight of Proteus rising from the sea;
Or hear old Triton blow his wreathèd horn.

<hr>

WILLIAM WORDSWORTH

"Lines Composed a Few Miles above Tintern Abbey"

Although Wordsworth wrote this poem at an early stage of his career (1798), it explores many of the subtle transactions between the human soul and the natural world that were to occupy him for the rest of his life. Which do we see more of in the world of this poem: the mind of the speaker at work on the natural world or the natural world at work on the mind of the speaker? And given that this is a poem, a creation of the human mind, can we always tell these two processes apart from one another? What is the significance of this difficulty?

In lines 103-112, the speaker makes some very complex and powerful claims about the capacity of nature and "the language of the senses" to

<hr>

"Lines Composed a Few Miles above Tintern Abbey, on Revisiting the Banks of the Wye during a Tour," in *The Poetical Works of Wordsworth*, ed. Henry Reed (Philadelphia: Porter & Coates, 1851), pp. 191-193.

shape the human soul, to fashion and sustain our identities. He says that the eye and the ear both "half create" and "perceive" the landscape, and that this process is "The anchor of my purest thoughts, the nurse,/The guide, the guardian of my heart, and soul/Of all my moral being." What are some of the ways in which the poem itself has dramatized or represented this process and its vital importance in the life of the speaker from the very beginning of the poem?

Notice and describe all of the different contexts, moments, and moods in which the speaker apprehends "the same" scene, for example as a young boy and an older man, through immediate sense perception and later memory. If the natural scene itself has so many different effects upon the soul of the speaker at different times and in different contexts, should we not wonder whether "nature" in and of itself has any formative role at all? Or is the speaker's identity forged simply by the work of the poet's mind upon itself? Why should nature be so important then? Could it be because when we stand in the presence of nature, we stand before those things that we did not ourselves create? Is our attitude before natural things different from our attitude toward those things we did create, toward the work of our own hands, for example?

FIVE years have past; five summers, with the length
Of five long winters! and again I hear
These waters, rolling from their mountain-springs
With a soft inland murmur. — Once again
Do I behold these steep and lofty cliffs,
That on a wild secluded scene impress
Thoughts of more deep seclusion; and connect
The landscape with the quiet of the sky.
The day is come when I again repose
Here, under this dark sycamore, and view   10
These plots of cottage-ground, these orchard-tufts,
Which at this season, with their unripe fruits,
Are clad in one green hue, and lose themselves
'Mid groves and copses. Once again I see
These hedge-rows, hardly hedge-rows, little lines
Of sportive wood run wild: these pastoral farms,
Green to the very door; and wreaths of smoke
Sent up, in silence, from among the trees!

With some uncertain notice, as might seem
Of vagrant dwellers in the houseless woods,   20
Or of some Hermit's cave, where by his fire
The Hermit sits alone.
                      These beauteous forms,
Through a long absence, have not been to me
As is a landscape to a blind man's eye:
But oft, in lonely rooms, and 'mid the din
Of towns and cities, I have owed to them
In hours of weariness, sensations sweet,
Felt in the blood, and felt along the heart;
And passing even into my purer mind,
With tranquil restoration: — feelings too   30
Of unremembered pleasure: such, perhaps,
As have no slight or trivial influence
On that best portion of a good man's life,
His little, nameless, unremembered, acts
Of kindness and of love. Nor less, I trust,
To them I may have owed another gift,
Of aspect more sublime; that blessed mood,
In which the burthen of the mystery,
In which the heavy and the weary weight
Of all this unintelligible world,   40
Is lightened: — that serene and blessed mood,
In which the affections gently lead us on, —
Until, the breath of this corporeal frame
And even the motion of our human blood
Almost suspended, we are laid asleep
In body, and become a living soul:
While with an eye made quiet by the power
Of harmony, and the deep power of joy,
We see into the life of things.
                         If this
Be but a vain belief, yet, oh! how oft —   50
In darkness and amid the many shapes
Of joyless daylight; when the fretful stir
Unprofitable, and the fever of the world,
Have hung upon the beatings of my heart —
How oft, in spirit, have I turned to thee,
O sylvan Wye! thou wanderer thro' the woods,

How often has my spirit turned to thee!
　　And now, with gleams of half-extinguished thought,
With many recognitions dim and faint,
And somewhat of a sad perplexity,　　　　　　　　　　　　　　60
The picture of the mind revives again:
While here I stand, not only with the sense
Of present pleasure, but with pleasing thoughts
That in this moment there is life and food
For future years. And so I dare to hope,
Though changed, no doubt, from what I was when first
I came among these hills; when like a roe
I bounded o'er the mountains, by the sides
Of the deep rivers, and the lonely streams,
Wherever Nature led: more like a man　　　　　　　　　　　　70
Flying from something that he dreads, than one
Who sought the thing he loved. For Nature then
(The coarser pleasures of my boyish days,
And their glad animal movements all gone by)
To me was all in all. — I cannot paint
What then I was. The sounding cataract
Haunted me like a passion: the tall rock,
The mountain, and the deep and gloomy wood,
Their colours and their forms, were then to me
An appetite; a feeling and a love,　　　　　　　　　　　　　80
That had no need of a remoter charm,
By thought supplied, nor any interest
Unborrowed from the eye. — That time is past,
And all its aching joys are now no more,
And all its dizzy raptures. Not for this
Faint I, nor mourn nor murmur; other gifts
Have followed; for such loss, I would believe,
Abundant recompence. For I have learned
To look on Nature, not as in the hour
Of thoughtless youth; but hearing oftentimes　　　　　　　　90
The still, sad music of humanity,
Nor harsh nor grating, though of ample power
To chasten and subdue. And I have felt
A presence that disturbs me with the joy
Of elevated thoughts; a sense sublime
Of something far more deeply interfused,

Whose dwelling is the light of setting suns,
And the round ocean and the living air,
And the blue sky, and in the mind of man;
A motion and a spirit, that impels   100
All thinking things, all objects of all thought,
And rolls through all things. Therefore am I still
A lover of the meadows and the woods,
And mountains; and of all that we behold
From this green earth; of all the mighty world
Of eye, and ear, — both what they half create,
And what perceive; well pleased to recognise
In Nature and the language of the sense,
The anchor of my purest thoughts, the nurse,
The guide, the guardian of my heart, and soul   110
Of all my moral being.

                  Nor perchance,
If I were not thus taught, should I the more
Suffer my genial spirits to decay:
For thou art with me here upon the banks
Of this fair river; thou my dearest Friend,
My dear, dear Friend; and in thy voice I catch
The language of my former heart, and read
My former pleasures in the shooting lights
Of thy wild eyes. Oh! yet a little while
May I behold in thee what I was once,   120
My dear, dear Sister! and this prayer I make,
Knowing that Nature never did betray
The heart that loved her; 'tis her privilege,
Through all the years of this our life, to lead
From joy to joy: for she can so inform
The mind that is within us, so impress
With quietness and beauty, and so feed
With lofty thoughts, that neither evil tongues,
Rash judgments, nor the sneers of selfish men,
Nor greetings where no kindness is, nor all   130
The dreary intercourse of daily life,
Shall e'er prevail against us, or disturb
Our cheerful faith, that all which we behold
Is full of blessings. Therefore let the moon
Shine on thee in thy solitary walk;

And let the misty mountain-winds be free
To blow against thee: and, in after years,
When these wild ecstasies shall be matured
Into a sober pleasure; when thy mind
Shall be a mansion for all lovely forms,   140
Thy memory be as a dwelling-place
For all sweet sounds and harmonies; oh! then,
If solitude, or fear, or pain, or grief,
Should be thy portion, with what healing thoughts
Of tender joy wilt thou remember me,
And these my exhortations! Nor, perchance —
If I should be where I no more can hear
Thy voice, nor catch from thy wild eyes these gleams
Of past existence — wilt thou then forget
That on the banks of this delightful stream   150
We stood together; and that I, so long
A worshipper of Nature, hither came
Unwearied in that service: rather say
With warmer love — oh! with far deeper zeal
Of holier love. Nor wilt thou then forget,
That after many wanderings, many years
Of absence, these steep woods and lofty cliffs,
And this green pastoral landscape, were to me
More dear, both for themselves and for thy sake!

LOVE

GILBERT MEILAENDER

"Friendship and Vocation"

In this chapter from his book *Friendship,* the Christian ethicist Gilbert Meilaender sharpens and deepens a distinction between two kinds of love: love of work in service to many neighbors who have been given to us (vocation) and reciprocal love of a few, carefully chosen, human beings (friendship). The chapter is not a developed case on behalf of the joys and importance of friendship, as Heschel's was for Sabbath or Wordsworth's for nature, though Meilaender does point in that direction. His emphasis, rather, is on the theological turns that led to the devaluation of friendship in comparison to work. He argues that Protestant Christians, from John Calvin and William Perkins to Dorothy Sayers (whose essay, which Meilaender quotes, is included earlier in this chapter) are responsible for "elevating work to a central place in life." And he contrasts this Protestant Christian view of life to the Classical view of life in which work was regarded as irksome and friendship was understood to be the primary source of human fulfillment. So we do not simply have two contrasting and conflicting loves here: we have two different views of what should give to a human life its meaning and significance.

Much of the middle portion of this selection reviews some of the material from Part I and the vocabulary of vocation. Notice, however, that Meilaender gives a friendly but critical account of this vocabulary, and he is especially careful to demonstrate how the Christian idea of vocation has been twisted to include notions of self-fulfillment that were

From Gilbert Meilaender, *Friendship: A Study in Theological Ethics* (Notre Dame: University of Notre Dame Press, 1981), pp. 86-103.

originally alien to it. And he sometimes sharpens the tension between vocation and friendship by offering concrete cases in which devotion to our work and devotion to our friends must result in painful conflicts. Do you think that his examples here, especially the one taken from a novel by Dorothy Sayers, suggest that we should never mix the worlds of work and friendship?

Though the Christian world of vocation and the Classical world of friendship, personified early in the essay by the figures of John Wesley and Samuel Johnson, do seem at times inimical to one another, Meilaender attempts to reconcile them or at least to show how work and friendship might be enjoyed together in the same life. When he suggests that Christians might very well reject Sayers's idea that we live in order to work and instead "work in order to live," seeking sources of fulfillment elsewhere (in friendship, for example), has he abandoned the Christian ideal of vocation? Or has he abandoned only what he calls the "pagan" ideal of vocation?

In our next chapter, on the balanced life, we will examine several other answers to the question of whether or not it is possible in today's world to assume multiple responsibilities and to enjoy several different sources of fulfillment in a life that matters.

There is an apocryphal tale of the chronic absentee colliery-worker who was asked by his exasperated manager why he worked only four shifts every week; "because," replied the man, "I can't live on three."

P. D. Anthony, *The Ideology of Work*

In order to commit ourselves to the well-being of our neighbors, we do not necessarily have to become Franciscans. There is an important strand of Christian tradition which has believed that love can remain nonpreferential and yet be fitted for society through commitment to vocation. This has, in particular, been a Protestant ideal. In our vocation we serve (some) neighbors and find our place in a whole system of vocations used by God to care for (many) neighbors.

There can be little doubt that the idea of vocation has had enormous social and cultural significance. It suggests, in fact, an ideal of life very different from the classical ideal in which persons found fulfillment and were assured of their own worth through a life shared with friends. By contrast, the idea of providence — when taken seriously in Christian thought — has suggested the related idea of the calling. God calls each of us to some work in life and by his providential governance uses our work to serve the needs of many neighbors. The classical ideal remains particularistic and concerned, to a large degree, with self-fulfillment. The Christian ideal suggests a more universalistic emphasis and, at least in its purer forms, seems to commend self-forgetfulness in service of one's vocation.

These contrasting styles of life mark more than a break between the two great cultures of the West, however; they suggest possible choices for anyone at any time. Boswell records that Dr. Johnson once said of John Wesley, the great Methodist preacher who logged thousands of miles on horseback while traveling around England to preach,

> John Wesley's conversation is good, but he is never at leisure. He is always obliged to go at a certain hour. This is very disagreeable to a man who loves to fold his legs and have out his talk, as I do.

It would, in the whole of our cultural history, be hard to find better paradigms of these two contrasting styles of life. No one took more pleasure in conversation among friends than Dr. Johnson. And few had a stronger sense of vocation than John Wesley (referred to by one biographer as "The Lord's Horseman"). And the tension between these two styles of life is noted in Dr. Johnson's comment. Wesley's conversation is good, but — driven as he is by the requirements of his calling — he can never just sit down, fold his legs, and have out his talk! Serious commitment to vocation means that one lives to work, and we should not forget that it is also possible to choose — as some have — to work to live, while seeking delight and fulfillment in the bond of friendship.

I

Although the concept of a calling as one's work in life has been of great importance in Christian thought, we could not say that it is particularly pronounced in the Bible. The biblical writings concern themselves more with God's calling of a people for himself or of a person to exercise a special function for the good of this people. Thus, Israel — and the new Israel — is called as a people holy unto God, and Christians are given different gifts fitting them for various tasks within the body of Christ. It is, therefore, something genuinely new when St. Paul writes, "let everyone lead the life which the Lord has assigned to him, and in which God has called him" (I Corinthians 7:17) — conflating the call to membership in God's people with the call to work of a certain sort. The impact of this passage, particularly in the hands of Luther and Calvin, was enormous. Of it Kenneth Kirk has written:

> The words "call" and "calling" here obviously have two meanings. There is the "call" to be a Christian, and the "calling" (as we say), or worldly avocation, already being followed when the call to Christianity comes. . . . Quite deliberately Paul places these secular conditions and circumstances — this profession in which a man happens to be at the time of his conversion — on the same spiritual level as that conversion itself. Each is a "call" or "calling" direct from God. . . . This "Oriental," this "ascetic," this Puritan who stands aloof from the everyday life of the world — it is to him we owe the great Christian truth that the most ordinary and secular employment can and should be regarded as a mission directly laid upon us by the Omnipotent God himself.

It is true that this view did not always prevail within Christendom before the great Reformers articulated it with depth and power. Although Protestant polemic can sometimes overdo the contrast, medieval Catholicism did think of a vocation primarily as the call to the monastic life — which, of course, leaves the majority of Christians without a specifically religious vocation. One can truthfully say, therefore, with Einar Billing that

> the more fully a Catholic Christian develops his nature, the more he becomes a stranger to ordinary life, the more he departs from the men and women who move therein. But . . . the evangelical church does not seek to create religious virtuosos, but holy and saintly men and women *in* the call.

For the Reformers, at least in theory, every Christian becomes a monk — except that, now, the serious Christian life is lived out within the world, and the whole of that life is offered up to God.

It is common, since Weber explored the Protestant Ethic, to note that Calvin's concept of the calling is more aggressive and disciplined than is Luther's. And though here again one could overdo the contrast, there is truth in this much of Weber's thesis. The Calvinist, if not Calvin himself, did want to master the world and reshape it to the glory of God. This task requires unresting activity and a disciplined life. Thus, as one author aptly puts it,

"Puritans discovered a utopia of men without leisure." We can see fairly clearly the ideas at work in the Protestant concept of the calling if we consider William Perkins's discussion. Perkins, certainly a serious and judicious Puritan divine, may well have been the most important Puritan thinker in England at the beginning of the seventeenth century.

A vocation or calling is, Perkins writes, *"a certain kind of life, ordained and imposed on man by God, for the common good."* That is, in good scholastic fashion we can say that the efficient cause of one's calling is God and the final cause is the common or public good. Each of these is important for Perkins's discussion. A calling implies a Caller — that is, God. And Perkins uses two metaphors to relate God as efficient cause to the system of human callings: a military and a mechanical metaphor. In an army camp, Perkins notes, the general appoints each man to his particular place, in which he is to remain against the enemy. And if each man fulfills his appointed task faithfully, the army will function well. Even so, Perkins suggests, "it is in humane societies: God the Generall, appointing to every man his particular calling. . . ." (It is worth noting in passing that, while military modes of organization may often be necessary in human life, few of us regard it as the most desirable way to live. Such organization may value insufficiently the distinctive characteristics of different persons.)

Perkins's other metaphor is mechanical. "Againe, in a clocke, made by the art and handy-worke of man, there be many wheeles, and everyone hath his severall motion, some turne this way, some that way, some goe softly, some apace: and they are all ordered by the motion of the watch." And Perkins finds a "notable resemblance" between this and the way in which God, in his special providence, allots to every person a particular calling. Well-oiled parts of a mechanism — that, it is not unfair to say, is what human beings become in such a system of vocations.

So much for the efficient cause. What of the final cause of our callings? The end of this system of vocations is the common good. Service in one's calling, if undertaken seriously and faithfully, will benefit others. One can be confident of that because God — the great General or, as we prefer, Clockmaker — has so arranged the system of callings with the welfare of humanity at heart. We could, of course, interpret this in a kind of *laissez-faire* manner: Everyone tends to his own knitting and God, like an invisible hand, sees to it that the system of callings fits together. But Perkins does not intend us to think of vocations in that way. Indeed, he explicitly rejects as wicked "that common saying, *Every man for himselfe, and God for us all.*" We are to look, in our callings, not to our own interests but to the common good. It is, of course, true that God could care for human beings simply through an immediate exercise of his power, but he chooses to work mediately. He chooses "that men should be his instruments, for the good of one another." It is in service of this end that we "joyne . . . our callings together." What we see very clearly here is the universalistic impulse built into this Christian understanding of vocation. Though any individual's vocation will, of course, be limited in focus, the system of callings as a whole — under the providential governance of God — serves the needs of many neighbors.

It is this universalistic impulse which permits a system of vocations to place our works of love in a more universally other-regarding context while still allowing special attachment to certain tasks and to needs of certain people. But again, this is not to suggest that individuals can settle contentedly into their routine tasks, assuming that God will care for distant neighbors. Einar Billing has suggested that "the call constantly has to struggle against two adversaries: stereotyped workmanship and unresponsible idealism." On the one hand, the person called by God must rigorously restrict his efforts to the actual task appointed by God. If this is not done, no one's needs are really served. At the same time, however, one must remain open to possibilities for "an infinite expansion of our work." God's call may, after all, lead in new directions, and "we must be prepared for each new assignment he may have for us." Thus, the universalistic impulse has a place directly within the life of each individual called; its place lies in the openness to possibilities for infinite expansion. But that is, I think, only a qualification, even if an important one. Universality is, in the main, a feature not of any particular vocation but of the whole system of vocations.

The consequences of this understanding of vocation are of great significance. To begin with, work is elevated to a central place in life. It is serious business, since, after all, we are called to our work by God and used by him to serve the needs of our fellows. Perkins, for example, makes this point at great length. The chief enemies of the calling are idleness and sloth, which Perkins, in all the seriousness with which an earlier age could invest such terms, calls "damnable sinnes." Indeed, to make his point Perkins uses a scriptural reference which was a Puritan favorite: "The servant that had received but one talent, is called an evillservant, because he was slouthfull in the use of it." We need only remember John Wesley, a man never at leisure to have out his talk, to understand what serious business a vocation could become. Such a calling leaves little place for self-indulgence within life. We may simply note, without in any way suggesting that folding one's legs and having out one's talk is unworthy, that wholehearted commitment to our calling may leave little time for such pleasures. The inevitable result is that deep personal relationships like friendship, without precisely being denigrated, become harder and harder to sustain. They are not so much criticized as they are squeezed out of life. Personal significance is found in one's calling — or it is not found at all.

Not only is little place left in life for the apparent self-indulgence of a bond like friendship, but something begins to happen to the work one does, as well. Whatever inadequacies Weber's thesis may contain, it is not hard to see with him that the idea of a system of callings is related to the idea of division of labor. At the same time that the worker is called upon to find personal significance in his work — it is, after all, God's call — the work itself becomes increasingly impersonal and subject to rational economic calculation. The worker is a soldier in the great army of which God is General, or a part in the machine constructed by God the Clockmaker. Each person should carry out faithfully and seriously his or her function in the system of callings. And one's place in that system is determined not by personal bonds like friendship but by considerations of efficiency and fairness. Devotion to the task at hand becomes of supreme importance.

Quite often, perhaps because we prefer not to think about it, we do not appreciate what commitment to a vocation really requires, how much like an overriding religious commitment it can be. Dorothy Sayers has illustrated this point brilliantly in *Gaudy Night*. The mystery which needs solving in this story results from a case of academic dishonesty. Sayers's plot revolves around a women's college at Oxford — a college which is suddenly subjected to various attacks on property and persons. The attacks, it is finally discovered, have been made by Annie, who works at the college. Years before these events Annie's husband had been driven from academic life because Miss de Vine — now teaching at Shrewsbury College where Annie works — discovered that he had suppressed evidence which would have disproven his thesis. Interestingly, one of Annie's acts of violence involved defacing a novel called *The Search* "at the exact point where the author upholds, or appears for the moment to uphold, the doctrine that loyalty to the abstract truth must over-ride all personal considerations." And it was, of course, precisely such commitment to the truth, understood as integral to her vocation, which had led Miss de Vine to expose Annie's husband. At one point in the story Miss de Vine, talking with Harriet, discusses her own view of what vocational commitment requires. She and Harriet agree that if we find a subject in which we're content with second-rate work, that cannot be where our commitment really lies.

> "No," said Miss de Vine. "If you are once sure what you do want, you find that everything else goes down before it like grass under a

roller — all other interests, your own and other people's. Miss Lydgate wouldn't like my saying that, but it's as true of her as of anybody else. She's the kindest soul in the world, in things she's indifferent about, like the peculations of Jukes. But she hasn't the slightest mercy on the prosodical theories of Mr. Elkbottom. She wouldn't countenance those to save Mr. Elkbottom from hanging. She'd say she couldn't. And she couldn't, of course. If she actually *saw* Mr. Elkbottom writhing in humiliation, she'd be sorry, but she wouldn't alter a paragraph. That would be treason. One can't be pitiful where one's own job is concerned. You'd lie cheerfully, I expect, about anything except — what?"

"Oh, anything!" said Harriet, laughing, "Except saying that somebody's beastly book is good when it isn't. I can't do that. It makes me a lot of enemies, but I can't do it."

"No, one can't," said Miss de Vine. "However painful it is, there's always one thing one has to deal with sincerely, if there's any root to one's mind at all. I ought to know, from my own experience. Of course, the one thing may be an emotional thing; I don't say it mayn't. One may commit all the sins in the calendar, and still be faithful and honest towards one person. If so, then that one person is probably one's appointed job. I'm not despising that kind of loyalty; it doesn't happen to be mine, that is all."

Clearly, Miss de Vine is a woman who knows what an overriding vocational commitment means and the way in which it may make purely personal concerns secondary. One must simply get on with the job — and getting on with it may leave no room even for pity, much less for friendship. Miss de Vine does grant that this kind of commitment might be given not to a vocation but to another person (as Annie gave it to her husband). She does not, she says, despise that kind of personal loyalty. Harriet presses the point.

> "Then you're all for the impersonal job?"
> "I am," said Miss de Vine.
> "But you say you don't despise those who make some other person their job?"
> "Far from despising them," said Miss de Vine, "I think they are dangerous."

In the context of the story her words are prophetic, since Annie — whose overriding commitment is one of loyalty to a person — is indeed dangerous. More to the point, though, such persons are dangerous because their commitment is so partial, so preferential. Commitment to a vocation is not like that. The vocation serves many people's needs; God sees to that. But the worker himself shows no particular preference; his commitment is to the work. Miss de Vine is, I think, correct to suggest that such commitment may be less dangerous than Annie's. But it exacts a price, and Harriet is not mistaken to suggest that it is "impersonal." Humanity has been greatly enriched by the Protestant concept of a system of callings in which each finds his or her place. Whether individual lives have been enriched by it is another, and harder, question.

II

"Dead matter leaves the factory ennobled and transformed, where men are corrupted and degraded," wrote Pius XI. And it may be that the Christian concept of vocation has fostered that corruption; at the very least, it can certainly obscure it. We noted above that the concept of the calling could invest work with the dimension of personal significance while at the same time turning work into an impersonal task and possibly (as a result of division of labor) a mindless task. In such circumstances, the affirmation that we can find personal significance in our work begins to sound a bit shrill — as if, just possibly, we were trying to convince ourselves.

To regard work as a calling is to suggest that we live to work, that our work is of central significance for our person. Still more, the calling gives to work a religious significance which it is not likely to acquire in any other way. Thus, Dorothy Sayers could suggest that work expresses something essential in human nature; for it is a natural function of human beings who are made in the image of their Creator. The worker gives full expression to an essential feature of our shared human nature. "His satisfaction comes, in the godlike manner, from looking upon what He has made and finding it very good." Sayers was no fool, of course, and she realized that it is not easy to say this about the work many, probably most, people spend their lives doing. But to realize that, and nevertheless keep on emphasizing the significance of work, is to risk obscuring something important. For the Greeks, friendship was clearly important for self-fulfillment. "No one," writes Aristotle, "would choose to live without friends, even if he had all other goods." In coming to know the friend as "another self," one came to know oneself as well and acquired a sense of one's personal significance. To suggest that we live to work — and to cloak this in the religious garb of the calling — is to try to have work play a similar role in our lives. It is to make work as central in our sense of who we are as friendship was for the Greeks.

It is crucial to see that when we take this step we have really distorted the significance of the calling as it was understood and developed by early Protestants like Perkins. The point of the calling was, quite simply, that it was appointed by God to serve neighbors. If along the way some self-fulfillment came as well, there was nothing wrong with that, but it was hardly the point of the calling. Our modern notion — into which even so independent a thinker as Sayers could be lured — that the point of work is to give meaning, purpose, and fulfillment to life is a degradation of the calling. It is a degradation against which we should have been guarded by both our experience and our theological tradition.

Our experience should surely have taught us that, although some people seem to find their work satisfying in itself, it is equally true that "work, for most people, has always been ugly, crippling, and dangerous." We may in good conscience recommend such work as service to the neighbor or even as an instrument of spiritual discipline, but it ought be cloaked in no other religious garb. When the system of vocations as we experience it today is described in terms which make work the locus of self-fulfillment, Christian ethics ought to object — on the empirical ground that this is far from true, and on the theological ground that vocation ought not make self-fulfillment central. When work as we know it emerges as the dominant idea in our lives — when we identify ourselves to others in terms of what we do for a living, work for which we are paid — and when we glorify such work in terms of self-fulfillment, it is time for Christian ethics to speak a good word for working simply in order to live. Perhaps we need to suggest today that it is quite permissible, even appropriate, simply to work in order to live and to seek one's fulfillment elsewhere — in personal bonds like friendship, for example.

Such a suggestion is likely to meet with disapproval from every side, and this disapproval is likely to use that magic word "alienation." Put most simply, "alienation means that the worker has little sense of personal investment in his or her work. We work at one thing — live for another. The alienated worker, we are told, understands his work only instrumentally — as a means to having the wherewithal and the opportunity to pursue other ends and values. And, the argument continues, such an alienated worker — one who works only to live — can scarcely live a fully human existence. Self-fulfillment is impossible in such circumstances. We are by now so accustomed to taking this purported fact of alienation for granted that it comes as something of a shock to be told, as P. D. Anthony has recently argued, that "man can be regarded as alienated from his work only when he has been subjected to an ideology which requires him to be devoted to it." Yet, Anthony is quite correct. Alienation becomes possible only when, first, work has been given central place in human life, and, second, it is assumed that we are to gain a sense of personal fulfillment from our work. The idea of the calling contributed to the first of these; degradation of that idea to the second. The end of this road becomes apparent in Marxist thought, where alienation has been such a central concept. According to Marx, human beings "begin to distinguish themselves from animals as soon as they begin to *produce* their means of subsistence." The human being is a worker — and once that is made central, alienation becomes a possibility, indeed, a likelihood. As the place and importance of work in human life are exaggerated, the undesirable characteristics of work become more glaring and objectionable. It is possible to be alienated from our work only if we first imagine that we were to find in it a high degree of personal fulfillment. Whatever its defects, it is one of the virtues of capitalism that it must allow people simply to work for money and seek fulfillment elsewhere. Indeed, we might say with Anthony that "capitalism represents an imperfect stage in development towards the absolute transcendency of economic values and an associated ideology of work, the fullest development of which is represented in Marxism."

If our experience should have warned us against making work an essential feature of human nature and the locus of self-fulfillment, so ought our theological tradition. I have already noted that the idea of the calling, in its pure form, had little to do with achieving personal fulfillment. For Luther and Calvin one worked in order not to become a burden to others and because God had appointed for one this particular calling as service to one's neighbors. Even with those qualifications, however, it remains true that the calling may have given work greater centrality in life than it should have, and it is not surprising that coupled with exhortations to faithfulness in one's calling were vigorous attacks on idleness and begging. And in the modern world, work has certainly begun to have the status of an idol. In such circumstances we need to reassert other aspects of our theological tradition. Karl Barth, arguing that human beings, for the most part, work to live rather than live to work, directed a much needed polemic against the idol of work.

It is of a piece with the rather feverish modern overestimation of work and of the process of production that particularly at the climax of the 19th century, and even more so in our own, it should be thought essential to man, or more precisely to the true nature of man, to have a vocation in this sense. On such a view it is forgotten that there are children and the sick and elderly and others for whom vocation in this sense can be only the object either of expectation and preparation or of recollection. It is also forgotten that there are the unemployed, though these are certainly not without a vocation. Finally, it is forgotten that there are innumerable active women who do not have this kind of vocation.

It is worth recalling that it was possible for biblical writers to speak of the promise of God for his people as *rest.* "So then, there remains a sabbath rest for the people of God; for whoever enters God's rest also ceases from his labors as God did from his" (Hebrews 4:9f.). And, indeed, that sabbath rest, as it even now recurs in the weekly cycle of Christian life, is already testimony to the fact that work offers no final fulfillment for human existence.

This is what we ought to have learned and what Christian ethics should call to mind: that work is not an essential feature of a human life, that the point of work is not our own fulfillment but service to others, that work has its limits and need not always make it impossible for us to fold our legs and have out our talk. The proper tone — which does not idolize work but which grants its necessity — was captured quite well by Calvin when he wrote of the calling: "each man will bear and swallow the discomforts, vexations, weariness, and anxieties in his way of life, when he has been persuaded that the burden was laid upon him by God."

III

The Christian concept of vocation becomes degraded whenever it is seen primarily as a source of self-fulfillment. In a world which thinks of work in that way there would seem to be good reason to prefer the bond of friendship to work; for, though the self is fulfilled in friendship, the bond is reciprocal, and others are truly loved for their own sakes. And even if work is understood properly and the calling seen only as a God-appointed means of serving the neighbor, there should be limits to what the calling can ask of us. Even if a system of callings has a universalistic impulse, the final responsibility for meeting those universal needs rests with God, who structures this system of callings. Faithfulness in our vocation, even faithfulness which is sensitive to the danger of "stereotyped workmanship" and alert to the possibilities for "infinite expansion" of the task, does not mean unlimited responsibility. The calling is a way of recognizing the legitimate claims of distant neighbors without imagining that any of us is responsible for meeting all of them and without driving out of life any place for special, preferential bonds of love like friendship. In this way, and unlike the Franciscan love which breaks through all normal bonds of life, the concept of the calling makes it possible for love to be universal yet "fitted for society."

We should not imagine, however, that the fit can ever be perfect — that the claims of friendship and the claims of vocation can be perfectly reconciled in this life. There are several reasons why this is not possible, some grounded in sociological observations about modern Western societies, others grounded more deeply in the structure of Christian theology. Even if our affirmation of vocation is a chastened one and our appreciation of the place of friendship cautious, we will find that a life which does justice to the claims of each is not easy to live.

A world in which vocation has become central must be a world in which preferential bonds like friendship become increasingly remote from large stretches of our life. We do not hire and fire people on the basis of friendship; indeed, to do so strikes many of us as more than a little suspect. Thus, in the world of vocation as in that of politics, we purchase fairness at the price of impersonality. Further, as Miss de Vine realized, serious commitment to a vocation may leave little time for personal concerns; the task has its own built-in necessities and momentum. More important still may be the fact that many vocations in our world require mobility. We may have to move at any time. And certainly any advancement in our work — advancement which may well put us in a position to serve more neighbors — will often require change of location. The result is predictable. "Deep personal bonds are discouraged by the knowledge of transcience," and we learn to keep our commitments tentative and provisional. One does not have to be concerned primarily with personal advancement to be affected in this way. We need only be seriously committed to our God-appointed task and open to the possibilities for "infinite expansion" of that task. The circle soon becomes a vicious one; for those who are enticed by vocational necessities to keep their personal commitments tentative become increasingly isolated and increasingly tempted to try to "live to work." In such a world, as William May has perceptively noted, "the Bell Telephone Company and the Hallmark card industry grow rich on the conscience of Americans uneasy about their overextended personal loyalties."

Thus, the tension between the claims of vocation and friendship is partly a result of certain characteristics of a society like ours, one which has been organized increasingly around the hub of vocation. But the roots of the difficulty go considerably deeper. We may discern this in a paradox which St. Anselm saw in the divine will. Anselm distinguished a divine *disposition* from a divine *distribution*. The divine disposition requires that we go where God wills, that we be obedient to his disposition, even if it should require separation from friends. At the same time, however, the divine distribution bestows the gift of friendship in our lives. This paradox, which Anselm finds in his own experience, is one of the central problems of the Christian life. Earthly affections like friendship are bestowed by the Creator and no fully human life can do without them; yet that same God may lay upon us a task which makes the enjoyment of such attachments difficult or impossible. "The cause of God," Adele Fiske writes, "may often run contrary to human affection. . . . Anselm says rather piteously: 'do not love me less because God does his will in me.'"

God gives both the earthly bond of friendship, which enriches life, and the calling, which serves the neighbor. Theories which rest content in preferential loves or, alternatively, which glorify the calling above all else fail to appreciate the paradox of the divine will which Anselm discerned. The tension between bonds of particular love and a love which is open to every neighbor (in the calling) cannot be overcome by any theory, however intricate. Our thinking can only warn against certain mistakes, certain wrong turnings which we might take. But this central problem of the Christian life must be lived, not just thought. This much, if Adele Fiske is correct, Anselm clearly realized. "St. Anselm soberly faces the fact that God's will often seems to work against itself, destroying the gift it has given. This problem is solved *ambulando*, or it is not solved; he suffers and admits it, but does not try to escape by turning away from human love to love 'God alone'." The tension between particular bonds and a more universally open love — of which the tension between friendship and vocation is an instance — cannot be eliminated for creatures whose lives are marked by the particularities of time and place but who yet are made to share with all others the praise of God. The tension between particular and universal love is "solved" only as it is lived out in a life understood as pilgrimage toward the God who gives both the friend and the neighbor.

If Christian commitment to vocation shattered forever the classical ideal of a unified life devoted to leisured conversation with friends and contemplation, this was not without loss. And Christian thought at its best has never pretended that vocation exacted no price. Only the glorification of vocation as self-fulfillment, which is simultaneously a degradation of the true concept of the calling, has led us to believe that no price was asked. We have, in a sense, sought once again to unify life. As the Greek found a unified life centered in friendship, so the modern pagan seeks it in vocation. But a proper Christian understanding will forego that unity in favor of a life which, recognizing that God gives both the friend and the neighbor, prefers to face the problem *ambulando*. It may be wise to allow the final word about friendship and vocation to St. Augustine, who, as much as anyone, shattered that classical ideal of a unified life. In Book XIX of his *City of God* Augustine considers whether the best life is one of leisure (and contemplation) or one of action — or some combination of these. After making all the appropriate qualifications — that one should not be so active as to have no need or time for God, that the active life is not to be sought for reasons of ambition — Augustine comes to terms with the life he himself would have loved, a life of leisured pursuit of truth among friends, and the life he actually lived as a bishop.

> We see then that it is love of truth that looks for sanctified leisure, while it is the compulsion of love that undertakes righteous engagement in affairs. If this latter burden is not imposed on us, we should employ our freedom from business in the quest for truth and its contemplation, while if it is laid upon us, it is to be undertaken because of the compulsion of love. Yet even in this case the delight in truth should not be utterly abandoned, for fear that we should lose this enjoyment and that compulsion should overwhelm us.

3

Is a Balanced Life Possible and Preferable to a Life Focused Primarily on Work?

Two years ago, a college senior left the office of her pre-med advisor in tears. She had finally mustered the courage to inform him that she had decided not to go to medical school. She was the top student in the class and had always wanted to be a doctor, and both the college she attended and her parents had invested large sums of money in her education on the assumption that she would someday become an outstanding physician. The more she learned about what the life of an MD was really like, however, the less she wanted to become one. From everything she had observed, she told her advisor, the life of a doctor seemed all consuming, with work weeks of sixty or even eighty hours not uncommon. She hoped someday to bear and raise children, and she was in love with a young man with whom she wanted to share her life. She wanted, she explained, a "balanced life" that was not so consumed by paid employment that she lacked time for her family, friends, church, and community.

Her advisor was not pleased. The young woman had already been admitted to two top medical schools. The pre-med program at her college had awarded her its top summer research opportunities. He urged her to finish medical school and *then* to determine whether her fears were based on fact or fiction. He reminded her that the school had given her a "full ride" based on the understanding that she would stay the course. He pointed out that she might change, that her boyfriend might abandon her, and that she might have second thoughts about children. All of this was to no avail. The pre-med advisor succeeded only in further upsetting the young woman, who had been anxiously weighing her decision for several months.

We, the editors of this book, and surely nearly all its readers, fully support the progress of women in the professions in recent decades, and we encourage all who feel called to become physicians or to embrace other challenging professions to do so. Yet there is no doubt that scenes like the one just described are increasingly common on college campuses and elsewhere, as both men and women experience the concerns about the world of work expressed by this student. Many young people have witnessed the hectic lives of their parents and other adults and have resolved not to repeat this pattern. In fact, already in college some find that the pressures to achieve in many areas become more than they want to bear and that their efforts to juggle academic work, paid work, artistic and athletic endeavors, and friendship bring more stress than satisfaction. Later, among those who enter "fast track" jobs after graduation, some grow dissatisfied and look for ways to shift gears to a different kind of employment so that they can have a more leisurely and fulfilling personal life. At the same time, many other people relish the experience of trying to meet multiple demands and don't worry about the conflicts that probably lie ahead.

Individual differences in physical energy, family experience, personal goals, and occupational focus surely exert great influence on decisions like the one made by the pre-med student. Economics also frame such decisions, which usually have significant financial consequences. But these decisions also require hard thinking and honest conversation, because what we decide reflects, at best, our convictions about what it means to lead a good life. Was this student simply fearful of taking on difficult challenges even though she might have realized, on further thought, that doing so would be worthwhile in the end? Or had she instead come to believe that a life that matters *should* be a balanced one, agreeing with Gilbert Meilaender's argument (in the previous chapter) that many of us must or should work primarily in order to live and then seek our sources of fulfillment and lasting achievement elsewhere — in family, friendship, neighborliness, and civic engagement?

Robert Reich, an economist who served as Secretary of Labor during the 1990s, tells of getting into just the sort of "unbalanced" pattern of life this student wanted to avoid. In his book *The Future of Success: Working and Living in the New Economy*, he describes a turning point in his own career. As one immersed in a very demanding but also intensely enjoyable job, Reich frequently stayed late at the office. One night, realizing he would not be home in time to tuck his young sons into bed for the fifth night in a row, he phoned to say good night. The younger of the two said that was okay, but asked please to be awakened for a hug when his father got home. Reich insisted that it would be too late and that the boy needed his sleep, but his son persisted. Asked why, he said he just wanted to know his dad was home. "To this day, I can't explain precisely what happened to me at that moment," Reich remembers. "Yet I suddenly knew I had to leave my job."[1]

While granting that his job was an unusual one and grateful that he had ample opportunities to find other satisfying employment, Reich links his own experience to the difficulties increasing numbers of Americans also have in "making a living and making a life." Finding a good balance really is getting harder, he argues, primarily because technological and economic innovation have made the marketplace far more turbulent and unpredictable than it was even a decade ago. Finding success in this changing and highly competitive economy requires constant hustle, and employers, universities, and other institutions have restructured in ways that elicit more and more work from those who want to have the impressive material benefits this new economy provides to those who do well. In this context, of course, personal relationships and patterns of life also become more unsettled and unpredictable.

In Reich's assessment, none of the life paths considered by our pre-med student is free of risks and obstacles, if only because of the turbulence of the economy in which she will work and, perhaps, raise a family. Yet he does not advise his readers to relinquish their longing for a balanced life. Instead, he encourages them to face up to choices of two kinds: those we can make personally, and those we must make as a nation by enacting policies that are more supportive of family and community life. Both kinds of choices are ultimately moral ones.

Delving into the moral questions surrounding the aspiration to have a balanced life, we find that not all of the challenges are the massive economic ones Reich describes. As our pre-med student discovered, those who actively seek to lead this kind of life are often discouraged by others, especially if these individuals are enormously talented in one particular area of human endeavor. People like this student are sometimes thought to have "let down the side" if they shrink back from a full development of their one special talent. They *could*, so the argument often runs, have made a real difference in the

---

1. Robert Reich, *The Future of Success* (New York: Vintage, 2001), p. 7.

world by finding the cure for multiple sclerosis or inventing a more fuel-efficient car or bringing peace to the Middle East or easing poverty. Instead, they settled for their own comfort over others' needs. They chose a life of self-satisfaction over a life of significance. They lacked virtues like courage and self-sacrifice; indeed, they might be said to be cowardly and selfish. And they surely preferred what Aristotle would have thought to be the less noble to the more noble, the long life of mild enjoyment to the short but splendid one. If we were to review the unsuccessful arguments of Achilles's friends and mentors in Book IX of the *Iliad* (see Chapter 1 of Part II, "Are Some Lives More Significant than Others?") when they sought to persuade him to do what he excelled at doing instead of nursing his own grievances and threatening to abandon the field of battle for an ordinary life back home, we would have a very good summary of the arguments advanced today by those who oppose the "balanced life" as the best example of a "life that matters."

Invoking Aristotle's argument and remembering the *Iliad* here should lead us to see that the problem of the "balanced life" may be the middle-class, democratic equivalent of the Greek problem of the brief life of sacrificial heroism as opposed to the long life of equable contentment. Most of the people who *do* have a choice in the kind of work they will do and the kind of lives they will lead (and we should always remember that this is a small minority of the people on the globe) will face this problem at one time or another. And the dilemma can be acute, as it was for the student. Even aside from the question of whether such a "balanced life" is possible within our current socioeconomic system, we must ask another question: Is such a life truly one of significance, one that is preferable to a life marked by single-minded devotion to a particular task, talent, cause, or job?

The selections in this chapter are chosen because they offer a variety of perspectives on how we might think about balance in our own lives and as an aspect of the communities within which we live. The path to the balanced life, if that is what one desires, is certainly not laid out in advance; there are no simple roadmaps to follow. However, several of the selections that follow provide images, and some also offer advice, about what balance might look like and how it might be attained. Alongside these selections are others that challenge the aspiration to a balanced life, depicting it as impossible or as less desirable than a life that is focused on important work.

The texts included here are

- a sociological study of the changing conditions of work (Wuthnow)
- a reflection on one couple's efforts to share equally in creative work outside the home and in the care of their family (Miller-McLemore)

- a description of everyday tensions between work and family life (Hochschild)
- an article on two, mutually exclusive ways of being a doctor (Zuger)
- a poem representing a balanced life (Longfellow)
- a chapter from a novel about a man who found a balanced life through immersion within a specific local community (Berry)
- two eulogies of a great statesman offered from very different perspectives, which together suggest a kind of balance
- a challenge to live one's life in an unbalanced, fiercely focused way (Dillard)
- a poem suggesting that a balanced life is impossible if one also seeks distinguished achievement (Yeats)
- an essay on how responding to great social issues demands a different, and difficult, kind of balance (Jane Addams)
- a conversation that places the longing for balance within the context of human finitude (Moyers and Nussbaum).

The first selection describes the economic and cultural landscape upon which our choices will be negotiated. Robert Wuthnow is a sociologist whose work combines survey research, in-depth conversations with ordinary people, and perceptive accounts of larger social changes over time. His reading of the contemporary situation is that most Americans "want it all." They think that they can excel at work, enjoy plenty of leisure time, nurture a happy family, create a comfortable living space for themselves, remain physically fit, cultivate several lasting friendships, volunteer in their communities, and deepen their spiritual lives. However, several features of contemporary society complicate our lives and usually impede the fulfillment of these hopes, according to Wuthnow, citing dual-career families, divorce, longevity, decreasing occupational security, and the growing divide between rich and poor. One result has been a major shift in the typical life cycle, as young adults increasingly postpone making decisions about both family and work. Balance between these two aspects of life is not all Americans mean when they speak of "wanting it all," however. Wuthnow's piece should make us wonder about how much of Americans' difficulties in attaining balance are due not so much to competition between work and love as to their desire to enjoy the high standard of living typified by, as he puts it, "the three-car garage."

Many would say that the choices people must make within this turbulent economic, social, and cultural climate fall with special weight on women. We do not know whether the boyfriend of the pre-med student in our story also rejected a high-status, lucrative profession for the sake of the quality of the life they hoped someday to share. We do know, however, that the pressure on families that makes the balanced life difficult has implications for both fathers and mothers, as well as for their children. In a chapter from her book *Also a Mother: Work and Family as Theological Dilemma*, Bonnie Miller-McLemore describes the reasons, the hopes, the strategies, and the difficulties that have attended the effort she and her husband have made to arrange their lives in ways that allow both of them to pursue interesting careers as well as to care for their three young sons. Doing this, Miller-McLemore insists, requires focused attention to gender, to the ways in which both she and her husband have been socialized into male and female roles that are now deeply internalized. In addition to providing a realistic portrait of one family's attempt at balance, this essay also introduces some insights from feminist thought into our thinking about the balanced life.

The author of the next selection, Arlie Russell Hochschild, is one of those who would argue that the difficulties in attaining the balance for which many people say they long have taken an especially hard toll upon women. One of her studies of the lives of married women who work outside the home demonstrated that most discover that after a hard day's work at the office they must then work a "second shift" in the home, since their spouses are for various reasons unwilling to shoulder their fair share of domestic responsibilities. More recently, Hochschild has made an even more startling and disturbing discovery. Given new management strategies in the workplace, increasing numbers of people, far from seeking a balanced life, now prefer the workplace to the home, escaping to the former to avoid the clamorous burdens of the latter.[2] Since Hochschild realizes that most of the women who work outside the home do so by necessity, her findings raise troubling questions about the conflicts between what people say they hope for and the situations within which they actually live.

The next essay also considers issues of balance by focusing primarily on the workplace. In her portrait of two medical interns, Dr. Abigail Zuger reflects on the character of a young man and a young woman who bring very different personal approaches to their work. One seems more likely to sustain a balanced life than the other, and Zuger's account suggests that the personal approaches we bring to demanding and difficult work, rather than simply the structure of the workplace and economy, can make a big differ-

---

2. Arlie Russell Hochschild, *The Second Shift* (New York: Viking Penguin, 1989), and *The Time Bind: When Work Becomes Home and Home Becomes Work* (New York: Henry Holt, 1997). The selection included in this chapter is based on the research Hochschild did for *The Time Bind*.

ence for those who aspire to a balanced life. Yet at the same time, this essay may raise questions about what may be lost when balance prevails.

Are the obstacles to leading a balanced life really so imposing in modern, post-industrial democracies, or are our appetites and expectations the root of the difficulty? Are our problems in this area primarily social and economic, or are they finally moral and spiritual? Literary portraits of attractive and significant balanced lives are often set in places either far away from the big cities where most people live or long ago when life seemed simpler. Longfellow's memorable portrait of a blacksmith was, after all, set in a nineteenth-century village. And Jayber Crow, the title character in Wendell Berry's novel, finds a life in which work and home seem wholly of a piece with one another only after he returns to a Kentucky village near where he was born and raised and settles into a not-very-lucrative life as a barber. He finds a balanced life when he finally rediscovers a genuine community.

Although Longfellow's blacksmith and Berry's barber may tempt us to think that a balanced life is possible only in worlds we have lost, we might wonder instead whether these portraits manifest basic virtues that one might cultivate anywhere, virtues like simplicity and loyalty to place. As one of the desert monastics of antiquity observed, we can be filled, even fulfilled, either by getting all that we want or by reducing our appetites to the point that whatever we get truly satisfies us. The American people have by and large chosen the first road to the full life. But should we? Loyalty to place, however desirable, is sometimes difficult to maintain, as Wuthnow's essay confirmed. Nevertheless, rootedness in a particular locale may be the one thing most needful for a balanced life. And the locale need not be a small town or an idyllic, pastoral village. It could just as well be a neighborhood in a vast metropolitan area.

Once we begin to think about the importance of place to the project of leading lives that matter, we soon realize how crucially important a sense of place has been to stories about destiny in the Classical tradition and vocation in the Christian tradition. Achilles' alternative destinies were framed in terms of both times and places: a *short* life on the foreign *battlefield* or a *long* life in the *homeland*. And the great call narratives of the Bible typically combine a future task with a summons to a place: Abraham from Ur to Canaan; Moses from Mt. Horeb to Egypt; Jonah from his home to Nineveh. By contrast, according to some contemporary accounts of vocation that draw upon the nuances of the etymology of the term, vocation is the *place* or space where we are stationed, and we are called to respond to the divine summons in *that* place, not somewhere else (see the selection by Bonhoeffer in Part I). Therefore, vocational discernment for some Christians involves primarily the study of how I should live where I am presently stationed (as a student, for example) rather than the discovery of what I should do and where I should go at some point in the future. And beyond these two distinct meanings of place, we might also consider how they relate one to another. For example, in our highly mobile society, some people feel more called to a specific place — for example, to their hometown or to a city or wilderness area they love — than to a specific occupation, and they adjust their work accordingly. Jayber Crow's life in Port William may help us to recognize some of the gifts that can come from sinking deeply into a specific place, in both senses of the word.

The possibility of a balanced life also looks very different if we enlarge the temporal perspective, considering a life *over time* rather than a life at just one of its several stages from youth to old age. As Wuthnow's essay shows, we bring different expectations to what we do at different ages, taking on various commitments, or not, sequentially. A snapshot of a human being's life on just one day is probably not the best way to evaluate that life. If we were to take that snapshot, however, perhaps the best time to take it would be at one's funeral, as survivors begin to assess a life that is finished and can finally be seen as a whole. This is what we glimpse in the eulogies included here, which were delivered at the funeral of Prime Minister Yitzhak Rabin of Israel by two people who knew and loved him in very different ways and from very different perspectives. That one man could win tributes from two such differently related people suggests a life that is balanced, though perhaps not in the way we usually mean that.

Although some of the readings in this chapter show how challenging it is to lead a balanced life, most of the ones up to this point honor the desire to do so and even suggest ways to pursue this desire. Yet, as we have already seen in Aristotle, not all agree that balance is what characterizes a good life. Indeed, some argue against this aspiration, advocating what they see as greater goods or insisting that those who think they can avoid the hard choices that so often tip the balance are deluded. Even if a balanced life is possible, the next four authors in this chapter believe, it may not be preferable to a life that includes extraordinary achievement in one theater of human endeavor or that responds to a great social need or a powerful vocational passion. Their voices force us to return to the desire to lead lives that *matter*, lives that are significant as well as good. Perhaps we should sacrifice some goodness for the sake of significance? Perhaps, if we are committed to a great cause, say, finding a vaccine for polio, we should be excused for neglecting our children? Should we automatically forgive the productive musical genius his thoughtless ineptitude in other areas of his life? Once we add the ambition for extraordinary achievement to the question of the possibility and relative merits of a balanced life over an unbalanced one, questions multiply and become more difficult.

The essay by Annie Dillard, "Living Like Weasels," would seem to offer encouragement to the musical genius, the great scientist, or, indeed, anyone who has an outstanding gift or love for just one thing. She does not explore the moral compromises that may or may not be made by those who embrace the fiercely focused approach she commends. However, her essay seems to disparage those of us who withhold any of our energy and attention from the one thing we love most because we wish to do other things as well.

William Butler Yeats's poem, "The Choice," explores some of the consequences of pursuing one's work with the kind of devotion Dillard seems to commend. We must choose "perfection of the life, or of the work," the poet seems to insist. We cannot have both. Perhaps an example of what he meant can be found in the selection about the two medical interns. One of them seems to be an excellent doctor, among the very best, but she appears to have had no life outside of her work. The other seems to lead a balanced life, but his teacher finds his devotion to medicine falling short of genuine excellence. We might wonder whether our pre-med student would have changed her mind had she read Yeats's poem alongside Dr. Zuger's article. She might have seen that one can be a reasonably capable doctor and still enjoy a balanced life. On the other hand, she might have had the highest standards for herself in whatever she chose to do. In that case, she might not have been able to lead the life of the male medical student featured in the article with a good conscience and with any sense of self-respect. Should we then think of the balanced life well led as a relatively mediocre one, or should we think of it as representing another kind of excellence, equally as worthy of praise as the excellence of the person who has chosen "perfection of the work"?

Jane Addams provides us with a different way of thinking about the whole matter by setting individual choice in the context of the great social movements of one's time. Writing a century ago, Addams believed that all people, men and women, should seek to lead lives of significance, lives that press beyond personal satisfaction and family sustenance to a public-spirited vision of the common good. For her, significance was a social value as much as an individual one, and she hoped that whole families would someday respond to "the social claim" to participate in great movements such as eliminating urban poverty. While she understood that young people often have to choose what to do in the face of considerable pressure from families who disagree, she dared to challenge them to answer to the summons to social engagement, which she saw as the higher priority.

Addams was a great social reformer who would become the first woman to win the Nobel Peace Prize, and it is not surprising that she hoped the conflict between family and "the social claim" would ultimately be resolved by changes in society. Martha Nussbaum, the philosopher whose ideas emerge in the conversation that ends this chapter, is less sanguine about the capacity of human beings to resolve this conflict. While making it clear that she supports social changes that would make it incrementally easier for people to balance work and family, she insists that no amount of social engineering will ever get to the root of the problem: we are finite beings.

All of us must sacrifice some goods for other goods every day, Nussbaum argues. We cannot be at our faculty meeting and at our daughter's piano recital at the same time. We are in this way like some of the tragic figures in the Greek tragedies. Instead of deluding ourselves into thinking that we can have it all, instead of pretending that a truly balanced life is possible, we should face unflinchingly the inherently tragic structure of our lives.

Although Nussbaum's vision may seem discouraging at first, she actually wants to encourage us to live in such a way that "it becomes a possibility that tragedy can happen to you." To withhold oneself from a range of deep and caring attachments would be to miss what is truly important in life. For the Greeks and for Nussbaum, the suffering experienced when human beings fail to balance their multiple commitments deepens their awareness of their attachments and, in a sense, ushers them into a more expansive understanding of what it means to be human. Suffering and failure, then, are not arguments against the aspiration to lead a balanced life. Nor, for that matter, are they arguments against centering one's life around the passionate pursuit of excellence in one thing, which will surely include suffering and failure of its own.

ROBERT WUTHNOW

"The Changing Nature of Work in the United States: Implications for Vocation, Ethics, and Faith"

The experiences of Americans who enter the labor force today are quite different from those of their parents and grandparents. In the essay below, Robert Wuthnow, who teaches sociology and directs the Center for the Study of American Religion at Princeton University, identifies ten trends that have reshaped the American economy and the patterns of employment it supports. According to Wuthnow, economic change has been accompanied by changes in how Americans think about their work and its place within the lives they hope to lead. In particular, he identifies a growing tendency for Americans to "want it all," even though the persistent uncertainty of most people's economic situation may make this wish difficult to satisfy. Is "wanting it all" the same thing as wanting to lead a balanced life? If not, how are these two desires related?

Wuthnow especially notes the emergence of a period of prolonged uncertainty about work and interpersonal commitments during young adulthood. He seems sympathetic to those who postpone making major life decisions during these years. But does this mean that increasing numbers of people can begin to lead lives that matter only in their thirties? Must people be settled in one place with one special friend into one life-long career before they can lead significant lives? Or can the flexibility and mobility Wuthnow describes make it easier to devote oneself to people and causes that are wider in scope and importance than is possible for those with settled commitments?

From *The Cresset* 67, no. 1 (Michaelmas [September] 2003): 5-13.

The question of trends in the nature of work is daunting. The long term effects of urbanization and the declining proportion of the population who farm or who are engaged in animal husbandry (noting even the rarity with which such terms as "animal husbandry" are now mentioned), and the effects of such technological innovations as the invention of the steam engine, the moldboard plow, electricity, the automobile, and the computer at various moments in our history are monumental. But for the sake of keeping our discussion within manageable limits, I will focus only on developments since the last half of the twentieth century and highlight fewer than a dozen of the most significant ways in which the American labor force has changed and what that means for us as we think about vocation.

First is the changing gender composition of the labor force. The question, "Do you work?" would have made little sense to women throughout most of human history. Women worked long hours tending crops or livestock, cooking and cleaning, raising children, and often taking their place alongside men in cotton mills, print shops, and retail stores. But in recent memory, this question has come to mean, "Are you gainfully employed in the paid labor force?" And, as we know, the answer for a growing proportion of American women over the past half century has been "yes." Figures compiled by the US Census Bureau show that in 1940, only 28 percent of American women were in the labor force, a figure that rose to 37 percent during World War II, but then fell back to about 30 percent immediately after the war; it rose gradually during the 1950s, but reached only 38 percent in 1960; after this, there has been a steady increase: to 43 percent of women in 1970; 52 percent in 1980; 58 percent in 1990; and an estimated 61 percent in 2000. Or, viewed another way, the American workforce in 1940 was composed of about three men for every woman, whereas now it is composed almost equally of women and men.

Why did this trend in female labor participation take place? One hypothesis is that it was a response to the feminist movement, and especially the writings and speeches of early (not suffragette, but 1950s and 60s) feminist thinkers, such as Kate Millett and Betty Friedan, who decried the gendered stigma that encouraged talented women to stay at home rather than pursuing careers. In retrospect, an alternative explanation appears more plausible, that is that the involvement of women in the paid labor force increased as a result of the shift away from heavy industry and manufacturing (which had shifted labor toward men, even more so than in the agricultural sector) to light industry, clerical work, to, as it was generally described, a service economy.

That is, jobs opened up for women as secretaries and clerks, in such semi-professions as hospital work and bookkeeping, and in the professions, starting with nursing and teaching and then spreading into law, medicine, engineering, and science. As mental labor replaced hard physical labor, women were able to enter the labor force in greater numbers. Indeed, there was high demand for their work and, in turn, the additional family wages they earned then spurred the economy by increasing the capacity of American families to spend money on labor-saving home devices and other consumer products.

But there is one important caveat to this interpretation. It is sometimes read as suggesting that white collar women — indeed, white women in the professions — led the way, as bright girls went to college and then pioneered women's work in the labor force. This view reflects the social class bias of those who have been in positions to write the history of women's work. More careful scholarship suggests that it was actually working class women — and indeed, minorities, especially African-American women — who were the true pioneers in women's inclusion in the labor force. This point could be shown with data from the US Census.

But let me illustrate it with data from a different source — data that I will want to come back to later in considering some implications of the changing nature of work. These data are from national surveys of twelfth graders conducted annually between 1976 and 1996. These teenagers were asked whether or not their mothers worked in the labor force outside the home. Among white teenagers there was a sharp increase: from 59 percent in 1976 who said their mothers worked to 81 percent in 1996.

But even at the end of this trend, the figure for white teens was below the figure for black teens. Already in 1976, 84 percent of black teens said their mothers were in the labor force, and this proportion rose to 91 percent by 1996. This should not surprise us. More often, women have worked when they had to, when their lower income families needed additional money, rather than when they simply chose to work. But, as we shall see, there are also some important implications associated with these different trends.

A second trend is the growing number of two income or "dual career" families. This trend is clearly related to the first trend, the growing inclusion of women in the paid labor force, because many women in the labor force are married, but they are not identical. This second trend is associated with two important changes in what social scientists call "the household economy." One change is that two-income families have higher family incomes than single-income families do. Indeed, some economists argue that the higher standard of living enjoyed by middle-class Americans in recent decades is almost completely attributable to the increasing number of two income families. And the economy has adjusted to this change, so that now two incomes are required in order for middle-class families to enjoy the standard of living to which they feel entitled: vacations, larger houses, second or third cars, daycare, college educations for their children, and the like.

The other change in household economy is that to a much greater extent than a generation ago, parents spend time in the workplace. Juliet Schor, in *The Overworked American*, has calculated that the average individual now spends nearly a month more on the job than in 1970. And if both spouses are considered, the fact that only one used to be in the labor force means that total parental time on the job has risen from about 35 to 40 hours a week to 75 or 80 hours a week. Thus, family schedules become more complicated and women increasingly experience what Arlie Hochschild has termed "the second shift" (in a book by this title), working all day outside the home and then returning home to the household chores and childrearing tasks.

A third trend is *the increasing proportion of single parents in the work force*. The divorce rate is currently about twice as high as it was in the 1950s and the proportion of divorced people in the US is about four times what it was then. More people are remaining single and yet having children, as well.

The rising divorce rate is a topic that would require separate treatment, but one plausible explanation (which bears mentioning here) is that the increasing inclusion of women in the labor force was partly responsible for the increasing number of people who became divorced — not, as some observers have suggested, because women found it hard to work and be good wives, but because having a job gave women a source of income independent from their husband's and thus made it possible to escape from an abusive or unsatisfactory marriage.

Whatever the case, a substantial number of young people, especially women, can now expect to be in the labor force as single parents. This means juggling work and parenting responsibilities on one's own. Except for wealthy or upper-class women who can afford daycare, it usually means a cut in earnings and fewer economic resources for their children. And, in recognition of these possibilities, more young people are postponing marriage and childrearing, or are cohabiting instead of marrying, as ways of avoiding some of the negative economic consequences of being a single parent. But for employers, the presence of single parents is often an economic boon because they can pay people less, knowing they are desperate to retain their jobs. As a personnel manager for a large company in Texas told me one time, "I try to hire divorced moms. They have to be dependable."

These considerations bring us to a fourth trend, which is *the increasing number of Americans who work in temporary positions and whose work experiences are governed by what has euphemistically become known as "outsourcing."* I wrote about this trend in my *Loose Connections,* in which I argued that the workplace (like other social institutions) has become more porous in response to changing market conditions. A porous workplace is the opposite of the stable, bureaucratic style of organization that social scientists studied in the first half of the twentieth century. Those organizations trained employees, supervised them carefully, and expected the good ones to stay, gradually moving up the hierarchy. That commitment can be costly in a rapidly changing economy, as Japanese firms discovered in the 1980s.

Today's firms minimize their fixed costs. They keep inventories low, using information technology to do so; they subcontract, rather than bringing functions under their own administrative umbrella; and they hire temp workers or rely heavily on consultants. Adjunct faculty in colleges and universities are a good example. People in temporary positions and with limited term contracts give organizations greater flexibility in responding to changing market conditions. These workers often do not accumulate retirement benefits and may not even receive health coverage. A growing proportion of the labor force can expect to work all or at least part of their careers in such temporary positions.

Along with temporary work and outsourcing, we need to mention a fifth trend: *the shift from work organized around a single, lifetime career to having multiple careers during one's lifetime.* In a national study I conducted a few years ago, I asked people who were currently in the labor force how many different lines of work they had been in since they entered the labor force as an adult. Among men and women past the age of 45, only 21 percent had been in just one line of work; 79 percent had been in at least two different lines of work; 55 percent had been in three different lines of work, and 31 percent had been in four different lines of work. I will talk about some of the implications of this kind of shifting careers in a moment, but for now, let me just say that it creates uncertainty in planning for a career, uncertainty in deciding how to invest scarce dollars on schooling, and uncertainty about what one's income may be and where one may live. It creates emotional difficulties for people as they make major career moves, and it often requires additional training, continuing education, and emotional and intellectual flexibility.

The likelihood of multiple careers is increased by a sixth trend: *the extended longevity of the population, and the increased health of the older population,* which in turn affect the age of retirement and, thus, the chances of people working longer, pursuing so-called second or third careers, or working part-time or as volunteers in later life. Since 1970, in the US average life expectancy at birth has increased by seven years for males (from 67.1 years to 74.1 years) and by five years for females (from 74.7 years to 79.7 years). Thus, among people who are currently age 21, the average male can expect to live to age 75 and the average female to age 80. For those who retire at age 65, then, there will be ten years for men and 15 years for women when they are not in the labor force, yet for the majority, their health will be good enough to remain active.

Knowing this may not have much of an effect on decisions about work when people are in college or in their twenties. But it will increasingly shape their thinking as they age. Their longevity demands hard choices between immediate consumption and saving for retirement, between saving for themselves and investing in their children's lives or education, and between working past age 65 and cultivating other interests.

Some people work harder and longer at their jobs, feeling they must do so in order to pay for their retirement and feeling that they will have opportunities later to do other things. For these people, as Robert Putnam has shown, volunteering and community service may be postponed only to increase dramatically after they retire.

Other people anticipate retiring earlier and think about pursuing second careers. Clergy, for instance, are increasingly being recruited from those in their forties or fifties who go to seminary at that age and then begin a second career that will take them to retirement.

A seventh trend is what some observers have termed *the shift to a "post-materialist" economy*. Ronald Inglehart, a political scientist at the University of Michigan, claims that most middle class people in the United States, and indeed in all industrialized countries, now live in sufficient abundance to have their basic needs for food, shelter, and other economic necessities fulfilled. As a result, people have more time, money, and freedom to pursue higher values, such as personal fulfillment, serving others, or expressing concern about the environment.

Other observers, such as economist Robert Fogel, suggest that this postmaterialist economy may result in a new spiritual awakening. Of course all of this is speculation, and it does not persuade me, at least not when I remember that spiritual awakenings are more often prompted by hard times rather than the soft life. Still, it is worth remembering that work is now conducted for most people in the United States in an atmosphere of abundance.

The post-materialist economy is associated with another trend (number eight), which involves higher education, the professions, and, once again, the service economy, *the increasingly older age at which individuals enter the work force*. This trend has been mentioned so often that we need not dwell on it. Young people now seldom enter the labor force full time, as my father did, after finishing eighth grade, or as my mother did, after finishing high school.

While there are opportunities for part-time jobs during school, usually to earn spending money, and so-called entry-level or first jobs that one may take after college to buy time before settling into a regular career, it is more common for people to postpone entering careers until their mid to late 20s. The expansion of professions and the service economy also means that people can choose careers in which their values, perhaps even their religious values, are expressed — as in helping the needy or overcoming social problems.

In emphasizing affluence and higher education, though, we should not ignore a ninth trend, namely, *the growing divide between rich and poor and, more generally, the continuing if not worsening condition of the underemployed, marginally employed, and unemployed.* Economists differ on these topics, but most agree that since about 1980 the net worth of people in the top 1 percent or so of the population has increased much more substantially than that of the rest of the population. At the bottom, as many as 20 to 25 percent of families continue to live in poverty. Public welfare provision, since the welfare reform legislation of 1996, has diminished. But many families with one or more members in the labor force earn the minimum hourly wage and thus are unable to afford housing, medical care, or adequate food. Decreasing unionization and poorly paid jobs in the service economy, from health workers to fast food chain employees, have contributed to the problem.

Finally, as a tenth trend, *the American labor force has become increasingly diverse — ethnically, racially, and religiously — as a result of significant immigration over the past three or four decades.* Since 1965, when immigration laws were amended to make coming to the United States easier, approximately 22 million new immigrants have been added to the population. This number is nearly as large as that between 1890 and 1920, which we regard as the most formative period in US history as far as ethnic and religious diversity is concerned. Even more consequential now is the fact that much of the recent immigration extends beyond the Christian and Jewish communities. . . .

One of the clearest implications of these trends is what I have termed in some of my writing as "wanting it all." Americans want it all: jobs (two jobs in the case of couples) that support a comfortable middle-class suburban lifestyle involving a house not only with a white picket fence but also with a three-car garage; jobs that are also personally fulfilling, meaningful, and relatively free of stress; a warm community of friends in their neighborhood or church with whom to share dinner parties and go bowling; lovely, well-mannered children who, as Garrison Keillor says of the children in Lake Wobegon, are "all above average"; and lots of free time in which to pursue their hobbies and serve the needy.

We are the products of what social scientists sometimes call a "revolution of rising expectations." We want it all. And we know that more is within our reach, at least if we are young, because we are better educated than our parents, subject to less discrimination if we are women or people of color, and securely situated within an economic safety net provided by our parents' savings, the government, or our own earning capacity.

Little wonder that it has become harder to choose and settle into a vocation. A job has to do much more than pay the bills and provide for our children's future or our retirement. It has to be just right for us, appealing to our interests, making use of our talents, keeping us from being bored, and giving us wonderful people with whom to associate. Little wonder that people change jobs, and whole careers, more often than in the past. A utopia like this is almost certainly going to be just beyond our grasp. And little wonder that people increasingly find it difficult to settle into a job or career until they are thirty or thirty-five.

That is perhaps too critical, though. Another way to look at the present work environment is that it is one of incredible uncertainty. For people who came of age during the 1950s or 60s, it was possible to anticipate, and thus prepare for, the career in which one would remain for a lifetime. An aspiring high school student with a knack for chemistry planned to become a chemist, majored in chemistry in college, perhaps did graduate work, and then got a job at DuPont or Bristol-Meyers that lasted for the next forty years.

That same person probably married right after college, dragged his housewife spouse along to Delaware or New Jersey, and raised 2.5 children on his salary as a chemist. For people coming of age today, those kinds of certainties are no longer present. Chemistry's topics change from year to year, and there may be no job openings in chemistry at all — despite six or eight years of training. Or, even if there are jobs, it may be hard to know whether one's aptitude lies in chemistry or in medicine or in teaching or in music.

Dating is less certain in this environment, too, partly because one knows about the high rates of divorce, and partly because the potential challenge of juggling two careers may lead a person to postpone serious relationships until his or her job prospects are pinned down. Add to this the uncertainty of where one will live, how much moving around may be required, whether there will be layoffs, and questions about sexuality, AIDS, health, compatibility, religion, values, and friendship, and the situation indeed becomes incredibly uncertain. Some observers, in fact, liken the results to "post-traumatic stress syndrome." People become immobilized by the shock of it all. Or they adopt a risk-averse strategy of coping. They refuse to make long-term or deep commitments, knowing that it is more rational in an uncertain job or marriage market to cultivate lots of shallow commitments so that one can move when the situation demands. Flexibility, rather than fidelity, becomes the watchword. . . .

BONNIE MILLER-McLEMORE

"Generativity Crises of My Own"

Bonnie Miller-McLemore teaches practical theology and pastoral care at Vanderbilt University. Her interest in "generativity" has roots in her study of the psychologist Erik Erikson, who used this term to describe the stage of human development in which an adult engages in promoting the well-being of future generations, whether through care of one's own offspring or through contributions to the larger society. As the mother of three sons as well as a productive scholar and teacher, Miller-McLemore was troubled by the "either/or" — work or children? — that so often frames how women understand and embrace generativity, an issue she believes has tremendous though less obvious implications for men as well.

In this passage from her book *Also a Mother: Work and Family as Theological Dilemma* (1994), Miller-McLemore reports honestly on the ways in which she and her husband have struggled to balance their love of their work with their love of their children and one another. No one could say that she makes this balancing act sound easy! Yet she and her husband appear to be firmly committed to persisting in their often lonely efforts to share equally in both creative work and family nurture, dimensions of life they take to be important for women and men alike. Why does Miller-McLemore give so much attention to gender and what she sees as its distortions in our society as she tells her story?

From Bonnie Miller-McLemore, *Also a Mother: Work and Family as Theological Dilemma* (Nashville: Abingdon Press, 1994), pp. 113-127.

Protected by the hallowed halls of learning, I could go through the motions of acquiring the credentials and sustain the demand for equality with my male peers. Once beyond those college walls, the realities were bleak. I did not see many relationships or work situations that embodied equality and a full life. I knew few stories that could serve as models for constructing a new identity as a working woman, or for determining alternative values. Few men seemed to feel the strain of value-laden questions about marriage and children. I did not hear many of them asking, How will I combine work and family; and which is more important now? Elite, isolated, age-restricted, child-free educational institutions could pretend to be nonsexist and gender-free. The rest of society was certainly not, and in more cases than I liked to admit, did not even bother pretending.

I joined the long history of "thousands of women" before me by beginning my life with the same question: Must I choose? Initially, according to [Nadya] Aisenberg and [Mona] Harrington, most refuse to choose, or even refuse to believe that such a choice is necessary. Then they create a vast variety of strategies to prove it. Aware of the paucity of cultural models, but naively distancing myself from the effort it would take, I held on to the two scripts: the picture of myself as a wife and mother and the relatively new picture of myself pursuing the kinds of achievements previously reserved for men. When I embarked upon graduate education a year after completing my college degree, my intent was clear: I wanted a Ph.D., and I wanted the sort of intimate, serious relationship that might eventuate in marriage. I carefully refrained from admitting either intention. Many who would have endorsed the one would not have liked the other.

My path since, a relationship which did lead to marriage, and graduate work that led to a Ph.D., appears steady. This misrepresents the inner turmoil, the overt conflicts, and the insidious veering and tacking. Role reversal, or taking turns with chores or job moves, proved to be shallow solutions. These strategies simply disguised the ways in which roles do not easily reverse, and taking turns seldom happens easily or fairly in complex lives. Even working out the petty details of an equal distribution of the domestic tasks proved to be a bigger challenge than either my husband Mark or I had anticipated. Dividing household chores, long before children complicated the workload, is an illustrative example of the unexpected cognitive dissonance and emotional discord we incurred because of our shared commitment to gender justice.

Living in the shadow of resilient rules about roles and tasks, I had to let go of an irrational but insidious guilt because I was not cleaning, cooking, and otherwise ordering the home, and suppress anger when friends and family praised Mark for his "extra" work and told me "how lucky" I was. (Imagine someone telling him how lucky *he* was!) He had his own share of grievances. He also worked in a world that continued to predicate its rewards upon the assumption that someone, a woman, was at home doing the wash, that resisted the idea that he, a man, might have such work to do. The strength of this discord, and the tenacity of conventional expectations within heterosexual marriage, is particularly apparent when set beside the contrasting strategies of same-sexed couples. Gay and lesbian couples often resist assigning either person the role of homemaker or economic provider. Moreover, they have long known the difficulties of sustaining an enduring mutual partnership in a society which is even less supportive of them than of heterosexual couples. As biblical scholar L. William Countryman argues, "If there are useful models to be had [for egalitarian partnerships], they will probably be found among [gay and lesbian] couples."

The cognitive dissonance and emotional discord in the household are not unrelated to the kind of discord experienced in the workplace. Despite good intentions and the changes that have occurred, people still feel uncomfortable when women assume positions of authority on par with men at work, when they assert divergent opinions in leadership roles and then ask for maternity leave, or, more to the point, when men ask for paternity leave, as my husband tried to do. How can we explain the resistance to changing these scripts and moving toward a model of shared opportunities for self-fulfillment and nurture of others, for both women and men? . . .

Gender distinctions, however distorted and unjust, remain a backbone of social order, undergirding not just society's reproductive arrangements, but more plainly, the way people see and understand the world. People and institutions have a heavy investment in perpetuating these distinctions. Ambiguity in gender identity, from mothers in the workplace to transsexuality, is amazingly "difficult to tolerate," observes Cynthia Fuchs Epstein in *Deceptive Distinctions.* As the movie *The Crying Game* proves so powerfully, people are terribly disturbed when known gender categories are disrupted. They are uncomfortable with the inconsistency, the lack of clarity, and the impossibilities of closure. Although adults learn far more sophisticated ways than do children to camouflage their uneasiness when a young father arrives at a preschool tea, and his wife comes and talks about her profession, they are just as uncomfortable. In the end, Epstein remarks, society tends to "punish those who deviate" from the general practice.

More complicated trials came when our children arrived. These trials test the boundaries of our imagination and stamina. They test our commitment to democratic values in our relationship and to the priority we place on family life in general. . . .

Caring for children consumes more energy than most people acknowledge. "Consider the facts," urges Virginia Woolf. "First there are nine months before the baby is born. Then the baby is born. Then there are three or four months spent in feeding the baby. After the baby is fed there are certainly five years spent in playing with the baby. You cannot, it seems, let children run about the streets. It is not a 'pleasant' sight." Woolf does not mention the unpleasant sights of the later years, such as weathering the adolescent storms or launching children into their adult lives. The tasks do not end as readily as some suppose.

Most people cannot fathom the facts about children until they happen. Cultural images, like the common picture in obstetrical offices of a mother dressed in white lace, beatifically cradling an acquiescent infant, do not help. The clutter of children's paraphernalia and their unscheduled interruptions in the home of my midwife turned out to be a far more realistic portrayal. A mother of two, Mary Guerrera Congo, a "feministically critical Catholic," recounts her saga:

> I also had not foreseen that, while becoming a parent would strengthen the trust and tie I shared with my husband, it would also erode our relationship as we both suffered exhaustion and frustration . . . within the bonds and responsibilities of parenthood. . . .
>
> I had not foreseen that my sacrifice of energy and time to parenting would result in a continually widening gap between my own ability to advance in a financially sustaining career and the comparable ability of my husband and some of our single women friends. . . .
>
> I was repeatedly frustrated in my attempts to "go back to work." I found it required constant reassessment of my priorities. The very ground beneath me seemed to shift and then shift again and again, as I tried to balance my work, my energy, my confidence, my own sense of purpose and direction, and of course the child-care needs of my children. What I finally have found is that trying to weave mothering together with work is an ongoing and nagging and unresolved puzzle in my life. . . .
>
> I had not anticipated that grappling with how to parcel myself out among my new responsibilities would finally demand of me a total reassessment of my identity, my talents, my strengths and weaknesses, and of all my relationships. I never dreamt that this reassess-

ment would require of me nothing less than the clearest truth about my deepest and most protected feelings and hurts.

As Guerrera Congo implies, becoming a parent requires nothing less than the clearest truth about one's deepest values. A person's self-concept and life commitments shift dramatically when children enter the picture. Robbie Davis-Floyd contends that pregnancy is perhaps the most "overlooked life-crisis rite of passage" in American society, thus denying people an informed awareness of its powerful transformative potential. According to theologian Penelope Washbourn, this stage of life raises "fundamental religious questions" about the meaning of life and one's place within it, and about what is most important, valuable, and holy.

Not only has the import of this stage been denied and often lost, the existential questions it raises have become more complex. As Guerrera Congo testifies, parenthood is a social construction under siege. With minimal institutional and ideological support to answer its complex, value-laden questions, people enter it at their own risk. For both my husband and me, childbirth pressed us to consider a generativity conflict that Erikson had not considered — how to integrate productivity in our work lives with procreativity in our family and community life. It was not a matter of "generativity vs. stagnation" and boredom. Far from it. It was a question of "generativity vs. fragmentation" and exhaustion.

Today the personal and the political is nowhere "experienced more powerfully than in the practice of mothering," Sally Purvis observes. Before our first son, I could compartmentalize work and love, expecting equal treatment at work and establishing an egalitarian partnership in private life that seldom impinged directly upon the world of work. Upon becoming parents, a personal commitment to fairness in the home and to the valued priorities of the home could no longer remain private. Suddenly, our individual home-based commitments and egalitarian standards disrupted our work lives, at times taking both of us away from work and causing us to ask for certain allowances. Definitions of equality at work, based upon an undifferentiated similarity between men and women, and predicated on the contributions of a full-time housekeeper, had to expand to include the desires and diversities of child bearing and rearing, and the increased demands of domestic maintenance. . . .

Almost immediately, between Mark and me, the physiological disparities of bearing and nursing children necessitated a reappraisal of the mutuality internal to our relationship. However, these differences did not lessen our commitment to a mutuality and partnership. Nor did the differences lessen my desire or need for "a work of one's own." Rather, it intensified the pursuit and began to teach us the complicated lessons of the arduous practice of a mutuality that embodies more fully the tension inherent in the biblical commandment to "love your neighbor as yourself" (Mark 12:31). In retrospect, the period of acute physical difference was relatively brief and gave way to the trickier problems of socialized gender differences. This phase did prove a worthy testing ground for the breadth and depth of our commitment to a joint participation in parenting.

It is important to name, rather than ignore these difficulties of achieving equality in child bearing by a simple act of will — not to excuse or rationalize the conflicts, but to ameliorate and work through them. As Mary Becker observes, it is silence that perpetuates inequality, not the recognition of the intensity of maternal involvement in the pains and pleasures of their children. "Failing to discuss how difficult it is to equalize the emotional attachment of mothers and fathers to their children will inevitably cause continuing inequality." Only by recognizing this can we move toward equalizing paternal involvement.

We discovered that the mutuality we wanted to maintain could not be spelled out as easily as kitchen duty but required a measured and steady response to the continually emerging, evolving needs of our children for love, and our needs to love ourselves as parents and otherwise. Actualizing this mutuality amidst the flux and disparities between us required compensation for the person who had given too much. It required flexibility, improvisation, and support. Daily, we tried to find ways to balance the inequities of the demands that my physical proximity created for both of us, and to build avenues for common participation often with little outside encouragement or support. This sometimes meant intentionally inverting and overriding what seemed our natural impulses. When it seemed right and necessary, it even meant overriding the real physical inclinations of the "gut" with an affirmation of the deeper realities which our socialization had denied us — Mark's physical experience of the lure of our children and my experience of a desire for creative work. . . .

Creative work involves self-absorption and sometimes extensive self-concern, and it rests on the support of someone else's nurture. Nurturing work involves a certain self-giving and sometimes self-sacrifice. Above all, Mark and I knew that at some level, each of us wanted and needed comparable measures of both to keep our mutuality honest. We improvised until we found ways to make this happen in a fair way, in response to the needs of our children and our own needs.

In other words, something more than a "revision of household rules and the alternation of household roles" is required for mutuality in contemporary families. William Countryman argues that complex moral and theological shifts also are necessary:

> It involves new understandings of manliness and womanliness that can come about only with some pain and anxiety as well as some sense of liberation and joy. If the husband gives up the image of himself as sole ruler . . . he must also give up its spiritual equivalent — the image of himself as the family's unique sacrificial sustainer, isolated in his moral strength and grandeur. If the wife gives up being the servant of all . . . she must also give up the spiritual vision of herself as the one who gives all for others' good. . . . None of this will be easy.

Learning new moral and religious values and virtues is never easy.

As the work of Carol Gilligan has suggested, for this familial rearrangement to occur, it is critical that a woman recognize her love of self — that it is legitimate to consider the interests of the self and that each self must claim a certain measure of moral agency. For men, it is not recognition of rights or choice — concepts that many men take for granted — but intimacy or a significant personal relationship that moves them to higher levels of moral development. We discovered that sometimes it was essential to put my desire for and commitment to creative work on a par with — heaven forbid — the needs of the infant. Recognizing that Mark had a need and obligation to engage in the moral practice of birth and attachment was equally important. Particularly when the larger public was not supportive, we depended heavily upon the support of each other and the reciprocal affirmation of our children.

Pregnancy and care of children present an opportunity to realize, perhaps for the first time, that sacrifice — responsiveness to others, and autonomy — responsiveness to oneself — are not mutually exclusive. To consider caring for a baby, or to choose between bearing or aborting a fetus within one's own body, forces women to differentiate and consider how they care for themselves. Like some of the women in Gilligan's study, I found that giving birth and considering Woolf's "facts" of child care moved me from a stage in which considering one's own needs and desires is equated with selfishness, to a stage in which to act responsibly toward myself and my needs was to further my ability to respond to the needs of others. We struggled to learn the difficult lessons of loving our children as we loved ourselves.

Through many battles, toils, and snares, we have haltingly come to a give-and-take that includes transitional moments of self-giving and self-fulfillment for both of us. Conflicts between us are characterized by an angry threat by one party that we should list how much we have done, and each of us is always sure we have done more than the other. However, despite the strife and, optimally, the recognition that there is too much to do, we know this to be a more genuine mutuality than alternative models of woman's love of others and man's self-love. In the end, we have never followed through on our threat to list our labors, but some kind of mental list of checks and balances is actually necessary; as is over-gracious recognition of how much these labors actually demand. . . .

So what are the rudimentary contours of the life that my husband and I have resurrected in what often has felt like a vacuum? The experience of becoming a parent has had a transformative impact upon our thinking and acting. Traditional solutions that others have used, such as prioritizing work over family, or family over work, or making a sharp separation between work and family, simply did not work. Motherhood heightened my resentment of women's lack of real power in a male-defined work force, at the same time that it heightened my awareness of the low status of mothers and children.

Neither of us has simply moved in some straightforward, chronological fashion from one identity to another, from youth to adult, unmarried to married, spouse to parent. Rather, we experience what one study calls "role proliferation," a coterminous, continuous, and additive combination of multiple but disparate roles (domestic, occupational, marital, parental), to each of which one has equally high commitments. In addition, I feel what Celia Gilbert describes, in her own experiences as a working mother — the cultural "taboo on work as powerful as the proscription against incest" — which forbids her to admit that she loves her work as much as she loves her husband and children. Conversely, there are equally powerful taboos which forbid my husband to love his children as much as his work, or to spend comparable time with them.

But we asked for it: We entered reproductive and child-care decisions with a high regard for the priority of a relational partnership, and with different standards for ourselves within that partnership. While traditional women's work brings little recognition, much of it is integrally valuable, particularly that which pertains to attending to the development of a child or another person, and to securing networks of community support. Putting this value into words that are not saccharine or superficial is a more difficult task.

Contrary to a public world, where the model male adult labors at work but spends little time with children, we find ourselves more child-centered than the work world usually expects or assumes. During many weeks, we fall short of the standard "forty hours" and add hours with our children. We miss meetings, decline responsibilities, forsake job opportunities, forfeit certain promotions; we leave work for parent-teacher conferences, special programs, field trips. On the other hand, we find ourselves less child-centered than the cookies-and-milk images of child rearing and, on another level, more demanding of our children and their resilient resources, which social mores also underestimate. Cookies are store-bought, baked at odd hours, or more likely, our kids drag their own stools over to the stove and "pitch in," to borrow one of my friend's favorite family phrases, to make them, or even the main course.

Is not the narrative of the "pitch in" family more wholesome than the cookies-and-milk narrative, even if it conjures up images of overt conflicts, rather than temporary tranquility? Embodied in this pithy phrase is the idea that given love, children also need daily exercise at the practice of loving others as they love themselves, and this means a family system in which their pitching in is also essential to the family's functioning. . . .

While not alone in our struggle over the values that guide our work and child rearing, we often feel like strangers in a strange land. Perhaps this is partly because we live in the midst of a more conservative community in the Chicago suburbs. Many of our neighbors — mostly the men — work in the corporate sector with its higher incomes, while both of us work in the service sector with lower clerical incomes. From a position on the outer peripheries of a white upper-middle-class suburb, I observe a struggle to retain the status quo that has been forfeited by the working and underclass. Mothers who have chosen not to work juggle school programs, extracurricular activities, and car pools. Even if only 8 percent of U.S. mothers and fathers maintain the 1950s arrangement of breadwinner-homemaker, most school and work schedules still assume such a division, and many enclaves of convention, like the one in which we live, would like to preserve it.

Alternative models of shared responsibility are still very fresh. Their failure is predicted by conventional society and their success lacks careful articulation. Although religious congregations offer potential, there are few forums to consider the changes. In the words of one of my colleagues, when time and energy are at a premium, "friendships are the first to go." So are genuine public conversations. . . .

The lack of support goes still further. It is hard to sustain equal regard between us in a society that does not recognize the importance of equal regard, the values of domestic labor, or the necessary dependencies and demands of family life, whether raising children, caring for the impaired, or providing for the aging. People involved in these acts cannot sustain the necessary self-giving without the help of supportive public structures.

These reflections raise a more important question for me. If I am finding it hard to adjudicate the demands of work and family life, what about those with less flexible steady jobs, fewer and poorer day-care options, lower irregular incomes, or abusive, destructive family situations, and minimal support systems? All people face pressures in a society that provides little support for the intricacies of combining the generative activities of family with the demands of work. But the penalties weigh most heavily upon those who do not have the means to survive. The greatest costs may indeed be for the children of this generation and generations to come, who grow up in a world that allows little time or place for them.

ARLIE RUSSELL HOCHSCHILD

"There's No Place Like Work"

The titles of two best-selling books by sociologist Arlie Russell Hochschild — *The Time Bind* (1997) and *The Second Shift* (1989) — crystallize her sense of the difficulties faced by contemporary workers who also seek to sustain a good family life. The research presented in this selection is based on her study of the lives of those who worked for a corporation she calls "Amerco." Hochschild notes uncertainties in family life not unlike (and surely not unrelated to) the vast economic changes Wuthnow describes, and she seems to agree with Bonnie Miller-McLemore that families need more structural support from the larger society if they are to thrive. Yet she also introduces the impact of changes in the workplace itself on the "balance" working parents are able to achieve, or not, pointing especially to the emergence of Total Quality Management (TQM) systems that make some workplaces more like homes used to be, even as homes are becoming more like most workplaces used to be under management systems organized with the single-minded purpose of promoting greater efficiency. Although Amerco has "family-friendly" policies that would allow

From *The New York Times Magazine*, April 20, 1997, pp. 50-55, 81, 84.

workers to choose to work shorter hours, few choose to accept these benefits, and Hochschild's evidence suggests that workers are opting for longer hours not because they need the money.

Hochschild's interpretation of what she observed raises serious doubts about whether either "having it all" or "leading a balanced life" is possible or even desirable in today's socioeconomic context. Instead of working to live, she argues, more and more people are living to work; and even beyond this, they are living at work. If this is so, is this a state of affairs that is good for individuals, for society, or for neither or both? Why or why not?

We are used to thinking that work is where most people feel like "just a number" or "a cog in a machine." It is where they have to be "on," have to "act," where they are least secure and most harried.

But new management techniques so pervasive in corporate life have helped transform the workplace into a more appreciative, personal sort of social world. Meanwhile, at home the divorce rate has risen, and the emotional demands have become more baffling and complex. In addition to teething, tantrums and the normal developments of growing children, the needs of elderly parents are creating more tasks for the modern family — as are the blending, unblending, reblending of new stepparents, stepchildren, exes and former in-laws.

This idea began to dawn on me during one of my first interviews with an Amerco worker. Linda Avery, a friendly, 38-year-old mother, is a shift supervisor at an Amerco plant. When I meet her in the factory's coffee-break room over a couple of Cokes, she is wearing blue jeans and a pink jersey, her hair pulled back in a long, blond ponytail. Linda's husband, Bill, is a technician in the same plant. By working different shifts, they manage to share the care of their 2-year-old son and Linda's 16-year-old daughter from a previous marriage. "Bill works the 7 A.M. to 3 P.M. shift while I watch the baby," she explains. "Then I work the 3 P.M. to 11 P.M. shift and he watches the baby. My daughter works at Walgreen's after school."

Linda is working overtime, and so I begin by asking whether Amerco required the overtime, or whether she volunteered for it. "Oh, I put in for it," she replies. I ask her whether, if finances and company policy permitted, she'd be interested in cutting back on the overtime. She takes off her safety glasses, rubs her face and, without answering my question explains: "I get home, and the minute I turn the key, my daughter is right there. Granted, she needs somebody to talk to about her day. . . . The baby is still up. He should have been in bed two hours ago, and that upsets me. The dishes are piled in the sink. My daughter comes right up to the door and complains about anything her stepfather said or did, and she wants to talk about her job. My husband is in the other room hollering to my daughter, 'Tracy, I don't ever get any time to talk to your mother, because you're always monopolizing her time before I even get a chance!' They all come at me at once."

Linda's description of the urgency of demands and the unarbitrated quarrels that await her homecoming contrast with her account of arriving at her job as a shift supervisor: "I usually come to work early, just to get away from the house. When I arrive, people are there waiting. We sit, we talk, we joke. I let them know what's going on, who has to be where, what changes I've made for the shift that day. We sit and chitchat for 5 or 10 minutes. There's laughing, joking, fun."

For Linda, home has come to feel like work and work has come to feel a bit like home. Indeed, she feels she can get relief from the "work" of being at home only by going to the "home" of work. Why has her life at home come to seem like this? Linda explains it this way: "My husband's a great help watching our baby. But as far as doing housework or even taking the baby when I'm at home, no. He figures he works five days a week; he's not going to come home and clean. But he doesn't stop to think that I work seven days a week. Why should I have to come home and do the housework without help from anybody else? My husband and I have been through this over and over again. Even if he would just pick up from the kitchen table and stack the dishes for me, that would make a big difference. He does nothing. On his weekends off, he goes fishing. If I want any time off, I have to get a sitter. He'll help out if I'm not here, but the minute I am, all the work at home is mine."

With a light laugh, she continues: "So I take a lot of overtime. The more I get out of the house, the better I am. It's a terrible thing to say, but that's the way I feel."

When Bill feels the need for time off, to relax, to have fun, to feel free, he climbs in his truck and takes his free time without his family. Largely in response, Linda grabs what she also calls "free time" — at work. Neither Linda nor Bill Avery wants more time together at home, not as things are arranged now.

How do Linda and Bill Avery fit into the broader picture of American family and work life? Current research suggests that however hectic their lives, women who do paid work feel less depressed, think better of themselves and are more satisfied than women who stay at home. One study reported that women who work outside the home feel more valued at home than housewives do. Meanwhile, work is where many women feel like "good mothers." As Linda reflects: "I'm a good mom at home, but I'm a better mom at work. At home, I get into fights with Tracy. I want her to apply to a junior college, but she's not interested. At work, I think I'm better at seeing the other person's point of view."

Many workers feel more confident they could "get the job done" at work than at home. One study found that only 59 percent of workers feel their "performance" in the family is "good or unusually good," while 86 percent rank their performance on the job this way.

Forces at work and at home are simultaneously reinforcing this "reversal." The lure of work has been enhanced in recent years by the rise of company cultural engineering — in particular, the shift from Frederick Taylor's principles of scientific management to the Total Quality principles originally set out by W. Edwards Deming. Under the influence of a Taylorist world view, the manager's job was to coerce the worker's mind and body, not to appeal to the worker's heart. The Taylorized worker was de-skilled, replaceable and cheap, and as a consequence felt bored, demeaned and unappreciated.

Using modern participative management techniques, many companies now train workers to make their own work decisions, and then set before their newly "empowered" employees moral as well as financial incentives. At Amerco, the Total Quality worker is invited to feel recognized for job accomplishments. Amerco regularly strengthens the familylike ties of co-workers by holding "recognition ceremonies" honoring particular workers or self-management production teams. Amerco employees speak of "belonging to the Amerco family," and proudly wear their "Total Quality" pins or "High Performance Team" T-shirts, symbols of their loyalty to the company and of its loyalty to them. . . .

If Total Quality calls for "re-skilling" the worker in an "enriched" job environment, technological developments have long been de-skilling parents at home. Over the centuries, store-bought goods have replaced homespun cloth, homemade soap and home-baked foods. Day care for children, retirement homes for the elderly, even psychotherapy are, in a way, commercial substitutes for jobs that a mother once did at home. Even family-generated entertainment has, to some extent, been replaced by television, video games and the VCR. I sometimes watched Amerco families sitting together after their dinners, mute but cozy, watching sitcoms in which television mothers, fathers and children related in an animated way to one another while the viewing family engaged in relational loafing.

The one "skill" still required of family members is the hardest one of all — the emotional work of forging, deepening or repairing family relationships. It takes time to develop this skill, and even then things can go awry. Family ties are complicated. People get hurt. Yet as broken homes become more common — and as the sense of belonging to a geographical community grows less and less secure in an age of mobility — the corporate world has created a sense of "neighborhood," of "feminine culture," of family at work. Life at work can be insecure; the company can fire workers. But workers aren't so secure at home, either. Many employees have been working for Amerco for 20 years but are on their second or third marriages or relationships. The shifting balance between these two "divorce rates" may be the most powerful reason why tired parents flee a world of unresolved quarrels and unwashed laundry for the orderliness, harmony and managed cheer of work. People are getting their "pink slips" at home.

Amerco workers have not only turned their offices into "home" and their homes into workplaces; many have also begun to "Taylorize" time at home, where families are succumbing to a cult of efficiency previously associated mainly with the office and factory. Meanwhile, work time, with its ever longer hours, has become more hospitable to sociability — periods of talking with friends on E-mail, patching up quarrels, gossiping. Within the long workday of many Amerco employees are great hidden pockets of inefficiency while, in the far smaller number of waking weekday hours at home, they are, despite themselves, forced to act increasingly time-conscious and efficient.

The Averys respond to their time bind at home by trying to value and protect "quality time." A concept unknown to their parents and grandparents, "quality time" has become a powerful symbol of the struggle against the growing pressures at home. . . .

Quality time holds out the hope that scheduling intense periods of togetherness can compensate for an overall loss of time in such a way that a relationship will suffer no loss of quality. But this is just another way of transferring the cult of efficiency from office to home. We must now get our relationships in good repair in less time. Instead of nine hours a day with a child, we declare ourselves capable of getting "the same result" with one intensely focused hour. . . .

Part of modern parenthood seems to include coping with the resistance of real children who are not so eager to get their cereal so fast. Some parents try desperately not to appease their children with special gifts or smooth-talking promises about the future. But when time is scarce, even the best parents find themselves passing a system-wide familial speed-up along to the most vulnerable workers on the line. Parents are then obliged to try to control the damage done by a reversal of worlds. They monitor mealtime, homework time, bedtime, trying to cut out "wasted" time.

In response, children often protest the pace, the deadlines, the grand irrationality of "efficient" family life. Children dawdle. They refuse to leave places when it's time to leave. They insist on leaving places when it's not time to leave. Surely, this is part of the usual stop-and-go of childhood itself, but perhaps, too, it is the plea of children for more family time, and more control over what time there is. This only adds to the feeling that life at home has become hard work.

Instead of trying to arrange shorter or more flexible work schedules, Amerco parents often avoid confronting the reality of the time bind. Some minimize their ideas about how much care a child, a partner or they themselves "really need." They make do with less time, less attention, less understanding and less support at home than they once imagined possible. They *emotionally downsize* life. In essence, they deny the needs of family members, and they themselves become emotional ascetics. If they once "needed" time with each other, they are now increasingly "fine" without it. . . .

Obviously, not everyone, not even a majority of Americans, is making a home out of work and a workplace out of home. But in the working world, it is a growing reality, and one we need to face. Increasing numbers of women are discovering a great male secret — that work can be an escape from the pressures of home, pressures that the changing nature of work itself [is] only intensifying. Neither men nor women are going to take up "family friendly" policies, whether corporate or governmental, as long as the current realities of work and home remain as they are. For a substantial number of time-bound parents, the stripped-down home and the neighborhood devoid of community are simply losing out to the pull of the workplace.

ABIGAIL ZUGER, M.D.

"Defining a Doctor"

Many Tuesdays in *The New York Times*'s science section, a guest physician writes about a particularly difficult or interesting aspect of treating one of his or her patients. In this essay, Dr. Zuger focuses not on a patient but rather on two young doctors and their very different ways of defining the place of work in their lives. One way of putting the difference might draw on terms already familiar to us from other readings: one doctor "works to live," while the other "lives to work." Clearly the difference between them on this point influences how they approach their patients, a matter that may evoke concern within those of us who, though not doctors, are quite likely to find ourselves in their care. Which doctor would you more likely be? Which would you rather have treating you if you were ill? Note that there is little evidence in the essay about which doctor's patients are more likely to get well. Something else is at stake here, for doctors and patients alike.

Dr. Zuger's account may prompt us to ponder whether a person can really be a first-rate doctor — or an excellent practitioner in any extremely demanding and potentially emotional field — if his or her life is not at least somewhat unbalanced. Might such changes as emphasizing teamwork and shared responsibility make balance, or at least rest, more available, as some medical educators apparently hope? What would be the costs — to practitioners or patients — of such measures?

I had two interns to supervise that month, and the minute they sat down for our first meeting, I sensed how the month would unfold.

The man's white coat was immaculate, its pockets empty save for a sleek Palm Pilot that contained his list of patients.

From *The New York Times*, November 2, 2004, p. D5.

The woman used a large loose-leaf notebook instead, every dog-eared page full of lists of things to do and check, consultants to call, questions to ask. Her pockets were stuffed, and whenever she sat down, little handbooks of drug doses, wadded phone messages, pens, highlighters and tourniquets spilled onto the floor.

The man worked the hours legally mandated by the state, not a minute more, and sometimes considerably less. He was seldom in the hospital before 8 in the morning, and left by 5 unless he was on call. He ate a leisurely lunch every day and was never late for rounds.

The woman got to the hospital around dawn and was on the move for the rest of the day. Sometimes she went home when she was supposed to, but sometimes, if one of her patients was particularly sick, she would sign out to the covering intern and keep working, often talking to patients' relatives long into the night.

"I am now breaking the law," she would announce cheerfully to no one in particular, then trot off to do just a few final chores.

The man had a strict definition of what it meant to be a doctor. He did not, for instance, "do nurses' work" (his phrase). When one of his patients needed a specimen sent to the lab and the nurse didn't get around to it, neither did he. No matter how important the job was, no matter how hard I pressed him, he never gave in. If I spoke sternly to him, he would turn around and speak just as sternly to the nurse.

The woman did everyone's work. She would weigh her patients if necessary (nurses' work), feed them (aides' work), find salt-free pickles for them (dietitians' work) and wheel them to X-ray (transporters' work).

The man was cheerful, serene and well rested. The woman was over-tired, hyperemotional and constantly late. The man was interested in his patients, but they never kept him up at night. The woman occasionally called the hospital from home to check on hers. The man played tennis on his days off. The woman read medical articles. At least, she read the beginnings; she tended to fall asleep halfway through.

I felt as if I was in a medieval morality play that month, living with two costumed symbols of opposing philosophies in medical education. The woman was working the way interns used to: total immersion seasoned with exhaustion and adrenaline. As far as she was concerned, her patients were her exclusive responsibility. The man was an intern of the new millennium. His hours and duties were delimited; he saw himself as part of a health care team, and his patients' welfare as a shared responsibility.

This new model of medical internship got some important validation in *The New England Journal of Medicine* last week, when Harvard researchers reported the effects of reducing interns' work hours to 60 per week from 80 (now the mandated national maximum). The shorter workweek required a larger staff of interns to spell one another at more frequent intervals. With shorter hours, the interns got more sleep at home, dozed off less at work and made considerably fewer bad mistakes in patient care.

Why should such an obvious finding need an elaborate controlled study to establish? Why should it generate not only two long articles in the world's most prestigious medical journal, but also three long, passionate editorials? Because the issue here is bigger than just scheduling and manpower.

The progressive shortening of residents' work hours spells nothing less than a change in the ethos of medicine itself. It means the end of Dr. Kildare, Superstar — that lone, heroic healer, omniscient, omnipotent and ever-present. It means a revolution in the complex medical hierarchy that sustained him. Willy-nilly, medicine is becoming democratized, a team sport.

We can only hope the revolution will be bloodless. Everything will have to change. Doctors will have to learn to work well with others. They will have to learn to write and speak with enough clarity and precision so that the patient's story remains accurate as care passes from hand to hand. They will have to stop saying "my patient" and begin to say "our patient" instead.

It may be, when the dust settles, that the system will be more functional, less error-prone. It may be that we will simply have substituted one set of problems for another.

We may even find that nothing much has changed. Even in the Harvard data, there was an impressive range in the hours that the interns under study worked. Some logged in over 90 hours in their 80-hour workweek. Some put in 75 instead.

Medicine has always attracted a wide spectrum of individuals, from the lazy and disaffected to the deeply committed. Even draconian scheduling policies may not change basic personality traits, or the kind of doctors that interns grow up to be.

My month with the intern of the past and the intern of the future certainly argues for the power of the individual work ethic. Try as I might, it was not within my power to modify the way either of them functioned. The woman cared too much. The man cared too little. She worked too hard, and he could not be prodded into working hard enough. They both made careless mistakes. When patients died, the man shrugged and the woman cried. If for no other reason than that one, let us hope that the medicine of the future still has room for people like her.

HENRY WADSWORTH LONGFELLOW

"The Village Blacksmith"

Often an image of how things used to be lies just beneath the surface as we consider and evaluate how things are today. The poem that follows takes us abruptly back from the late twentieth-century world of the corporation and the teaching hospital, described in the preceding readings, to the simpler world of the preindustrial village. In fact, the author, Henry Wadsworth Longfellow (1807-1882), lived in an era of rapid urbanization and industrialization and was already looking back to an earlier time as he wrote this poem, which portrays a "worthy" tradesman and the setting within which he works.

This poem has more than historical interest, however. Embedded in Longfellow's description of the "village smithy" are responses to questions about the balance between work, community life, and the family that are still alive today. Note the rhythms of work and rest evident in the poem, the flow of persons in and out of the workplace, and the attitude with which the blacksmith does his work. The speaker of the poem closes his description of the blacksmith's life with a word of gratitude for his teaching. What "lesson" has the blacksmith taught? What can we learn from him?

Under a spreading chestnut-tree
    The village smithy stands;
The smith, a mighty man is he,
    With large and sinewy hands;
And the muscles of his brawny arms
    Are strong as iron bands.

From *The Complete Poetical Works of Henry Wadsworth Longfellow* (Boston and New York: Houghton Mifflin Company, 1893), pp. 14-15.

His hair is crisp, and black, and long,
    His face is like the tan;
His brow is wet with honest sweat,
    He earns whate'er he can,
And looks the whole world in the face,
    For he owes not any man.

Week in, week out, from morn till night,
    You can hear his bellows blow;
You can hear him swing his heavy sledge,
    With measured beat and slow,
Like a sexton ringing the village bell,
    When the evening sun is low.

And children coming home from school
    Look in at the open door;
They love to see the flaming forge,
    And hear the bellows roar,
And catch the burning sparks that fly
    Like chaff from a threshing-floor.

He goes on Sunday to the church,
    And sits among his boys;
He hears the parson pray and preach,
    He hears his daughter's voice,
Singing in the village choir,
    And it makes his heart rejoice.

It sounds to him like her mother's voice,
    Singing in Paradise!
He needs must think of her once more,
    How in the grave she lies;
And with his hard, rough hand he wipes
    A tear out of his eyes.

Toiling, — rejoicing, — sorrowing,
    Onward through life he goes;
Each morning sees some task begin,
    Each evening sees it close;

Something attempted, something done,
    Has earned a night's repose.

Thanks, thanks to thee, my worthy friend,
    For the lesson thou hast taught!
Thus at the flaming forge of life
    Our fortunes must be wrought;
Thus on its sounding anvil shaped
    Each burning deed and thought.

WENDELL BERRY

"An Invisible Web"

"I never put up a barber pole or a sign, or even gave my shop a name. I didn't have to. The building was already called 'the barbershop.'" So begins the novel *Jayber Crow,* which is written in the voice of the man who from 1937 until 1969 was "the barber" in Port William, a small town near "The River." This fictional town on the Kentucky side of the Ohio bears a strong resemblance to the area where Berry himself has farmed for more than thirty years. Berry has written over forty volumes of poems, essays, and fiction, including several other stories and novels also set in Port William. Like his fictional Jayber Crow, Berry appreciates the quality of life that can emerge for those who put down roots and learn the ways of a "local culture," within a community where work and love and nature overlap rather than tugging against one another.[3]

    "After I had been there a while, the shop began to be called Jayber Crow's, or just Jayber's," our narrator continues. This barber's personal identification with his job is powerful, and yet his life seems to have a cer-

---

3. Wendell Berry, "The Work of Local Culture," in *What Are People For?* (New York: HarperCollins, 1990).

From Wendell Berry, *Jayber Crow* (Washington, D.C.: Counterpoint, 2000), pp. 121-132.

tain kind of balance. In the chapters preceding the one included here, we learn of Jayber's childhood in Port William and nearby Squires Landing and of his lonely college years, when he felt like "a theoretical ignorant person from the sticks, who one day would go to a theoretical somewhere and make a theoretical something of himself." He began to come to himself when he experienced "a motion of the heart toward my origins. Far from rising above them, I was longing to sink into them until I would know the fundamental things." After drifting back home (quite literally, being carried there by flood waters), he eventually found his place, his work, his community.

This chapter, "An Invisible Web," may be read as a profound medita-tion on the connections between work and life, self and community, and the things that we do and the significance we find in them or give to them. To what extent does the significance of Jayber's work depend upon what he actually does as distinct from how he does it or how he understands it? What are the "horizons of significance" within which Jayber locates the meaning and importance of his work? What exactly is the "invisible web"? Do you see it as restrictive, supportive, or both?

─────────

Ernest Finley used to say, at about the time I returned, "In Port William we don't distinguish the masses from the classes." And in a way that was true. People did freely mingle in the gathering places of the town. Even Joe Banion, the last black man ever to live in Port William, was a participant and subject in the town's ever-continuing conversation about itself. People loved and befriended one another and were loved and befriended, talked with and about one another, quarrelled with and resented and sometimes fought one another, all pretty much without thought of "special privilege." The only one in my time who might have been accused of putting on airs was Cecelia Overhold, and in her younger days even Cecelia didn't do it all the time.

And yet certain lines were drawn that weren't much spoken of or much noticed. You would be aware of them only if they were overstepped or if you came into the town as an outsider. I could see, for instance, that Joe Banion was treated pretty much as an equal in talk and in work and in other ways, but also that he never sat down with white people indoors. The white peo-ple, who called him "Nigger Joe" to identify him among the several other Joes who lived around, never did so to his face.

I pretty soon found out too that several lines were drawn around a bachelor barber who was known to take part in social events such as the Lit-tle Worter Dranking Party at the Grandstand. The barbershop, for one thing, was a precinct strictly masculine except on Saturday mornings, when mothers with small sons would bring them in for haircuts. At other times, the small boys would be brought in by their fathers and you would have been just as likely to find women in the poolroom. This was not my rule; it was just what the arrangement was and, I suppose, had always been. Anyhow, as the barber of the town, I was pretty effectively divided from its womanly life. I mingled a little, of course, when I went into the stores, and also when I would go out in the mornings and evenings with my buckets to get water at the town pump across the road.

As the barber I was placed also within economic limits that were generally recognized. The shop, as I had been told at the start, and as I had to agree, would not support a man with family responsibilities; it might support a bachelor, if he was careful. The barber lived on what would nowadays be called a "renewable resource" and so would never be out of work, if he could keep going on what his customers could reasonably be charged, but the resource itself was limited.

At times it could be severely limited. I nearly went under, for instance, in the first full month I was in Port William. Almost nobody came to the shop — for a haircut, that is; I had plenty of talkers — and I couldn't imagine what was the matter until I learned that a lot of the people thought it unlucky or unhealthy to get a haircut in February. My income varied also according to the weather, the stages of farmwork, and the state of the local economy. What I had, Grover Gibbs said, was a full-time part-time job.

Such jobs were not highly esteemed. One day I made the mistake, while cutting Mr. Milo Settle's hair, of referring to my "line of work."

"Boy," said Mr. Settle, "you ain't got what I call a *job*. You got what I call a *position*."

When I set up in Port William I was going on twenty-three years old. I was what I would prefer to call not-pretty, which is to say balding, long of face and frame, without resemblance to any movie actor or electable politician. Also I was a man of limited means and prospects, and a bachelor. By "bachelor" I mean, as was generally meant, a man old enough to be married who was not married and who had no visible chance to get married. A bachelor was, by nature, under suspicion. The women did not turn their backs as I passed along the street; they were, in fact, polite and friendly enough, as a rule. And I did learn (a little too late) to pursue my bachelor's aims and satisfactions with some discretion. But nobody ever told me pointedly or even casually that any eligible maiden was a good cook. I was not held up as an example to the young.

And so, in a society that was in some ways classless, I was in a class by myself. I was soon identified as a man who now and again wouldn't mind to take a drink, or join a nighttime party of fox or coon hunters, or attend a water-drinking party at the Grandstand or a roadhouse dance.

The biggest disadvantage, maybe, was that I remained a sort of bystander a lot longer than I remained a stranger. They were calling me "Jayber" a long time before I was *involved*. Most people treated me well from the start, and some a lot better than well. But it only takes one or two, like Cecelia Overhold, to keep you reminded of how you fit in. So far as she ever let me see, Cecelia never looked straight at me again in her life. I got so that when I met her in the street I would tip my hat to her, if I was wearing one; if not, I would make a little bow. She always went by without looking at me, her head tilted to indicate not that she did not see me but that she had *already* seen me, and once was enough.

As for advantages, they were there right from the start, and there were several of them.

One was, I felt at home. There is more to this than I can explain. I just *felt* at home. After I got to Port William, I didn't feel any longer that I needed to look around to see if there was someplace I would like better. I quit wondering what I was going to make of myself. A lot of my doubts and questions were settled. You could say, I guess, that I was glad at last to be classified. I was not a preacher or a teacher or a student or a traveler. I was Port William's bachelor barber, and a number of satisfactions were available to me as the perquisites of that office.

Burley Coulter was correct, for instance, about the goodness of having your dwelling place and your place of business right together. When I came down the stairs and into the shop I was "at work." When I went back upstairs I was "at home." This was handy in a lot of ways. The stove that heated the shop heated my bedroom-living-room-bathroom-kitchen (my "efficiency apartment") upstairs. Often, in the winter, while I was at work (which included loafing and talking) in the shop, I would have a pot of beans or soup or stew simmering on the stove.

People respected the difference. The shop was a public place, but the upstairs room was private. I've had people in the shop or down there banging on the door all hours of the day and night, for Port William never went altogether to sleep, but I expect I could count on my fingers the number of times anybody ever came to the door upstairs. And most of those times it was Burley Coulter, who, up there, would be mannerly and reserved, very formal — as opposed to his behavior in the shop where, like nearly everybody, he felt at home.

My occupancy of the ramshackle little building seemed to give him immense satisfaction, as if he had foreseen it all in a dream and was amazed that it had come to pass. He didn't harp on the subject, but if it came up he enjoyed talking about it. And he made occasions to review my situation and accomplishments.

One day he came in and walked all around the shop, looking at everything in it and out every window. He then sat down and rubbed his hands together. "Yessir," he said, "it's fine. You got your working and your living right here together."

And then the others took it up:

"Yessir, it's hard to tell whether he's working or living."

"Especially when he's working, it's hard to tell if he's living."

"When he's working it's hard to tell if he's alive."

And so on.

Burley Coulter himself was one of the best perquisites of my office. Burley was nineteen years older than I was, old enough to have been my father, and in fact he was the same age my father would have been if he had lived. He was the most interesting man I ever knew. He was in his way an adventurer. And something worthy of notice was always going on in his head. I found him to be a surprising man, unpredictable, and at the same time always true to himself and recognizable in what he did. I had lived in Port William several years before I realized that Burley was proud of me for being a reader of books; he was not himself a devoted reader, but he thought it was excellent that I should be. It must have been 1940 or 1941 when he first came all the way into my upstairs room and saw my books in my little bookcase.

"Do you read in them?"

"Yes," I said.

He gave the shelves a long study, not reading the titles, apparently just assaying in his mind the number and weight of the books, their varying sizes and colors, the printing on their spines. And then he nodded his approval and said, "Well, that's all right."

I knew him for forty years, about, and saw him endure the times and suffer the changes, and we were always friends.

Among the other perquisites of my office, I might as well say, were all my customers. I remembered a surprising number of them from the days when, for one reason or another, they would turn up at Uncle Othy's store at Squires Landing. And a surprising number of them sooner or later acknowledged that they had taken notice of me back in those old days. I liked them varyingly; some I didn't like at all. But all of them have been interesting to me; some I have liked and some I have loved. I have raked my comb over scalps that were dirty both above and beneath. I have lowered the ears of good men and bad, smart and stupid, young and old, kind and mean; of men who have killed other men (think of that) and of men who have been killed (think of *that*). I cut the hair of Tom Coulter and Virgil Feltner and Jimmy Chatham and a good many more who went away to the various wars and never came back, or came back dead.

I became, over the years, a pretty good student of family traits: the shapes of heads, ears, noses, hands, and so forth. This was sometimes funny, as when I would get a suspicion of a kinship that was, you might say, unauthorized. But it was moving too, after a while, to realize that under my very hands a generation had grown up and another passed away.

My most difficult times were the early hours of Saturday when the parents would bring in the littlest boys. You talk about a trial — it would come when a young mother would bring her first child for his first haircut. At best it was like shooting at a moving target. At worst the boy would be a high-principled little fellow who found haircuts to be against his religion, and whose mother was jumping half out of her chair all the time, saying things like "Be still, sugar — Mr. Crow's not going to *hurt* you."

About as bad were some of the old men. They would forget they had faces until their beard began to itch, and then would come in for a shave. They were good-mannered old men who thought that when they were in company they ought to have something to say and that they ought to look at the people they were talking to. While I shaved them they would talk and look around as if I was not even present, let alone working around their ears and noses and throats with a straight razor.

But I must say I always liked having the old ones around. I sort of had a way of collecting them. There was a long string of them who made a regular sitting place of my shop after they got too old to work; some came in every Saturday and some came in every day, depending on how close by they lived. Some of them were outlandish enough, like the one everybody called Old Man Profet who, when he talked, breathed fiercely through his false teeth, which he took out, he said, only to sleep and to eat. Mr. Profet was inclined toward boasting and self-dramatization and belief in whatever he said. To hear him recount the exploits of his youth (in love, work, and strife) with the wind whistling in and out between his gritted teeth, you would think yourself in the presence of some dethroned old warrior king.

Uncle Stanley Gibbs, Grover's father, had no teeth at all and talked like a bubbling spring, and would say anything at all — *anything* — that he thought of. And sometimes he said, as Grover put it, "things that he nor nobody else ever thought of."

"Did you know," said Uncle Stanley, "that they cut a rock out of old Mrs. Shoals's apparatix as big as a hen egg?"

"No," I said. "I did not."

"Well, they did."

Mr. Wayne Thripple, on the other hand, never said much at all. He was a loose-skinned old fellow who just sat and stared ahead, glassy-eyed, as if about to go to sleep, but he never went to sleep. He spent a lot of time clearing his throat, loudly. *"Humh!"* he would say. "Unnnh uh-*hum!* Uh-hum! Hmmmmh! Uh-hum, uh-hum, uh-hum! Uh-*hum*-ahum!"

But there were also men such as Uncle Isham Quail and Old Jack Beechum and, later, Athey Keith and Mat Feltner, intelligent men who knew things that were surpassingly interesting to me. They were rememberers, carrying in their living thoughts all the history that such places as Port William ever have. I listened to them with all my ears and have tried to remember what they said, though from remembering what I remember I know that much is lost. Things went to the grave with them that will never be known again.

Uncle Marce Catlett would ride in on horseback to get a haircut and a shave the first thing every other Saturday afternoon, hitching his mare to the sugar tree in front of my door. There came a time when I would have to help him off and back onto the mare. Uncle Dave Coulter, Burley's father, always walked in, to save his horse. Neither of them ever loafed.

I came to feel a tenderness for them all. This was something new to me. It gave me a curious pleasure to touch them, to help them in and out of the chair, to shave their weather-toughened old faces. They had known hard use, nearly all of them. You could tell it by the way they held themselves and moved. Most of all you could tell it by their hands, which were shaped by wear and often by the twists and swellings of arthritis. They had used their hands forgetfully, as hooks and pliers and hammers, and in every kind of weather. The backs of their hands showed a network of little scars where they had been cut, nicked, thornstuck, pinched, punctured, scraped, and burned. Their faces told that they had suffered things they did not talk about. Every one of them had a good knife in his pocket, sharp, the blades whetted narrow and concave, the horn of the handle worn smooth. The oldest ones spoke, like Uncle Othy, the old broad speech of the place; they said "ahrn" and "fahr" and "tard" for "iron" and "fire" and "tired"; they said "yorn" for "yours," "cheer" for "chair," "deesh" for "dish," "dreen" for "drain," "slide" for "sled," and "juberous" for "dubious." I loved to listen to them, for they spoke my native tongue.

Among the best things that could happen (and that happened less and less often as time went on) were the nights when we would have music. I never quite knew how these came about. In my early days in the shop and on for a good many years, Bill Mixter and his brother and his sons had a band that would go about playing at square dances and such. Maybe there would be times when they would be in need of a place to gather and play. Maybe they had taken notice of my habit of keeping the shop open at night as long as anybody was there.

Anyhow, there would be a night now and then when they would wander in, one after another, a little past a decent bedtime, carrying their instruments. Maybe Burley Coulter would take down his old fiddle and come too. They never said that they had come to play; the instruments seemed just to be along by accident.

They would come in and sit down as people did who had come in to loaf, and the conversation would begin about as usual.

"Good evening to you, Jayber."

"Good evening to you, Bill."

"Well, what do you reckon you been up to?"

"Oh, no good, as usual."

If I had no customer, as I probably would not have at that hour of the night, I would climb into the seat of my profession and make myself comfortable.

They would greet me and one another as they came in. They took chairs, sat down, commented on the weather and other events, smoked maybe.

And then one or another of them would pick up his fiddle or guitar or banjo (you could never tell who it would be) and begin to tune it, plucking at the strings individually and listening. And then another would begin, and another. It was done almost bashfully, as if they feared that the silence might not welcome their music. Little sequences of notes would be picked out randomly here and there. (Their instruments just happened to be in their hands. The power of music-making had overtaken them by surprise, and they had to grow used to it.)

Finally Bill Mixter would lower his head, lay his bow upon the strings, and draw out the first notes of a tune, and the others would come in behind him. The music, while it lasted, brought a new world into being. They would play some tunes they had learned off the radio, but their knowledge was far older than that and they played too the music that was native to the place, or that the people of the place were native to. Just the names of the tunes were a kind of music; they call back the music to my mind still, after so many

290

years: "Sand Riffle," "Last Gold Dollar," "Billy in the Low Ground," "Gate to Go Through," and a lot of others. "A fiddle, now, is an atmospheric thing," said Burley Coulter. The music was another element filling the room and pouring out through the cracks. When at last they'd had their fill and had gone away, the shop felt empty, the silence larger than before.

But you could not be where I was without experiencing many such transformations. One of your customers, one of your neighbors (let us say), is a man known to be more or less a fool, a big talker, and one day he comes into your shop and you have heard and you see that he is dying even as he is standing there looking at you, and you can see in his eyes that (whether or not he admits it) he knows it, and all of a sudden everything is changed. You seem no longer to be standing together in the center of time. Now you are on time's edge, looking off into eternity. And this man, your foolish neighbor, your friend and brother, has shed somehow the laughter that has followed him through the world, and has assumed the dignity and the strangeness of a traveler departing forever.

The generation that was old and dying when I settled in Port William had memories that went back to the Civil War. And now my own generation, that calls back to the First World War, is old and dying. And gray hair is growing on heads that had just looked over tabletops at the time of World War II. I can see how we grow up like crops of wheat and are harvested and carried away.

But as the year warmed in 1937, I was a young man. I hardly knew what I knew, let alone what I was going to learn. In March, Burley Coulter brought his breaking plow in to the blacksmith shop and, in passing, plowed my garden. It broke beautifully. There was, as Burley said, nothing wrong with it. The dark soil rolled off the moldboard and fell to pieces. In the early mornings and late evenings, and in the intervals between customers, I brought to life the useful things Aunt Cordie had taught me and became a gardener. I worked and manured the ground, and on Good Friday planted potatoes, onions, peas, salad stuff, and set out some cabbage plants. It was lovely, then, to see the green things sprigging up in my long, straight rows. The garden took up nearly all the space between the shop and the privy out by the back fence, a hundred and fifty feet or so, and was only about eighteen feet wide. Depending on how I spaced them, I could have seven or eight rows.

I became a sort of garden fanatic, and I am not over it yet. You can take a few seed peas, dry and dead, and sow them in a little furrow, and they will sprout into a row of pea vines and bear more peas — it may not be a miracle, but that is a matter of opinion. When the days were lengthening and getting warmer and the sun was shining, I would be back in my garden all the time, working or just looking. When it was warm and I could leave the back door open, I could hear when anybody came into the shop, and I would go in, accomplish the necessary haircut or shave or conversation, and come back out again as soon as I was alone. I knew better than to expect a visible difference in an hour, but I looked anyhow.

Another new thing that happened to me after I came back to Port William was the feeling of loss. I began to live in my losses. When I was taken away from Squires Landing and put into The Good Shepherd [orphanage], I think I was more or less taken away from my grief. I was just lifted up out of it, like a caught fish. The loss of all my life and all the places and people I had known I felt then as homesickness. After I got over my homesickness and learned in my fashion to live and get along at The Good Shepherd, I learned to think of myself as myself. The past was gone. I was unattached. I could put my whole life in a smallish cardboard box and carry it in my hand.

But when I recognized Burley Coulter on the water that morning and told him who I was, and he remembered me from that lost and gone and given-up old time and then introduced me to people as the boy Aunt Cordie and Uncle Othy took to raise — well, that changed me. After all those years of keeping myself aloof and alone, I began to feel tugs from the outside. I felt my life branching and forking out into the known world. In a way, I was almost sorry. It was as though I knew without exactly knowing, or felt, or smelled in the air, the already accomplished fact that nothing would ever be simple for me again. I never again would be able to put my life in a box and carry it away.

The place itself and its conversation surrounded me with remindings. Aunt Cordie and Uncle Othy and the Thripples and Put Woolfork and Dark Tom Cotman and Emmet Edge and Aunt Ellie and Uncle Ben Fewclothes — all the people of that early world I once thought would last forever, and then thought I had left forever — were always coming back to mind because of something I saw or heard. They would turn up in the conversation in my shop. They returned to my dreams. In my comings and goings I crossed their tracks, and my own earlier ones, many times a day, weaving an invisible web that was as real as the ground it was woven over, and as I went about I would feel my losses and my debts.

In those days I was always sticking money here and there for safekeeping. I stuck Sam Hanks's unrepayable five-dollar bill into a book where I would have it to use if I had to use it, but where as long as I might keep it I would always know it from any other five-dollar bill. I kept it to remind me that there are some accounts that cannot be settled.

With that in mind, I watched for the first warm Sunday morning. When it came, I left town early. I followed the road along the ridgetops, and down into the Katy's Branch valley and up the other side, and then across the fields and down through the woods until I came to the open hillside above Squires Landing. Just at the woods' edge, where I could look down at the house and the store and the other buildings, I found a good sitting place and leaned my back against a tree.

I sat there a long time. I looked at everything and remembered it, and let my memories come back and take place. I don't believe I was exactly thinking; my mind was too crowded and too everywhere touched. What would come, came. The child I had been came and made his motions, out and about and around, down to the store, down to the garden, down to the barn, up to the house, up to the henhouse, across the river in Uncle Othy's johnboat, up the river in the buggy, over to the Thripples, up to Port William on Sunday morning, down to the river to see the steam-boats land and unload and load, up into the woods — weaving over the ground a web of ways, as present and as passing as the spiders' webs in the grass that catch the dew early in the morning. All my steps had made the place a world and made me at home in it, and then I had gone, just as Aunt Cordie and Uncle Othy had been at home and then had gone.

And like a shadow within a shadow, the time before my time came to me. I was old enough by then to know and believe that the old had once been young. Once, Aunt Cordie had been Cordie Quail, a pretty girl. There had been a day when Uncle Othy and Aunt Cordie had come there, young, just married, to begin their life at the landing, to have their pleasures and to endure what had to be endured. There had been a time before they came, and a time before that. And always, from a time before anybody knew of time, the river had been there. From my sitting place where the woods stood up at the edge of the pasture, I could see the river, risen a little, swift and muddy from the spring rains, coming down the mile-long reach above the Willow Run bend, swerving through the bend and coming on down past the landing, carrying its load of drift. And I saw how all-of-a-piece it was, how never-ending — always coming, always there, always going.

When I was filled with knowledge and could not hold any more, I went back over the ridge and down to Katy's Branch and up along the creek road to Goforth. I went to the site of my parents' house — *our* house — now gone, and my father's shop, gone, the place overgrown with young box elders and elms and cedars and redbuds and all manner of weeds and vines. I pressed in amongst the tangle and stood by the still-standing chimney and thought, "This is my home itself, where I began." I thought of my young parents, Iona and Luther. My few memories of that place came to me, and I felt the presence of memories I could not remember. I remembered so plainly that I could *hear* the sound of a hammer shaping metal on an anvil, the hammer blows muted at first on the heat-softened iron and then ringing clearer as it cooled and hardened.

The sunlight now lay over the valley perfectly still. I went over to the graveyard beside the church and found them under the old cedars: Uncle Othy and Aunt Cordie, Iona and Luther, and round about were Quails and Cotmans, Proudfoots and Thigpens, my mother's and Aunt Cordie's people. I am finding it a little hard to say that I felt them resting there, but I did. I felt their completeness as whatever they had been in the world.

I knew I had come there out of kindness, theirs and mine. The grief that came to me then was nothing like the grief I had felt for myself alone, at the end of my stay in Lexington. This grief had something in it of generosity, some nearness to joy. In a strange way it added to me what I had lost. I saw that, for me, this country would always be populated with presences and absences, presences of absences, the living and the dead. The world as it is would always be a reminder of the world that was, and of the world that is to come.

———

KING HUSSEIN AND NOA BEN ARTZI-PELOSSOF

Two Eulogies for Yitzhak Rabin

The remarkable pair of eulogies that follows provides two intensely personal views of the same man by two very different speakers — a colleague in the work of international politics, and a granddaughter. Both were delivered at the funeral of Israeli Prime Minister Yitzhak Rabin, which took place in Jerusalem after Rabin's assassination by a Jewish ultra-nationalist. The first eulogy is from King Hussein of Jordan, who had once been Rabin's foe

Fron *The New York Times*, November 5, 1995, pp. A10 and A11.

but had become his partner in working for lasting peace in the Middle East. The second is from seventeen-year-old Noa Ben Artzi-Pelossof.

No one can doubt that Rabin (1922-1995) led a significant life, a life that mattered to millions then and now. These two very different eulogies, brief though they are, suggest when taken together that Rabin led a balanced life as well. The first eulogy, delivered by a former enemy and fellow statesman, speaks of friendship. The second eulogy, delivered by a family member, speaks of heroism. Perhaps work, family, friendship, and citizenship are not so segregated from one another as we suppose. Perhaps family life can support rather than impede one's capacity to respond to urgent social concerns, a hope that will be expressed by Jane Addams in a reading further on in this chapter. Could it be possible that the best way to be a good grandfather is to be an exemplary citizen or an admired professional? Could it be equally possible that, in some jobs at least, a capacity for the supposedly "private" practice of friendship is as important as any other skill? Or should we always be wary of a "confusion of realms," keeping work, family, and friendship quite separate from one another?

King Hussein

My friends, I had never thought that the moment would come, like this, when I would grieve the loss of a brother, a colleague and a friend, a man, a soldier, whom I trust on the opposite side of a divide, whom I respected as he respected us — a man I came to know because I realized, as he did, that we have to cross over the divide, establish a dialogue, get to know each other and strive to leave for those who follow us a legacy that is worthy of them. And so we did. And so we became brethren and friends.

I've never been used to standing, except with you next to me, speaking of peace, speaking of our dreams and the hopes of generations to come that must live in peace, enjoy human dignity, come together, work together to build a better future, which is our right.

Never in all my thoughts did it occur to me that my first visit to Jerusalem in response to your invitation, and the invitation of the Speaker of the Knesset, at the invitation of the President of Israel, would be on such an occasion.

You lived as a soldier, you died as a soldier for peace.

And I believe it is time for all of us to come out openly and to speak of peace. Not here today, but for all the times to come. We belong to the camp of peace. We believe in peace. We believe that our one God wishes us to live in peace, and wishes peace upon us, for these are His teachings to all the followers of the three great monotheistic religions, the children of Abraham.

Let's not keep silent. Let our voices rise high to speak of our commitment to peace for all times to come. And let us tell those who live in darkness, who are the enemies of life, and through faith and religion and the teachings of one God, this is where we stand. This is our camp. Maybe God will bless you with the realization that you must join it, and we'll pray that He will. But otherwise, we are not ashamed, nor are we afraid, nor are we anything but determined to fulfill the legacy for which my friend fell, as did my grandfather in this very city when I was with him and but a boy.

He was a man of courage . . . and he was endowed with one of the greatest virtues that any man can have. He was endowed with humility. He felt, with those around him, an evolution of responsibility. He placed himself, as I do, and have done often, in the place of the other partner to achieve a worthy goal. And we achieved peace, an honorable peace and a lasting peace.

He had courage, he had vision, and he had a commitment to peace. And standing here, I commit before you, before my people in Jordan, before the world, myself to continue to do my utmost to insure that we leave a similar legacy. And when my time comes, I hope it will be like my grandfather's and like Yitzhak Rabin's.

For his spirit — and I try and make sense for the people of Jordan, my family, the people of Israel — decent people throughout the world feel today. So many live and so many inevitably die. This is the will of God, this is the way of all, but those are fortunate and lucky in life, those who are great are those who leave something behind and you are such a man, my friend.

The faces in my country, among the majority of our people, and our armed forces and people who once were your enemies, are somber today and their hearts are heavy. Let's hope and pray that God will give us all guidance, each in his respective position, to do what he can for the better future that Yitzhak Rabin sought with determination and courage.

Noa Ben Artzi-Pelossof

Please excuse me for not wanting to talk about the peace. I want to talk about my grandfather.

You always awake from a nightmare, but since yesterday I was continually awakening to a nightmare. It is not possible to get used to the nightmare of life without you. The television never ceases to broadcast pictures of you, and you are so alive that I can almost touch you — but only almost, and I won't be able to anymore.

Grandfather, you were the pillar of fire in front of the camp and now we are left in the camp alone, in the dark; and we are so cold and so sad.

I know that people talk in terms of a national tragedy, and of comforting an entire nation, but we feel the huge void that remains in your absence when grandmother doesn't stop crying.

Few people really knew you. Now they will talk about you for quite some time, but I feel that they really don't know just how great the pain is, how great the tragedy is; something has been destroyed.

Grandfather, you were and still are our hero. I wanted you to know that every time I did anything, I saw you in front of me. Your appreciation and your love accompanied us every step down the road, and our lives were always shaped after your values. You, who never abandoned anything, are now abandoned. And here you are, my ever-present hero, cold, alone, and I cannot do anything to save you. You are missed so much.

Others greater than I have already eulogized you, but none of them ever had the pleasure I had to feel the caresses of your warm, soft hands, to merit your warm embrace that was reserved only for us, to see your half-smile that always told me so much, that same smile which is no longer, frozen in the grave with you.

I have no feelings of revenge because my pain and feelings of loss are so large, too large. The ground has been swept out from below us, and we are groping now, trying to wander about in this empty void, without any success so far.

I am not able to finish this; left with no alternative, I say good-bye to you, hero, and ask you to rest in peace, and think about us, and miss us, as down here we love you so very much. I imagine angels are accompanying you now and I ask them to take care of you, because you deserve their protection.

～～～

ANNIE DILLARD

"Living Like Weasels"

Annie Dillard has published several highly acclaimed works of nonfiction, memoir, poetry, and fiction. Her first and most widely known book, *Pilgrim at Tinker Creek* (1974), records what she saw and learned during a year of thoughtful and observant living in the woods. As the essay included here demonstrates, her work is nourished by a fierce attentiveness to nature, as well as by a willingness to grapple with the big questions human beings have about the character and meaning of our own lives.

"Living Like Weasels," which describes a sixty-second encounter near a littered suburban pond, may not at first seem to be about leading a life that matters. From this encounter, however, Dillard wrests a lesson that could be immensely helpful to someone who wonders what to do in life. What shape would the passionate and utterly focused manner of the weasel give to a human life? If a person were to take Dillard's advice to live like a weasel, could he or she have — or even want — a "balanced" life?

A weasel is wild. Who knows what he thinks? He sleeps in his underground den, his tail draped over his nose. Sometimes he lives in his den for two days without leaving. Outside, he stalks rabbits, mice, muskrats, and birds, killing more bodies than he can eat warm, and often dragging the carcasses home. Obedient to instinct, he bites his prey at the neck, either splitting the jugular vein at the throat or crunching the brain at the base of the skull, and he does not let go. One naturalist refused to kill a weasel who was socketed into his hand deeply as a rattlesnake. The man could in no way pry the tiny weasel off, and he had to walk half a mile to water, the weasel dangling from his palm, and soak him off like a stubborn label.

And once, says Ernest Thompson Seton — once, a man shot an eagle

---

From Annie Dillard, *Teaching a Stone to Talk* (New York: Harper and Row, 1983), pp. 11-16.

out of the sky. He examined the eagle and found the dry skull of a weasel fixed by the jaws to his throat. The supposition is that the eagle had pounced on the weasel and the weasel swiveled and bit as instinct taught him, tooth to neck, and nearly won. I would like to have seen that eagle from the air a few weeks or months before he was shot: was the whole weasel still attached to his feathered throat, a fur pendant? Or did the eagle eat what he could reach, gutting the living weasel with his talons before his breast, bending his beak, cleaning the beautiful airborne bones?

I have been reading about weasels because I saw one last week. I startled a weasel who startled me, and we exchanged a long glance.

Twenty minutes from my house, through the woods by the quarry and across the highway, is Hollins Pond, a remarkable piece of shallowness, where I like to go at sunset and sit on a tree trunk. Hollins Pond is also called Murray's Pond; it covers two acres of bottomland near Tinker Creek with six inches of water and six thousand lily pads. In winter, brown-and-white steers stand in the middle of it, merely dampening their hooves; from the distant shore they look like miracle itself, complete with miracle's nonchalance. Now, in summer, the steers are gone. The water lilies have blossomed and spread to a green horizontal plane that is terra firma to plodding blackbirds, and tremulous ceiling to black leeches, crayfish, and carp.

This is, mind you, suburbia. It is a five-minute walk in three directions to rows of houses, though none is visible here. There's a 55 mph highway at one end of the pond, and a nesting pair of wood ducks at the other. Under every bush is a muskrat hole or a beer can. The far end is an alternating series of fields and woods, fields and woods, threaded everywhere with motorcycle tracks — in whose bare clay wild turtles lay eggs.

So. I had crossed the highway, stepped over two low barbed-wire fences, and traced the motorcycle path in all gratitude through the wild rose and poison ivy of the pond's shoreline up into high grassy fields. Then I cut down through the woods to the mossy fallen tree where I sit. This tree is excellent. It makes a dry, upholstered bench at the upper, marshy end of the pond, a plush jetty raised from the thorny shore between a shallow blue body of water and a deep blue body of sky.

The sun had just set. I was relaxed on the tree trunk, ensconced in the lap of lichen, watching the lily pads at my feet tremble and part dreamily over the thrusting path of a carp. A yellow bird appeared to my right and flew behind me. It caught my eye; I swiveled around — and the next instant, inexplicably, I was looking down at a weasel, who was looking up at me.

Weasel! I'd never seen one wild before. He was ten inches long, thin as a curve, a muscled ribbon, brown as fruitwood, soft-furred, alert. His face was fierce, small and pointed as a lizard's; he would have made a good arrowhead. There was just a dot of chin, maybe two brown hairs' worth, and then the pure white fur began that spread down his underside. He had two black eyes I didn't see, any more than you see a window.

The weasel was stunned into stillness as he was emerging from beneath an enormous shaggy wild rose bush four feet away. I was stunned into stillness twisted backward on the tree trunk. Our eyes locked, and someone threw away the key.

Our look was as if two lovers, or deadly enemies, met unexpectedly on an overgrown path when each had been thinking of something else: a clearing blow to the gut. It was also a bright blow to the brain, or a sudden beating of brains, with all the charge and intimate grate of rubbed balloons. It emptied our lungs. It felled the forest, moved the fields, and drained the pond; the world dismantled and tumbled into that black hole of eyes. If you and I looked at each other that way, our skulls would split and drop to our shoulders. But we don't. We keep our skulls. So.

He disappeared. This was only last week, and already I don't remember what shattered the enchantment. I think I blinked, I think I retrieved my brain from the weasel's brain, and tried to memorize what I was seeing, and the weasel felt the yank of separation, the careening splash-down into real life and the urgent current of instinct. He vanished under the wild rose. I waited motionless, my mind suddenly full of data and my spirit with pleadings, but he didn't return.

Please do not tell me about "approach-avoidance conflicts." I tell you I've been in that weasel's brain for sixty seconds, and he was in mine. Brains are private places, muttering through unique and secret tapes — but the weasel and I both plugged into another tape simultaneously, for a sweet and shocking time. Can I help it if it was a blank?

What goes on in his brain the rest of the time? What does a weasel think about? He won't say. His journal is tracks in clay, a spray of feathers, mouse blood and bone: uncollected, unconnected, loose-leaf, and blown.

I would like to learn, or remember, how to live. I come to Hollins Pond not so much to learn how to live as, frankly, to forget about it. That is, I don't think I can learn from a wild animal how to live in particular — shall I suck warm blood, hold my tail high, walk with my footprints precisely over the prints of my hands? — but I might learn something of mindlessness, something of the purity of living in the physical senses and the dignity of living without bias or motive. The weasel lives in necessity and we live in choice, hating necessity and dying at the last ignobly in its talons. I would like to live as I should, as the weasel lives as he should. And I suspect that for me the way is like the weasel's: open to time and death painlessly, noticing everything, remembering nothing, choosing the given with a fierce and pointed will.

I missed my chance. I should have gone for the throat. I should have lunged for that streak of white under the weasel's chin and held on, held on through mud and into the wild rose, held on for a dearer life. We could live under the wild rose wild as weasels, mute and uncomprehending. I could very calmly go wild. I could live two days in the den, curled, leaning on mouse fur, sniffing bird bones, blinking, licking, breathing musk, my hair tangled in the roots of grasses. Down is a good place to go, where the mind is single. Down is out, out of your ever-loving mind and back to your careless senses. I remember muteness as a prolonged and giddy fast, where every moment is a feast of utterance received. Time and events are merely poured, unremarked, and ingested directly, like blood pulsed into my gut through a jugular vein. Could two live that way? Could two live under the wild rose, and explore by the pond, so that the smooth mind of each is as everywhere present to the other, and as received and as unchallenged, as falling snow?

We could, you know. We can live any way we want. People take vows of poverty, chastity, and obedience — even of silence — by choice. The thing is to stalk your calling in a certain skilled and supple way, to locate the most tender and live spot and plug into that pulse. This is yielding, not fighting. A weasel doesn't "attack" anything; a weasel lives as he's meant to, yielding at every moment to the perfect freedom of single necessity.

I think it would be well, and proper, and obedient, and pure, to grasp your one necessity and not let it go, to dangle from it limp wherever it takes you. Then even death, where you're going no matter how you live, cannot you part. Seize it and let it seize you up aloft even, till your eyes burn out and drop; let your musky flesh fall off in shreds, and let your very bones unhinge and scatter, loosened over fields, over fields and woods, lightly, thoughtless, from any height at all, from as high as eagles.

WILLIAM BUTLER YEATS

"The Choice"

The Irish poet William Butler Yeats (1865-1939) is widely regarded as one of the best poets of the twentieth century. The short poem below addresses the question of whether it is possible and desirable to have a balanced life by setting up a radical choice between "the life" and "the work." The poem is particularly suggestive about what consequences may attend the selection of either alternative.

As you reflect on this poem, remember that Yeats chose each word with great deliberation, pursuing, in a sense, the perfection of this particular piece of work, this poem. Why is it "the intellect" that is forced to make the choice between life and work? And what difference does it make that the choice, as Yeats puts it, is between "perfection of the life, or of the work"? Is the quest for perfection — or even for highly distinguished accomplishment — essential for a life of significance? In your view, would it be acceptable to settle for less outstanding performance if balance were thereby attainable?

The intellect of man is forced to choose
Perfection of the life, or of the work,
And if it take the second must refuse
A heavenly mansion, raging in the dark.
When all that story's finished, what's the news?
In luck or out the toil has left its mark:
That old perplexity an empty purse,
Or the day's vanity, the night's remorse.

From *The Complete Poems of W. B. Yeats* (New York: Macmillan, 1933), p. 242.

JANE ADDAMS

"Filial Relations"

Jane Addams (1860-1935) was the founder of one of the first settlement houses in North America, a pioneer in the field of social work, and a political reformer and antiwar activist who was awarded the Nobel Peace Prize. She came to these accomplishments as a member of the first generation of American women to attend college, and thus as one whose educational advantages opened new doors while also raising new and perplexing questions about what to do with her life. In her autobiography, *Twenty Years at Hull House,* she depicts the eight years following her own graduation as full of illness and heartache, so intense was her desire to discover what she should do that was more important and meaningful than the travel and leisure activities her family thought appropriate. She found her vocation after recognizing that serving the urban poor — first in East London, as mentioned here, and then in Chicago, where she would spend the rest of her life — offered a way to express her "enlarged interest in life" and to participate in "the social movements around us."

Unlike Miller-McLemore, Addams's dilemma was not how to balance marriage with work but rather how to balance the "social claim" — the urgent summons to be engaged in service to a world in need — with the expectations of her family of origin and their sense of the primacy of private life. In this excerpt, Addams is concerned to find a "healing compromise" among a number of claims and opportunities, each of which she acknowledges has some legitimacy. When claims conflict or compete, however, she argues that we should honor the higher claim, which to her resides with the larger life of society rather than in the family. At the same time, she advocates ways of reformulating the relationship between family and society that might both serve society well and make such choices less wrenching for individuals.

From Jane Addams, *Democracy and Social Ethics* (New York: The Macmillan Company, 1902; Urbana and Chicago: University of Illinois Press, 2002), pp. 35-47.

Over her decades in Hull House, Addams was a mentor to many young adults who came to Hull House seeking paths of usefulness. What summons or challenge is she offering here? How might you respond to the priorities she proposes?

There are many people in every community who have not felt the "social compunction," who do not share the effort toward a higher social morality, who are even unable to sympathetically interpret it. Some of these have been shielded from the inevitable and salutary failures which the trial of new powers involve because they are content to attain standards of virtue demanded by an easy public opinion, and others of them have exhausted their moral energy in attaining to the current standard of individual and family righteousness.

Such people, who form the bulk of contented society, demand that the radical, the reformer, shall be without stain or question in his personal and family relations, and judge most harshly any deviation from the established standards. There is a certain justice in this: it expresses the inherent conservatism of the mass of men, that none of the established virtues which have been so slowly and hardly acquired shall be sacrificed for the sake of making problematic advance; that the individual, in his attempt to develop and use the new and exalted virtue, shall not fall into the easy temptation of letting the ordinary ones slip through his fingers.

This instinct to conserve the old standards, combined with a distrust of the new standard, is a constant difficulty in the way of those experiments and advances depending upon the initiative of women, both because women are the more sensitive to the individual and family claims, and because their training has tended to make them content with the response to these claims alone.

There is no doubt that, in the effort to sustain the moral energy necessary to work out a more satisfactory social relation, the individual often sacrifices the energy which should legitimately go into the fulfillment of personal and family claims, to what he considers the higher claim. . . .

The mind of each one of us reaches back to our first struggles as we emerged from self-willed childhood into a recognition of family obligations. We have all gradually learned to respond to them, and yet most of us have had at least fleeting glimpses of what it might be to disregard them and the elemental claim they make upon us. We have yielded at times to the temptation of ignoring them for selfish aims, of considering the individual and not the family convenience, and we remember with shame the self-pity which inevitably followed. But just as we have learned to adjust the personal and family claims, and to find an orderly development impossible without recognition of both, so perhaps we are called upon now to make a second adjustment between the family and the social claim, in which neither shall lose and both be ennobled.

The attempt to bring about a healing compromise in which the two shall be adjusted in proper relation is not an easy one. It is difficult to distinguish between the outward act of him who in following one legitimate claim has been led into the temporary violation of another, and the outward act of him who deliberately renounces a just claim and throws aside all obligation for the sake of his own selfish and individual development. The man, for instance, who deserts his family that he may cultivate an artistic sensibility, or acquire what he considers more fullness of life for himself, must always arouse our contempt. Breaking the marriage tie as Ibsen's "Nora" did, to obtain a larger self-development, or holding to it as George Eliot's "Romola" did, because of the larger claim of the state and society, must always remain two distinct paths. The collision of interests, each of which has a real moral basis and a right to its own place in life, is bound to be more or less tragic. It is the struggle between two claims, the destruction of either of which would bring ruin to the ethical life. Curiously enough, it is almost exactly this contradiction which is the tragedy set forth by the Greek dramatist, who asserted that the gods who watch over the sanctity of the family bond must yield to the higher claims of the gods of the state. The failure to recognize the social claim as legitimate causes the trouble; the suspicion constantly remains that woman's public efforts are merely selfish and captious, and are not directed to the general good. This suspicion will never be dissipated until parents, as well as daughters, feel the democratic impulse and recognize the social claim.

Our democracy is making inroads upon the family, the oldest of human institutions, and a claim is being advanced which in a certain sense is larger than the family claim. The claim of the state in time of war has long been recognized, so that in its name the family has given up sons and husbands and even the fathers of little children. If we can once see the claims of society in any such light, if its misery and need can be made clear and urged as an explicit claim, as the state urges its claims in the time of danger, then for the first time the daughter who desires to minister to that need will be recognized as acting conscientiously. This recognition may easily come first through the emotions, and may be admitted as a response to pity and mercy long before it is formulated and perceived by the intellect.

The family as well as the state we are all called upon to maintain as the highest institutions which the race has evolved for its safeguard and protection. But merely to preserve these institutions is not enough. There come periods of reconstruction, during which the task is laid upon a passing generation, to enlarge the function and carry forward the ideal of a long-established institution. There is no doubt that many women, consciously and unconsciously, are struggling with this task. The family, like every other element of human life, is susceptible of progress, and from epoch to epoch its tendencies and aspirations are enlarged, although its duties can never be abrogated and its obligations can never be cancelled. It is impossible to bring about the higher development by any self-assertion or breaking away of the individual will. The new growth in the plant swelling against the sheath, which at the same time imprisons and protects it, must still be the truest type of progress. The family in its entirety must be carried out into the larger life. Its various members together must recognize and acknowledge the validity of the social obligation. When this does not occur we have a most flagrant example of the ill-adjustment and misery arising when an ethical code is applied too rigorously and too conscientiously to conditions which are no longer the same as when the code was instituted, and for which it was never designed. We have all seen parental control and the family claim assert their authority in fields of effort which belong to the adult judgment of the child and pertain to activity quite outside the family life. Probably the distinctively family tragedy, of which we all catch glimpses now and then, is the assertion of this authority through all the entanglements of wounded affection and misunderstanding. We see parents and children acting from conscientious motives and with the tenderest affection, yet bringing about a misery which can scarcely be hidden.

Such glimpses remind us of that tragedy enacted centuries ago in Assisi, when the eager young noble cast his very clothing at his father's feet, dramatically renouncing his filial allegiance, and formally subjecting the narrow family claim to the wider and more universal duty. All the conflict of tragedy ensued which might have been averted, had the father recognized the higher claim, and had he been willing to subordinate and adjust his own claim to it. The father considered his son disrespectful and hard-hearted, yet we know St. Francis to have been the most tender and loving of men, responsive to all possible ties, even to those of inanimate nature. We know that by his affections he freed the frozen life of his time. The elements of tragedy lay in the narrowness of the father's mind; in his lack of comprehension and his lack of sympathy with the power which was moving his son, and which was but part of the religious revival which swept Europe from end to end in the early part of the thirteenth century; the same power which built the cathedrals of the North, and produced the saints and sages of the South. But the father's situation was nevertheless genuine; he felt his heart sore and angry, and his dignity covered with disrespect. He could not, indeed, have felt otherwise, unless he had been touched by the fire of the same revival, and lifted out of and away from the contemplation of himself and his narrower claim. It is another proof that the notion of a larger obligation can only come through the response to an enlarged interest in life and in the social movements around us. . . .

One summer the writer went from a two weeks' residence in East London, where she had become sick and bewildered by the sights and sounds encountered there, directly to Switzerland. She found the beaten routes of travel filled with young English men and women who could walk many miles a day, and who could climb peaks so inaccessible that the feats received honorable mention in Alpine journals, — a result which filled their families with joy and pride. These young people knew to a nicety the proper diet and clothing which would best contribute toward endurance. Everything was very fine about them save their motive power. The writer does not refer to the hard-worked men and women who were taking a vacation, but to the leisured young people, to whom this period was the most serious of the year, and filled with the most strenuous exertion. They did not, of course, thoroughly enjoy it, for we are too complicated to be content with mere exercise. Civilization has bound us too closely with our brethren for anyone of us to be long happy in the cultivation of mere individual force or in the accumulation of mere muscular energy.

With Whitechapel [an impoverished section of London] constantly in mind, it was difficult not to advise these young people to use some of this muscular energy of which they were so proud, in cleaning neglected alleys and paving soggy streets. Their stores of enthusiasm might stir to energy the listless men and women of East London and utilize latent social forces. The exercise would be quite as good, the need of endurance as great, the care for proper dress and food as important; but the motives for action would be turned from selfish ones into social ones. Such an appeal would doubtless be met with a certain response from the young people, but would never be countenanced by their families for an instant. . . .

Wounded affection there is sure to be, but this could be reduced to a modicum if we could preserve a sense of the relation of the individual to the family, and of the latter to society, and if we had been given a code of ethics dealing with these larger relationships, instead of a code designed to apply so exclusively to relationships obtaining only between individuals.

Doubtless the clashes and jars which we all feel most keenly are those which occur when two standards of morals, both honestly held and believed in, are brought sharply together. The awkwardness and constraint we experience when two standards of conventions and manners clash but feebly prefigure this deeper difference.

<hr />

BILL MOYERS

Interview with Martha Nussbaum

Martha Nussbaum is a philosopher who teaches at the University of Chicago. In *The Fragility of Goodness: Luck and Ethics in Greek Tragedy and Philosophy* (1986), she argues that ancient Greek dramas were works of philosophy insofar as they investigated ideas that could not be presented and explored as well in any other way. The emotions that tragedies arouse, Nussbaum believes, have cognitive significance. There are some things we cannot learn without feeling our way through them.

In the conversation below, which was broadcast on public television in 1988, she shows how Aeschylus's tragedy *Agamemnon* speaks directly to questions about the balanced life. Agamemnon's unbearable but unavoidable choice between his daughter and his army, Nussbaum argues, shows how impossible it is to find easy resolutions to the dilemmas that arise when two important commitments conflict. We are all like Agamemnon, she argues, in that we must daily renounce some goods for the sake of other goods, sacrificing things or people that we love for other things or people we also love. Nussbaum argues against several objections to this view, insisting that we give up efforts to deny that "tragedy" — on a small daily scale or in great matters — is a real possibility for those who "live their lives with a deep seriousness of commitment." Indeed, she claims, tragedy happens "*only* to those who seek to live well."

What does Nussbaum see as the alternatives to tragedy and the suf-

<hr />

From Bill Moyers, *A World of Ideas* (New York: Doubleday, 1989), pp. 449-452.

fering it entails? What case does she make for the benefits of a life that is vulnerable to tragedy? Do you agree that "you should care about things in a way that makes it a possibility that tragedy will happen to you"?

————————————

MOYERS: You write about these ancient Greeks — Aristotle, Hecuba, Antigone, Creon — as if they were next-door neighbors. Are they really so vivid to you?

NUSSBAUM: They are. The big problems haven't changed all that much, and the Greek works face these problems head-on, with a courage and eloquence that I don't always find in modern works on moral philosophy.

MOYERS: What kinds of problems?

NUSSBAUM: Take the problem of moral conflict: In Aeschylus' *Agamemnon*, a king is trying to do his best to lead his army off to Troy. Suddenly he finds that his expedition is becalmed, and he's told that the reason is that the gods are demanding a sacrifice. He has to kill his own daughter in order to complete that expedition.

So here we have two deep and entirely legitimate commitments coming into a terrible conflict in which there's not anything the king can do that will be without wrongdoing. On the one hand, if he doesn't sacrifice his daughter, he's disobeying the gods, and his entire expedition is probably going to perish; on the other hand, he's got to kill his own daughter. Thinking about this, as the play says, with tears in his eyes, he says, "A heavy doom is disobedience, but heavy too if I shall rend my own child, the pride of my house, polluting my father's hands with streams of slaughtered maiden's blood close by the altar. Which of these is without evils?"

Often, when you care deeply about more than one thing, the very course of life will bring you round to a situation where you can't honor both of the commitments. It looks like anything you do will be wrong, perhaps even terrible, in some way.

MOYERS: Do you think it's true for the taxi driver out there on the street right now? He doesn't see himself as a King making those horrific choices. Life doesn't present itself to him that way.

NUSSBAUM: Oh, but I think it does, on a smaller basis. Just take a person who has a career and who also has children, and who has to juggle those two responsibilities every day. Nothing will guarantee that in some event you can't prevent from arising, you'll have to neglect one of those commitments and neglect something that's really ethically important because the very course of life has produced a terrible conflict.

 I face this every day myself as a mother who has to juggle career and child-raising. So often, just on a very mundane level, you've got a meeting, and your child's acting in a school play, and you can't do both things. Whatever you do, you're going to be neglecting something that's really important.

MOYERS: So that's what you meant when you wrote that daycare is a modern version of an old Greek tragedy.

NUSSBAUM: If you realize that people face these conflicts, there's an awful lot society can do to provide institutions that make those conflicts arise a little less often. But no social situation, however ideal, is going to make those conflicts just go away.

MOYERS: No, but we were taught to rank obligations — you know the old term, choose priorities — and not to make of every conflict of competing goods a great moral drama.

NUSSBAUM: I think that moral philosophy has had a very bad influence here in two areas. One traditional moral view is that there are no conflicts of obligations, that that's an illogical view. Immanuel Kant and Thomas Aquinas said, in different ways, that any conflict of obligation is really only apparent, that it's a violation of logic to think that there could be a genuine conflict of this kind. I think that view is just a misdescription of what actually happens in people's lives. There is nothing illogical about saying, "I am going to care deeply about my work and my writing; I'm also going to care deeply about my family, my child." That's not illogical. That's perfectly coherent. Over the course of a life, not only can you combine these things, but they actually enrich each other and make the life of each of them better. But that doesn't prevent these terrible situations that you can't entirely foresee.

MOYERS: Is this what you meant when you wrote once that "Tragedy is trying to live well"?

NUSSBAUM: Tragedy happens *only* when you are trying to live well, because for a heedless person who doesn't have deep commitments to others Agamemnon's conflict isn't a tragedy. Somebody who's a bad person could go in and slaughter that child with equanimity or could desert all the men and let them die. But it's when you are trying to live well, and you deeply care about the things you're trying to do, that the world enters in, in a particularly painful way. It's in that struggle with recalcitrant circumstances that a lot of the value of the moral life comes in.

Now the lesson certainly is not to try to maximize conflict or to romanticize struggle and suffering, but it's rather that you should care about things in a way that makes it a possibility that tragedy will happen to you. If you hold your commitments lightly, in such a way that you can always divest yourself from one or the other of them if they conflict, then it doesn't hurt you when things go badly. But you want people to live their lives with a deep seriousness of commitment: not to adjust their desires to the way the world actually goes, but rather to try to wrest from the world the good life that they desire. And sometimes that does lead them into tragedy.

If you really feel what it is to love someone or some commitment and be bound to that, then, when a conflict arises, you will feel deep pain, and you will feel what Agamemnon felt. Even at a smaller level you will feel, "Which of these is without evils?"

MOYERS: And the good life is the life lived according to your moral values, the life that is trying to find an ethical path through the wilderness.

NUSSBAUM: It's a life that is trying to live well toward friends, toward fellow citizens, and toward one's own capabilities and their development.

MOYERS: There are so many conflicting obligations for an individual today: religion, family, friends, state, country, party, neighborhood.

NUSSBAUM: Sometimes people find this so messy that it can't be tolerated, and they retreat into some simplifying view. Either they say, "We know that obligations have to be consistent, and so if there's an apparent conflict, it's not really conflict, and all I have to do is find out which one takes precedence, and the other one just simply drops away and ceases to exert a claim on me"; or they might say, "Well, yes, it's a sort of conflict, but really we see that all values are commensurable, so that if I measure up the quantities of goodness that are here and the quantities of goodness that are over here, then all I need to do is ask myself, 'Where is there a greater quantity of goodness?' and then I go in that direction, and missing out on the other one is sort of like missing out on fifty dollars when what I'm doing is getting two hundred dollars" — and it doesn't seem very painful any more when you look at it that way.

Very often people take up some such way of looking at things because to see that they are really two altogether different things here, both of them seriously worthwhile, both of them things to which you have made a commitment in your own heart, and you can't follow both in this particular circumstance — that is very painful. What the tragedies show us is that temptation to flee into some sort of simplifying theory is a very old temptation, and it probably is going to be around as long as human beings are faced with these problems.

MOYERS: I asked you about the moral lesson, and you said what the tragedies show us. In one sense there is no lesson and no moral, is there? It's simply the revelation of life as seen through the artist, the philosopher, the sufferer, the pilgrim. There's no effort to instruct.

NUSSBAUM: But you know, sometimes just to see the complexity that's there and see it honestly without flinching and without redescribing it in the terms of some excessively simple theory — that is itself progress. It's progress for public life as well as private life, because it's only when we've done that step that we can then ask ourselves, "How can our institutions make it less likely that those conflicts will happen to people? How can we create schemes of child care, for example, that will make this tragic conflict of obligations less of a daily fact of women's lives and perhaps more of a rare and strange occurrence?"

MOYERS: Do you say, "Well, philosophy has helped me to see that this is a natural part of life, and I'll accept the stress and the strain and the conflict, and I'll walk on the tightrope with the balancing rod and hope to get to the other side"?

NUSSBAUM: Sometimes it's pretty clear which one you ought to choose, but it's very, very important to separate the question, "Which is the better choice?" from the question, "Is there any choice available to me here that's free of wrongdoing?" Agamemnon has to sacrifice his daughter because it's clear the gods are going to kill everyone, including the daughter, if he doesn't. Looked at that way, he had better make that choice. Still, he has not got the right to think that just because he's made the right choice, everything is well. In the play, he says, "May all be for the best," and the chorus says that he's mad. You don't accept an artificial, easy solution to this, but the hope would be that through that kind of pain, you understand better what your commitments are and how deep they are. That's what Aeschylus means when he says that through suffering comes a kind of learning — a grace that comes by violence from the gods.

4

Should I Follow My Talents as I Decide What to Do to Earn a Living?

≡≡≡

Suppose that Shakespeare had a sister as talented and as stage-struck as he. Throughout her childhood, the best days of each year were those on which traveling players performed in the village square. How deeply she longed to be up there on the stage with them! How wonderful it would be to hear them speaking the lines she composed! After years of invention and practice with her brother, she knew that she would be good at these things. As the time neared when she would have to marry or enter some great household as a servant, she could think of little but London, that bright city of glorious theaters and crowded bookshops of which her brother had spoken. Longing to act and already full of ideas for the plays she would write, she ignored her parents' protests and made her way to the great city. Once there, however, she could not find honorable work. Her family never heard from her again.

Shakespeare's sister first appeared in the musings of Virginia Woolf, the great English novelist and essayist of the early twentieth century, who included the story in her book *A Room of One's Own* as an example of how impossible it had long been for a woman to support herself by her writing. But Woolf's story also suggests another problem faced by talented artists like this one. Even in the centuries after work in the theater became available to women, including our own time, it seems clear that far more young women have abandoned the relative safety of their hometowns in the hope of acting on the stage than have ever found success in that field. And the same is surely true of men who have aspired to become actors or playwrights. How many have taken huge financial and personal risks to pursue this dream, passing up other opportunities that would have carried many rewards yet failing in the end to secure the jobs they so desired? Were they foolish to let the praise they earned with great performances in high school and college productions go to their heads? Were they unwise to ignore their mothers' worries about how the culturally unorthodox world they were about to enter would affect their moral life, or their fathers' advice to be sure to keep up their payments for health care coverage?

Matt Damon, who is now a hugely successful film actor as well as a writer (we shall read part of a screenplay he wrote later in this chapter), dropped out of Harvard because he was so eager to start working as a professional actor. For him, this risk turned out well, though there were a few years early on when he wondered if it would. Perhaps success finally came because Damon really is more talented than all the others who have done the same thing and failed. The convergence of desire, talent, and luck is rare, however, and only in exceptional cases is it possible to predict what an individual's success will be. Similarly, there are many who have hoped to be professional baseball players who have simply struck out, either because their own talent was an infinitesimal and unpredictable bit short or because they pulled a muscle at just the wrong time.

In our society, athletes and actors are the high-profile figures whose success is most often attributed to their talent. Yet almost everyone who has what the philosopher Immanuel Kant called "fortunate natural aptitudes" is liable to face difficult choices about whether to base the pursuit of specific jobs on these aptitudes. As we shall see in one of the examples below, someone with exceptional mathematical ability might have to leave the place and community he loves if he is to work at a suitably challenging level and contribute his special insights to an important project. Should the fact that he has great talent override his other desires? This problem, of course, is related to the one we explored in the previous chapter: If one has all the personal and intellectual abilities needed to become, say, an outstanding physician, must one agree to undergo the strenuous demands of training and practice even though one desires to lead a more balanced life? Musicians face similar dilemmas: many are forced to spend years on the road, filling in in orchestras for a year at a time or playing small jazz venues all over the country until a permanent position is found or a big record contract is signed — something that never happens for many, in spite of their obvious talent and hard work.

Lest this picture seem to discourage the ambitions that often lie very close to the hearts of those who possess great talents, we should also notice that many other factors do encourage them to cultivate their talents. First, for many exceptionally gifted people choosing *not* to do so is simply unthinkable. As for Sonny, the musician in the story by James Baldwin that concludes this chapter, the gift and the person seem to be one. In addition, strong currents in Western culture press in favor of the cultivation of talents, even in the face of the rather gloomy prospects we have sketched above. As some of the readings in this chapter make plain, it is widely presumed that talent is a strong indication of what kind of work we should pursue. Those who prefer to do something that leaves an outstanding talent undeveloped can be accused of "burying their treasure" (in a common interpretation of a biblical passage), or of self-indulgence (in the judgment of the influential philosopher Immanuel Kant), or of "hiding her gift in a napkin" (by a path-breaking woman novelist of the nineteenth century). Talents are given, in this common judgment, to be used. Even this set of arguments leaves some questions open, however. Must talents be used to provide income? Could a gifted pianist not enjoy playing for her family and friends in the same way that the man in Robert Frost's poem "Two Tramps in Mud Time" (see Chapter 2) enjoys chopping his own firewood?

The selections in this chapter fall into two groups. The first group contains four short texts that wrestle in one way or another with the belief that one must develop one's talents, a belief that has had considerable influence in Western cultures:

- Matthew 25:14-30, The Parable of the Talents
- a sonnet by John Milton
- a passage from Immanuel Kant's *Grounding for the Metaphysics of Morals*
- a selection from *The Life of Charlotte Brontë*, by Elizabeth Gaskell.

A key source of the Western belief that one ought to develop one's talents is a widespread interpretation of a parable of Jesus in the Gospel of Matthew, the parable of the talents. The parable itself is somewhat puzzling, as is typically true of parables; as we shall see, it is not at all clear whether it is really about what we are to do with the kind of "talents" that concern us in this chapter. Nonetheless, the idea that "the Master," presumably God, will punish those who "bury" their "talents" has been for centuries one source of the conviction that if you can do something exceptionally well, then you should make it the focus of your efforts in life.

In the sonnet that follows, the great English poet John Milton draws on this parable's imagery as he tries to come to terms with his blindness, which has robbed him of his ability to invest the "Talent" God has given him. The next reading sets forth the judgment of the philosopher Immanuel Kant about whether it is one's duty to cultivate one's talent. While Milton *cannot* exercise his talent because of disability, Kant imagines a man who *will not* exercise his because he prefers to indulge his ease and pleasure — a choice Kant finds impossible for a rational being to condone. Finally, Elizabeth Gaskell, one of the first successful women authors, reflects on the life of another, Charlotte Brontë, arguing that a gifted woman has a duty to develop her talents, even though this may be nearly impossible because of the weight of unavoidable family duties.

Together, these texts display how strong the pressure to develop one's talent can be, at least among highly educated Europeans such as the last three authors. Milton's poem proposes that God's grace can cover our failure to do so in special cases, but on the whole these literary and philosophical texts seek to persuade those with natural gifts to exercise them.

The second group of readings contains two works of fiction, each of which is not only longer than each text in the first group but also more ambiguous in its response to the question we are considering. These are:

- two scenes from the screenplay of *Good Will Hunting*
- "Sonny's Blues," a short story by James Baldwin.

Both of these readings invite us to ponder the choices faced by young men from working-class urban backgrounds who happen to possess remarkable gifts. For Will, a mathematics genius from South Boston, deciding to accept a job that will use his immense talent means leaving his friends and neighborhood. For Sonny, a musical genius from Harlem, finding work as a jazz pianist means entering a dangerous subculture that is also remote from the support he has known earlier in life. We meet Will in the midst of his decision; we see Sonny after his is made. In each case, we will want to ask what these characters should do or should have done. Is doing work that draws fully on their remarkable talents the best path to a life that matters?

MATTHEW 25:14-30

The Parable of the Talents

In this parable of Jesus, the word translated as "talent" obviously refers to a unit of money, not to an aptitude or a special ability. Nevertheless, within the Christian tradition of interpretation the parable has been read as a metaphor for the proper use of talent in the latter sense of the word. Just as Aristotle broadened the definition of "wealth" by saying that it includes anything that can be measured by money, some Christians have broadened the meaning of "talent" here by saying that it refers not just to treasure but also to the use of time and ability.

Read in this way, the parable raises questions about whether native abilities or aptitudes should ever be "buried." If we do have a special talent, would it be wrong for us to fail to use it for the welfare of others? Do we have a duty to cultivate the talent? If so, what if we have many talents? Must all of them be cultivated? If so, must our paid employment be the only or the principal place where we develop our special gifts?

"For it is as if a man, going on a journey, summoned his slaves and entrusted his property to them; to one he gave five talents, to another two, to another one, to each according to his ability. Then he went away. The one who had received the five talents went off at once and traded with them, and made five more talents. In the same way, the one who had the two talents made two more talents. But the one who had received the one talent went off and dug a hole in the ground and hid his master's money. After a long time the master of those slaves came and settled accounts with them. Then the one who had received the five talents came forward, bringing five more talents,

---

From the New Revised Standard Version of the Bible.

saying, 'Master, you handed over to me five talents; see, I have made five more talents.' His master said to him, 'Well done, good and trustworthy slave; you have been trustworthy in a few things, I will put you in charge of many things; enter into the joy of your master.' And the one with the two talents also came forward, saying, 'Master, you handed over to me two talents; see, I have made two more talents.' His master said to him, 'Well done, good and trustworthy slave; you have been trustworthy in a few things, I will put you in charge of many things; enter into the joy of your master.' Then the one who had received the one talent also came forward, saying, 'Master, I knew that you were a harsh man, reaping where you did not sow, and gathering where you did not scatter seed; so I was afraid, and I went and hid your talent in the ground. Here you have what is yours.' But his master replied, 'You wicked and lazy slave! You knew, did you, that I reap where I did not sow, and gather where I did not scatter? Then you ought to have invested my money with the bankers, and on my return I would have received what was my own with interest. So take the talent from him, and give it to the one with the ten talents. For to all those who have, more will be given, and they will have an abundance; but from those who have nothing, even what they have will be taken away. As for this worthless slave, throw him into the outer darkness, where there will be weeping and gnashing of teeth.'"

JOHN MILTON

"On His Blindness"

John Milton (1608-1674) is widely considered one of the greatest poets of the English language. Like his epic poems *Paradise Lost* and *Paradise Regained*, this sonnet arises from profound reflection on the meaning of Christian Scriptures — here, the parable of the talents. If it is "death" to

From *The Complete Poems of John Milton*, The Harvard Classics (New York: P. F. Collier, 1909), p. 86.

hide one's "Talent," as the Master in the parable declares, what is Milton to make of the fact that due to his blindness his talent is "lodged with me useless"? He imagines talking back to God in protest against this injustice, but "Patience" suggests an alternative, more gracious account of God's expectations.

This poem was written in 1655, as Milton's eyesight failed. In fact, his greatest writing lay ahead of him; his "Talent" would not long be useless. Nonetheless, the sonnet raises a genuine question that has caused many to despair about whether they can lead significant lives: What are we to do with a talent that cannot be cultivated because of disability or some other powerful obstacle? Do you agree that "they also serve who only stand and wait"?

When I consider how my light is spent
Ere half my days in this dark world and wide,
And that one Talent which is death to hide
Lodged with me useless, though my soul more bent
To serve therewith my Maker, and present
My true account, lest he returning chide,
"Doth God exact day-labour, light denied?"
I fondly ask. But Patience, to prevent
That murmur, soon replies, "God does not need
Either man's work or his own gifts. Who best
Bear his mild yoke, they serve him best. His state
Is kingly: thousands at his bidding speed,
And post o'er land and ocean without rest;
They also serve who only stand and wait."

IMMANUEL KANT

Grounding for the Metaphysics of Morals

Immanuel Kant (1724-1804) is one of the most influential philosophers in the Western tradition. The following reading comes from a section of his work in which he is considering the duties we owe to ourselves or to one another. His argument builds on the "categorical imperative," an ethical principle that is central to his thought: "Act as if the maxim from which you act were to become through your will a universal law." When we are deciding what it is our duty to do, in other words, we should decide to act in a way that would be good if all persons were to take the same action. What does this principle lead Kant to conclude is our duty with regard to cultivating our "fortunate natural aptitudes"? What would he think of someone who chose not to do so? Do you agree?

3e. A third finds in himself a talent whose cultivation could make him a man useful in many respects. But he finds himself in comfortable circumstances and prefers to indulge in pleasure rather than to bother himself about broadening and improving his fortunate natural aptitudes. But he asks himself further whether his maxim of neglecting his natural gifts, besides agreeing of itself with his propensity to indulgence, might agree also with what is called duty. He then sees that a system of nature could indeed always subsist according to such a universal law, even though every man . . . should let his talents rust and resolve to devote his life entirely to idleness, indulgence, propagation, and, in a word, to enjoyment. But he cannot possibly will that this should become a universal law of nature or be implanted in us as such a law by a natural instinct. For as a rational being he necessarily wills that all his faculties should be developed, inasmuch as they are given him for all sorts of possible purposes.

From Immanuel Kant, *Grounding for the Metaphysics of Morals*, trans. James W. Ellington (Indianapolis: Hackett Publishing Company, Inc., 1993), p. 31.

ELIZABETH GASKELL

The Life of Charlotte Brontë

In this reading, first published in 1857, one gifted woman reflects on the challenges faced by another in a society where women had little social support in developing their talents, and indeed where it was widely assumed that women were unlikely to have noteworthy talents in any case. The successful English novelist Elizabeth Gaskell (1810-1865) befriended Charlotte Brontë (1816-1855) when the latter was disclosed to be the astonishing new novelist "Currer Bell" (the male pseudonym Brontë had adopted), the author of *Jane Eyre*. Gaskell's biography of Brontë, though not always fully accurate, provides a vivid and sympathetic account of the difficulties the younger author had to overcome in cultivating her talent as a writer. Among the difficulties Brontë faced was reconciling the "separate duties" that belonged to the "two parallel currents — her life as Currer Bell, the author; her life as Charlotte Brontë, the woman," as Gaskell put it just before the passage below.

Because this reading concerns Brontë's effort to reconcile these two currents, it would also fit as a response to Question Three of this anthology: Is a balanced life possible and preferable to one focused on one thing? Yet here we note especially Gaskell's then countercultural insistence that a gifted woman "must not hide her gift in a napkin." On what basis does Gaskell make a case for cultivating the talents of women who have outstanding aptitudes? Has social change since 1857 made her views seem antiquated, or is Gaskell's insistence that a woman "should do what is not impossible" still forward-looking today? And what do you make of her comments about men and their talents? Might this passage now have more relevance to the lives of men than she could have foreseen?

From Elizabeth C. Gaskell, *The Life of Charlotte Brontë* (1857; London: Oxford University Press, 1919), p. 279.

When a man becomes an author, it is probably merely a change of employment to him. He takes a portion of that time which has hitherto been devoted to some other study or pursuit; he gives up something of the legal or medical profession, in which he has hitherto endeavoured to serve others, or relinquishes part of the trade or business by which he has been striving to gain a livelihood; and another merchant, or lawyer, or doctor, steps into his vacant place, and probably does as well as he. But no other can take up the quiet, regular duties of the daughter, the wife, or the mother, as well as she whom God has appointed to fill that particular place: a woman's principal work in life is hardly left to her own choice; nor can she drop the domestic charges devolving on her as an individual, for the exercise of the most splendid talents that were ever bestowed. And yet she must not shrink from the extra responsibility implied by the very fact of her possessing such talents. She must not hide her gift in a napkin; it was meant for the use and service of others. In an humble and faithful spirit must she labour to do what is not impossible, or God would not have set her to do it.

———

MATT DAMON AND BEN AFFLECK

Good Will Hunting

The title of this 1997 film is a pun. On the one hand it refers to the title character, whose name is Will Hunting. On the other hand it implies that the film is about this character's hunt for something — for his vocation or, in a larger sense, for his identity — that he can accept with good will.

Will Hunting is a genius. He can work out problems in mathematics that baffle the professors who teach at MIT, where he works as a janitor. For complicated reasons that he does not himself fully understand, Will simultaneously hides and displays his prodigious ability by sneaking around the halls of the school at night and writing the solutions to complicated

From Matt Damon and Ben Affleck, *Good Will Hunting: A Screenplay* (New York: Miramax Books, 1997), pp. 125-134.

problems others cannot solve on chalkboards in the hallways. Will claims that he simply wants to be a manual laborer — a custodian or a bricklayer — instead of a code breaker for the government, the job he has been offered. As the scene unfolds between Will and Sean, his therapist, do you think Will really means what he says, or is he troubled by, or even afraid of, his own genius? Have you ever failed to develop a talent for fear of what might be expected or required of you if you did so?

The second series of exchanges in the screenplay takes place between Will and his friend Chuckie, both of whom are doing construction work. Chuckie thinks that he will be and probably should be a construction worker for his entire life. Like Sean, however, he recognizes Will's talent and hopes that Will will use it. Sometimes our teachers and friends can recognize and appreciate our talents more than we can. If several of our acquaintances urge us to pursue a particular vocation on the basis of our extraordinary aptitudes for that calling, are we obliged to follow their advice? Why or why not? In his exchange with Chuckie, Will suggests that he values place — the neighborhood and his friends — over career, desire over talent. Gary Badcock (see Part I) argued that it is often quite legitimate to prefer place over occupation, desire over talent. What do you think?

Damon and Affleck won an Academy Award for writing the screenplay for this film, in which they also starred as Will and Chuckie. Robin Williams played Sean, Will's therapist.

INT. SEAN'S OFFICE — NIGHT

Will sits across from Sean.

SEAN   So you might be working for Uncle Sam.

WILL   I don't know.

SEAN   Gerry says the meeting went well.

WILL   I guess.

SEAN   What did you think?

WILL   What did I think?

A beat. Will has obviously been stewing on this.

WILL   *(cont'd)*
Say I'm working at N.S.A. Somebody puts a code on my desk, something nobody else can break. So I take a shot at it and maybe I break it. And I'm real happy with myself, 'cause I did my job well. But maybe that code was the location of some rebel army in North Africa or the Middle East. Once they have that location, they bomb the village where the rebels were hiding and fifteen hundred people I never had a problem with get killed.

(rapid fire)

Now the politicians are sayin' "send in the Marines to secure the area" 'cause they don't give a shit. It won't be their kid over there, gettin' shot. Just like it wasn't them when their number got called, 'cause they were pullin' a tour in the National Guard. It'll be some guy from Southie takin' shrapnel in the ass. And he comes home to find that the plant he used to work at got exported to the country he just got back from. And the guy who put the shrapnel in his ass got his old job, 'cause he'll work for fifteen cents a day and no bathroom breaks.

Meanwhile my buddy from Southie realizes the only reason he was over there was so we could install a government that would sell us oil at a good price.

And of course the oil companies used the skirmish to scare up oil prices so they could turn a quick buck. A cute, little ancillary benefit for them but it ain't helping my buddy at two-fifty a gallon. And naturally they're takin' their sweet time bringin' the oil back and maybe even took the liberty of hiring an alcoholic skipper who likes to drink seven and sevens and play slalom with the icebergs and it ain't too long 'til he hits one, spills the oil, and kills all the sea-life in the North Atlantic. So my buddy's out of work and he can't afford to drive so he's got to walk to the job interviews which sucks 'cause the shrapnel in his ass is givin' him chronic hemorrhoids. And meanwhile he's starvin' 'cause every time he tries to get a bite to eat the only blue-plate special they're servin' is North Atlantic scrod with Quaker State.

A beat.

WILL   *(cont'd)*
So what'd I think? I'm holdin' out for somethin' better. I figure

I'll eliminate the middle man. Why not just shoot my buddy, take his job and give it to his sworn enemy, hike up gas prices, bomb a village, club a baby seal, hit the hash pipe and join the National Guard? Christ, I could be elected President.

SEAN   Do you think you're alone?

WILL   What?

SEAN   Do you have a soul-mate?

WILL   Define that.

SEAN   Someone who challenges you in every way. Who takes you places, opens things up for you. A soul-mate.

WILL   Yeah.

Sean waits.

WILL   (cont'd)
Shakespeare, Neitzche [sic], Frost, O'Connor, Chaucer, Pope, Kant —

SEAN   They're all dead.

WILL   Not to me, they're not.

SEAN   But you can't give back to them, Will.

WILL   Not without a heater and some serious smelling salts, no . . .

SEAN   That's what I'm saying, Will. You'll never have that kind of relationship in a world where you're afraid to take the first step because all you're seeing are the negative things that might happen ten miles down the road.

WILL   Oh, what? You're going to take the professor's side on this?

SEAN   Don't give me your line of shit.

WILL   I didn't want the job.

SEAN   It's not about that job. I'm not saying you should work for the government. But, you could do anything you want. And there are people who work their whole lives layin' brick so their kids have a chance at the kind of opportunity you have. What do you want to do?

WILL   I didn't ask for this.

SEAN   Nobody gets what they ask for, Will. That's a cop-out.

WILL   Why is it a cop-out? I don't see anythin' wrong with layin'
            brick, that's somebody's home I'm buildin'. Or fixin' some-
            body's car, somebody's gonna get to work the next day 'cause
            of me. There's honor in that.

SEAN   You're right, Will. Any man who takes a forty minute train ride
            so those college kids can come in in the morning and their
            floors will be clean and their trash cans will be empty is an hon-
            orable man.

            A beat. Will says nothing.

SEAN   *(cont'd)*
            And when they get drunk and puke in the sink, they don't have
            to see it the next morning because of you. That's real work,
            Will. And there is honor in that. Which I'm sure is why you
            took the job.

            A beat.

SEAN   *(cont'd)*
            I just want to know why you decided to sneak around at night,
            writing on chalkboards and lying about it.

            (beat)

            'Cause there's no honor in that.

            Will is silent.

SEAN   *(cont'd)*
            Something you want to say?

            Sean gets up, goes to the door and opens it.

SEAN   *(cont'd)*
            Why don't you come back when you have an answer for me.

WILL   What?

SEAN   If you won't answer my questions, you're wasting my time.

WILL   What?

            Will loses it, slams the door shut.

WILL   *(cont'd)*
Fuck you!

Sean has finally gotten to Will.

WILL   *(cont'd)*
Who the fuck are you to lecture me about life? You fuckin'
burnout! Where's your "soul-mate"?!

Sean lets this play out.

WILL   *(cont'd)*
Dead! She dies and you just cash in your chips. That's a fuckin'
cop-out!

SEAN   I been there. I played my hand.

WILL   That's right. And you fuckin' lost! And some people would
have the sack to lose a big hand like that and still come back
and ante up again!

SEAN   Look at me. What do you want to do?

A beat. Will looks up.

SEAN   *(cont'd)*
You and your bullshit. You got an answer for everybody. But I
asked you a straight question and you can't give me a straight
answer. Because you don't know.

Sean goes to the door and opens it. Will walks out.

CUT TO:
INT. MAGGIORE BUILDER'S CONSTRUCTION SITE — DAY

*Will and Chuckie take crowbars to a wall. This is what they do for a
living. As they routinely hammer away, Will becomes more involved in
his battle with the wall. Plaster and lathing fly as Will vents his rage.
Chuckie, noticing, stops working and takes a step back, watching Will.
Will is oblivious. . . .*

EXT. HANRAHAN'S PACKAGE STORE — LATER

*Will walks out carrying a brown bag. He is filthy, having just knocked
off work.*

CUT TO:
EXT. MAGGIORE BUILDER'S CONSTRUCTION SITE — PARKING LOT

Chuckie is sitting on the hood of his Cadillac, watching Will across the street. Chuckie is covered in grime as well. Will starts walking towards Chuckie. As he draws closer, he heaves a can of Budweiser a good thirty yards, to Chuckie, who handles it routinely.

Will takes a seat next to Chuckie and they crack open their beers. Other workers file out of the site. They drink.

CHUCKIE   How's the woman?

WILL   Gone.

CHUCKIE   What?

WILL   She went to Medical school in California.

CHUCKIE   Sorry, brother.

(beat)

I don't know what to tell ya. You know all the girls I been with. You been with 'em too, except for Cheryl McGovern which was a big mistake on your part brother . . .

WILL   Oh I'm sure, that's why only one of us has herpes.

CHUCKIE   Some shows are worth the price of admission, partner.

This gets a small laugh from Will.

CHUCKIE   *(cont'd)*
My fuckin' back is killin' me.

A passing SHEET METAL WORKER overhears this.

SHEET METAL WORKER
That's why you should'a gone to college.

WILL   Fuck you.

CHUCKIE   Suck my crank. Fuckin' sheet metal pussy.

(beat)

So, when are you done with those meetin's?

WILL   Week after I'm twenty-one.

CHUCKIE   Are they hookin' you up with a job?

WILL   Yeah, sit in a room and do long division for the next fifty years.

CHUCKIE   Yah, but it's better than this shit.
At least you'd make some nice bank.

WILL   Yeah, be a fuckin' lab rat.

CHUCKIE   It's a way outta here.

WILL   What do I want a way outta here for? I want to live here the rest of my life. I want to be your next door neighbor. I want to take our kids to little league together up Foley Field.

CHUCKIE   Look, you're my best friend, so don't take this the wrong way, but in 20 years, if you're livin' next door to me, comin' over watchin' the fuckin' Patriots' games and still workin' construction, I'll fuckin' kill you. And that's not a threat, that's a fact. I'll fuckin' kill you.

WILL   Chuckie, what are you talkin' . . .

CHUCKIE   Listen, you got somethin' that none of us have.

WILL   Why is it always this? I owe it to myself? What if I don't want to?

CHUCKIE   Fuck you. You owe it to me. Tomorrow I'm gonna wake up and I'll be fifty and I'll still be doin' this. And that's all right 'cause I'm gonna make a run at it. But you, you're sittin' on a winning lottery ticket and you're too much of a pussy to cash it in. And that's bullshit 'cause I'd do anything to have what you got! And so would any of these guys. It'd be a fuckin' insult to us if you're still here in twenty years.

WILL   You don't know that.

CHUCKIE   Let me tell you what I do know. Every day I come by to pick you up, and we go out drinkin' or whatever and we have a few laughs. But you know what the best part of my day is? The ten seconds before I knock on the door 'cause I let myself think I might get there, and you'd be gone. I'd knock on the door and you wouldn't be there. You just left.

    A beat.

CHUCKIE   *(cont'd)*
Now, I don't know much. But I know that.

JAMES BALDWIN

"Sonny's Blues"

James Baldwin (1924-1987), a leading American novelist of the mid-twentieth century, grew up in circumstances much like those of the characters we meet in this story. The story's narrator has survived the hazards that threaten the well-being of young men in Harlem and has become a happily married high school teacher, in spite of considerable loss and hardship along the way. His younger brother, Sonny, has apparently been less fortunate.

This story raises the question of whether Sonny's exceptional musical talent, which he has cultivated under very difficult circumstances, is partly to blame for his suffering. The title "Sonny's Blues" could refer either to the immense pain Sonny has endured or to the wonderful music he is able to create. Or does Baldwin mean to suggest that the two are inseparably interwoven? Would a life of greater safety be preferable to the creative but tortured life Sonny has led?

I read about it in the paper, in the subway, on my way to work. I read it, and I couldn't believe it, and I read it again. Then perhaps I just stared at it, at the newsprint spelling out his name, spelling out the story. I stared at it in the swinging lights of the subway car, and in the faces and bodies of the people, and in my own face, trapped in the darkness which roared outside.

It was not to be believed and I kept telling myself that, as I walked from the subway station to the high school. And at the same time I couldn't doubt it. I was scared, scared for Sonny. He became real to me again. A great block of ice got settled in my belly and kept melting there slowly all day long, while I taught my classes algebra. It was a special kind of ice. It kept melting, sending trickles of ice water all up and down my veins, but it never got less.

From James Baldwin, *Going to Meet the Man* (New York: Dial Press, 1965), pp. 103-141.

Sometimes it hardened and seemed to expand until I felt my guts were going to come spilling out or that I was going to choke or scream. This would always be at a moment when I was remembering some specific thing Sonny had once said or done.

When he was about as old as the boys in my classes his face had been bright and open, there was a lot of copper in it; and he'd had wonderfully direct brown eyes, and great gentleness and privacy. I wondered what he looked like now. He had been picked up, the evening before, in a raid on an apartment downtown, for peddling and using heroin.

I couldn't believe it: but what I mean by that is that I couldn't find any room for it anywhere inside me. I had kept it outside me for a long time. I hadn't wanted to know. I had had suspicions, but I didn't name them, I kept putting them away. I told myself that Sonny was wild, but he wasn't crazy. And he'd always been a good boy, he hadn't ever turned hard or evil or disrespectful, the way kids can, so quick, so quick, especially in Harlem. I didn't want to believe that I'd ever see my brother going down, coming to nothing, all that light in his face gone out, in the condition I'd already seen so many others. Yet it had happened and here I was, talking about algebra to a lot of boys who might, every one of them for all I knew, be popping off needles every time they went to the head. Maybe it did more for them than algebra could.

I was sure that the first time Sonny had ever had horse, he couldn't have been much older than these boys were now. These boys, now, were living as we'd been living then, they were growing up with a rush and their heads bumped abruptly against the low ceiling of their actual possibilities. They were filled with rage. All they really knew were two darknesses, the darkness of their lives, which was now closing in on them, and the darkness of the movies, which had blinded them to that other darkness, and in which they now, vindictively, dreamed, at once more together than they were at any other time, and more alone.

When the last bell rang, the last class ended, I let out my breath. It seemed I'd been holding it for all that time. My clothes were wet — I may have looked as though I'd been sitting in a steam bath, all dressed up, all afternoon. I sat alone in the classroom a long time. I listened to the boys outside, downstairs, shouting and cursing and laughing. Their laughter struck me for perhaps the first time. It was not the joyous laughter which — God knows why — one associates with children. It was mocking and insular, its intent was to denigrate. It was disenchanted, and in this, also, lay the authority of their curses. Perhaps I was listening to them because I was thinking about my brother and in them I heard my brother. And myself.

One boy was whistling a tune, at once very complicated and very simple, it seemed to be pouring out of him as though he were a bird, and it sounded very cool and moving through all that harsh, bright air, only just holding its own through all those other sounds.

I stood up and walked over to the window and looked down into the courtyard. It was the beginning of the spring and the sap was rising in the boys. A teacher passed through them every now and again, quickly, as though he or she couldn't wait to get out of that courtyard, to get those boys out of their sight and off their minds. I started collecting my stuff. I thought I'd better get home and talk to Isabel.

The courtyard was almost deserted by the time I got downstairs. I saw this boy standing in the shadow of a doorway, looking just like Sonny. I almost called his name. Then I saw that it wasn't Sonny, but somebody we used to know, a boy from around our block. He'd been Sonny's friend. He'd never been mine, having been too young for me, and, anyway, I'd never liked him. And now, even though he was a grown-up man, he still hung around that block, still spent hours on the street corners, was always high and raggy. I used to run into him from time to time and he'd often work around to asking me for a quarter or fifty cents. He always had some real good excuse, too, and I always gave it to him, I don't know why.

But now, abruptly, I hated him. I couldn't stand the way he looked at me, partly like a dog, partly like a cunning child. I wanted to ask him what the hell he was doing in the school courtyard.

He sort of shuffled over to me, and he said, "I see you got the papers. So you already know about it."

"You mean about Sonny? Yes, I already know about it. How come they didn't get you?"

He grinned. It made him repulsive and it also brought to mind what he'd looked like as a kid. "I wasn't there. I stay away from them people."

"Good for you." I offered him a cigarette and I watched him through the smoke. "You come all the way down here just to tell me about Sonny?"

"That's right." He was sort of shaking his head and his eyes looked strange, as though they were about to cross. The bright sun deadened his damp dark brown skin and it made his eyes look yellow and showed up the dirt in his kinked hair. He smelled funky. I moved a little away from him and I said, "Well, thanks. But I already know about it and I got to get home."

"I'll walk you a little ways," he said. We started walking. There were a couple of kids still loitering in the courtyard and one of them said good-night to me and looked strangely at the boy beside me.

"What're you going to do?" he asked me. "I mean, about Sonny?"

"Look. I haven't seen Sonny for over a year, I'm not sure I'm going to do anything. Anyway, what the hell *can* I do?"

"That's right," he said quickly, "ain't nothing you can do. Can't much help old Sonny no more, I guess."

It was what I was thinking and so it seemed to me he had no right to say it.

"I'm surprised at Sonny, though," he went on — he had a funny way of talking, he looked straight ahead as though he were talking to himself — "I thought Sonny was a smart boy, I thought he was too smart to get hung."

"I guess he thought so too," I said sharply, "and that's how he got hung. And now about you? You're pretty goddamn smart, I bet."

Then he looked directly at me, just for a minute. "I ain't smart," he said. "If I was smart, I'd have reached for a pistol a long time ago."

"Look. Don't tell *me* your sad story, if it was up to me, I'd give you one." Then I felt guilty — guilty, probably, for never having supposed that the poor bastard *had* a story of his own, much less a sad one, and I asked, quickly, "What's going to happen to him now?"

He didn't answer this. He was off by himself some place. "Funny thing," he said, and from his tone we might have been discussing the quickest way to get to Brooklyn, "when I saw the papers this morning, the first thing I asked myself was if I had anything to do with it. I felt sort of responsible."

I began to listen more carefully. The subway station was on the corner, just before us, and I stopped. He stopped, too. We were in front of a bar and he ducked slightly, peering in, but whoever he was looking for didn't seem to be there. The juke box was blasting away with something black and bouncy and I half watched the barmaid as she danced her way from the juke box to her place behind the bar. And I watched her face as she laughingly responded to something someone said to her, still keeping time to the music. When she smiled one saw the little girl, one sensed the doomed, still-struggling woman beneath the battered face of the semi-whore.

"I never *give* Sonny nothing," the boy said finally, "but a long time ago I come to school high and Sonny asked me how it felt." He paused, I couldn't bear to watch him, I watched the barmaid, and I listened to the music which seemed to be causing the pavement to shake. "I told him it felt great." The music stopped, the barmaid paused and watched the juke box until the music began again. "It did."

All this was carrying me some place I didn't want to go. I certainly didn't want to know how it felt. It filled everything, the people, the houses, the music, the dark, quicksilver barmaid, with menace; and this menace was their reality.

333

"What's going to happen to him now?" I asked again.

"They'll send him away some place and they'll try to cure him." He shook his head. "Maybe he'll even think he's kicked the habit. Then they'll let him loose" — he gestured, throwing his cigarette into the gutter. "That's all."

"What do you mean, that's *all?*"

But I knew what he meant.

"I *mean*, that's *all*." He turned his head and looked at me, pulling down the corners of his mouth. "Don't you know what I mean?" he asked, softly.

"How the hell *would* I know what you mean?" I almost whispered it, I don't know why.

"That's right," he said to the air, "how would *he* know what I mean?" He turned toward me again, patient and calm, and yet I somehow felt him shaking, shaking as though he were going to fall apart. I felt that ice in my guts again, the dread I'd felt all afternoon; and again I watched the barmaid, moving about the bar, washing glasses, and singing. "Listen. They'll let him out and then it'll just start all over again. That's what I mean."

"You mean — they'll let him out. And then he'll just start working his way back in again. You mean he'll never kick the habit. Is that what you mean?"

"That's right," he said, cheerfully. "*You* see what I mean."

"Tell me," I said at last, "why does he want to die? He must want to die, he's killing himself, why does he want to die?"

He looked at me in surprise. He licked his lips. "He don't want to die. He wants to live. Don't nobody want to die, ever."

Then I wanted to ask him — too many things. He could not have answered, or if he had, I could not have borne the answers. I started walking. "Well, I guess it's none of my business."

"It's going to be rough on old Sonny," he said. We reached the subway station. "This is your station?" he asked. I nodded. I took one step down. "Damn!" he said, suddenly. I looked up at him. He grinned again. "Damn it if I didn't leave all my money home. You ain't got a dollar on you, have you? Just for a couple of days, is all."

All at once something inside gave and threatened to come pouring out of me. I didn't hate him any more. I felt that in another moment I'd start crying like a child.

"Sure," I said. "Don't sweat." I looked in my wallet and didn't have a dollar, I only had a five. "Here," I said. "That hold you?"

He didn't look at it — he didn't want to look at it. A terrible, closed look came over his face, as though he were keeping the number on the bill a secret from him and me. "Thanks," he said, and now he was dying to see me go. "Don't worry about Sonny. Maybe I'll write him or something."

"Sure," I said. "You do that. So long."

"Be seeing you," he said. I went on down the steps.

And I didn't write Sonny or send him anything for a long time. When I finally did, it was just after my little girl died, he wrote me back a letter which made me feel like a bastard.

Here's what he said:

Dear brother,

You don't know how much I needed to hear from you. I wanted to write you many a time but I dug how much I must have hurt you and so I didn't write. But now I feel like a man who's been trying to climb up out of some deep, real deep and funky hole and just saw the sun up there, outside. I got to get outside.

I can't tell you much about how I got here. I mean I don't know how to tell you. I guess I was afraid of something or I was trying to escape from something and you know I have never been very strong in the head (smile). I'm glad Mama and Daddy are dead and can't see what's happened to their son and I swear if I'd known what I was doing I would never have hurt you so, you and a lot of other fine people who were nice to me and who believed in me.

I don't want you to think it had anything to do with me being a musician. It's more than that. Or maybe less than that. I can't get anything straight in my head down here and I try not to think about what's going to happen to me when I get outside again. Sometime I think I'm going to flip and *never* get outside and sometime I think I'll come straight back. I tell you one thing, though, I'd rather blow my brains out than go through this again. But that's what they all say, so they tell me. If I tell you when I'm coming to New York and if you could meet me, I sure would appreciate it. Give my love to Isabel and the kids and I was sure sorry to hear about little Gracie. I wish I could be like Mama and say the Lord's will be done, but I don't know it seems to me that trouble is the one thing that never does get stopped and I don't know what good it does to blame it on the Lord. But maybe it does some good if you believe it.

Your brother,
Sonny

Then I kept in constant touch with him and I sent him whatever I could and I went to meet him when he came back to New York. When I saw him many things I thought I had forgotten came flooding back to me. This was because I had begun, finally, to wonder about Sonny, about the life that Sonny lived inside. This life, whatever it was, had made him older and thinner and it had deepened the distant stillness in which he had always moved. He looked very unlike my baby brother. Yet, when he smiled, when we shook hands, the baby brother I'd never known looked out from the depths of his private life, like an animal waiting to be coaxed into the light.

"How you been keeping?" he asked me.

"All right. And you?"

"Just fine." He was smiling all over his face. "It's good to see you again."

"It's good to see you."

The seven years' difference in our ages lay between us like a chasm: I wondered if these years would ever operate between us as a bridge. I was remembering, and it made it hard to catch my breath, that I had been there when he was born; and I had heard the first words he had ever spoken. When he started to walk, he walked from our mother straight to me. I caught him just before he fell when he took the first steps he ever took in this world.

"How's Isabel?"

"Just fine. She's dying to see you."

"And the boys?"

"They're fine, too. They're anxious to see their uncle."

"Oh, come on. You know they don't remember me."

"Are you kidding? Of course they remember you."

He grinned again. We got into a taxi. We had a lot to say to each other, far too much to know how to begin.

As the taxi began to move, I asked, "You still want to go to India?"

He laughed. "You still remember that. Hell, no. This place is Indian enough for me."

"It used to belong to them," I said.

And he laughed again. "They damn sure knew what they were doing when they got rid of it."

Years ago, when he was around fourteen, he'd been all hipped on the idea of going to India. He read books about people sitting on rocks, naked, in all kinds of weather, but mostly bad, naturally, and walking barefoot through hot coals and arriving at wisdom. I used to say that it sounded to me as though they were getting away from wisdom as fast as they could. I think he sort of looked down on me for that.

"Do you mind," he asked, "if we have the driver drive alongside the park? On the west side — I haven't seen the city in so long."

"Of course not," I said. I was afraid that I might sound as though I were humoring him, but I hoped he wouldn't take it that way.

So we drove along, between the green of the park and the stony, lifeless elegance of hotels and apartment buildings, toward the vivid, killing streets of our childhood. These streets hadn't changed, though housing projects jutted up out of them now like rocks in the middle of a boiling sea. Most of the houses in which we had grown up had vanished, as had the stores from which we had stolen, the basements in which we had first tried sex, the rooftops from which we had hurled tin cans and bricks. But houses exactly like the houses of our past yet dominated the landscape, boys exactly like the boys we once had been found themselves smothering in these houses, came down into the streets for light and air and found themselves encircled by disaster. Some escaped the trap, most didn't. Those who got out always left something of themselves behind, as some animals amputate a leg and leave it in the trap. It might be said, perhaps, that I had escaped, after all, I was a school teacher; or that Sonny had, he hadn't lived in Harlem for years. Yet, as the cab moved uptown through streets which seemed, with a rush, to darken with dark people, and as I covertly studied Sonny's face, it came to me that what we both were seeking through our separate cab windows was that part of ourselves which had been left behind. It's always at the hour of trouble and confrontation that the missing member aches.

We hit 110th Street and started rolling up Lenox Avenue. And I'd known this avenue all my life, but it seemed to me again, as it had seemed on the day I'd first heard about Sonny's trouble, filled with a hidden menace which was its very breath of life.

"We almost there," said Sonny.

"Almost." We were both too nervous to say anything more.

We live in a housing project. It hasn't been up long. A few days after it was up it seemed uninhabitably new, now, of course, it's already rundown. It looks like a parody of the good, clean, faceless life — God knows the people who live in it do their best to make it a parody. The beat-looking grass lying around isn't enough to make their lives green, the hedges will never hold out the streets, and they know it. The big windows fool no one, they aren't big enough to make space out of no space. They don't bother with the windows, they watch the TV screen instead. The playground is most popular with the children who don't play at jacks, or skip rope, or roller skate, or swing, and they can be found in it after dark. We moved in partly because it's not too far from where I teach, and partly for the kids; but it's really just like the houses in which Sonny and I grew up. The same things happen, they'll have the same things to remember. The moment Sonny and I started into the house I had the feeling that I was simply bringing him back into the danger he had almost died trying to escape.

Sonny has never been talkative. So I don't know why I was sure he'd be dying to talk to me when supper was over the first night. Everything went fine, the oldest boy remembered him, and the youngest boy liked him, and Sonny had remembered to bring something for each of them; and Isabel, who is really much nicer than I am, more open and giving, had gone to a lot of trouble about dinner and was genuinely glad to see him. And she's always been able to tease Sonny in a way that I haven't. It was nice to see her face so vivid again and to hear her laugh and watch her make Sonny laugh. She wasn't, or, anyway, she didn't seem to be, at all uneasy or embarrassed. She chatted as though there were no subject which had to be avoided and she got Sonny past his first, faint stiffness. And thank God she was there, for I was filled with that icy dread again. Everything I did seemed awkward to me, and everything I said sounded freighted with hidden meaning. I was trying to re-member everything I'd heard about dope addiction and I couldn't help watching Sonny for signs. I wasn't doing it out of malice. I was trying to find out something about my brother. I was dying to hear him tell me he was safe.

"Safe!" my father grunted, whenever Mama suggested trying to move to a neighborhood which might be safer for children. "Safe, hell! Ain't no place safe for kids, nor nobody."

He always went on like this, but he wasn't, ever, really as bad as he sounded, not even on weekends, when he got drunk. As a matter of fact, he was always on the lookout for "something a little better," but he died before he found it. He died suddenly, during a drunken weekend in the middle of the war, when Sonny was fifteen. He and Sonny hadn't ever got on too well. And this was partly because Sonny was the apple of his father's eye. It was because he loved Sonny so much and was frightened for him, that he was al-ways fighting with him. It doesn't do any good to fight with Sonny. Sonny just moves back, inside himself, where he can't be reached. But the principal reason that they never hit it off is that they were so much alike. Daddy was big and rough and loud-talking, just the opposite of Sonny, but they both had — that same privacy.

Mama tried to tell me something about this, just after Daddy died. I was home on leave from the army.

This was the last time I ever saw my mother alive. Just the same, this pic-ture gets all mixed up in my mind with pictures I had of her when she was younger. The way I always see her is the way she used to be on a Sunday af-ternoon, say, when the old folks were talking after the big Sunday dinner. I always see her wearing pale blue. She'd be sitting on the sofa. And my father would be sitting in the easy chair, not far from her. And the living room would be full of church folks and relatives. There they sit, in chairs all around the living room, and the night is creeping up outside, but nobody knows it yet. You can see the darkness growing against the windowpanes and you hear the street noises every now and again, or maybe the jangling beat of a tambourine from one of the churches close by, but it's real quiet in the room. For a moment nobody's talking, but every face looks darkening, like the sky outside. And my mother rocks a little from the waist, and my father's eyes are closed. Everyone is looking at something a child can't see. For a minute they've forgotten the children. Maybe a kid is lying on the rug, half asleep. Maybe somebody's got a kid in his lap and is absent-mindedly stroking the kid's head. Maybe there's a kid, quiet and big-eyed, curled up in a big chair in the corner. The silence, the darkness coming, and the darkness in the faces frightens the child obscurely. He hopes that the hand which strokes his forehead will never stop — will never die. He hopes that there will never come a time when the old folks won't be sitting around the living room, talking about where they've come from, and what they've seen, and what's happened to them and their kinfolk.

But something deep and watchful in the child knows that this is bound to end, is already ending. In a moment someone will get up and turn on the light. Then the old folks will remember the children and they won't talk any more that day. And when light fills the room, the child is filled with darkness. He knows that every time this happens he's moved just a little closer to that darkness outside. The darkness outside is what the old folks have been talking about. It's what they've come from. It's what they endure. The child knows that they won't talk any more because if he knows too much about what's happened to *them,* he'll know too much too soon, about what's going to happen to *him.*

The last time I talked to my mother, I remember I was restless. I wanted to get out and see Isabel. We weren't married then and we had a lot to straighten out between us.

There Mama sat, in black, by the window. She was humming an old church song, *Lord, you brought me from a long ways off.* Sonny was out somewhere. Mama kept watching the streets.

"I don't know," she said, "if I'll ever see you again, after you go off from here. But I hope you'll remember the things I tried to teach you."

"Don't talk like that," I said, and smiled. "You'll be here a long time yet."

She smiled, too, but she said nothing. She was quiet for a long time. And I said, "Mama, don't you worry about nothing. I'll be writing all the time, and you be getting the checks. . . ."

"I want to talk to you about your brother,'" she said, suddenly. "If anything happens to me he ain't going to have nobody to look out for him."

"Mama," I said, "ain't nothing going to happen to you *or* Sonny. Sonny's all right. He's a good boy and he's got good sense."

"It ain't a question of his being a good boy," Mama said, "nor of his having good sense. It ain't only the bad ones, nor yet the dumb ones that gets sucked under." She stopped, looking at me. "Your Daddy once had a brother," she said, and she smiled in a way that made me feel she was in pain. "You didn't never know that, did you?"

"No," I said, "I never knew that," and I watched her face.

"Oh, yes," she said, "your Daddy had a brother." She looked out of the window again. "I know you never saw your Daddy cry. But *I* did — many a time, through all these years."

I asked her, "What happened to his brother? How come nobody's ever talked about him?"

This was the first time I ever saw my mother look old.

"His brother got killed," she said, "when he was just a little younger than you are now. I knew him. He was a fine boy. He was maybe a little full of the devil, but he didn't mean nobody no harm."

Then she stopped and the room was silent, exactly as it had sometimes been on those Sunday afternoons. Mama kept looking out into the streets.

"He used to have a job in the mill," she said, "and, like all young folks, he just liked to perform on Saturday nights. Saturday nights, him and your father would drift around to different places, go to dances and things like that, or just sit around with people they knew, and your father's brother would sing, he had a fine voice, and play along with himself on his guitar. Well, this particular Saturday night, him and your father was coming home from some place, and they were both a little drunk and there was a moon that night, it was bright like day. Your father's brother was feeling kind of good, and he was whistling to himself, and he had his guitar slung over his shoulder. They was coming down a hill and beneath them was a road that turned off from the highway. Well, your father's brother, being always kind of frisky, decided to run down this hill, and he did, with that guitar banging and clanging behind him, and he ran across the road, and he was making water behind a tree. And your father was sort of amused at him and he was still coming down the hill, kind of slow. Then he heard a car motor and that same minute his brother stepped from behind the tree, into the road, in the moonlight. And he started to cross the road. And your father started to run down the hill, he says he don't know why. This car was full of white men. They was all drunk, and when they seen your father's brother they let out a great whoop and holler and they aimed the car straight at him. They was having fun, they just wanted to scare him, the way they do sometimes, you know. But they was drunk. And I guess the boy, being drunk, too, and scared, kind of lost his head. By the time he jumped it was too late. Your father says he heard his brother scream when the car rolled over him, and he heard the wood of that guitar when it give, and he heard them strings go flying, and he heard them white men shouting, and the car kept on a-going and it ain't stopped till this day. And, time your father got down the hill, his brother weren't nothing but blood and pulp."

Tears were gleaming on my mother's face. There wasn't anything I could say.

"He never mentioned it," she said, "because I never let him mention it before you children. Your Daddy was like a crazy man that night and for many a night thereafter. He says he never in his life seen anything as dark as that road after the lights of that car had gone away. Weren't nothing, weren't nobody on that road, just your Daddy and his brother and that busted guitar. Oh, yes. Your Daddy never did really get right again. Till the day he died he weren't sure but that every white man he saw was the man that killed his brother."

She stopped and took out her handkerchief and dried her eyes and looked at me.

"I ain't telling you all this," she said, "to make you scared or bitter or to make you hate nobody. I'm telling you this because you got a brother. And the world ain't changed."

I guess I didn't want to believe this. I guess she saw this in my face. She turned away from me, toward the window again, searching those streets.

"But I praise my Redeemer," she said at last, "that He called your Daddy home before me. I ain't saying it to throw no flowers at myself, but, I declare, it keeps me from feeling too cast down to know I helped your father get safely through this world. Your father always acted like he was the roughest, strongest man on earth. And everybody took him to be like that. But if he hadn't had *me* there — to see his tears!"

She was crying again. Still, I couldn't move. I said, "Lord, Lord, Mama, I didn't know it was like that."

"Oh, honey," she said, "there' a lot that you don't know. But you are going to find it out." She stood up from the window and came over to me. "You got to hold on to your brother," she said, "and don't let him fall, no matter what it looks like is happening to him and no matter how evil you gets with him. You going to be evil with him many a time. But don't you forget what I told you, you hear?"

"I won't forget," I said. "Don't you worry, I won't forget. I won't let nothing happen to Sonny."

My mother smiled as though she were amused at something she saw in my face. Then, "You may not be able to stop nothing from happening. But you got to let him know you's *there*."

Two days later I was married, and then I was gone. And I had a lot of things on my mind and I pretty well forgot my promise to Mama until I got shipped home on a special furlough for her funeral.

And, after the funeral, with just Sonny and me alone in the empty kitchen, I tried to find out something about him. "What do you want to do?" I asked him.

"I'm going to be a musician," he said.

For he had graduated, in the time I had been away, from dancing to the juke box to finding out who was playing what, and what they were doing with it, and he had bought himself a set of drums.

"You mean, you want to be a drummer?" I somehow had the feeling that being a drummer might be all right for other people but not for my brother Sonny.

"I don't think," he said, looking at me very gravely, "that I'll ever be a good drummer. But I think I can play a piano."

I frowned. I'd never played the role of the older brother quite so seriously before, had scarcely ever, in fact, *asked* Sonny a damn thing. I sensed myself in the presence of something I didn't really know how to handle, didn't understand. So I made my frown a little deeper as I asked: "What kind of musician do you want to be?"

He grinned. "How many kinds do you think there are?"

"Be *serious*," I said.

He laughed, throwing his head back, and then looked at me. "I *am* serious."

"Well, then, for Christ's sake, stop kidding around and answer a serious question. I mean, do you want to be a concert pianist, you want to play classical music and all that, or — or what?" Long before I finished he was laughing again. "For Christ's *sake*, Sonny!"

He sobered, but with difficulty. "I'm sorry. But you sound so — *scared!*" and he was off again.

"Well, you may think it's funny now, baby, but it's not going to be so funny when you have to make your living at it, let me tell you *that*." I was furious because I knew he was laughing at me and I didn't know why.

"No," he said, very sober now, and afraid, perhaps, that he'd hurt me, "I don't want to be a classical pianist. That isn't what interests me. I mean" — he paused, looking hard at me, as though his eyes would help me to understand, and then gestured helplessly, as though perhaps his hand would help — "I mean, I'll have a lot of studying to do, and I'll have to study *everything,* but, I mean, I want to play *with* — jazz musicians." He stopped. "I want to play jazz," he said.

Well, the word had never before sounded as heavy, as real, as it sounded that afternoon in Sonny's mouth. I just looked at him and I was probably frowning a real frown by this time. I simply couldn't see why on earth he'd want to spend his time hanging around nightclubs, clowning around on bandstands, while people pushed each other around a dance floor. It seemed — beneath him, somehow. I had never thought about it before, had never been forced to, but I suppose I had always put jazz musicians in a class with what Daddy called "good-time people."

"Are you *serious?*"

"Hell, *yes,* I'm serious."

He looked more helpless than ever, and annoyed, and deeply hurt.

I suggested, helpfully: "You mean — like Louis Armstrong?"

His face closed as though I'd struck him. "No. I'm not talking about none of that old-time, down home crap."

"Well, look, Sonny, I'm sorry, don't get mad. I just don't altogether get it, that's all. Name somebody — you know, a jazz musician you admire."

"Bird."

"Who?"

"Bird! Charlie Parker! Don't they teach you nothing in the goddamn army?"

I lit a cigarette. I was surprised and then a little amused to discover that I was trembling. "I've been out of touch," I said. "You'll have to be patient with me. Now. Who's this Parker character?"

"He's just one of the greatest jazz musicians alive," said Sonny, sullenly, his hands in his pockets, his back to me. "Maybe *the* greatest," he added, bitterly, "that's probably why *you* never heard of him."

"All right," I said, "I'm ignorant. I'm sorry. I'll go out and buy all the cat's records right away, all right?"

"It don't," said Sonny, with dignity, "make any difference to me. I don't care what you listen to. Don't do me no favors."

I was beginning to realize that I'd never seen him so upset before. With another part of my mind I was thinking that this would probably turn out to be one of those things kids go through and that I shouldn't make it seem important by pushing it too hard. Still, I didn't think it would do any harm to ask: "Doesn't all this take a lot of time? Can you make a living at it?"

He turned back to me and half leaned, half sat, on the kitchen table. "Everything takes time," he said, "and — well, yes, sure, I can make a living at it. But what I don't seem to be able to make you understand is that it's the only thing I want to do."

"Well, Sonny," I said, gently, "you know people can't always do exactly what they *want* to do — "

"*No,* I don't know that," said Sonny, surprising me. "I think people *ought* to do what they want to do, what else are they alive for?"

"You getting to be a big boy," I said desperately, "it's time you started thinking about your future."

"I'm thinking about my future," said Sonny, grimly. "I think about it all the time."

I gave up. I decided, if he didn't change his mind, that we could always talk about it later. "In the meantime," I said, "you got to finish school." We had already decided that he'd have to move in with Isabel and her folks. I knew this wasn't the ideal arrangement because Isabel's folks are inclined to be dicty and they hadn't especially wanted Isabel to marry me. But I didn't know what else to do. "And we have to get you fixed up at Isabel's."

There was a long silence. He moved from the kitchen table to the window. "That's a terrible idea. You know it yourself."

"Do you have a *better* idea?"

He just walked up and down the kitchen for a minute. He was as tall as I was. He had started to shave. I suddenly had the feeling that I didn't know him at all.

He stopped at the kitchen table and picked up my cigarettes. Looking at me with a kind of mocking, amused defiance, he put one between his lips. "You mind?"

"You smoking already?"

He lit the cigarette and nodded, watching me through the smoke. "I just wanted to see if I'd have the courage to smoke in front of you." He grinned and blew a great cloud of smoke to the ceiling. "It was easy." He looked at my face. "Come on, now. I bet you was smoking at my age, tell the truth."

I didn't say anything but the truth was on my face, and he laughed. But now there was something very strained in his laugh. "Sure. And I bet that ain't all you was doing."

He was frightening me a little. "Cut the crap," I said. "We already decided that you was going to go and live at Isabel's. Now what's got into you all of a sudden?"

"You decided it," he pointed out. "I didn't decide nothing." He stopped in front of me, leaning against the stove, arms loosely folded. "Look, brother. I don't want to stay in Harlem no more, I really don't." He was very earnest. He looked at me, then over toward the kitchen window. There was something in his eyes I'd never seen before, some thoughtfulness, some worry all his own. He rubbed the muscle of one arm. "It's time I was getting out of here."

"Where do you want to *go,* Sonny?"

"I want to join the army. Or the navy, I don't care. If I say I'm old enough, they'll believe me."

Then I got mad. It was because I was so scared. "You must be crazy. You goddamn fool, what the hell do you want to go and join the *army* for?"

"I just told you. To get out of Harlem."

"Sonny, you haven't even finished *school.* And if you really want to be a musician, how do you expect to study if you're in the *army?*"

He looked at me, trapped, and in anguish. "There's ways. I might be able to work out some kind of deal. Anyway, I'll have the G.I. Bill when I come out."

"If you come out." We stared at each other. "Sonny, please. Be reasonable. I know the setup is far from perfect. But we got to do the best we can."

"I ain't learning nothing in school," he said. "Even when I go." He turned away from me and opened the window and threw his cigarette out into the narrow alley. I watched his back. "At least, I ain't learning nothing you'd want me to learn." He slammed the window so hard I thought the glass would fly out, and turned back to me. "And I'm sick of the stink of these garbage cans!"

"Sonny," I said, "I know how you feel. But if you don't finish school now, you're going to be sorry later that you didn't." I grabbed him by the shoulders. "And you only got another year. It ain't so bad. And I'll come back and I swear I'll help you do *whatever* you want to do. Just try to put up with it till I come back. Will you please do that? For me?"

He didn't answer and he wouldn't look at me.

"Sonny. You hear me?"

He pulled away. "I hear you. But you never hear anything *I* say."

I didn't know what to say to that. He looked out of the window and then back at me. "OK," he said, and sighed. "I'll try."

Then I said, trying to cheer him up a little, "They got a piano at Isabel's. You can practice on it."

And as a matter of fact, it did cheer him up for a minute. "That's right," he said to himself. "I forgot that." His face relaxed a little. But the worry, the thoughtfulness, played on it still, the way shadows play on a face which is staring into the fire.

But I thought I'd never hear the end of that piano. At first, Isabel would write me, saying how nice it was that Sonny was so serious about his music and how, as soon as he came in from school, or wherever he had been when he was supposed to be at school, he went straight to that piano and stayed there until suppertime. And, after supper, he went back to that piano and stayed there until everybody went to bed. He was at the piano all day Saturday and all day Sunday. Then he bought a record player and started playing records. He'd play one record over and over again, all day long sometimes, and he'd improvise along with it on the piano. Or he'd play one section of the record, one chord, one change, one progression, then he'd do it on the piano. Then back to the record. Then back to the piano.

Well, I really don't know how they stood it. Isabel finally confessed that it wasn't like living with a person at all, it was, like living with sound. And the sound didn't make any sense to her, didn't make any sense to any of them — naturally. They began, in a way, to be afflicted by this presence that was living in their home. It was as though Sonny were some sort of god, or monster. He moved in an atmosphere which wasn't like theirs at all. They fed him and he ate, he washed himself, he walked in and out of their door; he certainly wasn't nasty or unpleasant or rude, Sonny isn't any of those things; but it was as though he were all wrapped up in some cloud, some fire, some vision all his own; and there wasn't any way to reach him.

At the same time, he wasn't really a man yet, he was still a child, and they had to watch out for him in all kinds of ways. They certainly couldn't throw him out. Neither did they dare to make a great scene about that piano because even they dimly sensed, as I sensed, from so many thousands of miles away, that Sonny was at that piano playing for his life.

But he hadn't been going to school. One day a letter came from the school board and Isabel's mother got it — there had, apparently, been other letters but Sonny had torn them up. This day, when Sonny came in, Isabel's mother showed him the letter and asked where he'd been spending his time. And she finally got it out of him that he'd been down in Greenwich Village, with musicians and other characters, in a white girl's apartment. And this scared her and she started to scream at him and what came up, once she began — though she denies it to this day — was what sacrifices they were making to give Sonny a decent home and how little he appreciated it.

Sonny didn't play the piano that day. By evening, Isabel's mother had calmed down but then there was the old man to deal with, and Isabel herself. Isabel says she did her best to be calm but she broke down and started crying. She says she just watched Sonny's face. She could tell, by watching him, what was happening with him. And what was happening was that they penetrated his cloud, they had reached him. Even if their fingers had been a thousand times more gentle than human fingers ever are, he could hardly help feeling that they had stripped him naked and were spitting on that nakedness. For he also had to see that his presence, that music, which was life or death to him, had been torture for them and that they had endured it, not at all for his sake, but only for mine. And Sonny couldn't take that. He can take it a little better today than he could then but he's still not very good at it and, frankly, I don't know anybody who is.

The silence of the next few days must have been louder than the sound of all the music ever played since time began. One morning, before she went to work, Isabel was in his room for something and she suddenly realized that all of his records were gone. And she knew for certain that he was gone. And he was. He went as far as the navy would carry him. He finally sent me a postcard from some place in Greece and that was the first I knew that Sonny was still alive. I didn't see him any more until we were both back in New York and the war had long been over.

He was a man by then, of course, but I wasn't willing to see it. He came by the house from time to time, but we fought almost every time we met. I didn't like the way he carried himself, loose and dreamlike all the time, and I didn't like his friends, and his music seemed to be merely an excuse for the life he led. It sounded just that weird and disordered.

Then we had a fight, a pretty awful fight, and I didn't see him for months. By and by I looked him up, where he was living, in a furnished room in the Village, and I tried to make it up. But there were lots of other people in the room and Sonny just lay on his bed, and he wouldn't come downstairs with me, and he treated these other people as though they were his family and I weren't. So I got mad and then he got mad, and then I told him that he might just as well be dead as live the way he was living. Then he stood up and he told me not to worry about him any more in life, that he *was* dead as far as I was concerned. Then he pushed me to the door and the other people looked on as though nothing were happening, and he slammed the door behind me. I stood in the hallway, staring at the door. I heard somebody laugh in the room and then the tears came to my eyes. I started down the steps, whistling to keep from crying, I kept whistling to myself, *You going to need me, baby, one of these cold, rainy days.*

I read about Sonny's trouble in the spring. Little Grace died in the fall. She was a beautiful little girl. But she only lived a little over two years. She died of polio and she suffered. She had a slight fever for a couple of days, but it didn't seem like anything and we just kept her in bed. And we would certainly have called the doctor, but the fever dropped, she seemed to be all right. So we thought it had just been a cold. Then, one day, she was up, playing, Isabel was in the kitchen fixing lunch for the two boys when they'd come in from school, and she heard Grace fall down in the living room. When you have a lot of children you don't always start running when one of them falls, unless they start screaming or something. And, this time, Grace was quiet. Yet, Isabel says that when she heard that *thump* and then that silence, something happened in her to make her afraid. And she ran to the living room and there was little Grace on the floor, all twisted up, and the reason she hadn't screamed was that she couldn't get her breath. And when she did scream, it was the worst sound, Isabel says, that she'd ever heard in all her life, and she still hears it sometimes in her dreams. Isabel will sometimes wake me up with a low, moaning, strangled sound and I have to be quick to awaken her and hold her to me and where Isabel is weeping against me seems a mortal wound.

I think I may have written Sonny the very day that little Grace was buried. I was sitting in the living room in the dark, by myself, and I suddenly thought of Sonny. My trouble made his real.

One Saturday afternoon, when Sonny had been living with us, or, anyway, been in our house, for nearly two weeks, I found myself wandering aimlessly about the living room, drinking from a can of beer, and trying to work up the courage to search Sonny's room. He was out, he was usually out whenever I was home, and Isabel had taken the children to see their grandparents. Suddenly I was standing still in front of the living room window, watching Seventh Avenue. The idea of searching Sonny's room made me still. I scarcely dared to admit to myself what I'd be searching for. I didn't know what I'd do if I found it. Or if I didn't.

On the sidewalk across from me, near the entrance to a barbecue joint, some people were holding an old-fashioned revival meeting. The barbecue cook, wearing a dirty white apron, his conked hair reddish and metallic in the pale sun, and a cigarette between his lips, stood in the doorway, watching them. Kids and older people paused in their errands and stood there, along with some older men and a couple of very tough-looking women who watched everything that happened on the avenue, as though they owned it, or were maybe owned by it. Well, they were watching this, too. The revival was being carried on by three sisters in black, and a brother. All they had were their voices and their Bibles and a tambourine. The brother was testifying and while he testified two of the sisters stood together, seeming to say, amen, and the third sister walked around with the tambourine outstretched and a couple of people dropped coins into it. Then the brother's testimony ended and the sister who had been taking up the collection dumped the coins into her palm and transferred them to the pocket of her long black robe. Then she raised both hands, striking the tambourine against the air, and then against one hand, and she started to sing. And the two other sisters and the brother joined in.

It was strange, suddenly, to watch, though I had been seeing these street meetings all my life. So, of course, had everybody else down there. Yet, they paused and watched and listened and I stood still at the window. *"Tis the old ship of Zion,"* they sang, and the sister with the tambourine kept a steady, jangling beat, *"it has rescued many a thousand!"* Not a soul under the sound of their voices was hearing this song for the first time, not one of them had been rescued. Nor had they seen much in the way of rescue work being done around them. Neither did they especially believe in the holiness of the three sisters and the brother, they knew too much about them, knew where they lived, and how. The woman with the tambourine, whose voice dominated the air, whose face was bright with joy, was divided by very little from the woman who stood watching her, a cigarette between her heavy, chapped lips, her hair a cuckoo's nest, her face scarred and swollen from many beatings, and her black eyes glittering like coal. Perhaps they both knew this, which was why, when, as rarely, they addressed each other, they addressed each other as Sister. As the singing filled the air the watching, listening faces underwent a change, the eyes focusing on something within; the music seemed to soothe a poison out of them; and time seemed, nearly, to fall away from the sullen, belligerent, battered faces, as though they were fleeing back to their first condition, while dreaming of their last. The barbecue cook half shook his head and smiled, and dropped his cigarette and disappeared into his joint. A man fumbled in his pockets for change and stood holding it in his hand impatiently, as though he had just remembered a pressing appointment further up the avenue. He looked furious. Then I saw Sonny, standing on the edge of the crowd. He was carrying a wide, flat notebook with a green cover, and it made him look, from where I was standing, almost like a schoolboy. The coppery sun brought out the copper in his skin, he was very faintly smiling, standing very still. Then the singing stopped, the tambourine turned into a collection plate again. The furious man dropped in his coins and vanished, so did a couple of the women, and Sonny dropped some change in the plate, looking directly at the woman with a little smile. He started across the avenue, toward the house. He has a slow, loping walk, something like the way Harlem hipsters walk, only he's imposed on this his own half-beat. I had never really noticed it before.

I stayed at the window, both relieved and apprehensive. As Sonny disappeared from my sight, they began singing again. And they were still singing when his key turned in the lock.

"Hey," he said.

"Hey, yourself. You want some beer?"

"No. Well, maybe." But he came up to the window and stood beside me, looking out. "What a warm voice," he said.

They were singing *If I could only hear my mother pray again!*

"Yes," I said, "and she can sure beat that tambourine."

"But what a terrible song," he said, and laughed. He dropped his notebook on the sofa and disappeared into the kitchen. "Where's Isabel and the kids?"

"I think they went to see their grandparents. You hungry?"

"No." He came back into the living room with his can of beer. "You want to come some place with me tonight?"

I sensed, I don't know how, that I couldn't possibly say no. "Sure. Where?"

He sat down on the sofa and picked up his notebook and started leafing through it. "I'm going to sit in with some fellows in a joint in the Village."

"You mean, you're going to play, tonight?"

"That's right." He took a swallow of his beer and moved back to the window. He gave me a sidelong look. "If you can stand it."

"I'll try," I said.

He smiled to himself and we both watched as the meeting across the way broke up. The three sisters and the brother, heads bowed, were singing *God be with you till we meet again.* The faces around them were very quiet. Then the song ended. The small crowd dispersed. We watched the three women and the lone man walk slowly up the avenue.

"When she was singing before," said Sonny, abruptly, "her voice reminded me for a minute of what heroin feels like sometimes — when it's in your veins. It makes you feel sort of warm and cool at the same time. And distant. And — and sure." He sipped his beer, very deliberately not looking at me. I watched his face. "It makes you feel — in control. Sometimes you've got to have that feeling."

"Do you?" I sat down slowly in the easy chair.

"Sometimes." He went to the sofa and picked up his notebook again. "Some people do."

"In order," I asked, "to play?" And my voice was very ugly, full of contempt and anger.

"Well" — he looked at me with great, troubled eyes, as though, in fact, he hoped his eyes would tell me things he could never otherwise say — "they *think* so. And *if* they think so — !"

350

"And what do *you* think?" I asked.

He sat on the sofa and put his can of beer on the floor. "I don't know," he said, and I couldn't be sure if he were answering my question or pursuing his thoughts. His face didn't tell me. "It's not so much to *play*. It's to *stand* it, to be able to make it at all. On any level." He frowned and smiled: "In order to keep from shaking to pieces."

"But these friends of yours," I said, "they seem to shake themselves to pieces pretty goddamn fast."

"Maybe." He played with the notebook. And something told me that I should curb my tongue, that Sonny was doing his best to talk, that I should listen. "But of course you only know the ones that've gone to pieces. Some don't — or at least they haven't *yet* and that's just about all *any* of us can say." He paused. "And then there are some who just live, really, in hell, and they know it and they see what's happening and they go right on. I don't know." He sighed, dropped the notebook, folded his arms. "Some guys, you can tell from the way they play, they on something *all* the time. And you can see that, well, it makes something real for them. But of course," he picked up his beer from the floor and sipped it and put the can down again, "they *want* to, too, you've got to see that. Even some of them that say they don't — *some,* not all."

"And what about you?" I asked — I couldn't help it. "What about you? Do *you* want to?"

He stood up and walked to the window and remained silent for a long time. Then he sighed. "Me," he said. Then: "While I was downstairs before, on my way here, listening to that woman sing, it struck me all of a sudden how much suffering she must have had to go through — to sing like that. It's *repulsive* to think you have to suffer that much."

I said: "But there's no way not to suffer — is there, Sonny?"

"I believe not," he said and smiled, "but that's never stopped anyone from trying." He looked at me. "Has it?" I realized, with this mocking look, that there stood between us, forever, beyond the power of time or forgiveness, the fact that I had held silence — so long! — when he had needed human speech to help him. He turned back to the window. "No, there's no way not to suffer. But you try all kinds of ways to keep from drowning in it, to keep on top of it, and to make it seem — well, like *you*. Like you did something, all right, and now you're suffering for it. You know?" I said nothing. "Well you know," he said, impatiently, "why *do* people suffer? Maybe it's better to do something to give it a reason, *any* reason."

"But we just agreed," I said, "that there's no way not to suffer. Isn't it better, then, just to — take it?"

"But nobody just takes it," Sonny cried, "that's what I'm telling you! Ev-

erybody tries not to. You're just hung up on the *way* some people try — it's not *your* way!"

The hair on my face began to itch, my face felt wet. "That's not true," I said, "that's not true. I don't give a damn what other people do, I don't even care how they suffer. I just care how *you* suffer." And he looked at me. "Please believe me," I said, "I don't want to see you — die — trying not to suffer."

"I won't," he said, flatly, "die trying not to suffer. At least, not any faster than anybody else."

"But there's no need," I said, trying to laugh, "is there? in killing yourself."

I wanted to say more, but I couldn't. I wanted to talk about will power and how life could be — well, beautiful. I wanted to say that it was all within; but was it? or, rather, wasn't that exactly the trouble? And I wanted to promise that I would never fail him again. But it would all have sounded — empty words and lies.

So I made the promise to myself and prayed that I would keep it.

"It's terrible sometimes, inside," he said, "that's what's the trouble. You walk these streets, black and funky and cold, and there's not really a living ass to talk to, and there's nothing shaking, and there's no way of getting it out — that storm inside. You can't talk it and you can't make love with it, and when you finally try to get with it and play it, you realize *nobody's* listening. So *you've* got to listen. You got to find a way to listen."

And then he walked away from the window and sat on the sofa again, as though all the wind had suddenly been knocked out of him. "Sometimes you'll do *anything* to play, even cut your mother's throat." He laughed and looked at me. "Or your brother's." Then he sobered. "Or your own." Then: "Don't worry. I'm all right now and I think I'll *be* all right. But I can't forget — where I've been. I don't mean just the physical place I've been, I mean where I've *been*. And *what* I've been."

"What have you been, Sonny?" I asked.

He smiled — but sat sideways on the sofa, his elbow resting on the back, his fingers playing with his mouth and chin, not looking at me. "I've been something I didn't recognize, didn't know I could be. Didn't know anybody could be." He stopped, looking inward, looking helplessly young, looking old. "I'm not talking about it now because I feel *guilty* or anything like that — maybe it would be better if I did, I don't know. Anyway, I can't really talk about it. Not to you, not to anybody," and now he turned and faced me. "Sometimes, you know, and it was actually when I was most *out* of the world, I felt that I was in it, that I was *with* it, really, and I could play or I didn't really have to *play*, it just came out of me, it was there. And I don't know how I played, thinking about it now, but I know I did awful things, those times, sometimes, to people.

Or it wasn't that I *did* anything to them — it was that they weren't real." He picked up the beer can; it was empty; he rolled it between his palms: "And other times — well, I needed a fix, I needed to find a place to lean, I needed to clear a space to *listen* — and I couldn't find it, and I — went crazy, I did terrible things to *me*, I was terrible *for* me." He began pressing the beer can between his hands, I watched the metal begin to give. It glittered, as he played with it, like a knife, and I was afraid he would cut himself, but I said nothing. "Oh well. I can never tell you. I was all by myself at the bottom of something, stinking and sweating and crying and shaking, and I smelled it, you know? my stink, and I thought I'd die if I couldn't get away from it and yet, all the same, I knew that everything I was doing was just locking me in with it. And I didn't know," he paused, still flattening the beer can, "I didn't know, I still *don't* know, something kept telling me that maybe it was good to smell your own stink, but I didn't think that *that* was what I'd been trying to do — and — who can stand it?" and he abruptly dropped the ruined beer can, looking at me with a small, still smile, and then rose, walking to the window as though it were the lodestone rock. I watched his face, he watched the avenue. "I couldn't tell you when Mama died — but the reason I wanted to leave Harlem so bad was to get away from drugs. And then, when I ran away, that's what I was running from — really. When I came back, nothing had changed, I hadn't changed, I was just — older." And he stopped, drumming with his fingers on the windowpane. The sun had vanished, soon darkness would fall. I watched his face. "It can come again," he said, almost as though speaking to himself. Then he turned to me. "It can come again," he repeated. "I just want you to know that."

"All right," I said, at last. "So it can come again, All right."

He smiled, but the smile was sorrowful. "I had to try to tell you," he said.

"Yes," I said. "I understand that."

"You're my brother," he said, looking straight at me, and not smiling at all.

"Yes," I repeated, "yes. I understand that."

He turned back to the window, looking out. "All that hatred down there," he said, "all that hatred and misery and love. It's a wonder it doesn't blow the avenue apart."

We went to the only nightclub on a short, dark street, downtown. We squeezed through the narrow, chattering, jam-packed bar to the entrance of the big room, where the bandstand was. And we stood there for a moment, for the lights were very dim in this room and we couldn't see. Then, "Hello, boy," said a voice and an enormous black man, much older than Sonny or myself, erupted out of all that atmospheric lighting and put an arm around Sonny's shoulder. "I been sitting right here," he said, "waiting for you."

He had a big voice, too, and heads in the darkness turned toward us.

Sonny grinned and pulled a little away, and said, "Creole, this is my brother. I told you about him."

Creole shook my hand. "I'm glad to meet you, son," he said, and it was clear that he was glad to meet me *there,* for Sonny's sake. And he smiled, "You got a real musician in *your* family," and he took his arm from Sonny's shoulder and slapped him, lightly, affectionately, with the back of his hand.

"Well. Now I've heard it all," said a voice behind us. This was another musician, and a friend of Sonny's, a coal-black, cheerful-looking man, built close to the ground. He immediately began confiding to me; at the top of his lungs, the most terrible things about Sonny, his teeth gleaming like a lighthouse and his laugh coming up out of him like the beginning of an earthquake. And it turned out that everyone at the bar knew Sonny, or almost everyone; some were musicians, working there, or nearby, or not working, some were simply hangers-on, and some were there to hear Sonny play. I was introduced to all of them and they were all very polite to me. Yet, it was clear that, for them, I was only Sonny's brother. Here, I was in Sonny's world. Or, rather: his kingdom. Here, it was not even a question that his veins bore royal blood.

They were going to play soon and Creole installed me, by myself, at a table in a dark corner. Then I watched them, Creole, and the little black man, and Sonny, and the others, while they horsed around, standing just below the bandstand. The light from the bandstand spilled just a little short of them and, watching them laughing and gesturing and moving about, I had the feeling that they, nevertheless, were being most careful not to step into that circle of light too suddenly: that if they moved into the light too suddenly, without thinking, they would perish in flame. Then, while I watched, one of them, the small, black man, moved into the light and crossed the bandstand and started fooling around with his drums. Then — being funny and being, also, extremely ceremonious — Creole took Sonny by the arm and led him to the piano. A woman's voice called Sonny's name and a few hands started clapping. And Sonny, also being funny and being ceremonious, and so touched, I think, that he could have cried, but neither hiding it nor showing it, riding it like a man, grinned, and put both hands to his heart and bowed from the waist.

Creole then went to the bass fiddle and a lean, very bright-skinned brown man jumped up on the bandstand and picked up his horn. So there they were, and the atmosphere on the bandstand and in the room began to change and tighten. Someone stepped up to the microphone and announced them. Then there were all kinds of murmurs. Some people at the bar shushed others. The waitress ran around, frantically getting in the last orders, guys and chicks got closer to each other, and the lights on the bandstand, on the quartet, turned to a kind of indigo. Then they all looked different there. Creole looked about him for the last time, as though he were making certain that all his chickens were in the coop, and then he jumped and struck the fiddle. And there they were.

All I know about music is that not many people ever really hear it. And even then, on the rare occasions when something opens within, and the music enters, what we mainly hear, or hear corroborated, are personal, private, vanishing evocations. But the man who creates the music is hearing something else, is dealing with the roar rising from the void and imposing order on it as it hits the air. What is evoked in him, then, is of another order, more terrible because it has no words, and triumphant, too, for that same reason. And his triumph, when he triumphs, is ours. I just watched Sonny's face. His face was troubled, he was working hard, but he wasn't with it. And I had the feeling that, in a way, everyone on the bandstand was waiting for him, both waiting for him and pushing him along. But as I began to watch Creole, I realized that it was Creole who held them all back. He had them on a short rein. Up there, keeping the beat with his whole body, wailing on the fiddle, with his eyes half closed, he was listening to everything, but he was listening to Sonny. He was having a dialogue with Sonny. He wanted Sonny to leave the shoreline and strike out for the deep water. He was Sonny's witness that deep water and drowning were not the same thing — he had been there, and he knew. And he wanted Sonny to know. He was waiting for Sonny to do the things on the keys which would let Creole know that Sonny was in the water.

And, while Creole listened, Sonny moved, deep within, exactly like someone in torment. I had never before thought of how awful the relationship must be between the musician and his instrument. He has to fill it, this instrument, with the breath of life, his own. He has to make it do what he wants it to do. And a piano is just a piano. It's made out of so much wood and wires and little hammers and big ones, and ivory. While there's only so much you can do with it, the only way to find this out is to try; to try and make it do everything.

And Sonny hadn't been near a piano for over a year. And he wasn't on much better terms with his life, not the life that stretched before him now. He and the piano stammered, started one way, got scared, stopped; started another way, panicked, marked time, started again; then seemed to have found a direction, panicked again, got stuck. And the face I saw on Sonny I'd never seen before. Everything had been burned out of it, and, at the same time, things usually hidden were being burned in, by the fire and fury of the battle which was occurring in him up there.

Yet, watching Creole's face as they neared the end of the first set, I had the feeling that something had happened, something I hadn't heard. Then they finished, there was scattered applause, and then, without an instant's warning, Creole started into something else, it was almost sardonic, it was *Am I Blue*. And, as though he commanded, Sonny began to play. Something began to happen. And Creole let out the reins. The dry, low, black man said something awful on the drums, Creole answered, and the drums talked back. Then the horn insisted, sweet and high, slightly detached perhaps, and Creole listened, commenting now and then, dry, and driving, beautiful and calm and old. Then they all came together again, and Sonny was part of the family again. I could tell this from his face. He seemed to have found, right there beneath his fingers, a damn brand-new piano. It seemed that he couldn't get over it. Then, for awhile, just being happy with Sonny, they seemed to be agreeing with him that brand-new pianos certainly were a gas.

Then Creole stepped forward to remind them that what they were playing was the blues. He hit something in all of them, he hit something in me, myself, and the music tightened and deepened, apprehension began to beat the air. Creole began to tell us what the blues were all about. They were not about anything very new. He and his boys up there were keeping it new, at the risk of ruin, destruction, madness, and death, in order to find new ways to make us listen. For, while the tale of how we suffer, and how we are delighted, and how we may triumph is never new, it always must be heard. There isn't any other tale to tell, it's the only light we've got in all this darkness.

And this tale, according to that face, that body, those strong hands on those strings, has another aspect in every country, and a new depth in every generation. Listen, Creole seemed to be saying, listen. Now these are Sonny's blues. He made the little black man on the drums know it, and the bright, brown man on the horn. Creole wasn't trying any longer to get Sonny in the water. He was wishing him Godspeed. Then he stepped back, very slowly, filling the air with the immense suggestion that Sonny speak for himself.

Then they all gathered around Sonny and Sonny played. Every now and again one of them seemed to say, amen. Sonny's fingers filled the air with life, his life. But that life contained so many others. And Sonny went all the way back, he really began with the spare, flat statement of the opening phrase of the song. Then he began to make it his. It was very beautiful because it wasn't hurried and it was no longer a lament. I seemed to hear with what burning he had made it his, with what burning we had yet to make it ours, how we could cease lamenting. Freedom lurked around us and I understood, at last, that he could help us to be free if we would listen, that he would never be free until we did. Yet, there was no battle in his face now. I heard what he had gone through, and would continue to go through until he came to rest in earth. He had made it his: that long line, of which we knew only Mama and Daddy. And he was giving it back, as everything must be given back, so that, passing through death, it can live forever. I saw my mother's face again, and felt, for the first time, how the stones of the road she had walked on must have bruised her feet. I saw the moonlit road where my father's brother died. And it brought something else back to me, and carried me past it, I saw my little girl again and felt Isabel's tears again, and I felt my own tears begin to rise. And I was yet aware that this was only a moment, that the world waited outside, as hungry as a tiger, and that trouble stretched above us, longer than the sky.

Then it was over. Creole and Sonny let out their breath, both soaking wet, and grinning. There was a lot of applause and some of it was real. In the dark, the girl came by and I asked her to take drinks to the bandstand. There was a long pause, while they talked up there in the indigo light and after awhile I saw the girl put a Scotch and milk on top of the piano for Sonny. He didn't seem to notice it, but just before they started playing again, he sipped from it and looked toward me, and nodded. Then he put it back on top of the piano. For me, then, as they began to play again, it glowed and shook above my brother's head like the very cup of trembling.

5

To Whom Should I Listen?

When you face a major decision, to whom do you turn for advice? Do you turn to your friends? To your religious leader? To books? To those appointed to be your "adviser" or "counselor" by your college, company, or health care system? Or do you try to figure things out on your own?

Throughout *Leading Lives That Matter* we have encountered people who either sought to give advice or were the recipients of advice, welcome and otherwise. William James, lecturing to his students, did not seek to guide each one into a specific path. However, he did have strong convictions about ideals and effort that he very much wanted to share with them all, in the hope that they would make worthy and challenging life choices. We first met Albert Schweitzer, on the other hand, as the recipient of advice. As a young man who longed to offer direct service to others, he found life-shaping guidance in a magazine article about the need for doctors in Africa. Later, after he sent a letter about his plans to his friends and relatives, they uniformly sought to dissuade him from this course. He chose to reject their counsel.

Whether to seek advice, and then whether to take the advice others offer, can become an urgent question for those who are deciding what to do in life. The fact that we live in a society where what we do is seen as an important indicator of who we are raises the stakes as we determine how to answer this question. And the likelihood that we will receive different advice from different sources can make the prospect of listening to a range of voices seem only a path to further perplexity. Moreover, most modern individuals place a high value on making independent choices about what they will do, as the philosopher Charles Taylor argued in the selection from his work included in Part I of this anthology. The ideal that Taylor calls "authenticity" makes many of us extremely wary about asking others for help in making important life choices.

At the same time, there can be little doubt that other people matter immensely in the choices we make. When we look within ourselves, we find a medley of voices from important others in our lives — parents, grandparents, siblings, teachers, pastors, and friends — that we have internalized. Taylor argues that the distinctive individuality so prized by contemporary people is in fact fashioned in a lifelong series of conversations with significant others such as these. Moreover, he insists that individual identity makes sense only when it is oriented to a horizon of meaning that is more generally shared. If Taylor is right, even when we are not explicitly turning to others to help us decide what we should do and what kind of person we want to become, we are still taking their voices into account.

Those of us who are teachers often talk with students about what they should do in life. Most of the time we are, as Taylor would predict, reluctant to be too directive: we do indeed place high value on helping each individual make a decision she can claim as distinctively her own. Often, then, our task becomes one of helping a given student to identify and respond appropriately to the many voices she has encountered and internalized over the years that might steer her in one direction or another. Among these might be voices that say no to certain aspirations because of prejudice based on gender, race, or class; voices that encourage ideals of service; voices that insist that money is the most important factor to consider; voices that point important decisions toward a horizon defined by religious faith.

To whom should we listen? For those in the midst of making important choices, sorting out the character and worth of many voices is a crucial matter. This is true not only for students but also for those during times of transition that come later in life, for the voices in conversation with which our identities are formed will continue to be present all our lives long.

Every reading in this chapter focuses on an individual who must come to terms with voices such as these as he or she decides what to do in life. The mixture of fiction and autobiography in this chapter will allow us to share, in imagination, the experience of a variety of persons as they determine which voices to heed. The selections are:

- a short story by Will Weaver, "The Undeclared Major"
- a chapter entitled "Two Kinds," from *The Joy Luck Club,* a novel by Amy Tan
- a selection from *The Autobiography of Malcolm X*
- two chapters from Lois Lowry's young adult novel *The Giver*
- an autobiographical essay by Vincent Harding, "I Hear Them . . . Calling"
- a selection from a novel by Willa Cather, *The Song of the Lark*
- a chapter from *A Dresser of Sycamore Trees,* a memoir by Garret Keizer.

For most of us, our parents are the earliest and strongest influence on what we do and who we become. The first two selections in this chapter are works of fiction, both written in the first person, which invite us into the imagination and thinking of two young people as they come to terms with the expectations of their parents. In "The Undeclared Major," twenty-year-old Walter Hansen comes home for a visit to his family's wheat farm in the Upper Midwest, deeply uncertain about how his parents will receive his decision not to major in a subject that will lead directly to a practical job in agriculture or business. It is evident that Walter's return home, even though only for a short visit, also draws him into internal conversation with a larger community — with uncles and cousins and townspeople, indeed with all those who surrounded and nurtured him over the years. Walter's sense of the extent to which he belongs to and among these people expands during the course of the story. "The Undeclared Major" may well elicit thoughts in all of us about how much the approval of our families and communities of origin matters as we consider what we shall be. Would Walter, or would we, declare a different major, so to speak, if met with strong opposition from those among whom we grew up?

The next selection depicts a parent-child relationship that is more conflicted than the one Walter and his father enjoy. The title refers to a declaration the mother in the story makes in condemnation of her daughter's efforts at independence. "Only two kinds of daughters," the mother shouts in Chinese. "Those who are obedient and those who follow their own mind." Most of the story focuses on a generational battle of wills that took place during the narrator's childhood. By the end, however, when she has become an adult and her mother has died, she can begin to perceive ways in which her mother's voice has become part of her own identity in spite of the struggles they experienced. This story may help all of us to imagine ways of acknowledging our parents' influence even when we have resisted or opposed some of our parents' wishes. We should also note that in both stories the parents are making decisions about how forcefully to try to mould the lives of their children, even as the children figure out what to embrace from their parents' legacy.

Another group of powerful adults who are authorized by society to guide young people in deciding what they will do is teachers. In the third reading, an excellent eighth-grade student who is African American receives advice from a white teacher who proves to be a most unworthy guide. This selection from *The Autobiography of Malcolm X*, a classic in its genre written by the Muslim leader in collaboration with Alex Haley, thus provides an instructive example of when *not* to listen to certain voices. Looking back on the teacher's appalling remark, the adult Malcolm realizes that this overt manifestation of white racism became a turning point in his life. This selection concludes as the author considers the alternative futures he might have experienced if this turning point had not occurred. What gave him the strength to resist the teacher's disparagement? How might even painful experiences and ugly voices be appropriated in ways that can be helpful in the long run?

The question we are considering, of course, presumes that one may choose whose advice to follow or to ignore. In the fictional community depicted in Lois Lowry's novel *The Giver*, there is no space for this question or, indeed, for other difficult questions about life or work. There, a committee of adults simply assigns each young person to an occupation at the age of twelve. The fact that these and other adults obviously attend with great care to the gifts and temperament of each child before making each assignment gives us something to admire, especially when we contrast that to the racist disdain showed by Malcolm's teacher. (In an imaginary remedy for racism, in Lowry's society — a utopia? a dystopia? — color itself has been abolished.) Assigning occupations also has the benefit of clarity and efficiency; readers who have experienced what it feels like to be paralyzed by indecision might conclude that a process such as this could be in some ways a comfort. Most contemporary Americans would find the process described here unacceptable, of course. But might it nonetheless offer something of value that is missing in the way most of us now find our way into one or another kind of work?

In the final three selections we encounter individuals who learn to listen to voices that transcend the immediate situations in which they find themselves. In "I Hear Them . . . Calling," Vincent Harding tells of how he listened, across the years, to an ever-expanding chorus of voices that eventually summoned him into his work as a leader in the civil rights movement, a peace activist, a husband and father, and a religious scholar, author, and teacher.

Some of these voices were near at hand in his family and home congregation, but others spoke to him out of the history of the African American struggle for freedom. Next, the great American novelist Willa Cather tells of how a burned-out singer, Thea Kronborg, found her strength and her art renewed by opening herself to an ancient landscape and the people who once inhabited it. Finally we have Garret Keizer's account of how he turned to prayer and fasting in a monastery in hopes of deciding which of three professions to pursue. The voices that called to Harding usually found him in the midst of the busy places where he worked and studied over the years, while Cather's heroine and Keizer found clarity in a place apart, only later returning to active lives in the world. For all three, however, the capacity to listen was indispensable; one wonders how many others might hear similar voices from the past, indeed from the divine, but never take the time or pay the necessary attention. For both Thea Kronborg and Garret Keizer, a deliberate retreat into a secluded space of listening was of great importance.

These seven readings, when taken together, challenge each of us to listen with care to and for those voices we believe to be trustworthy, within and beyond ourselves. They also challenge those who are in a position to advise others, as almost all of us are at one time or another, to do so with care, compassion, and close attention to the needs, gifts, and circumstances of those who entrust us with their yearning to lead significant and fulfilling lives. The stories set on the Minnesota farm and in the California household invite parents as well as children, no matter what their age, to consider together the weighty expectations we have of one another. And teachers as well as students have much to learn from the anger of the young man who was assaulted by his teacher's words. Malcolm's story is not just about how to listen; it is also about how to speak. In addition, all of us would do well to become more alert to the distinctive gifts that belong to members of our neighborhoods and communities of faith, so that we might become more deliberate about calling a young Vincent Harding into the good work he longs to do, to his own satisfaction and for the well-being of all. And when confusion sets in, as it may for those who are older as well as for young adults, we might offer spaces for contemplation and renewal such as those found by Thea Kronborg and Garret Keizer.

To whom should I listen?, then, suggests a parallel question: How best may I speak? In the readings that follow, some speak abysmally, but a few characters acquit themselves very well indeed.

WILL WEAVER

"The Undeclared Major"

From the very beginning of this story, we are in the presence of a young person who is thinking deeply about what he will do as his life's work and what the implications of his choice will be. As Walter returns to the land, family, and community where he was raised, he wonders how much he still belongs there and whether the people among whom he grew up will accept him as he grows in new directions. This story portrays — explicitly and in more subtle ways — the ties Walter actually has to this community. Notice how Walter's own sense of these ties changes over the course of the story.

The concern of this chapter of *Leading Lives That Matter* — "To whom should I listen?" — is one to which Walter has given lots of thought and worry, because he has gone against what he imagines as the advice of his family, friends, and acquaintances. Have you or others you know done something similar? Do you admire Walter's apparent refusal to heed the counsel of those who know him best? Is it necessary to refuse such advice in order to "become ourselves"? Or does the story challenge this way of putting the question?

Will Weaver, who grew up on a farm in northern Minnesota, now teaches English in the same region, at Bemidji State University.

―――――――――――――――――

In his gloomy periods Walter Hansen saw himself as one large contradiction. He was still twenty, yet his reddish hair was in full retreat from the white plain of his forehead. He had small and quick-moving blue eyes, eyes

From Will Weaver, *A Gravestone Made of Wheat* (New York: Simon and Schuster, 1989), pp. 169-175.

that tended skyward, eyes that noted every airplane that passed overhead; his hands and feet were great, heavy shovels. As Walter shambled between his classes at the University of Minnesota in Minneapolis, he sometimes caught unexpected sight of himself in a tall glass doorway or window. He always stopped to stare: there he was, the big farm kid with a small handful of books. Walter Hansen, the only twenty-year-old Undeclared Major on the whole campus.

But even that wasn't true. Walter Hansen had declared a major some time ago; he just hadn't felt up to telling anyone what it was.

At present Walter sat in the last, backward-facing seat of the Greyhound bus, reading *The Collected Stories of John Cheever*. Occasionally he looked up to stare at the blue-tinted fields, which in their passing pulled him, mile by mile, toward home. Toward his twenty-first birthday this very weekend.

By the third hour of the trip Walter had a headache from reading. He put away Cheever and began to watch the passing farms. It was a sunny, wet April in central Minnesota. Farmers were trying to spread manure. Their tractors left black ruts in the yellow corn stubble, and once Walter saw two tractors chained together straining, the big rear wheels spinning, throwing clods in the air, as they tried to pull free a third spreader sunk to its hubs beneath an overenthusiastic load of dung.

At the end of the fourth hour Walter's hometown came onto the horizon. It was low and scattered, and soon began to flash by in the windows of the slowing bus like a family slide show that was putting to sleep even the projector operator. A junkyard with a line of shining hubcaps nailed on the fence. A combination deer farm and aquarium with its stuffed black bear wearing a yellow hula skirt, and wheels that stood by the front door. Then the tall and narrow white wooden houses. The square red brick buildings of Main Street, where the bus sighed to a stop at the Shell station. Ducking his head, Walter clambered down the bus steps and stood squinting in the sunlight.

Main Street was three blocks long. Its two-story buildings were fronted with painted tin awnings or cedar shake shingles to disguise the brick and make the buildings look lower and more modern. At the end of Main Street was the taller, dull gray tower of the feed mill. A yellow drift of cornmeal lay on its roof. A blue wheel of pigeons turned overhead. At the stoplight a '57 Chevy chirped its tires, accelerated rapidly for half a block, then braked sharply to turn down Main Street.

Which Walter planned to avoid. On Main Street he would have to speak to people. They would ask him things.

"Walt — so how's the rat race?"

"Walt — where does a person park down there?"

"So Walt, what was it you're going into again? Business? Engineering? Vetinary?"

Carrying his small suitcase, and looking neither left nor right, Walter slipped undetected across Main Street. He walked two blocks to the railroad crossing where he set out east.

The iron rails shone blue. Between the rails, tiny agates glinted red from their bed of gravel, and the flat, sun-warmed railroad ties exhaled a faint breath of creosote. On Walter's right, a robin dug for worms on the sunny south embankment; on the north side, the dirty remnant of a snowbank leaked water downhill. Walter stopped to poke at the snowbank with a stick. Beneath a black crust and mud and leaves, the snow was freshly white and sparkling — but destined, of course, to join the muddy pond water below. Walter thought about that. About destiny. He stood with the chill on his face from the old snowbank and the sun warm on his neck and back. There was a poem buried somewhere in that snowbank. Walter waited, but the first line would not visit him. He walked on.

Walter was soon out of town and into woods and fields. Arms outstretched, suitcase balanced atop his head, he walked one rail for twenty-two ties, certainly a record of some sort. Crows called. A redheaded woodpecker flopped from east to west across the rails. The bird was ridiculously heavy for the length of its wings, a fact which made Walter think of Natural Science. Biology. Veterinary Medicine and other majors with names as solid and normal as fork handles.

Animal Husbandry.

Technical Illustration.

Mechanical Engineering.

Ahead on Walter's left was a twenty-acre field of new oat seeding, brown in the low spots, dusty chartreuse on the higher crowns of the field.

Plant Science.

He could tell people he was developing new wheat strains for Third World countries, like Norman Borlaug.

He walked on, slower now, for around a slight bend he could see, a half mile ahead, the gray dome of his father's silo and the red shine of the dairy barn. He neared the corner post of the west field, where his father's land began. Half the field was gray, the other half was freshly black. He slowed further. A meadowlark called from a fence post. Walter stopped to pitch a rock at the bird.

Then he heard a tractor. From behind a broad swell in the field rose his father's blue cap, tan face, brown shirt, then the red snout of the Massey-

Ferguson. The Massey pulled their green four-row corn planter. His father stood upright on the platform of the tractor. He stood that way to sight down the tractor's nose, to keep its front tires on the line scuffed in the dirt by the corn planter's marker on the previous round. Intermittently Walter's father swiveled his neck for a glance back at the planter. He looked, Walter knew, for the flap of a white rag tied around the main shaft; if the white flag waved, the main shaft turned, the planter plates revolved, pink kernels fell — Walter knew all that stuff.

He stopped walking. There were bushes along the fencerow, and he stooped to lower his profile, certain that his father hadn't seen him. First Walter wanted to go home, talk to his mother, have a cup of coffee. Two cups, maybe. A cinnamon roll. A bowl of bing cherries in sauce, with cream. Maybe one more splash of coffee. Then. Then he'd come back to the field to speak with his father.

Nearing the field's end, his father trailed back his right arm, found the cord, which he pulled at the same moment as he turned hard to left. Brakes croaked. Tripped, the marker arms rose, the Massey came hard around with its front wheels reaching for their new track, the planter straightened behind, the right arm with its shining disk fell, and his father, back to Walter, headed downfield.

Except that brakes croaked again and the tractor came to a stop. His father turned to Walter and held up a hand.

Walter waved once. He looked briefly behind him to the rails that led back toward town, then crossed the ditch and swung his suitcase over the barbed wire.

His father shut off the tractor. "Hey, Walt — " his father called.

Walter waved again.

His father waited by the corn planter. He smiled, his teeth white against the tan skin, the dust. Walter came up to him.

"Walt," his father said.

They stood there grinning at each other. They didn't shake hands. Growing up, Walter believed people shook hands only in the movies or on used-car lots. None of his relatives ever shook hands. Their greeting was to stand and grin at each other and raise their eyebrows up and down. At the university Walter and his circle of friends shook hands coming and going, European style.

"How's it going?" Walter said, touching his boot to the corn planter.

"She's rolling," his father said. "Got one disk that keeps dragging, but other than that."

People in Walter's family often did not complete their sentences.

"A disk dragging," Walter said.

"Yep," his father said. He squinted at Walter, looked down at his clean clothes. "What would you do for a stuck disk?" he asked.

"I'd take out the grease zerk and run a piece of wire in there. That failing, I'd take off the whole disk and soak it in a pan of diesel fuel overnight," Walter said.

Father and son grinned at each other.

His father took off his hat. His forehead was white, his hair coppery.

"So how's the rat race, son?"

"Not so bad," Walter said.

His father paused a moment. "Any . . . decisions yet?" his father said.

Walter swallowed. He looked off toward town. "About . . . a major, you mean?" Walter said.

His father waited.

"Well," Walter said. His mouth went dry. He swallowed twice.

"Well," he said, "I think I'm going to major in English."

His father pursed his lips. He pulled off his work gloves one finger at a time. "English," he said.

"English," Walter nodded.

His father squinted. "Son, we already know English."

Walter stared. "Well, yessir, that's true. I mean, I'm going to study literature. Books. See how they're written. Maybe write one of my own some day."

His father rubbed his brown neck and stared downfield.

Two white sea gulls floated low over the fresh planting.

"So what do you think?" Walter said.

His father's forehead wrinkled and he turned back to Walter. "What could a person be, I mean with that kind of major? An English major," his father said, testing the phrase on his tongue and his lips.

"Be," Walter said. He fell silent. "Well, I don't know, I could be a . . . writer. A teacher maybe, though I don't think I want to teach. At least not for a while. I could be . . ." Then Walter's mind went blank. As blank and empty as the fields around him.

His father was silent. The meadowlark called again.

"I would just be myself, I guess," Walter said.

His father stared a moment at Walter. "Yourself, only smarter," he added.

"Yessir," Walter said quickly, "that's it."

His father squinted downfield at the gulls, then back at Walter. "Nobody talked you into this?"

Walter shook his head no.

"You like it when you're doing it?" his father asked. He glanced across his own field, at what he had planted.

Walter nodded.

His father looked back to Walter and thought another moment. "You think you can make a living at it?"

"Somehow," Walter said.

His father shrugged. "Then I can't see any trouble with it myself," he said. He glanced away, across the fields to the next closest set of barns and silos. "Your uncles, your grampa, they're another story, I suppose."

"They wouldn't have to know," Walter said quickly.

His father looked back to Walter and narrowed his eyes. "They ask me, I'll tell them," he said.

Walter smiled at his father. He started to take a step closer, but at that moment his father looked up at the sun. "We better keep rolling here," he said. He tossed his gloves to Walter. "Take her around once or twice while I eat my sandwich."

Walter climbed onto the tractor and brought up the RPMs. In another minute he was headed downfield. He stood upright on the platform and held tightly to the wheel. The leather gloves were still warm and damp from his father's hands. He sighted the Massey's radiator cap on the thin line in the dirt ahead, and held it there. Halfway downfield he remembered to check the planter flag; in one backward glance he saw his father in straight brown silhouette against the chartreuse band of the fencerow bushes, saw the stripe of fresh dirt unrolling behind, the green seed canisters, and below, the white flag waving. He let out a breath.

After two rounds, Walter began to relax. He began to feel the warm thermals from the engine, the cool breath of the earth below. Gulls hovered close over the tractor, their heads cocked earthward as they waited for the disks to turn up yellow cutworms. A red agate passed underneath and was covered by dirt. The corn planter rolled behind, and through the trip rope, a cotton cord gone smoothly black from grease and dusty gloves, Walter felt the shafts turning, the disks wheeling, the kernels dropping, the press wheel tamping the seed into four perfect rows.

Well, not entirely perfect rows.

Walter, by round four, had begun to think of other things. That whiteness beneath the old snowbank. The blue shine of the iron rails. The damp warmth of his father's gloves. The heavy, chocolate-layer birthday cake that he knew, as certain as he knew the sun would set tonight and rise tomorrow, his mother had hidden in the pantry. Of being twenty-one and the limitless destiny, the endless prospects before him, Walter Hansen, English Major.

As he thought about these and other things, the tractor and its planter drifted a foot to the right, then a foot to the left, centered itself, then drifted again. At field's end his father stood up. He began to wave at Walter first with one hand, then both. But Walter drove on, downfield, smiling slightly to himself, puzzling over why it was he so seldom came home.

AMY TAN

"Two Kinds"

The first-person narrative below describes a conflict that is at once generational and cultural. The mother who expends every effort to shape her daughter's identity and to evoke her gifts is Chinese; the daughter, partly as the result of her mother's actions, is becoming increasingly American. The narrator is Jing-Mei Woo, one of the main characters in Amy Tan's novel *The Joy Luck Club*. Like Tan herself, these characters were born in America to parents who had emigrated from China, though each responds differently to her cultural heritage and context.

For most of us, the most formative influences in our lives, shaping both who we become and what we wind up doing to earn a living, are our parents. What does the narrator learn in the course of her conflicts with her mother? What does she hope for and expect from her mother? Are these hopes and expectations reasonable? Typical or unusual? Moderate or excessive? The narrator's most important lesson in the story is something that she learns, only after her mother's death, in the act of playing once again the piano that had been the occasion and the scene of a formidable test of wills. What is that lesson? What can it teach us about how to learn from our parents without being crushed by their influence?

From Amy Tan, *The Joy Luck Club* (New York: G. P. Putnam's Sons, 1989), pp. 132-144.

My mother believed you could be anything you wanted to be in America. You could open a restaurant. You could work for the government and get good retirement. You could buy a house with almost no money down. You could become rich. You could become instantly famous.

"Of course you can be prodigy, too," my mother told me when I was nine. "You can be best anything. What does Auntie Lindo know? Her daughter, she is only best tricky."

America was where all my mother's hopes lay. She had come here in 1949 after losing everything in China: her mother and father, her family home, her first husband, and two daughters, twin baby girls. But she never looked back with regret. There were so many ways for things to get better.

We didn't immediately pick the right kind of prodigy. At first my mother thought I could be a Chinese Shirley Temple. We'd watch Shirley's old movies on TV as though they were training films. My mother would poke my arm and say, *"Ni kan"* — You watch. And I would see Shirley tapping her feet, or singing a sailor song, or pursing her lips into a very round O while saying, "Oh my goodness."

"Ni kan," said my mother as Shirley's eyes flooded with tears. "You already know how. Don't need talent for crying!"

Soon after my mother got this idea about Shirley Temple, she took me to a beauty training school in the Mission district and put me in the hands of a student who could barely hold the scissors without shaking. Instead of getting big fat curls, I emerged with an uneven mass of crinkly black fuzz. My mother dragged me off to the bathroom and tried to wet down my hair.

"You look like Negro Chinese," she lamented, as if I had done this on purpose.

The instructor of the beauty training school had to lop off these soggy clumps to make my hair even again. "Peter Pan is very popular these days," the instructor assured my mother. I now had hair the length of a boy's, with straight-across bangs that hung at a slant two inches above my eyebrows. I liked the haircut and it made me actually look forward to my future fame.

In fact, in the beginning, I was just as excited as my mother, maybe even more so. I pictured this prodigy part of me as many different ages, trying each one on for size. I was a dainty ballerina girl standing by the curtains, waiting to hear the right music that would send me floating on my tiptoes. I was like the Christ child lifted out of the straw manger, crying with holy indignity. I was Cinderella stepping from her pumpkin carriage with sparkly cartoon music filling the air.

In all of my imaginings, I was filled with a sense that I would soon become *perfect*. My mother and father would adore me. I would be beyond reproach. I would never feel the need to sulk for anything.

But sometimes the prodigy in me became impatient. "If you don't hurry up and get me out of here, I'm disappearing for good," it warned. "And then you'll always be nothing."

Every night after dinner, my mother and I would sit at the Formica kitchen table. She would present new tests, taking her examples from stories of amazing children she had read in *Ripley's Believe It or Not,* or *Good Housekeeping, Reader's Digest,* and a dozen other magazines she kept in a pile in our bathroom. My mother got these magazines from people whose houses she cleaned. And since she cleaned many houses each week, we had a great assortment. She would look through them all, searching for stories about remarkable children.

The first night she brought out a story about a three-year-old boy who knew the capitals of all the states and even most of the European countries. A teacher was quoted as saying the little boy could also pronounce the names of the foreign cities correctly.

"What's the capital of Finland?" my mother asked me, looking at the magazine story.

All I knew was the capital of California, because Sacramento was the name of the street we lived on in Chinatown. "Nairobi!" I guessed, saying the most foreign word I could think of. She checked to see if that was possibly one way to pronounce "Helsinki" before showing me the answer.

The tests got harder — multiplying numbers in my head, finding the queen of hearts in a deck of cards, trying to stand on my head without using my hands, predicting the daily temperatures in Los Angeles, New York, and London.

One night I had to look at a page from the Bible for three minutes and then report everything I could remember. "Now Jehoshaphat had riches and honor in abundance and . . . that's all I remember, Ma," I said.

And after seeing my mother's disappointed face once again, something inside of me began to die. I hated the tests, the raised hopes and failed expectations. Before going to bed that night, I looked in the mirror above the bathroom sink and when I saw only my face staring back — and that it would always be this ordinary face — I began to cry. Such a sad, ugly girl! I made high-pitched noises like a crazed animal, trying to scratch out the face in the mirror.

And then I saw what seemed to be the prodigy side of me because I had never seen that face before. I looked at my reflection, blinking so I could see more clearly. The girl staring back at me was angry, powerful. This girl and I were the same. I had new thoughts, willful thoughts, or rather thoughts filled with lots of won'ts. I won't let her change me, I promised myself. I won't be what I'm not.

So now on nights when my mother presented her tests, I performed listlessly, my head propped on one arm. I pretended to be bored. And I was. I got so bored I started counting the bellows of the foghorns out on the bay while my mother drilled me in other areas. The sound was comforting and reminded me of the cow jumping over the moon. And the next day, I played a game with myself, seeing if my mother would give up on me before eight bellows. After a while I usually counted only one, maybe two bellows at most. At last she was beginning to give up hope.

Two or three months had gone by without any mention of my being a prodigy again. And then one day my mother was watching *The Ed Sullivan Show* on TV. The TV was old and the sound kept shorting out. Every time my mother got halfway up from the sofa to adjust the set, the sound would go back on and Ed would be talking. As soon as she sat down, Ed would go silent again. She got up, the TV broke into loud piano music. She sat down. Silence. Up and down, back and forth, quiet and loud. It was like a stiff embraceless dance between her and the TV set. Finally she stood by the set with her hand on the sound dial.

She seemed entranced by the music, a little frenzied piano piece with this mesmerizing quality, sort of quick passages and then teasing lilting ones before it returned to the quick playful parts.

"*Ni kan*," my mother said, calling me over with hurried hand gestures, "Look here."

I could see why my mother was fascinated by the music. It was being pounded out by a little Chinese girl, about nine years old, with a Peter Pan haircut. The girl had the sauciness of a Shirley Temple. She was proudly modest like a proper Chinese child. And she also did this fancy sweep of a curtsy, so that the fluffy skirt of her white dress cascaded slowly to the floor like the petals of a large carnation.

In spite of these warning signs, I wasn't worried. Our family had no piano and we couldn't afford to buy one, let alone reams of sheet music and piano lessons. So I could be generous in my comments when my mother bad-mouthed the little girl on TV.

"Play note right, but doesn't sound good! No singing sound," complained my mother.

"What are you picking on her for?" I said carelessly. "She's pretty good. Maybe she's not the best, but she's trying hard."

I knew almost immediately I would be sorry I said that.

"Just like you," she said. "Not the best. Because you not trying." She gave a little huff as she let go of the sound dial and sat down on the sofa.

The little Chinese girl sat down also to play an encore of "Anitra's Dance" by Grieg. I remember the song, because later on I had to learn how to play it.

Three days after watching *The Ed Sullivan Show*, my mother told me what my schedule would be for piano lessons and piano practice. She had talked to Mr. Chong, who lived on the first floor of our apartment building. Mr. Chong was a retired piano teacher and my mother had traded housecleaning services for weekly lessons and a piano for me to practice on every day, two hours a day, from four until six.

When my mother told me this, I felt as though I had been sent to hell. I whined and then kicked my foot a little when I couldn't stand it anymore.

"Why don't you like me the way I am? I'm *not* a genius! I can't play the piano. And even if I could, I wouldn't go on TV if you paid me a million dollars!" I cried.

My mother slapped me. "Who ask you be genius?" she shouted. "Only ask you be your best. For you sake. You think I want you be genius? Hnnh! What for! Who ask you!"

"So ungrateful," I heard her mutter in Chinese. "If she had as much talent as she has temper, she would be famous now."

Mr. Chong, whom I secretly nicknamed Old Chong, was very strange, always tapping his fingers to the silent music of an invisible orchestra. He looked ancient in my eyes. He had lost most of the hair on top of his head and he wore thick glasses and had eyes that always looked tired and sleepy. But he must have been younger than I thought, since he lived with his mother and was not yet married.

I met Old Lady Chong once and that was enough. She had this peculiar smell like a baby that had done something in its pants. And her fingers felt like a dead person's, like an old peach I once found in the back of the refrigerator; the skin just slid off the meat when I picked it up.

I soon found out why Old Chong had retired from teaching piano. He was deaf. "Like Beethoven!" he shouted to me. "We're both listening only in our head!" And he would start to conduct his frantic silent sonatas.

Our lessons went like this. He would open the book and point to different things, explaining their purpose: "Key! Treble! Bass! No sharps or flats! So this is C major! Listen now and play after me!"

And then he would play the C scale a few times, a simple chord, and then, as if inspired by an old, unreachable itch, he gradually added more notes and running trills and a pounding bass until the music was really something quite grand.

I would play after him, the simple scale, the simple chord, and then I just played some nonsense that sounded like a cat running up and down on top of garbage cans. Old Chong smiled and applauded and then said, "Very good! But now you must learn to keep time!"

So that's how I discovered that Old Chong's eyes were too slow to keep up with the wrong notes I was playing. He went through the motions in half-time. To help me keep rhythm, he stood behind me, pushing down on my right shoulder for every beat. He balanced pennies on top of my wrists so I would keep them still as I slowly played scales and arpeggios. He had me curve my hand around an apple and keep that shape when playing chords. He marched stiffly to show me how to make each finger dance up and down, staccato like an obedient little soldier.

He taught me all these things, and that was how I also learned I could be lazy and get away with mistakes, lots of mistakes. If I hit the wrong notes because I hadn't practiced enough, I never corrected myself. I just kept playing in rhythm. And Old Chong kept conducting his own private reverie.

So maybe I never really gave myself a fair chance. I did pick up the basics pretty quickly, and I might have become a good pianist at that young age. But I was so determined not to try, not to be anybody different that I learned to play only the most ear-splitting preludes, the most discordant hymns.

Over the next year, I practiced like this, dutifully in my own way. And then one day I heard my mother and her friend Lindo Jong both talking in a loud bragging tone of voice so others could hear. It was after church, and I was leaning against the brick wall wearing a dress with stiff white petticoats. Auntie Lindo's daughter, Waverly, who was about my age, was standing farther down the wall about five feet away. We had grown up together and shared all the closeness of two sisters squabbling over crayons and dolls. In other words, for the most part, we hated each other. I thought she was snotty. Waverly Jong had gained a certain amount of fame as "Chinatown's Littlest Chinese Chess Champion."

"She bring home too many trophy," lamented Auntie Lindo that Sunday. "All day she play chess. All day I have no time do nothing but dust off her winnings." She threw a scolding look at Waverly, who pretended not to see her.

"You lucky you don't have this problem," said Auntie Lindo with a sigh to my mother.

And my mother squared her shoulders and bragged: "Our problem worser than yours. If we ask Jing-mei wash dish, she hear nothing but music. It's like you can't stop this natural talent."

And right then, I was determined to put a stop to her foolish pride.

A few weeks later, Old Chong and my mother conspired to have me play in a talent show which would be held in the church hall. By then, my parents had saved up enough to buy me a secondhand piano, a black Wurlitzer spinet with a scarred bench. It was the showpiece of our living room.

For the talent show, I was to play a piece called "Pleading Child" from Schumann's *Scenes from Childhood*. It was a simple, moody piece that sounded more difficult than it was. I was supposed to memorize the whole thing, playing the repeat parts twice to make the piece sound longer. But I dawdled over it, playing a few bars and then cheating, looking up to see what notes followed. I never really listened to what I was playing. I daydreamed about being somewhere else, about being someone else.

The part I liked to practice best was the fancy curtsy: right foot out, touch the rose on the carpet with a pointed foot, sweep to the side, left leg bends, look up and smile.

My parents invited all the couples from the Joy Luck Club to witness my debut. Auntie Lindo and Uncle Tin were there. Waverly and her two older brothers had also come. The first two rows were filled with children both younger and older than I was. The littlest ones got to go first. They recited simple nursery rhymes, squawked out tunes on miniature violins, twirled Hula Hoops, pranced in pink ballet tutus, and when they bowed or curtsied, the audience would sigh in unison, "Awww," and then clap enthusiastically.

When my turn came, I was very confident. I remember my childish excitement. It was as if I knew, without a doubt, that the prodigy side of me really did exist. I had no fear whatsoever, no nervousness. I remember thinking to myself, This is it! This is it! I looked out over the audience, at my mother's blank face, my father's yawn, Auntie Lindo's stiff-lipped smile, Waverly's sulky expression. I had on a white dress layered with sheets of lace, and a pink bow in my Peter Pan haircut. As I sat down I envisioned people jumping to their feet and Ed Sullivan rushing up to introduce me to everyone on TV.

And I started to play. It was so beautiful. I was so caught up in how lovely I looked that at first I didn't worry how I would sound. So it was a surprise to me when I hit the first wrong note and I realized something didn't sound quite right. And then I hit another and another followed that. A chill started at the top of my head and began to trickle down. Yet I couldn't stop playing, as though my hands were bewitched. I kept thinking my fingers would adjust themselves back, like a train switching to the right track. I played this strange jumble through two repeats, the sour notes staying with me all the way to the end.

When I stood up, I discovered my legs were shaking. Maybe I had just been nervous and the audience, like Old Chong, had seen me go through the right motions and had not heard anything wrong at all. I swept my right foot out, went down on my knee, looked up and smiled. The room was quiet, except for Old Chong, who was beaming and shouting, "Bravo! Bravo! Well done!" But then I saw my mother's face, her stricken face. The audience clapped weakly, and as I walked back to my chair, with my whole face quivering as I tried not to cry, I heard a little boy whisper loudly to his mother, "That was awful," and the mother whispered back, "Well, she certainly tried."

And now I realized how many people were in the audience, the whole world it seemed. I was aware of eyes burning into my back. I felt the shame of my mother and father as they sat stiffly throughout the rest of the show.

We could have escaped during intermission. Pride and some strange sense of honor must have anchored my parents to their chairs. And so we watched it all: the eighteen-year-old boy with a fake mustache who did a magic show and juggled flaming hoops while riding a unicycle. The breasted girl with white makeup who sang from *Madama Butterfly* and got honorable mention. And the eleven-year-old boy who won first prize playing a tricky violin song that sounded like a busy bee.

After the show, the Hsus, the Jongs, and the St. Clairs from the Joy Luck Club came up to my mother and father.

"Lots of talented kids," Auntie Lindo said vaguely, smiling broadly.

"That was somethin' else," said my father, and I wondered if he was referring to me in a humorous way, or whether he even remembered what I had done.

Waverly looked at me and shrugged her shoulders. "You aren't a genius like me," she said matter-of-factly. And if I hadn't felt so bad, I would have pulled her braids and punched her stomach.

But my mother's expression was what devastated me: a quiet, blank look that said she had lost everything. I felt the same way, and it seemed as if everybody were now coming up, like gawkers at the scene of an accident, to see what parts were actually missing. When we got on the bus to go home, my father was humming the busy-bee tune and my mother was silent. I kept thinking she wanted to wait until we got home before shouting at me. But when my father unlocked the door to our apartment, my mother walked in and then went to the back, into the bedroom. No accusations. No blame. And in a way, I felt disappointed. I had been waiting for her to start shouting, so I could shout back and cry and blame her for all my misery.

I assumed my talent-show fiasco meant I never had to play the piano again. But two days later, after school, my mother came out of the kitchen and saw me watching TV.

"Four clock," she reminded me as if it were any other day. I was stunned, as though she were asking me to go through the talent-show torture again. I wedged myself more tightly in front of the TV.

"Turn off TV," she called from the kitchen five minutes later. I didn't budge. And then I decided. I didn't have to do what my mother said anymore. I wasn't her slave. This wasn't China. I had listened to her before and look what happened. She was the stupid one.

She came out from the kitchen and stood in the arched entryway of the living room. "Four clock," she said once again, louder.

"I'm not going to play anymore," I said nonchalantly. "Why should I? I'm not a genius."

She walked over and stood in front of the TV. I saw her chest was heaving up and down in an angry way.

"No!" I said, and I now felt stronger, as if my true self had finally emerged. So this was what had been inside me all along.

"No! I won't!" I screamed.

She yanked me by the arm, pulled me off the floor, snapped off the TV. She was frighteningly strong, half pulling, half carrying me toward the piano as I kicked the throw rugs under my feet. She lifted me up and onto the hard bench. I was sobbing by now, looking at her bitterly. Her chest was heaving even more and her mouth was open, smiling crazily as if she were pleased I was crying.

"You want me to be someone that I'm not," I sobbed. "I'll never be the kind of daughter you want me to be!"

"Only two kinds of daughters," she shouted in Chinese. "Those who are obedient and those who follow their own mind! Only one kind of daughter can live in this house. Obedient daughter!"

"Then I wish I wasn't your daughter. I wish you weren't my mother," I shouted. As I said these things I got scared. It felt like worms and toads and slimy things crawling out of my chest, but it also felt good, as if this awful side of me had surfaced, at last.

"Too late change this," said my mother shrilly.

And I could sense her anger rising to its breaking point. I wanted to see it spill over. And that's when I remembered the babies she had lost in China, the ones we never talked about.

"Then I wish I'd never been born!" I shouted. "I wish I were dead! Like them."

It was as if I had said the magic words. Alakazam! — and her face went blank, her mouth closed, her arms went slack, and she backed out of the room, stunned, as if she were blowing away like a small brown leaf, thin, brittle, lifeless.

It was not the only disappointment my mother felt in me. In the years that followed, I failed her so many times, each time asserting my own will, my right to fall short of expectations. I didn't get straight As. I didn't become class president. I didn't get into Stanford. I dropped out of college.

For unlike my mother, I did not believe I could be anything I wanted to be. I could only be me.

And for all those years, we never talked about the disaster at the recital or my terrible accusations afterward at the piano bench. All that remained unchecked, like a betrayal that was now unspeakable. So I never found a way to ask her why she had hoped for something so large that failure was inevitable.

And even worse, I never asked her what frightened me the most: Why had she given up hope?

For after our struggle at the piano, she never mentioned my playing again. The lessons stopped. The lid to the piano was closed, shutting out the dust, my misery, and her dreams.

So she surprised me. A few years ago, she offered to give me the piano, for my thirtieth birthday. I had not played in all those years. I saw the offer as a sign of forgiveness, a tremendous burden removed.

"Are you sure?" I asked shyly. "I mean, won't you and Dad miss it?"

"No, this your piano," she said firmly. "Always your piano. You only one can play."

"Well, I probably can't play anymore," I said. "It's been years."

"You pick up fast," said my mother, as if she knew this was certain. "You have natural talent. You could been genius if you want to."

"No I couldn't."

"You just not trying," said my mother. And she was neither angry nor sad. She said it as if to announce a fact that could never be disproved. "Take it," she said.

But I didn't at first. It was enough that she had offered it to me. And after that, every time I saw it in my parents' living room, standing in front of the bay windows, it made me feel proud, as if it were a shiny trophy I had won back.

Last week I sent a tuner over to my parents' apartment and had the piano reconditioned, for purely sentimental reasons. My mother had died a few months before and I had been getting things in order for my father, a little bit at a time. I put the jewelry in special silk pouches. The sweaters she had knitted in yellow, pink, bright orange — all the colors I hated — I put those in moth-proof boxes. I found some old Chinese silk dresses, the kind with little slits up the sides. I rubbed the old silk against my skin, then wrapped them in tissue and decided to take them home with me.

After I had the piano tuned, I opened the lid and touched the keys. It sounded even richer than I remembered. Really, it was a very good piano. Inside the bench were the same exercise notes with handwritten scales, the same secondhand music books with their covers held together with yellow tape.

I opened up the Schumann book to the dark little piece I had played at the recital. It was on the left-hand side of the page, "Pleading Child." It looked more difficult than I remembered. I played a few bars, surprised at how easily the notes came back to me.

And for the first time, or so it seemed, I noticed the piece on the right-hand side. It was called "Perfectly Contented." I tried to play this one as well. It had a lighter melody but the same flowing rhythm and turned out to be quite easy. "Pleading Child" was shorter but slower; "Perfectly Contented" was longer, but faster. And after I played them both a few times, I realized they were two halves of the same song.

MALCOLM X WITH ALEX HALEY

The Autobiography of Malcolm X

This reading provides a testimony to the importance of *not* listening to those whose prejudgments keep them from being trustworthy guides. *The Autobiography of Malcolm X,* which is imbued with righteous anger at oppression, traces Malcolm's journey from childhood to prison, where he was converted to the Nation of Islam, and then to his discovery of global Islam as a movement that transcended racial divisions. A great orator and powerful voice in the movement for the empowerment of African American people, Malcolm X was assassinated by Nation of Islam activists while delivering a speech in Harlem in 1965. His autobiography, which has become an American classic, was written in collaboration with Alex Haley, who later wrote *Roots,* which tells the story of Haley's ancestors in Africa, in slavery, and in freedom.

This selection appears fairly early in the book and describes what Malcolm would later realize was a "turning point" in his life. What gave him the courage and determination to reject his teacher's advice, especially when this limiting advice was not just that of an individual teacher, but the script of an entire society? He concludes this chapter with a series of "what ifs" — other futures that might have been his apart from one fortunate turn of events. What limiting social scripts bear in upon Americans of different races, genders, and backgrounds today? Upon you? Where do you, and others, turn for the strength to resist these scripts?

That summer of 1940, in Lansing, I caught the Greyhound bus for Boston with my cardboard suitcase, and wearing my green suit. If someone had hung a sign, "HICK," around my neck, I couldn't have looked much more ob-

From Alex Haley, *The Autobiography of Malcolm X* (orig. New York: Grove Press, 1965; repr. Ballantine Books, 1973), pp. 41-46.

vious. They didn't have the turnpikes then; the bus stopped at what seemed every corner and cowpatch. From my seat in — you guessed it — the back of the bus, I gawked out of the window at white man's America rolling past for what seemed a month, but must have been only a day and a half.

When we finally arrived, Ella met me at the terminal and took me home. The house was on Waumbeck Street in the Sugar Hill section of Roxbury, the Harlem of Boston. I met Ella's second husband, Frank, who was now a soldier; and her brother Earl, the singer who called himself Jimmy Carleton; and Mary, who was very different from her older sister. It's funny how I seemed to think of Mary as Ella's sister, instead of her being, just as Ella is, my own half-sister. It's probably because Ella and I always were much closer as basic types; we're dominant people, and Mary has always been mild and quiet, almost shy.

Ella was busily involved in dozens of things. She belonged to I don't know how many different clubs; she was a leading light of local so-called "black society." I saw and met a hundred black people there whose big-city talk and ways left my mouth hanging open.

I couldn't have feigned indifference if I had tried to. People talked casually about Chicago, Detroit, New York. I didn't know the world contained as many Negroes as I saw thronging downtown Roxbury at night, especially on Saturdays. Neon lights, nightclubs, poolhalls, bars, the cars they drove! Restaurants made the streets smell — rich, greasy, down-home black cooking! Jukeboxes blared Erskine Hawkins, Duke Ellington, Cootie Williams, dozens of others. If somebody had told me then that some day I'd know them all personally, I'd have found it hard to believe. The biggest bands, like these, played at the Roseland State Ballroom, on Boston's Massachusetts Avenue — one night for Negroes, the next night for whites.

I saw for the first time occasional black-white couples strolling around arm in arm. And on Sundays, when Ella, Mary, or somebody took me to church, I saw churches for black people such as I had never seen. They were many times finer than the white church I had attended back in Mason, Michigan. There, the white people just sat and worshipped with words; but the Boston Negroes, like all other Negroes I had ever seen at church, threw their souls and bodies wholly into worship.

Two or three times, I wrote letters to Wilfred intended for everybody back in Lansing. I said I'd try to describe it when I got back.

But I found I couldn't.

My restlessness with Mason — and for the first time in my life a restlessness with being around white people — began as soon as I got back home and entered eighth grade.

I continued to think constantly about all that I had seen in Boston, and about the way I had felt there. I know now that it was the sense of being a real part of a mass of my own kind, for the first time.

The white people — classmates, the Swerlins, the people at the restaurant where I worked — noticed the change. They said, "You're acting so strange. You don't seem like yourself, Malcolm. What's the matter?"

I kept close to the top of the class, though. The topmost scholastic standing, I remember, kept shifting between me, a girl named Audrey Slaugh, and a boy named Jimmy Cotton.

It went on that way, as I became increasingly restless and disturbed through the first semester. And then one day, just about when those of us who had passed were about to move up to 8-A, from which we would enter high school the next year, something happened which was to become the first major turning point of my life.

Somehow, I happened to be alone in the classroom with Mr. Ostrowski, my English teacher. He was a tall, rather reddish white man and he had a thick mustache. I had gotten some of my best marks under him, and he had always made me feel that he liked me. He was, as I have mentioned, a natural-born "advisor," about what you ought to read, to do, or think — about any and everything. We used to make unkind jokes about him: why was he teaching in Mason instead of somewhere else, getting for himself some of the "success in life" that he kept telling us how to get?

I know that he probably meant well in what he happened to advise me that day. I doubt that he meant any harm. It was just in his nature as an American white man. I was one of his top students, one of the school's top students — but all he could see for me was the kind of future "in your place" that almost all white people see for black people.

He told me, "Malcolm, you ought to be thinking about a career. Have you been giving it thought?"

The truth is, I hadn't. I never have figured out why I told him, "Well, yes, sir, I've been thinking I'd like to be a lawyer." Lansing certainly had no Negro lawyers — or doctors either — in those days, to hold up an image I might have aspired to. All I really knew for certain was that a lawyer didn't wash dishes, as I was doing.

Mr. Ostrowski looked surprised, I remember, and leaned back in his chair and clasped his hands behind his head. He kind of half-smiled and said, "Malcolm, one of life's first needs is for us to be realistic. Don't misunderstand me, now. We all here like you, you know that. But you've got to be realistic about being a nigger. A lawyer — that's no realistic goal for a nigger. You need to think about something you *can* be. You're good with your hands

— making things. Everybody admires your carpentry shop work. Why don't you plan on carpentry? People like you as a person — you'd get all kinds of work."

The more I thought afterwards about what he said, the more uneasy it made me. It just kept treading around in my mind.

What made it really begin to disturb me was Mr. Ostrowski's advice to others in my class — all of them white. Most of them had told him they were planning to become farmers. But those who wanted to strike out on their own, to try something new, he had encouraged. Some, mostly girls, wanted to be teachers. A few wanted other professions, such as one boy who wanted to become a county agent; another, a veterinarian; and one girl wanted to be a nurse. They all reported that Mr. Ostrowski had encouraged what they had wanted. Yet nearly none of them had earned marks equal to mine.

It was a surprising thing that I had never thought of it that way before, but I realized that whatever I wasn't, I *was* smarter than nearly all of those white kids. But apparently I was still not intelligent enough, in their eyes, to become whatever I wanted to be.

It was then that I began to change — inside.

I drew away from white people. I came to class, and I answered when called upon. It became a physical strain simply to sit in Mr. Ostrowski's class.

Where "nigger" had slipped off my back before, wherever I heard it now, I stopped and looked at whoever said it. And they looked surprised that I did.

I quit hearing so much "nigger" and "What's wrong?" — which was the way I wanted it. Nobody, including the teachers, could decide what had come over me. I knew I was being discussed.

In a few more weeks, it was that way, too, at the restaurant where I worked washing dishes, and at the Swerlins'.

One day soon after, Mrs. Swerlin called me into the living room and there was the state man, Maynard Allen. I knew from the faces that something was about to happen. She told me that none of them could understand why — after I had done so well in school, and on my job, and living with them, and after everyone in Mason had come to like me — I had lately begun to make them all feel that I wasn't happy there anymore.

She said she felt there was no need for me to stay at the detention home any longer, and that arrangements had been made for me to go and live with the Lyons family, who liked me so much.

She stood up and put out her hand. "I guess I've asked you a hundred times, Malcolm — do you want to tell me what's wrong?"

I shook her hand, and said, "Nothing, Mrs. Swerlin." Then I went and got my things, and came back down. At the living room door I saw her wiping her eyes. I felt very bad. I thanked her and went out in front to Mr. Allen, who took me over to the Lyons'.

Mr. and Mrs. Lyons, and their children, during the two months I lived with them — while finishing eighth grade — also tried to get me to tell them what was wrong. But somehow I couldn't tell them, either.

I went every Saturday to see my brothers and sisters in Lansing, and almost every other day I wrote to Ella in Boston. Not saying why, I told Ella that I wanted to come there and live.

I don't know how she did it, but she arranged for official custody of me to be transferred from Michigan to Massachusetts, and the very week I finished the eighth grade, I again boarded the Greyhound bus for Boston.

I've thought about that time a lot since then. No physical move in my life has been more pivotal or profound in its repercussions.

If I had stayed on in Michigan, I would probably have married one of those Negro girls I knew and liked in Lansing. I might have become one of those state capitol building shoeshine boys, or a Lansing Country Club waiter, or gotten one of the other menial jobs which, in those days, among Lansing Negroes, would have been considered "successful" — or even become a carpenter.

Whatever I have done since then, I have driven myself to become a success at it. I've often thought that if Mr. Ostrowski had encouraged me to become a lawyer, I would today probably be among some city's professional black bourgeoisie, sipping cocktails and palming myself off as a community spokesman for and leader of the suffering black masses, while my primary concern would be to grab a few more crumbs from the groaning board of the two-faced whites with whom they're begging to "integrate."

All praise is due to Allah that I went to Boston when I did. If I hadn't, I'd probably still be a brainwashed black Christian.

LOIS LOWRY

The Giver

The Giver, which falls into the category known as "young adult fiction," is popular among middle schoolers and older adults alike, for it probes ethical issues of enduring interest. It is set in a seemingly utopian, futuristic world organized in ways that are meant to remove pain and conflict from everyday life. Yet there are evidently a few cracks in the system; Jonas, the novel's protagonist, has begun to notice unusual things and to have some questions about the society in which he lives.

This selection describes an annual community ceremony in which young people are assigned to the work the adults believe will be most fitting for them. Clearly, the process leading up to this ceremony is proof that the adults have paid careful attention to the gifts of each child in the community as well as to the community's need for certain kinds of work to be done. Does this ceremony therefore embody Frederick Buechner's definition of vocation (see Part I)? And in what ways does the Assignments ceremony fulfill Russell Muirhead's proposal that everyone should have "fitting" work (see Chapter 2)? How might Buechner and Muirhead criticize this process?

Chapter Seven

Now Jonas's group had taken a new place in the Auditorium, trading with the new Elevens, so that they sat in the very front, immediately before the stage.

They were arranged by their original numbers, the numbers they had been given at birth. The numbers were rarely used after the Naming. But each child knew his number, of course. Sometimes parents used them in ir-

---

From Lois Lowry, *The Giver* (New York: Dell Laurel-Leaf, 1993), pp. 50-64.

ritation at a child's misbehavior, indicating that mischief made one unworthy of a name. Jonas always chuckled when he heard a parent, exasperated, call sharply to a whining toddler, "That's *enough,* Twenty-three!"

Jonas was Nineteen. He had been the nineteenth new child born his year. It had meant that at his Naming, he had been already standing and bright-eyed, soon to walk and talk. It had given him a slight advantage the first year or two, a little more maturity than many of his groupmates who had been born in the later months of that year. But it evened out, as it always did, by Three.

After Three, the children progressed at much the same level, though by their first number one could always tell who was a few months older than others in his group. Technically, Jonas's full number was Eleven-nineteen, since there were other Nineteens, of course, in each age group. And today, now that the new Elevens had been advanced this morning, there were two Eleven-nineteens. At the midday break he had exchanged smiles with the new one, a shy female named Harriet.

But the duplication was only for these few hours. Very soon he would not be an Eleven but a Twelve, and age would no longer matter. He would be an adult, like his parents, though a new one and untrained still.

Asher was Four, and sat now in the row ahead of Jonas. He would receive his Assignment fourth.

Fiona, Eighteen, was on his left; on his other side sat Twenty, a male named Pierre whom Jonas didn't like much. Pierre was very serious, not much fun, and a worrier and tattletale, too. "Have you checked the rules, Jonas?" Pierre was always whispering solemnly. "I'm not sure that's within the rules." Usually it was some foolish thing that no one cared about — opening his tunic if it was a day with a breeze; taking a brief try on a friend's bicycle, just to experience the different feel of it.

The initial speech at the Ceremony of Twelve was made by the Chief Elder, the leader of the community who was elected every ten years. The speech was much the same each year: recollection of the time of childhood and the period of preparation, the coming responsibilities of adult life, the profound importance of Assignment, the seriousness of training to come.

Then the Chief Elder moved ahead in her speech.

"This is the time," she began, looking directly at them, "when we acknowledge differences. You Elevens have spent all your years till now learning to fit in, to standardize your behavior, to curb any impulse that might set you apart from the group.

"But today we honor your differences. They have determined your futures."

She began to describe this year's group and its variety of personalities, though she singled no one out by name. She mentioned that there was one who had singular skills at caretaking, another who loved newchildren, one with unusual scientific aptitude, and a fourth for whom physical labor was an obvious pleasure. Jonas shifted in his seat, trying to recognize each reference as one of his groupmates. The caretaking skills were no doubt those of Fiona, on his left; he remembered noticing the tenderness with which she had bathed the Old. Probably the one with scientific aptitude was Benjamin, the male who had devised new, important equipment for the Rehabilitation Center.

He heard nothing that he recognized as himself, Jonas.

Finally the Chief Elder paid tribute to the hard work of her committee, which had performed the observations so meticulously all year. The Committee of Elders stood and was acknowledged by applause. Jonas noticed Asher yawn slightly covering his mouth politely with his hand.

Then, at last, the Chief Elder called number One to the stage, and the Assignments began.

Each announcement was lengthy, accompanied by a speech directed at the new Twelve. Jonas tried to pay attention as One, smiling happily, received her Assignment as Fish Hatchery Attendant along with words of praise for her childhood spent doing many volunteer hours there, and her obvious interest in the important process of providing nourishment for the community.

Number One — her name was Madeline — returned, finally, amidst applause, to her seat, wearing the new badge that designated her Fish Hatchery Attendant. Jonas was certainly glad that *that* Assignment was taken; he wouldn't have wanted it. But he gave Madeline a smile of congratulation.

When Two, a female named Inger, received her Assignment as Birthmother, Jonas remembered that his mother had called it a job without honor. But he thought that the Committee had chosen well. Inger was a nice girl though somewhat lazy, and her body was strong. She would enjoy the three years of being pampered that would follow her brief training; she would give birth easily and well; and the task of Laborer that would follow would use her strength, keep her healthy, and impose self-discipline. Inger was smiling when she resumed her seat. Birthmother was an important job, if lacking in prestige.

Jonas noticed that Asher looked nervous. He kept turning his head and glancing back at Jonas until the group leader had to give him a silent chastisement, a motion to sit still and face forward.

Three, Isaac, was given an Assignment as Instructor of Sixes, which obviously pleased him and was well deserved. Now there were three Assignments gone, none of them ones that Jonas would have liked — not that he could have been a Birthmother, anyway, he realized with amusement. He tried to sort through the list in his mind, the possible Assignments that remained. But there were so many he gave it up; and anyway, now it was Asher's turn. He paid strict attention as his friend went to the stage and stood self-consciously beside the Chief Elder.

"All of us in the community know and enjoy Asher," the Chief Elder began. Asher grinned and scratched one leg with the other foot. The audience chuckled softly.

"When the committee began to consider Asher's Assignment," she went on, "there were some possibilities that were immediately discarded. Some that would clearly not have been right for Asher.

"For example," she said, smiling, "we did not consider for an instant designating Asher an Instructor of Threes."

The audience howled with laughter. Asher laughed, too, looking sheepish but pleased at the special attention. The Instructors of Threes were in charge of the acquisition of correct language.

"In fact," the Chief Elder continued, chuckling a little herself, "we even gave a little thought to some retroactive chastisement for the one who had been *Asher's* Instructor of Threes so long ago. At the meeting where Asher was discussed, we retold many of the stories that we all remembered from his days of language acquisition.

"Especially," she said, chuckling, "the difference between snack and smack. Remember, Asher?"

Asher nodded ruefully, and the audience laughed aloud. Jonas did, too. He remembered, though he had been only a Three at the time himself.

The punishment used for small children was a regulated system of smacks with the discipline wand: a thin, flexible weapon that stung painfully when it was wielded. The Childcare specialists were trained very carefully in the discipline methods: a quick smack across the hands for a bit of minor misbehavior; three sharper smacks on the bare legs for a second offense.

Poor Asher, who always talked too fast and mixed up words, even as a toddler. As a Three, eager for his juice and crackers at snacktime, he one day said "smack" instead of "snack" as he stood waiting in line for the morning treat.

Jonas remembered it clearly. He could still see little Asher, wiggling with impatience in the line. He remembered the cheerful voice calling out, "I want my smack!"

The other Threes, including Jonas, had laughed nervously. "Snack!" they corrected. "You meant snack, Asher!" But the mistake had been made. And precision of language was one of the most important tasks of small children. Asher had asked for a smack.

The discipline wand, in the hand of the Childcare worker, whistled as it came down across Asher's hands. Asher whimpered, cringed, and corrected himself instantly. "Snack," he whispered.

But the next morning he had done it again. And again the following week. He couldn't seem to stop, though for each lapse the discipline wand came again, escalating to a series of painful lashes that left marks on Asher's legs. Eventually, for a period of time, Asher stopped talking altogether, when he was a Three.

"For a while," the Chief Elder said, relating the story, "we had a silent Asher! But he learned."

She turned to him with a smile. "When he began to talk again, it was with greater precision. And now his lapses are very few. His corrections and apologies are very prompt. And his good humor is unfailing." The audience murmured in agreement. Asher's cheerful disposition was well known throughout the community.

"Asher." She lifted her voice to make the official announcement. "We have given you the Assignment of Assistant Director of Recreation."

She clipped on his new badge as he stood beside her, beaming. Then he turned and left the stage as the audience cheered. When he had taken his seat again, the Chief Elder looked down at him and said the words that she had said now four times, and would say to each new Twelve. Somehow she gave it special meaning for each of them.

"Asher," she said, "thank you for your childhood."

The Assignments continued, and Jonas watched and listened, relieved now by the wonderful Assignment his best friend had been given. But he was more and more apprehensive as his own approached. Now the new Twelves in the row ahead had all received their badges. They were fingering them as they sat, and Jonas knew that each one was thinking about the training that lay ahead. For some — one studious male had been selected as Doctor, a female as Engineer, and another for Law and Justice — it would be years of hard work and study. Others, like Laborers and Birthmothers, would have a much shorter training period.

Eighteen, Fiona, on his left, was called. Jonas knew she must be nervous; but Fiona was a calm female. She had been sitting quietly, serenely, throughout the Ceremony.

Even the applause, though enthusiastic, seemed serene when Fiona was given the important Assignment of Caretaker of the Old. It was perfect for such a sensitive, gentle girl, and her smile was satisfied and pleased when she took her seat beside him again.

Jonas prepared himself to walk to the stage when the applause ended and the Chief Elder picked up the next folder and looked down to the group to call forward the next new Twelve. He was calm now that his turn had come. He took a deep breath and smoothed his hair with his hand.

"Twenty," he heard her voice say clearly. "Pierre." *She skipped me,* Jonas thought, stunned. Had he heard wrong? No. There was a sudden hush in the crowd, and he knew that the entire community realized that the Chief Elder had moved from Eighteen to Twenty, leaving a gap. On his right, Pierre, with a startled look, rose from his seat and moved to the stage.

A mistake. She made a mistake. But Jonas knew, even as he had the thought, that she hadn't. The Chief Elder made no mistakes. Not at the Ceremony of Twelve.

He felt dizzy, and couldn't focus his attention. He didn't hear what Assignment Pierre received, and was only dimly aware of the applause as the boy returned, wearing his new badge. Then: Twenty-one. Twenty-two.

The numbers continued in order. Jonas sat, dazed, as they moved into the Thirties and then the Forties, nearing the end. Each time, at each announcement, his heart jumped for a moment, and he thought wild thoughts. Perhaps now she would call his name. Could he have forgotten his own number? No. He had always been Nineteen. He was sitting in the seat marked Nineteen.

But she had *skipped* him. He saw the others in his group glance at him, embarrassed, and then avert their eyes quickly. He saw a worried look on the face of his group leader.

He hunched his shoulders and tried to make himself smaller in the seat. He wanted to disappear, to fade away, not to exist. He didn't dare to turn and find his parents in the crowd. He couldn't bear to see their faces darkened with shame.

Jonas bowed his head and searched through his mind. *What had he done wrong?*

Chapter Eight

The audience was clearly ill at ease. They applauded at the final Assignment; but the applause was piecemeal, no longer a crescendo of united enthusiasm. There were murmurs of confusion.

Jonas moved his hands together, clapping, but it was an automatic, meaningless gesture that he wasn't even aware of. His mind had shut out all of the earlier emotions: the anticipation, excitement, pride, and even the happy kinship with his friends. Now he felt only humiliation and terror.

The Chief Elder waited until the uneasy applause subsided. Then she spoke again.

"I know," she said in her vibrant, gracious voice, "that you are all concerned. That you feel I have made a mistake."

She smiled. The community, relieved from its discomfort very slightly by her benign statement, seemed to breathe more easily. It was very silent.

Jonas looked up.

"I have caused you anxiety," she said. "I apologize to my community." Her voice flowed over the assembled crowd.

"We accept your apology," they all uttered together.

"Jonas," she said, looking down at him, "I apologize to you in particular. I caused you anguish."

"I accept your apology," Jonas replied shakily.

"Please come to the stage now."

Earlier that day, dressing in his own dwelling, he had practiced the kind of jaunty, self-assured walk that he hoped he could make to the stage when his turn came. All of that was forgotten now. He simply willed himself to stand, to move his feet that felt weighted and clumsy, to go forward, up the steps and across the platform until he stood at her side.

Reassuringly she placed her arm across his tense shoulders.

"Jonas has not been assigned," she informed the crowd, and his heart sank.

Then she went on. "Jonas has been *selected*."

He blinked. What did that mean? He felt a collective, questioning stir from the audience. They, too, were puzzled.

In a firm, commanding voice she announced, "Jonas has been selected to be our next Receiver of Memory."

Then he heard the gasp — the sudden intake of breath, drawn sharply in astonishment, by each of the seated citizens. He saw their faces; the eyes widened in awe.

And still he did not understand.

"Such a selection is very, very rare," the Chief Elder told the audience. "Our community has only one Receiver. It is he who trains his successor.

"We have had our current Receiver for a very long time," she went on. Jonas followed her eyes and saw that she was looking at one of the Elders. The Committee of Elders was sitting together in a group; and the Chief Elder's eyes were now on one who sat in the midst but seemed oddly separate from them. It was a man Jonas had never noticed before, a bearded man with pale eyes. He was watching Jonas intently.

"We failed in our last selection," the Chief Elder said solemnly. "It was ten years ago, when Jonas was just a toddler. I will not dwell on the experience because it causes us all terrible discomfort."

Jonas didn't know what she was referring to, but he could sense the discomfort of the audience. They shifted uneasily in their seats.

"We have not been hasty this time," she continued. "We could not afford another failure."

"Sometimes," she went on, speaking now in a lighter tone, relaxing the tension in the Auditorium, "we are not entirely certain about the Assignments, even after the most painstaking observations. Sometimes we worry that the one assigned might not develop, through training, every attribute necessary. Elevens are still children, after all. What we observe as playfulness and patience — the requirements to become Nurturer — could, with maturity, be revealed as simply foolishness and indolence. So we continue to observe during training, and to modify behavior when necessary.

"But the Receiver-in-training cannot be observed, cannot be modified. That is stated quite clearly in the rules. He is to be alone, apart, while he is prepared by the current Receiver for the job which is the most honored in our community."

Alone? Apart? Jonas listened with increasing unease.

"Therefore the selection must be sound. It must be a unanimous choice of the Committee. They can have no doubts, however fleeting. If, during the process, an Elder reports a dream of uncertainty, that dream has the power to set a candidate aside instantly.

"Jonas was identified as a possible Receiver many years ago. We have observed him meticulously. There were no dreams of uncertainty.

"He has shown all of the qualities that a Receiver must have."

With her hand still firmly on his shoulder, the Chief Elder listed the qualities.

"*Intelligence*," she said. "We are all aware that Jonas has been a top student throughout his school days.

"*Integrity*," she said next. "Jonas has, like all of us, committed minor transgressions." She smiled at him. "We expect that. We hoped, also, that he would present himself promptly for chastisement, and he has always done so.

"*Courage*," she went on. "Only one of us here today has ever undergone the rigorous training required of a Receiver. He, of course, is the most important member of the Committee: the current Receiver. It was he who re-minded us, again and again, of the courage required.

"Jonas," she said, turning to him, but speaking in a voice that the entire community could hear, "the training required of you involves pain. Physical pain."

He felt fear flutter within him.

"You have never experienced that. Yes, you have scraped your knees in falls from your bicycle. Yes, you crushed your finger in a door last year."

Jonas nodded, agreeing, as he recalled the incident, and its accompany-ing misery.

"But you will be faced, now," she explained gently, "with pain of a mag-nitude that none of us here can comprehend because it is beyond our expe-rience. The Receiver himself was not able to describe it, only to remind us that you would be faced with it, that you would need immense courage. We cannot prepare you for that.

"But we feel certain that you are brave," she said to him.

He did not feel brave at all. Not now.

"The fourth essential attribute," the Chief Elder said, "is *wisdom*. Jonas has not yet acquired that. The acquisition of wisdom will come through his training.

"We are convinced that Jonas has the ability to acquire wisdom. That is what we looked for.

"Finally, The Receiver must have one more quality, and it is one which I can only name, but not describe. I do not understand it. You members of the community will not understand it, either. Perhaps Jonas will, because the current Receiver has told us that Jonas already has this quality. He calls it the Capacity to See Beyond."

The Chief Elder looked at Jonas with a question in her eyes. The audi-ence watched him, too. They were silent.

For a moment he froze, consumed with despair. He *didn't* have it, the whatever-she-had-said. He didn't know what it was. Now was the moment when he would have to confess, to say, "No, I don't. I *can't*," and throw him-self on their mercy, ask their forgiveness, to explain that he had been wrongly chosen, that he was not the right one at all.

But when he looked out across the crowd, the sea of faces, the thing happened again. The thing that had happened with the apple.

They *changed*.

He blinked, and it was gone. His shoulders straightened slightly. Briefly he felt a tiny sliver of sureness for the first time.

She was still watching him. They all were.

"I think it's true," he told the Chief Elder and the community. "I don't understand it yet. I don't know what it is. But sometimes I see something. And maybe it's beyond."

She took her arm from his shoulders.

"Jonas," she said, speaking not to him alone but to the entire community of which he was a part, "you will be trained to be our next Receiver of Memory. We thank you for your childhood."

Then she turned and left the stage, left him there alone, standing and facing the crowd, which began spontaneously the collective murmur of his name.

"Jonas." It was a whisper at first: hushed, barely audible. "Jonas. Jonas."

Then louder, faster. "JONAS. JONAS. JONAS."

With the chant, Jonas knew, the community was accepting him and his new role, giving him life, the way they had given it to the newchild Caleb. His heart swelled with gratitude and pride.

But at the same time he was filled with fear. He did not know what his selection meant. He did not know what he was to become.

Or what would become of him.

VINCENT HARDING

"I Hear Them . . . Calling"

Vincent Harding has been involved throughout his adult life in domestic and international movements for peace and justice. This essay was written fairly early in his career, as he was writing the path-breaking book *There Is a River: The Black Struggle for Freedom in America* (1981). Presently Professor Emeritus of Religion and Social Transformation at Iliff School of Theology in Denver, Harding continues to be an inspiring speaker and writer.

Placing this essay just after the selection from *The Giver* allows us to

---

From *Callings!* ed. James Y. Holloway and Will D. Campbell (New York: Paulist Press, 1974), pp. 57-69.

envision another, quite different example of a community that noticed the gifts of a young person and sought to shape his future. How does Harding's sense of the scope and needs of the community that is "calling" to him change over time? Do his relationship to this community and his various ways of responding to the call of his people deepen or threaten what we might call, with Charles Taylor, his "authenticity"?

Callings are strange things. I think I've heard a fair number in my time, perhaps fewer than I was supposed to — or maybe it was more; I'm not certain now. Sometimes they proved to be nothing more than echoes bouncing off from other lives (lives I sometimes thought were mine) and passed on their way. Others puzzled me, and led me into ways I do not yet understand. Some I understand and fear. A few — perhaps more than I know — I have followed as far as they led; and some are still moving. Still moving, preparing to join themselves to the sounds of the new summons, and I suspect there are yet borders to cross.

Callings are strange things. The first I remember (or want to remember?) came through the Black believers who were my extended family in a Harlem congregation. I felt their loving, often demanding grip on my life at an early time — maybe 6 or 7 — and heard the call through all their voices and fiercely possessive hopes.

Up there on platforms and stages, at all the church programs, reciting the poems and Bible verses, I heard them set me apart: "He's going to be a preacher," that call said (really meaning, he is going to be *our* preacher, ours, to assure the continuance of our hopes beyond the borders of our lives), and it was a while before I understood that it was supposed to be *my* calling, that I should hear it and respond.

It took a while for that to happen, for I was hearing other calls as well — or thought I was, though I'm sure I didn't name them that — and was trying to move with them. Like the calling to be an athlete. (This was before Jackie Robinson, so I'm not sure where I thought that road would lead. Perhaps I simply thought that a man should be able to spend his life doing what he really liked, and I liked everything that had to do with balls and bats and running and jumping and falling and feeling the strength of bodies against each other. I liked them far more than the violin and then the piano lessons that my mother hoped in vain I'd like.) That lasted for a while, but I wasn't growing as tall as I thought an athlete ought to be — especially one who thought he was called to play first base, among other things — and I began to hear other calls.

Somehow I got involved with building model airplanes, partly, I suppose, because no one had bothered to mass produce television sets yet (and we probably wouldn't have been able to afford one) and partly because there were no brothers and sisters to share the sometimes lonely days with. That's when the call came to be an aeronautical engineer (whatever that is), and I hadn't found out that Black folks weren't supposed to be aeronautical engineers. What I did find out was that my mathematical skills weren't good enough to pass the test for the high school where all the really bright, aeronautical engineer–types were supposed to attend; so that call too was pressed aside. I think the model airplanes were pretty good, though.

Meanwhile, the loving, tightly gripping community was pressing me forward — not entirely against the sometimes showmanship of my will — into minor church offices, and other responsibilities. And I continued to be up in front at the programs (we, education-oriented folks that we were, mostly of West Indian heritage on the way from Africa, we called them *Lyceum* programs, following traditions of self-improvement deeply instilled in the African people of this country and elsewhere), reciting, only now it was a kind of quasi-acting we used to call Dramatic Reading. That was how I met James Weldon Johnson and Paul Lawrence Dunbar (not really knowing who I was meeting, not really hearing many things they were calling to me), and Walt Whitman and Alfred Lord Tennyson and a lot of even stranger people. Then on youth days I would periodically be the preacher, and that was enough to assure my extended family — and I think my mother too — that the call they heard was authentic, needing only the seasoning of time and the deepening of commitment, much seasoning and deepening — because I had some ways about me that they weren't quite sure were supposed to go with preaching in a Biblically-immersed community of saints.

But I hadn't stopped hearing the callings from other sources. In high school the teachers were the media, and I heard the call to high school teaching. Then one odd teacher told me I'd never pass the oral examination with such a wide space between my two front teeth. And high school teaching was put aside for a time.

Now, this thing with writing is part of the strangeness of the callings. I have not yet moved deeply enough into the chambers of the past to be certain about where and how it came. Perhaps the church community was the voice here too, encouraging my terrible poetry and acting as if my quarterly reports or my summaries and homilies on the Bible lessons were great documents (arousing, of course, certain contrary feelings among the younger members of my family-tribe at Victory Tabernacle Seventh Day Christian Church). That original voice is at least temporarily lost to me, but I know it existed, and if it was the community of believers, they likely did not know then that they had helped open me to one of the major tensions of my world of callings, a sometimes fierce stretching between writing and speaking, between writing and preaching, between scholarship and ministry in the midst of the people.

And by the time I got to college — somehow I think I always knew I had to go to college; and since there was absolutely no money for such a thing, I had to go to the only college I knew where you could at once attend without tuition and also have all the teachers and the loving tribe beam and say, "how wonderful, City College, that's a *hard* school to get into" — the loudest calling was towards writing, pressing me deeply into short story courses, journalism courses (finally majoring in History because there weren't enough writing courses), still experimenting with poetry, mostly devoted to working with the weekly campus newspaper, eventually becoming the inevitable FIRST NEGRO editor of that ancient institution of wisdom and scandal.

At City College, the calling towards writing meant another tension, pressed me towards a period of largely white friends and co-workers who vied with the ancestral community for my loyalties and my attention, led me into certain strange pathways which shut out voices I should have heard, led to great pain. But callings are strange things.

Some of the Tribe was likely worried when, after college, I went off to something else that wasn't really preaching, to graduate work in Journalism. (With all due respect to *their* worries, I was more worried about the Army then. That was a call I hoped to avoid for as long as possible.) Again the tensions of college were there, perhaps multiplied, as I was clearly being groomed for another FIRST NEGRO position. The serious and painful double voices were there, raising questions about the callings of the believers down the hill, through the park, in Harlem, and the callings which sometimes seemed so right and noble and GOOD FOR THE RACE) up at City College and over at Morningside Heights — and the worlds were deeply in tension. Callings will sometimes do that.

When I finally had to answer the call of the draft board, it was 1953. Knowing of no movement, lacking courage and desire to go the path of a C.O., which I did know a bit about — but didn't really hear that call, perhaps didn't want to — I went in. I wanted desperately to be sent to Germany or Japan or even Korea, any place outside of this country — for "education," not from alienation, yet. By then I thought I had filtered out the central call among the callings, and prepared for the next FIRST NEGRO experience, at some liberal newspaper, my preference, of course, being the New York *Times.* So, my post-Army movement seemed fairly well established as I went in, hearing all the raucous sounds of death and animality which substitute for life in the Army, but determining to be a good soldier, perhaps even an officer, getting overseas somewhere.

But in the strangeness that has surrounded so much of my life (coming, I know now, from deep sounding sources in the surrounding ancestral company of saints), I also decided, perhaps for the first time, to try to listen consciously, with anticipation, for the callings. I think I wanted to see if I would hear confirmations of the voices which had come through the believers or the teachers, seeking some release from the tension, suspecting perhaps that I might be pressed across new borders, following, listening. And in a place I never expected, under circumstances I would not have chosen, a brother spoke and asked me if I had ever thought of teaching; and for reasons far too complex and too far away to speak of now, I knew that I had heard the voice, the calling for that time.

(Strange about the Army. It never sent me anywhere, except Fort Dix, N.J. and Fort Benjamin Harrison, Indiana — partly because I knew how to type and play handball. Strange, too, that time of listening. I ended up rejecting all my inclinations towards the good soldier, became a C.O. in my heart. Strange, too: I had decided to engage in a very serious and sustained study of the Bible, partly for the listening, partly to prove to my girlfriend that she ought to be a Seventh Day Adventist like me. I did not know that in those long wrestlings with text and spirit I would be engaging in a major step on my journey beyond the borders of the loving family-tribe of believers at Victory Tabernacle [but like all tribal partings, of course, never being able to leave them].)

It was strange about the call. I still had the words of the odd high school teacher in my mind, and decided that if I were going to teach it might be better to try college, where I assumed that spaces between teeth didn't count. But I knew nothing about graduate schools, and finally, when pressed to choose among the ones where I had been accepted, opened myself with fear and trembling to the voice of the tribe/community/church, and went to Chicago — two weeks after discharge from the Army — where I could be of assistance as interim, part-time pastor of a little mission congregation that Victory Tabernacle sponsored there. That made the graduate school acceptable, worldly as they knew it was. Now, I would be anchored in an extension of the tribe; so they thought the calls and prayers had finally drawn me out of the strange and various paths I had explored.

How do you explain it? Callings are strange things. In Chicago, for the first time — after having grown up in Harlem and the Bronx — strangely it was in Chicago that I finally heard and saw the Black urban condition in

399

America. On the Southside, I heard its singing and its screams, saw its determination and its terror, sensed its freedom and its captivity. And while there was much I did not then understand about such calls, I knew this was calling me.

One day I shall try to understand and speak more fully of the painful calling which took me away from the little mission congregation — and ultimately away from my immediate (but not my ultimate) relationship to the tribe of my childhood and my youth. That calling is not fully clear to me yet, and even if it were, it is not yet time to speak of it. This much can be said: the move to an interracial congregation as a lay pastor of a team ministry seemed to allow me to hold the tension of Blackness and whiteness (it was, of course, a time when such things seemed most urgent), the tension of teaching and preaching, of study and ministry. But those are only superficial statements, and should be received as such for now.

Nor is it yet time to speak fully of the ultimately transforming call that led to marriage, a call far different than any I had known, a call I was in too many ways unprepared to understand in all the richness of its meanings and its summons. But I know it is a calling, mine.

Then, before graduate work had ended, the call of the Southern Freedom Movement became overwhelming, pressing aside almost every other voice. There was no escaping it. It possessed me during my first, exploring journey into the South (grasped me there sitting on Martin King's bed in Montgomery where he rested recovering from his stabbing). It came to Chicago in the body of the students and found me. While sit-ins and freedom-rides were still sweeping across the South, we left Chicago and went South, hearing, following a call.

We shall understand it better by and by, and also speak more clearly of it, that calling. Now let it suffice to say that it was then that all the fiercely gripping, special callings of the South began, calls of the Movement, of Southwest Georgia (home of my wife's parents, repository of so many memories of hope and fear), of all the stretching land upon which my people walked, and worked, and ran, and stood, and died. Then it began, all the callings of Birmingham and Tuskegee, of Montgomery and Mobile, of Jackson and Meridian, of Gulfport and Greenwood, of New Orleans and Charleston, of Hickory and Atlanta, of Ella Baker and Amzie Moore, of Ralph Abernathy and Bill Shields, of Bob Moses Parris and Annelle Ponder, of Jim and Diane, of Septima Clark and Slater King, of Clarence Jordan and Staughton Lynd — this was the beginning of new callings.

And when, after four years that encompassed a generation of struggle, when the Movement had passed its height, it was possible to hear strange callings through personal tragedy, and there were endings and beginnings again. Then finally the finishing of graduate work and the beginning of teaching — still with a space between the front two teeth.

There the latest callings began. From somewhere — had Buddha visited? — there was an urgent aching to understand the meaning of Vietnam, and on the 20th anniversary of Hiroshima, that need plunged me past the superficial surfaces of my knowing, brought me in touch with the meaning of that brutal tale, that heroic defense of life, and provided new impetus for my continuing movement away from this America, towards a radically transformed society.

Teaching, spaces and all. There the latest callings began. Teaching history I was called to understand how little I knew of history. Teaching Black students, I learned how little this Black student, this FIRST NEGRO, had been taught, especially about the truth of his own long pilgrimage, about his people's struggles against the powers of death, about their determined movement towards new life. And when I knew that, I began — as in the Army, only a different army now — to listen again, hearing some things that I had let slip by in the days of the Tribe, understanding things I had only seen in the Movement. I began to hear voices more loudly than ever before, and they will not be silent, for they are me.

I hear all the varied sounds of my homeland, all its human sounds, all its animals, its spirit-filled rivers and lakes, its waterfalls, its mountains, its grass and trees playing with the wind. I hear them all.

I hear all the screaming of my homeland, all the mournful pacing down to the slave baracoons, all the piercing, dying shouts, all the parting wailing sounds. I hear children, crying children, I hear men, I hear women, calling, now desiring only to be remembered, and vindicated. I hear them between the decks of the ships called *Jesus* and *St. John*, and *Liberty*, and *Justice*. I hear their whispers and then their bursting yells as they come on decks prepared to die, and, if necessary, to kill for their freedom. I hear them calling, falling on the decks, thrown, often leaping to their ending — but not ending — in the waters. I hear them singing as they go under the waves — free.

I hear my people. I hear them calling from Virginia to San Francisco, I hear their songs and their cries and their defiant shouts and their long silences through all the horrors called slavery. I hear them lost in the wilderness, I hear them moving, seeking the North Star, determined to make their way to freedom.

I hear them in preaching and praying, holding one another through hunger and parting, through torture and sickness, through childbirth and dying, I hear them calling.

I hear my people, lurching, flooding towards freedom during the Civil War, seizing their own liberty. I hear them fighting and falling, rising and hoping again. I hear them in all the halcyon hopeful first days of Reconstruction, in all the bloody years that followed, when hope was crushed by the force of white arms and the power of white betrayals.

I hear them, mourning, weeping, wailing, prostrate around the thousands of trees where brothers and sisters were hung and burned and mutilated beyond recognition by a savage people. I hear them vowing never to give in, never to turn back, to endure, to resist, to live, to go on. I hear their calling.

I hear them coming North, I hear them in the armies, I hear them in the mills, I hear them in the railroads, I hear them in the fires, I hear them in the waters, I hear Nat Turner and David Walker, I hear Douglass and Delaney, I hear Harriet and Sojourner, I hear Ida B. Wells and Bishop Turner, I hear Garvey and DuBois, I hear Bessie Smith. I hear them calling.

I hear them in depression, picking their way through garbage piles, sharing even that with one another. I hear them calling for Robeson, for Father, for Daddy, for Adam, for Solidarity, for help.

I hear them in war, dying for a land that will not protect them. I hear them coming beyond war to struggle for truth. I hear them in court. I hear them in the streets. I hear ladies walking in Montgomery. I hear Martin preaching in the churches, hear his footsteps on the road. I hear old folks singing in churches, standing before dogs. I hear students risking their lives, freezing in jail, singing while hungry, laughing when afraid, not being overcome. I hear them calling.

I hear my people marching, refusing to stop, refusing to be quiet, refusing to be satisfied, refusing to die.

I hear Malcolm, I hear Stokely, I hear Rap and Feather, I hear Ruby and Jim. I hear Jonathan. I hear Angela. I hear Attica. I hear dying Panthers and preachers. I hear living men and women. I hear them. I hear voices, and I know what it means.

Callings are a strange thing. I know what it means: I am a witness, in spite of myself, beyond myself, and their voices must be heard.

I am a witness (teacher, preacher, ranter, raver, dissident, resistant, radical, revolutionary, silent carrier), witness to their truth and power, pressed forward by the force of their being, by the integrity of their struggle, by the silent roaring of their voices. No turning back.

I know what it means: I am historian — now recognizing all the long ago callings — summoned to tell their story, for them, for myself, for our children. They shall not be forgotten.

It means I am now of them, deep calling unto deep. Their voice has entered so profoundly into me that I am flesh of their flesh, bone of their bone, song of their song, pain of their pain, hope of their hope. Forever lost to scholarly "objectivity," forever seared by the passion of their fiery movement, unwilling and unable to be detached from their struggle. Bound by cords of life and death and love — and intimations of the morning. Privileged, permitted, summoned to join them, their struggle is mine, and I am called forward into tomorrow, searching for the way to carry the struggle, to break the bonds, to build the new land of their hopes.

(Callings are strange things. They find you in the midst of your own family.)

I hear my mother, sighing, scrubbing all the floors in all the white homes, bearing with love and pain and anxious prayer the burden that I was/am. (I would like to hear my father, and one day I suspect I shall.) I know it means I am still son, hope, strength, promise for tomorrow, beyond all the pain and death.

I hear voices — of my children, Rachel Sojourner and Jonathan DuBois. I believe that ancient rivers of our people flow in them. I hear their voices, and I know what it means. It means I am called to be father, rock and strength, encourager for the struggles of tomorrow, baptizer in the rivers of their past.

I hear a voice, of my wife, Rosemarie. I know what it means. I am to be husband and man, strength and solace, lover and companion in the way, resting place and summons to joy in the morning.

Callings are strange things. I think I have heard many voices in many times and places, but it may be that I have heard only One.

WILLA CATHER

"The Ancient People"

The novel from which this selection comes tells the story of Thea Kronborg, a woman born in a small town in the desert West who eventually goes on to a luminous international career as an opera singer. As this section of the novel begins, Thea is at a low point, having failed to attain the success of which she had dreamed. At a friend's suggestion, she goes on what we might today call a retreat, placing herself in a situation that allows her to view herself, the world, and her future in a different way. What are the sources of the renewed strength and confidence that Thea gradually attains? What does the place to which she has come for respite enable her to recover in herself and to understand about her own art?

These four chapters of *The Song of the Lark*, by the American novelist Willa Cather (1873-1947), belong to a section of the novel entitled "The Ancient People."

I

The San Francisco Mountain lies in Northern Arizona, above Flagstaff, and its blue slopes and snowy summit entice the eye for a hundred miles across the desert. About its base lie the pine forests of the Navajos, where the great red-trunked trees live out their peaceful centuries in that sparkling air. The *piñons* and scrub begin only where the forest ends, where the country breaks into open, stony clearings and the surface of the earth cracks into deep canyons. The great pines stand at a considerable distance from each other. Each tree grows alone, murmurs alone, thinks alone. They do not intrude upon each other. The Navajos are not much in the habit of giving or of asking help. Their language is not a communicative one, and they never attempt an

From Willa Cather, *The Song of the Lark* (Boston: Houghton Mifflin Co., 1915), pp. 295-308.

404

interchange of personality in speech. Over their forests there is the same inexorable reserve. Each tree has its exalted power to bear.

That was the first thing Thea Kronborg felt about the forest, as she drove through it one May morning in Henry Biltmer's democrat wagon — and it was the first great forest she had ever seen. She had got off the train at Flagstaff that morning, rolled off into the high, chill air when all the pines on the mountain were fired by sunrise, so that she seemed to fall from sleep directly into the forest.

Old Biltmer followed a faint wagon trail which ran southeast, and which, as they traveled, continually dipped lower, falling away from the high plateau on the slope of which Flagstaff sits. The white peak of the mountain, the snow gorges above the timber, now disappeared from time to time as the road dropped and dropped, and the forest closed behind the wagon. More than the mountain disappeared as the forest closed thus. Thea seemed to be taking very little through the wood with her. The personality of which she was so tired seemed to let go of her. The high, sparkling air drank it up like blotting-paper. It was lost in the thrilling blue of the new sky and the song of the thin wind in the *piñons*. The old, fretted lines which marked one off, which defined her, — made her Thea Kronborg, Bowers's accompanist, a soprano with a faulty middle voice, — were all erased.

So far she had failed. Her two years in Chicago had not resulted in anything. She had failed with Harsanyi, and she had made no great progress with her voice. She had come to believe that whatever Bowers had taught her was of secondary importance, and that in the essential things she had made no advance. Her student life closed behind her, like the forest, and she doubted whether she could go back to it if she tried. Probably she would teach music in little country towns all her life. Failure was not so tragic as she would have supposed; she was tired enough not to care.

She was getting back to the earliest sources of gladness that she could remember. She had loved the sun, and the brilliant solitudes of sand and sun, long before these other things had come along to fasten themselves upon her and torment her. That night, when she clambered into her big German feather bed, she felt completely released from the enslaving desire to get on in the world. Darkness had once again the sweet wonder that it had in childhood.

II

Thea's life at the Ottenburg ranch was simple and full of light, like the days themselves. She awoke every morning when the first fierce shafts of sunlight darted through the curtainless windows of her room at the ranch house. After breakfast she took her lunch-basket and went down to the canyon. Usually she did not return until sunset.

Panther Canyon was like a thousand others — one of those abrupt fissures with which the earth in the Southwest is riddled; so abrupt that you might walk over the edge of any one of them on a dark night and never know what had happened to you. This canyon headed on the Ottenburg ranch, about a mile from the ranch house, and it was accessible only at its head. The canyon walls, for the first two hundred feet below the surface, were perpendicular cliffs, striped with even-running strata of rock. From there on to the bottom the sides were less abrupt, were shelving, and lightly fringed with *piñons* and dwarf cedars. The effect was that of a gentler canyon within a wilder one. The dead city lay at the point where the perpendicular outer wall ceased and the V-shaped inner gorge began. There a stratum of rock, softer than those above, had been hollowed out by the action of time until it was like a deep groove running along the sides of the canyon. In this hollow (like a great fold in the rock) the Ancient People had built their houses of yellowish stone and mortar. The over-hanging cliff above made a roof two hundred feet thick. The hard stratum below was an everlasting floor. The houses stood along in a row, like the buildings in a city block, or like a barracks.

In both walls of the canyon the same streak of soft rock had been washed out, and the long horizontal groove had been built up with houses. The dead city had thus two streets, one set in either cliff, facing each other across the ravine, with a river of blue air between them.

The canyon twisted and wound like a snake, and these two streets went on for four miles or more, interrupted by the abrupt turnings of the gorge, but beginning again within each turn. The canyon had a dozen of these false endings near its head. Beyond, the windings were larger and less perceptible, and it went on for a hundred miles, too narrow, precipitous, and terrible for man to follow it. The Cliff Dwellers liked wide canyons, where the great cliffs caught the sun. Panther Canyon had been deserted for hundreds of years when the first Spanish missionaries came into Arizona, but the masonry of the houses was still wonderfully firm; had crumbled only where a landslide or a rolling boulder had torn it.

All the houses in the canyon were clean with the cleanness of sun-baked, wind-swept places, and they all smelled of the tough little cedars that twisted themselves into the very doorways. One of these rock-rooms Thea took for her own. Fred had told her how to make it comfortable. The day after she came old Henry brought over on one of the pack-ponies a roll of Navajo blankets that belonged to Fred, and Thea lined her cave with them. The room was not more than eight by ten feet, and she could touch the stone roof with her finger-tips. This was her old idea: a nest in a high cliff, full of sun. All morning long the sun beat upon her cliff, while the ruins on the opposite side of the canyon were in shadow. In the afternoon, when she had the shade of two hundred feet of rock wall, the ruins on the other side of the gulf stood out in the blazing sunlight. Before her door ran the narrow, winding path that had been the street of the Ancient People. The yucca and niggerhead cactus grew everywhere. From her doorstep she looked out on the ocher-colored slope that ran down several hundred feet to the stream, and this hot rock was sparsely grown with dwarf trees. Their colors were so pale that the shadows of the little trees on the rock stood out sharper than the trees themselves. When Thea first came, the chokecherry bushes were in blossom, and the scent of them was almost sickeningly sweet after a shower. At the very bottom of the canyon, along the stream, there was a thread of bright, flickering, golden-green, — cottonwood seedlings. They made a living, chattering screen behind which she took her bath every morning.

Thea went down to the stream by the Indian water trail. She had found a bathing-pool with a sand bottom, where the creek was dammed by fallen trees. The climb back was long and steep, and when she reached her little house in the cliff she always felt fresh delight in its comfort and inaccessibility. By the time she got there, the woolly red-and-gray blankets were saturated with sunlight, and she sometimes fell asleep as soon as she stretched her body on their warm surfaces. She used to wonder at her own inactivity. She could lie there hour after hour in the sun and listen to the strident whir of the big locusts, and to the light, ironical laughter of the quaking asps. All her life she had been hurrying and sputtering, as if she had been born behind time and had been trying to catch up. Now, she reflected, as she drew herself out long upon the rugs, it was as if she were waiting for something to catch up with her. She had got to a place where she was out of the stream of meaningless activity and undirected effort.

Here she could lie for half a day undistracted, holding pleasant and incomplete conceptions in her mind — almost in her hands. They were scarcely clear enough to be called ideas. They had something to do with fragrance and color and sound, but almost nothing to do with words. She was singing very little now, but a song would go through her head all morning, as a spring keeps welling up, and it was like a pleasant sensation indefinitely prolonged. It was much more like a sensation than like an idea, or an act of remembering. Music had never come to her in that sensuous form before. It had always been a thing to be struggled with, had always brought anxiety and exaltation and chagrin — never content and indolence. Thea began to wonder whether people could not utterly lose the power to work, as they can lose their voice or their memory. She had always been a little drudge, hurrying from one task to another — as if it mattered! And now her power to think seemed converted into a power of sustained sensation. She could become a mere receptacle for heat, or become a color, like the bright lizards that darted about on the hot stones outside her door; or she could become a continuous repetition of sound, like the cicadas.

III

The faculty of observation was never highly developed in Thea Kronborg. A great deal escaped her eye as she passed through the world. But the things which were for her, she saw; she experienced them physically and remembered them as if they had once been a part of herself. The roses she used to see in the florists' shops in Chicago were merely roses. But when she thought of the moonflowers that grew over Mrs. Tellamantez's door, it was as if she had been that vine and had opened up in white flowers every night. There were memories of light on the sand hills, of masses of prickly-pear blossoms she had found in the desert in early childhood, of the late afternoon sun pouring through the grape leaves and the mint bed in Mrs. Kohler's garden, which she would never lose. These recollections were a part of her mind and personality. In Chicago she had got almost nothing that went into her subconscious self and took root there. But here, in Panther Canyon, there were again things which seemed destined for her.

Panther Canyon was the home of innumerable swallows. They built nests in the wall far above the hollow groove in which Thea's own rock chamber lay. They seldom ventured above the rim of the canyon, to the flat, wind-swept tableland. Their world was the blue air-river between the canyon walls. In that blue gulf the arrow-shaped birds swam all day long, with only an occasional movement of the wings. The only sad thing about them was their timidity; the way in which they lived their lives between the echoing cliffs and never dared to rise out of the shadow of the canyon walls. As they swam past her door, Thea often felt how easy it would be to dream one's life out in some cleft in the world.

From the ancient dwelling there came always a dignified, unobtrusive sadness; now stronger, now fainter, — like the aromatic smell which the dwarf cedars gave out in the sun, — but always present, a part of the air one breathed. At night, when Thea dreamed about the canyon, — or in the early morning when she hurried toward it, anticipating it, — her conception of it was of yellow rocks baking in sunlight, the swallows, the cedar smell, and that peculiar sadness — a voice out of the past, not very loud, that went on saying a few simple things to the solitude eternally.

Standing up in her lodge, Thea could with her thumb nail dislodge flakes of carbon from the rock roof — the cooking-smoke of the Ancient People. They were that near! A timid, nest-building folk, like the swallows. How often Thea remembered Ray Kennedy's moralizing about the cliff cities. He used to say that he never felt the hardness of the human struggle or the sadness of history as he felt it among those ruins. He used to say, too, that it made one feel an obligation to do one's best. On the first day that Thea climbed the water trail she began to have intuitions about the women who had worn the path, and who had spent so great a part of their lives going up and down it. She found herself trying to walk as they must have walked, with a feeling in her feet and knees and loins which she had never known before, — which must have come up to her out of the accustomed dust of that rocky trail. She could feel the weight of an Indian baby hanging to her back as she climbed.

The empty houses, among which she wandered in the afternoon, the blanketed one in which she lay all morning, were haunted by certain fears and desires; feelings about warmth and cold and water and physical strength. It seemed to Thea that a certain understanding of those old people came up to her out of the rock shelf on which she lay; that certain feelings were transmitted to her, suggestions that were simple, insistent, and monotonous, like the beating of Indian drums. They were not expressible in words, but seemed rather to translate themselves into attitudes of body, into degrees of muscular tension or relaxation; the naked strength of youth, sharp as the sun-shafts; the crouching timorousness of age, the sullenness of women who waited for their captors. At the first turning of the canyon there was a half-ruined tower of yellow masonry, a watch-tower upon which the young men used to entice eagles and snare them with nets. Sometimes for a whole morning Thea could see the coppery breast and shoulders of an Indian youth there against the sky; see him throw the net, and watch the struggle with the eagle.

Old Henry Biltmer, at the ranch, had been a great deal among the Pueblo Indians who are the descendants of the Cliff-Dwellers. After supper he used to sit and smoke his pipe by the kitchen stove and talk to Thea about them. He had never found any one before who was interested in his ruins. Every Sunday the old man prowled about in the canyon, and he had come to know a good deal more about it than he could account for. He had gathered up a whole chestful of Cliff-Dweller relics which he meant to take back to

Germany with him some day. He taught Thea how to find things among the ruins: grinding-stones, and drills and needles made of turkey-bones. There were fragments of pottery everywhere. Old Henry explained to her that the Ancient People had developed masonry and pottery far beyond any other crafts. After they had made houses for themselves, the next thing was to house the precious water. He explained to her how all their customs and ceremonies and their religion went back to water. The men provided the food, but water was the care of the women. The stupid women carried water for most of their lives; the cleverer ones made the vessels to hold it. Their pottery was their most direct appeal to water, the envelope and sheath of the precious element itself. The strongest Indian need was expressed in those graceful jars, fashioned slowly by hand, without the aid of a wheel.

When Thea took her bath at the bottom of the canyon, in the sunny pool behind the screen of cottonwoods, she sometimes felt as if the water must have sovereign qualities, from having been the object of so much service and desire. That stream was the only living thing left of the drama that had been played out in the canyon centuries ago. In the rapid, restless heart of it, flowing swifter than the rest, there was a continuity of life that reached back into the old time. The glittering thread of current had a kind of lightly worn, loosely knit personality, graceful and laughing. Thea's bath came to have a ceremonial gravity. The atmosphere of the canyon was ritualistic.

One morning, as she was standing upright in the pool, splashing water between her shoulder-blades with a big sponge, something flashed through her mind that made her draw herself up and stand still until the water had quite dried upon her flushed skin. The stream and the broken pottery: what was any art but an effort to make a sheath, a mould in which to imprison for a moment the shining, elusive element which is life itself, — life hurrying past us and running away, too strong to stop, too sweet to lose? The Indian women had held it in their jars. In the sculpture she had seen in the Art Institute, it had been caught in a flash of arrested motion. In singing, one made a vessel of one's throat and nostrils and held it on one's breath, caught the stream in a scale of natural intervals.

IV

Thea had a superstitious feeling about the potsherds, and liked better to leave them in the dwellings where she found them. If she took a few bits back to her own lodge and hid them under the blankets, she did it guiltily, as if she were being watched. She was a guest in these houses, and ought to behave as such. Nearly every afternoon she went to the chambers which contained the most interesting fragments of pottery, sat and looked at them for a while. Some of them were beautifully decorated. This care, expended upon vessels that could not hold food or water any better for the additional labor put upon them, made her heart go out to those ancient potters. They had not only expressed their desire, but they had expressed it as beautifully as they could. Food, fire, water, and something else — even here, in this crack in the world, so far back in the night of the past! Down here at the beginning that painful thing was already stirring; the seed of sorrow, and of so much delight.

There were jars done in a delicate overlay, like pine cones; and there were many patterns in a low relief, like basket-work. Some of the pottery was decorated in color, red and brown, black and white, in graceful geometrical patterns. One day, on a fragment of a shallow bowl, she found a crested serpent's head, painted in red on terra-cotta. Again she found half a bowl with a broad band of white cliff-houses painted on a black ground. They were scarcely conventionalized at all; there they were in the black border, just as they stood in the rock before her. It brought her centuries nearer to these people to find that they saw their houses exactly as she saw them.

Yes, Ray Kennedy was right. All these things made one feel that one ought to do one's best, and help to fulfill some desire of the dust that slept there. A dream had been dreamed there long ago, in the night of ages, and the wind had whispered some promise to the sadness of the savage. In their own way, those people had felt the beginnings of what was to come. These potsherds were like fetters that bound one to a long chain of human endeavor.

Not only did the world seem older and richer to Thea now, but she herself seemed older. She had never been alone for so long before, or thought so much. Nothing had ever engrossed her so deeply as the daily contemplation of that line of pale-yellow houses tucked into the wrinkle of the cliff. Moonstone and Chicago had become vague. Here everything was simple and definite, as things had been in childhood. Her mind was like a ragbag into which she had been frantically thrusting whatever she could grab. And here she must throw this lumber away. The things that were really hers separated themselves from the rest. Her ideas were simplified, became sharper and clearer. She felt united and strong.

When Thea had been at the Ottenburg ranch for two months, she got a letter from Fred announcing that he "might be along at almost any time now." The letter came at night, and the next morning she took it down into the canyon with her. She was delighted that he was coming soon. She had never felt so grateful to any one, and she wanted to tell him everything that had

411

happened to her since she had been there — more than had happened in all her life before. Certainly she liked Fred better than any one else in the world. There was Harsanyi, of course — but Harsanyi was always tired. Just now, and here, she wanted some one who had never been tired, who could catch an idea and run with it.

She was ashamed to think what an apprehensive drudge she must always have seemed to Fred, and she wondered why he had concerned himself about her at all. Perhaps she would never be so happy or so good-looking again, and she would like Fred to see her, for once, at her best. She had not been singing much, but she knew that her voice was more interesting than it had ever been before.

She had begun to understand that — with her, at least — voice was, first of all, vitality; a lightness in the body and a driving power in the blood. If she had that, she could sing. When she felt so keenly alive, lying on that insensible shelf of stone, when her body bounded like a rubber ball away from its hardness, then she could sing. This, too, she could explain to Fred. He would know what she meant.

Another week passed. Thea did the same things as before, felt the same influences, went over the same ideas; but there was a livelier movement in her thoughts, and a freshening of sensation, like the brightness which came over the underbrush after a shower. A persistent affirmation — or denial — was going on in her, like the tapping of the woodpecker in the one tall pine tree across the chasm. Musical phrases drove each other rapidly through her mind, and the song of the cicada was now too long and too sharp. Everything seemed suddenly to take the form of a desire for action.

It was while she was in this abstracted state, waiting for the clock to strike, that Thea at last made up her mind what she was going to try to do in the world, and that she was going to Germany to study without further loss of time. Only by the merest chance had she ever got to Panther Canyon. There was certainly no kindly Providence that directed one's life; and one's parents did not in the least care what became of one, so long as one did not misbehave and endanger their comfort. One's life was at the mercy of blind chance. She had better take it in her own hands and lose everything than meekly draw the plough under the rod of parental guidance. She had seen it when she was at home last summer, — the hostility of comfortable, self-satisfied people toward any serious effort. Even to her father it seemed indecorous. Whenever she spoke seriously, he looked apologetic. Yet she had clung fast to whatever was left of Moonstone in her mind. No more of that! The Cliff-Dwellers had lengthened her past. She had older and higher obligations.

GARRET KEIZER

A Dresser of Sycamore Trees

Like the preceding selection, this reading tells the story of a person who is unsure of what to do in life and who therefore undertakes a period of retreat and reflection. In this case, a young man seeks an answer from God during several days of prayer, conversation, and reflection in a Christian monastery. Does he find there what he had expected? Why is Psalm 118:5 an appropriate epigraph for this essay?

For nearly two decades, Garret Keizer served as the part-time priest of a small Episcopal parish in northern Vermont, while also teaching English at a nearby high school, an experience he has described in a wonderful book, *No Place but Here: A Teacher's Vocation in a Rural Community*. He still lives in that area but is now a full-time writer. As the passage shows, all three occupations — ministry, teaching, writing — were already in his mind when he made the retreat described here.

I called to the Lord in my distress;
the Lord answered by setting me free.

Psalm 118:5

If I tend to my driving, and put off getting milk and gas until tomorrow, I can be home before my wife goes to bed. She will ask me how it went, and I will tell her I am happy with the visit. I took Communion to one person, had supper with another, met someone on the street who is "thinking about coming to church," and wound up the steeple clock enough to last until Sunday. Actually, I am intoxicated with the visit. The image of an old woman taking the wafer reverently in arthritic hands overwhelms me as I

From Garret Keizer, *A Dresser of Sycamore Trees: The Finding of a Ministry* (Boston: David R. Godine, 1991), pp. 1-16.

round a mountain and the full moon appears blessing the branches of a great dead elm. The ionosphere has come down in the night, like St. Peter's visionary sheetful of clean and unclean animals, and my car radio is a feast of stations. A little more volume, a little more speed — I give thanks for my family, my church, the Supremes. Next week, without fail, I will stop at the farm which it is too late to visit now, but passing by I pray for the family who live there. I pray for their cows and the land. And I tell myself by way of exultation what I now tell my reader by way of warning: it won't get much better than this.

The story of how I came to be the lay minister of a small Episcopal parish in an old railroad junction town in the northeast corner of Vermont could begin in a number of places. It could begin in a city where I used to work, at a lunch-hour church service, after which a young priest approached me and asked, "Who are you, and how do you come to be here?" Or it could begin at the small Church of St. John in the Wilderness, built over a century ago by a wealthy woman in memory of her husband, who had died on their honeymoon. In spite of that ominous precedent, my wife and I were married there, because her Catholic parents and my Protestant ones could each claim their share of the Episcopal tradition, and because, quite frankly, we liked the way the building looked.

If I wanted more drama, more sense of destiny, I suppose I could begin with a great-grandfather, a Dutch Reformed minister, who according to the legend in my family had lost his wife and children no one remembered how — and had cursed God, and left the ministry, and then returned later in life to serve until he died. More simply and to the point, I could begin with my baptism, the ordination rite of all Christian lay ministers.

But instead, I start out at an Anglican monastery, on the bank of a great American river, where I went eleven years ago, at the age of twenty-six, because I wasn't yet sure what I wanted to be when I grew up.

I was two months away from moving to Vermont's Northeast Kingdom and embarking on my first and present job as a high school English teacher. Signing the contract was probably what forced the issue. I was sure I didn't want to do *that* for very long. Believing that serious problems call for drastic remedies, I did the most sensibly drastic thing I could think of: I ran off to pray and fast in a monastery, just about vowing in imitation of the Buddha not to rise from my meditations until I was enlightened, but also asking that, if possible, enlightenment not take longer than several days. I was driving a rented car.

I had been thinking of returning to graduate school for a Ph.D. I had already taken my master's in English, writing my thesis on the poetry of George Herbert, the unofficial patron saint of Episcopal poets, priests, and graduate students. I would eventually make the pilgrimage to his church in Bemerton, England, and was just then beginning to correspond with his venerable biographer, Amy Charles, who had already cast her ballot in favor of my choosing an academic path.

But I was also thinking of the law. Law school occurs to most English majors as inevitably as suicide occurs to all of us. With most it's just a passing thought; a few try, and botch it up (one suspects that some of these are really crying out for help), and a few others actually carry it off. With a law degree, I reasoned, I could shore up the proletariat, defend the oppressed, put the fear of God into racists, expropriators, and polluters. And if I tired of all that, I could make enough money to *own* the car I was renting and to buy a new one like it every year.

Yes, I also wanted "to be a writer." I had wanted "to be a writer" since adolescence. I was just far enough beyond adolescence to begin asking exactly what I meant by the phrase. And of course I was thinking, like Mr. Herbert and my great-grandfather before me, of becoming an ordained minister. That was on my mind most of all. That was why I was going to a monastery to ask my question.

In my dilemma over vocations I was like so many others of my generation, with greater choices and higher expectations for a life's work, and therefore with greater anxiety about it, too. It's hard to imagine another society on earth for which this issue was or is so consuming. Was this the angst of my parents and their friends as they sat talking and listening to the radio before, during, or after the war? To have a job, yes, to have one that paid well, that had "some kind of future," that enabled you to "be your own boss" — all practical or even idealistic matters, but not quite *religious* ones. And for many of their children, I think, the issue is virtually religious. I think you can hear echoes of the question "What must I do to be saved?" whenever you listen to people of my approximate age talk about work. So I think there may be subtler explanations for my going to the monastery besides the facts of my religious affiliation and the ecclesiastical nature of one of my "career" choices.

Interestingly enough, very religious people do not always see the vocational quest as a monumentally sacred one — in spite of or perhaps because of the claim that all honest work can be holy. In a book about Lubavitcher Hasidim entitled *Holy Days*, Liz Harris tells how a convert named Moshe found his life's work. An obviously learned man, he thought of becoming a teacher. He sought the advice of his rebbe. Why not become a metal engraver? the rebbe suggested. No explanation on his part, no qualms on

Moshe's. Apparently, the Hasidim feel that individuals are no more capable of finding happiness through their own vocational choices than they are at finding wedded bliss through courtship. So such things are largely arranged for them. I don't say now, nor did I say then, that vocations ought to be arranged. And yet I suppose my only real difference from Moshe was that I sought an unquestionably divine arrangement. I wanted God, no one less, to make the decision for me. Believing that vocations were made in heaven, I wanted the matchmaker to speak from that height. I came to the monastery hoping things might be quiet enough for me to hear my answer.

It was indeed a tranquil place. Its brick cloisters, guest house, chapel, and library sat on a gently sloping hill overlooking the river. One could easily walk to the shore through a small wood at the foot of the hill. Well-kept lawns and gardens made up the grounds. The monks were wise enough to know that visitors to such places have traditionally expected to revel in a little bogus asceticism, and so the rooms in the guest house were appropriately Spartan, though the refectory and reading rooms were as comfortable as those of any country inn.

The center of life there was, of course, the chapel, to which the monastic community came for matins at six, Eucharist at nine, diurnum at noon, vespers at five, and compline at seven. It was arranged in the monastic style, with opposing rows of choir stalls for the monks running from the altar to the rear of the church, where pews accommodated guests who wanted to attend services. The bells at the altar, the red votive light, and the life-size, dusky wooden crucifix hanging on the stucco wall all exhaled "Cath-lick" in an incense-reeking breath that could make a man raised on Calvinism just about swoon. The sultry July weather added a disturbingly Mediterranean ambience to the whole effect. Like every other attempt to join eternity and time, this place was an enclosed garden, a fragment of Eden full of possibilities in which one vaguely heard a serpentine hissing. The impulse to fall to one's knees coexisted in a visitor like me with the impulse to head for the parking lot screaming.

Instead, I set about following the routine of the house, with details of my own regimen thrown in. I goofed almost from the start. Between wake-up and matins, the house was supposed to be in silence. I had no complaints about that. In fact there's a great liberty, especially in a dormitory-style bathroom like the one in the guest house, to be able to shave, shower, and pee without the need for any small talk — monastic small talk at that. But no sooner had I lathered my face when in walked a half-dressed middle-aged man with one of the worst cases of cerebral palsy I'd ever seen and something to tell me about his cigarette lighter.

After some difficulty, I understood that he wanted me to put in a new flint. I set to work, but, not being a smoker myself, I needed some instruction about the lighter. At this point the guestmaster stuck his head in the doorway and curtly reminded us that "the house is supposed to be in silence!" The other man grinned at me with an expression that seemed to say "We've been very naughty — and we'll probably be very naughty again" and headed back to his room with agonizing difficulty. I've been here for just a little while, I thought, and already I've violated the rule. I had been there just a little while, I see now, and how swiftly God had sent me an angel.

"We can talk now," he said to me when I met him after the service. He was a little easier to understand now that he wasn't trying to hide his voice from the guestmaster, though he continued to drool steadily. He was here after a brief stint in an Episcopal seminary. He had been visiting the monastery "since before you were born." His name was Jeffrey.

He asked a series of questions about my employment and education which inevitably revealed my reasons for being there. He even managed, without any hints from me as I recall, to guess some of the options I was considering. Of course, none of this was as strange as I probably took it to be. It would not surprise me to learn that I was one of dozens of young men who visited the monastery that summer, and other summers, with roughly the same questions on their minds. If Jeffrey had indeed been coming there for more than forty years, he could probably spot one of us a mile away — the sneakers, the notepad, the "man of the desert" beard, the constipated expression at prayer. Still, what is not unusual may nevertheless be uncanny. And there was something uncanny in the way he put his finger on so many of my concerns. It was like sitting down with a police artist who began sketching a true-to-life portrait of my assailant — without much help from me.

Nothing struck me so much as the fact that he was "back" from a place I might be heading to. "Seminary," he said, was not his "cup of tea." It was "overrated." Theology was "sanctified bullshit." It did not take an especially perceptive mind to realize that something very painful had happened to him there, something that nevertheless did not rule out his returning to the monastery or asserting, "I would die for this place. . . . I would die for the Episcopal Church."

Near the end of the conversation, after he had been naming great writers with not-so-great educations, he asked me, "Who was the greatest failure that ever lived?"

"Jesus Christ," I answered.

"That's right," he said. "Yet he conquered the world."

Then he offered me a cigarette and, when I declined, asked me to light his. He said he was glad he'd met me.

No conversation could last too long if one expected to attend all the prayer services of the community — and especially if one also had things to write, read, see, and prayers to say on his own. I saw even then a real benefit in that forced halting of the day, throughout the day, to "do the work" which was the monks' main job. How many times are we in the secular world saved from some destructively stupid decision or impulse simply by having to break for lunch? "Saved by the bell," we say. Yet what a long and murderous fight it is when the bell rings but once or twice a working day, and that to eat, or drink coffee. What would it be like if we were all on monastery time? The disadvantages of such a stop-and-go schedule would have to be placed alongside gains such as a more humane pace, a more thoughtful production, a less ill-tempered work force, a less immodest consumption of the world's resources.

Services — and meals, too — provided one with occasions to see the community. Other times, many of the monks were in the cloistered areas. There was quite an array of men, from a princely African novice who served at the altar, to an ancient white-haired monk who filled the church with his consumption-like coughing. The abbot was a stern and virile-looking man; in the secular world he might have been a narcotics cop or a claims adjuster. He ran a tight ship, too; I heard some murmured complaints about his having changed the time of matins to an hour earlier, and once, after what was a less than flawless performance of the liturgy, he demanded "to see all of the brothers immediately after the service." Across from him sat a monk, one of the "culprits" in the incident above, with the unflappably beatific countenance one would expect to find in a monastery — or at some kind of group encounter weekend. There was also a slight, nervous man whom I liked almost on sight, an Alice-in-Wonderland sort of character who perpetually appeared to have lost something very important, unable to recall where he'd left it. Does it explain anything to add that he was the monastery librarian? Of every man there I wanted to ask the question put to me by that young priest when I'd shown up like a stray cat at an Episcopal cathedral: "Who are you, and how did you come to be here?"

However a monk had come to be there, his coming had meant a giving up of something — and that made all of the brothers fascinating and in some ways awesome. All of them had refused to believe that "you can have it all." In other words, all of them were challenging what has become the virtual battle cry of "yuppie" culture in the decade since I made my retreat.

418

That battle cry is also the complete antithesis of any notion of social or ecological responsibility, even though people who claim "you can have it all" often affect to care about such things — why not, when you can "have it all"? Quietly the monks were saying, and have been saying for twenty centuries, "That won't work." If other persons, peoples, species, and generations are to have justice, no one can "have it all." There are choices to make and prices to pay for those choices.

If that had been their only message, their only reason for being, they would have been of supreme value to a young man who was wondering if he might not skirt the vocational question altogether by doing every worthy thing that occurred to him. Eleven years later, and quite settled into "my work," I still need a reminder of those monks and their sacrifices every single day. I am still tempted to believe that with good "time management" I can have all the pearls, including the Pearl of Great Price.

With so many men dedicated to prayer, it was natural that I ask one of them to pray for me in my dilemma. I chose Brother Philip, the old cougher, in part because his age might have meant a greater experience with prayer, and in part because I guessed his duties at the monastery were now quite limited, and so I might in a way be helping him by asking for his help. He accepted. "How old are you?" he asked. When he heard my age he said, somewhat wearily, "You still have plenty of time," and that was the end of our discussion. I did not tell him that I had stopped feeling as though I had plenty of time on my twenty-fifth birthday, and especially after taking that teaching job.

The next day, after Sunday Communion, Brother Philip rushed past me toward the refectory with a purposeful energy that, in him, seemed nearly supernatural. For an instant I think I may have wondered if he had some prophetic thing to shout into the abbot's face. He burst past several other monks and guests before stopping abruptly at the breakfast buffet, where he filled his plate with an almost obscene helping of bacon. Over the years I have grown increasingly fond of this image, the memory of this monk, and bacon. At the time I saw nothing but irony — that young man's sense of "Ah-ha, I see you!" For people such as I was, and have all I can do to resist being now, life is ablaze with epiphanies revealing the falseness all around us, when often nothing is revealed so much as our own immaturity. What we take for another eruption of the painful truth is just another pimple breaking out on our young soul's face. Perhaps Brother Philip was teaching me an important lesson, the corollary to renunciation, that when you have chosen asceticism for your life's work, and find yourself feeble and close to death, and the Lord deigns to provide you with some bacon, load up.

At that same meal I ended my own fasting. One of my most vivid memories of the monastery is the way my fast had renewed the taste of Cheerios, and how cool and sweet the milk was as the sun shone on my face through the refectory windows. Austerity will give you sensations like that, and I had come with a mind to be austere. My first night I planned to "keep watch" till dawn in the chapel. After an hour or so, I modified the plan to remaining in the chapel until dawn and sleeping on a bench if I could. Late in the night a monk came in and asked if I were all right. I said yes, and he left — perhaps, as I later realized, putting off his own reason for coming there in order to honor mine. Shortly thereafter, I went back to my room and slept. One of the psalms appointed for the next day contained the verse:

> It is in vain that you rise up early
>   and go late to rest . . .
> for he gives to his beloved sleep.

God also gave me an especially tight and fraternal embrace from that same brother when the kiss of peace was shared at Communion the next day. Though the monk and I hardly spoke to one another again, there was a definite sense of closeness, a shared understanding, whenever we took the Sacrament together.

Nevertheless, it was to Jeffrey that I grew closest. It was with him that I spent much of my time. I was quite conscious that he liked an audience, and a little suspicious that he liked to stretch a story somewhat. His contradictions were numerous. But in all he said was evidence of a genuine heart, and a profound hurt — the wounds of his handicap, and the wounds of his time in seminary.

"In my life," he told me, "I have learned to accept rejection. I have learned to do without all normal human desires, sex, friendship. . . . I have learned to love people without accepting love in return. The only regret I have is setting foot in seminary." It was hard for me to believe that was his only regret, though I didn't say so. He seemed to guess anyway. "What if 95 percent of the people in this world had cerebral palsy? To get a job or a girl you'd have to go like *this*" — but the cruel caricature of his own condition, all the more grotesque because he had to exaggerate an extreme disability, belied his point. Nevertheless, he did seem to have reconciled his fate with his faith. "If I were cured tomorrow at seven-fifteen, it would be the greatest tragedy of my life. Because knowing my weakness, I know I would forget about God by four."

What he certainly would *not* forget was what he regarded as the cruelty of certain officials at his former seminary. In his most bitter outburst, he exclaimed: "I have more respect for the Mafia than for the Episcopal Church. The Mafia is more honest about what it is doing." Apparently, the blow had come in the form of a controversy over a room. Jeffrey was told that if he came back for another semester, he would have to find his own apartment. I knew nothing of the details, of course, but Jeffrey was convinced that the crux of the whole matter was the unwillingness of the church to ordain someone in his condition. They were simply throwing up obstacles. "I'd have more respect if they'd said, 'Jeffrey, you're a paralytic, and you look like a monkey.'"

Eleven years later I can still hear him say "look like a monkey." In one of our talks, he abruptly asked me to write a letter as he dictated. The letter was to me.

> Dear Gary,
>
> It is about five months before Christmas. I like to think of Christmas in this way. I am very fond of dogs. I wonder how I would feel if God Almighty said to me: "I'm going to make you into a dog. And you're going to look like a dog, and eat like a dog, and sleep like a dog." You know, that is just what happened at the Incarnation when God Almighty became a man in Jesus Christ.
>
> But I suppose one of the best ways to really get the significance and the joy of Christmas is to be heartbroken. Because when your heart is broken, then and only then can Christ come in. And a strange thing happens; our lust turns into love, our hatred turns into humility, our greed turns into gratitude, and suddenly we are surprised by joy.

Surprised by joy, okay — but what struck me most was the terrible juxtaposition of Christ as dog and Jeffrey as monkey. As with the Cross itself, there was an implied redemption in these images, but also the evidence of dreadful humiliation and heartbreak. I suppose that by now a reader may be asking, "This is all quite interesting, but what does it have to do with your going to the monastery to seek your vocation?" I ask myself that question again and again. Why, when I turned aside to consider the ordained ministry more seriously than at any time before or since, why was I confronted with this chain-smoking, drooling, hurting, pontificating, self-taught, iconoclastic, and perhaps heroic refugee from seminary? Was this a warning? A challenge? A reflection? An incarnation? A howling case of absurd irrelevancy to anything I can think of? I still don't know.

But I do know that I shall never forget him. And I also know from re-peated experience that often when we pray for a "solution" to our dilemmas we receive instead an icon for our prayers.

At the end of Georges Bernanos's novel, *The Diary of a Country Priest*, the pro-tagonist says, "[I]f pride could die in us, the supreme grace would be to love oneself in all simplicity — as one would love anyone of those who them-selves have suffered and loved in Christ."

As I reread the journal I kept in those days, I am sometimes moved by an impulse to love "in all simplicity" the man I was, if not the one I am. To be sure, I can get awfully annoyed with him, *too*. Should I phone my wife, he wondered, or endure the solitude for another day? "Call her, you jerk!" I shout across the decade. The angels turn to me with frowns of disapproval. "I don't care. He's an idiot. He never should have gone away in the first place." Perhaps I was more fit to be a minister when I asked if I should be one than I am now.

But it is that "fitness" — rather, the burning desire to *be* fit — that I am able to love. I paid attention to everything, conversations, psalms, dreams, the flight of mating butterflies, believing it was necessary to note every de-tail and sift them all later in the hope of discovering a few nuggets of mean-ing. At times everything seemed meaningful, which of course everything is, but as Eliot noted, "Human kind cannot bear very much reality."

There were parables everywhere. Returning from a stay on the bank of the river, I happened on a cluster of black raspberry bushes. My first impulse was to strip them clean, hand to mouth. But the experiences of the past days made me want to share the berries with someone, even if there were only a few. I went back to the monastery kitchen for a colander. In the enthusiasm of my decision, however, I had forgotten to note where the bushes were. I searched for them in vain, until, frustrated and tired, I discovered another cluster of bushes, several times larger, and picked enough berries to share with the entire house. A pretty mundane incident perhaps, but in my state of mind at the time, it was as numinous and shining as the feeding of the five thousand.

A lot of my journal is simply the copying of certain passages from the Scriptures, which were read during the daily offices. When you come to the Bible in any state of agitation, its words seem to be activated — and I was coming to portions of the lectionary no fewer than five times a day. At its lowest level, this sense of activated Scripture is akin to augury; the Bible be-comes a Ouija board over which the ego slides to its own conclusions while pretending that the power of God has moved its attention this way and that.

Notwithstanding the temptation, I believe something supernatural *does* occur in any earnest encounter with Scripture. It is impossible not to find the marks of your life engraved among its details.

Of all the lessons, I found myself most drawn to the story of the Gerasene demoniac. He is the man possessed by a "legion" of devils, crying and cutting himself among the tombs. Jesus exorcises the demons and sends them into a herd of swine. I had read the story many times, but this may have been the first time, speaking both literally and figuratively, that I actually heard it out loud. I immediately identified with the man tormented by a legion of voices. He broke the fetters brought to restrain him — he could damage the arguments of any professional guide or caregiver — but he could not silence the pandemonium within. I loved Jesus for rebuking the demons when they proclaimed him the Son of God: he cared more for health than praise; he preferred a man "clothed and in his right mind" to the accolades of a tormented religious neurotic. And his compassion extended to the demons themselves; he even answered their prayer not to return them to "the abyss." "Send us to the swine, let us enter them." Wouldn't he answer mine?

Finally, I was impressed by Jesus' refusal to allow the cured man to follow him as a disciple.

> And as he was getting into the boat, the man who had been possessed with demons begged him that he might be with him. But he refused, and said to him, "Go home to your friends, and tell them how much the Lord has done for you, and how he has had mercy on you."

Along with the call to go into all the world, was there also a call to go home? Maybe, I thought, that question could be put more simply: was there a call to stay out of seminary?

The theme that seemed to recur in the lessons, in my reading, in my conversations with Jeffrey, and thus throughout the journal I kept, was that God respected my freedom. "Only you can decide what will bring you fulfillment," Jeffrey said. "Love God, and do as you please," St. Augustine had written. "I called to the Lord in my distress," one of the psalms proclaimed; "the Lord answered by setting me free." That was beginning to sound like my answer, too, though it was not without a distress of its own.

At roughly the midpoint of my time at the monastery and of my journal, I attempted to clarify the situation this way:

I have come here to ask God what my vocation should be. And yet I almost think I hear him asking me what I want it to be. Do I know? If a voice thundered overhead, "Garret, choose your vocation, and whatever it is I will accept your choice, prosper it, sanctify it . . . ," could I answer? Do I really know what I in my heart of hearts want to do?

Is there some dishonesty in claiming to desire the will of God when one does not know his own will? Do I desire submission to God, or do I simply want to avoid the struggle and the risk involved in finding out what I want? Jesus asks that God's will, not his, be done — but only after he has made his own will perfectly clear: "Father, if it be possible, let this cup be passed from me."

So now I stand before God and say, "Should I be a priest?" Perhaps I should be saying "Father, I want to be a priest, yet thy will be done" or "Father, I dread that vocation, yet thy will be done."

I was not even sure which of those two petitions fit my case. But of the few things I did know with certainty, one in which my own desires and my sense of "God's will" seemed to converge was my talks with Jeffrey. Whatever I was meant to do after leaving the monastery, I was sure I was meant to talk with him as long as I stayed. During one of his diatribes against the seminary, when he said, "They ruined my goal of serving the Church," I interrupted to say that was impossible. He was indeed serving the Church, for he had helped at least one member of it — he had helped me. He seemed touched.

With Jeffrey's intercession I hoped to gain access to the monks' own library. This was not usually permitted, at least according to Jeffrey. He maintained that book stealing was a great occupational vice among priests, and that the monastery library had suffered accordingly. Even religious lay people were prone to the weakness. He told me he used to work in a library frequented by Pentecostals. They invited him to one of their prayer meetings, at which there was a display of glossolalia, speaking in tongues. "I wish the Holy Spirit would tell you to bring your books back!" he had spouted. Anyway, permission was granted, and one of the last things we did together was to walk slowly — part of the way arm in arm — to the library within the cloisters.

Years afterward, when I read Umberto Eco's *The Name of the Rose* with its labyrinthine monastic library, I would recall the library at my retreat, not because it was so large or its denizens so sinister, but because it was a mildly forbidden place, and a forbidding and fascinating place, too, full of literature, theology, hagiography, ascetics, and the bowel-churning thrill that comes to me in any sizable collection of books. I suppose if I want to push the theme of providence to extremes, I could say that there was something providential in my making this little trip so close to the end of my visit.

Jeffrey had taken me where *any* vocational choice I was likely to make would also take me — to a place where books were stored, and read, and sometimes written.

The last words my journal records Jeffrey's having said to me were "Pray for me, a sinner." I did not remember until later that these are also the last words an Episcopal priest says to a penitent after pronouncing him or her absolved.

My eagerness to go home — one of the most powerful recurring emotions of my adult life — was now even stronger than my wish that something would be "settled" by my prayers and meditations. I missed my wife terribly. One of the monks said that I should have taken her along, and certainly should do so in future, adding, "We'd even give you a room together, and, if you wanted, we'd give you a double bed, too." I was perhaps too distracted by the thought of putting a double bed to its best use smack in the middle of a monastery to grasp the import of what he was saying. Unless I could take my home to this spiritual place, or bring this spiritual place home, my "retreat" was just that — no more.

And maybe it *was* no more. I am at a distance where I can write about this; I am not yet where I can measure its value. It has occurred to me that I may have gone to that monastery with no more virtue than many a young man has taken to a whorehouse. At a very manageable cost, I was hoping to seize a significant experience that would confirm my "manhood," maybe change my life, at least make me feel better. Perhaps I am unkind to myself. Certainly God was kinder. For I had called to the Lord in my distress, and the Lord answered by setting me free — rather, by letting me know, in what I now hear as a virtual choir of voices, that I was free; free to watch or sleep, to fast or eat bacon, to stay at the guest house alone or with my wife; free, if I could leaven freedom with faith, to accept my own handicapping limitations as part of "my way" rather than obstacles in my way; free, finally, to ignore a legion of the voices that said I was letting God down if I didn't become a priest, or letting myself down if I taught high school, or letting go too easily if I turned my back on both vocations to write down the story of my turning. This was God's answer. It was not the answer I had been looking for, but that was because God, also, was free. God was not subject to the terms of my question.

And as it turned out, the more specific and directive answer I had been seeking was on its way. I would very soon be presented with a ministry I could freely accept, or refuse. But first I would have to move to a wonderful place, and make the acquaintance of an extraordinary person.

6

Can I Control What I Shall
Do and Become?

Just as we began to write this chapter, the people of New Orleans endured a catastrophe that changed the life of almost everyone it touched. Images of flooded streets, crumbled buildings, and thousands of lost and hurting people filled our newspapers and television screens day after day, and gradually a sense of the overwhelming human cost of this event began to emerge. Before long the ripples of loss reached our own vicinity, a thousand miles to the north. A few students from New Orleans transferred into our university, where they had to start over on the semester's work while also dealing with the loss of the friends, campus, and city they had known and loved. One of our friends, who administers a large organization in New Orleans, told us when we finally reached him about his frantic, ongoing efforts to restore communication with hundreds of scattered employees, each one now not only out of work but probably homeless as well, and perhaps also suffering injury or bereavement. Another friend, a New Orleans native who moved north years ago, told us of how the lives of her relatives had been suddenly turned upside down. These disruptions within our own circle of acquaintance were only a tiny piece of the nearly unimaginable whole.

In the aftermath of Hurricane Katrina, who among the seriously affected could believe that they control their own destiny? And what about the rest of us, who were impacted less directly? Should the storm not serve as an important reality check for us as well?

Great events like this storm, which force highly visible changes on whole cities or nations, alter the lives of countless people. Wars, natural disasters, acts of terrorism: in the face of these, the question of whether or not we can control who we shall become and what we shall do is hard to answer with a straightforward "yes, we can." Even the smaller-scale catastrophes that come upon almost all of us at one time or another — cancer, crime, the loss of a loved one — make us realize that control is often not a fact of life.

Even so, many of the voices Americans are likely to hear as they grow up insist that we have a very significant degree of control over what we shall become. "You can be anything you want if you work hard enough," youngsters are told. "Plan ahead to meet your goals and secure your future," guidance counselors, investment brokers, placement officers, and self-help books urge, repeating similar warning-filled encouragements from elementary school to retirement. The content of the advice changes somewhat as we age, but its tone and tenor remain fairly consistent. And such advice does bear a certain amount of truth. Although the great majority of us cannot become "anything" we might wish — an NBA star? a successful actress? — planning and preparation do increase the likelihood that we can reach some of our more realistic goals.

The tug of war between planning what we shall become and acknowledging that in many cases we cannot control what will happen to us reflects one of the points of tension between the two traditions that inform this book and, indeed, American culture as a whole. Democracy encourages an interpretation of the world and our own prospects within it that is open-ended, with outcomes significantly shaped by the desires and actions of individuals. The stories that foster the notion that we can be anything we want to be flourish in the soil of this tradition: Ben Franklin's carefully planned rise from a tradesman's family to wealth and fame, Horace Greeley's "young man" heading West to make his fortune, Horatio Alger's impoverished orphan who pulls himself up by his bootstraps. Here, the sources of success are good character, hard work, and careful planning — at least two of which would seem to be within one's own control. By contrast, the tradition of Christianity, while not univocally disputing Democracy's vision, seeks to keep its adherents mindful that their own powers are always contingent. "Thy will be done," Christians pray daily to God, whom they see as their constant source of life and strength. Remembering that all of us will someday die is not only realistic, Christians affirm; as C. S. Lewis points out in the sermon included earlier in this book (see Chapter 1 of Part II), Christians think that remembering that we will die is actually good for us. Confessing that we are finite and therefore *not* finally in control of our own destinies becomes the source of a different kind of freedom than that offered by Democracy: the freedom to face one's perils confident that one belongs to God, who will surely prevail in the end. A prayer by Thomas Merton, which concludes this chapter, is an expression of just this kind of freedom.

Few Christians today renounce hard work and careful planning in pursuit of one's goals. Similarly, few who stand in the tradition of Democracy would deny that hard, intelligent work is sometimes unrewarded, or would argue that the fruits of such work are invulnerable to destruction. Beyond this, moreover, the adherents of both traditions should readily agree that when unjust social structures prevent people from having any control over what they will become, both Democracy and Christianity are violated. Inequities of opportunity and resources such as those made plain by Hurricane Katrina rob far too many people of significant control over what they will become. We hope that Americans will draw on both great traditions as New Orleans is rebuilt, so that it will be a more just and equitable place for all its residents.

In many important ways, then, the two traditions do not stand in stark opposition to one another on the question at issue here. Still, the fact that they have been so intertwined complicates our efforts to figure out what to do. If I remain aware of how contingent things are, does it really make sense to lay out careful plans? If I make careful plans and work very hard to advance in my chosen career and do indeed succeed, am I really just benefiting from prior advantages I did nothing to earn? To what extent *can* I actually control whether or not my life will be one that is significant and choice-worthy?

The selections below address the question of whether we can control what we shall do or become from a number of angles. Only rarely does an author make a direct argument that yes, we can, or no, we cannot. Instead, most of these texts are reflections on specific situations within which the authors become aware of the openness or the boundedness of human choice and control. Included here are:

- the nineteenth-century British poem "Invictus," which has become an anthem of self-determination (Henley)
- a meditation by a contemporary undertaker on how his father entered the profession he has now taken on as his own and passed on to his children as well (Lynch)

- "The Last Hours," a poem about a man who chooses a future different from the one prescribed by his job (Dunn)
- the Book of Jonah, the biblical story of a man who says no to what God wants him to do
- a letter written by a soldier in the Civil War to his wife (Ballou)
- a twentieth-century Russian poem that also places human control in the shadow of war (Yevtushenko)
- a prayer for God's help in relinquishing control (Merton).

The two readings that stand in sharpest contrast are the first and the last. Neither author, we should note, claims control over such matters as what occupation he will pursue or how long he will live. However, each suggests a manner of inhabiting the world and forming relationships within it that could have bearing upon how one approaches one's important life choices.

"Invictus," a poem by William Ernest Henley, a nineteenth-century British editor, opens the series of documents with a strong claim that one *can* control one's own destiny. The poet does not by any means deny that circumstances may turn against him and that he may suffer injury and every manner of outward defeat. Indeed, his claim to self-determination seems to refer more to his "unconquerable soul" than to his winning a place of honor within the structures of human society. What he seems to advocate is an attitude of utter independence from divine or human ties beyond the self. The poem's final lines have become, perhaps unfairly, clichés for such an attitude: "I am the captain of my fate: I am the master of my soul."

The final reading, a prayer written by Thomas Merton, a Christian monk, could hardly be more different. Its tone is one of humility. It is offered by one who confesses that he knows almost nothing about the future, the world, himself, or even God's will. It addresses a Being thought to be both almighty and loving; trust is the key feeling here. Far from defying gods or fate or other persons for the sake of his own goals, Merton simply thanks God for God's constant care and expresses confidence that this will be sufficient, no matter what may lie ahead.

Although Henley, who died in 1903, can hardly be blamed for the bombing of the Oklahoma City Federal Building in 1995, his poem became associated with that crime after it was reported to be a favorite of Timothy McVeigh, the bomber. Many observers thought they perceived McVeigh coldly adopting the posture of defiance the poem depicts even while he was awaiting his execution. If violence is an effort to seize control of events without regard for others, do you see this poem as one that would encourage violence such as that used by McVeigh? Or, stepping back from that unfortunate connection, would it be fair to see other forms of disregard for others in the poem's bold assertions? Note, by contrast, Merton's effort to acknowledge the incompleteness of his own view of things, including even his theology. Perhaps Henley would consider Merton's stance a form of passivity unworthy of humankind. What do you think?

It is not surprising that questions of human control often lead to meditations on natural disasters, wars, or other forms of violence, for in the presence of overwhelming threats such as these we who are mortal cannot avoid acknowledging our finitude. As C. S. Lewis noted in his wartime sermon, war simply makes visible what is always true; and so do hurricanes and acts of terrorism, we might add today. Yet if we were to think that we could control what we shall do and become if it were not for such cataclysmic interventions, we would still be mistaken. What of the more subtle, often benign forces that shape us in ways beyond our comprehension, defining the choices that lie before us and shaping us to "fit" one kind of work rather than another, as Russell Muirhead might say (see Chapter 2)?

The next text, by Thomas Lynch, portrays how influences of this kind converge in a life of meaningful work. The story Lynch tells is a simple one centered on a scene in his father's life, more than sixty years earlier. As it turns out, this scene would prove to be the inception of Lynch's own life work, as well as that of his children. There is nothing so mysterious here, in a sense: just the story of a large Catholic family that starts a business and passes it down from one generation to the next and then the next. However, Lynch, who has found the work his father "passed on" to him deeply satisfying, sees more in these events. "All things work together toward some good," he quotes St. Paul. "God works in strange ways," he quotes his mother. He sees, in other words, God's providence, God's hidden but effective work of caring for the Lynch family and for those whom they would serve. Even for those of us who do not enter the same business as our parents, this story should make us wonder how the legacy they have bestowed upon us — interests, dispositions, opportunities, even personal quirks — may influence what we will do.

In earlier times, of course, the question of control over what we shall do in life would have been unthinkable precisely because almost everyone entered the family business. Blacksmiths' sons became blacksmiths, midwives' daughters became midwives. The workplace depicted in the next document — the high rise office building — belongs to an economy in which individuals arrive at work by themselves rather than in family groups. This arrangement sounds like it would provide more freedom, and on the whole it probably does. And yet what significant choices really exist for those who work in cubicles in the offices of vast corporations? What kinds of jobs are actually available? How free are those who need jobs to choose one or another? How are we likely to be shaped as persons by the jobs we keep or do not keep? Just such questions lie beneath the surface of this recent poem by Stephen Dunn. The white-collar worker depicted here has more freedom than many workers, in all likelihood. Perhaps, as he hopes, he has by the end of the poem expanded his control over what he will do and become.

The next text, a short story that is now part of Jewish and Christian Scripture, is also about a man who walked away from his job — or rather who tried to. Today, many of those who feel undecided about what they should do with their lives say they wish God would speak to them and make the answer clear. Jonah was given exactly this kind of clarity, and his pious speeches and even his argument with God demonstrate that he did not doubt the source of the call he received. He simply did not want to answer it; it was not something he would have *chosen*. But it was nevertheless his call, and God repeatedly made it impossible for him to evade it. Reading this story in our own time, with choice as an exalted cultural value, we would do well to ask whether, even today, our callings sometimes choose us more than we choose our callings. Might Thomas Lynch or his father have felt this way? What about Will, the young man in the film *Good Will Hunting* (see Chapter 4)? As he repeatedly tried to run away from the path opened to him by his amazing mathematical ability, his friend and his therapist argued back, refusing to let him say no.

Jonah's calling led him to Nineveh, an ancient capital on the Tigris River, just across from the present-day city of Mosul in northern Iraq. As we write this chapter, our country is at war in that very vicinity. The next two texts remind us once again of how war lays bare the contingency of human plans and, indeed, of human life itself. The first document is a letter written by a soldier to his wife on the eve of battle, a letter he knows will be delivered to her if he dies in the conflict. The second is a poem about a wedding, an occasion shadowed by the fact that the groom will soon depart for the front. While Sullivan Ballou seems to embrace the possibility of his death as something he has chosen freely, the Russians at the wedding feast seem reluctant to face up to the fact of impending separation and violence. Which approach seems to you the more accurate way of understanding human contingency in wartime? Which seems more worthy?

Thomas Merton, who wrote the prayer that ends this chapter, spent most of his adult life in the Abbey of Gethsemane, a Trappist monastery in Kentucky. Though physically removed from violence like that suffered by Sullivan Ballou or the Russian bridegroom, he meditated often on the violence that has pervaded human history and became a leading advocate for peace during the 1960s. His prayer expresses longing for a form of security that renders irrelevant one's ability to "control" what one will do and become. Merton knows that "perils" whose character cannot yet be specified lie ahead, for him as for everyone, and that there will be times when "I may seem to be lost and in the shadow of death." Yet he accepts the finitude all of the texts in this chapter allude to in one way or another — or, at least, he asks for God's help in doing so.

The sharp contrast between "Invictus" and Merton's prayer puts a vivid frame around the question explored in this chapter. As much as these two texts disagree, both also use phrases and express sentiments that can be encountered in any college, congregation, or community today. In a culture deeply shaped by Democracy and also by "choice" as an engine of the consumer economy, we rightly seek some degree of control over what we shall do and become. At the same time, as mortal human beings who know that we are vulnerable to storms, illness, and violence of many kinds, we acknowledge our contingency, as not only Christianity but other religious traditions teach us to do.

Taken as a whole, the readings in this chapter place more emphasis on the contingency of our plans and the vulnerability of our efforts at "control" than they do on the planning and foresight encouraged by career counselors. However, the choices in even these texts — to become an undertaker, to quit an office job, to volunteer for the Union Army — disclose that people do say yes or no at specific points, even within circumscribed contexts. These readings also invite us to be alert to those moments when the "givens" that shape our finite lives open paths that become life-giving and fruitful. Even though Jonah refused to enjoy the work God gave him, he did participate in saving "a hundred and twenty thousand persons who do not know their right hand from their left, and also many animals." And the members of the extended Lynch family, drawn by a little boy's epiphany into an occupation they might not otherwise have found, discovered both satisfaction and service in the work he bequeathed to them.

It is just possible that some of the people whose lives were disrupted by Hurricane Katrina will discover during the recovery process callings they would not have anticipated or chosen before the storm. To notice this is not to say that this awful cloud has a silver lining or that the devastation that occurred was in any sense a good thing. Rather, it is to remind ourselves that our callings always come to us within specific contexts, and that even the present scene of devastation is an arena within which there is much significant and choice-worthy work to be done.

433

WILLIAM ERNEST HENLEY

"Invictus"

William Ernest Henley (1849-1903) suffered ill health as a boy and young man but eventually became an influential man of letters in Victorian England. A poet, playwright, and essayist, he also served as editor of several periodicals over the course of his career. In this capacity he introduced to the public such writers as H. G. Wells and William Butler Yeats, whose work is included in other chapters of *Leading Lives That Matter*.

"Invictus," which means "unconquered," is a cry of defiance; the poet insists that he alone is "the master of my fate . . . the captain of my soul." This assertion is made even though he has experienced "the bludgeonings of chance" and even though his head is "bloody." Moreover, the darkness with which the poem begins is persistent, and the world in which it is set is bleak. The speaker's mastery, in other words, does not seem to be over events. Against whom or what, then, is he declaring his independence? What is the character of the "mastery" he claims to have?

Out of the night that covers me,
Black as the Pit from pole to pole,
I thank whatever gods may be
For my unconquerable soul.

In the fell clutch of circumstance
I have not winced nor cried aloud.
Under the bludgeonings of chance
My head is bloody, but unbowed.

From *Modern British Poetry*, ed. Louis Untermeyer (1885-1977). See http://www.bartleby.com/103/

Beyond this place of wrath and tears
Looms but the Horror of the shade,
And yet the menace of the years
Finds, and shall find, me unafraid.

It matters not how strait the gate,
How charged with punishments the scroll,
I am the master of my fate:
I am the captain of my soul.

〰〰〰

THOMAS LYNCH

"Passed On"

Thomas Lynch grew up in Michigan, where his father ran a funeral home. He also became an undertaker, work he has found both significant and meaningful. In addition to this work, he writes poems and essays filled with wisdom about the human condition gleaned from his years of dealing with the dead and those who mourn for them. His books include *The Undertaking; Still Life in Milford;* and *Bodies in Motion and at Rest.* He now spends part of each year in Ireland in a cottage once inhabited by his grandparents.

The reading below could have been included in several different parts of this book. It uses the vocabulary of vocation. It gives us a glimpse into a family that balances life with work. It shows how one boy, and then many of his descendants, chose the work they would do. It is included here because Lynch brings the vocational choice about which he is writing around to a conclusion that gives one important answer to the question of whether we can control what we shall do and become. As his mother puts it, "God works in strange ways." To what extent does Lynch attribute the

From *Christian Century*, July 13, 2004, p. 29.

outcome to God? What other factors beyond his own control shaped his father's choice, and his own?

The photo of the new priest among his people is an old one. "First Solemn High Mass," it reads in white handprint in the top right corner, "of Rev. Thomas P. Lynch," and on the next line, "St. John's Church, Jackson, Mich., June 10, 1934." It is a panoramic, 17″ × 7′ black-and-white glossy.

Up on the steps in the middle background at the arching doorway of the church stands the celebrant, flanked by deacon and sub deacon, vested in albs and chasubles, with two cassocked and surpliced men off to the right who must have been the altar servers on the day. They are surrounded by a crescent of family and well-wishers, five dozen or more, the front row seated on folding chairs in the foreground, all posed, looking at the photographer with that same grin folks get on their faces when they say, "Cheese!"

Thomas P. Lynch is two months shy of his 30th birthday. Though he survived the Spanish flu in 1918, he's been sickly and susceptible ever since. He has been to seminary in Detroit, but because he was croupy and tubercular, his archbishop sent him to Denver and then Santa Fe to finish his training in those high, dry western climates. He has come home at long last, fully fledged, anointed and ordained, to say a solemn high mass for his people — the family and neighbors of his childhood. He will die in two years of influenza and pneumonia, ten days short of his 32nd birthday.

In front of him, smack in the middle of this assemblage, seated at the right hand of my grandfather, is my father, the priest's only nephew. It is the second Sunday in June, the middle of the Great Depression and my father is ten years old, the only young boy in the frame, dressed in saddle shoes, knee britches, white shirt and tie, looking for all the world like his grandson, my eldest boy, when he was ten.

Father Lynch will be stationed in Taos, New Mexico, at Neutral Senora de Guadalupe. He will marry and bury and baptize and teach young Apache and Hispanic children how to play baseball and avoid the deadly sins. After two years his health will turn and he'll be taken to Santa Fe where, after three days in St. Vincent's Sanatorium, he will die on July 31, 1936. His body will be sent home in a box by train to Jackson, Michigan, where the people in this photo will follow him back into this church for the funeral mass and out to St. John's Cemetery where he'll be buried next to his father and mother.

When his brother, my grandfather, E. J. Lynch, goes to the funeral home to organize the local obsequies, he takes my father, now 12 years old, along for the ride. While the men talk, the boy wanders through the old house until he makes it to the basement where he sees his uncle, the dead priest, being dressed in his liturgical vestments by two men in shirtsleeves, black slacks and gray-striped ties. They lift the priest's body into a casket, place his biretta in the corner of the casket lid and turn to find the young boy, standing in the doorway, watching.

It is to this moment in the first week of August 1936, standing in the basement of Desnoyer Funeral Home in Jackson, Michigan, that my father will always trace his decision to become a funeral director.

"I knew right away," he would always recount it, "that was the thing I was meant to do."

Why, I've often wondered, did he not decide to be a priest? But speaking for my brothers and my sisters, we're pleased he chose the course in life he did.

In the next ten years my father will play right tackle for the St. Francis de Sales High School, learn to drive a car, fall in love with the red-headed Rosemary O'Hara, enlist in the Marine Corps and spend four years in the South Pacific shooting a light machine gun at Japanese foot soldiers. He will return, a skinny and malarial hero, to Detroit, wed Rosemary, enroll in mortuary school at Wayne State University and go to work for a local funeral home. He promises his new bride that someday, just wait and see, they'll have a funeral home of their own, a house in the suburbs, "and maybe a couple of junior partners!" Within two months she is pregnant with the first of nine children.

Two generations later, their grandsons and granddaughters are graduating from mortuary school and joining the family firm of funeral directors that operates five mortuaries in the suburbs of Detroit, serving more than a thousand families a year. They trace their calling to their parents. Their parents trace their calling to their father, who traced his calling to the priest in this photo, who died young and was sent home to Michigan and prepared for burial. Such are the oddities of chance and happenstance. Or such are the workings of the will of God.

Lately I've been thinking about vocations — the calling we were always told to listen for — that would tell us what God had in mind for us. I wonder if the young priest heard it, or my father, or if, out of the ordinary silence, they discerned by faith just what it was God wanted them to do. In this, I think we are fellow pilgrims, we sometimes doubting Thomas's who wonder still, but live our lives by faith.

"All things work together toward some good" is what St. Paul has to say about such things. "God works in strange ways," my mother said.

～

STEPHEN DUNN

"The Last Hours"

This poem, like Lynch's essay, reflects on a young man's decision about whether to follow his father's career path, this time a path that leads into the corporate world. Now, years later, the poet recalls an afternoon on which he did exercise some control over what he would become. This is not to say that he knew what lay ahead: "I know only what I don't want," he thinks.

What does the poem tell us about the context within which he made this choice? Note the historical moment, his family connections, and the purpose of the company for which he works. How might these affect his ability to act? How do parallel factors in your own context liberate you, or not, to exert influence on what you will become?

"The Last Hours" was published in the book that won the 2001 Pulitzer Prize for Poetry. Stephen Dunn teaches creative writing at Stockton College in New Jersey as well as in workshops around the country.

There's some innocence left,
and these are the last hours of an empty afternoon
at the office, and there's the clock
on the wall, and my friend Frank
in the adjacent cubicle selling himself
on the phone.
 I'm twenty-five, on the shaky
ladder up, my father's son, corporate,
clean-shaven, and I know only what I don't want,
which is almost everything I have.
 A meeting ends.

From *Different Hours* (New York: W. W. Norton, 2002), p. 55.

Men in serious suits, intelligent men
who've been thinking hard about marketing snacks,
move back now to their window offices, worried
or proud. The big boss, Horace,
had called them in to approve this, reject that —
the big boss, a first-name, how's-your-family
kind of assassin, who likes me.
    It's 1964.
The sixties haven't begun yet. Cuba is a larger name
than Vietnam. The Soviets are behind
everything that could be wrong. Where I sit
it's exactly nineteen minutes to five. My phone rings.
Horace would like me to stop in
before I leave. *Stop in.* Code words,
leisurely words, that mean *now.*
    Would I be willing
to take on this? Would X's office, who by the way
is no longer with us, be satisfactory?
About money, will this be enough?
I smile, I say yes and yes and yes,
but — I don't know from what calm place
this comes — I'm translating
his beneficence into a lifetime, a life
of selling snacks, talking snack strategy,
thinking snack thoughts.
    On the elevator down
it's a small knot, I'd like to say, of joy.
That's how I tell it now, here in the future,
the fear long gone.
By the time I reach the subway it's grown,
it's outsized, an attitude finally come round,
and I say it quietly to myself: *I quit,*
and keep saying it, knowing I will say it, sure
of nothing else but.

The Book of Jonah

Many children first encounter Jonah as a somewhat silly character in a Bible story that reaches its climax when Jonah is swallowed by a great fish. However, when we come to this story as adults, we recognize Jonah as someone driven to distraction by a severe vocational crisis. Even though the path before him is fairly plain, he resists going down it — a response that is not all that uncommon. Have any of us tried to flee our callings? Perhaps we resist because we don't believe we have a calling; what we are doing now may not seem important enough to take so seriously. Perhaps we suspect we do have a calling but aren't very happy about it — it just looks too demanding or is too poorly paid to appeal to us. Jonah's example challenges the notion that self-fulfillment and happiness are reliable indicators of a true calling; after all, his comes directly from God and is, within the terms of this story, at least a *true* calling. Even so, it does not live up to Frederick Buechner's definition of "vocation" as "the place where your deep gladness and the world's deep hunger meet" (see Part I).

Jonah is not a bad person on the whole. God does choose him, after all, and Jonah speaks words of sound biblical theology; his prayer from the belly of the fish is beautiful, and he piously acknowledges that God is "slow to anger, and abounding in steadfast love." Yet his behavior is persistently disobedient and ungrateful. Would it be better for Jonah — and similarly, for us — to attain closer congruence between what we say we believe and what we do in life?

Now the word of the LORD came to Jonah son of Amittai, saying, "Go at once to Nineveh, that great city, and cry out against it; for their wickedness has come up before me." But Jonah set out to flee to Tarshish from the presence of the LORD. He went down to Joppa and found a ship going to

---

From the New Revised Standard Version of the Bible.

Tarshish; so he paid his fare and went on board, to go with them to Tarshish, away from the presence of the LORD.

But the LORD hurled a great wind upon the sea, and such a mighty storm came upon the sea that the ship threatened to break up. Then the mariners were afraid, and each cried to his god. They threw the cargo that was in the ship into the sea, to lighten it for them. Jonah, meanwhile, had gone down into the hold of the ship and had lain down, and was fast asleep. The captain came and said to him, "What are you doing sound asleep? Get up, call on your god! Perhaps the god will spare us a thought so that we do not perish."

The sailors said to one another, "Come, let us cast lots, so that we may know on whose account this calamity has come upon us." So they cast lots, and the lot fell on Jonah. Then they said to him, "Tell us why this calamity has come upon us. What is your occupation? Where do you come from? What is your country? And of what people are you?"

"I am a Hebrew," he replied. "I worship the LORD, the God of heaven, who made the sea and the dry land." Then the men were even more afraid, and said to him, "What is this that you have done!" For the men knew that he was fleeing from the presence of the LORD, because he had told them so.

Then they said to him, "What shall we do to you, that the sea may quiet down for us?" For the sea was growing more and more tempestuous. He said to them, "Pick me up and throw me into the sea; then the sea will quiet down for you; for I know it is because of me that this great storm has come upon you." Nevertheless the men rowed hard to bring the ship back to land, but they could not, for the sea grew more and more stormy against them. Then they cried out to the LORD, "Please, O LORD, we pray, do not let us perish on account of this man's life. Do not make us guilty of innocent blood; for you, O LORD, have done as it pleased you." So they picked Jonah up and threw him into the sea; and the sea ceased from its raging. Then the men feared the LORD even more, and they offered a sacrifice to the LORD and made vows.

But the LORD provided a large fish to swallow up Jonah; and Jonah was in the belly of the fish three days and three nights.

Then Jonah prayed to the LORD his God from the belly of the fish, saying,

"I called to the LORD out of my distress,
    and he answered me;
out of the belly of Sheol I cried,
    and you heard my voice.

You cast me into the deep,
    into the heart of the seas,
    and the flood surrounded me;
all your waves and your billows
    passed over me.
Then I said, 'I am driven away
from your sight;
how shall I look again
    upon your holy temple?'
The waters closed in over me;
    the deep surrounded me;
weeds were wrapped around my head
    at the roots of the mountains.
I went down to the land
    whose bars closed upon me forever;
yet you brought up my life from the Pit,
    O LORD my God.
As my life was ebbing away,
    I remembered the LORD;
and my prayer came to you,
    into your holy temple.
Those who worship vain idols
    forsake their true loyalty.
But I with the voice of thanksgiving
    will sacrifice to you;
what I have vowed I will pay.
    Deliverance belongs to the LORD!"

Then the LORD spoke to the fish, and it spewed Jonah out upon the dry land.

The word of the LORD came to Jonah a second time, saying, "Get up, go to Nineveh, that great city, and proclaim to it the message that I tell you." So Jonah set out and went to Nineveh, according to the word of the LORD. Now Nineveh was an exceedingly large city, a three days' walk across. Jonah began to go into the city, going a day's walk. And he cried out, "Forty days more, and Nineveh shall be overthrown!" And the people of Nineveh believed God; they proclaimed a fast, and everyone, great and small, put on sackcloth.

When the news reached the king of Nineveh, he rose from his throne, removed his robe, covered himself with sackcloth, and sat in ashes. Then he had a proclamation made in Nineveh: "By the decree of the king and his nobles: No human being or animal, no herd or flock, shall taste anything. They shall not feed, nor shall they drink water. Human beings and animals shall be covered with sackcloth, and they shall cry mightily to God. All shall turn from their evil ways and from the violence that is in their hands. Who knows? God may relent and change his mind; he may turn from his fierce anger, so that we do not perish."

When God saw what they did, how they turned from their evil ways, God changed his mind about the calamity that he had said he would bring upon them; and he did not do it.

But this was very displeasing to Jonah, and he became angry. He prayed to the LORD and said, "O LORD! Is not this what I said while I was still in my own country? That is why I fled to Tarshish at the beginning; for I knew that you are a gracious God and merciful, slow to anger, and abounding in steadfast love, and ready to relent from punishing. And now, O LORD, please take my life from me, for it is better for me to die than to live." And the LORD said, "Is it right for you to be angry?" Then Jonah went out of the city and sat down east of the city, and made a booth for himself there. He sat under it in the shade, waiting to see what would become of the city.

The LORD God appointed a bush, and made it come up over Jonah, to give shade over his head, to save him from his discomfort; so Jonah was very happy about the bush. But when dawn came up the next day, God appointed a worm that attacked the bush, so that it withered. When the sun rose, God prepared a sultry east wind, and the sun beat down on the head of Jonah so that he was faint and asked that he might die. He said, "It is better for me to die than to live."

But God said to Jonah, "Is it right for you to be angry about the bush?" And he said, "Yes, angry enough to die." Then the LORD said, "You are concerned about the bush, for which you did not labor and which you did not grow; it came into being in a night and perished in a night. And should I not be concerned about Nineveh, that great city, in which there are more than a hundred and twenty thousand persons who do not know their right hand from their left, and also many animals?"

~~~~~

SULLIVAN BALLOU

A Letter to His Wife, 1861

As we have noted, times of war often force people to acknowledge the limits of their control over what they shall be and do. Soldiers preparing for battle, who must face the imminent possibility of their own death, have long observed the custom of writing a letter to loved ones before major engagements, to be delivered only if they die. The following selection is one such letter. Here a young officer writes to his twenty-four-year-old wife, who is at home in New England with their five-year-old and two-year-old sons. This letter, found among his belongings, has become a well-known record of what this particular war meant to supporters of the Union, as well as a powerful statement of the losses sustained in any war.

Ballou (March 28, 1829–July 21, 1861) met his death in the First Battle of Bull Run, one of the earliest engagements of the Civil War. Enthusiasts on both sides thought the war would be swift and easy, though in fact it would grind on for nearly four more years, becoming what is still the bloodiest war in U.S. history. Ballou, a supporter of Lincoln who was active in Rhode Island politics and one of the first to enlist, was clear about the ideals for which he was fighting. Notice, however, his acknowledgment to his wife that his actions are also "hazarding the happiness of those I love" — herself and their sons. His enlistment influenced not only what he would do and become, but also their futures. How does the question of control over who one person will be and become necessarily become related to the destinies of others, whether family members or strangers, such as, in this case, enemy troops?

From http://usinfo.state.gov/usa/infousa/facts/democrac/23.htm

July 14, 1861

Camp Clark, Washington [D.C.]

My very dear Sarah:

The indications are very strong that we shall move in a few days — perhaps tomorrow. Lest I should not be able to write you again, I feel impelled to write lines that may fall under your eye when I shall be no more.

Our movement may be one of a few days duration and full of pleasure — and it may be one of severe conflict and death to me. Not my will, but thine O God, be done. If it is necessary that I should fall on the battlefield for my country, I am ready. I have no misgivings about, or lack of confidence in, the cause in which I am engaged, and my courage does not halt or falter. I know how strongly American Civilization now leans upon the triumph of the Government, and how great a debt we owe to those who went before us through the blood and suffering of the Revolution. And I am willing — perfectly willing — to lay down all my joys in this life, to help maintain this Government, and to pay that debt.

But, my dear wife, when I know that with my own joys I lay down nearly all of yours, and replace them in this life with cares and sorrows — when, after having eaten for long years the bitter fruit of orphanage myself, I must offer it as their only sustenance to my dear little children — is it weak or dishonorable, while the banner of my purpose floats calmly and proudly in the breeze, that my unbounded love for you, my darling wife and children, should struggle in fierce, though useless, contest with my love of country?

I cannot describe to you my feelings on this calm summer night, when two thousand men are sleeping around me, many of them enjoying the last, perhaps, before that of death — and I, suspicious that Death is creeping behind me with his fatal dart, am communing with God, my country, and thee.

I have sought most closely and diligently, and often in my breast, for a wrong motive in thus hazarding the happiness of those I loved and I could not find one. A pure love of my country and of the principles I have often advocated before the people and "the name of honor that I love more than I fear death" have called upon me, and I have obeyed.

Sarah, my love for you is deathless, it seems to bind me to you with mighty cables that nothing but Omnipotence could break; and yet my love of Country comes over me like a strong wind and bears me irresistibly on with all these chains to the battlefield.

The memories of the blissful moments I have spent with you come creeping over me, and I feel most gratified to God and to you that I have enjoyed them so long. And hard it is for me to give them up and burn to ashes the hopes of future years, when God willing, we might still have lived and loved together, and seen our sons grow up to honorable manhood around us. I have, I know, but few and small claims upon Divine Providence, but something whispers to me — perhaps it is the wafted prayer of my little Edgar — that I shall return to my loved ones unharmed. If I do not, my dear Sarah, never forget how much I love you, and when my last breath escapes me on the battlefield, it will whisper your name.

Forgive my many faults, and the many pains I have caused you. How thoughtless and foolish I have oftentimes been! How gladly would I wash out with my tears every little spot upon your happiness, and struggle with all the misfortune of this world, to shield you and my children from harm. But I cannot. I must watch you from the spirit land and hover near you, while you buffet the storms with your precious little freight, and wait with sad patience till we meet to part no more.

But, O Sarah! If the dead can come back to this earth and flit unseen around those they loved, I shall always be near you; in the garish day and in the darkest night — amidst your happiest scenes and gloomiest hours — always, always; and if there be a soft breeze upon your cheek, it shall be my breath; or the cool air fans your throbbing temple, it shall be my spirit passing by.

Sarah, do not mourn me dead; think I am gone and wait for thee, for we shall meet again.

As for my little boys, they will grow as I have done, and never know a father's love and care. Little Willie is too young to remember me long, and my blue-eyed Edgar will keep my frolics with him among the dimmest memories of his childhood. Sarah, I have unlimited confidence in your maternal care and your development of their characters. Tell my two mothers his and hers I call God's blessing upon them. O Sarah, I wait for you there! Come to me, and lead thither my children.

Sullivan

YEVGENY YEVTUSHENKO

"Weddings"

This poem by the Russian poet Yevgeny Yevtushenko also affords a glimpse into life on the precipice of war. Its perspective is different from that of Sullivan Ballou, however. There are no odes to ideals or discussions of the reasons to fight, though we do learn from the reference to Hitler that this scene takes place during World War II. In addition, the one writing is not the one who will himself be going into battle, at least not any time soon. How do these differences and others you may notice affect the quite different tone of this poem?

The job of the one who is speaking provides him with a specific point of vision into the human finitude on display at each wedding. And this poem is, in fact, very much about his job; even, we might say, about his calling or vocation, since we see him being called or summoned to his work by drunken wedding guests. Moreover, he seems to understand that he has a certain vocation in this situation. Do you agree with what he says about his job, his calling, in the last sentence?

Weddings in days of war,
false cheating comfort,
those hollow phrases:
"He won't get killed . . ."
On a snowbound winter road,
slashed by a cruel wind,
I speed to a hasty wedding
in a neighboring village.
Gingerly I enter

From *Early Poems by Yevgeny Yevtushenko,* trans. George Reavey (London: Marion Boyars Publishers, 1997).

a buzzing cottage,
I, a folk dancer of repute,
with a forelock dangling
from my forehead.
All spruced up,
    disturbed,
among relatives
    and friends
the bridegroom sits, just mobilized,
distraught.
Sits
    with Vera — his bride —
but in a day or two
he'll pull on a gray soldier's coat
and, wearing it, leave for the front.
Then with a rifle he will go,
tramping over alien
    soil;
a German bullet, perhaps,
will lay him low . . .
A glass of foaming home brew
he's not able yet to drink.
Their first night together
will likely be their last.
Chagrined, the bridegroom stares,
and with all his soul in anguish
cries to me across the table:
"Well, go on, why don't you dance!"
They all forget their drinking,
all fix me with goggling eyes,
and I slide and writhe,
beating a rhythm with my hooves.
Now I drum a tattoo,
    now drag my toes
across the floor.
Whistling shrilly,
    I clap my hands,
leap up near the ceiling.
Slogans on the wall fly past,
"Hitler will be kaput!"

But the bride
    scalds
her face
    with tears.
I'm already a wet rag,
barely catch my breath . . .
"Dance!" —
    they shout in desperation,
and I dance again . . .
Back home, my ankles
feel as stiff as wood;
but from yet another wedding
    drunken guests
come knocking at the door once more.
Soon as mother lets me go,
I'm off to weddings once again,
and round the tablecloth anew
I stamp my feet and bend my knees.
The bride sheds bitter tears,
friends are tearful too.
I'm afraid for everyone.
    I've no desire to dance,
but you can't
    not dance.

THOMAS MERTON

Thoughts in Solitude

After an excellent and cosmopolitan education in Europe and the United
States, Thomas Merton (1915-1968) converted to Roman Catholicism in

From Thomas Merton, *Thoughts in Solitude* (New York: Farrar, Straus & Cudahy, 1958), p. 83.

1938 and entered a strict monastic community in 1941. His writing from the monastery — first and most notably his autobiography, *The Seven Storey Mountain* (1948), but also dozens of other books as well as extensive correspondence with other spiritual leaders — made him an influential voice for Catholic Christianity, and his works continue to be widely read today. Though residing in a contemplative community in a rural area, Merton prayed and wrote about pressing social issues such as race relations, war, and economic injustice, and he also encouraged Western Christians to give attention to the religions of the East.

This prayer, widely known as the Thomas Merton prayer, provides a classic Christian answer to the question of whether we can control what we shall do and become. Does Merton's profession of ignorance seem to you a realistic description of the human ability to shape the future? Does his trust in God seem to you a daring venture, a sign of weakness, or something else?

My Lord God, I have no idea where I am going. I do not see the road ahead of me. I cannot know for certain where it will end. Nor do I really know myself, and the fact that I think that I am following your will does not mean that I am actually doing so. But I believe that the desire to please you does in fact please you. And I hope I have that desire in all that I am doing. I hope that I will never do anything apart from that desire. And I know that if I do this you will lead me by the right road though I may know nothing about it. Therefore will I trust you always though I may seem to be lost and in the shadow of death. I will not fear, for you are ever with me, and you will never leave me to face my perils alone.

7

How Shall I Tell
the Story of My Life?

───≈≈≈───

The first reading featured in this chapter, Robert Frost's "The Road Not Taken," surely numbers among the five or ten most familiar and beloved poems in all of American literature. Most people, including some famous writers who have used phrases from the poem as titles for their books, believe that the poem is about life's major choices and their consequences. For them, the whole poem reduces to its last two lines: "I took the [road] less traveled by/ And that has made all the difference."

Several of the readings in the previous sections of this anthology go far to explain why Americans, of all people, would be disposed to read Frost's poem this way. As Charles Taylor argued in Part I, Americans may value free choice above almost everything else. Indeed, many citizens believe that choice by itself confers significance upon the object of choice. Russell Muirhead taught us in Part II, Chapter 2, that a complete account of "just work" in a democratic society should provide for an element of choice. We believe that our work is "just" in part because we have chosen to do it. Gilbert Meilaender reminded us, also in Chapter 2, that our friends are people we have chosen, not people with whom we've suddenly become smitten or who have been forced into our company. We've read about the reasons for choosing one kind of life over another one, about whom we should heed when we are making decisions, and about how and why so many of the things that shape our identities are at one and the same time free and constrained. Leading a life that matters surely involves making good choices.

Though these deep and legitimate concerns about the place of free choice in our lives may explain why "The Road Not Taken" has been "taken" to be about choice, the poem is not mainly about choice at all. It instead explores the shape of the stories we tell to ourselves and others about ourselves over the course of our lives. The poem is also about how and why these stories change. The poem teaches us that there are two things of roughly equal importance in determining the quality of the lives we lead: the choices we make and what we make of those choices. Our interpretations of what we have chosen to do and of what has happened to us often take the form of stories, and these narratives in turn constitute our inner sense of ourselves, which includes feelings of meaning, purpose, and significance. To put this a bit differently, our imagination is just as important as our reason in shaping our identities and in making for lives of significance and substance. The widespread misreading of "The Road Not Taken" may indicate that as a people we do not rightly appreciate the importance of the imagination in shaping our efforts to lead lives that matter.

When we come to Frost's poem with these latter ideas in our minds, we notice right away that the whole poem consists of two very different stories of the "same" event. The first story is relatively long (the first fifteen lines), quite indecisive about whether the two roads encountered by the speaker on an autumn morning differed from one another at all, and concluded by a resolution to keep one of the roads for some other time. The second story is much shorter (the final three lines), much more resolute about the differences between the two roads, and concluded by a resolution to take that one "less traveled." The speaker tells the first story sometime soon after the event and then imagines how he will tell the story differently "ages and ages hence." The speaker knows that his perspective on life will change over time and that he will be a different kind of person in old age than he was when he first came upon the two roads. He (or she) even knows how he will be different: he'll be surer in his judgments and more dramatic in narrating certain particular choices in his life. Memory, the thread of continuity in his identity, will serve to some extent his sense of himself even as the changing shape of his life's story will serve to change his sense of the significance of his past. One choice will have made "all the difference," and his literally "self"-serving memory will move him to claim that he once chose a "less traveled" way, even though he was not at all clear about this matter in the immediate aftermath of the moment of choice.

Like the speaker in this poem, all of us revise our own life stories all of the time. Unlike the speaker in the poem, many of us are not as aware of this as we should be. Sometimes we revise our stories depending on our audience. Would not most of us tell the story of an embarrassing experience somewhat differently to our parents, our siblings, our lovers, and our employers? But we undertake our work of revision more often for the sake of our primary audience, ourselves. The readings that follow "The Road Not Taken" will help us to understand the complexities and the vital importance of this constant process of "composing our lives." Two of these readings are from creative artists who make their living telling stories, and two are by social scientists who study the importance of the stories we fashion for ourselves to our identities and personalities. The last reading reminds us that, just as we cannot fully control those things that we remember and shape into our stories, we cannot fully control how others will remember us. The five readings are as follows:

- Mary Catherine Bateson, "Composing a Life Story"
- Wendell Berry, from *Jayber Crow*
- John Steinbeck, from *East of Eden*
- Dan McAdams, "An American Life Story"
- Michael T. Kaufman, "Robert McG. Thomas, 60, Chronicler of Unsung Lives"

Mary Catherine Bateson has lived most of her life on the boundary between creative writing and social science. She is an anthropologist who has told true stories about the lives of other people. In her essay below, which is based on her book *Composing a Life,* she shows why we should attend as much to what we make of our choices as we do to the choices we make. Learning to become more imaginative and resourceful in composing our own pasts can enable us to lead more significant lives in the future. We can discover that what appear to be sudden ruptures in our lives really connect at a deeper level to skills and interests that we have always had, thereby helping us draw upon our past selves in facing some new challenge that has suddenly come upon us. Someone, for example, might have been a teacher in New Orleans for many years prior to Hurricane Katrina only to find herself living with relatives in Boise, Idaho, where the only job available to her is in the development office for a local hospital. If she can understand development work as a kind of education, she might discover more continuity than discontinuity between the kind of work she was doing as an English teacher in a high school and the kind of work she will be doing in attempting to enlist community support for a new health care facility. This discovery might in turn enable her to become a very effective fund raiser. Her success, in this case, would be directly linked to her imaginative capacity to shape a story of continuity from what first seemed to her a broken and disconnected narrative.

Bateson's essay uses three senses of the word "compose," drawn from the three arts of painting, music, and creative writing, to explicate the complexities involved in shaping the narratives of our lives. This work of composition touches upon all of the topics and questions raised in the previous chapters of this anthology. For example, if we think of composing our life as a painter might think of composition on a canvas, we will attend with great care to achieving balance and harmony among the several elements in our lives. Balance, in this view, consists less of walking a tightrope so as to give equal attention to our work, our home, and our community so that we do not take a tumble, and more of creatively imagining the ways in which these several parts of our lives might constitute a whole, might complement one another, and might be assigned our own special proportions to produce a distinctive life of harmony and integrity. If, on the other hand, we view our life as a musical composition, a tonal structure unfolding over time, we are apt to look for harmonies over the course of our life rather than expecting perfect harmony at each and every moment.

Bateson is well aware of the fact that when we compose our lives as a creative writer might, we invariably choose from a repertoire of plots, characters, and themes that we have inherited from our culture. We may be reminded here of Russell Muirhead's discussion in Chapter 2 of how our choice of work is both free and constrained. We may be free to choose from a menu of several possible jobs, but we did not ourselves create the menu. Just so with the stories that we fashion about ourselves. We are free to emplot our narratives as comedies or tragedies, but we did not ourselves invent comedy and tragedy. We absorb from our culture without realizing it a host of narrative possibilities from the films we see, the books we read, and the stories that we hear other people tell about themselves. The shape that we give at any moment to our own life's story will therefore resemble the shape of other people's stories, some of them "real" and others "fictional." Part of the work of coming to know ourselves involves our ability to choose from a repertoire of characters and plots those that most truly capture who we are and what we can reasonably aspire to become.

The excerpt from Wendell Berry's novel *Jayber Crow* shows us the title character in the midst of this "work of knowing." Jayber interrupts the telling of his own life's story to consider the shape of that story. We get to watch him consider and reject several plot lines, drawn from some of the great works of world literature he read when he was a student. Though he admires the plots and the central characters in some of these books and even wishes that his own life's story could credibly be told in their terms, he realizes that some of the narratives drawn from this repertoire don't quite fit him. Thus, though he sometimes wishes that the shape of his life could honestly be charted as a straight line of progress, he discovers that it more often resembles a circle. He seems to settle at times for mystery over clarity, for trust in providence over rational plot resolution. But this interpretation itself has precedents, and Jayber knows it. The story of a life told as a series of accidents that seem best represented as a sometimes confused and confusing pilgrimage, often marked by ironic twists and turns, resembles one of the great stories that Catherine Bateson alludes to in her essay. St. Augustine, in his *Confessions*, composed his own life as a sometimes ironic pilgrimage suffused throughout with a "feeling that he had been led."

The efforts all of us make to impose narrative order of some kind upon the teeming variety of our experiences often yield a sense of meaning and coherence but not always a corresponding sense of significance. Our story might make sense, but did it matter after all? And if so, how and why? Whereas the project of making sense of our lives often involves our imitating other plot lines or characters in the fashioning of our autobiographies, the project of discovering and creating significance often involves interpreting our own life stories as parts of larger stories to which they contribute. John Steinbeck's novel *East of Eden* is an epic story of two families over the course of several generations. The significance of the families' story, as the title of the novel suggests, comes from its being a part of one of the oldest stories in the world. In the middle of that novel, the narrator speaks directly to the readers, stating that there really is only *one* story in the world and that our lives are more or less significant, more or less choice-worthy, depending upon what part we play in that larger story. The story of the world, says the narrator, is a kind of eternal struggle between good and evil, between the good and the bad within us, and between people who are on balance good and people who are on balance evil.

Dan McAdams, a personality psychologist at Northwestern University, has spent much of his life studying the "good" people. And he has discerned a complex connection between such people and the kind of stories they tell about their lives. By "good" people, McAdams means "generative" people, to use the more technical and precise vocabulary of his discipline. Such people are for the most part virtuous, in Aristotle's sense, but in addition they show an unusual amount of interest in and devotion to the welfare of the next generation. So, in the terms of this anthology, their lives are meaningful, virtuous, *and* significant. These people really do make a difference in the world. And the majority of them have a tendency to tell the story of their own lives in a particular way, according to a particular kind of plot. McAdams calls these stories "narratives of redemption."

The connection between the "goodness" of these people and the shape of their stories is not a causal one exactly. Generative people do not become good because they see their life stories as narratives of redemption, nor do they tell such stories because they are good. Instead, a tendency to discern "redemption" in their own stories and in the larger story of the world of which they are a part is very frequently, though not always, an important mark of a generative personality. Identity and story are linked here, but more in terms of a revealing statistical correlation than in terms of a causal sequence. Discerning redemptive patterns is part of what it means to lead a significant life. Christian practical theologians would be pleased with McAdams's findings, since many of them believe that the Christian life at its best includes the ability to discover and interpret redemption in the world and to participate in the great story of redemption embodied in the life and death of Jesus of Nazareth.

McAdams's research does not suggest, however, that the disposition to interpret one's life as a narrative of redemption is a distinctively Christian phenomenon. Though many of the generative people McAdams studied are religious, a large number are not. And among the ones who are religious, not all are Christian. Some international reactions to his work, however, have made him suspect that a different correlation exists: a correlation with nationality based on the possibility that, by comparison to Europeans, Americans may be unusually disposed to see their life stories in redemptive terms. In other words, like the idea of vocation, the idea of redemption has extended its provenance well beyond religious communities, lying at the intersection of religious and democratic traditions.

Many of McAdams's generative people likely will be remembered very warmly by their friends and neighbors when the stories of their lives are complete. But can any of them be sure of this? The narrator of *East of Eden* urged us to "remember our dying and try so to live that our death brings no pleasure to the world." The soundness of such advice depends to some extent upon our being able to predict even if we cannot control how we will be remembered by others. The last reading in this chapter reminds us that, however important the stories we fashion about our lives might be, the final versions, the ones that will largely determine how we will be remembered in this world, will be written by others. At the end of Chapter 1, after we had presented some examples of the different literary forms used to remember the lives of others — obituaries, eulogies, and elegies — we suggested that readers might, as a good spiritual and intellectual exercise, write their own obituary notices. This recommendation is akin to the counsel of Steinbeck's narrator, for it invites us to view our present aspirations and choices from the vantage point of a whole life. But it differs from Steinbeck's counsel in one vitally important respect: it emphasizes the question of what we ourselves wish to do and to be, not what we imagine will win us the love and admiration of "the world."

The obituary of Robert McG. Thomas, who was himself a writer of obituaries, should remind us that the stories we invent about ourselves can be of limited importance. Thomas had a special gift for discovering the one revealing anecdote or detail that illuminated the dominant theme of an entire life. He could capture the essence of a whole life in a few telling moments of it. It seems doubtful that we could do this so well for ourselves. In other words, in order to lead lives that matter it is probably just as important to listen to the stories that others are telling about us as it is to imagine our own. The truth of our lives, as the proverbial saying goes, may lie "somewhere in between."

ROBERT FROST

"The Road Not Taken"

The life and work of Robert Frost (1874-1963) spanned the entire first half of the twentieth century. As we noted in the introduction to another one of his poems, "Two Tramps in Mud Time" (Chapter 2), the deceptive simplicity of much of his work has tempted many readers to offer interpretations that are superficial at best or altogether mistaken at worst. To avoid such interpretations here, it is best to begin thinking about this poem by comparing the two accounts of the "same" event that exist within the poem. We have indicated some of the differences between the two stories in the general introduction to this chapter above.

For our purposes in this chapter, we want to use the poem to help us understand the process by which we ourselves revise our own life stories. So we need to ask ourselves what kind of person the speaker is, based upon the kind of story that he tells and the way in which he tells it in lines 1-15. For example, he seems constantly to second-guess himself and his judgments. How else would you characterize him?

When the speaker imagines what he *will* be telling about the same event many years later, he offers an account interrupted by a sigh (that dash at the end of line 18). Is this a sigh of regret or resignation or fatigue? The feat that the speaker accomplishes is quite remarkable. To see how and why this is so, think of the story you would now tell about why you made a certain decision — for example, about why you chose to attend one college rather than another one. Now try to imagine how that story will be different when you tell it again "ages and ages hence." Now compare the two. What does that comparison teach you about how you expect to develop over time?

From *Collected Poems of Robert Frost* (New York: Henry Holt and Company, 1930), p. 131.

Two roads diverged in a yellow wood,
And sorry I could not travel both
And be one traveler, long I stood
And looked down one as far as I could
To where it bent in the undergrowth;   5

Then took the other, as just as fair,
And having perhaps the better claim,
Because it was grassy and wanted wear;
Though as for that the passing there
Had worn them really about the same,   10

And both that morning equally lay
In leaves no step had trodden black.
Oh, I kept the first for another day!
Yet knowing how way leads on to way,
I doubted if I should ever come back.   15

I shall be telling this with a sigh
Somewhere ages and ages hence:
Two roads diverged in a wood, and I —
I took the one less traveled by,
And that has made all the difference.   20

MARY CATHERINE BATESON

"Composing a Life Story"

Mary Catherine Bateson is a writer and anthropologist who has spent many years studying how human beings grow and change over time. One of her best-known books, *Composing a Life* (1989), is a comparative bio-

From Mary Catherine Bateson, *Willing to Learn: Passages of Personal Discovery* (Hanover, NH: Steerforth Press, 2004), pp. 66-74.

graphical study of five very different, creative women. In observing their lives and listening to their life stories, in remembering the lives of her famous parents, Gregory Bateson and Margaret Mead, and in thinking about the different ways she had thought about her own life, she came to think of life as a kind of improvisational art form. The essay below is about the importance of our imaginative ability to compose our own lives in multiple and resourceful ways. It suggests that if we become skilled in telling stories to ourselves about ourselves, we will be more likely to lead actual lives that matter, more likely to discover and maintain a constancy of purpose beneath a surface of many changes, more likely to achieve some kind of balance among our sometimes competing obligations, even more likely to learn from the generation before us and to teach the generation following. In other words, the capacity to "compose" our lives affects all of the several aspects of our identities and our life's work that we have thus far considered.

Bateson also suggests that though there is always a good deal of invention in our life compositions, there is also some discovery as well. Moreover, we do not very often invent new plot lines; we typically absorb them from our culture. When you think of the shape of your own life, do you do so in terms of one of the story lines that Bateson mentions — for example, as a conversion narrative? Finally, do we live our lives first and then retrospectively compose them, or do we first compose them and seek to live according to the plotline we have constructed or chosen from the repertoire offered to us by our culture?

There are three meanings that "composing a life," as a phrase, has to me. Two of those meanings compare living to different arts, in that I see the way people live their lives as, in itself, an artistic process. An artist takes ingredients that may seem incompatible, and organizes them into a whole that is not only workable, but finally pleasing and true, even beautiful. As you get up in the morning, as you make decisions, as you spend money, make friends, make commitments, you are creating a piece of art called: your life. The word *compose* helps me look at two aspects of that process.

Very often in the visual arts, you put together components to find a way that they fit together and balance each other in space. You make a visual composition of form and color. One thing that you do in composing a life is to put together disparate elements that need to be in some kind of balance, like a still life with tools, fruit, and musical instruments. This sense of balance is something that women have been especially aware of in recent years because they cannot solve the problem of composing the different elements of their lives simply by making them separate, as men have.

Of course, less and less are men able to compartmentalize their lives. For a long time it was possible for men to think in terms of a line between the public and the private. A man would go to the workplace, and then, at a certain point, he would switch that part of the day off and go home to a world where the atmosphere was different. He could switch gears from one aspect of his life to the other.

But it hasn't been possible for women to separate their commitments in quite the same way. It is one thing in the traditional nuclear family for the husband to go to the office and stop thinking about his family during the day because he has left his wife in charge. It is quite a different thing for both parents to go off and feel that they can completely forget what is happening with the family. Many women have the sense that the combining of different areas in their lives is a problem that is with them all the time.

What this has meant is that women have lived their lives experiencing multiple simultaneous demands from multiple directions. Increasingly men are also living that way. So thinking about how people manage this is becoming more and more important. One way to approach the situation is to think of how a painter composes a painting: by synchronously putting elements together and finding a pattern in how they fit.

But of course *compose* has another meaning in music. Music is an art in which you create something that happens *over time* that goes through various transitions. Examining your life in this way, you have to look at the change that occurs within a lifetime — discontinuities, transitions, and the growth of various sorts — and the artistic unity, like that of a symphony with very different movements, that can characterize a life.

In addition to these two meanings of composing a life — one that relates to the visual arts and the other that relates to music — I want to emphasize a third meaning, one that has to do with the ways in which you compose your own *versions* of your life. I'm referring to the stories you make about your life, the stories you tell first to yourself and then to other people, the stories you use as lenses for interpreting experience as it comes along. What I want to say is that you can play with, compose, multiple versions of a life.

There are advantages in having access to multiple versions of your life story. I am not referring to a true version versus a false version, or to one that works in a given therapeutic context as opposed to others, or to one that will sell to *People* magazine as opposed to ones that won't. I am referring to the freedom that comes not only from owning your memory and your life story but also from knowing that you make creative choices in how you look at your life.

In the postmodern environment in which we live, it is easy to say that no version is fixed, no version is completely true. I want to push beyond that awareness and encourage you to think about the creative responsibility involved in the fact that there are different ways to tell your stories. It's not that one is true and another is not true. It's a matter of emphasis and context. For example, one of the things that people do at meetings is to introduce themselves. I was at a conference recently where, in the course of two days, I introduced myself three times in different breakout groups. One person who had been there all three times came up to me and said, "You know, you said something completely different every time." Of course I did. The contexts were different.

Imagine the choices you have in saying things about yourself and about other people. These are real choices, but they are made in the presence of a set of conventions. Think of a self-introduction as a literary genre. There are things you include and things you don't. Those decisions are related to who you're talking to and where you are, as well as who you're talking about.

You can do the same with versions of your life history. For instance, most people can tell a version that emphasizes the continuities in their lives to make a single story that goes in a clear direction. But the same people can also tell their life stories as if they were following on this statement: "After lots of surprises and choices, or interruptions and disappointments, I have arrived someplace I could never have anticipated." Every one of us has a preference for one of these versions, but if we try, we can produce both. My guess is that there are a lot of people reading this who think of themselves as growing and developing and moving on smoothly. That's part of the intellectual context many of us are in. But some of us experience our lives as discontinuous, interrupted processes.

For example, one version of my life story goes like this: I already thought of myself as a writer when I was in high school, and there hasn't been a year since college that I haven't published something. Now I spend half the year writing full-time and half the year writing and teaching. Many of my students are future writers.

That's one version of me. The other version goes like this: I planned in high school to be a poet. But I gave up writing poetry in college. The only writing I did for years was academic publish-or-perish writing. When I became unemployed because of the Iranian revolution, shortly after my mother died, I dealt with unemployment by starting to write a memoir. I suddenly found that I could write nonfiction. Now I'm considering switching again and writing a novel.

Both of these are true stories. But they are very different stories. One person told me there had been so much discontinuity in her life that it wasn't hard to think of a discontinuous version, but it was painful to tell it. I think that's a problem many people have. Because our society has preferred continuous versions of stories, discontinuities seem to indicate that something is wrong with you. A discontinuous story becomes a very difficult story to claim.

I would say that the most important effect of my recent book *Composing a Life* has been to give people who feel that they've been bumped from one thing to another, with no thread of continuity, a way of positively interpreting their experience. You might be uncomfortable with your life if it has been like *The Perils of Pauline*, yet many of us have lives like that. One strategy for working with that kind of life is to make a story that *interprets change as continuity*. One of my favorites was someone who said, "My life is like surfing, with one wave coming after another." He unified his whole life with that single simile.

The choice you make affects what you can do next. Often people use the choice of emphasizing either continuity or discontinuity as a way of preparing for the next step. They interpret the present in a way that helps them construct a particular future. . . .

When I started *Composing a Life,* the issue I wanted to explore was discontinuity. Part of my interest was based on two events in my own life. One was that I had just gone through the experience of losing, in a rather painful way, a job I cared about. I had been forced to change jobs before, because of my husband changing jobs, and I had had to adapt to that situation. So what I set out to do was to look at a group of women who had been through a lot of transitions and who were able to cope with the changes. I was asking the question "How on earth does one survive this kind of interruption?"

The other circumstance that made me focus on the issue of discontinuity had to do with my experiences in Iran. At the time of the Iranian revolution, my husband and I had been living and working there for seven years. We, and a great many of our friends, had to make fresh starts; many Iranians became refugees. The way they interpreted their situation was absolutely critical to their adjustment. I could see very clearly, among them, that there were those who came into the refugee situation with a sense that they had skills and adaptive patterns they could transfer to the new situation. They were emphasizing continuity. Other people came into the refugee situation feeling that their lives had ended and they had to start from zero. You could see that the choices people made about how to interpret the continuities and discontinuities in their lives had great implications for the way they approached the future.

Much of coping with discontinuity has to do with discovering threads of continuity. You cannot adjust to change unless you can recognize some analogy between your old situation and your new situation. Without that analogy you cannot transfer learning. You cannot apply skills. If you can recognize a problem that you've solved before, in however different a guise, you have a much greater chance of solving that problem in the new situation. That recognition is critical to the transfer of learning.

It can be very difficult to recognize the ways in which one situation or event in your life is linked to others. When I was working on my memoir of my parents, *With a Daughter's Eye*, I found an example of this in my father's life. Some of you may know my father, Gregory Bateson, as a great anthropologist, a great thinker. But in the middle of his life, he went through a difficult period that lasted for some time. From year to year he didn't know whether he would have a salary, whether there would be anything to live on.

His career at that time must have seemed totally discontinuous. First he was a biologist. Then he got interested in anthropology and went to New Guinea. He made a couple of field trips that he never wrote up. Then to Bali. During World War II he wrote an analysis of propaganda films and worked in psychological warfare. Then he did a study of communication in psychotherapy. Then he worked on alcoholism and schizophrenia, and then on dolphins and octopuses. Somehow he turned into a philosopher.

One of the things that I realized while I was putting together the memoir is that only when he drew together a group of his articles — all written in very different contexts for very different audiences, with apparently different subject matter — to put them into the book called *Steps to an Ecology of Mind* did it become clear to him that he had been working on the same kind of question all his life: The continuous thread through all of his work was an interest in the relationships between ideas.

The interruptions that forced him to change his research focus were absolutely critical to pushing him up the ladder of logical types, so that ultimately he could see continuity at a very abstract level. His insight, his understanding of what he had been working on all his life, was a result of a sometimes desperate search for a continuity beyond the discontinuities. So even when I was working on the memoir, I was picking at this question of continuity and discontinuity, and examining the incredible gains that can come from reconstruing a life history by combining both interpretations.

Of course, in composing any life story, there is a considerable weight of cultural pressure. Narratives have canonical forms. One of the stories that we, as a culture, respond to is the story in which the hero's or heroine's end is contained in the beginning. . . .

One of my favorite examples is a story from the life of St. Teresa of Avila, a Counter-Reformation saint. When she was a child, part of Spain was still controlled by the Moors: part of the country was Catholic, and part was Muslim. When she was ten or so, she set out, with her younger brother, for the territory controlled by the Moors in order to be martyred and go to heaven. This becomes an appropriate story to prefigure a life of self-sacrifice and dedication to God. Many biographies and autobiographies have this pattern. . . .

Another popular form is one that we can think of as the conversion narrative. It's a simple plot. Lives that in reality have a lot of zigzags in them get reconstructed into before-and-after narratives with one major disconti-nuity. One very interesting example is the *Confessions of St. Augustine,* which tells the story of his life before and after his conversion to Christianity. The narrative structure requires that he depict himself before conversion as a terrible sinner, that he devalues all he did before he was converted, and that he dredge up sins to talk about so he can describe a total turnaround. . . .

A more complicated conversion story is *The Autobiography of Malcolm X.* Much of the book tells of how Malcolm X, who had been a small-time crook, was converted in prison to the Nation of Islam, Elijah Muhammad's American Black Muslim movement. About two-thirds of the book is writ-ten as a conventional conversion narrative: "I was deep in sin and then I was saved by Elijah Muhammad."

But then another big discontinuity occurs. Malcolm X becomes disillu-sioned with the corruption within the Nation of Islam and isolated by the politics around Elijah Muhammad. He separates from them, making a pil-grimage to Mecca and converting to orthodox Islam, and starts his own Muslim organization in the United States. So in this book you have the im-age of somebody who developed an interpretation of his life to support the validity of one particular message of salvation and then had to flip over into another one. It's an extraordinarily interesting and unusual story because the conversion happens not once but twice.

One very common example of the uses of the conversion story shows up in Twelve-Step programs. Twelve-Step programs essentially convey the message that if you can construe your life in such a way as to support a turnaround, we will help you construct a new life. But you have to define yourself, as St. Augustine had to define himself, as a sinner, or as Malcolm X had to define himself for his second conversion, as having been duped. An emphasis on a turnaround becomes the condition for moving on to the next stage.

The conversion narrative can be a very empowering way of telling your story, because it allows you to make a fresh start. The more continuous story, in which the end is prefigured in the beginning, is powerful in different ways. But what I want to emphasize are the advantages of choosing a particular interpretation at a particular time, and the even greater advantage of using *multiple* interpretations.

The availability of multiple interpretations of a life story is particularly important in how the generations communicate with each other. When we, as parents, talk to our children about our lives, there is a great temptation to edit out the discontinuities, to reshape our histories so that they look more coherent than they are. But when we tell stories to our children with the zig-zags edited out, it causes problems for many of those children. A lot of young people have great difficulty committing themselves to a relationship or to a career because of the feeling that once they do, they're trapped for a long, long time. They feel they've got to get on the right "track" because, after all, this is a long and terrifying commitment. I think it is very liberating for college students when an older person says to them, "Your first job after college need not be the beginning of an ascending curve that's going to take you through your life. It can be a zigzag. You might be doing something different in five years." That's something young people need to hear: that the continuous story, where the whole of a person's life is prefigured very early on, is often a cultural creation, not a reflection of life as it is really lived.

The ways in which we interpret our life stories have a great effect on how our children come to define their own identities. An example of this occurred in my own life when my daughter was about to become a teenager. She said to me, "Gee, Mom, it must be awfully hard on you and Daddy that I'm not interested in any of the things you're interested in." I said, "What do you mean?" She said, "Well, you're professors. You write books about social science. I'm an actress. I care about theater." I said a secret prayer because it was clearly a very tricky moment. Maybe she needed to believe in that discontinuity. Maybe it was worrying her and she needed to get away from that discontinuity.

But what I said to her was "Well, to be a social scientist, to be an anthropologist, you have to be a good observer of human behavior. You have to try and understand how people think and why they behave as they do. It strikes me that that's pretty important for a good actor." She has been telling that story ever since because it gave her permission to pursue what she deeply wanted to pursue without feeling she was betraying me and her father. But it also gave her permission to use anything she might pick up from us by giving her a way of construing the cross-generational relationship as a continuity. . . .

***

WENDELL BERRY

Jayber Crow

Wendell Berry is a poet, essayist, and novelist who lives on a small, working farm in Kentucky. In the short passage below from his novel *Jayber Crow*, which is about the life of a barber in a Kentucky hamlet, Berry raises important questions about the relationship between our actual lives and the stories we might be tempted to tell ourselves about them. Bateson makes a powerful case for our lives as improvisational art forms, but to what extent should we be free to improvise? Every life story omits some details and exaggerates others, selects some incidents as crucial and tries to diminish the importance of embarrassing moments. But to what extent should we be constrained by faithfulness to the record?

Here, Jayber Crow finds himself wishing that his life had been emplotted one way rather than another. But he seems constrained by what he actually did or failed to do, by what actually happened to him and by what he made of those events at the time, to tell his life's story in a way that is perhaps less coherent and admirable than he would hope. Bateson shows us how important it is to be resourceful in formulating our life's stories. To what extent is it also important that we be truthful? What does "truthfulness" mean in the context of our autobiographies?

Note that the first sentences of the selection refer to Dante's *Divine Comedy*, which begins in the Dark Wood of Error, and John Bunyan's *Pilgrim's Progress*, which follows the King's Highway.

From Wendell Berry, *Jayber Crow* (Washington, DC: Counterpoint, 2000), p. 133.

If you could do it, I suppose, it would be a good idea to live your life in a straight line — starting, say, in the Dark Wood of Error, and proceeding by logical steps through Hell and Purgatory and into Heaven. Or you could take the King's Highway past appropriately named dangers, toils, and snares, and finally cross the River of Death and enter the Celestial City. But that is not the way I have done it, so far. I am a pilgrim, but my pilgrimage has been wandering and unmarked. Often what has looked like a straight line to me has been a circle or a doubling back. I have been in the Dark Wood of Error any number of times. I have known something of Hell, Purgatory, and Heaven, but not always in that order. The names of many snares and dangers have been made known to me, but I have seen them only in looking back. Often I have not known where I was going until I was already there. I have had my share of desires and goals, but my life has come to me or I have gone to it mainly by way of mistakes and surprises. Often I have received better than I have deserved. Often my fairest hopes have rested on bad mistakes. I am an ignorant pilgrim, crossing a dark valley. And yet for a long time, looking back, I have been unable to shake off the feeling that I have been led — make of that what you will.

JOHN STEINBECK

East of Eden

By contrast to Bateson, who argues that there are many narrative forms available to us when we compose our own lives, the narrator of John Steinbeck's (1902-1968) novel *East of Eden* claims that there "is one story in the world, and only one." That story is a melodrama, the unfolding struggle between good and evil. And the narrator believes that our lives take on substance, meaning, and significance only in terms of the world's *one* story, in which we all are necessarily actors.

In the midst of this argument, the narrator offers us this rather star-

---

From John Steinbeck, *East of Eden* (New York: The Viking Press, 1952), pp. 413-415.

tling piece of advice about how we should lead our lives: "if you or I must choose between two courses of thought or action, we should remember our dying and try so to live that our death brings no pleasure to the world." The cogency of the advice would seem to depend in part on what the narrator means by "the world," a realm that in some vocabularies refers to those who are wicked or self-indulgent. What do you think the narrator means by the term? He has, after all, divided people into those who have led good lives on the whole and those who have led evil ones. Suppose that the narrator is referring only to those who have led lives that are choice-worthy and significant when he speaks of "the world." Is his advice sound under that interpretation?

A child may ask, "What is the world's story about?" And a grown man or woman may wonder, "What way will the world go? How does it end and, while we're at it, what's the story about?"

I believe that there is one story in the world, and only one, that has frightened and inspired us, so that we live in a Pearl White serial of continuing thought and wonder. Humans are caught — in their lives, in their thoughts, in their hungers and ambitions, in their avarice and cruelty, and in their kindness and generosity too — in a net of good and evil. I think this is the only story we have and that it occurs on all levels of feeling and intelligence. Virtue and vice were warp and woof of our first consciousness, and they will be the fabric of our last, and this despite any changes we may impose on field and river and mountain, on economy and manners. There is no other story. A man, after he has brushed off the dust and chips of his life, will have left only the hard, clean questions: Was it good or was it evil? Have I done well — or ill?

Herodotus, in the Persian War, tells a story of how Croesus, the richest and most-favored king of his time, asked Solon the Athenian a leading question. He would not have asked it if he had not been worried about the answer. "Who," he asked, "is the luckiest person in the world?" He must have been eaten with doubt and hungry for reassurance. Solon told him of three lucky people in old times. And Croesus more than likely did not listen, so anxious was he about himself. And when Solon did not mention him, Croesus was forced to say, "Do you not consider me lucky?"

Solon did not hesitate in his answer. "How can I tell?" he said. "You aren't dead yet."

And this answer must have haunted Croesus dismally as his luck disappeared, and his wealth and his kingdom. And as he was being burned on a tall fire, he may have thought of it and perhaps wished he had not asked or not been answered.

And in our time, when a man dies — if he has had wealth and influence and power and all the vestments that arouse envy, and after the living take stock of the dead man's property and his eminence and works and monuments — the question is still there: Was his life good or was it evil? — which is another way of putting Croesus's question. Envies are gone, and the measuring stick is: "Was he loved or was he hated? Is his death felt as a loss or does a kind of joy come of it?"

I remember clearly the deaths of three men. One was the richest man of the century, who, having clawed his way to wealth through the souls and bodies of men, spent many years trying to buy back the love he had forfeited and by that process performed great service to the world and, perhaps, had much more than balanced the evils of his rise. I was on a ship when he died. The news was posted on the bulletin board, and nearly everyone received the news with pleasure. Several said, "Thank God that son of a bitch is dead."

Then there was a man, smart as Satan, who, lacking some perception of human dignity and knowing all too well every aspect of human weakness and wickedness, used his special knowledge to warp men, to buy men, to bribe and threaten and seduce until he found himself in a position of great power. He clothed his motives in the names of virtue, and I have wondered whether he ever knew that no gift will ever buy back a man's love when you have removed his self-love. A bribed man can only hate his briber. When this man died the nation rang with praise and, just beneath, with gladness that he was dead.

There was a third man, who perhaps made many errors in performance but whose effective life was devoted to making men brave and dignified and good in a time when they were poor and frightened and when ugly forces were loose in the world to utilize their fears. This man was hated by the few. When he died the people burst into tears in the streets and their minds wailed, "What can we do now? How can we go on without him?"

In uncertainty I am certain that underneath their topmost layers of frailty men want to be good and want to be loved. Indeed, most of their vices are attempted short cuts to love. When a man comes to die, no matter what his talents and influence and genius, if he dies unloved his life must be a failure to him and his dying a cold horror. It seems to me that if you or I must choose between two courses of thought or action, we should remember our dying and try so to live that our death brings no pleasure to the world.

We have only one story. All novels, all poetry, are built on the never-ending contest in ourselves of good and evil. And it occurs to me that evil must constantly respawn, while good, while virtue, is immortal. Vice has always a new fresh young face, while virtue is venerable as nothing else in the world is.

———

DAN McADAMS

"An American Life Story"

Personality psychologist Dan McAdams, a professor at Northwestern University, adds one very important narrative form to the cultural repertoire of stories Mary Catherine Bateson describes in her essay and from which we may choose when we seek to compose our own lives. In this essay drawn from the prologue of his recent book, *The Redemptive Self* (2005), McAdams summarizes findings that are especially pertinent to our concerns about leading lives that matter.

McAdams has spent many years studying Americans who are leading lives that matter according to almost every standard we have encountered in the other readings. They are people of good character who have "made a positive difference" in the world. And if they are Americans, they are much more disposed than others anywhere to construe their lives in redemptive terms, to cast the stories they tell themselves about themselves into a particular narrative form.

Why do you think that people of noble character who do make a difference in the world are so drawn to narratives of redemption when they talk about their lives? Does McAdams think that such an affinity is always a salutary thing? In other words, does a tendency to think of your life in redemptive terms make you a better person? Two features of redemptive narratives are an early conviction that one has been specially blessed and

---

From Dan P. McAdams, *The Redemptive Self: Stories Americans Live By* (New York: Oxford University Press, 2005).

that others have suffered. Do you think that those who have been specially blessed in fact have an obligation to serve those who have not been similarly fortunate? Why or why not?

Beginning September 11, 2001, William Langewiesche spent nine months at the site of the World Trade Center disaster. He observed and interviewed firefighters, construction workers, engineers, police officers, and paid volunteers who cleared the debris and dug through the rubble in search of survivors. "Within hours of the collapse [of the towers], as rescuers rushed in and resources were marshaled," Langewiesche later wrote, "the disaster was smothered in an *exuberant and distinctively American embrace.*" The workers were convinced that something good would arise from the carnage. "Despite the apocalyptic nature of the scene," Langewiesche suggested, "the response was unhesitant and almost childishly optimistic: *it was simply understood* that you would find survivors, and then that you would find the dead, and that this would help their families to get on with their lives, and that your resources were unlimited, and that you would work night and day to clean up the mess, and that this would allow the world's greatest city to rebuild quickly, and maybe even to make itself into something better than before."

Put differently, it was simply understood that there would be *redemption*.

An exuberant and distinctively American response, unhesitant, almost childish. The workers were convinced that the death and the destruction of September 11 would give way to new life, new growth, new power, and a new reality that, in some fundamental sense, would prove better than what came before. Their faith reflected the hopes of many American citizens — men and women who have never known a foreign attack on American soil but who feel deep in their bones that bad things, even things this bad, ultimately lead to good outcomes, that suffering is ultimately redeemed.

Maybe there *is* something childish (and even arrogant) about this response, this expectation that we will be delivered from our pain and suffering no matter what, that we will overcome in the long run, that we will rise from the depths of the present, that things will get better and that we will eventually grow and find fulfillment in the world. But I am not talking here about the naiveté of children. I am talking instead about mature men and women who, like many of the workers at the World Trade Center site, are committed to making a positive difference in the world. As unfashionable as this may seem, I am talking about *good people,* for the most part, productive and caring, socially responsible, hard-working adults who try to pay their bills and their taxes, try to provide for their families, and try to make something good out of their lives, even as they fail and get distracted along the way. I am talking about the kinds of people who support the institutions that are necessary to create and sustain what the sociologist Robert Bellah calls a "good society." These may be the kinds of people that the framers of the U.S. Constitution had in mind when they identified the ultimate authors of their document as "We the people." For the framers, we the people aimed to "form a more perfect union, establish justice, insure domestic tranquility, provide for the common defense, promote the general welfare, and secure the blessings of liberty to ourselves and our posterity."

It is with *good people* that I begin this book. Who are the good people? I am no moral philosopher, so I do not have a rigorous definition to give you. Let me, instead, take a cue from the U.S. Constitution, and from an eminent psychologist, the late Erik H. Erikson, who wrote provocatively about psychological health, adaptation, and goodness across the human lifespan. The Constitution suggests that we the people should strive to assure justice, peace, security, and freedom not just for us today — but for *our posterity,* our children and our children's children. The good society must work to promote the well-being of future generations. Erikson claimed that good *people* — especially in their middle-adult years — should do the same. Erikson had a word for this. He called it *generativity.*

Generativity is the adult's concern for and commitment to promoting the welfare and development of future generations. The most obvious and natural expression of generativity is the care that parents provide for their children. But generativity can be expressed in many other ways, too, including teaching, mentoring, leadership, and even citizenship. Generative adults seek to give something back to society. They work to make their world a better place, not just for themselves but for future generations, as well. They try to take the long view. Whether they consciously think about it this way or not, generative adults work for the good of posterity. A good society depends on the generative efforts of adults. For this reason (among others), Erikson believed that generativity was more than simply a psychological standard for adult mental health. He also saw it as the prime *virtue* of adulthood.

Different people have different virtues. Some people are more honest than others. Some may be more courageous, faithful, or self-disciplined. And so it is with generativity, as Erikson well knew. Most adults are moderately generative on the average, focusing most of their generative inclinations on their families. A few adults show virtually no generativity in their lives. And some, on the other end of the spectrum, are extraordinarily generative in many different ways. Think of them as generativity superstars.

For many years now, I have been studying the superstars. Who are the especially generative people in our society? What are their lives like? In the summer of 2000, I was presenting some of this research at a scientific conference in the Netherlands when I received a comment from a woman in the audience that eventually gave birth to this book. The main point of my talk was that highly generative adults tend to tell a certain kind of *story* about their lives, a story that emphasizes the themes of suffering, *redemption,* and personal destiny. The comment I received went something like this: "Professor McAdams, this is very interesting, but these life stories you describe, they seem so, well, *American.*" Initially, I heard this as a criticism of the work. After all, I had been assuming that my findings applied to very generative adults *in general,* regardless of their backgrounds. To say the life stories I described all sounded very "American" was to suggest that my research findings were too limited, that they were not "generalizable," as we social scientists often say.

After thinking longer about the woman's comment, however, I came to realize two things. First, she was probably right, at least in part. My results about Americans might not generalize completely to other societies. Second, I think I like the fact that she may have been right. Her comment suggests an important insight: The life stories of highly generative American adults may reveal as much about American society and culture as they do about the generative adults themselves. It is as if these well-meaning American people who dedicate their lives to promoting the well-being of the next generation are *walking embodiments of some of the most cherished (and contested) ideas in our American heritage.* Yet they probably don't even know it.

What is the story these adults tell? Everybody has a unique life story to tell. But if you listen to many life stories, as I and my students have over the past 20 years, you begin to recognize some common patterns. The pattern that I will focus on in this book is the one that tends to distinguish the life stories told by highly generative American adults from those told by less generative American adults. Research findings suggest that highly generative American adults are statistically more likely than their less generative counterparts to make sense of their own lives through an idealized story script that emphasizes, among other themes, the power of human redemption. In the most general sense, redemption is *a deliverance from suffering to a better world.* Religious conceptions of redemption imagine it as a divine intervention or sacred process, and the better world may mean heaven, a state of grace, or some other transcendent status. The general idea of redemption can be found in all of the world's major religions and many cultural traditions.

It is important to realize, however, that redemption carries many secular meanings that have nothing to do with religion. Everyday talk is filled with redemptive metaphors. People often speak of "putting the past behind" them in order to move away from something negative to a positive future. Adages such as "every dark cloud has a silver lining," "it's always darkest before dawn," and "no pain, no gain" suggest that suffering in life can often lead to growth or fulfillment. "When life gives you lemons, make lemonade," we are told. Try to transform the negative into some kind of positive. We all know expressions like these, and we can all probably find a few instances in our own lives when this general idea seemed to take hold. Furthermore, we are encouraged to think about our lives in redemptive terms. As just one example, many high-school counselors in the United States today strongly urge their college-bound seniors to write personal essays that document the ways they have overcome adversity. College admissions officers appear to value these redemptive accounts quite highly, sometimes even assigning extra points to an applicant's file for especially compelling stories of resilience, recovery, defying the odds, and the like.

When they take stock of their own lives, highly generative American adults tend to *narrate* them around the theme of redemption. They are more likely than the rest of us to see redemptive patterns in their lives. Most everybody can find some kind of redemption in their life stories. But highly generative American adults tend to see more of it and to attribute more significance or meaning to the redemptive scenes and situations they do recall. They also expect more redemptive scenes for the future. In the prototypical life story told by the highly generative American adult, the protagonist encounters many setbacks and experiences a great deal of pain in life, but over time these negative scenes lead to especially positive outcomes, outcomes that might not have occurred had the suffering never happened in the first place. Thus, redemption helps to move the life story forward.

Let me say more about this story.

How does the story begin? In the beginning is a blessing, a special advantage, a sense of personal destiny. Highly generative adults are much more likely than less generative adults to emphasize in their autobiographies ways in which they felt lucky or *advantaged* early on in life. The advantage they think they enjoyed is typically not economic or material. Perhaps, instead, mom liked them the best. Perhaps, they had a special skill. Perhaps, they had a teacher or an uncle who sought them out for special treatment. Whatever, they believe they were fortunate in some way. At the same time, the story suggests, certain *other* characters were *not* fortunate. Highly generative adults are much more likely than less generative adults to recall *scenes in early life in which they witnessed the suffering or disadvantage of other people.* "I remember the retarded kid on our street, how the boys used to pick on him," one highly generative adult recalls. "Our church bus was re-routed so it wouldn't pick up the black kids," recalls another, as he remembers how it dawned on him as a young white boy that all people in American society are not treated equally.

The implicit message in the beginning of the story is clear: *I am blessed; others suffer.* This stark contrast sets up a moral challenge: Because I (the main character in the story) am advantaged in some way, I have the opportunity/responsibility to help improve the lives of those who may not be so blessed. I may even feel that I am *called* to do this, that it is my special fate or personal destiny to be of service to others. "I have some basic gifts," says one highly generative adult, "and I think the purpose of life is to take the gifts you're given and leave the world better for them." Asked what life's most important value is, another says: "Finding your own personal gift and utilizing it the best you can for your personal welfare and for the welfare of everybody else."

How does the plot develop? Early on (typically in adolescence), the protagonist in this story takes in (or develops) a system of beliefs, often rooted in a religious tradition, which serves to guide him or her for the rest of the story. Although the protagonist will go through many changes as the plot unfolds over the life course, the core of this belief system is not likely to change much at all. It is a steadfast foundation for the person's identity. What will change, though, are motivations — the wants and needs and strivings of the story's main character. During certain chapters of my life story, I may want to change the world in a powerful and positive way. At other times, I may want to be loved and cherished by others. Sometimes I want to stand out as different; after all, I am special, blessed. At other times, I want to be accepted as an equal in a community of caring people. I want to be strong, but I want to be loved. I want to be free, but I want to belong. The tension between individual self-expression and human belongingness is arguably a universal feature of social life. But the tension is especially pronounced in the life stories of highly generative American adults. On the one hand, they have clear and compelling belief systems that have convinced them that they know what is right, what is true in life. On the other hand, they do not always know what they want, or they may want things that seem mutually incompatible — like power and love, perhaps, or freedom and community.

Guided by a clear personal belief system and striving to attain goals that express both power and love, the main character in this story encounters expected and unexpected obstacles and challenges as the plot unfolds. The protagonist will encounter friends and enemies, heroes and villains. There will be scenes of joy, excitement, sadness, fear, shame, and most any other emotion that may be imagined. But a recurrent pattern will hold: Negative emotional scenes will often lead directly to positive outcomes. Suffering will consistently be redeemed. Redemptive sequences will help to move the plot forward and ultimately help give the story its *progressive* form. As one generative adult puts it, "When dealing with anything negative, I was taught to swing the door and make something positive out of it." Another highly generative adult sees his life mission as "confounding ignorance with good works." Many scenes in his life story begin with an expression of ignorance, but this gives way (is redeemed) by a positive action that proves to enlighten others. Despite many setbacks, things get better over time in these kinds of life stories. There is growth and improvement.

How does the story end? The stories people tell about their own lives are works in progress. Still, people can imagine what the future will hold and how, ultimately, things may or may not work out in the end. Highly generative adults see continued progress and growth in the story, even if they anticipate daunting obstacles ahead and even if they are pessimistic about the overall future of the world. They see their contributions to others as having enduring impact, even if only in small ways. Through their children often, but often also through many other projects and endeavors in their lives, they see themselves as leaving a legacy for the future. The imagery of growth and progress is very common in these stories. The protagonist gives birth to many things and people, cares for them and provides for their well-being, and eventually lets them go so that they can move forward in life with the generative blessings they have received. One highly generative adult put it this way: "When I die, I guess the chemicals in my body, well, they'll go to fertilize some plants, you know, some ears of corn, and the good deeds I do will live through my children and through the people I love."

In sum, then, here is the general script of the life story I have described: *I learn in childhood that I have a special gift. At the same time, I see (and am moved by) suffering and injustice in my world. As a result, I come to believe that my personal destiny is to have some positive impact on others. In adolescence I internalize a belief system that sustains my commitment to improving the world. I will never abandon these core beliefs. Over the course of my adult life, I struggle to reconcile my strong needs for power and independence with my equally strong needs for love and community. Bad things happen to me, but often good outcomes follow. My suffering is usually redeemed, as I continue to progress, to learn, to improve. Looking to the future, I expect the things I have generated will continue to grow and flourish, even in a dangerous world.*

What does this life story mean? Why does this kind of story appear so often in the lives of very generative American adults? What is so great about this story? *And what is wrong with it?* My central goal in this book is to explore the psychological and cultural meaning of redemptive stories in American lives. The great American novelist Robert Penn Warren has written that to be an American is not a matter of blood or birth; it is a matter of an idea. That idea is large and "contains multitudes," as Walt Whitman said, but at the heart of it are stories that Americans have traditionally told about themselves and about their nation. Highly generative American adults tell life stories that unconsciously rework deep and vexing issues in our cultural heritage. These same stories, furthermore, address thorny new problems we face as Americans living at the dawn of the 21st century. As I move back and forth in this book between psychology and American culture, I will affirm and defend six key points. Taken together, these six points make up my book's essential argument:

1. Generativity is the central psychological and moral challenge adults face, especially in their 30s, 40s, and 50s.
2. Generative adults tend to see their lives as redemptive stories that emphasize related themes such as early advantage, the suffering of others, moral clarity, the conflict between power and love, and leaving a legacy of growth.
3. Redemptive life stories promote psychological health and maturity, and they provide narrative guidelines for living a good life.
4. Redemptive life stories reflect and rework such quintessentially American ideas as *manifest destiny, the chosen people,* and the ambivalence Americans have traditionally felt about our most cherished of all values — *freedom.* Expressions of these themes can be found not only in the life stories of highly generative American adults but in a wide range of American cultural texts, from Puritan conversion stories and the Gettysburg Address to contemporary self-help books and *People* magazine.
5. Redemptive life stories in America are profoundly shaped by two American peculiarities: (a) the fact that this is one of the most *religious* industrialized societies in the world and (b) that this society has been torn asunder, from its inception, by the issue of *race*. Some of the most redemptive texts in the American tradition may be found in the African-American heritage and in the life stories of highly generative black adults.
6. For all their psychological and moral strength, redemptive life stories sometimes fail, and they may reveal dangerous shortcomings and blind spots in Americans' understandings of themselves and the world. After all, is it not presumptuous to expect deliverance from all suffering? Is it

not an affront to those who have suffered the greatest calamities and heartaches to expect, even to suggest, that things will work out nice and happy in the end? In this sense, there may indeed be something "almost childish" about the redemptive self — something a bit too naïve and Pollyanna for a world where tragedy often seems more common and compelling than redemption. And is it not arrogant to imagine one's life as the full manifestation of an inner destiny? You can sometimes detect an entitled, "true believer" quality in the life stories of many highly generative American adults — an assuredness regarding the goodness and the power of the individual self that may seem off-putting and can sometimes prove destructive. We will see, then, that redemptive narratives sometimes condone and reinforce social isolation and a kind of psychological *American exceptionalism*. Redemptive narratives may support, intentionally or unconsciously, a naïve optimism about the world, excessive moral fervor, and self-righteous aggression, even war, in the service of self-centered ends. The rhetoric of redemption makes it easy for Americans to see ourselves as superior to the rest of the world, and to identify our enemies as the axis of evil. While redemptive life narratives affirm hope and human progress, therefore, we must also face up to the dark side of American redemption.

*   *   *

Almost 20 years ago, the sociologist Robert Bellah and his colleagues published an influential book, *Habits of the Heart*, that examined the ways Americans have traditionally talked about their strivings for personal fulfillment and interpersonal community. In the 18th and 19th centuries, figures like Thomas Jefferson and Abraham Lincoln personified uniquely American *character types*, the authors argued, who inspired Americans to live good lives. These types no longer work for us, however. *Habits of the Heart* showed that Americans today have a very difficult time finding an appropriate language to express desires for living together in harmony, helping each other, and committing themselves to meaningful, long-term life projects beyond the self. It is not so much that we are selfish people as we are incapable of expressing the desires we do have to go beyond self-interest. Bellah and his colleagues challenged their readers to imagine new character types who might inspire future generations of Americans to live caring and productive lives.

From a psychological standpoint, the authors of *Habits of the Heart* may have been asking for too much. Research in personality and developmental psychology suggests that most people are too complex to fit into the kind of neat character types that Bellah described. Human lives are messy and filled with contradictions. Each person shows a wide range of different traits; different traits get expressed in different situations; people change in important ways over time. Nonetheless, Bellah and his colleagues were definitely on to something important in focusing so much attention on how Americans *talk* about their lives. When people talk about their lives, *they tell stories.* It is through stories that we often learn the greatest lessons for our lives — lessons about success and failure, good and evil, what makes a life worth living, what makes a society good. It is through stories, furthermore, that we define who we are. Stories provide us with our identities.

Highly generative American adults may not fit neatly into any single character type, but they do seem to have a *type of story* to tell about life. The redemptive stories that highly generative American adults tell recapture some of the ideas espoused in moral character types from long ago, but they also speak in the very contemporary language of 21st-century America. Redemptive stories provide images, scenes, plots, and themes that we might wish to borrow and rework into our own lives. I will never be just like my most admired hero from history or the movies, or my most beloved high school coach. But I may borrow pieces of their *stories* and work them into my own. . . .

My research is part of an emerging movement in the social sciences called the *narrative study of lives.* The central idea in this movement is that human lives are cultural texts that can be interpreted as stories. People create stories to make sense of their lives. These evolving stories — or *narrative identities* — provide our lives with some semblance of meaning, unity, and purpose. Along with our dispositional traits and our motives and goals, internalized life stories make up important aspects of our personality. Our stories are implicated in determining what we do and how we make sense of what we do. As a *narrative psychologist,* I systematically analyze the texts of people's life stories to obtain a better understanding of both the people who tell the stories and the culture within which those stories (and those people) are born. "We tell ourselves stories in order to live," writes the American essayist Joan Didion. By examining life stories, we may learn more about how Americans live, and how we might live better.

MICHAEL T. KAUFMAN

"Robert McG. Thomas, 60, Chronicler of Unsung Lives"

The reading below is most unusual; it is an obituary of a writer of obituaries. As such, it enables us to witness, on two levels at once, the processes by which others make sense of human lives. The value, we might even say the virtue, of stories that we tell about ourselves during our lifetimes derives in part from their serviceability. How well do these stories enable us to lead lives that matter, to feel that we possess a solid sense of identity and purpose? But this cannot be the virtue of a good obituary, since the subject of the obituary is no longer living. It would seem that the virtue of a good obituary is its "truthfulness," its capacity to be faithful to the actual life of its subject.

But perhaps this contrast between the serviceability of the life's story told by the subject and the truthfulness of the obituary written about the subject is misleading. We might wonder whom the obituary writer is serving: the dead subject or the living survivors? Or is the obituary writer serving the memory of the dead for the sake of posterity? If the obituary writer serves primarily the living, why is truthfulness important?

Robert McG. Thomas Jr., a reporter for *The New York Times* who extended the possibilities of the conventional obituary form, shaking the dust from one of the most neglected areas of daily journalism, died on Thursday at his family's summer home in Rehoboth Beach, Del. He was 60 and also had a home in Manhattan.

The cause was abdominal cancer, said his wife, Joan.

Mr. Thomas began writing obituaries full time in 1995 after serving as a police reporter, a rewrite man, a society news reporter and a sports writer. He developed a fresh approach to the genre, looking for telling details to il-

From *The New York Times*, January 8, 2000.

luminate lives that might otherwise have been overlooked or under-reported.

Mr. Thomas saw himself as the sympathetic stranger at the wake listening to the friends and survivors of the deceased, alert for the moment when one of them would tell a memorable tale that could never have made its way into *Who's Who* or a resume but that just happened to define a life.

In 1995, when *The Times* proposed him for a Pulitzer Prize in the category of spot news, the nomination began: "Every week, readers write to *The New York Times* to say they were moved to tears or laughter by an obituary of someone they hadn't known until that morning's paper. Invariably, the obituary is the work of Robert McG. Thomas Jr., who hadn't known the subject, either, until the assignment landed on his desk a few hours before deadline."

The gallery of portraits that Mr. Thomas compiled covered an impressive range. Among them were Howard C. Fox, "the Chicago clothier and sometime big-band trumpeter who claimed credit for creating and naming the zoot suit with the reet pleat, the reave sleeve, the ripe stripe, the stuff cuff and the drape shape that was the stage rage during the boogie-woogie rhyme time of the early 1940's," and Russell Colley, a mechanical engineer who became "the Calvin Klein of space" and was known to a generation of astronauts as the "father of the space suit." There were Rose Hamburger, a 105-year-old racing handicapper; Marion Tinsley, a checker champion unbeaten by man or machine, and a vivacious woman who started out as a showgirl and ended up a princess ("Honeychile Wilder is dead, and if the '21' Club is not in actual mourning, it is because the venerable former speakeasy on West 52nd Street was closed for vacation last week when word got around that one of its most memorable former patrons had died on Aug. 11 at Memorial Sloan-Kettering Cancer Center").

Mr. Thomas, a tall man with wavy hair who spoke in a voice soft with traces of his native Tennessee, was an extremely gregarious and social man. Last week he officiated at the annual New Year's Eve party he first started giving at the family home in Shelbyville 32 years ago. About 5 percent of the town's 12,000 people attended, and Mr. Thomas, wearing a blue silk shirt with embroidered sun and moon that he bought for the occasion, cheered his guests and the new century. As in past years, he expressed hopes that the fireworks he had ordered would not set fire to the Presbyterian church across the road.

He was fond of writing about people who became legendary as a result of a single exploit, like Douglas Corrigan, who took off from New York in a tiny overloaded plane bound for California (he said) in 1938 and landed in Dublin some 28 hours later. He became an instant hero, forever to be known as Wrong Way Corrigan, but in his obituary, Mr. Thomas went beyond recapitulation to suggest that Mr. Corrigan was more cunning than befuddled. He wrote:

"Although he continued to claim with a more or less straight face that he had simply made a wrong turn and been led astray by a faulty compass, the story was far from convincing, especially to the American aviation authorities who had rejected his repeated requests to make just such a flight because his modified 1929 Curtiss-Robin monoplane was judged unworthy."

In a similar vein, he wrote of Johnny Sylvester, who died in 1990, 64 years after he came to fame as a bedridden boy who inspired Babe Ruth. Here is how Mr. Thomas began his obituary, which was included in "The Last Word: The New York Times Book of Obituaries and Farewells" (William Morrow): "There are those who will tell you that little Johnny Sylvester was never that sick and certainly not dying. They will tell you that Babe Ruth never promised to hit a home run for him in Game 4 of the 1926 World Series, and that the three home runs that the Babe did hit in that game in no way saved the 11-year-old youngster's life.

"Any representations to the contrary, these people will tell you, were simply embellishments of a trivial incident by an oversentimental press in a hypersentimental age.

"Such people are known as cynics."

There was something mythic, too, about Sylvia Weinberger, Mr. Thomas wrote, "who used a sprinkling of matzoh meal, a pinch of salt and a dollop of schmaltzmanship to turn chopped liver into a commercial success."

Robert McGill Thomas Jr. was born and grew up in Shelbyville, Tenn., where chopped liver is rare and schmaltz is not part of the vernacular. He spent his 15th year cheering for a distant relative, Senator Estes Kefauver, as Kefauver ran for vice president on the Democratic ticket with Adlai E. Stevenson. Three years later Mr. Thomas went to Yale, where he worked on the student newspaper and flunked out as a result of a decision, he said, "to major in New York rather than anything academic."

After joining *The Times* as a copyboy in 1959, Mr. Thomas spent the next four decades in a variety of reporting assignments, often prowling police stations and working the phones in the late hours to produce fast-breaking stories. With his fondness for anomalies, Mr. Thomas might have described his own journalistic career as more circuitous than meteoric.

Always regarded as a stylish writer by his colleagues, he sometimes ran into career turbulence because of an acknowledged tendency to carry things like sentences, paragraphs, ideas and enthusiasms further than at least some editors preferred. Indeed, he went beyond acknowledging this trait to defending it. "Of course I go too far," he used to say. "But unless you go too far how are you ever going to find out how far you can go?"

All of this may explain the sympathy he showed in his obituaries of underachievers and late bloomers.

There was certainly no sense of superiority in his account of the life choice made by Steven Slepack, a man who gave up a promising career in marine biology to become Professor Bendeasy, "the man in the beribboned tuxedo jacket who delighted a generation of schoolchildren by twisting balloons into animals in Central Park." He described a character actor named Jack Weston as "the quintessential New Yorker, which is to say he was born in Cleveland and lived in Los Angeles for 18 years, hating every minute of it he wasn't actually in front of the camera."

In writing about Anton Rosenberg, a painter and jazz musician, Mr. Thomas said he "embodied the Greenwich Village hipster ideal of 1950's cool to such a laid-back degree and with such determined detachment that he never amounted to much of anything."

For some admirers, for whom Mr. Thomas's work came to be known as "McG's," a favorite was his obituary of Edward Lowe, which revealed how Mr. Lowe, a sawdust merchant from Cassopolis, Mich., found a new use for some kiln-dried granulated clay he had been selling as a sop for grease spills in industrial plants and created a million-dollar market for the product he named and marketed as Kitty Litter.

Mr. Thomas provided the antecedent action to the tale in a second paragraph that established the historical significance of Mr. Lowe's achievement: "Cats have been domesticated since ancient Egypt, but until a fateful January day in 1947, those who kept them indoors full time paid a heavy price. For all their vaunted obsession with paw-licking cleanliness, cats, whose constitutions were adapted for arid desert climes, make such an efficient use of water that they produce a highly concentrated urine that is one of the most noxious effluences of the animal kingdom. Boxes filled with sand, sawdust or wood shavings provided a measure of relief from the resulting stench, but not enough to make cats particularly welcome in discriminating homes."

One of his admirers was Joseph Epstein, the literary essayist. "I have noted an interesting general-assignment obituary writer with the somewhat overloaded name of Robert McG. Thomas Jr., who occasionally gets beyond the facts and the rigid formula of the obit to touch on — of all things to find in *The New York Times* — a deeper truth," Mr. Epstein wrote.

"Thus Thomas on one Fred Rosenstiel, 'who spent his life planting gardens to brighten the lives of his fellow New Yorkers, and to alleviate an abiding sadness in his heart. . . .' The sadness, we learn later in the obituary, derived from Mr. Rosenstiel's inability to 'forgive himself for surviving the Holocaust.' A fine touch."

In addition to his wife, Mr. Thomas is survived by their twin sons, Andrew, of Lewes, Del., and David, of Manhattan; a sister, Carey Gates Thomas Hines of Birmingham, Ala., and two grandchildren.

Epilogue

In the funeral scene early in *The Death of Ivan Ilych,* one of Ilych's associates looks at him lying in his casket. He notices the expression on the dead man's face, which showed that "what was necessary" had been "accomplished rightly": the body had been "rightly" prepared for burial by the professionals charged with that responsibility. But beneath the proprieties, "there was in that expression a reproach and a warning to the living." We readers are among the living who must reckon with the expression on Ivan Ilych's face. What, we should wonder as we read Leo Tolstoy's great story, do Ilych's life and Ilych's death say to us about what it means to live a life that matters?

Answering this question carefully will require us to revisit in a serious and enlightening way most of the issues raised in this anthology. *Leading Lives That Matter* has demonstrated time and time again that the question of what it means to lead a significant and choice-worthy life needs to be explored from many vantage points within thickly described contexts. We learned in Part I that people in our society have different ways of speaking and thinking about what makes for a life that matters. The chapters in Part II then provided a variety of readings about several of the concerns that are part of the larger inquiry into what a significant and meaningful life might look like, including especially the complicated relationship between what we do to earn a living and who we are as human beings. Often, we found that we made better progress in this investigation when we focused upon particular characters in well-defined situations, such as the young Albert Schweitzer as he was deciding to become a jungle doctor or the singer Thea Kronborg, the character in Willa Cather's novel who was trying to figure out whether she should continue her musical career. When we examined and compared short sketches of whole lives — obituaries, eulogies, and biographical essays — we found that we were able to focus and clarify our own thinking about how and why we ourselves might choose one kind of life over another one.

More often than not, however, we wanted to know more about a particular life before we were prepared to pass judgment upon it. What options did the person really have available to her? What was the person like in all areas of life, not just the one portrayed? What really motivated someone to act as he did? What kinds of advice was he receiving? What support did he receive from family and friends? What were the social or religious norms that had shaped him? Thanks to the genius of Leo Tolstoy, we can have the answers to all of these questions and more in the case of Ivan Ilych, if we read his story closely. We can take the measure of his life both as he lived it and as he interpreted it retrospectively just before his death. And though the novel is quite short by comparison to the ones for which Tolstoy is best known, *War and Peace* (1865-1869) and *Anna Karenina* (1873-1877), we will grow to feel as we read that we have access to Ilych's entire life, that nothing that we need to understand this man, his living, and his dying has been omitted.

Curiously, the novel both begins and ends with the death of Ivan Ilych. Rather, to be more precise, the novel begins with a funeral notice and a subsequent dramatization of how Ilych's family and friends respond to his death, and it closes with the death itself, dramatizing how Ivan Ilych finally responds to his own dying. By beginning with the funeral, Tolstoy allows us to examine Ilych's society before we meet Ilych himself. This enables us to determine how much Ilych was himself the product of that society, how much his own character, aspirations, and values were those of his family, his friends, and his professional associates. *Leading Lives That Matter* has been organized in a similar way, attending first to the ways in which various voices within our own culture think and speak about matters of life and death before turning to the examination of the lives of particular people. Readers should therefore be especially attentive in the first part of the novel to what the several characters most value about their own lives and Ilych's, to how they think and speak about what matters in a human life.

The second and third parts of the novel tell the story of Ivan Ilych's life within the two domains that have most often occupied us in this anthology — work and family. From the very beginning, the narrator characterizes Ilych as "intelligent, polished, lively, and agreeable" and soon after as "capable, cheerful, good-natured, and sociable." These attributes certainly seem admirable, but we might wonder about the differences between them and the adjectives that Aristotle would have used to describe a human being of good character — wise, temperate, just, courageous, and generous. We should consider Ilych in his two primary settings and ask ourselves what kind of a lawyer and judge, and what kind of a husband and father, he was. How did he understand the relationship between love and work, or between home and the office? One way to study this relationship would be to think about how Ilych went about purchasing and furnishing his home. We must wonder, too, about which was more important and significant to him, professional ambition or familial intimacy. Consider, for example, that the narrator tells us about the death of one of his children almost in passing, yet Ilych's "hardest year" involved a professional setback, not a personal loss.

The fourth part of the novel begins with the onset of Ilych's illness and then traces the progress of his reaction to it. At first, he seems to deal with his disease in the same manner that he has dealt with the rest of his "life." But a subtle process of discovery and reversal begins to take place. For example, when he becomes a patient, the ministrations and the demeanor of the doctors remind him of his own behavior toward those who have come before him on the bench. Indeed, the nature of professional work constitutes one of the minor themes of the novel, giving us a chance to review some of the questions we considered regarding the relationship between what we do for a living and who we are. Does Ilych's story suggest that Russell Muirhead was right? Has Ilych's work formed his character or at least reinforced some aspects of his personality while diminishing others? And if so, has this process ennobled him? Ilych sometimes seems to live out scrupulously the kind of separation between work and friendship, between the professional and the personal, that Gilbert Meilaender partially espoused in Chapter 2. Does the narrator present this separation favorably or unfavorably? Does Ilych himself admire it in his own doctors?

Ilych grows to regard one person in the story with larger and larger measures of gratitude, admiration, and affection: the butler's young assistant, Gerasim. As a way of thinking again about what a vocation might be by comparison to a job, we might compare the various professionals in the book to Gerasim and ponder the differences between the way the doctors and lawyers work and the way Gerasim works. Gerasim, in the judgment of the narrator and in the judgment of Ivan Ilych, seems to be living rightly and truly. But exactly what is it about his character, the manner in which he carries out his tasks, and the nature of his relationship to Ilych that makes Gerasim a positive example of what it means to live a human life worthy of choice and admiration? The people around him are certainly better educated, more "successful," and more solidly established in the world. What does Gerasim know that they do not?

From the beginning of the fifth section of the novel through most of the rest of the story, Ivan Ilych's growing conviction that he is dying leads him to ask these very questions. And he then begins, over and over again, to review and revision his own life and to direct similar questions to himself. Soon he is tormented by them. "Maybe I did not live as I ought to have done," it suddenly occurs to him. "But how could that be, when I did everything properly?" This question is part of a dialogue that goes on within Ivan Ilych almost to the point of his death. One of the voices is clearly his own, but we should ask ourselves where the other one comes from. And we should wonder especially about what Ilych lacked that Gerasim had.

On what basis does Ivan Ilych come to believe that his life has been a failure? At times he seems to speak in the vocabulary of authenticity. He says he lived a "false life" as opposed to a "true one." His most pleasant memories, his *only* pleasant memories, seem to be those of his childhood. And he seems to resemble exactly the kind of people who Charles Taylor says have "missed the point of their lives" (Part I). At other times, one of the voices within him seems to speak the vocabulary of virtue. He seems to believe that he failed to live "rightly" according to certain standards and in accordance with certain virtues. At still other times, he seems to think in the vocabulary of vocation. Like Dietrich Bonhoeffer, he comes to realize that he should have challenged the socially prescribed boundaries of his duties as a lawyer and judge. Having objectified death as an "*It*" that he cannot escape, he seems at times also to be looking for another "it," the one thing that would have given his life significance and substance. But what was it? This is his question, as it remains ours.

No one can read the ending of this story without wondering whether and how it is a credible "narrative of redemption," to use Dan McAdams's phrase from Chapter 7. Can a life that has been almost entirely "false" or "wrong" or "unreal" be redeemed by a certain kind of death? If so, how? Answers to these questions will depend upon how we regard some of Ilych's last feelings and acts toward his wife and young son. They will depend as well on how we interpret his seeming "denial of death" at the end, compared to his earlier efforts to deny It. They will depend most importantly upon what exactly about his life we think required "redemption." Was it something missing that needed to be acquired, something lost that needed to be restored, or something sinful that needed to be forgiven? And what of death itself? Was death something that happened to Ilych, or was it the last act of his life?

Epilogue

The Death of Ivan Ilych was the first piece of fiction that Tolstoy wrote after his conversion to a rather idiosyncratic form of Christianity. He had himself been rather dissolute and self-indulgent in his early life, and he had for a time been convinced that human life and destiny were totally determined by impersonal historical forces. Most critics have argued that the power of *The Death of Ivan Ilych* derives in part from tensions within the story between Tolstoy's Christian and non-Christian self. Whatever the case may be, Tolstoy was in many ways very much like his exact contemporary, William James, and like the other great figure featured in the prologue to this anthology, Albert Schweitzer. (Indeed, both James and Schweitzer mention Tolstoy in the selections included in the Prologue.) These three all belonged a century ago, as most of us do today, to several sometimes conflicting traditions of human thought, religious as well as secular.

For Tolstoy, some of these conflicts were at one and the same time a source of terrible agony and wonderful genius. As one of the most astute students of his life and work, Isaiah Berlin, has written, Tolstoy "had the eyes of a fox and the heart of a hedgehog." Like a fox, he saw the many and various and irreconcilable ways of living in the world, the endlessly diverse ways that human beings have chosen to lead lives of substance and significance. With artistic skill unmatched among novelists, he faithfully dramatized these many ways to truth. But like a hedgehog, he longed his whole life for *one* truth that would unify human experience and that might provide a clear and compelling answer for everyone about how they should live. His torment came from the fact that his gifts and his longings were often deeply at odds. His vocation was to represent in nearly inexhaustible detail many lives in such a way that his readers could gain greater clarity about the issues that mattered so deeply to him. The same spirit and purpose have guided this anthology, so it is altogether fitting that it should end with a work by the great Russian master.

LEO TOLSTOY

The Death of Ivan Ilych

i

During an interval in the Melvinski trial in the large building of the Law Courts, the members and public prosecutor met in Ivan Egorovich Shebek's private room, where the conversation turned on the celebrated Krasovski case. Fëdor Vasilievich warmly maintained that it was not subject to their jurisdiction, Ivan Egorovich maintained the contrary, while Peter Ivanovich, not having entered into the discussion at the start, took no part in it but looked through the *Gazette* which had just been handed in.

"Gentlemen," he said, "Ivan Ilych has died!"

"You don't say so!"

"Here, read it yourself," replied Peter Ivanovich, handing Fëdor Vasilievich the paper still damp from the press. Surrounded by a black border were the words: "Praskovya Fëdorovna Golovina, with profound sorrow, informs relatives and friends of the demise of her beloved husband Ivan Ilych Golovin, Member of the Court of Justice, which occurred on February the 4th of this year 1882. The funeral will take place on Friday at one o'clock in the afternoon."

Ivan Ilych had been a colleague of the gentlemen present and was liked by them all. He had been ill for some weeks with an illness said to be incurable. His post had been kept open for him, but there had been conjectures that in case of his death Alexeev might receive his appointment, and that either Vinnikov or Shtabel would succeed Alexeev. So on receiving the news

From *The Death of Ivan Ilych and Other Stories*, trans. Aylmer Maude (New York: Signet Classic, 2003), pp. 93-152.

of Ivan Ilych's death the first thought of each of the gentlemen in that private room was of the changes and promotions it might occasion among themselves or their acquaintances.

"I shall be sure to get Shtabel's place or Vinnikov's," thought Fëdor Vasilievich. "I was promised that long ago, and the promotion means an extra eight hundred rubles a year for me besides the allowance."

"Now I must apply for my brother-in-law's transfer from Kaluga," thought Peter Ivanovich. "My wife will be very glad, and then she won't be able to say that I never do anything for her relations."

"I thought he would never leave his bed again," said Peter Ivanovich aloud. "It's very sad."

"But what really was the matter with him?"

"The doctors couldn't say — at least they could, but each of them said something different. When last I saw him I thought he was getting better."

"And I haven't been to see him since the holidays. I always meant to go."

"Had he any property?"

"I think his wife had a little — but something quite trifling."

"We shall have to go to see her, but they live so terribly far away."

"Far away from you, you mean. Everything's far away from your place."

"You see, he never can forgive my living on the other side of the river," said Peter Ivanovich, smiling at Shebek. Then, still talking of the distances between different parts of the city, they returned to the Court.

Besides considerations as to the possible transfers and promotions likely to result from Ivan Ilych's death, the mere fact of the death of a near acquaintance aroused, as usual, in all who heard of it the complacent feeling that, "it is he who is dead and not I."

Each one thought or felt, "Well, he's dead but I'm alive!" But the more intimate of Ivan Ilych's acquaintances, his so-called friends, could not help thinking also that they would now have to fulfil the very tiresome demands of propriety by attending the funeral service and paying a visit of condolence to the widow.

Fëdor Vasilievich and Peter Ivanovich had been his nearest acquaintances. Peter Ivanovich had studied law with Ivan Ilych and had considered himself to be under obligations to him.

Having told his wife at dinner-time of Ivan Ilych's death and of his conjecture that it might be possible to get her brother transferred to their circuit, Peter Ivanovich sacrificed his usual nap, put on his evening clothes, and drove to Ivan Ilych's house.

At the entrance stood a carriage and two cabs. Leaning against the wall in the hall downstairs near the cloak-stand was a coffin-lid covered with cloth of gold, ornamented with gold cord and tassels, that had been polished up with metal powder. Two ladies in black were taking off their fur cloaks. Peter Ivanovich recognized one of them as Ivan Ilych's sister, but the other was a stranger to him. His colleague Schwartz was just coming downstairs, but on seeing Peter Ivanovich enter he stopped and winked at him, as if to say: "Ivan Ilych has made a mess of things — not like you and me."

Schwartz's face, with his Piccadilly whiskers and his slim figure in evening dress, had as usual an air of elegant solemnity which contrasted with the playfulness of his character and had a special piquancy here, or so it seemed to Peter Ivanovich.

Peter Ivanovich allowed the ladies to precede him and slowly followed them upstairs. Schwartz did not come down but remained where he was, and Peter Ivanovich understood that he wanted to arrange where they should play bridge that evening. The ladies went upstairs to the widow's room, and Schwartz with seriously compressed lips but a playful look in his eyes, indicated by a twist of his eyebrows the room to the right where the body lay.

Peter Ivanovich, like everyone else on such occasions, entered feeling uncertain what he would have to do. All he knew was that at such times it is always safe to cross oneself. But he was not quite sure whether one should make obeisances while doing so. He therefore adopted a middle course. On entering the room he began crossing himself and made a slight movement resembling a bow. At the same time, as far as the motion of his head and arm allowed, he surveyed the room. Two young men — apparently nephews, one of whom was a high-school pupil — were leaving the room, crossing themselves as they did so. An old woman was standing motionless, and a lady with strangely arched eyebrows was saying something to her in a whisper. A vigorous, resolute Church Reader, in a frock-coat, was reading something in a loud voice with an expression that precluded any contradiction. The butler's assistant, Gerasim, stepping lightly in front of Peter Ivanovich, was strewing something on the floor. Noticing this, Peter Ivanovich was immediately aware of a faint odour of a decomposing body.

The last time he had called on Ivan Ilych, Peter Ivanovich had seen Gerasim in the study. Ivan Ilych had been particularly fond of him and he was performing the duty of a sick nurse.

Peter Ivanovich continued to make the sign of the cross slightly inclining his head in an intermediate direction between the coffin, the Reader, and the icons on the table in a corner of the room. Afterwards, when it seemed to him that this movement of his arm in crossing himself had gone on too long, he stopped and began to look at the corpse.

The dead man lay, as dead men always lie, in a specially heavy way, his rigid limbs sunk in the soft cushions of the coffin, with the head forever bowed on the pillow. His yellow waxen brow with bald patches over his sunken temples was thrust up in the way peculiar to the dead, the protruding nose seeming to press on the upper lip. He was much changed and had grown even thinner since Peter Ivanovich had last seen him, but, as is always the case with the dead, his face was handsomer and above all more dignified than when he was alive. The expression on the face said that what was necessary had been accomplished, and accomplished rightly. Besides this there was in that expression a reproach and a warning to the living. This warning seemed to Peter Ivanovich out of place, or at least not applicable to him. He felt a certain discomfort and so he hurriedly crossed himself once more and turned and went out of the door — too hurriedly and too regardless of propriety, as he himself was aware.

Schwartz was waiting for him in the adjoining room with legs spread wide apart and both hands toying with his top-hat behind his back. The mere sight of that playful, well-groomed, and elegant figure refreshed Peter Ivanovich. He felt that Schwartz was above all these happenings and would not surrender to any depressing influences. His very look said that this incident of a church service for Ivan Ilych could not be a sufficient reason for infringing the order of the session — in other words, that it would certainly not prevent his unwrapping a new pack of cards and shuffling them that evening while a footman placed four fresh candles on the table: in fact, that there was no reason for supposing that this incident would hinder their spending the evening agreeably. Indeed he said this in a whisper as Peter Ivanovich passed him, proposing that they should meet for a game at Fëdor Vasilievich's. But apparently Peter Ivanovich was not destined to play bridge that evening. Praskovya Fëdorovna (a short, fat woman who despite all efforts to the contrary had continued to broaden steadily from her shoulders downwards and who had the same extraordinarily arched eyebrows as the lady who had been standing by the coffin), dressed all in black, her head covered with lace, came out of her own room with some other ladies, conducted them to the room where the dead body lay, and said: "The service will begin immediately. Please go in."

Schwartz, making an indefinite bow, stood still, evidently neither accepting nor declining this invitation. Praskovya Fëdorovna, recognizing Peter Ivanovich, sighed, went close up to him, took his hand, and said: "I know you were a true friend to Ivan Ilych . . ." and looked at him awaiting some suitable response. And Peter Ivanovich knew that, just as it had been the right thing to cross himself in that room, so what he had to do here was to press her hand, sigh, and say, "Believe me. . . ." So he did all this and as he did it felt that the desired result had been achieved: that both he and she were touched.

"Come with me. I want to speak to you before it begins," said the widow. "Give me your arm."

Peter Ivanovich gave her his arm and they went to the inner rooms, passing Schwartz, who winked at Peter Ivanovich compassionately.

"That does for our bridge! Don't object if we find another player. Perhaps you can cut in when you do escape," said his playful look.

Peter Ivanovich sighed still more deeply and despondently, and Praskovya Fëdorovna pressed his arm gratefully. When they reached the drawing-room, upholstered in pink cretonne and lighted by a dim lamp, they sat down at the table — she on a sofa and Peter Ivanovich on a low pouffe, the springs of which yielded spasmodically under his weight. Praskovya Fëdorovna had been on the point of warning him to take another seat, but felt that such a warning was out of keeping with her present condition and so changed her mind. As he sat down on the pouffe Peter Ivanovich recalled how Ivan Ilych had arranged this room and had consulted him regarding this pink cretonne with green leaves. The whole room was full of furniture and knick-knacks, and on her way to the sofa the lace of the widow's black shawl caught on the carved edge of the table. Peter Ivanovich rose to detach it, and the springs of the pouffe, relieved of his weight, rose also and gave him a push. The widow began detaching her shawl herself, and Peter Ivanovich again sat down, suppressing the rebellious springs of the pouffe under him. But the widow had not quite freed herself and Peter Ivanovich got up again, and again the pouffe rebelled and even creaked. When this was all over she took out a clean cambric handkerchief and began to weep. The episode with the shawl and the struggle with the pouffe had cooled Peter Ivanovich's emotions and he sat there with a sullen look on his face. This awkward situation was interrupted by Sokolov, Ivan Ilych's butler, who came to report that the plot in the cemetery that Praskovya Fëdorovna had chosen would cost two hundred rubles. She stopped weeping and, looking at Peter Ivanovich with the air of a victim, remarked in French that it was very hard for her. Peter Ivanovich made a silent gesture signifying his full conviction that it must indeed be so.

"Please smoke," she said in a magnanimous yet crushed voice, and turned to discuss with Sokolov the price of the plot for the grave.

Peter Ivanovich while lighting his cigarette heard her inquiring very circumstantially into the prices of different plots in the cemetery and finally decide which she would take. When that was done she gave instructions about engaging the choir. Sokolov then left the room.

"I look after everything myself," she told Peter Ivanovich, shifting the albums that lay on the table; and noticing that the table was endangered by his cigarette-ash, she immediately passed him an ash-tray, saying as she did so: "I consider it an affectation to say that my grief prevents my attending to practical affairs. On the contrary, if anything can — I won't say console me, but — distract me, it is seeing to everything concerning him." She again took out her handkerchief as if preparing to cry, but suddenly, as if mastering her feeling, she shook herself and began to speak calmly. "But there is something I want to talk to you about."

Peter Ivanovich bowed, keeping control of the springs of the pouffe, which immediately began quivering under him.

"He suffered terribly the last few days."

"Did he?" said Peter Ivanovich.

"Oh, terribly! He screamed unceasingly, not for minutes but for hours. For the last three days he screamed incessantly. It was unendurable. I cannot understand how I bore it; you could hear him three rooms off. Oh, what I have suffered!"

"Is it possible that he was conscious all that time?" asked Peter Ivanovich.

"Yes," she whispered. "To the last moment. He took leave of us a quarter of an hour before he died, and asked us to take Volodya away."

The thought of the sufferings of this man he had known so intimately, first as a merry little boy, then as a school-mate, and later as a grown-up colleague, suddenly struck Peter Ivanovich with horror, despite an unpleasant consciousness of his own and this woman's dissimulation. He again saw that brow, and that nose pressing down on the lip, and felt afraid for himself.

"Three days of frightful suffering and then death! Why, that might suddenly, at any time, happen to me," he thought, and for a moment felt terrified. But — he did not himself know how — the customary reflection at once occurred to him that this had happened to Ivan Ilych and not to him, and that it should not and could not happen to him, and that to think that it could would be yielding to depression which he ought not to do, as Schwartz's expression plainly showed. After which reflection Peter Ivanovich felt reassured, and began to ask with interest about the details of Ivan Ilych's death, as though death was an accident natural to Ivan Ilych but certainly not to himself.

After many details of the really dreadful physical sufferings Ivan Ilych had endured (which details he learnt only from the effect those sufferings had produced on Praskovya Fëdorovna's nerves) the widow apparently found it necessary to get to business.

"Oh, Peter Ivanovich, how hard it is! How terribly, terribly hard!" and she again began to weep.

Peter Ivanovich sighed and waited for her to finish blowing her nose. When she had done so he said, "Believe me . . ." and she again began talking and brought out what was evidently her chief concern with him — namely, to question him as to how she could obtain a grant of money from the government on the occasion of her husband's death. She made it appear that she was asking Peter Ivanovich's advice about her pension, but he soon saw that she already knew about that to the minutest detail, more even than he did himself. She knew how much could be got out of the government in consequence of her husband's death, but wanted to find out whether she could not possibly extract something more. Peter Ivanovich tried to think of some means of doing so, but after reflecting for a while and, out of propriety, condemning the government for its niggardliness, he said he thought that nothing more could be got. Then she sighed and evidently began to devise means of getting rid of her visitor. Noticing this, he put out his cigarette, rose, pressed her hand, and went out into the ante-room.

In the dining-room where the clock stood that Ivan Ilych had liked so much and had bought at an antique shop, Peter Ivanovich met a priest and a few acquaintances who had come to attend the service, and he recognized Ivan Ilych's daughter, a handsome young woman. She was in black and her slim figure appeared slimmer than ever. She had a gloomy, determined, almost angry expression, and bowed to Peter Ivanovich as though he were in some way to blame. Behind her, with the same offended look, stood a wealthy young man, an examining magistrate, whom Peter Ivanovich also knew and who was her fiancé, as he had heard. He bowed mournfully to them and was about to pass into the death-chamber, when from under the stairs appeared the figure of Ivan Ilych's schoolboy son, who was extremely like his father. He seemed a little Ivan Ilych, such as Peter Ivanovich remembered when they studied law together. His tear-stained eyes had in them the look that is seen in the eyes of boys of thirteen or fourteen who are not pure-minded. When he saw Peter Ivanovich he scowled morosely and shamefacedly. Peter Ivanovich nodded to him and entered the death-chamber. The service began: candles, groans, incense, tears, and sobs. Peter Ivanovich stood looking gloomily down at his feet. He did not look once at the dead man, did not yield to any depressing influence, and was one of the first to leave the room. There was no one in the anteroom, but Gerasim darted out of the dead man's room, rummaged with his strong hands among the fur coats to find Peter Ivanovich's and helped him on with it.

"Well, friend Gerasim," said Peter Ivanovich, so as to say something. "It's a sad affair, isn't it?"

"It's God's will. We shall all come to it some day," said Gerasim, displaying his teeth — the even, white teeth of a healthy peasant — and, like a man in the thick of urgent work, he briskly opened the front door, called the coachman, helped Peter Ivanovich into the sledge, and sprang back to the porch as if in readiness for what he had to do next.

Peter Ivanovich found the fresh air particularly pleasant after the smell of incense, the dead body, and carbolic acid. "Where to, sir?" asked the coachman.

"It's not too late even now. . . . I'll call round on Fëdor Vasilievich."

He accordingly drove there and found them just finishing the first rubber, so that it was quite convenient for him to cut in.

ii.

Ivan Ilych's life had been most simple and most ordinary and therefore most terrible.

He had been a member of the Court of Justice, and died at the age of forty-five. His father had been an official who after serving in various ministries and departments in Petersburg had made the sort of career which brings men to positions from which by reason of their long service they cannot be dismissed, though they are obviously unfit to hold any responsible position, and for whom therefore posts are specially created, which though fictitious carry salaries of from six to ten thousand rubles that are not fictitious, and in receipt of which they live on to a great age.

Such was the Privy Councillor and superfluous member of various superfluous institutions, Ilya Epimovich Golovin.

He had three sons, of whom Ivan Ilych was the second. The eldest son was following in his father's footsteps only in another department, and was already approaching that stage in the service at which a similar sinecure would be reached. The third son was a failure. He had ruined his prospects in a number of positions and was now serving in the railway department. His father and brothers, and still more their wives, not merely disliked meeting him, but avoided remembering his existence unless compelled to do so. His sister had married Baron Greff, a Petersburg official of her father's type. Ivan Ilych was *le phénix de la famille* as people said. He was neither as cold and formal as his elder brother nor as wild as the younger, but was a happy mean between them — an intelligent, polished, lively and agreeable man. He had studied with his younger brother at the School of Law, but the latter had failed to complete the course and was expelled when he was in the fifth class. Ivan Ilych finished the course well. Even when he was at the School of Law he was just what he remained for the rest of his life: a capable, cheerful, good-natured, and sociable man, though strict in the fulfilment of what he considered to be his duty: and he considered his duty to be what was so considered by those in authority. Neither as a boy nor as a man was he a toady, but from early youth was by nature attracted to people of high station as a fly is drawn to the light, assimilating their ways and views of life and establishing friendly relations with them. All the enthusiasms of childhood and youth passed without leaving much trace on him; he succumbed to sensuality, to vanity, and latterly among the highest classes to liberalism, but always within limits which his instinct unfailingly indicated to him as correct.

At school he had done things which had formerly seemed to him very horrid and made him feel disgusted with himself when he did them; but when later on he saw that such actions were done by people of good position and that they did not regard them as wrong, he was able not exactly to regard them as right, but to forget about them entirely or not be at all troubled at remembering them.

Having graduated from the School of Law and qualified for the tenth rank of the civil service, and having received money from his father for his equipment, Ivan Ilych ordered himself clothes at Scharmer's, the fashionable tailor, hung a medallion inscribed *respice finem* on his watch-chain, took leave of his professor and the prince who was patron of the school, had a farewell dinner with his comrades at Donon's first-class restaurant, and with his new and fashionable portmanteau, linen, clothes, shaving and other toilet appliances, and a traveling rug, all purchased at the best shops, he set off for one of the provinces where, through his father's influence, he had been attached to the Governor as an official for special service.

In the province Ivan Ilych soon arranged as easy and agreeable a position for himself as he had had at the School of Law. He performed his official tasks, made his career, and at the same time amused himself pleasantly and decorously. Occasionally he paid official visits to country districts, where he behaved with dignity both to his superiors and inferiors, and performed the duties entrusted to him, which related chiefly to the sectarians, with an exactness and incorruptible honesty of which he could not but feel proud.

In official matters, despite his youth and taste for frivolous gaiety, he was exceedingly reserved, punctilious, and even severe; but in society he was often amusing and witty, and always good-natured, correct in his manner, and *bon enfant,* as the governor and his wife — with whom he was like one of the family — used to say of him.

In the province he had an affair with a lady who made advances to the elegant young lawyer, and there was also a milliner; and there were carousals with aides-de-camp who visited the district, and after-supper visits to a certain outlying street of doubtful reputation; and there was too some obsequiousness to his chief and even to his chief's wife, but all this was done with such a tone of good breeding that no hard names could be applied to it. It all came under the heading of the French saying: *"Il faut que jeunesse se passe."* [*"Youth must have its fling."*] It was all done with clean hands, in clean linen, with French phrases, and above all among people of the best society and consequently with the approval of people of rank.

So Ivan Ilych served for five years and then came a change in his official life. The new and reformed judicial institutions were introduced, and new men were needed. Ivan Ilych became such a new man. He was offered the post of examining magistrate, and he accepted it though the post was in another province and obliged him to give up the connexions he had formed and to make new ones. His friends met to give him a send-off; they had a group-photograph taken and presented him with a silver cigarette-case, and he set off to his new post.

As examining magistrate Ivan Ilych was just as *comme il faut* and decorous a man, inspiring general respect and capable of separating his official duties from his private life, as he had been when acting as an official on special service. His duties now as examining magistrate were far more interesting and attractive than before. In his former position it had been pleasant to wear an undress uniform made by Scharmer, and to pass through the crowd of petitioners and officials who were timorously awaiting an audience with the governor, and who envied him as with free and easy gait he went straight into his chief's private room to have a cup of tea and a cigarette with him. But not many people had then been directly dependent on him — only police officials and the sectarians when he went on special missions — and he liked to treat them politely, almost as comrades, as if he were letting them feel that he who had the power to crush them was treating them in this simple, friendly way. There were then but few such people. But now, as an examining magistrate, Ivan Ilych felt that everyone without exception, even the most important and self-satisfied, was in his power, and that he need only write a few words on a sheet of paper with a certain heading, and this or that important, self-satisfied person would be brought before him in the role of an accused person or a witness, and if he did not choose to allow him to sit down, would have to stand before him and answer his questions. Ivan

Ilych never abused his power; he tried on the contrary to soften its expression, but the consciousness of it and of the possibility of softening its effect, supplied the chief interest and attraction of his office. In his work itself, especially in his examinations, he very soon acquired a method of eliminating all considerations irrelevant to the legal aspect of the case, and reducing even the most complicated case to a form in which it would be presented on paper only in its externals, completely excluding his personal opinion of the matter, while above all observing every prescribed formality. The work was new and Ivan Ilych was one of the first men to apply the new Code of 1864 [a judicial reform following the emancipation of the serfs in 1861].

On taking up the post of examining magistrate in a new town, he made new acquaintances and connexions, placed himself on a new footing, and assumed a somewhat different tone. He took up an attitude of rather dignified aloofness towards the provincial authorities, but picked out the best circle of legal gentlemen and wealthy gentry living in the town and assumed a tone of slight dissatisfaction with the government, of moderate liberalism, and of enlightened citizenship. At the same time, without at all altering the elegance of his toilet, he ceased shaving his chin and allowed his beard to grow as it pleased.

Ivan Ilych settled down very pleasantly in this new town. The society there, which inclined towards opposition to the Governor, was friendly, his salary was larger, and he began to play *vint* [a form of bridge], which he found added not a little to the pleasure of life, for he had a capacity for cards, played good-humouredly, and calculated rapidly and astutely, so that he usually won.

After living there for two years he met his future wife, Praskovya Fëdorovna Mikhel, who was the most attractive, clever, and brilliant girl of the set in which he moved, and among other amusements and relaxations from his labours as examining magistrate, Ivan Ilych established light and playful relations with her.

While he had been an official on special service he had been accustomed to dance, but now as an examining magistrate it was exceptional for him to do so. If he danced now, he did it as if to show that though he served under the reformed order of things, and had reached the fifth official rank, yet when it came to dancing he could do it better than most people. So at the end of an evening he sometimes danced with Praskovya Fëdorovna, and it was chiefly during these dances that he captivated her. She fell in love with him. Ivan Ilych had at first no definite intention of marrying, but when the girl fell in love with him he said to himself: "Really, why shouldn't I marry?"

Praskovya Fëdorovna came of a good family, was not bad looking, and had some little property. Ivan Ilych might have aspired to a more brilliant match, but even this was good. He had his salary, and she, he hoped, would have an equal income. She was well connected, and was a sweet, pretty, and thoroughly correct young woman. To say that Ivan Ilych married because he fell in love with Praskovya Fëdorovna and found that she sympathized with his views of life would be as incorrect as to say that he married because his social circle approved of the match. He was swayed by both these considerations: the marriage gave him personal satisfaction, and at the same time it was considered the right thing by the most highly placed of his associates.

So Ivan Ilych got married.

The preparations for marriage and the beginning of married life, with its conjugal caresses, the new furniture, new crockery, and new linen, were very pleasant until his wife became pregnant — so that Ivan Ilych had begun to think that marriage would not impair the easy, agreeable, gay and always decorous character of his life, approved of by society and regarded by himself as natural, but would even improve it. But from the first months of his wife's pregnancy, something new, unpleasant, depressing, and unseemly, and from which there was no way of escape, unexpectedly showed itself.

His wife, without any reason — *de gaieté de cœur* as Ivan Ilych expressed it to himself — began to disturb the pleasure and propriety of their life. She began to be jealous without any cause, expected him to devote his whole attention to her, found fault with everything, and made coarse and ill-mannered scenes.

At first Ivan Ilych hoped to escape from the unpleasantness of this state of affairs by the same easy and decorous relation to life that had served him heretofore: he tried to ignore his wife's disagreeable moods, continued to live in his usual easy and pleasant way, invited friends to his house for a game of cards, and also tried going out to his club or spending his evenings with friends. But one day his wife began upbraiding him so vigorously, using such coarse words, and continued to abuse him every time he did not fulfil her demands, so resolutely and with such evident determination not to give way till he submitted — that is, till he stayed at home and was bored just as she was — that he became alarmed. He now realized that matrimony — at any rate with Praskovya Fëdorovna — was not always conducive to the pleasures and amenities of life, but on the contrary often infringed both comfort and propriety, and that he must therefore entrench himself against such infringement. And Ivan Ilych began to seek for means of doing so. His official duties were the one thing that imposed upon Praskovya Fëdorovna, and by means of his official work and the duties attached to it he began struggling with his wife to secure his own independence.

With the birth of their child, the attempts to feed it and the various failures in doing so, and with the real and imaginary illnesses of mother and child, in which Ivan Ilych's sympathy was demanded but about which he understood nothing, the need of securing for himself an existence outside his family life became still more imperative.

As his wife grew more irritable and exacting and Ivan Ilych transferred the centre of gravity of his life more and more to his official work, so did he grow to like his work better and became more ambitious than before.

Very soon, within a year of his wedding, Ivan Ilych had realized that marriage, though it may add some comforts to life, is in fact a very intricate and difficult affair towards which in order to perform one's duty, that is, to lead a decorous life approved of by society, one must adopt a definite attitude just as towards one's official duties.

And Ivan Ilych evolved such an attitude towards married life. He only required of it those conveniences — dinner at home, housewife, and bed — which it could give him, and above all that propriety of external forms required by public opinion. For the rest he looked for light-hearted pleasure and propriety, and was very thankful when he found them, but if he met with antagonism and querulousness he at once retired into his separate fenced-off world of official duties, where he found satisfaction.

Ivan Ilych was esteemed a good official, and after three years was made Assistant Public Prosecutor. His new duties, their importance, the possibility of indicting and imprisoning anyone he chose, the publicity his speeches received, and the success he had in all these things, made his work still more attractive.

More children came. His wife became more and more querulous and ill-tempered, but the attitude Ivan Ilych had adopted towards his home life rendered him almost impervious to her grumbling.

After seven years' service in that town he was transferred to another province as Public Prosecutor. They moved, but were short of money and his wife did not like the place they moved to. Though the salary was higher the cost of living was greater, besides which two of their children died and family life became still more unpleasant for him.

Praskovya Fëdorovna blamed her husband for every inconvenience they encountered in their new home. Most of the conversations between husband and wife, especially as to the children's education, led to topics which recalled former disputes, and those disputes were apt to flare up again at any moment. There remained only those rare periods of amorousness which still came to them at times but did not last long. These were islets at which they anchored for a while and then again set out upon that ocean of veiled hostility which showed itself in their aloofness from one another. This aloofness might have grieved Ivan Ilych had he considered that it ought not to exist, but he now regarded the position as normal, and even made it the goal at which he aimed in family life. His aim was to free himself more and more from those unpleasantnesses and to give them a semblance of harmlessness and propriety. He attained this by spending less and less time with his family, and when obliged to be at home he tried to safeguard his position by the presence of outsiders. The chief thing however was that he had his official duties. The whole interest of his life now centred in the official world and that interest absorbed him. The consciousness of his power, being able to ruin anybody he wished to ruin, the importance, even the external dignity of his entry into court, or meetings with his subordinates, his success with superiors and inferiors, and above all his masterly handling of cases, of which he was conscious — all this gave him pleasure and filled his life, together with chats with his colleagues, dinners, and bridge. So that on the whole Ivan Ilych's life continued to flow as he considered it should do — pleasantly and properly.

So things continued for another seven years. His eldest daughter was already sixteen, another child had died, and only one son was left, a schoolboy and a subject of dissension. Ivan Ilych wanted to put him in the School of Law, but to spite him Praskovya Fëdorovna entered him at the High School. The daughter had been educated at home and had turned out well: the boy did not learn badly either.

iii.

So Ivan Ilych lived for seventeen years after his marriage. He was already a Public Prosecutor of long standing, and had declined several proposed transfers while awaiting a more desirable post, when an unanticipated and unpleasant occurrence quite upset the peaceful course of his life. He was expecting to be offered the post of presiding judge in a University town, but Happe somehow came to the front and obtained the appointment instead. Ivan Ilych became irritable, reproached Happe, and quarrelled both with him and with his immediate superiors — who became colder to him and again passed him over when other appointments were made.

This was in 1880, the hardest year of Ivan Ilych's life. It was then that it became evident on the one hand that his salary was insufficient for them to live on, and on the other that he had been forgotten, and not only this, but that what was for him the greatest and most cruel injustice appeared to others a quite ordinary occurrence. Even his father did not consider it his duty to help him. Ivan Ilych felt himself abandoned by everyone, and that they regarded his position with a salary of 3,500 rubles as quite normal and even fortunate. He alone knew that with the consciousness of the injustices done him, with his wife's incessant nagging, and with the debts he had contracted by living beyond his means, his position was far from normal.

In order to save money that summer he obtained leave of absence and went with his wife to live in the country at her brother's place.

In the country, without his work, he experienced *ennui* for the first time in his life, and not only *ennui* but intolerable depression, and he decided that it was impossible to go on living like that, and that it was necessary to take energetic measures.

Having passed a sleepless night pacing up and down the veranda, he decided to go to Petersburg and bestir himself, in order to punish those who had failed to appreciate him and to get transferred to another ministry.

Next day, despite many protests from his wife and her brother, he started for Petersburg with the sole object of obtaining a post with a salary of five thousand rubles a year. He was no longer bent on any particular department, or tendency, or kind of activity. All he now wanted was an appointment to another post with a salary of five thousand rubles, either in the administration, in the banks, with the railways, in one of the Empress Marya's Institutions, or even in the customs — but it had to carry with it a salary of five thousand rubles and be in a ministry other than that in which they had failed to appreciate him.

And this quest of Ivan Ilych's was crowned with remarkable and unexpected success. At Kursk an acquaintance of his, F. I. Ilyin, got into the first-class carriage, sat down beside Ivan Ilych, and told him of a telegram just received by the Governor of Kursk announcing that a change was about to take place in the ministry: Peter Ivanovich was to be superseded by Ivan Semënovich.

The proposed change, apart from its significance for Russia, had a special significance for Ivan Ilych, because by bringing forward a new man, Peter Petrovich, and consequently his friend Zachar Ivanovich, it was highly favourable for Ivan Ilych, since Zachar Ivanovich was a friend and colleague of his.

In Moscow this news was confirmed, and on reaching Petersburg Ivan Ilych found Zachar Ivanovich and received a definite promise of an appointment in his former department of Justice.

A week later he telegraphed to his wife: "Zachar in Miller's place. I shall receive appointment on presentation of report."

Thanks to this change of personnel, Ivan Ilych had unexpectedly obtained an appointment in his former ministry which placed him two stages above his former colleagues besides giving him five thousand rubles salary and three thousand five hundred rubles for expenses connected with his removal. All his ill humour towards his former enemies and the whole department vanished, and Ivan Ilych was completely happy.

He returned to the country more cheerful and contented than he had been for a long time. Praskovya Fëdorovna also cheered up and a truce was arranged between them. Ivan Ilych told of how he had been fêted by everybody in Petersburg, how all those who had been his enemies were put to shame and now fawned on him, how envious they were of his appointment, and how much everybody in Petersburg had liked him.

Praskovya Fëdorovna listened to all this and appeared to believe it. She did not contradict anything, but only made plans for their life in the town to which they were going. Ivan Ilych saw with delight that these plans were his plans, that he and his wife agreed, and that, after a stumble, his life was regaining its due and natural character of pleasant lightheartedness and decorum.

Ivan Ilych had come back for a short time only, for he had to take up his new duties on the 10th of September. Moreover, he needed time to settle into the new place, to move all his belongings from the province, and to buy and order many additional things: in a word, to make such arrangements as he had resolved on, which were almost exactly what Praskovya Fëdorovna too had decided on.

Now that everything had happened so fortunately, and that he and his wife were at one in their aims and moreover saw so little of one another, they got on together better than they had done since the first years of marriage. Ivan Ilych had thought of taking his family away with him at once, but the insistence of his wife's brother and her sister-in-law, who had suddenly become particularly amiable and friendly to him and his family, induced him to depart alone.

So he departed, and the cheerful state of mind induced by his success and by the harmony between his wife and himself, the one intensifying the other, did not leave him. He found a delightful house, just the thing both he and his wife had dreamt of. Spacious, lofty reception rooms in the old style, a convenient and dignified study, rooms for his wife and daughter, a study for his son — it might have been specially built for them. Ivan Ilych himself superintended the arrangements, chose the wallpapers, supplemented the furniture (preferably with antiques which he considered particularly *comme il faut*), and supervised the upholstering. Everything progressed and progressed and approached the ideal he had set himself: even when things were only half completed they exceeded his expectations. He saw what a refined and elegant character, free from vulgarity, it would all have when it was ready. On falling asleep he pictured to himself how the reception-room would look. Looking at the yet unfinished drawing-room he could see the fireplace, the screen, the what-not, the little chairs dotted here and there, the dishes and plates on the walls, and the bronzes, as they would be when everything was in place. He was pleased by the thought of how his wife and daughter, who shared his taste in this matter, would be impressed by it. They were certainly not expecting as much. He had been particularly successful in finding, and buying cheaply, antiques which gave a particularly aristocratic character to the whole place. But in his letters he intentionally understated everything in order to be able to surprise them. All this so absorbed him that his new duties — though he liked his official work — interested him less than he had expected. Sometimes he even had moments of absent-mindedness during the Court Sessions, and would consider whether he should have straight or curved cornices for his curtains. He was so interested in it all that he often did things himself, rearranging the furniture, or rehanging the curtains. Once when mounting a stepladder to show the upholsterer, who did not understand, how he wanted the hangings draped, he made a false step and slipped, but being a strong and agile man he clung on and only knocked his side against the knob of the window frame. The bruised place was painful but the pain soon passed, and he felt particularly bright and well just then. He wrote: "I feel fifteen years younger." He thought he would have everything ready by September, but it dragged on till mid-October. But the result was charming not only in his eyes but to everyone who saw it.

In reality it was just what is usually seen in the houses of people of moderate means who want to appear rich, and therefore succeed only in resembling others like themselves: there were damasks, dark wood, plants, rugs, and dull and polished bronzes — all the things people of a certain class have in order to resemble other people of that class. His house was so like the others that it would never have been noticed, but to him it all seemed to be quite exceptional. He was very happy when he met his family at the station and brought them to the newly furnished house all lit up, where a footman in a white tie opened the door into the hall decorated with plants, and when they went on into the drawing-room, and the study uttering exclamations of delight. He conducted them everywhere, drank in their praises eagerly, and beamed with pleasure. At tea that evening, when Praskovya Fëdorovna among other things asked him about his fall, he laughed and showed them how he had gone flying and had frightened the upholsterer.

"It's a good thing I'm a bit of an athlete. Another man might have been killed, but I merely knocked myself, just here; it hurts when it's touched, but it's passing off already — it's only a bruise."

So they began living in their new home — in which, as always happens, when they got thoroughly settled in they found they were just one room short — and with the increased income, which as always was just a little (some five hundred rubles) too little, but it was all very nice.

Things went particularly well at first, before everything was finally arranged and while something had still to be done: this thing bought, that thing ordered, another thing moved, and something else adjusted. Though there were some disputes between husband and wife, they were both so well satisfied and had so much to do that it all passed off without any serious quarrels. When nothing was left to arrange it became rather dull and something seemed to be lacking, but they were then making acquaintances, forming habits, and life was growing fuller.

Ivan Ilych spent his mornings at the law court and came home to dinner, and at first he was generally in a good humour, though he occasionally became irritable just on account of his house. (Every spot on the tablecloth or the upholstery, and every broken window-blind string, irritated him. He had devoted so much trouble to arranging it all that every disturbance of it distressed him.) But on the whole his life ran its course as he believed life should do: easily, pleasantly, and decorously.

He got up at nine, drank his coffee, read the paper, and then put on his undress uniform and went to the law courts. There the harness in which he worked had already been stretched to fit him and he donned it without a hitch: petitioners, inquiries at the chancery, the chancery itself, and the sittings public and administrative. In all this the thing was to exclude everything fresh and vital, which always disturbs the regular course of official business, and to admit only official relations with people, and then only on official grounds. A man would come, for instance, wanting some information. Ivan Ilych, as one in whose sphere the matter did not lie, would have nothing to do with him: but if the man had some business with him in his official capacity, something that could be expressed on officially stamped paper, he would do everything, positively everything he could within the limits of such relations, and in doing so would maintain the semblance of friendly human relations, that is, would observe the courtesies of life. As soon as the official relations ended, so did everything else. Ivan Ilych possessed this capacity to separate his real life from the official side of affairs and not mix the two, in the highest degree, and by long practice and natural aptitude had brought it to such a pitch that sometimes, in the manner of a virtuoso, he would even allow himself to let the human and official relations mingle. He let himself do this just because he felt that he could at any time he chose resume the strictly official attitude again and drop the human relation. And he did it all easily, pleasantly, correctly, and even artistically. In the intervals between the sessions he smoked, drank tea, chatted a little about politics, a little about general topics, a little about cards, but most of all about official appointments. Tired, but with the feelings of a virtuoso — one of the first violins who has played his part in an orchestra with precision — he would return home to find that his wife and daughter had been out paying calls, or had a visitor, and that his son had been to school, had done his homework with his tutor, and was duly learning what is taught at High Schools. Everything was as it should be. After dinner, if they had no visitors, Ivan Ilych sometimes read a book that was being much discussed at the time, and in the evening settled down to work, that is, read official papers, compared the depositions of witnesses, and noted paragraphs of the Code applying to them. This was neither dull nor amusing. It was dull when he might have been playing bridge, but if no bridge was available it was at any rate better than doing nothing or sitting with his wife. Ivan Ilych's chief pleasure was giving little dinners to which he invited men and women of good social position, and just as his drawing-room resembled all other drawing-rooms so did his enjoyable little parties resemble all other such parties.

Once they even gave a dance. Ivan Ilych enjoyed it and everything went off well, except that it led to a violent quarrel with his wife about the cakes and sweets. Praskovya Fëdorovna had made her own plans, but Ivan Ilych insisted on getting everything from an expensive confectioner and ordered too many cakes, and the quarrel occurred because some of those cakes were left over and the confectioner's bill came to forty-five rubles. It was a great and disagreeable quarrel. Praskovya Fëdorovna called him "a fool and an imbecile," and he clutched at his head and made angry allusions to divorce.

But the dance itself had been enjoyable. The best people were there, and Ivan Ilych had danced with Princess Trufonova, a sister of the distinguished founder of the Society "Bear my Burden."

The pleasures connected with his work were pleasures of ambition; his social pleasures were those of vanity; but Ivan Ilych's greatest pleasure was playing bridge. He acknowledged that whatever disagreeable incident happened in his life, the pleasure that beamed like a ray of light above everything else was to sit down to bridge with good players, not noisy partners, and of course to four-handed bridge (with five players it was annoying to have to stand out, though one pretended not to mind), to play a clever and serious game (when the cards allowed it) and then to have supper and drink a glass of wine. After a game of bridge, especially if he had won a little (to win a large sum was unpleasant), Ivan Ilych went to bed in specially good humour.

So they lived. They formed a circle of acquaintances among the best people and were visited by people of importance and by young folk. In their views as to their acquaintances, husband, wife and daughter were entirely agreed, and tacitly and unanimously kept at arm's length and shook off the various shabby friends and relations who, with much show of affection, gushed into the drawing-room with its Japanese plates on the walls. Soon these shabby friends ceased to obtrude themselves and only the best people remained in the Golovins' set.

Young men made up to Lisa, and Petrishchev, an examining magistrate and Dmitri Ivanovich Petrishchev's son and sole heir, began to be so attentive to her that Ivan Ilych had already spoken to Praskovya Fëdorovna about it, and considered whether they should not arrange a party for them, or get up some private theatricals.

So they lived, and all went well, without change, and life flowed pleasantly.

iv.

They were all in good health. It could not be called ill health if Ivan Ilych sometimes said that he had a queer taste in his mouth and felt some discomfort in his left side.

But this discomfort increased and, though not exactly painful, grew into a sense of pressure in his side accompanied by ill humour. And his irritability became worse and worse and began to mar the agreeable, easy, and correct life that had established itself in the Golovin family. Quarrels between husband and wife became more and more frequent, and soon the ease and amenity disappeared and even the decorum was barely maintained. Scenes again became frequent, and very few of those islets remained on which husband and wife could meet without an explosion. Praskovya Fëdorovna now had good reason to say that her husband's temper was trying. With characteristic exaggeration she said he had always had a dreadful temper, and that it had needed all her good nature to put up with it for twenty years. It was true that now the quarrels were started by him. His bursts of temper always came just before dinner, often just as he began to eat his soup. Sometimes he noticed that a plate or dish was chipped, or the food was not right, or his son put his elbow on the table, or his daughter's hair was not done as he liked it, and for all this he blamed Praskovya Fëdorovna. At first she retorted and said disagreeable things to him, but once or twice he fell into such a rage at the beginning of dinner that she realized it was due to some physical derangement brought on by taking food, and so she restrained herself and did not answer, but only hurried to get the dinner over. She regarded this self-restraint as highly praiseworthy. Having come to the conclusion that her husband had a dreadful temper and made her life miserable, she began to feel sorry for herself, and the more she pitied herself the more she hated her husband. She began to wish he would die; yet she did not want him to die because then his salary would cease. And this irritated her against him still more. She considered herself dreadfully unhappy just because not even his death could save her, and though she concealed her exasperation, that hidden exasperation of hers increased his irritation also.

After one scene in which Ivan Ilych had been particularly unfair and after which he had said in explanation that he certainly was irritable but that it was due to his not being well, she said that if he was ill it should be attended to, and insisted on his going to see a celebrated doctor.

He went. Everything took place as he had expected and as it always does. There was the usual waiting and the important air assumed by the doctor, with which he was so familiar (resembling that which he himself assumed in court), and the sounding and listening, and the questions which called for answers that were foregone conclusions and were evidently unnecessary, and the look of importance which implied that "if only you put yourself in our hands we will arrange everything — we know indubitably how it has to be done, always in the same way for everybody alike." It was all just as it was in the law courts. The doctor put on just the same air towards him as he himself put on towards an accused person.

The doctor said that so-and-so indicated that there was so-and-so inside the patient, but if the investigation of so-and-so did not confirm this, then he must assume that and that. If he assumed that and that, then . . . and so on. To Ivan Ilych only one question was important: was his case serious or not? But the doctor ignored that inappropriate question. From his point of view it was not the one under consideration, the real question was to decide between a floating kidney, chronic catarrh, or appendicitis. It was not a question of Ivan Ilych's life or death, but one between a floating kidney and appendicitis. And that question the doctor solved brilliantly, as it seemed to Ivan Ilych, in favour of the appendix, with the reservation that should an examination of the urine give fresh indications the matter would be reconsidered. All this was just what Ivan Ilych had himself brilliantly accomplished a thousand times in dealing with men on trial. The doctor summed up just as brilliantly, looking over his spectacles triumphantly and even gaily at the accused. From the doctor's summing up Ivan Ilych concluded that things were bad, but that for the doctor, and perhaps for everybody else, it was a matter of indifference, though for him it was bad. And this conclusion struck him painfully, arousing in him a great feeling of pity for himself and of bitterness towards the doctor's indifference to a matter of such importance.

He said nothing of this, but rose, placed the doctor's fee on the table, and remarked with a sigh: "We sick people probably often put inappropriate questions. But tell me, in general, is this complaint dangerous, or not? . . ."

The doctor looked at him sternly over his spectacles with one eye, as if to say: "Prisoner, if you will not keep to the questions put to you, I shall be obliged to have you removed from the court."

"I have already told you what I consider necessary and proper. The analysis may show something more." And the doctor bowed.

Ivan Ilych went out slowly, seated himself disconsolately in his sledge, and drove home. All the way home he was going over what the doctor had said, trying to translate those complicated, obscure, scientific phrases into plain language and find in them an answer to the question: "Is my condition bad? Is it very bad? Or is there as yet nothing much wrong?" And it seemed to him that the meaning of what the doctor had said was that it was very bad. Everything in the streets seemed depressing. The cabmen, the houses, the passers-by, and the shops were dismal. His ache, this dull gnawing ache that never ceased for a moment, seemed to have acquired a new and more serious significance from the doctor's dubious remarks. Ivan Ilych now watched it with a new and oppressive feeling.

He reached home and began to tell his wife about it. She listened, but in the middle of his account his daughter came in with her hat on, ready to go out with her mother. She sat down reluctantly to listen to this tedious story, but could not stand it long, and her mother too did not hear him to the end.

"Well, I am very glad," she said. "Mind now to take your medicine regularly. Give me the prescription and I'll send Gerasim to the chemist's." And she went to get ready to go out.

While she was in the room Ivan Ilych had hardly taken time to breathe, but he sighed deeply when she left it.

"Well," he thought, "perhaps it isn't so bad after all."

He began taking his medicine and following the doctor's directions, which had been altered after the examination of the urine. But then it happened that there was a contradiction between the indications drawn from the examination of the urine and the symptoms that showed themselves. It turned out that what was happening differed from what the doctor had told him, and that he had either forgotten, or blundered, or hidden something from him. He could not, however, be blamed for that, and Ivan Ilych still obeyed his orders implicitly and at first derived some comfort from doing so.

From the time of his visit to the doctor, Ivan Ilych's chief occupation was the exact fulfilment of the doctor's instructions regarding hygiene and the taking of medicine, and the observation of his pain and his excretions. His chief interests came to be people's ailments and people's health. When sickness, deaths, or recoveries were mentioned in his presence, especially when the illness resembled his own, he listened with agitation which he tried to hide, asked questions, and applied what he heard to his own case.

The pain did not grow less, but Ivan Ilych made efforts to force himself to think that he was better. And he could do this so long as nothing agitated him. But as soon as he had any unpleasantness with his wife, any lack of success in his official work, or held bad cards at bridge, he was at once acutely sensible of his disease. He had formerly borne such mischances, hoping soon to adjust what was wrong, to master it and attain success, or make a grand slam. But now every mischance upset him and plunged him into despair. He would say to himself: "There now, just as I was beginning to get better and the medicine had begun to take effect, comes this accursed misfortune, or unpleasantness. . . ." And he was furious with the mishap, or with the people who were causing the unpleasantness and killing him, for he felt that this fury was killing him but could not restrain it. One would have thought that it should have been clear to him that this exasperation with circumstances and people aggravated his illness, and that he ought therefore to ignore unpleasant occurrences. But he drew the very opposite conclusion: he said that he needed peace, and he watched for everything that might disturb it and became irritable at the slightest infringement of it. His condition was rendered worse by the fact that he read medical books and consulted doctors. The progress of his disease was so gradual that he could deceive himself when comparing one day with another — the difference was so slight. But when he consulted the doctors it seemed to him that he was getting worse, and even very rapidly. Yet despite this he was continually consulting them.

That month he went to see another celebrity, who told him almost the same as the first had done but put his questions rather differently, and the interview with this celebrity only increased Ivan Ilych's doubts and fears. A friend of a friend of his, a very good doctor, diagnosed his illness again quite differently from the others, and though he predicted recovery, his questions and suppositions bewildered Ivan Ilych still more and increased his doubts. A homoeopathist diagnosed the disease in yet another way, and prescribed medicine which Ivan Ilych took secretly for a week. But after a week, not feeling any improvement and having lost confidence both in the former doctor's treatment and in this one's, he became still more despondent. One day a lady acquaintance mentioned a cure effected by a wonder-working icon. Ivan Ilych caught himself listening attentively and beginning to believe that it had occurred. This incident alarmed him. "Has my mind really weakened to such an extent?" he asked himself. "Nonsense! It's all rubbish. I mustn't give way to nervous fears but having chosen a doctor must keep strictly to his treatment. That is what I will do. Now it's all settled. I won't think about it, but will follow the treatment seriously till summer, and then we shall see. From now there must be no more of this wavering!" This was easy to say but impossible to carry out. The pain in his side oppressed him and seemed to grow worse and more incessant, while the taste in his mouth grew stranger and stranger. It seemed to him that his breath had a disgusting smell, and he was conscious of a loss of appetite and strength. There was no deceiving himself: something terrible, new, and more important than anything before in his life, was taking place within him of which he alone was aware. Those about him did not understand or would not understand it, but thought everything in the world was going on as usual. That tormented Ivan Ilych more than anything. He saw that his household, especially his wife and daughter who were in a perfect whirl of visiting, did not understand anything of it and were annoyed that he was so depressed and so exacting, as if he were to blame for it. Though they tried to disguise it he saw that he was an obstacle in their path, and that his wife had adopted a definite line in regard to his illness and kept to it regardless of anything he said or did. Her attitude was this: "You know," she would say to her friends, "Ivan Ilych can't do as other people do, and keep to the treatment prescribed for him. One day he'll take his drops and keep strictly to his diet and go to bed in good time, but the next day unless I watch him he'll suddenly forget his medicine, eat sturgeon — which is forbidden — and sit up playing cards till one o'clock in the morning."

"Oh, come, when was that?" Ivan Ilych would ask in vexation. "Only once at Peter Ivanovich's."

"And yesterday with Shebek."

"Well, even if I hadn't stayed up, this pain would have kept me awake."

"Be that as it may you'll never get well like that, but will always make us wretched."

Praskovya Fëdorovna's attitude to Ivan Ilych's illness, as she expressed it both to others and to him, was that it was his own fault and was another of the annoyances he caused her. Ivan Ilych felt that this opinion escaped her involuntarily — but that did not make it easier for him.

At the law courts too, Ivan Ilych noticed, or thought he noticed, a strange attitude towards himself. It sometimes seemed to him that people were watching him inquisitively as a man whose place might soon be vacant. Then again, his friends would suddenly begin to chaff him in a friendly way about his low spirits, as if the awful, horrible, and unheard-of-thing that was going on within him, incessantly gnawing at him and irresistibly drawing him away, was a very agreeable subject for jests. Schwartz in particular irritated him by his jocularity, vivacity, and *savoir-faire,* which reminded him of what he himself had been ten years ago.

Friends came to make up a set and they sat down to cards. They dealt, bending the new cards to soften them, and he sorted the diamonds in his hand and found he had seven. His partner said "No trumps" and supported him with two diamonds. What more could be wished for? It ought to be jolly and lively. They would make a grand slam. But suddenly Ivan Ilych was conscious of that gnawing pain, that taste in his mouth, and it seemed ridiculous that in such circumstances he should be pleased to make a grand slam.

He looked at his partner Mikhail Mikhaylovich, who rapped the table with his strong hand and instead of snatching up the tricks pushed the cards courteously and indulgently towards Ivan Ilych that he might have the pleasure of gathering them up without the trouble of stretching out his hand for them. "Does he think I am too weak to stretch out my arm?" thought Ivan Ilych, and forgetting what he was doing he over-trumped his partner, missing the grand slam by three tricks. And what was most awful of all was that he saw how upset Mikhail Mikhaylovich was about it but did not himself care. And it was dreadful to realize why he did not care.

They all saw that he was suffering, and said: "We can stop if you are tired. Take a rest." Lie down? No, he was not at all tired, and he finished the rubber. All were gloomy and silent. Ivan Ilych felt that he had diffused this gloom over them and could not dispel it. They had supper and went away, and Ivan Ilych was left alone with the consciousness that his life was poisoned and was poisoning the lives of others, and that this poison did not weaken but penetrated more and more deeply into his whole being.

With this consciousness, and with physical pain besides the terror, he must go to bed, often to lie awake the greater part of the night. Next morning he had to get up again, dress, go to the law courts, speak, and write; or if he did not go out, spend at home those twenty-four hours a day each of which was a torture. And he had to live thus all alone on the brink of an abyss, with no one who understood or pitied him.

V.

So one month passed and then another. Just before the New Year his brother-in-law came to town and stayed at their house. Ivan Ilych was at the law courts and Praskovya Fëdorovna had gone shopping. When Ivan Ilych came home and entered his study he found his brother-in-law there — a healthy, florid man — unpacking his portmanteau himself. He raised his head on hearing Ivan Ilych's footsteps and looked up at him for a moment without a word. That stare told Ivan Ilych everything. His brother-in-law opened his mouth to utter an exclamation of surprise but checked himself, and that action confirmed it all.

"I have changed, eh?"

"Yes, there is a change."

And after that, try as he would to get his brother-in-law to return to the subject of his looks, the latter would say nothing about it. Praskovya Fëdorovna came home and her brother went out to her. Ivan Ilych locked the door and began to examine himself in the glass, first full face, then in profile. He took up a portrait of himself taken with his wife, and compared it with what he saw in the glass. The change in him was immense. Then he bared his arms to the elbow, looked at them, drew the sleeves down again, sat down on an ottoman, and grew blacker than night.

"No, no, this won't do!" he said to himself, and jumped up, went to the table, took up some law papers and began to read them, but could not continue. He unlocked the door and went into the reception-room. The door leading to the drawing-room was shut. He approached it on tiptoe and listened.

"No, you are exaggerating!" Praskovya Fëdorovna was saying.

"Exaggerating! Don't you see it? Why, he's a dead man! Look at his eyes — there's no light in them. But what is it that is wrong with him?"

"No one knows. Nikolaevich [that was another doctor] said something, but I don't know what. And Leshchetitsky [this was the celebrated specialist] said quite the contrary. . . ."

Ivan Ilych walked away, went to his own room, lay down, and began musing: "The kidney, a floating kidney." He recalled all the doctors had told him of how it detached itself and swayed about. And by an effort of imagination he tried to catch that kidney and arrest it and support it. So little was needed for this, it seemed to him. "No, I'll go to see Peter Ivanovich again." [That was the friend whose friend was a doctor.] He rang, ordered the carriage, and got ready to go.

"Where are you going, Jean?" asked his wife, with a specially sad and exceptionally kind look.

This exceptionally kind look irritated him. He looked morosely at her. "I must go to see Peter Ivanovich."

He went to see Peter Ivanovich, and together they went to see his friend, the doctor. He was in, and Ivan Ilych had a long talk with him.

Reviewing the anatomical and physiological details of what in the doctor's opinion was going on inside him, he understood it all.

There was something, a small thing, in the vermiform appendix. It might all come right. Only stimulate the energy of one organ and check the activity of another, then absorption would take place and everything would come right. He got home rather late for dinner, ate his dinner, and conversed cheerfully, but could not for a long time bring himself to go back to work in his room. At last, however, he went to his study and did what was necessary, but the consciousness that he had put something aside — an important, intimate matter which he would revert to when his work was done — never left him. When he had finished his work he remembered that this intimate matter was the thought of his vermiform appendix. But he did not give himself up to it, and went to the drawing-room for tea. There were callers there, including the examining magistrate who was a desirable match for his daughter, and they were conversing, playing the piano, and singing. Ivan Ilych, as Praskovya Fëdorovna remarked, spent that evening more cheerfully than usual, but he never for a moment forgot that he had postponed the important matter of the appendix. At eleven o'clock he said good-night and went to his bedroom. Since his illness he had slept alone in a small room next to his study. He undressed and took up a novel by Zola, but instead of reading it he fell into thought, and in his imagination that desired improvement in the vermiform appendix occurred. There was the absorption and evacuation and the re-establishment of normal activity. "Yes, that's it!" he said to himself. "One need only assist nature, that's all." He remembered his medicine, rose, took it, and lay down on his back watching for the beneficent action of the medicine and for it to lessen the pain. "I need only take it regularly and avoid all injurious influences. I am already feeling better, much better." He began touching his side: it was not painful to the touch. "There, I really don't feel it. It's much better already." He put out the light and turned on his side. . . . "The appendix is getting better, absorption is occurring." Suddenly he felt the old, familiar, dull, gnawing pain, stubborn and serious. There was the same familiar loathsome taste in his mouth. His heart sank and he felt dazed. "My God! My God!" he muttered. "Again, again! and it will never cease." And suddenly the matter presented itself in a quite different aspect. "Vermiform appendix! Kidney!" he said to himself. "It's not a question of appendix or kidney, but of life and . . .

death. Yes, life was there and now it is going, going and I cannot stop it. Yes. Why deceive myself? Isn't it obvious to everyone but me that I'm dying, and that it's only a question of weeks, days . . . it may happen this moment. There was light and now there is darkness. I was here and now I'm going there! Where?" A chill came over him, his breathing ceased, and he felt only the throbbing of his heart.

"When I am not, what will there be? There will be nothing. Then where shall I be when I am no more? Can this be dying? No, I don't want to!" He jumped up and tried to light the candle, felt for it with trembling hands, dropped candle and candlestick on the floor, and fell back on his pillow.

"What's the use? It makes no difference," he said to himself, staring with wide-open eyes into the darkness. "Death. Yes, death. And none of them know or wish to know it, and they have no pity for me. Now they are playing." (He heard through the door the distant sound of a song and its accompaniment.) "It's all the same to them, but they will die too! Fools! I first, and they later, but it will be the same for them. And now they are merry . . . the beasts!"

Anger choked him and he was agonizingly, unbearably miserable. "It is impossible that all men have been doomed to suffer this awful horror!" He raised himself.

"Something must be wrong. I must calm myself — must think it all over from the beginning." And he again began thinking. "Yes, the beginning of my illness: I knocked my side, but I was still quite well that day and the next. It hurt a little, then rather more. I saw the doctors, then followed despondency and anguish, more doctors, and I drew nearer to the abyss. My strength grew less and I kept coming nearer and nearer, and now I have wasted away and there is no light in my eyes. I think of the appendix — but this is death! I think of mending the appendix, and all the while here is death! Can it really be death?" Again terror seized him and he gasped for breath. He leant down and began feeling for the matches, pressing with his elbow on the stand beside the bed. It was in his way and hurt him, he grew furious with it, pressed on it still harder, and upset it. Breathless and in despair he fell on his back, expecting death to come immediately.

Meanwhile the visitors were leaving. Praskovya Fëdorovna was seeing them off. She heard something fall and came in.

"What has happened?"

"Nothing. I knocked it over accidentally."

She went out and returned with a candle. He lay there panting heavily, like a man who has run a thousand yards, and stared upwards at her with a fixed look.

"What is it, Jean?"

"No . . . o . . . thing. I upset it." ("Why speak of it? She won't understand," he thought.)

And in truth she did not understand. She picked up the stand, lit his candle, and hurried away to see another visitor off. When she came back he still lay on his back, looking upwards.

"What is it? Do you feel worse?"

"Yes."

She shook her head and sat down.

"Do you know, Jean, I think we must ask Leshchetitsky to come and see you here."

This meant calling in the famous specialist, regardless of expense. He smiled malignantly and said "No." She remained a little longer and then went up to him and kissed his forehead.

While she was kissing him he hated her from the bottom of his soul and with difficulty refrained from pushing her away.

"Good-night. Please God you'll sleep."

"Yes."

vi.

Ivan Ilych saw that he was dying, and he was in continual despair.

In the depth of his heart he knew he was dying, but not only was he not accustomed to the thought, he simply did not and could not grasp it.

The syllogism he had learnt from Kiezewetter's Logic: "Caius is a man, men are mortal, therefore Caius is mortal," had always seemed to him correct as applied to Caius, but certainly not as applied to himself. That Caius — man in the abstract — was mortal, was perfectly correct, but he was not Caius, not an abstract man, but a creature quite, quite separate from all others. He had been little Vanya, with a mamma and a papa, with Mitya and Volodya, with the toys, a coachman and a nurse, afterwards with Katenka and with all the joys, griefs, and delights of childhood, boyhood, and youth. What did Caius know of the smell of that striped leather ball Vanya had been so fond of? Had Caius kissed his mother's hand like that, and did the silk of her dress rustle so for Caius? Had he rioted like that at school when the pastry was bad? Had Caius been in love like that? Could Caius preside at a session as he did? "Caius really was mortal, and it was right for him to die; but for me, little Vanya, Ivan Ilych, with all my thoughts and emotions, it's altogether a different matter. It cannot be that I ought to die. That would be too terrible."

Such was his feeling.

"If I had to die like Caius I should have known it was so. An inner voice would have told me so, but there was nothing of the sort in me and I and all my friends felt that our case was quite different from that of Caius. And now here it is!" he said to himself. "It can't be. It's impossible! But here it is. How is this? How is one to understand it?"

He could not understand it, and tried to drive this false, incorrect, morbid thought away and to replace it by other proper and healthy thoughts. But that thought, and not the thought only but the reality itself, seemed to come and confront him.

And to replace that thought, he called up a succession of others, hoping to find in them some support. He tried to get back into the former current of thoughts that had once screened the thought of death from him. But strange to say, all that had formerly shut off, hidden, and destroyed his consciousness of death, no longer had that effect. Ivan Ilych now spent most of his time in attempting to re-establish that old current. He would say to himself: "I will take up my duties again — after all I used to live by them." And banishing all doubts he would go to the law courts, enter into conversation with his colleagues, and sit carelessly as was his wont, scanning the crowd with a thoughtful look and leaning both his emaciated arms on the arms of his oak chair; bending over as usual to a colleague and drawing his papers nearer he would interchange whispers with him, and then suddenly raising his eyes and sitting erect would pronounce certain words and open the proceedings. But suddenly in the midst of those proceedings the pain in his side, regardless of the stage the proceedings had reached, would begin its own gnawing work. Ivan Ilych would turn his attention to it and try to drive the thought of it away, but without success. *It* would come and stand before him and look at him, and he would be petrified and the light would die out of his eyes, and he would again begin asking himself whether *It* alone was true. And his colleagues and subordinates would see with surprise and distress that he, the brilliant and subtle judge, was becoming confused and making mistakes. He would shake himself, try to pull himself together, manage somehow to bring the sitting to a close, and return home with the sorrowful consciousness that his judicial labours could not as formerly hide from him what he wanted them to hide, and could not deliver him from *It*. And what was worst of all was that *It* drew his attention to itself not in order to make him take some action but only that he should look at *It*, look it straight in the face: look at it and without doing anything, suffer inexpressibly.

And to save himself from this condition Ivan Ilych looked for consolations — new screens — and new screens were found and for a while seemed to save him, but then they immediately fell to pieces or rather became transparent, as if It penetrated them and nothing could veil It.

In these latter days he would go into the drawing-room he had arranged — that drawing-room where he had fallen and for the sake of which (how bitterly ridiculous it seemed) he had sacrificed his life — for he knew that his illness originated with that knock. He would enter and see that something had scratched the polished table. He would look for the cause of this and find that it was the bronze ornamentation of an album that had got bent. He would take up the expensive album which he had lovingly arranged, and feel vexed with his daughter and her friends for their untidiness — for the album was torn here and there and some of the photographs turned upside down. He would put it carefully in order and bend the ornamentation back into position. Then it would occur to him to place all those things in another corner of the room, near the plants. He could call the footman, but his daughter or wife would come to help him. They would not agree, and his wife would contradict him, and he would dispute and grow angry. But that was all right, for then he did not think about It. It was invisible.

But then, when he was moving something himself, his wife would say: "Let the servants do it. You will hurt yourself again." And suddenly It would flash through the screen and he would see it. It was just a flash, and he hoped it would disappear, but he would involuntarily pay attention to his side. "It sits there as before, gnawing just the same!" And he could no longer forget It, but could distinctly see it looking at him from behind the flowers. "What is it all for?"

"It really is so! I lost my life over that curtain as I might have done when storming a fort. Is that possible? How terrible and how stupid. It can't be true! It can't, but it is."

He would go to his study, lie down, and again be alone with It: face to face with It. And nothing could be done with It except to look at it and shudder.

vii.

How it happened it is impossible to say because it came about step by step, unnoticed, but in the third month of Ivan Ilych's illness, his wife, his daughter, his son, his acquaintances, the doctors, the servants, and above all he himself, were aware that the whole interest he had for other people was whether he would soon vacate his place, and at last release the living from the discomfort caused by his presence and be himself released from his sufferings.

He slept less and less. He was given opium and hypodermic injections of morphine, but this did not relieve him. The dull depression he experienced in a somnolent condition at first gave him a little relief, but only as something new, afterwards it became as distressing as the pain itself or even more so.

Special foods were prepared for him by the doctors' orders, but all those foods became increasingly distasteful and disgusting to him.

For his excretions also special arrangements had to be made, and this was a torment to him every time — a torment from the uncleanliness, the unseemliness, and the smell, and from knowing that another person had to take part in it.

But just through this most unpleasant matter, Ivan Ilych obtained comfort. Gerasim, the butler's young assistant, always came in to carry the things out. Gerasim was a clean, fresh peasant lad, grown stout on town food and always cheerful and bright. At first the sight of him, in his clean Russian peasant costume, engaged in that disgusting task embarrassed Ivan Ilych.

Once when he got up from the commode too weak to draw up his trousers, he dropped into a soft armchair and looked with horror at his bare, enfeebled thighs with the muscles so sharply marked on them.

Gerasim with a firm light tread, his heavy boots emitting a pleasant smell of tar and fresh winter air, came in wearing a clean Hessian apron, the sleeves of his print shirt tucked up over his strong bare young arms; and refraining from looking at his sick master out of consideration for his feelings, and restraining the joy of life that beamed from his face, he went up to the commode.

"Gerasim!" said Ivan Ilych in a weak voice.

Gerasim started, evidently afraid he might have committed some blunder, and with a rapid movement turned his fresh, kind, simple young face which just showed the first downy signs of a beard.

"Yes, sir?"

"That must be very unpleasant for you. You must forgive me. I am helpless."

"Oh, why, sir," and Gerasim's eyes beamed and he showed his glistening white teeth, "what's a little trouble? It's a case of illness with you, sir."

And his deft strong hands did their accustomed task, and he went out of the room stepping lightly. Five minutes later he as lightly returned.

Ivan Ilych was still sitting in the same position in the armchair.

"Gerasim," he said when the latter had replaced the freshly-washed utensil. "Please come here and help me." Gerasim went up to him. "Lift me up. It is hard for me to get up, and I have sent Dmitri away."

Gerasim went up to him, grasped his master with his strong arms deftly but gently, in the same way that he stepped — lifted him, supported him with one hand, and with the other drew up his trousers and would have set him down again, but Ivan Ilych asked to be led to the sofa. Gerasim, without an effort and without apparent pressure, led him, almost lifting him, to the sofa and placed him on it.

"Thank you. How easily and well you do it all!"

Gerasim smiled again and turned to leave the room. But Ivan Ilych felt his presence such a comfort that he did not want to let him go.

"One thing more, please move up that chair. No, the other one — under my feet. It is easier for me when my feet are raised."

Gerasim brought the chair, set it down gently in place, and raised Ivan Ilych's legs on to it. It seemed to Ivan Ilych that he felt better while Gerasim was holding up his legs.

"It's better when my legs are higher," he said. "Place that cushion under them."

Gerasim did so. He again lifted the legs and placed them, and again Ivan Ilych felt better while Gerasim held his legs. When he set them down Ivan Ilych fancied he felt worse.

"Gerasim," he said. "Are you busy now?"

"Not at all, sir," said Gerasim, who had learnt from the townsfolk how to speak to gentlefolk.

"What have you still to do?"

"What have I to do? I've done everything except chopping the logs for tomorrow."

"Then hold my legs up a bit higher, can you?"

"Of course I can. Why not?" And Gerasim raised his master's legs higher and Ivan Ilych thought that in that position he did not feel any pain at all.

"And how about the logs?"

"Don't trouble about that, sir. There's plenty of time."

Ivan Ilych told Gerasim to sit down and hold his legs, and began to talk to him. And strange to say it seemed to him that he felt better while Gerasim held his legs up.

After that Ivan Ilych would sometimes call Gerasim and get him to hold his legs on his shoulders, and he liked talking to him. Gerasim did it all easily, willingly, simply, and with a good nature that touched Ivan Ilych. Health, strength, and vitality in other people were offensive to him, but Gerasim's strength and vitality did not mortify but soothed him.

What tormented Ivan Ilych most was the deception, the lie, which for some reason they all accepted, that he was not dying but was simply ill, and that he only need keep quiet and undergo a treatment and then something very good would result. He however knew that do what they would nothing would come of it, only still more agonizing suffering and death. This deception tortured him — their not wishing to admit what they all knew and what he knew, but wanting to lie to him concerning his terrible condition, and wishing and forcing him to participate in that lie. Those lies — lies enacted over him on the eve of his death and destined to degrade this awful, solemn act to the level of their visitings, their curtains, their sturgeon for dinner — were a terrible agony for Ivan Ilych. And strangely enough, many times when they were going through their antics over him he had been within a hairbreadth of calling out to them: "Stop lying! You know and I know that I am dying. Then at least stop lying about it!" But he had never had the spirit to do it. The awful, terrible act of his dying was, he could see, reduced by those about him to the level of a casual, unpleasant, and almost indecorous incident (as if someone entered a drawing-room diffusing an unpleasant odour) and this was done by that very decorum which he had served all his life long. He saw that no one felt for him, because no one even wished to grasp his position. Only Gerasim recognized it and pitied him. And so Ivan Ilych felt at ease only with him. He felt comforted when Gerasim supported his legs (sometimes all night long) and refused to go to bed, saying: "Don't you worry, Ivan Ilych. I'll get sleep enough later on," or when he suddenly became familiar and exclaimed: "If you weren't sick it would be another matter, but as it is, why should I grudge a little trouble?" Gerasim alone did not lie; everything showed that he alone understood the facts of the case and did not consider it necessary to disguise them, but simply felt sorry for his emaciated and enfeebled master. Once when Ivan Ilych was sending him away he even said straight out: "We shall all of us die, so why should I grudge a little trouble?" — expressing the fact that he did not think his work burdensome, because he was doing it for a dying man and hoped someone would do the same for him when his time came.

Apart from this lying, or because of it, what most tormented Ivan Ilych was that no one pitied him as he wished to be pitied. At certain moments after prolonged suffering he wished most of all (though he would have been ashamed to confess it) for someone to pity him as a sick child is pitied. He longed to be petted and comforted. He knew he was an important functionary, that he had a beard turning grey, and that therefore what he longed for was impossible, but still he longed for it. And in Gerasim's attitude towards him there was something akin to what he wished for, and so that attitude comforted him. Ivan Ilych wanted to weep, wanted to be petted and cried over, and then his colleague Shebek would come, and instead of weeping and being petted, Ivan Ilych would assume a serious, severe, and profound air, and by force of habit would express his opinion on a decision of the Court of Cassation and would stubbornly insist on that view. This falsity around him and within him did more than anything else to poison his last days.

viii.

It was morning. He knew it was morning because Gerasim had gone, and Peter the footman had come and put out the candles, drawn back one of the curtains, and begun quietly to tidy up. Whether it was morning or evening, Friday or Sunday, made no difference, it was all just the same: the gnawing, unmitigated, agonizing pain, never ceasing for an instant, the consciousness of life inexorably waning but not yet extinguished, the approach of that ever dreaded and hateful Death which was the only reality, and always the same falsity. What were days, weeks, hours, in such a case?

"Will you have some tea, sir?"

"He wants things to be regular, and wishes the gentlefolk to drink tea in the morning," thought Ivan Ilych, and only said "No."

"Wouldn't you like to move onto the sofa, sir?"

"He wants to tidy up the room, and I'm in the way. I am uncleanliness and disorder," he thought, and said only:

"No, leave me alone."

The man went on bustling about. Ivan Ilych stretched out his hand. Peter came up, ready to help.

"What is it, sir?"

"My watch."

Peter took the watch which was close at hand and gave it to his master.

"Half-past eight. Are they up?"

"No, sir, except Vladimir Ivanich" (the son) "who has gone to school. Praskovya Fëdorovna ordered me to wake her if you asked for her. Shall I do so?"

"No, there's no need to." "Perhaps I'd better have some tea," he thought, and added aloud: "Yes, bring me some tea."

Peter went to the door, but Ivan Ilych dreaded being left alone. "How can I keep him here? Oh yes, my medicine." "Peter, give me my medicine." "Why not? Perhaps it may still do me some good." He took a spoonful and swallowed it. "No, it won't help. It's all tomfoolery, all deception," he decided as soon as he became aware of the familiar, sickly, hopeless taste: "No, I can't believe in it any longer. But the pain, why this pain? If it would only cease just for a moment!" And he moaned. Peter turned towards him. "It's all right. Go and fetch me some tea."

Peter went out. Left alone Ivan Ilych groaned not so much with pain, terrible though that was, as from mental anguish. Always and for ever the same, always these endless days and nights. If only it would come quicker! If only *what* would come quicker? Death, darkness? . . . No, no! Anything rather than death!

When Peter returned with the tea on a tray, Ivan Ilych stared at him for a time in perplexity, not realizing who and what he was. Peter was disconcerted by that look and his embarrassment brought Ivan Ilych to himself.

"Oh, tea! All right, put it down. Only help me to wash and put on a clean shirt."

And Ivan Ilych began to wash. With pauses for rest, he washed his hands and then his face, cleaned his teeth, brushed his hair, and looked in the glass. He was terrified by what he saw, especially by the limp way in which his hair clung to his pallid forehead.

While his shirt was being changed he knew that he would be still more frightened at the sight of his body, so he avoided looking at it. Finally he was ready. He drew on a dressing-gown, wrapped himself in a plaid, and sat down in the armchair to take his tea. For a moment he felt refreshed, but as soon as he began to drink the tea he was again aware of the same taste, and the pain also returned. He finished it with an effort, and then lay down stretching out his legs, and dismissed Peter.

Always the same. Now a spark of hope flashes up, then a sea of despair rages, and always pain; always pain, always despair, and always the same. When alone he had a dreadful and distressing desire to call someone, but he knew beforehand that with others present it would be still worse. "Another dose of morphine — to lose consciousness. I will tell him, the doctor, that he must think of something else. It's impossible, impossible, to go on like this."

An hour and another pass like that. But now there is a ring at the door bell. Perhaps it's the doctor? It is. He comes in fresh, hearty, plump, and cheerful, with that look on his face that seems to say: "There now, you're in a panic about something, but we'll arrange it all for you directly!" The doctor knows this expression is out of place here, but he has put it on once for all and can't take it off — like a man who has put on a frock-coat in the morning to pay a round of calls.

The doctor rubs his hands vigorously and reassuringly.

"Brr! How cold it is! There's such a sharp frost; just let me warm myself!" he says, as if it were only a matter of waiting till he was warm, and then he would put everything right.

"Well now, how are you?"

Ivan Ilych feels that the doctor would like to say: "Well, how are our affairs?" but that even he feels that this would not do, and says instead: "What sort of a night have you had?"

Ivan Ilych looks at him as much as to say: "Are you really never ashamed of lying?" But the doctor does not wish to understand this question, and Ivan Ilych says: "Just as terrible as ever. The pain never leaves me and never subsides. If only something . . ."

"Yes, you sick people are always like that. . . . There, now I think I am warm enough. Even Praskovya Fёdorovna, who is so particular, could find no fault with my temperature. Well, now I can say good-morning," and the doctor presses his patient's hand.

Then, dropping his former playfulness, he begins with a most serious face to examine the patient, feeling his pulse and taking his temperature, and then begins the sounding and auscultation.

Ivan Ilych knows quite well and definitely that all this is nonsense and pure deception, but when the doctor, getting down on his knee, leans over him, putting his ear first higher then lower, and performs various gymnastic movements over him with a significant expression on his face, Ivan Ilych submits to it all as he used to submit to the speeches of the lawyers, though he knew very well that they were all lying and why they were lying.

The doctor, kneeling on the sofa, is still sounding him when Praskovya Fёdorovna's silk dress rustles at the door and she is heard scolding Peter for not having let her know of the doctor's arrival.

She comes in, kisses her husband, and at once proceeds to prove that she has been up a long time already, and only owing to a misunderstanding failed to be there when the doctor arrived.

Ivan Ilych looks at her, scans her all over, sets against her the whiteness and plumpness and cleanness of her hands and neck, the gloss of her hair, and the sparkle of her vivacious eyes. He hates her with his whole soul. And the thrill of hatred he feels for her makes him suffer from her touch.

Her attitude towards him and his disease is still the same. Just as the doctor had adopted a certain relation to his patient which he could not abandon, so had she formed one towards him — that he was not doing something he ought to do and was himself to blame, and that she reproached him lovingly for this — and she could not now change that attitude.

"You see he doesn't listen to me and doesn't take his medicine at the proper time. And above all he lies in a position that is no doubt bad for him — with his legs up."

She described how he made Gerasim hold his legs up.

The doctor smiled with a contemptuous affability that said: "What's to be done? These sick people do have foolish fancies of that kind, but we must forgive them."

When the examination was over the doctor looked at his watch, and then Praskovya Fëdorovna announced to Ivan Ilych that it was of course as he pleased, but she had sent today for a celebrated specialist who would examine him and have a consultation with Michael Danilovich (their regular doctor).

"Please don't raise any objections. I am doing this for my own sake," she said ironically, letting it be felt that she was doing it all for his sake and only said this to leave him no right to refuse. He remained silent, knitting his brows. He felt that he was so surrounded and involved in a mesh of falsity that it was hard to unravel anything.

Everything she did for him was entirely for her own sake, and she told him she was doing for herself what she actually was doing for herself, as if that was so incredible that he must understand the opposite.

At half-past eleven the celebrated specialist arrived. Again the sounding began and the significant conversations in his presence and in another room, about the kidneys and the appendix, and the questions and answers, with such an air of importance that again, instead of the real question of life and death which now alone confronted him, the question arose of the kidney and appendix which were not behaving as they ought to and would now be attacked by Michael Danilovich and the specialist and forced to amend their ways.

The celebrated specialist took leave of him with a serious though not hopeless look, and in reply to the timid question Ivan Ilych, with eyes glistening with fear and hope, put to him as to whether there was a chance of recovery, said that he could not vouch for it but there was a possibility. The look of hope with which Ivan Ilych watched the doctor out was so pathetic that Praskovya Fëdorovna, seeing it, even wept as she left the room to hand the doctor his fee.

The gleam of hope kindled by the doctor's encouragement did not last long. The same room, the same pictures, curtains, wall-paper, medicine bottles, were all there, and the same aching suffering body, and Ivan Ilych began to moan. They gave him a subcutaneous injection and he sank into oblivion.

It was twilight when he came to. They brought him his dinner and he swallowed some beef tea with difficulty, and then everything was the same again and night was coming on.

After dinner, at seven o' clock, Praskovya Fëdorovna came into the room in evening dress, her full bosom pushed up by her corset, and with traces of powder on her face. She had reminded him in the morning that they were going to the theatre. Sarah Bernhardt was visiting the town and they had a box, which he had insisted on their taking. Now he had forgotten about it and her toilet offended him, but he concealed his vexation when he remembered that he had himself insisted on their securing a box and going because it would be an instructive and aesthetic pleasure for the children.

Praskovya Fëdorovna came in, self-satisfied but yet with a rather guilty air. She sat down and asked how he was, but, as he saw, only for the sake of asking and not in order to learn about it, knowing that there was nothing to learn — and then went on to what she really wanted to say: that she would not on any account have gone but that the box had been taken and Helen and their daughter were going, as well as Petrishchev (the examining magistrate, their daughter's fiancé) and that it was out of the question to let them go alone; but that she would have much preferred to sit with him for a while; and he must be sure to follow the doctor's orders while she was away.

"Oh, and Fëdor Petrovich" (the fiancé) "would like to come in. May he? And Lisa?"

"All right."

Their daughter came in in full evening dress, her fresh young flesh exposed (making a show of that very flesh which in his own case caused so much suffering), strong, healthy, evidently in love, and impatient with illness, suffering, and death, because they interfered with her happiness.

Fëdor Petrovich came in too, in evening dress, his hair curled *à la Capoul*, a tight stiff collar round his long sinewy neck, an enormous white shirt-front and narrow black trousers tightly stretched over his strong thighs. He had one white glove tightly drawn on, and was holding his opera hat in his hand.

Following him the schoolboy crept in unnoticed, in a new uniform; poor little fellow, and wearing gloves. Terribly dark shadows showed under his eyes, the meaning of which Ivan Ilych knew well.

His son had always seemed pathetic to him, and now it was dreadful to see the boy's frightened look of pity. It seemed to Ivan Ilych that Vasya was the only one besides Gerasim who understood and pitied him.

They all sat down and again asked how he was. A silence followed: Lisa asked her mother about the opera-glasses, and there was an altercation between mother and daughter as to who had taken them and where they had been put. This occasioned some unpleasantness.

Fëdor Petrovich inquired of Ivan Ilych whether he had ever seen Sarah Bernhardt. Ivan Ilych did not at first catch the question, but then replied: "No, have you seen her before?"

"Yes, in *Adrienne Lecouvreur*."

Praskovya Fëdorovna mentioned some roles in which Sarah Bernhardt was particularly good. Her daughter disagreed. Conversation sprang up as to the elegance and realism of her acting — the sort of conversation that is always repeated and is always the same.

In the midst of the conversation Fëdor Petrovich glanced at Ivan Ilych and became silent. The others also looked at him and grew silent. Ivan Ilych was staring with glittering eyes straight before him, evidently indignant with them. This had to be rectified, but it was impossible to do so. The silence had to be broken, but for a time no one dared to break it and they all became afraid that the conventional deception would suddenly become obvious and the truth become plain to all. Lisa was the first to pluck up courage and break that silence, but by trying to hide what everybody was feeling, she betrayed it.

"Well, if we are going it's time to start," she said, looking at her watch, a present from her father, and with a faint and significant smile at Fëdor Petrovich relating to something known only to them. She got up with a rustle of her dress.

They all rose, said good-night, and went away.

When they had gone it seemed to Ivan Ilych that he felt better; the falsity had gone with them. But the pain remained — that same pain and that same fear that made everything monotonously alike, nothing harder and nothing easier. Everything was worse.

Again minute followed minute and hour followed hour. Everything remained the same and there was no cessation. And the inevitable end of it all became more and more terrible.

"Yes, send Gerasim here," he replied to a question Peter asked.

ix.

His wife returned late at night. She came in on tiptoe, but he heard her, opened his eyes, and made haste to close them again. She wished to send Gerasim away and to sit with him herself, but he opened his eyes and said: "No, go away."

"Are you in great pain?"

"Always the same."

"Take some opium."

He agreed and took some. She went away.

Till about three in the morning he was in a state of stupefied misery. It seemed to him that he and his pain were being thrust into a narrow, deep black sack, but though they were pushed further and further in they could not be pushed to the bottom. And this, terrible enough in itself, was accompanied by suffering. He was frightened yet wanted to fall through the sack, he struggled but yet co-operated. And suddenly he broke through, fell, and regained consciousness. Gerasim was sitting at the foot of the bed dozing quietly and patiently, while he himself lay with his emaciated stockinged legs resting on Gerasim's shoulders; the same shaded candle was there and the same unceasing pain.

"Go away, Gerasim," he whispered.

"It's all right, sir. I'll stay awhile."

"No. Go away."

He removed his legs from Gerasim's shoulders, turned sideways onto his arm, and felt sorry for himself. He only waited till Gerasim had gone into the next room and then restrained himself no longer but wept like a child. He wept on account of his helplessness, his terrible loneliness, the cruelty of man, the cruelty of God, and the absence of God.

"Why hast Thou done all this? Why hast Thou brought me here? Why, why dost Thou torment me so terribly?"

He did not expect an answer and yet wept because there was no answer and could be none. The pain again grew more acute, but he did not stir and did not call. He said to himself: "Go on! Strike me! But what is it for? What have I done to Thee? What is it for?"

Then he grew quiet and not only ceased weeping but even held his breath and became all attention. It was as though he were listening not to an audible voice but to the voice of his soul, to the current of thoughts arising within him.

"What is it you want?" was the first clear conception capable of expression in words, that he heard.

"What do you want? What do you want?" he repeated to himself.

"What do I want? To live and not to suffer," he answered. And again he listened with such concentrated attention that even his pain did not distract him.

"To live? How?" asked his inner voice.

"Why, to live as I used to — well and pleasantly."

"As you lived before, well and pleasantly?" the voice repeated.

And in imagination he began to recall the best moments of his pleasant life. But strange to say none of those best moments of his pleasant life now seemed at all what they had then seemed — none of them except the first recollections of childhood. There, in childhood, there had been something really pleasant with which it would be possible to live if it could return. But the child who had experienced that happiness existed no longer, it was like a reminiscence of somebody else.

As soon as the period began which had produced the present Ivan Ilych, all that had then seemed joys now melted before his sight and turned into something trivial and often nasty.

And the further he departed from childhood and the nearer he came to the present the more worthless and doubtful were the joys. This began with the School of Law. A little that was really good was still found there — there was lightheartedness, friendship, and hope. But in the upper classes there had already been fewer of such good moments. Then during the first years of his official career, when he was in the service of the Governor, some pleasant moments again occurred: they were the memories of love for a woman. Then all became confused and there was still less of what was good; later on again there was still less that was good, and the further he went the less there was. His marriage, a mere accident, then the disenchantment that followed it, his wife's bad breath and the sensuality and hypocrisy: then that deadly official life and those preoccupations about money, a year of it, and two, and ten, and twenty, and always the same thing. And the longer it lasted the more deadly it became. "It is as if I had been going downhill while I imagined I was going up. And that is really what it was. I was going up in public opinion, but to the same extent life was ebbing away from me. And now it is all done and there is only death."

"Then what does it mean? Why? It can't be that life is so senseless and horrible. But if it really has been so horrible and senseless, why must I die and die in agony? There is something wrong!"

"Maybe I did not live as I ought to have done," it suddenly occurred to him. "But how could that be, when I did everything properly?" he replied, and immediately dismissed from his mind this, the sole solution of all the riddles of life and death, as something quite impossible.

"Then what do you want now? To live? Live how? Live as you lived in the law courts when the usher proclaimed 'The judge is coming!' The judge is coming, the judge!" he repeated to himself. "Here he is, the judge. But I am not guilty!" he exclaimed angrily. "What is it for?" And he ceased crying, but turning his face to the wall continued to ponder on the same question: Why, and for what purpose is there all this horror? But however much he pondered he found no answer. And whenever the thought occurred to him, as it often did, that it all resulted from his not having lived as he ought to have done, he at once recalled the correctness of his whole life and dismissed so strange an idea.

x.

Another fortnight passed. Ivan Ilych now no longer left his sofa. He would not lie in bed but lay on the sofa, facing the wall nearly all the time. He suffered ever the same unceasing agonies and in his loneliness pondered always on the same insoluble question: "What is this? Can it be that it is Death?" And the inner voice answered: "Yes, it is Death."

"Why these sufferings?" And the voice answered, "For no reason — they just are so." Beyond and besides this there was nothing.

From the very beginning of his illness, ever since he had first been to see the doctor, Ivan Ilych's life had been divided between two contrary and alternating moods: now it was despair and the expectation of this uncomprehended and terrible death, and now hope and an intently interested observation of the functioning of his organs. Now before his eyes there was only a kidney or an intestine that temporarily evaded its duty, and now only that incomprehensible and dreadful death from which it was impossible to escape.

These two states of mind had alternated from the very beginning of his illness, but the further it progressed the more doubtful and fantastic became the conception of the kidney, and the more real the sense of impending death.

He had but to call to mind what he had been three months before and what he was now, to call to mind with what regularity he had been going downhill, for every possibility of hope to be shattered.

Latterly during that loneliness in which he found himself as he lay facing the back of the sofa, a loneliness in the midst of a populous town and surrounded by numerous acquaintances and relations but that yet could not have been more complete anywhere — either at the bottom of the sea or under the earth — during that terrible loneliness Ivan Ilych had lived only in memories of the past. Pictures of his past rose before him one after another. They always began with what was nearest in time and then went back to what was most remote — to his childhood — and rested there. If he thought of the stewed prunes that had been offered him that day, his mind went back to the raw shrivelled French plums of his childhood, their peculiar flavour and the flow of saliva when he sucked their stones, and along with the memory of that taste came a whole series of memories of those days: his nurse, his brother, and their toys. "No, I mustn't think of that. . . . It is too painful," Ivan Ilych said to himself, and brought himself back to the present — to the button on the back of the sofa and the creases in its morocco. "Morocco is expensive, but it does not wear well: there had been a quarrel about it. It was a different kind of quarrel and a different kind of morocco that time when we tore father's portfolio and were punished, and mamma brought us some tarts. . . ." And again his thoughts dwelt on his childhood, and again it was painful and he tried to banish them and fix his mind on something else.

Then again together with that chain of memories another series passed through his mind — of how his illness had progressed and grown worse. There also the further back he looked the more life there had been. There had been more of what was good in life and more of life itself. The two merged together. "Just as the pain went on getting worse and worse, so my life grew worse and worse," he thought. "There is one bright spot there at the back, at the beginning of life, and afterwards all becomes blacker and blacker and proceeds more and more rapidly — in inverse ratio to the square of the distance from death," thought Ivan Ilych. And the example of a stone falling downwards with increasing velocity entered his mind. Life, a series of increasing sufferings, flies further and further towards its end — the most terrible suffering. "I am flying. . . ." He shuddered, shifted himself, and tried to resist, but was already aware that resistance was impossible, and again with eyes weary of gazing but unable to cease seeing what was before them, he stared at the back of the sofa and waited — awaiting that dreadful fall and shock and destruction.

"Resistance is impossible!" he said to himself. "If I could only understand what it is all for! But that too is impossible. An explanation would be possible if it could be said that I have not lived as I ought to. But it is impossible to say that," and he remembered all the legality, correctitude, and propriety of his life. "That at any rate can certainly not be admitted," he thought, and his lips smiled ironically as if someone could see that smile and be taken in by it. "There is no explanation! Agony, death. . . . What for?"

xi.

Another two weeks went by in this way and during that fortnight an event occurred that Ivan Ilych and his wife had desired. Petrishchev formally proposed. It happened in the evening. The next day Praskovya Fëdorovna came into her husband's room considering how best to inform him of it, but that very night there had been a fresh change for the worse in his condition. She found him still lying on the sofa but in a different position. He lay on his back, groaning and staring fixedly straight in front of him.

She began to remind him of his medicines, but he turned his eyes towards her with such a look that she did not finish what she was saying; so great an animosity, to her in particular, did that look express.

"For Christ's sake let me die in peace!" he said.

She would have gone away, but just then their daughter came in and went up to say good morning. He looked at her as he had done at his wife, and in reply to her inquiry about his health said dryly that he would soon free them all of himself. They were both silent and after sitting with him for a while went away.

"Is it our fault?" Lisa said to her mother. "It's as if we were to blame! I am sorry for papa, but why should we be tortured?"

The doctor came at his usual time. Ivan Ilych answered "Yes" and "No," never taking his angry eyes from him, and at last said: "You know you can do nothing for me, so leave me alone."

"We can ease your sufferings."

"You can't even do that. Let me be."

The doctor went into the drawing-room and told Praskovya Fëdorovna that the case was very serious and that the only resource left was opium to allay her husband's sufferings, which must be terrible.

It was true, as the doctor said, that Ivan Ilych's physical sufferings were terrible, but worse than the physical sufferings were his mental sufferings, which were his chief torture.

His mental sufferings were due to the fact that that night, as he looked at Gerasim's sleepy, good-natured face with its prominent cheek-bones, the question suddenly occurred to him: "What if my whole life has really been wrong?"

It occurred to him that what had appeared perfectly impossible before, namely that he had not spent his life as he should have done, might after all be true. It occurred to him that his scarcely perceptible attempts to struggle against what was considered good by the most highly placed people, those scarcely noticeable impulses which he had immediately suppressed, might have been the real thing, and all the rest false. And his professional duties and the whole arrangement of his life and of his family, and all his social and official interests, might all have been false. He tried to defend all those things to himself and suddenly felt the weakness of what he was defending. There was nothing to defend.

"But if that is so," he said to himself, "and I am leaving this life with the consciousness that I have lost all that was given me and it is impossible to rectify it — what then?"

He lay on his back and began to pass his life in review in quite a new way. In the morning when he saw first his footman, then his wife, then his daughter, and then the doctor, their every word and movement confirmed to him the awful truth that had been revealed to him during the night. In them he saw himself — all that for which he had lived — and saw clearly that it was not real at all, but a terrible and huge deception which had hidden both life and death. This consciousness intensified his physical suffering tenfold. He groaned and tossed about, and pulled at his clothing which choked and stifled him. And he hated them on that account.

He was given a large dose of opium and became unconscious, but at noon his sufferings began again. He drove everybody away and tossed from side to side.

His wife came to him and said:

"Jean, my dear, do this for me. It can't do any harm and often helps. Healthy people often do it."

He opened his eyes wide.

"What? Take communion? Why? It's unnecessary! However. . . ."

She began to cry.

"Yes, do, my dear. I'll send for our priest. He is such a nice man."

"All right. Very well," he muttered.

When the priest came and heard his confession, Ivan Ilych was softened and seemed to feel a relief from his doubts and consequently from his sufferings, and for a moment there came a ray of hope. He again began to think of the vermiform appendix and the possibility of correcting it. He received the sacrament with tears in his eyes.

When they laid him down again afterwards he felt a moment's ease, and the hope that he might live awoke in him again. He began to think of the operation that had been suggested to him. "To live! I want to live!" he said to himself.

His wife came in to congratulate him after his communion, and when uttering the usual conventional words she added:

"You feel better, don't you?"

Without looking at her he said "Yes."

Her dress, her figure, the expression of her face, the tone of her voice, all revealed the same thing. "This is wrong, it is not as it should be. All you have lived for and still live for is falsehood and deception, hiding life and death from you." And as soon as he admitted that thought, his hatred and his agonizing physical suffering again sprang up, and with that suffering a consciousness of the unavoidable, approaching end. And to this was added a new sensation of grinding shooting pain and a feeling of suffocation.

The expression of his face when he uttered that "yes" was dreadful. Having uttered it, he looked her straight in the eyes, turned on his face with a rapidity extraordinary in his weak state and shouted:

"Go away! Go away and leave me alone!"

xii.

From that moment the screaming began that continued for three days, and was so terrible that one could not hear it through two closed doors without horror. At the moment he answered his wife he realized that he was lost, that there was no return, that the end had come, the very end, and his doubts were still unsolved and remained doubts.

"Oh! Oh! Oh!" he cried in various intonations. He had begun by screaming, "I won't!" and continued screaming on the letter O.

For three whole days, during which time did not exist for him, he struggled in that black sack into which he was being thrust by an invisible, resistless force. He struggled as a man condemned to death struggles in the hands of the executioner, knowing that he cannot save himself. And every moment he felt that despite all his efforts he was drawing nearer and nearer to what terrified him. He felt that his agony was due to his being thrust into that black hole and still more to his not being able to get right into it. He was hindered from getting into it by his conviction that his life had been a good one. That very justification of his life held him fast and prevented his moving forward, and it caused him most torment of all.

Suddenly some force struck him in the chest and side, making it still harder to breathe, and he fell through the hole and there at the bottom was a light. What had happened to him was like the sensation one sometimes experiences in a railway carriage when one thinks one is going backwards while one is really going forwards and suddenly becomes aware of the real direction.

"Yes, it was all not the right thing," he said to himself, "but that's no matter. It can be done. But what *is* the right thing?" he asked himself, and suddenly grew quiet.

This occurred at the end of the third day, two hours before his death. Just then his schoolboy son had crept softly in and gone up to the bedside. The dying man was still screaming desperately and waving his arms. His hand fell on the boy's head, and the boy caught it, pressed it to his lips, and began to cry.

At that very moment Ivan Ilych fell through and caught sight of the light, and it was revealed to him that though his life had not been what it should have been, this could still be rectified. He asked himself, "What *is* the right thing?" and grew still, listening. Then he felt that someone was kissing his hand. He opened his eyes, looked at his son, and felt sorry for him. His wife came up to him and he glanced at her. She was gazing at him open-mouthed, with undried tears on her nose and cheek and a despairing look on her face. He felt sorry for her too.

"Yes, I am making them wretched," he thought. "They are sorry, but it will be better for them when I die." He wished to say this but had not the strength to utter it. "Besides, why speak? I must act," he thought. With a look at his wife he indicated his son and said: "Take him away . . . sorry for him . . . sorry for you too. . . ." He tried to add, "forgive me," but said "forgo" and waved his hand, knowing that He whose understanding mattered would understand.

And suddenly it grew clear to him that what had been oppressing him and would not leave him was all dropping away at once from two sides, from ten sides, and from all sides. He was sorry for them, he must act so as not to hurt them: release them and free himself from these sufferings.

"How good and how simple!" he thought. "And the pain?" he asked himself. "What has become of it? Where are you, pain?"

He turned his attention to it.

"Yes, here it is. Well, what of it? Let the pain be."

"And death . . . where is it?"

He sought his former accustomed fear of death and did not find it. "Where is it? What death?" There was no fear because there was no death.

In place of death there was light.

"So that's what it is!" he suddenly exclaimed aloud. "What joy!"

To him all this happened in a single instant, and the meaning of that instant did not change. For those present his agony continued for another two hours. Something rattled in his throat, his emaciated body twitched, then the gasping and rattle became less and less frequent.

"It is finished!" said someone near him.

He heard these words and repeated them in his soul.

"Death is finished," he said to himself. "It is no more!"

He drew in a breath, stopped in the midst of a sigh, stretched out, and died.

Index